230·2 MAY

This book is due for return on or before the last date shown below.

Contemporary Catholic Theology – a Reader

edited by

Michael A. Hayes
and
Liam Gearon

GRACEWING

First published in 1998
Reprinted 2001

Gracewing
2 Southern Avenue, Leominster
Herefordshire HR6 0QF

UK ISBN 0 85244 488 5

Typesetting by
Action Publishing Technology Ltd, Gloucester, GL1 1SP

Printed by Antony Rowe Ltd,
Chippenham SN14 6LH

Contents

Foreword

Working in the field of Religious Education in the 1970s, one of my happiest tasks was to tutor teachers for what was then the Catholic Teachers Certificate, now the Catholic Certificate in Religious Studies (CCRS). I lost count of the number who acknowledged that it had turned out to be so much more than simply a professional study, indeed a key growth point in their own faith.

Managed and awarded by the Board of Religious Studies of the Bishops' Conference of England and Wales, the Catholic Certificate in Religious Studies is now the most widely used foundation course in the Catholic Church in England and Wales. It attracts not only student and graduate teachers but very many others who are involved in ministry in the Church as well as those who study simply for personal growth.

Many of its students are eager readers, others can be persuaded! But the constant search is for suitable and affordable material on the various topics. I have no doubt at all that there will be a warm and relieved welcome for this new Reader which Michael Hayes and Liam Gearon have put together. The authors from whom they have drawn the material are all well known and highly regarded theologians who write clearly and attractively and whose work will, I hope, move our students to want to read more, perhaps even to build on their present studies to more advanced levels.

Because of the make up of the CCRS, in serving its students with this new Reader, the compilers have composed a book of Catholic theology which will undoubtedly and deservedly find a very wide readership.

I thank both of them for their skill in choosing and their patient perseverance in persuading authors.

†John Rawsthorne
Bishop of Hallam

Preface

The contents of this volume offer the reader a broad insight into
Catholic theology. It does not claim to be a definitive work, simply
a reader, a sample of writers, many of whom have an international
reputation in their field. The difficulty we had as editors was not
what to include in the collection, rather what to leave out, for we
truly discovered that there is a vast range of excellent material
available, much of which we would have loved to have included.
The genesis of this Reader was to provide access to material for
students studying for the Catholic Certificate in Religious Studies
(CCRS), awarded by the Bishops' Conference of England and
Wales. The Reader covers the six main subject areas studied for the
Certificate. We hope that this collection will be a useful introduction to these six areas: The Old Testament, The New Testament,
The Person of Jesus, The Church, Christian Morality, and The
Sacraments. While this was the genesis of the volume we hope it
might be of interest to a wider audience. The volume is divided
into two sections, Section I on Scripture, and Section II on
Theology. This format corresponds to the Catholic Church's teaching that the one source of Revelation has two channels, Scripture
and Tradition.[1]

Section I begins with an introduction to the scriptures. Raymond
Brown's chapter on 'The Church and the Bible: a New
Understanding' gives a survey of the history of changes that have
taken place within the Catholic Church since the mid-twentieth
century with regard to its understanding of the scriptures. We have
also included here sections from the Instruction of the Pontifical
Biblical Commission on 'The Historical Truth of the Gospels'
pertaining to the formation of the Gospels, together with some
contextualising remarks by Brown. Robert Murray's chapter is an

[1] Vatican Council II, *Dei Verbum*, 18 November 1965.

appraisal of the Vatican Council II document 'On Divine Revelation (*Dei Verbum*)'. Murray highlights the fundamental importance theologically of this document and how 'it both undergirds and touches most of the council documents'. He questions whether its influence as a document has been in proportion to its importance. The chapter gives an outline of the document, then sketches 'the main lines of theological comment and response, and then liturgical, practical and ecumenical developments; then some "growing points" and problems in areas both of praxis and of theological reflection'.[2] The chapter on 'Historical-Critical Exegesis of the Bible in Roman Catholicism', also by Raymond Brown, shows how recent a phenomenon a historical-critical approach to biblical exegesis is. He highlights in particular the 1943 encyclical of Pope Pius XII, *Divino Afflante Spiritu*, and Pope Paul VI's Roman Pontifical Biblical Commision of 1964 as two important steps in this development. He also examines a 'revisionist' criticism of the historical-critical method of biblical scholarship.

Daniel Smith-Christopher's 'Returning to the Sources: The Hebrew Bible is an accessible chapter written specifically as an introduction for students. He argues for the use of the term 'The Hebrew Bible' rather than 'The Old Testament' for the former title 'reminds us of the language and culture of its origins (semitic, ancient near east) and reminds us that these writings are "holy" to both Jews and Christians – something we overlook to our disadvantage'. The unifying theological theme in these texts he identifies as a relationship between God and God's people. He surveys both the three distinct sections of the Hebrew Canon: Torah, Prophets, and Writings, and some of the problems of biblical analysis. He concludes by offering the reader some useful study questions. 'The Canon of the Old Testament' is the subject of the chapter by J. H. Hayes who surveys the long history of the development of the Canon of Scriptures and points out its semitic origin as 'reed', 'rod', 'rule', 'norm', and how it came to be used during the fourth century AD. The concept of a canon applies to writings which are accepted as authoritative, unchangeable and normative for religious faith and practice. Jean-Pierre Prévost's chapter 'What

---

[2] In preparation for this Reader Robert Murray drew the editors' attentions to his critical discussion of the section on Revelation in M.J.Walsh (ed.), *Commentary on the Catechism of the Catholic Church* (London: Geoffrey Chapman, 1994), 6-35. This analyses the section in the Catechism in detail, comparing it with the text of *Dei Verbum*, which at first sight seems to follow fairly closely, but which at key points it reinterprets in a more authoritarian sense than the conciliar text itself implies.

is a Prophet?', beginning with a biblical definition, provides an overview of both the major and minor prophets.

The chapters on the New Testament begin with Jeffrey Siker's 'Introduction to the Study of the New Testament' clearly showing that the writings of the New Testament express the faith commitments of the earliest Christian communities. He uses the term 'collage' as a way of seeing the overlapping but distinct images that the texts provide of Jesus and the meaning of Christian faith. The chapter begins with an overview of the New Testament as a whole, then discusses the formation of the New Testament canon. This is followed with a survey of various forms of criticism helping the reader to gain greater insight into the richness of the texts. Siker also highlights some distinctive aspects of the Gospels and the writings of Paul. Gideon Goosen and Margaret Tomlinson's 'Studying the Gospels: An Introduction' gives an overview of the four Gospel narratives highlighting in particular the Infancy Narratives of Matthew and Luke. They take us through the background to each Gospel in terms of authorship, date, place, intended community, background of the community, sources, structure, style, and theological slant. Joseph Fitzmyer's 'Spiritual Journey of Paul the Apostle' explores the etymology of the names Saul and Paul, the Jewish and cultural heritage of Paul. This is followed by an analysis of the most important element in the spiritual journey of Paul, the Damascus experience. Fitzmyer concludes this chapter by showing how Paul uses ten different images drawn from his Jewish or Hellenistic background to attempt to describe the implications of the Christ-event.

Section II opens with chapters on The Person of Jesus beginning with John O'Grady's thorough analysis of 'The Present State of Christology' which not only provides a clear overview of recent thinking in this area but provides critical links between christology, contemporary Catholic biblical studies and ecclesiology. O'Grady argues that just as contemporary theology maintains different models of the Church, so too we need to hold in tension different models of Jesus while retaining Jesus' paradigmatic status as Second Person in the Trinity. Dermot Lane's 'The Doctrine of the Incarnation: Human and Cosmic Considerations' provides a stimulating juxtaposition of classical and contemporary theologies of the Incarnation. His chapter examines the christological teachings deriving from the early Councils such as Nicea, Ephesus and Chalcedon and their place in modern day thinking about our world. More particularly, Lane argues powerfully for the need to re-evaluate our christologies in the light of modern discoveries in cosmology. Monika Hellwig's critical survey of the early period in the Church's history of christological reflection concludes with an analysis of the importance of Chalcedon in determining christology from the sixth century onwards. Enda Lyons' 'His Own Person or Divine Puppet?' presents the real questions of christology as still very much a living concern for Christians today, focusing especially upon the central christological question of the relation of Jesus' humanity to his divinity.

The Second Vatican Council's teachings provide an important backdrop to the chapters on The Church, thus expressing a major concern of the Church's theological quest at this time in its history: her understanding of herself and her relationship to the world. We begin with an overview and a context provided by Thomas Rausch's 'The Church and the Council'. This is followed by a more indepth and critical examination of what Richard McBrien calls 'the two twin pillars' of the Church's ecclesiogy: the document on 'The Church'[3] and the document on 'The Church in the Modern World'[4] by Richard McBrien and Enda McDonagh respectively. The two chapters by Francis Sullivan complement McBrien's and McDonagh's chapters and explore how the documents of the Second Vatican Council are to be evaluated and interpreted. Christopher Butler's chapter provides insights on how the Decree on Ecumenism provides insight into this developing ecclesiology.[5]

'What's Special About Christian Morality?' is a short article by Denis O'Callaghan and it introduces the chapters on Christian Morality. In 'Approaching Christian Morality', Vincent MacNamara highlights the distinctiveness of the Christian moral worldview. Timothy O'Connell's 'The History of Moral Theology' presents a brief and highly readable overview of all the major periods of development in Christian moral thinking. Thomas Rausch's challenging 'Sexual Morality and Social Justice' extends the discussion on the distinctiveness of Christian morality. Providing a most useful overview of the Church's teaching on sexual morality and social justice, while highlighting the controversial aspects of and links between both, Rausch concludes with some insightful comments on conscience and morality.[6]

[3] Vatican Council II, *Lumen Gentium*, 21 November 1964.
[4] Vatican Council II, *Gaudium et Spes*, 7 December 1965.
[5] Vatican Council II, *Unitatis Redintegratio*, 21 November 1964.
[6] Pope John Paul II, *Veritatis Splendour* (1993) is a key source here, as is the Catholic Bishops' Conference of England and Wales' (1996) statement *The Common Good and the Church's Social Teaching*.

Tad Guzie examines some conceptual, and specifically linguistic issues in the study of the sacraments in a consideration of familiar but theologically complex words. Aidan Kavanagh's commentary on the Vatican Council II's document on The Liturgy contextualises contemporary sacramental theology within this tradition.[7] The chapters by Joseph Martos, Philippe Bégurie and Claude Duchesneau focus upon the develement of the sacraments in the tradition of the Catholic Church.

---

[7] Vatican Council II, *Sacrosanctum Concilium*, 4 December 1963.

Abbreviations

AS	*Acta Synodalia Concilii Vaticani II*, Vatican City, 1970 ff.
AAS	*Acta Apostolicae Sedis*
BRCFC	R.E. Brown, *Biblical Reflections on Crises Facing the Church* (New York: Paulist, 1975)
CCL	*Corpus Christianorum, series Latina, Turnholt*, 1953 ff.
CELEM	Episcopal Conference of Latin America
CMHB	S.Z. Leiman, ed., *The Canon and Masorah of the Hebrew Bible* (New York: KTAV, 1974)
CP	Classical Philosophy
CMB	R.E. Brown, *The Critical Meaning of the Bible* (New York: Paulist, 1981)
CSEL	Corpus scriptorum ecclesiasticorum latinorum
CQB	*Catholic Biblical Quarterly*
DBS	H. Denzinger, C. Bannwart, and A. Schönmetzer, eds., *Enchiridion Symbolorum* (32nd ed.; Freiburg: Herder, 1963)
DH	*Dignitatis Humanae*
DS	Dezinger-Schönmetzer
DV	*Dei Verbum*
Exp Tem	*Expository Times*
GS	*Gaudium et Spes*
HTR	*Harvard Theological Review*
HUCA	*Hebrew Union College Annual*
IDB	G. A. Buttrick, ed., *The Interpreter's Dictionary of the Bible* (4 vols.; Nashville, TN: Abington, 1962)
JBR	*Journal of Bible and Religion*
JCB	R.E. Brown, J. A. Fitzmeyer, and R.E. Murphy, eds., *The Jerome Biblical Commentary* (Englewood Cliffs, NJ: Prentice Hall, 1968)
LG	*Lumen Gentium*
LXX	Septuagint (Greek translation of the Old Testament)

Mansi	J.D. Mansi, ed., *Sacrorum Conciliorum nova collectio*, Florence, 1759ff., continued by L.Petit and J. Martin, Paris and Leipzig, 1901–27
MQ	*McCormick Quarterly*
NA	Nostra Aetate
NAB	New American Bible
ND	Neuner-Dupuis
NedTTs	*Nederlands theologisch Tijdschrift*
NRSV	New Revised Standard Version
NT	New Testament
NTS	*New Testament Studies*
OCTBI	J.J. Megivern, ed., *Offical Catholic Teachings: Bible Interpretations* (Consortium Book; Wilmington, NC: McGrath, 1978)
OT	Old Testament
PAAJR	*Proceedings of the American Academy for Jewish Research*
PAHT	J.A. Fitzmyer, *Paul and His Theology: A Brief Sketch* (2nd ed., Englewood Cliffs, NJ: Prentice Hall, 1989)
PL	P.J. Migne, ed., *Patrologiae cursus completus, series latina*, Paris, 1844 ff.
ResQ	*Restoration Quarterly*
RSS	*Rome and the Study of Scripture* (7th ed.; St. Meinard, IN: Grail 1962)
RSV	Revised Standard Version
SBLDS	Society of Biblical Literature Dissertation Series
SC	*Sacrosanctum Concilium*
SE II	*Studia evangelica* (TU 87, 1964)
TDNT	G. Kittel and G. Friedrich, *Theological Dictionary of the New Testament* (10 vols.; Grand Rapids, MI: Eerdmans, 1964–76)
UR	*Unitatis Redintegratio*
USCC	United States Catholic Conference
WCFBA	World Catholic Federation for Biblical Apostolate
WWC	World Council of Churches
ZNW	*Zeitschrift für die neutestamentliche Wissenschaft*

Section I
Scripture

Chapter 1

The Church and the Bible:
A New Understanding

Raymond E. Brown SS

Very often when older Catholics hear at Mass a presentation about the Bible they are puzzled. In their youth they were probably never encouraged to read the Bible, and what is now being said about biblical stories (for instance, about Adam and Eve) bears little resemblance to what they heard when they were growing up. A similar confusion sometimes occurs when youngsters come home and report to their parents what they were taught about the Bible in religion class. The parents wonder whether this can be correct.

A simple answer to part of the confusion is that in the mid-twentieth century the Catholic Church drastically changed its position on the Scriptures. It did so because it saw how new methods greatly increased the understanding of the Bible and made its wealth more accessible and spiritually helpful.

The end of the nineteenth century

Our story begins in the last quarter of the nineteenth century, which was a very active period in the study of the Bible. The movement to submit the scriptural books to the same kind of historical and literary analysis as other ancient literature had been gaining force in Protestant circles, especially in Germany. It was now leading to solutions startlingly different from those held in the tradition. For instance, the Pentateuchal section of the Old Testament (the first five books) had been attributed to Moses by both Christians and Jews. In the 1870s and 1880s, however, a famous scholar, Julius Wellhausen, argued that these books were composed from four documents written four to eight hundred years after Moses.

Discoveries of Assyrian, Babylonian and Egyptian writings suggested that some biblical stories (like that of the flood), law codes and collections of wisdom had been borrowed from other nations. Anglican scholars, recognizing that the King James translation of the New Testament had been based on an inferior Greek manuscript tradition, used ancient manuscripts to print a superior Greek version on which new English translations were subsequently based.

We are accustomed today to receive encyclicals from the pope or directives from Vatican offices on controverted questions. But that was not always so. This ferment about new biblical methods and discoveries brought the papacy for the first time directly into Catholic discussions of the Bible with the encyclical *Providentissimus Deus* of Pope Leo XIII (1893).

Personally a very learned man, the pope recognized the value of some scholarly advances and spoke with considerable nuance about the situation. Nevertheless, he insisted on the Latin version (not the original Greek or Hebrew) as a basis of translation and on the traditional interpretations of scriptural passages. Happily, his encyclical spared Catholics a problem that would trouble many pious Protestants in relation to human evolution. It pointed out that the biblical authors, who shared the 'scientific' views of their times, do not teach answers to problems raised by the natural sciences of our times.

The first third of the twentieth century

On the academic scene, the turn of the century and the early 1900s saw among scholars an even more rapid acceptance of modern approaches to the Bible, often with a radical twist. Many scholars were saying that the Bible was not simply a history. For some, that meant calling into doubt the truth and important biblical affirmations like God's creation of the world, miracles, the divinity of Jesus, the Incarnation and the Resurrection, and so on. Recognizing that the Judeo-Christian faith was being undermined, conservative Protestants in the United States banded together to protect 'the fundamentals' by insisting on the literal historicity of everything described in the Scriptures – whence the name 'Fundamentalism'.

About the same time (more precisely, between 1905 and 1915), fearing that the radical Protestant scholarship would make its way into Catholic circles, the Roman Pontifical Biblical Commission issued a series of cautionary, conservative decrees rejecting most of the positions taken by contemporary Protestant academics. The Commission affirmed that Moses was substantially the author of the Pentateuch; Isaiah was one book; essentially, Matthew wrote the first Gospel and the apostle John the fourth; Paul wrote the Letters to Timothy and Titus. In the 1920s the Vatican Holy Office took vigorous action against any Catholic deviations from traditional positions on the Bible. These directives shaped textbooks and classroom teaching for decades to come (and that means what many of us were taught in classes dealing with Bible stories in Catholic grammar schools).

Thus, for the first third of the twentieth century one may speak of three trends in biblical interpretation. At most major Protestant divinity schools (universities and seminaries) the professors, recognizing the very real problems detected by modern historical and literary methods, advocated an approach that called into question the traditional authorship of the biblical books and recognized that many of them were far from exact histories of what they described. In reaction, fundamentalist and evangelist preachers and Bible colleges, in varying ways, contradicted such an approach by insisting on the literal inerrancy of the scriptures. Catholics, a third and isolated group ignored by both Protestant camps, held onto the traditional Christian doctrines by absolute fidelity to the positions inculcated by the Pontifical Biblical Commission.

The period of change: 1940–1965

Suddenly, in the 1940s during the pontificate of Pope Pius XII, the Catholic position changed. Here was a pope whose personal experience showed how wonderfully enriching Bible reading could be for the spiritual life. Change was now opportune because the mainstream of scholarly Protestant research had shifted back toward the centre, as radical positions were challenged by recent discoveries. For instance, the view that John's Gospel was written about AD 175 had been shown untenable by the dating of a small papyrus fragment of that Gospel to about 135, so that the traditional assignment of the composition of the Gospel to the 90s again became likely. Clay tablets discovered at Ugarit in Syria revealed a Canaanite language akin to Hebrew and suggested to scholars that some Old Testament poetry should be dated before 1000 BC, thus contradicting the late dating proposed by Wellhausen.

Consequently, in his encyclical *Divino Afflante Spiritu* (1943), Pius XII judged that it was safe for Catholic scholars to take up the methods that were previously forbidden. Translations from the original Hebrew and Greek were now encouraged. A particular aspect of the encyclical definitively steered Catholics away from fundamentalism: namely, the recognition that the Bible includes many different literary forms or genres, not just history. One might exemplify this by thinking of the Bible as the library both of ancient Israel and of the early Church, containing different kinds of history, poetry, drama, dramatized parables and so on. It is a bad mistake to wander into a modern library, pick up a historical novel or a play and read it as if it were exact history – the kind of mistake that literalists tend to make in dealing with the biblical books.

After the end of the Second World War, *Divino Afflante Spiritu* sparked an enormous growth in Catholic biblical scholarship. New teachers were trained, and the results of the changed approach to the Scriptures were gradually communicated to the people – the very steps the pope had urged. A statement of the Pontifical Biblical Commission to Cardinal Suhard of Paris in 1948 documented a change in Church attitudes toward the Pentateuch. Rather than being composed at one time by Moses, these first Old Testament books were composed from sources and developed in the course of history. While the early chapters of Genesis (including the Adam and Eve story) relate fundamental truths, they do so in figurative language and do not contain history in a modern sense.

By 1955 the secretary of the Pontifical Biblical Commission could declare that now Catholic scholars had complete liberty with regard to the 1905–1915 decrees of that Commission except where they touched on faith and morals (and very few of them did). This meant that Catholic scholars were free to adopt positions of authorship and dating that other Christians had come to hold under the pressure of evidence.

A crucial moment occurred at the beginning of the Second Vatican Council in 1962. Pius XII had died, and it soon became evident that not everyone in Rome approved of the biblical changes he had introduced. The preliminary document on the sources of revelation, sent out by the Holy Office before the Council as a basis for discussion, appealed to positions taken in the early 1900s and would have turned the clock back. This document was rejected by nearly two-thirds of the Council participants and sent back by Pope John XXIII for thorough rewriting.

As part of the rewriting, the important 'The Historical Truth of the Gospels' – *Instruction* of the Roman Pontifical Biblical Commission (1964) – became the basis of the final Vatican II document pertinent to Scripture (*Dogmatic Constitution on Divine Revelation*, promulgated in 1965). The Commission held that the Gospels, while retaining the sense of the sayings of Jesus, were not necessarily expressing them literally. The truth and historicity of the Gospels must be judged from the fact that the doctrine and life of Jesus were not reported for the purpose of being remembered but were preached so as to offer the Church a basis of faith and morals.

This Biblical Commission approach, which steers Catholics away from a literalist approach to the Gospels, was fortified by Vatican II's position on inerrancy: 'The books of Scripture must be acknowledged as teaching firmly, faithfully, and without error that truth which God wanted put into the sacred writings for the sake of our salvation' (*Divine Revelation, II*). That is a far cry from assuming that every statement in Scripture has to be literally accurate.

From 1965 till today: consolidation and new problems

In the last third of the century, since the end of the Second Vatican Council, Church needs have shaped developments in the Catholic approach to the Bible. A new set of liturgical books provided three years of Sunday Mass readings, involving not only the Old Testament (a most important innovation), but almost the complete texts of Mark, Matthew and Luke (one for each year; John is read every year, mostly in the Lenten and Easter seasons). The method of not mixing passages from one Gospel with those from another reflects the view that each evangelist had his own theology and viewpoint that guided not only what he narrated but how he did so. For liturgical purposes, translations from the original languages were made into the vernacular languages of the world – translations done according to modern standards of scholarship.

The Vatican Council had encouraged ecumenical relations, and Catholic and Protestant biblical specialists started to work together on some of these translations, as well as on sensitive issues that divided the Churches (like the biblical presentation of Peter and of Mary). Academics from the different confessions began to teach on the others' university and seminary faculties, for Catholic biblical scholarship and middle-of-the-road Protestant scholarship could agree on the meaning of much of the Scriptures. Within a remarkably short time Catholic scholarly production had reached equality in the eyes of all.

Where are we today? Inevitably, there are both encouraging and discouraging factors. Fortunately, Catholic biblical scholarship has remained remarkably untroubled in its relationship to Church authority, and directives from Rome have remained positive. The decline in the number of Catholic clergy means that in the fore-seeable future lay biblical scholars will become a majority on the Catholic scene. That can be very helpful in terms of new endeavor and perspective, but some of them will not have the general background in theology and Church history given to priests in the seminary. There may be difficulties in combining the scientific and the pastoral aspects of scriptural presentation.

The general biblical scene is complicated. The historical analysis so prominent at the beginning of the nineteenth century has remained important, but new methods of analysis have come into prominence. Indeed, in 1993 the Pontifical Biblical Commission produced a documentary stressing how these approaches could be complementary – a salutary reaction to a tendency to make one or the other the only important way to read Scripture.

New discoveries have also produced mixed benefits. The Dead Sea Scrolls, uncovered in Palestine beginning in 1947, are very helpful in supplying information on the text of the Hebrew Bible, on noncanonical biblical books and on the theology of a group of Jews who flourished from the second century BC to the first century AD. The delay in publishing some fragments, however, has fueled bizarre conspiracy theories about the suppression of damaging facts and fantastic claims that Christian leaders are described figuratively in the scrolls.

In 1945 a library of Coptic documents stemming from the fourth century AD was discovered in Egypt. Many of them exhibit a Gnostic vein of thought regarded as heretical by the Church Fathers. Some were translated from earlier Greek originals, and a number of radical scholars would exalt them as more original than our canonical New Testament.

Radio and TV often complicate a balanced approach to such issues. On the one hand, particularly in the southern and south-western United States, fundamentalist and literalist preachers occupy a good deal of the media time defending the word-for-word historicity of the Bible and issuing predictions based on the misunderstanding that Daniel and Revelation are exact prophecies of the future. They reject much modern Catholic and centrist Protestant exegesis.

On the other hand, hypotheses based on little evidence (such as some of those promoted by the 'Jesus Seminar') propose extravagant reinterpretations of Christian origins and are presented in the media as the latest scholarship. It is difficult to find on the radio or TV a presentation of the centrist approach to Scripture, which is actually the most commonly taught and held. Fortunately, a good number of books, Catholic and Protestant, embody that approach.

Perhaps the most encouraging element in the present Catholic picture is the number of people interested in the Bible. One hundred years ago it was almost axiomatic that Catholics did not read the Bible; the twentieth century has changed that picture dramatically.

Appendix

'The Historical Truth of the Gospel' – Instruction of the Roman Pontifical Biblical Commission (1964)

Prefatory remarks

As explained above, the occasion for this *Instruction* was the defeat of a very conservative preliminary document on *The Sources of Divine Revelation* submitted to the Second Vatican Council in late 1962. That *schema* had been drawn up by forces in Rome hoping to repeal the biblical reforms of Pope Pius XII. After its defeat, a new drafting committee was commissioned. Their work was considerably facilitated by the issuance of this *Instruction* by Biblical Commission with the approval of Pope Paul VI. It is a long document, and I quote here only from the sections (VI–X) pertaining to the formation of the Gospels.

These sections correspond to the majority view of centrist scholars, Protestant as well as Catholic, about Gospel origins. (For the translation of the whole and a commentary by J.A. Fitzmyer, who himself has served on the Biblical Commission, see *Theological Studies* 25 [1964], pages 386–408, from which translation I have adapted below.) To facilitate finding one's way in my own discussion, I have added headings in italics and italicized certain key affimations.

The text of the instruction

V1,2: To judge properly concerning the reliability of what is transmitted in the Gospels, the interpreter should pay diligent attention to the three stages of tradition by which the doctrine and the life of Jesus have come down to us.

Stage One: the ministry of Jesus

VII: Christ our Lord joined to himself chosen disciples who followed him from the begining, saw his deeds, heard his words, and in this way were equipped to be witnesses of his life and doctrine. When the Lord was orally explaining his doctrine, *he followed the modes of reasoning and exposition that were in vogue at the time. He accommodated himself to the mentality of his listeners* and saw to it that what he taught was firmly impressed on the mind and easily remembered by the disciples. These men understood the miracles and other events of the life of Jesus correctly: as deeds performed or designed that people might believe in Christ through them, and embrace with faith the doctrine of salvation.

Stage two: the preaching of the apostles

VIII: The apostles proclaimed above all the death and resurrection of the Lord, as they bore witness to Jesus. They faithfully explained his life and words, while taking into account in their method of preaching the cirumstances in which their listeners found themsleves. *After Jesus rose from the dead and his divinity was clearly perceived,* faith, far from destroying the memory of what had transpired, rather confirmed it, because their faith rested on the things that Jesus did and taught. Nor was he changed into a 'mythical' person and his teaching deformed in consequences of the worship that the desciples from that time on paid Jesus as the Lord and the Son of God. On the other hand there is no reason to deny that *the apostles passed on to their listeners what was really said and done by the Lord with that fuller understanding that they enjoyed,* having been instructed by the glorious events of the Christ and taught by the light of the Spirit of Truth. And so just as Jesus himself after his resurrection 'interpreted to them' the words of the Old Testement as well as his own, *they too interpreted his words and deeds according to the needs of their listeners.* 'Devoting themselves to the ministry of the word', they preached and made use of the various modes of speaking that were suited to their own purpose and the mentality of their listeners. For they were debtors 'to Greeks and barbarians, to the wise and foolish'. But these modes of speaking with which the preachers proclaimed Christ must be distinguished and (properly) assessed: catecheses, stories, testimonia, hymns, doxologies, prayers – and other *literary forms* of this sort which were in Sacred Scripture and accustomed to be used by people of the time.

Stage three: the writing by the evangelists

IX: This primitive instruction, which was at first passed on by word of mouth and then in writing – for it soon happened that many tried 'to compile a narrative of things' that concerned the Lord Jesus – was committed to writing by the sacred authors in four Gospels for the benfit of the Churches, with a method suited to the particular purpose which each (author) set for himself. *From the many things handed down they selected some things, reduced others to a synthesis, (still) others they explicated as they kept in mind the situation of the Churches.* With every (possible) means they sought that their readers might become aware of the reliability of those words by which they had been instructed. Indeed, from what they had received the sacred writers above all selected the things that were suited to the various situations of the faithful and to the purpose. Since the meaning of a statement also depends on the sequence, the evangelists, in passing on the words and deeds of our Saviour, explained these now in one context, now in another, depending on (their) usefulness to the reader. Consequently, let the exegete seek out the meaning intended by the evangelist in narrating a saying or a deed in a certain way or in placing it in a certain context. *For the truth of the story is not at all affected by the fact that the evangelists relate the words and deeds of the Lord in a different order, and express his saying not literally but differently, while preserving (their) sense.* For, as St Augustine says, 'It is quite probable that each evangelist believed it to have been his duty to recount what he had to in order, whether it be this or that, detracts in nothing from the truth and authority of the Gospel. But why the Holy Spirit, who apportions individually to each one as He wills, and who therefore undoubtedly also governed and ruled the minds of the holy (writers) in recalling what they were to write because of the preeminent authority that the books were to enjoy, permitted one to compile his narrative in this way and another in that, anyone with pious diligence may seek the reason and with divine aid will be able to find it.'

X: Unless exegetes pay attention to all these things that pertain to the origin and composition of the Gospels and make proper use of all the laudable achievements of recent research, they will not fulfill their task of probing into what the sacred writers intended and what they really said. From the results of the new investigation it is apparent that *the doctrine and life of Jesus were not simply reported for the sole purpose of being remembered, but were 'preached' so as to offer the Church a basis of faith and morals.* The interpreter (them), by tirelessly scrutinizing the testimony of the evangelists, will be able to illustrate more profoundly the perennial theological value of the Gospel and bring out clearly how necessary and important the Church's interpretation is.

Chapter 2

Revelation (*Dei Verbum*)

Robert Murray SJ

Dei Verbum is theologically the most fundamental of the documents of Vatican II. Of the four Constitutions, only it and *Lumen Gentium* are called 'Dogmatic', indicating a more formal doctrinal authority. There are many important links between them, as also with the Constitution on the Liturgy. These three correspond most to the expectations and hopes previously voiced by bishops and theological faculties. The nature of the Church and its tradition were central to the unfinished business from Vatican I; Modernism and the Roman reaction to it had left serious questions about the inspiration and inerrancy of the Bible and about the development of doctrine; the Liturgical Movement was already revealing both the need for major pastoral renewal and a vision of what its fruits could be, not merely inside the Catholic Church but also in its ecumenical relations.

Of the four Constitutions, *Dei Verbum* is the most theologically concentrated; but in its wider relevance it both undergirds and touches most of the Council documents – obviously those on the Church and the liturgy, but also all those with a mainly pastoral thrust. This wider outreach makes the opening words, 'The Word of God', perhaps more arresting than the more technical title 'On Divine Revelation'. But if *Dei Verbum* is so important, has its influence been proportionately great? A number of factors make it a complex task to estimate the degree of success in twenty-five years. Before we can try, it will be helpful to recall the issues that were at stake, the aims of the Council in this document, and the main emphases in its teachings and recommendations.

The history of *Dei Verbum*, (abbreviated to DV throughout this chapter), as one of the focal points of tension and conflict between theological viewpoints at the Council, is well known. It was when the draft for a document on revelation was presented in November 1962 that the council really began to experience the creative polarization that was to shape its whole history. No other theme was more suited to bring this about. On one side were found churchmen set on defending the truth (seen in a mainly static and propositional way), on condemning error, and on protecting Catholics against ideas of development and change. The draft on revelation (and a companion, 'On preserving the deposit of faith in its purity', also rejected) were prepared mainly by theologians of this tendency, who had been brought up to think of modernism as the most fundamental, comprehensive and insidious of all heresies.

On the other side were many who voiced optimism and trust in the Holy Spirit rather than defensiveness, saw more need for encouragement than for condemnations, and were convinced that there was a new opportunity for liturgical and pastoral use of the Bible which must not be missed. Here there were probably more pastors than scholars, especially from the third world, but there was a significant number of biblical scholars and theologians who looked back on decades in which loyal Catholic scholars had been harassed and impeded by an obsessive witch hunt against Modernism. They were convinced that the Catholic Church needed a credible account of how God's word acts in history, from the first formulation in human language through the gradual process of understanding, under changing historical conditions and as the Holy Spirit gives new insights. After three years of redrafting and hard debate, a large majority in the Council was able to welcome a text reflecting both the ideas and the spirit of the more 'pastoral' tendency.

The main features and emphasis of Dei Verbum

The Prologue (DV 1) sets the tone for the whole document. In the Latin, 'the Word of God' stands first, as object of the Church's *listening* and then proclamation. The order is important. Only subordinate to this order are references to Trent and Vatican I tucked in, with the promise of doctrinal guidance on revelation and its transmission. This order of values in the Prologue is reflected in the whole Constitution.

Chapter 1, 'Divine Revelation Itself' (DV 2–6), maintains the note of proclamation in mainly biblical language, and only towards its end does it reaffirm teachings of Vatican I on the human response to God's self-revelation. Before this, however, important new emphases have appeared. The pregnant sentence 'The economy of Revelation is realized by deeds and words, which are intrinsically bound up with each other' (DV 2) challenges two basic 'conservative' positions: the fear of allowing historical development in our understanding of divine truth, and the theory of separate sources of revelation. History is not merely the theatre in which God's self-revelation becomes known, but is itself a mode of revelation. All understanding is guided by the Holy Spirit, whose manifold activity is emphasized (whereas the first draft had practically restricted it to biblical inspiration).

In chapter 2, 'The Transmission of Divine Revelation' (DV 7–10), the sense of historical revelation continues, with repeated emphasis on the Holy Spirit, in relation not only to the apostles but also to the Church as a whole. The teaching role of the bishops, as successors to the apostles, is described as a service to the whole Church. The faith is a living Tradition (in a comprehensive sense, made clearer by capital T). It grows and develops: all members play their part in this, as they feed their understanding of the revealed message by their 'contemplation and study' and by experience of 'spiritual realities' (DV 8; cf. *Lumen Gentium* 12 on the 'prophetic function' in the whole people of God). It is by this living and developing Tradition that the canon of Scripture is recognized and its inner power made actual for believers, guided by the Holy Spirit. This passage, the tone of which reminds one of Newman, goes far beyond the timid language of the first draft and its companion with its static view of the 'deposit'.

In this way the dispute about Scripture and Tradition as distinct sources of revelation can be resolved (DV 9). The insistence on separate sources had been an ill-judged reaction to the Reformation *Scriptura sola*; now, by viewing both Scripture and Tradition as dynamic realities, they can be seen as intimately connected, gifts of the one Spirit, in a way that satisfied not only almost all the Council's members, but even the Reformed observers (Schutz and Thurian, 1968, ch. 2). A final section (DV 10) describes how the Church holds, and is helped to interpret rightly, this single deposit of God's Word which is formed by Scripture and Tradition together. The ideal (expressed in words again reminiscent of Newman) is a harmonious consensus of the faithful and the bishops; but authority in interpretation of the Word of God is vested in the 'living teaching office' entrusted to the bishops. However, this is no autonomous authority; it 'is not superior to the Word of God, but is its servant', bound to listen to it and expound it faithfully (DV 10). This was well symbolized by the enthronement of the gospel book at the Council, though more could have been made of it. The responsibilities of *magisterium* remain an issue to which we shall return.

Chapters 3–5 deal in turn with the inspiration and interpretation of Scripture and with the two Testaments. These chapters are comparatively less weighty, and are perhaps most valuable for what they do not say, if we remember the pressure for definitions and anathemas. Chapter 3 (DV 11–13) deals quietly with two ancient *questions mal posées* that were still causing storms: the question of 'inspiration' (or how human authors wrote 'God's Word') and the 'inerrancy' (or how far everything they wrote must be God's truth). There is a touch of 'learned ignorance' about the disarmingly simple solutions proposed, but they succeeded in breaking the impasse. The treatment of the principles of interpretation (DV 12) reaffirms the teaching of Pius XII's encyclical *Divino Afflante Spiritu* (1943) – very necessarily, since it was still being attacked, even by an Italian cardinal, as late as 1961 (XR 1, pp. 54–5). *Dei Verbum* 12 may seem very elementary today, but it gave needed encourage-ment to long-suffering Catholic exegetes.

Chapter 4, on the Old Testament (DV 14–16), is the least substan-tial part of *Dei Verbum*; it mainly repeats traditional Christian formulas, with no sensitivity towards Judaism as is called for in *Nostra Aetate* 4. Chapter 5, on the New Testament (DV 17–20), like-wise partly consists of rather conventional summaries; but it does deal, firmly yet flexibly, with questions of the historicity of the Gospels, and agrees that the development of the Gospel tradition was influenced by oral transmission and preaching (for allowing which, responsible scholars had been accused of heresy). The tone is reassuring to conservative piety yet far from fundamentalism, and it pronounces neither censures nor warnings to inhibit scholarly research. Today this chapter may seem almost too anodyne to be significant, but it gave much-needed relief and encouragement to Catholic New Testament scholars (see Fitzmyer, 1982, pp. 97–142).

Chapter 6, on Scripture in the life of the Church (DV 21–6), develops the main intention expressed in the Prologue and outlines a pastoral policy for liturgy (21; cf. *Sacrosanctum Concilium* 7, 24, 35, 51–2, 92), and for provision of Bible translations (22, including by co-operation with other Christian Bible Societies) with encouragement to reading, study and meditation by every section of the Church (23–5). Watchfulness and guidance by the 'magisterium' are mentioned several times, but the condescending and protective tone of the first draft has happily gone.

After twenty-five years

The question was posed above: If *Dei Verbum* is so important, has its influence been proportionately great? In terms of continuing public notice and practical effectiveness, the truthful answer has to be 'no'. Perhaps too much of it is a text for skilled professionals. And yet, if we look for signs of the biblical revival that the Council wanted to awaken, in many ways and in many parts of the Catholic world the answer is indeed 'yes', and all the more so if we remember how much leeway there was to be made up in knowledge and use of the Bible by Catholics. It is not easy to survey the many areas in which there has been not only response to *Dei Verbum*, but also developments traceable to its influence, yet going far beyond what most of the Council's members could have foreseen. After looking at first reactions I shall sketch the main lines of theological comment and response, and then liturgical, practical and ecumenical developments; then some 'growing points' and problems in areas both of praxis and of theological reflection.

The promulgation of *Dei Verbum*, in November 1965, was welcomed with widespread enthusiasm by Catholics and other Christians alike. Catholic biblical scholars, theologians and many active lay groups had good reasons to be grateful. Among the 'observers', the Orthodox now had something more like their own teaching on Tradition than from any previous Western Council. Anglicans and Protestants now not only heard the first systematic teaching on the word of God in the Church ever formulated by a Catholic Council (for Trent had only dealt with particular points at issue with the Reformers), but also admired it. Most remarkable of all, Karl Barth, having been unable to serve as an observer, later published his reflections (1967, 1969), asking himself such questions as 'How would things look if Rome (without ceasing to be Rome) were one day simply to overtake us and place us in the shadows, so far as the renewing of the Church through the Word and Spirit of the gospel is concerned?' (Barth, 1969, p. 75).

Dei Verbum invited Catholics to see God's revelation and human response to it less in merely propositional terms, but more as dynamic operations guided by the Holy Spirit. For many seminary-trained churchmen this was a radical change in both direction and spirit after some eighty years of official censures and directives, which too often saw a danger of heresy whenever the human part in the dialogue of revelation and the development of doctrine were explored. (To appreciate the reorientation that was called for after this period, see Latourelle, 1968, pp. 207–309; on Tradition, see Congar, 1966, especially pp. 196–221; on the trials of biblical scholars, see Levie, 1961.) As the Council proceeded, theologians had a fair idea of what kind of text was coming, and were prepared to explain its teaching and its practical implications. Among the commentaries that appeared, several were by participants in the Council as members, *periti* or observers. Perhaps the most distinguished and rich in content is that edited by Alonso Schökel (1969). Though this is in Spanish, the contributors were international, reflecting the work of the Pontifical Biblical Institute in Rome. This volume goes far beyond mere commentary, but ranks with more systematic works on the theological areas dealt with in *Dei Verbum* which appeared in the 1960s. Theologians were constantly in demand to speak and write for a wide public which was eager to understand the Council's message and importance. (The scene was surveyed regularly in *Concilium*: during the years 1965–72, when its issues were arranged in volumes, the successive parts of volume 1 (Dogma) and volume 10 (Scripture) contain many valuable articles.)

What Karl Rahner achieved in those years can hardly be summarized (but see his *Foundations of Christian Faith*, 1978, ch. V). However, his former colleague, Hans Urs von Balthasar, though a comparable (but contrasting) giant in the theology of revelation, hardly took any part in the Council or in the subsequent work of exposition and discussion. Not that he was remote from the Council's concerns; his long-standing dialogue with Karl Barth makes him no exception to the keen and growing ecumenical awareness that characterizes almost all Catholic theological writing since the 1960s.

Out of many systematic works from this period we may select for mention two, both titled *Theology of Revelation*: that by Latourelle (1968), which is more historically based, and that by Moran (1967), which focuses more on the experience of revelations as personal communion. The various possible emphases in thinking about revelation are illuminatingly analysed by Dulles (1983), using the method of 'models' which he had previously applied to ecclesiology. On the other main themes of *Dei Verbum*, Congar's monumental *Tradition and Traditions* (1966), though finished before the end of the Council, remains unsurpassed. On the Bible as the word of God, the balance achieved by *Dei Verbum* is worked out in comprehensive works such as those by Grelot (1968) and L. Alonso Schökel (1967). Since the study by Vawter (1972), the old problems of inspiration and inerrancy have largely been given a rest by Catholic theologians; perhaps for sheer weariness and relief, but perhaps also because from the late 1960s many of them were theologizing in exciting new university contexts and learning the arcane language of philosophical hermeneutics.

The most fundamental aspects of the liturgical renewal for which the Council called are all related to the biblical element in liturgy and to making it more accessible to all in the vernacular: the enormous enrichment of the lectionary, the emphasis on preaching the Word that has been read, the revelation of how biblically based the Eucharistic prayers and other sacramental actions are, and the restoration of the 'divine office' as the 'prayer of the Church'. Huge tasks had to be undertaken, and much has been achieved. The readings and psalms in the vernacular (often helped by clearer new versions, on which see below) and the call for more biblical sermons have already brought appreciable changes in Catholic worship and attitudes. But there are continuing blockages and problems, many of them practical. In many large Churches, built to enable the greatest possible numbers to attend Sunday Mass, the circumstances of worship too often hinder an effective liturgy of the Word. In contrast, in smaller and more informal gatherings such as house Masses, the power this can release has often been experienced so impressively that one wonders whether the new liturgy was not given to the Church prophetically, with a view to new circumstances which were to come, but which till now have been realized only unevenly.

The reform of the lectionary, despite experiment and evaluation before the contents were fixed, has also left serious problems. One arises from the increase in the sheer quantity of texts to be read, heard and (ideally) expounded, some of them very difficult both for preachers and for their congregations. Too often, public readers are not trained, either in technique or in appreciation of their role, for this important ministry of mediating the power of the word.

The problem of unrenewed attitudes is most acute among older clergy trained before the Council. Besides insecurity, there is a theological cause due to an unbalanced view of the relationship of Word and sacrament. *Sacrosanctum Concilium* speaks of the presence of Christ both in the sacraments and in the liturgical reading of the Word (SC 7); *Dei Verbum* likewise speaks of 'the one table of the Word of God and the Body of Christ' (DV 21). Though this doctrine is patristic, some 'conservatives' at the Council saw a threat to faith in the Eucharistic real presence. This reveals a mentality for which the Word is metaphorical and therefore less 'real'. The truth is that *all* sacramental thinking and language are symbolic, and precisely thereby, they work in a way not weaker but actually stronger than the way the naïve realist calls 'real'. The Council was clearly implying that (as Newman saw) Scripture itself works *sacramentally*, especially when it is made actual by effective reading and preaching in the liturgy. Whenever the liturgy of the word remains formal and lifeless, it shows that these fundamental sacramental and liturgical principles have yet to be learnt (see Bianchi, 1987, pp. 120–2).

While training for preaching has happily improved since the Council, other factors have sadly hampered and slowed down the work of theological re-education. A tragic number of those best equipped to explain the Council's teaching retired from the clergy in the later 1960s and 1970s, and thereafter were disqualified from teaching as a ministry in the Church, though there is no moral justification for a general judgment that such persons become unworthy to teach. The right to preach within the Mass is jealously reserved to the clergy, whereas members of the laity often prove to be endowed with this charism. To see the biblical renewal of liturgy successful in Europe, one still has to seek out certain Churches. The greatest renewal is elsewhere.

The Council's encouragement in the field of Bible translation and inter-confessional co-operation (DV 22) has borne abundant fruit. The key figure here was Cardinal A. Bea, the veteran biblical scholar whose experience and contacts fitted him uniquely to head the Secretariat for Christian Unity, to develop sensitive relations with both Christians and Jews, to bring all this manifold competence to the redrafting of *Dei Verbum* and the production of *Nostra Aetate*, and to foster the desired biblical renewal both pastorally within the Church and by ecumenical co-operation. The World Catholic Federation for the Biblical Apostolate (WCFBA) was formed in 1969, both to co-ordinate Catholic projects and to be the appropriate organ to work in partnership with the United Bible Societies. This world-wide structure and partnership has developed remarkably. In many countries the Bible really has proved, as the Latin American bishops said at Puebla in 1979, 'the soul of evangelization' and of religious education. Ecumenical pooling of resources for translation work is now normal; in 1984, out of 590 translation projects in progress, 390 were inter-confessional involving Catholics. There is equally fruitful ecumenical co-operation in activities such as the production of aids to daily Bible reading.

The encouragement to Bible study in *Dei Verbum* (23–5) speaks in turn of scholarly work, of the training and spiritual formation of the clergy, and of reading by the laity. Though there has been good response to the first two areas, it is in the third that the brief hints in the text have been totally transcended through the amazing growth of lay groups meeting for prayer or study, representing various degrees of organization or none, some purely Catholic but most of them ecumenically open. The best-known developments of this kind are the 'basic ecclesial communities' in Latin America, but comparable movements have appeared in all continents, varying according to social structure and tradition. In these new communities Christians have developed their own way of listening to the Word and responding to it from their own situation. Typical methods are described by Mesters (1980, 1989) and discussed by Rowland (1988, pp. 130–5). The members may be without education, or able to use handbooks such as those of Abesamis in the Philippines (1988) or of Tamez in Costa Rica (1982). These communities were discussed by Pope Paul VI in *Evangelii Nuntiandi* 58 (1975; Flannery 2, pp. 738–40), appreciatively though with some warnings: there is a danger of manipulation of the Word through ideological pressure and too selective reading (cf. Bianchi, 1987, pp. 132–6); but the vitality of this movement surely surpasses all other responses to *Dei Verbum*.

The Council's message to those engaged in biblical and theological research was encouraging and trustful. In this atmosphere Catholic scholarship has flourished, increasingly in an ecumenical setting and moving in directions not yet envisaged by *Dei Verbum*. Its chapter (4) on the Old Testament reflected the 'biblical theology' of the 1950s and the patristic viewpoint as enshrined in the liturgy. Catholic teachers turned with new confidence to biblical criticism, but by the 1980s many of its presuppositions were being questioned and its power to generate real understanding doubted. The ideal of 'listening to the text' and allowing different possible 'readings' has come to the fore, helped by a new appreciation of Jewish exegesis, often through joint study with Jews (as was recommended in *Nostra Aetate* 4), and by refreshing contributions from students of other literatures. This 'new look' need not, of course, exclude older interpretations; but it may well rejuvenate preaching.

New Testament studies have flowered to an extent too rich to summarize; let one work stand for all: Brown's magisterial commentary on the Fourth Gospel (1971). The relationship of Christology to New Testament study has remained a crucial area of study and debate. A useful contribution to this, entitled *Scripture and Christology*, appeared in 1984 from the Pontifical Biblical Commission in its new character since its reconstitution in 1971. This text, without carrying official papal authority, truly maintains the spirit of *Dei Verbum*. It surveys eleven contemporary approaches, evaluating them fairly and positively sketching the *desiderata* for an integral Christology (see Fitzmyer, 1986).

This document is significant not only for New Testament studies. In the ecclesiological context of *Dei Verbum* 10, it represents an exemplary exercise of magisterium as the ministry of teaching in the Church. This term always had this broader sense until, in the mid-nineteenth century, it began to have a capital M and a personified sense restricted to the episcopate, or more often just the papacy, as holders of teaching authority (see Congar, 1976; Hill, 1988, pp. 75–88). *Dei Verbum* 10 describes the magisterium as subordinate to the Word, but follows this with a problematic image of Scripture, Tradition and the Magisterium as a kind of trinity. The propriety of this depends on how inclusively or exclusively magisterium is being used. The third member is only commensurate with the two modes of revelation if it means a charism, constantly in action throughout the Church, guiding true understanding and teaching it. It is always to be hoped that this charism will be active in popes and bishops, but it is not, nor can it be, reduced solely to their authority. The more inclusive, 'small m' sense of magisterium has the main weight both of history and of Tradition behind it, and it is in this direction that the most vital movements in the Church – especially the increasing witness of women – are developing (cf. Metz and Schillebeeckx, 1985).

In the open intellectual milieu where Catholic exegetes and theologians now move among colleagues or other traditions of faith or of none, the traditional term 'hermeneutics' (the art and the principles of interpretation) has been taken over for a mode of philosophical discussion so technical that its products are usually baffling even to a well-educated reader. This is a tragedy, for biblical hermeneutics concerns the problems facing any ordinary person who wants to find meaning in texts coming from a remote past, and to understand in what sense they can be 'the Word of God'. The traditional doctrines of 'inspiration' and 'inerrancy' were posed in terms and actually added to the problems. Yet they were attempts to answer real questions, and not simply for fundamentalists. There is a ministry here that theologians and biblical scholars owe to the Church, to develop a hermeneutics more widely accessible to ordinary intelligent people today. This is done outstandingly by Mesters (1989).

One other critical feature of the present situation for maintaining the ministry of the word should be mentioned: it concerns the study of the biblical languages (Hebrew, Aramaic and Greek) and those of the classical ancient versions, at a level sufficient to assure that there will be enough scholars able to serve as fully competent exegetes and, therefore, as active tradents of Tradition. The primacy of classical studies in their chief base (Europe) came to an end about the middle of this century. What was a broadly based culture has become a field of specialization. This must be a matter of serious concern for the Church. Training scholars will not physically feed the hungry, but failing to train enough of them will mean clogging the springs from which we drink.

After twenty-five years we can indeed see much response to *Dei Verbum*, but it is still limited. Bishops at the Synod of 1985 and Pope John Paul II himself in 1986 complained that the message has not yet been heard. In 1984 the WCFBA Plenary Assembly asked for a Synod entirely on the biblical apostolate in the Church. The desired agenda would include the relation between the Word and the Eucharist; the liberating power of the Word of God; the Bible and the laity; the various ministries of the Word and their relation to exegesis; the danger of fundamentalism; the Bible and ecumenism; inculturation of the Word of God; the Bible and other sacred scriptures. This summary list indicates the amount of work still to be done.

Note
In 1989 the WCFBA was renamed more simple the Catholic Biblical Federation (CBF).

Bibliography
Abesamis, C. H. (1988) *A Third Look at Jesus*. Quezon City, Philippines, Claretian Publications.
Barth, K. (1969) *Ad Limina Apostolorum* (1967). Edinburgh, St. Andrew Press.
Bianchi, E. (1987) 'The Centrality of the Word of God', in G. Alberigo and J-P Jossua, pp. 115–36, *The Reception of Vatican II*. London, Burns & Oates.
Brown, R. E. (1971) *The Gospel According to John*. Garden City, NY, Doubleday, 1966; London, Geoffrey Chapman.
Congar, Y. (1966) *Tradition and Traditions*. London, Burns & Oates.
Congar, Y. (1976) 'Pour une histoire sémantique du terme magisterium', RSPT, vol. 60, pp. 85–98.
De Maio, R. (1963) *The Book of the Gospels at the Oecumenical Councils*. Vatican City.
Dodd, C. (1989) *Making Scripture Work: a practical guide to using Scripture in the local Church*. London, Geoffrey Chapman.
Dulles, A. (1983) *Models of Revelation*. Dublin, Gill & Macmillan.

Flannery OP, A. (1975) *Vatican Council II: The Conciliar and Post-Conciliar Documents.* New York, Costello Publishing Company: Dublin, Dominican Publications.

Fitzmyer, J. A. (1982) *A Christological Catechism.* New York, Paulist Press.

Fitzmyer, J. A. (1986) *Scripture and Christology.* New York, Paulist Press; London, Geoffrey Chapman.

Grelot, P. (1968) *The Bible, Word of God* (1965). New York, Desclee.

Hill, E. (1988) *Ministry and Authority in the Catholic Church.* London, Geoffrey Chapman.

Latourelle, R. (1968) *Theology of Revelation.* Cork, Mercier.

Levie, J. (1961) *The Bible, Word of God in Words of Men* (1958). London, Geoffrey Chapman.

Mesters, C. (1980) 'How the Bible Is Interpreted in Some Basic Christian Communities in Brazil', *Concilium,* no. 138, pp. 41–6.

Mesters, C. (1989) *Defenseless Flower: A New Reading of the Bible* (1983) Maryknoll, NY, Orbis Books; London, CIIR.

Metz, J. B. and Schillebeeckx, E., eds. (1985) 'The Teaching Authority of Believers,' *Concilium,* no. 180.

Moran, G. (1967) *Theology and Revelation.* London, Burns & Oates.

Rahner, K. (1978) *Foundations of Christian Faith.* London, Darton, Longman and Todd.

Rowland, C. (1988) *Radical Christianity.* Cambridge, Polity Press.

Schökel, L. Alonso (1967) *The Inspired Word.* London, Burns & Oates.

Schökel, L. Alonso ed. (1969) *Concilio Vaticano II: Comentarios a la Constitución Dei Verbum.* Madrid, BAC.

Schutz, R. and Thurian, M. (1968) *Revelation: A Protestant View (La parole vivante au Concile,* 1966). Philadelphia, Westminster.

Tamez, E. (1982) *Bible of the Oppressed* (1979). Maryknoll, New York, Orbis Books.

Vawter, B. (1972) *Biblical Inspiration.* Philadelphia, Westminster; London, Hutchinson.

Chapter 3

Historical-Critical Exegesis of the Bible in Roman Catholicism

Raymond E. Brown SS

Both elements in the designation 'historical-critical' are important. Although it may seem obvious that one must deal seriously with *historical* factors involved in the Scriptures, an intensive historical approach is really a recent phenomenon. That the Bible is inspired with God as its author had seemed previously to make irrelevant such historical questions as: Was a given biblical book written at one time and by one author? What traditions or sources did the human author(s) draw upon? What was the author's background and point of view? What were the problems of his time and community, and how did they affect his work? Does his message agree with that of other biblical authors? Have there been additions and even corrections added since the principal author first wrote?

Still more recent is the concept that various types of '*criticism*' or analysis might help to understand the biblical book, even aside from historical questions. These would include an analysis of a book in terms of its form(s) or genre(s) or type(s) of literature – each form has its own patterns which give us probabilities in determining how a particular piece of literature developed and should be interpreted. A knowledge of how literary features function in narration, poetry, drama, etc., is useful, as is a close study of overall structure in a work. With composite works, the signs of disparate material help to show the history of composition. In studying various forms of the text of a biblical book, one must know something about the patterns of scribal copying – a copying that influenced the transmission of the text from the time it was written to our extant manuscripts. All these aspects of 'criticism' affect how we read biblical books composed 2000 to 3000 years ago; and their implications are not to be easily dismissed even by someone who says, 'I read the Scriptures simply to let God speak to me.' Inevitably that reader will pose questions to the Scriptures, and both the questions that are posed and the answers that are found will be shaped by the time in which the reader lives. Every reader today, no matter how professedly 'simple', is consciously or unconsciously shaped by attitudes reflecting a critical sense – the critical sense by which we judge all that is communicated by modern media. Assumptions about historicity or science *will* be made by a reader who has any form of general education; and a basic grasp of what is involved in 'the historical-critical' reading of the Scriptures will prevent the assumptions or presuppositions from being naïve.

In a sense, historical criticism was developed through the recognition that the biblical accounts describe things that 'ain't necessarily so'. By the late 1600s the French scholar Richard Simon was pointing out that Moses was not the author of the whole Pentateuch; this led to the recognition of differences in the accounts of genesis of the world, of the human race, and of Israel. By the late 1700s differences among the Gospels were leading to the realization that Jesus in his lifetime was in some degree different from the full-blown scriptural portraits of him. Unfortunately, a tinge of skepticism and even of rationalism marred the work of many earlier historical critics who reduced the Bible to a fallible account of primitive religious beliefs. Thus a major issue has been the debate about how historical criticism is reconcilable with and even beneficial to a faith stance in which the Bible is venerated as the inspired word of God.

Roman Catholicism came to grips with this problem more slowly than some of the Protestant Churches but has now approved historical criticism more officially than almost any other Church. The first hesitant step was taken by Pope Leo XIII in 1893 who, although seeing dangers in the 'higher criticism' of his era, recognized that the biblical authors had the scientific vocabulary and outlook of primitive times and so could not be easily invoked in the modern debates about science – a statement with obvious implications for the whole creation/evolution discussion.[1] Much change in Church thinking occurred in the next 75 years before Pope Paul VI in 1968 could firmly laud critical scholars of the Bible: 'It is your honour that you dedicate yourselves in a professional and scientific way to employ all the means given you by modern technology in the literary, historical, and archaeological fields, and to use them

---

[1]   Encyclical *Providentissimus Deus* (RSS #122; DBS #3289).

in order to increase our knowledge.'[2] The history of this change in ecclesiastical outlook has been narrated many times,[3] but for the purposes of this chapter and this book let me concentrate on *the two basic steps* taken by Rome that led Catholicism away from a literalism or fundamentalism about everything described in the Bible. These two steps made it official Church teaching that the whole Bible is not history and the Gospels are not necessarily literal accounts of the ministry of Jesus.

The first step was made in the 1943 encyclical of Pope Pius XII, *Divino Afflante Spiritu*, with its insistence that there are different literary 'forms' in the Bible.[4] The Bible may be said to be a library (of Israel and of the Church);[5] so that historical writing is only one part of the larger collection which includes poetry, drama, epic, parable, preaching, etc. This principle has implications for the factual questions which will surely be asked by inquisitive minds: Was Jonah really swallowed by a large fish? Were there magi who came from the East to Jerusalem because they saw a star that symbolized the birth of the King of the Jews? One cannot answer such questions simply by saying: 'Yes, that is what the Bible says.' Nor can one answer such questions by stressing inspiration. The issue is whether the inspired section of the Bible that reports such an event is inspired parable, or inspired history, or a type of inspired literature that lies between history and imaginative presentation. The determination of history in the Bible, like the determination of history in other ancient literature and libraries, thus becomes a much more complex task.

Even after the guidance laid down by Pius XII another step needed to be taken, for the historical truth of the Gospels remained a particularly sensitive issue. Under Pope Paul VI in 1964 the Roman Pontifical Biblical Commission tackled that problem with a subtle answer, replete with implicit and explicit qualifications.[6] The basic thrust of the response is that, while the Gospels are substantially historical, they are not literally historical in every word and detail. Before being written down, the Gospel material passed through three stages of development which thoroughly modified it: (1) Jesus did and said things (2) which eyewitness

---

[2] Address to OT experts on April 19, 1968 (OCTBI #993).
[3] Article 'Church Pronouncements' in JBC 72:3–9.
[4] Paragraphs 35-39 (RSS #558–60).
[5] Vatican Library address of Pope Paul VI on March 25, 1972: 'The Bible is not just a book; it is a library in itself, a set of books of every different literary genre' (OCTBI #1036).
[6] The crucial section of the document may be found in BRCFC pp. 111–15.

disciples later incorporated into their preaching, and (3) still later this preaching became the source of the writers who gave us the Gospels.

Each stage in this process had its own goal and its own modality. *First*, Jesus himself spoke and acted in the context of his own place and time. I have often sought to express this concretely by insisting that people take seriously that Jesus was a Palestinian Jew of the first third of the first century – a limitation that curiously seems to offend some. *Second*, the apostles adapted Jesus' message to the people of their time (the second third of the first century), an adaptation involving translation into another language (Greek) and an effort at comprehensibility in other circumstances (the large cities of the Roman Empire). Moreover, they brought to the memories of what Jesus had said and done the transforming enlightenment of their post-resurrectional faith in Jesus. *Third*, from the preaching the writers or evangelists (who may have been composing their works 10 to 30 years apart in different areas) selected stories and sayings that fitted their purpose in presenting Jesus to audiences of their time (the last third of the first century, for most scholars). Accordingly, they reorganized the material so that often it was presented more logically than chronologically; and they expanded it through necessary clarifications. None of this development need be seen as a distortion if it be remembered that the Gospels were not written simply as records to aid remembrance but as encouragements to belief and life. The historicity of the Gospels, then, is that of preaching, faithfully transmitting a message.

This explicit teaching of the 1964 Biblical Commission document, which in a brave but positive way affirmed that the Gospels are not necessarily literal accounts, had two implicit corollaries that have often been missed. Although the document refers to the Gospels as a whole, it is clear on careful reading that those who composed it were thinking only of that part of Jesus' activity for which the apostolic preachers were witnesses, namely, the public ministry from the baptism to the resurrection. That the historicity of the narratives of Jesus' birth and infancy was another matter was understood by the Biblical Commission which planned but never completed a further study. The historicity of the infancy narratives has remained a debated subject among Catholic scholars, but occasionally one encounters a naïve attempt to solve it on the basis of the 1964 statement which dealt with a section of the Gospels for which much clearer witness was assured. Secondly, although the Biblical Commission's statement (and the Vatican II document on

Divine Revelation which used the Commission's statement as a guide) allows continued respect for the ancient terminology of 'apostles and apostolic men' in reference to the Gospel writers, the Commission made a clear distinction between the apostles who preached and those who wrote the Gospels in dependency on that preaching. Implicitly, then, the Commission allowed for the view of most scholars today that no one of the evangelists was an eyewitness of the ministry of Jesus. Rather the evangelists were 'second-generation' Christians drawing their knowledge from the earlier apostolic generation that had seen him and had shaped the tradition. This clarification does not undermine the value of the Gospels but explains their wide variations in reporting sequence and locations for which the evangelists had no personal remembrance. (By way of example, if the evangelists were not apostolic eyewitnesses, it is far easier to explain how Matthew's Gospel could report the cleansing of the Temple at the end of the ministry and John's Gospel report it at the very beginning.)

These developments in the Catholic approach to Bible historicity have beneficially effected an intelligent understanding of the Scriptures. Much less time and effort has been wasted on fundamentalist attempt to defend every detail and to explain away every historical difficulty. More attention has been given to the purpose of the author, and a greater realism has marked our understanding of how Christianity grew and adapted to challenges. Of course, with a departure from absolute historicity, there is always the danger of moving too far in the other direction of minimalizing historical content. Yet relatively little of that has occurred among Catholic biblical scholars. Having found Church authority a help in changing previous positions, they were not 'angry young men' launching out on a crusade to overthrow. The best-known Catholic NT scholars in the world today would be regarded as moderates or centrists by their Protestant colleagues (who would have practical knowledge of radicalism and would be able to detect it).

Hostility toward historical criticism

Granted these facts of Church support and of caution shown by Catholic biblical scholars, one may well be puzzled by occasional references to historical criticism as barren, passé, and wrong, at times accompanied by the glib assertion that the historical-critical approach is now questioned by 'many scholars'. With the understanding that the term 'revisionism' can describe an effort to prove that the majority view of an issue is wrong, let me examine the various motives behind the revisionist attempts directed against the historical-critical method that is so widely attested in Catholic scholarship today. I shall separate the revisionists who reject or challenge historical-critical exegesis into two major groups.

I Revisionists of a literalist or fundamentalist tendency

(1) Those who are annoyed by biblical criticism because it underlines the human elements in the Bible, i.e., that the biblical books were written at a particular time, under particular circumstances, and in histor-ically-conditioned language and outlook. As pointed out above, this issue is the heart of the whole historical approach to the Scriptures. Rejection of historical criticism on this core reflects a fear that biblical critics detract from the divine authority of the Bible. If the rationalist originators of historical criticism did not respect sufficiently the 'of God' element in the Bible, the literalist rejectors of historical criticism do not respect sufficiently the fact that human beings spoke and wrote the 'word' element of the Bible. I would maintain, however, that the weakening of either element in the 'word of God' destroys the essential two-fold char-acter of the Scriptures.[7]

Most Catholic readers of the Bible have had little training in this whole question of criticism. Because in the past the Bible has been very conservatively treated in the Catholic Church and because of the influence from media fundamentalist preaching, they will tend to assume that everything described in the Bible actually happened. The first step in education may be the insistence that it is now perfectly correct within Catholic teaching to recognize that not everything in the Bible is historical.

Another step is to acquaint Catholic readers with the rationale behind the historical-critical questions that scholars ask, especially if those questions are *prima facie* disturbing. There is no way to prevent ordinary people from becoming aware of the kinds of questions that are being asked in scholarship today; for, whether the scholars consent or not, their views are picked up by the media and often sensationalized. The instinctive reaction of many Catholics will be annoyance at the presumption of the scholars unless somehow they can see that scholarly probing is approved by

---

[7] See a discussion of this in 'The Human Word of the Almighty God', CMB pp. 1–22.

the official Church and is not threatening to faith. For instance, scholars have asked whether a star really shone in the East to reveal to magi the birth of the King of the Jews, a star that came to rest over a house in Bethlehem. One must consider whether such questioners are rationalistically denying the miraculous or simply examining whether the infancy narrative of Matthew necessarily belongs to the same category of developed eyewitness tradition that is involved in Matthew's account of the public ministry. A decision that the infancy narrative belongs to some other literary form which allows a freer use of OT symbolism may cause the scholar to think that the star need not be a historical phenomenon. The decision is not a matter of rationalism and lies perfectly within the lines of investigation encouraged by Church authority.

Inevitably, it will be objected that such a historical-critical approach takes away from the absolute authority of the Bible. But Roman Catholics have traditionally insisted that biblical authority comes to expression in the context of the believing and teaching Church. Some Catholic defenders of biblical literalism would impose attitudes more often associated with ultraconservative Protestants who deny the need for an interpreting Church. If everything in the Bible is not necessarily historical, Catholics are *not* left without the guidance of the Church as to what they must believe. This last observation brings me to a second type of literalist revisionist.

(2) Those who claim historical-critical exegesis leads to a denial of Catholic dogmas. 'Fundamentalism' is a term that had its origins among Protestants who saw biblical literalism as the only way to preserve certain fundamentals of the Christian faith, and some Catholics continue to promote literalism for the same reason. Let me make three observations in reference to this issue. *First,* in Catholicism dogma expresses divine revelation as interpreted by the teaching Church. Therefore, it is perfectly possible to claim that the Bible, historically-critically considered, does not offer sufficient proof for a doctrine and still think the dogma must be accepted as infallibly taught because of Church tradition. Sometimes such an approach has been dismissed as fideism. It would be fideism if one held that the Church teaching was to be maintained even though the biblical evidence denied the dogma, or if there was no intelligible argument for a position of the Church which goes beyond the biblical evidence. But in the examples I am thinking of, Catholic exegetes are not suggesting that the limited biblical evidence contradicts Church dogma or that the Church has no reason for

going beyond the biblical evidence. They are simply placing the responsibility for the dogma where it belongs, not in the Scriptures, but in the complementary developments of subsequent Church tradition – developments that stem from reflection upon the Scriptures in context of Church life. Nothing in these remarks suggests a theory of '*two* sources of revelation': the basic witness of the Christian revelation is the tradition of the Church, but NT Scripture represents only the first-century phase of that tradition.

Second, one must be precise about what is Catholic dogma and what is popular understanding of that dogma. In other words, one must distinguish between a nuanced and a naïve presentation of the dogma. It is now official Catholic teaching (*Mysterium Ecclesiae* [1973]) that frequently doctrine has been phrased in 'the change-able conceptions of a given epoch' and that one must distinguish between the truth infallibly taught and the way that truth has been phrased.[8] I would maintain that there is *no irreconcilable conflict* between the results of Catholic historical-critical exegesis and a nuanced understanding of Catholic dogma. Rather, literalists who attack such exegesis as undermining the faith are often identifying the dogma with their own naïve understanding of it. For instance, there is a Catholic dogma about God's creating the world, in the sense of God's bringing the world into being by His absolute power; but there is no Catholic dogma about how creation took place, or how long it took. There is a Catholic dogma that bishops are the successors of the apostles, in the sense that the pastoral care of the Churches once exercised by the apostles ultimately passed into the hands of the bishops; but there is no Catholic dogma that the Twelve Apostles laid hands on immediate succes-sors appointing one bishop in each Church. Many more examples of the distinction between nuanced and naïve understandings could be offered; and in each of them it would be the naïve under-standing, which is not really part of the dogma, that is being challenged by historical-critical exegesis.

Third, one must be very accurate in reporting the precise results of Catholic historical-critical exegesis. I think I have a reasonably good grasp of what the best-known NT exegetes propose in refer-ence to the virginal conception of Jesus, the bodily resurrection, the divinity of Jesus Christ, Christ's founding the Church and insti-tuting the sacraments, the position of Peter in reference to the later papacy, etc. In no instance do *most* Catholic historical-critical exegetes contradict Catholic dogma properly understood. I do not

---

[8] The crucial section of this document may be found in BRCFC pp. 116–18.

mean that there is not an occasional Catholic NT exegete, for instance, who denies the virginal conception or the bodily resurrection. I judge, however, that this is a minority view, to be traced not to historical-critical exegesis as such but to one person's practice of that exegesis – a practice that I regard as incorrect. I do not mean that there are not Catholic systematic theologians who deny Church dogmas, citing historical-critical exegesis as support for their position. In such instances, however, one must be very careful to ascertain whether they cite *Catholic* exegetes and cite them *correctly*. Conservative critics may wish to hold Catholic exegetes responsible for the misuse of their exegesis by others, but that is pure nonsense: the misuse of a discipline never vitiates the discipline.

If one takes into account the three points I have just made, one will realize that the underlying dislike of historical-critical exegesis in this type of revisionism is related to the effect that such exegesis has in making one rethink Catholic dogma, as to what is the core of the dogma and what is the time-conditioned expression of it. That rethinking produces uneasiness on either end of the Catholic spectrum. Historical criticism should not be made to pay the price for those who have their own axes to grind.

II. Revisionists for hermeneutical purposes

There is a type of revisionist who does not espouse a fundamentalist or literalist approach either to the Bible or to doctrine, but who has another set of interests in relation to the Bible, interest to which historical criticism may seem an obstacle. Once again, there are subdivisions:

(a) *Those who have found biblical criticism barren,* providing little results for spirituality, preaching, or theology. Protest is sometimes raised against a biblical criticism that is totally immersed in recondite historical questions or in attributing verses to sources so that it overlooks the living word of God. A more nuanced evaluation faults biblical criticism because its practitioners make no relationship between their research and theology or Church life. Yet, in point of fact, today historical critics often do *not* confine their overall studies (as distinct from highly specialized articles or monographs, which remain essential) to source analysis or to nontheological interpretation of the text. Increasingly, commentaries and topical works written by exegetes seek to understand the

whole world of thought (historical, comparative, ideological, sociological, religious) that comes to light in the biblical text.
Stereotypes of biblical criticism, based on rationalist efforts of the
19th century, are increasingly unfair; for historical critics do not do
their duty if in interpreting a religious text they do not show what
it meant religiously to those who wrote and read it. True, theological categories discovered by biblical critics may not be the same as
those of systematic theologians, but the proper relationship
between the discoveries of the biblical critic and the world of the
systematic theologians is often between two different theological
interests rather than between the nontheological and the theological. Surely, more needs to be done in discovering how these two
different theological domains, biblical and systematic, are related;
but there is far less cause for despairing that the twain will never
meet.

Thus the overall charge that historical criticism is barren is over-
done; and the proper remedy for whatever truth there may be in
the charge is to join to historical criticism spiritual concerns, theological interests, and indications on how to preach from the Bible.
No one with a proper sense of hermeneutics claims that historical
criticism is the only or the total approach to the Bible. It is an even
greater exaggeration, however, to claim that spiritual, theological,
and preaching interests can dispense with the contributions of
historical criticism – that attitude creates the danger of building
castles in the air. Above all, historical questions must be answered
by historical means. The biblical opinions of Church Fathers or
spiritual writers are extremely valuable to the development of
overall Catholic thought; but unless those writers had historical
information they cannot answer historical questions. The effort of
a few in their rhetorical overkill to demean historical criticism
because it is not all-sufficient represents a danger of the recrudes-
cence of the disdain for the historical that has too often marked
theoretical thought.

(b) Literary critics who insist that biblical works, once written, have a life
of their own, so that questions of sources, author's intention, and
community setting become irrelevant. Similar reactions may come
from the advocates of structuralism or semiotics more concerned
with the inner structure of the text than with the author's background. A type of revisionism related to such interests might
ignore historical questions as totally useless to interpretation.

Here less arrogance is necessary on both sides of the question.
Many historical critics understand well that their work grasps only

part of the meaning of the text, precisely because that text has its own identity as a body of literature and as a section of the larger canon of Scripture. I stressed this strongly in CMB (especially pp. 23–24) even as I was ardently defending the importance of biblical criticism. There I insisted that hermeneutics or the discovery of biblical meaning goes beyond historical criticism and that the historical critic has no reason to denigrate the importance of contributions from other forms of hermeneutical investigation. But on the opposite side, the advocates of other types of biblical criticism (literary criticism, narrative criticism, rhetorical criticism, structuralism, etc.), despite their enthusiasm at the novel insights gathered by their methodologies, should also learn modesty. Too often a new approach is hailed as dispensing with all that has gone before instead of adding to what has gone before. No matter what import these other approaches may have, there is *one question that will always be fundamental*: What was the biblical author trying consciously to communicate to his readers and how did those readers grasp what he wrote? Obviously we have only limited means to discover that, but any approach which ignores it wanders too far from our basic criteria of meaning.

In this light I want to add a particular comment about 'canonical criticism', particularly as phrased recently by B. S. Childs.[9] This criticism involves a recognition that the NT books as they left the quill of their authors did not stop their theological journey. The canon is the normative collection of Scriptures, which in the case of the NT reached its most widely accepted form in the 4th century. The canonical process may be seen as the collecting, ordering, and transmitting of the tradition which had been phased in first-century writings in such a way as to enable that tradition to function as Sacred Scripture for a community of faith and practice (Childs, 25). The process was not uniform or unilinear, but involved a basic continuity between the early stages of NT formation and the effecting of an authoritative collection. It loosened the individual texts that constitute the NT from their first-century

---

[9] *The New Testament as Canon: An Introduction* (Philadelphia: Fortress, 1985). Childs is wide-swinging in his critique of contemporary NT exegetes. Theorists (and abstract critics) of hermeneutical method should be forced to write a substantial commentary or an individual biblical book, so that by their fruits, and not by their theory, they can be judged. Few are as brave as Childs in doing this. Others can evaluate the OT commentary he produced (and that is his field of expertise); his suggestions about the NT are often so lopsided that they could produce commentaries with insufficient relation to what the biblical author intended.

historical setting and enabled them to address every future believer – a reinterpretation for new situations that involved considerable freedom (Childs, 23). This means that paradoxically 'the witness of Jesus Christ has been given its normative shape through an interpretative process of the post-Apostolic age' (Childs, 28). All this I agree with, having written myself strongly in the same direction in CMB pp. 23–44. *Biblical* hermeneutics or the search for the meaning of the *Scriptures* cannot be content with the literal sense (the meaning that the book had when it was first composed); it must look to the meaning that the book had when it became scriptural or part of the Bible, i.e., part of the canon.

Nevertheless, the issue remains about the role given to a search for the literal sense in such a large hermeneutical process, a search that heavily involves historical criticism. Theoretically Childs does not deny the importance of historical criticism; it is 'here to stay' (Childs, 45). Practically, however, in his evaluation of NT exegetical commentaries, Childs decries any priority given to the literal sense and deplores the attempt to distinguish between the literal and canonical levels of meaning pertinent to the Bible. Thus, for instance, in Childs' view the historical situation faced by the author of I John becomes totally subordinate to the fact that the Church has read this letter as a universal or catholic epistle to all Christians (Childs, 487). The search for canonical meaning becomes almost the sole goal of the interpreter. I agree that the canonical meaning of Scripture is more normative for Christian living; but the biblical scholar (in a role distinct from the role of Church preacher and teacher) must uncover the literal sense in order that the ancient dialogue which took place in the canon-forming process – the dialogue between the particularistic first-century meaning and the more universalistic later meaning – may remain open. Through the universalizing thrust of the canonical process, the Scriptures became 'a living vehicle through which the Lord of the Church continued to address his people' (Childs, 29). But how do we stop the Church insight from being frozen when the canon was substantially formed (4th century) or at any other moment, thus terminating the dialogue? How do we make certain that the Scriptures remain 'a word from the ever-present Saviour', and not the Church talking to itself? And since the NT text of this 'word' was written in the first century, how do we stop a Church interpretation from becoming so free that really another 'word' has been substituted and the continuity of the process broken? Historical-critical exegesis in its quest for the literal sense is an ally in preventing such abuses. It does not give us the normative sense of

Scripture but challenges the Church by its discoveries (which change and grow as the techniques of investigation improve). The literal sense serves as an obstacle toward substituting a self-composed word for the word given so long ago. Childs (47) agrees with me that the essence of canon is a fundamental dialectic between what a text meant and what it means. Alas, by sending the exegete almost exclusively to search for the canonical meaning, he tends to obliterate the importance and distinctiveness of the literal level uncovered by historical exegesis. In his method, what it meant will soon no longer be able to speak to what it means.

My final word, then, in reference to the importance of other forms of criticism is the insistence that historical criticism must be allowed to make its major contribution toward answering the question of biblical meaning. The maxim of Pope Pius XII (*Divino Afflante Spiritu* 23 [RSS 550]) remains valid: 'Let the interpreters bear in mind that their foremost and greatest endeavor should be to discern and define clearly that sense of the biblical words which is called literal.'

(c) *Those who seek to use Scripture in support of a cause.* Sometimes advocates of particular causes can be quite vituperative about historical criticism as distracting from a hermeneutic or principle of interpretation more relevant to the cause they are advocating. Liberation theologians often think that the issue of the oppressed and poor is the only optic through which Scriptures may be read; accordingly, they may look on the majority of exegetes as remote from the real issue of the Third World and as oppressors who are depriving the readers of the Bible of a cutting tool for societal change. Feminists may argue that historical-critical exegesis is an instrument of a patriarchal scholarship insensitive to the women's movement. There have been Marxist interpretations of Scripture – again, quite different from the results of historical-critical exegesis.

A modern issue may well raise important questions that have been neglected in previous exegesis and thus enrich scholarship. For instance, when biblical scholars are asked to study about the oppressed, or about women, they sometimes discover in the text aspects previously overlooked. Often, historical-critical study is an effective tool in working out such new insights, so that there need be no contradiction between this form of exegesis and 'relevant' issues. On the other hand, a monolithic attempt to make the Scripture serve one modern cause may easily become counterproductive and lead to a distorted exegesis, i.e., reading things into the text. Rightly, complaints have been raised against an older proof-text optic whereby a doctrine became the eyeglass through which Scriptures were read, and passages were sought out that might be ingeniously interpreted in support of that doctrine, no matter what the original author meant. Prooftexting in support of modern causes is just as one-sided; and historical-critical exegesis may be a healthy antidote in reminding us that the biblical authors were often ignorant of, or uninterested in, issues that seem important to us. That does not make those issues less important, but it sets them in the context of history. If some issues that mattered to Paul or Matthew (like the Jew–Gentile conversion matter) seem irrelevant to us today (even when interpreted intelligently as to their underlying significance), that may constitute a salutary warning that our burning issues may seem irrelevant several decades or a century from now. A Scripture read solely through the modern-issue optic could also seem irrelevant in the future.

***

As a conclusion to my remarks about the various forms of biblical revisionism hostile to historical-critical exegesis, let me make the following observations. The number of such revisionists is small, despite attempts, mostly by ultraconservatives, to make it seem a vast movement. The demise of historical criticism is 'exaggerated', as Mark Twain observed upon reading his own obituary. The various revisionists who work from very different principles might dislike one another's exegesis even more than they dislike historical-critical exegesis, so that the revisionist movement is not of one mind. Imagine what a strange bedfellows the fundamentalist I have discussed under I above would make with the liberationists and feminists described under IIc.

One thing that many of these revisionists have in common is their dislike of a relatively unimpassioned, hard-headed look at history, a look that seeks to serve no particular cause. (I recognize that no scholarship is totally objective or disinterested, but in principle historical criticism tries to be descriptive.) If this outlook on history is *contemptuous* of interests foreign to the historical-critical discipline (dogmatic, spiritual, social, literary, etc.), then the historical-critical discipline is being poorly practised. But, if *without contempt*, historical-critical exegesis shows that the interests of the original author were different from what we might have expected, the resultant dialogue with those who would use the text for their own interests can be fruitful in keeping the use both sober and balanced. No other method has been devised that will answer purely historical questions better; and we are on dangerous ground when we decide that historical answers (even when they are disturbing) are irrelevant or must be changed precisely because they upset our outlook. Once again, I am not saying that historical answers need tyrannize our views so that our views of present realities are incorrect because they do not agree with past views of that reality. I am insisting that our views will be stronger and more persuasive if we have not sought to bend the past to suit us, but have entered into dialogue with past contributions to the total picture.

The future lies not with a rejection of the historical-critical method (which I regard as a permanent contribution to human knowledge), but in a refinement of the method, so that it will answer appropriately posed questions even more accurately, and its contributions to the larger picture of biblical interpretation can be seen in better perspective.

Chapter 4

Returning to the Sources:
The Hebrew Bible

Daniel L. Smith-Christopher

How can we describe any unity found among thirty-nine different books written over a period of about 850 years? Perhaps the answer lies in the fact that this collection of books describes a long-standing relationship. Indeed, the Hebrew Bible could be said to describe a stormy romance between very strong-willed lovers.

Although the metaphor of a romance is perhaps unusual, it is hardly original. The prophet Hosea in the eighth century BC had already used this image to great effect, contrasting the true love of Yahweh for the Hebrew people against the 'cheap lust' of the same community when they worshipped the local agricultural gods whom they believed might guarantee fertility and fruitful crops (Hos 2).

The description of a *relationship* between Israel and God is a major theme that ties an otherwise very diverse body of writings into a coherent whole. All the great unifying theological themes that have been suggested for the Hebrew Bible – 'salvation history', 'covenant', 'the Kingdom of God' – all are arguably secondary to the primacy of a basic relationship between God and God's people.

This relationship is described by various Hebrew writers in very human terms (frequently as lovers, but also as parent and child – see Hos 11) as they struggle to express their understanding of their God, 'Yahweh'. Like all relationships, so this divine-human one described in the Hebrew Bible has its dramatic episodes of jealous rage and angry disappointment, but perhaps most impressive in Hebrew faith, a very moving intimacy of love, compassion, and forgiveness. The spell that the Hebrew Bible casts on those who study it is thus not unlike the fascination with a beloved, whose new wonders provide occasional surprises, disappointments and with it all, great joy. It comes as no surprise, then, that the study of Scripture is compared to the love of 'Lady Wisdom' (Prov 3:13-18). For modern theological studies, and our own relationship with God, it is as necessary to re-read the previous words spoken between us as it is to continue to find new words to speak and new skills for listening to God today. In short, it is essential to return to the source.

The Hebrew sources

To begin, it is important to speak of 'The Hebrew Bible' rather than 'The Old Testament'. 'The Hebrew Bible' reminds us of the language and culture of its origins (semitic, ancient near east) *and* reminds us that these writings are 'holy' to both Jews and Christians – something we overlook to our disadvantage. Hebrew is a semitic language, related to other modern and ancient semitic languages, such as Arabic.

The Hebrew Bible is a collection of books written over nearly a millennium, roughly between 1000 BC and 150 BC. Counting Samuel, Kings, and Chronicles as two books each, the thirty-nine books were written predominantly in Hebrew. The early Christian Church, however, differed with early Judaism in the decision about the canon (that is, the authoritative collection of books that form our Bible), and decided to include a number of works written predominantly late (after 250 BC) and in Greek. This collection is known as 'the Apocrypha' (by Protestants, who do not consider them part of the biblical canon) or the 'Deutero-Canonical' books (by Roman Catholics who accept them). In addition, there are a large number of books that have survived, mostly from the Hellenistic Period (e.g., 333 BC through about AD 250) known as the 'Pseudepigrapha'. These books are of considerable historical, literary, and religious interest for the study of the Jewish people, but they are not of direct interest to the study of Hebrew history previous to the Hellenistic age.

The books of the Hebrew Canon are traditionally divided into three distinct sections: Torah ('Law' or 'Instruction'), Prophets, and Writings. These sections contain the following books:

Torah: Genesis, Exodus, Leviticus, Numbers, Deuteronomy

Prophets: Joshua, Judges, 1 & 2 Samuel, 1 & 2 Kings, Isaiah, Jeremiah, Ezekiel, Nahum, Habakkuk, Amos, Hosea, Joel, Micah, Malachi, Haggai, Zechariah, Zephaniah, Obadiah, and Jonah.

Writings: Psalms, Proverbs, Song of Solomon, Lamentations, Job, Esther, Ecclesiastes, Ezra-Nehemiah, Chronicles, Ruth, and Daniel.

The 'Deutero-Canonical' Books: Ecclesiasticus, Wisdom, Tobit, Judith, 1 & 2 Maccabees, and Baruch.

In order to understand these books, it is essential to have some basic familiarity with the outline of ancient Hebrew history. It is to this that we now turn, followed by a brief survey of the written materials, and finishing with an introduction to methods of biblical analysis.

Ancient Hebrew history

The following twelve dates represent important milestones in the history of the Hebrew people and provide a basic orientation that will allow us to relate specific books to specific events and time period. It should be understood that these dates are often only estimates, especially the early ones.

1280 BC   The Exodus of the Jewish slaves from Egypt under the leadership of Moses.

1020 BC   The beginning of the monarchy after the period of the Judges: Saul, followed by David and Solomon.

922 BC   The death of Solomon and the division of the land into two states, Judah in the south and Israel in the north.

722 BC   The Fall of the northern kingdom to the invading Assyrians from northwest Mesopotamia.

640 BC   King Josiah. The 'Deuteronomic Reforms' and the historical writings, Joshua through 2 Kings.

587 BC   The final defeat of Judah by the Babylonians, who deport many Judean citizens. Jerusalem temple is destroyed.

539 BC   Cyrus the Persian defeats Babylon and allows captive peoples to begin returning to their homelands.

520 BC   Most probable date for the rebuilding of the destroyed temple in Jerusalem.

450 BC   Approximate time of the missions of Nehemiah and Ezra.

333 BC   Alexander the Great's invasions of Palestine and the Near East; beginning of the influence of Hellenism.

167 BC   Antiochus IV (Epiphanes) attempts to unite his terri-
          tory through forced Hellenism. Oppression of Jews.
          Maccabean resistance begins.
 64 BC   Palestine under Roman control.
          * * * (After the birth of Jesus) * * *
 AD 70   Destruction of the second temple by the Romans.

It is not wise to separate the Hebrew Bible from the people who
produced it and the land where these people lived. Recent scholarship has begun to emphasize the importance of the
socio-economic and political context of the rise of the Israelite
confederation in the thirteenth and twelfth centuries BC. The land
of Canaan was by then already a long-disputed territory that acted
as a bridge between the Egyptians to the south, the Hittites centred
largely in Asia Minor, and the rising powers to the east in
Mesopotamia (see Map No. 1). Seen in this way, biblical history
takes place in an ancient 'Grand Central Station'.

From Egyptian reports, it appears that Canaan was populated by
'city-states' run by the local elite; they lived off the surplus
provided by agricultural peasants who farmed grains in the plain
and maintained small orchards in the hills (olives, figs and grapes).
The ideological support for this system was a religion based on
insuring agricultural and human fertility and respecting the established order or authority based on provision of sacrifice for gods.
The main gods were the storm god Baal, a feminine god Asherah,
and the father-god, El. Canaanite religion was supported by a
priesthood which maintained various temples and cult-centres.
This was the situation in Canaan when the Jews who were former
slaves arrived from Egypt.

The precise circumstances of the 'Exodus' are difficult to determine from biblical traditions. For example, Exodus 10:28–29 ends
the tradition which suggests an 'escape' from Egypt, while Exodus
11–12 supports an 'expulsion' of the Jews after a tenth and final
plague which caused the death of all Egyptian first-born children.
The book of Exodus blends the two by portraying Pharaoh as
changing his mind and chasing the Jews, giving rise to the traditions of the delivery of the Jews by the sea. But here again, there
are two traditions, one which portrays the Jews as escaping across
slightly muddy marshlands that rendered the Egyptian chariots
useless (a more natural explanation), and the later editing which
turned the episode into a miraculous parting of a large body of
water, clearly intended to magnify the theological importance of
God's assistance of the Jewish people in times of trouble.

Map No. 1

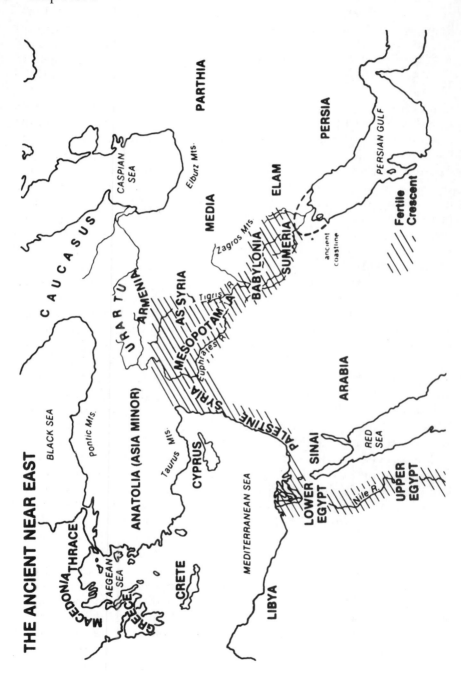

THE ANCIENT NEAR EAST

In any case, a group of former slaves in Egypt arrived in Canaan about 1250 BC with a religion about a God who liberated them from Egyptian slavery. This religion, in its early form, is closely associated with Moses. Early Israelite faith was based on basic moral expectations ('laws'); worship in a movable shrine or tent; and worship of a god known by the name of 'Yahweh'. The main feature of this religion, as far as the Canaanite peasantry was concerned, however, was the fact that this God Yahweh was a god who liberated slaves, and was thus a god who spoke to their condition. This religion had explosive impact upon arrival in Canaan, and the vast majority of those people who became the 'twelve tribes of Israel' were Canaanites who converted to the new religion.

This conversion to the religion of Yahweh, however, was uneven, and there was a persistent problem of mixing Canaanite and Yahwist religious ideas throughout the era of the Kings of Israel and Judah, from about 1000 BC to the Deuteronomic Reforms of 640–609 BC. There have been a number of recent archaeological discoveries that reveal the extent of syncretism (that is, the blending of two or more religious traditions) in this era. For example, prayers inscribed on pieces of clay were found in a small shrine near the Sinai desert which addressed 'Yahweh' and 'his consort/wife Asherah'. Such a prayer gives evidence that people were mixing Israelite and Canaanite religious ideas. The Bible's condemnation of many of the Israelite and Judean kings who abandoned pure Yahweh worship reveals that the kings often found the conservatism of Canaanite religion more to their liking than the reformist zeal of Yahweh worship. These kings were severely criticized by the radical advocates of Yahweh worship, the prophets.

It appears then, that Yahweh worship began as a 'minority' religion among former Egyptian slaves and converted Canaanites which eventually gained ascendancy late in the monarchy (especially in Josiah's reign). By this time, however, the fate of the independent Israelite nations was sealed by the rise of world empires based in Mesopotamia, and the worship of Yahweh would develop towards Judaism among a people who were politically and economically subordinate to these empires. In other words, the emerging identity of 'Israelites' took a decisive turn away from a *political* identity when these massive empires (first the Assyrians, then the Babylonians, and then the Persians) began to extend their influence westward into the Palestinian coastlands.

The Israelite monarchy began about 1000 BC. David was the most significant early leader who managed to unite the disparate Hebrew/Canaanite peoples against the immediate threat of the coastal invaders known as Philistines. David also established a capital city, Jerusalem, and extended Israelite political influence across the Jordan into the territories of Ammon, Moab, Edom and northward into Syria (see Map No. 2).

The son who eventually succeeded David (Solomon) engaged in further campaigns of consolidation, including the construction of a national shrine modeled on Canaanite temple architecture. But despite Solomon's reputation for diplomacy and 'wisdom', the human toll of his building campaigns was considered oppressive by the peoples, especially in the northern territory (1 Kgs 9:22, but see 1 Kgs 5:27; 11:28 and 1 Kgs 12).

Palestine/Canaan was not a homogeneous environment, and agricultural differences led to social differences, exacerbated by the requirements for Solomon's construction in both labour and taxes. When Solomon died, the northern peoples broke from the Jerusalem dynasty (involving territory from ten of the twelve tribes), and established a new 'Israelite' state in 922 BC. Hence, the Hebrew Bible refers to the northern state as 'Israel', and the southern state as 'Judah'. Judah maintained the Davidic family dynasty, while Israel was ruled by a succession of monarchs, none of whom were ultimately able to establish a rival dynastic family. It therefore appears that the northern state was more unstable. In the north, the Prophets would occasionally lead coups by proclaiming that God had chosen a new king while the old king still sat on the throne!

In the latter half of the eighth century BC, the northern state joined a coalition of states in an attempt to resist the increasing pressure of the Assyrian Empire. When the southern monarch, Ahaz, refused to join the coalition, the coalition members determined to force Ahaz's hand, and initiated a war. In response, Ahaz called on the Assyrians for assistance, who responded with an invasion in the west. The coalition was destroyed by the invading Assyrians, including the northern state of Israel in 722 BC.

The Assyrian Empire practised a martial technique that guaranteed that conquered territories would not be able to muster resistance. This involved deporting large segments of the newly conquered population, and exchanging this body of people with a group taken from another part of the empire. But the Assyrian Empire was eventually defeated by the rise of a rival Mesopotamian power based in the southern part of the Tigris–Euphrates basin, the Babylonians (so-called because they based themselves in the ancient religious capital of Babylon, near modern day Baghdad, Iraq).

Between 640-609, that is, between the decline of the Assyrian

Empire and the Babylonian ascendancy, King Josiah reigned in Jerusalem. Josiah is credited with initiating a major reform, centralizing all worship in Jerusalem (thus ending worship in local shrines, which may have contributed to syncretism with Canaanite religious practices) and restoring a purer form of Yahweh worship, probably in league with some of the prophets. His movement was based on the laws contained in the book of Deuteronomy, and therefore it is referred to as the 'Deuteronomic Reform'. This movement also inspired further literary production. After the tragic death of Josiah in a campaign against the Egyptians (609 BC), the 'Deuteronomic History' was composed, beginning with Joshua and carrying on to the Babylonian conquest described at the end of 2 Kings.

The Babylonians were eventually able to defeat the Assyrian armies in 609 BC. After becoming King, Nebuchadnezzar led the Babylonians further south on the Canaanite coastlands, consolidating his control of the area as a buffer zone against the Egyptians. In 597, the young king Jehoiachin surrendered to Nebuchadnezzar, who accepted Judah as a vassal state, and placed a ruler of his own choosing as a client-ruler in Jerusalem. Nebuchadnezzar renamed this man 'Zedekiah' (name changing often symbolized political control), placed him on the throne, and then returned to Babylon with a small number of exiles, including the young king Jehoiachin. This was the beginning of the Exile, and apparently involved only the 'upper layers' of Judean society – anyone who might pose an immediate threat to the rule of Babylon.

Zedekiah was the client ruler for ten years, but during this time became ambitious about ruling Judah as an independent state. It is probable that he was encouraged in this bold folly by promises of Egyptian assistance, since prophets like Jeremiah bitterly condemned the idea that Egypt would provide any credible assistance in a bid for independence. When Zedekiah ceased paying tribute to the Babylonians, this was tantamount to a declaration of independence, and it wasn't long before Nebuchadnezzar arrived back in the west with his armies to reassert control. Jerusalem was destroyed in 587–576 BC after a long siege, and Zedekiah's sons were killed. Zedekiah himself was tortured and taken to Babylon. The temple was destroyed, and temple implements and furnishing were taken 'captive' along with a very large number of the population. This exile was more widespread than ten years before, and involved a significant number of the population. Estimates vary from twenty thousand to over seventy thousand, but in any case a significant percentage of the population.

Map No. 2

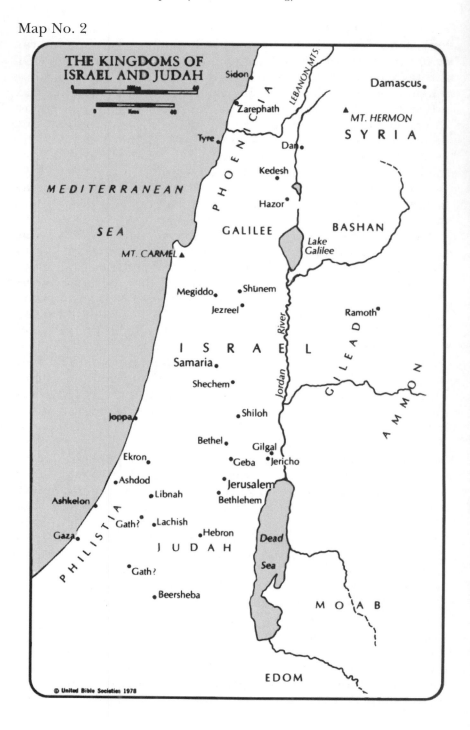

This 'Babylonian Exile' represents one of the most decisive changes of destiny for the Jewish people; yet the exilic community survived and reconstructed their faith. When the Persians finally conquered Babylon in 539, the Emperor Cyrus allowed Jews to return to Palestine. Although a sizable Jewish community remained in Babylon, various 'returns' (described in Ezra) of Jews to Palestine allowed the reconstruction of faith, community, and even temple worship.

We know very little about post-Exilic Judean society. There are only a few books that are confidently dated to this era, such as Haggai, Zechariah, Malachi and Ezra-Nehemiah. This lack of information continues to the Hellenistic Period (post 333 BC) when we once again begin to have historical/literary sources such as the Apocryphal Books [Deutero-Canonical Books] and various Pseudepigraphic works. What we can surmise is that the Jewish community formed a strong communal identity and faith under the leadership of priests, who emerged as the primary leaders in place of the Davidic royal dynasty. Hopes for a restored Davidic ruler became the basis for a future age, occasionally inspiring nationalist activity among some Jews in Palestine. But in this time, many Jews were living in a 'Diaspora' (that is, in lands other than Palestine/Israel) that extended from Egypt far into the East beyond Babylon and Persian territory. For them, faith no longer meant national existence, but inward spiritual identity as well as resistance to cultural assimilation. From these communities we have stories of faithful Jews in foreign lands such as Daniel and Esther.

From the time of the exile until the twentieth century, with only a relatively brief time before the Roman occupation in 64 BC, the Jewish people were to remain politically and economically subordinate to non-Jews. Judaism and Christianity, therefore, are religions whose roots are to be found in people who were politically 'occupied'. Yahweh, a God of liberated slaves, would then become the God of the powerless and the God of judgment on the oppressor, the rich, and the powerful.

If we keep in mind that virtually *all* of the Hebrew Bible was edited and arranged (if not entirely written) by a politically powerless people, then the biblical hymns to a 'God of war' take on somewhat different nuances. Such ideas take on an entirely different (and non-biblical) meaning when self-servingly quoted by the powerful, or used to adorn the halls of modern pentagonal symbols of world power. All of these insights, however, come to us form a variety of kinds of religious literature in the Hebrew Bible, each contributing different perspectives. Let us briefly survey some of these and also some of the issues raised by the modern study of these books.

The books of the Hebrew Bible

The Pentateuch and the Deuteronomic History: history and law

Israelite history is typified by its overt moralism. If it is true that writing history is never merely a description of events, Hebrew historiography is surely an excellent example of history written with a clear motive and goal in mind.

The main task of the historical writers of ancient Israel was to illustrate their understanding of God, and how God was involved in their lives. In short, it is *religious* literature and not royal archives or historical annals. A great deal of needless misunderstanding is avoided by maintaining such a perspective. The study of the primeval history of Genesis (chs 1–11), for example, is deeply enhanced if students realize that these stories are to be read mainly as important religious and philosophical instruction, and not as 'scientific' guidelines on the origin of species. It seems, then, that the proper response to the creation and/or flood narratives of Genesis is an appreciation of the religious lessons of moral responsibility, God's preference for the just, God's involvement with and care for humanity, and humanity's stubborn resistance. Mounting an expedition to find 'pieces of the ark' on Mount Ararat in modern Turkey, then, is not the most appropriate response to the biblical texts because it misses their central message and attempts to make these texts into something that they are not.

Furthermore, such notions perpetuate a false notion that modern students must somehow suspend their critical faculties in order to read, understand, and appreciate the Hebrew Bible. The primeval history tells us about ancient Hebrew understanding of the nature of human folly, and God's persistent love and attention.

The primeval history is followed by stories of the 'Patriarchs and Matriarchs' of Ancient Israel: Abraham and Sarah, Isaac and Rebekah, Jacob and his sons, and Joseph in Egypt. Scholars were more confident of the historicity of the patriarchal stories as recent as thirty to fifty years ago, but recent work in both archaeology and textual analysis has raised serious doubt as to whether any of the material in Genesis can be used to reconstruct ancient history in any significant way. It seems best to treat Genesis as a religiously motivated story of the origin of the Hebrew people and their arrangement in 'clans' named for figures discussed in Genesis stories (e.g., the 'twelve tribes' as the twelve sons of Jacob). This provided a unifying history for the peoples of Canaan in the twelfth to tenth centuries BC who converted to Yahweh worship. The patriarchal stories also carry on the theme of God's persistent attention, despite the constant failures of the humans represented in these stories.

The most prominent feature of the first five books of the Bible, however, is not history writing, but law. Virtually *all* of the religious laws, civil laws, and moral principles of ancient Israel are codified in three collections contained in the first five books. The earliest of these collections is known as the 'Covenant Code', contained in the book of Exodus (roughly chs 19–24). This collection was supplemented at least twice, by a major collection of law from the late seventh century in Deuteronomy (the very name means 'second law') which is thus named the 'Deuteronomic Code'. The final collection of laws consists mainly of priestly or religious laws (although not exclusively) which were added by the priests in the post-exilic period. These laws can be found in Exodus 25–31, but also throughout Leviticus. The oldest layer of this priestly law is probably located in Leviticus 17–26 (called 'The Holiness Code' from the recurring phrase, 'you shall be holy ...'), but surrounded by later commentary and additional laws in Leviticus and Numbers.

The frequent repetition of laws and legal themes (e.g., the fact that the 'ten commandments' are found twice) is explained by this history of supplementing the legal codes with later legal material from different eras. Interestingly, this history of supplementing the texts allows modern students to do comparative work on the development of the status of women and slaves, to take two instances, in Israelite law. Scholars have long noted the progressive 'humanization' of the status of slaves, between the Covenant Code (Exod 21), and the Deuteronomic Code (Deut 15:12–18). The later code, for example, specifically delineates the provisions to be provided to released slaves, and furthermore prohibits the return of escaped slaves to masters (Deut 23:16), etc. Most impressive of all, perhaps, is the somewhat utopian expectation of social justice provided by the priests in Leviticus 25, where the 'Jubilee Year' was to provide for the return of all purchased land to the original tribal owners, thus preventing a growing rift between rich and poor by redistributing the land every fifty years! Law, in ancient Israel, was clearly both normative and prescriptive.

The Prophets

It is unfortunate that popular ideas about the prophets tend to focus on the notion that prophets 'predict the future'. In fact, the main activities of the prophets were (1) to be a 'messenger' of God, delivering messages very much like a royal emissary or message runner, (2) to be 'God's prosecutor', delivering judgments on sinful acts on behalf of God and God's laws, and (3) to make known God's will, either when consulted for specific information, or given unsolicited in public forums such as at the city gates. Any suggestions about future events were always in the prior context of these other main activities. The prophets' words were intended for their own time, and represented God's continued involvement in history. To suggest that the words of the prophets were for a distant future not only removes the prophets from history (thus misrepresenting the main point of God's involvement in the history of the people), but also invites irresponsible attempts to 'interpret' the prophets' words 'for the modern times' as if they are hidden predictions. In fact, to paraphrase Mark Twain, the prophets' words were feared not because they were cryptic messages for future times, but because they were understood only too well and spoke of real events in the lives of the kings and people who heard them.

The prophets of ancient Israel were mysterious and charismatic men and women who were feared as well as respected. From occasional references in 1 and 2 Samuel, it appears that prophecy had its origins in travelling bands of charismatics who would speak out of a self-imposed, trance-like state (1 Sam 10:9ff). In time, however, great prophets became individually noted, and would gather traditions and/or legends around them, as well as bands of disciples. The best example of this later development are the stories about Elijah and Elisha in the Deuteronomic History (1 Kgs 17–21; 2 Kgs 2–13), but also the books of Isaiah and Jeremiah.

Each of the prophets is a unique figure with an interesting difference in outlook and perspective, although in the case of some of the shorter books it is hard to determine a perspective on the basis of so little material: (Obadiah is only twenty-one verses long; Nahum and Malachi only three chapters.) We probably owe the existence of prophetic writings to disciples (or in the case of Jeremiah, a companion who was a scribe) who maintained a tradition of repeating, studying, and commenting on the traditions of their teacher.

The first prophet for whom we have writings is Amos, himself a somewhat enigmatic man whose prophecies consist of unrelenting judgment against many nations, not simply Israel and Judah. In fact, some scholars believe that the final few verses which offer some hope didn't even come from Amos!

In contrast to Amos, Hosea used intimate and romanticized images of God as lover and parent of the people of Israel to describe his sadness at Israel's disobedience (which he compared to adultery or rejecting a parent). Hosea even carries his message to the point of giving his children names that are symbolic of God's anger for the people (e.g. Lo-Ammi equals you are 'not my people').

Not long after Hosea and Amos were active in the north, the traditions surrounding the prophet Isaiah began in the south. The book of Isaiah is a good example of the continued tradition that major prophetic figures can inaugurate. The prophet himself was active from about 740 BC, and his words are largely recalled in chapters 1–39 of the present book of Isaiah. Chapters 40–55 however, come from a nameless prophet active toward the end of the Babylonian Exile (so dated because of the references to Cyrus the Persian, see Isa 45:1). The similarities to Isaiah chapters 1–39 has led many scholars to suspect the presence of an Isaiah 'tradition' within which this nameless prophet worked.

The most interesting element of this prophet, whom scholars refer to as 'Second Isaiah' (sometimes Deutero-Isaiah), it is the use of the image of the 'suffering servant'. This figure is most likely a collective reference to the Israelite exiles, but was deeply influential among early Christians in their struggle for ways to interpret the events and meaning of the life, death, and resurrection of Jesus (see esp. Isa 42:1–4; 49:1–6; 50:4–9 and 52:13–53:12). The image of suffering for the sake of righteousness and righteous suffering earning favour is therefore a prophetic Jewish, and not uniquely Christian, notion. The final chapters, 56–66, often called 'Trito-Isaiah,' are collections of sayings, perhaps by disciples of the prophet Deutero-Isaiah. It also appears that the peaceful hopes of this third collection influenced the editing of passages in the first section, such as parts of Isaiah 2, 4, 9, 11 and perhaps the most powerful peace vision in the entire Bible, the later section of Isaiah 19.

Jeremiah was outspokenly involved in the politics surrounding the Deuteronomic reform and the fall of the southern state to the Babylonians. He is perhaps best known for his unusual conviction that the conquest by the Babylonians was God's will, and that the Judeans therefore must 'bend their necks' to the yoke of Babylon for a period of time. No doubt Jeremiah shared the general

Deuteronomic perspective that the exilic events were punishment for the previous period of rejection of the laws of God. The book of Jeremiah is composed in two main sections, the poetic sayings of Jeremiah himself and prose sections of biographical information about Jeremiah. Both are attributed to the scribe and companion of Jeremiah, Baruch.

Ezekiel, on the other hand, was active among the Babylonian exiles. He was given to occasionally bizarre acts of public theater to illustrate his prophetic messages. His main concern was to be the spiritual well-being of the exiled people, but also their continued relationship to the religious life that the exiles left behind in Palestine.

Prophetic books continued to be produced in the post-exilic community as well. Haggai, for example, is concerned mainly with the restoration of religious life in the post exilic community, particularly the importance of rebuilding the temple. Similarly, Zechariah is typified by issues of faith and practice in the post-exilic community.

In conclusion, prophecy represents a phenomenon that is central to our understanding of ancient Hebrew religion, but we shouldn't forget what marginalized and controversial figures these people were. The prophets, therefore, have been more influential in retrospect than in their own era. The prophets became central to the understanding of Hebrew faith, and that is what led to the preservation and continued study of their messages.

Apocalyptic Literature and Its Relationship to Prophecy

A question that has fascinated both students and scholars is the ultimate fate of prophetic activity. Did prophecy die out? Did it evolve into something else? Recently scholars have worked on various theories connecting the changes in late prophetic activity to the rise of apocalyptic visionaries.

Apocalyptic literature typically contains a description of an extended, highly symbolic vision, or visions. The vision is usually described in graphic, often bizarre detail and is accompanied by the narration of an angel or godly figure. Apocalyptic literature became very popular in the Hellenistic period, and continued to be influential in the Roman period among both Jews and early Christians. Although we have only two major examples of apocalyptic literature in the Bible (Dan 7–12 in the Hebrew Bible and Revelation in the New Testament), many examples of nonbiblical apocalyptic writings have survived from this period. It seems that prophetic activity was replaced by the apocalyptic visionaries who described, in symbolic visions from God, references to the coming judgment on the oppressive rules and events of their times.

Apocalyptic literature remains deeply involved in contemporary events. By envisioning God's intervention on behalf of the oppressed, Jewish apocalyptic writers were calling for an activism of resistance to Greek and Roman culture and rule. The visions of Daniel, after all, are attached to stories of Jewish figures in foreign courts who are vindicated for their faithful persistence or, in other words, their spiritual resistance. Indeed, after three months of Bible reading in a South African jail, Mahatma Gandhi emerged proclaiming Daniel to be 'one of the greatest nonviolent resistors in history'. Apocalyptic literature, then, illustrates a central concern of post-exilic Hebrew faith, maintaining faith and identity in circumstances of powerlessness and even oppression.

The Writings

The last major section of the Hebrew Bible is a general category into which an interesting variety of texts are grouped. Generally known as the 'Writings', it includes poetic religious hymns, stories, and Wisdom literature.

Poetry

The largest body of religious poetry in the Bible is the Psalms. Ever popular as devotional literature, the Psalms were written over a large span of Jewish history. The nature of Hebrew poetry is controversial. There are debates, for example, about whether Hebrew poetry does or does not have a discernible meter, and if not, what other elements are unique to its form and mechanics. Nevertheless, there are some general statements that can be made even with regard to Hebrew poetry in English. Hebrew poetry, like Canaanite poetry, is typified by parallelism. Parallelism simply means that the first line of the poem ('A') is somehow echoed in the second line ('B') and, less often, in the third line as well ('C'). Attempts to be specific about various kinds of parallelism have foundered on the fact that as the descriptive categories increase, the value of such a complex explanation is questionable. For beginning students, it is only necessary to pay attention to what relation the second, and possibly third, lines have to the first line, in order to see parallelism at work.

As for the content of psalms, it is important to see that there are many different kinds of psalms dealing with different subjects.

Psalm 29 and other psalms reveal so many linguistic and literary similarities to Canaanite literature that most scholars believe it was virtually a Canaanite hymn to Baal that was taken over and only slightly changed to a Yahweh hymn. Other Psalms have their origin in ceremonies of the enthronement of the King and/or the celebration of the new year (Pss 72, 89, 2, 100). Others, clearly referring to the events of the exile, reveal a very late origin (Pss 126, 137).

Most scholars believe that the psalms were originally five separate collections that have been edited together. This would explain not only the occasional repetition of a psalm, but also the fact that at the end of each of the five presumed originally separate books is a stylized doxology, 'Amen, Amen' (see the end of Pss 41, 72, 89, 106, 150).

The frustrating aspect of psalms study, as a part of the larger problem of the study of Israelite religion, is that we have only a very vague notion of how worship in ancient Israel actually worked. Scholars presume, for example, that changes between first person singular and plural in psalms might represent antiphonal worship, or that psalms of a prayerful, personal nature were mainly for personal devotion; but these are all speculations. There is, unfortunately, no 'order of service' or description of worship for the ancient temple, and we have as little an idea about worship in the second temple. Yet it is clear that the adaptability of psalms to both corporate as well as personal worship, is at the heart of the modern popularity of this book.

Wisdom Literature

Wisdom literature, which includes books such as Proverbs, Job, Ecclesiastes, and Wisdom, is not unique to Israel. We have examples of collections of wise sayings frequently written as if an elder father is advising his son or a teacher advising a student from all over the ancient near east. Indeed, part of the book of Proverbs, our main Wisdom book, is drawn directly from Egyptian wisdom literature (Prov 22:17–24:22). This is surely because the main themes of wisdom literature: relationships, diplomacy, watching one's tongue, money and frugality, the dangers of adultery or of strong drink, and the gaining of knowledge are basic human issues. Indeed, it has been argued that wisdom literature, based as it is on the observation of the human condition, is really secular literature. It most certainly is literature from the upper classes of society. This is clear when comparing wisdom literature's attitude to wealth as a sign of God's blessing to prophetic condemnation of the wealthy as virtually outside of God's blessing.

But wisdom literature, based as it is on human observation, is also the basis for rationalism, and ultimately, scientific thought. Wisdom literature, for example Ecclesiastes, is steadfast against empty hope or false idealism, preferring the often depressing reality of how the observed world, and the people in it, really are. Thus, it is significant that wisdom literature is represented in the Hebrew Bible at all, perhaps indicating that all of human thought is to be a part of the reality of faith. But wisdom literature is not without its detractors within the Bible. The enigmatic book of Job has often been described as 'antiwisdom' literature because wisdom fails to provide answers to Job's agonizing questions about why the righteous suffer (as our human wisdom continues to fail us on this question!).

Finally, there are important little stories in the Bible, such as the book of Esther and the book of Jonah. Each of these books represent a genre of Hebrew literature that is also represented within other books (Joseph in Genesis, Dan 1–6), now known as 'Diaspora stories'. These are important stories that reflect the conditions of the Jewish people in the post-exilic communities in Palestine and outside Palestine. Their main purpose is to teach steadfast devotion to faith in times of stress and political subordination.

Of course, much more could be said about the varieties of literature of the Hebrew Bible. We have surveyed some of the more well known genres and books pointing out some of the most interesting and popular issues and problems involved with each. But biblical studies become interesting only when students begin to learn the tools, methods, and skills for analysis so that they can explore the text themselves. Let us consider some basic forms of analysis of the Hebrew Bible, considering along the way the sorts of questions that need to be asked.

Biblical scholarship

Now that we have surveyed the three main sections of the Bible, it is important to survey some of the problems of biblical analysis. A good example of biblical analysis at work is the study of the first five books of the Bible, and the theory which has evolved in that study known as 'the Documentary Hypothesis'.

The Documentary Hypothesis

Even the most casual readers of Genesis will find themselves somewhat perplexed by a series of interesting literary phenomena. For example, there are *two* creation stories, which differ in the described order of creation, among other things (plants, then animals, then people in 1:1–2:4a; people, plants, then animals, in 2:4b–3:24). There are other stories, such as the 'Threat to the Patriarch's Wife' that are repeated no less than three times in the text (12:10–20; 20; 26:1–11) and others that are told twice (the banishment of Hagar in ch. 16 and again in ch. 21). Already in the eighteenth century, scholars noticed inconsistency between these two different series of stories. One of the two versions of repeated stories, for example, would use the name 'Elohim' for God, while the other consistently used 'Yahweh'. One of the versions would present God more anthropomorphically (in human-like form as a person who walked and spoke to people), while the other would maintain a majestic view of God removed from humanity and speaking from heaven or in dreams.

These observations led to 'the Documentary Hypothesis'. Its basic outlines are rather simple, and even though the idea is constantly under review and challenge, it remains a basic foundation for analysis of the first books of the Bible.

According to the Documentary Hypothesis, an early collection of laws and oral traditions were gathered together in the time of Solomon in order to provide a history for the regime. These traditions, which consistently used the name 'Yahweh', formed a coherent collection of material that extended from creation to the early monarchy. This early collection is referred to by the letter 'J'. Scholars who engage in 'form criticism' try to identify and isolate the small pieces of texts or stories that may have originated in oral tradition. Perhaps a few lines of poetry, or preliterary form of a story, can be identified, and from this, we can determine how that tradition or text has been used and elaborated on as time passed. By paying careful attention to forms of folklore, for example, it may be possible to see how some of the patriarchal stories were originally oral stories told long before Solomon's scribes brought them together in their collection. Furthermore, some idea of their original form may show us how those scribes altered the stories, or used the older oral traditions for their own purposes.

After their break from the united monarchy (922 BC), the northern kingdom probably fashioned their own history, using the word 'Elohim' for God, and these materials are thus designated as 'E'. Again, form criticism may show us the 'form' of the materials that the 'E' writers introduced into the text, and what purpose they serve in the text.

The J and E documents were then further supplemented during

the Deuteronomic Reforms (after 640 BC) by the addition of
Deuteronomy (called 'D'). Furthermore, these editors wrote an
extended commentary on Israelite history from the perspective of
the Deuteronomic laws. This history was written from the time of
the conquest (Joshua) until the beginning of the Babylonian Exile
(at the end of 2 Kgs), and was mainly interested in teaching the
moral lessons of Deuteronomy by illustrating the folly of the
Israelite/Judean kings who consistently ignored the laws of Moses.

Finally, during and after the Exile, the leadership of the Jewish
people passed from the royal family exclusively, to a shared royal-
priestly rulership, and finally the priesthood exclusively. During
this time, the priestly leadership engaged in a final gathering and
editing of the biblical material. The materials that they added
throughout the first five books of the Bible are thus designated 'P'.
P material can be found throughout the first five books, beginning
with the first creation story (which, as one would expect from
priests, gives prominence to the importance of the Sabbath, when
even God 'rested'). The 'P' editors seem concerned to clarify religious matters and details at various points, and introduced large
amounts of material in Leviticus and Numbers. Finally, however, it
is just as important to realize that we now read the first five books
of the Bible as a unit *because* of the work of the priests. By separating Deuteronomy from Joshua, for example, the priestly editors
left Moses at the entrance to the promised land at the end of the
most sacred collection of books, the Torah. Could this be influenced by the condition of Exile, and the realization that they, too,
live in the hope of seeing the promised land again?

With this general outline of the Documentary Hypothesis [(J + E
+ D) + P] in mind, it is clear that any serious analysis of any passage
from the Pentateuch, and indeed from the Deuteronomic historian, must begin with a preliminary location of the passage within
the work of one of the 'sources'. This process is called 'source criticism'.

Once we have identified the 'source' to which a certain passage
ought to be assigned, it is interesting to see how the editors of the
text have brought the sources together. This form of criticism is
called 'redaction' criticism (from the German for 'editing').
Consider the way in which the addition of the first creation story
(by the P writers) affects the way we read the second version starting at 2:4b. *Now,* the second story reads as if it is a commentary of
the first story, so much so that most students don't even realize that
they are two different stories until they look more carefully at
them.

The attraction of biblical studies is its constant freshness because of the new questions that are constantly being asked. Recently, students and scholars have begun to borrow questions and methods from other disciplines and are bringing them to biblical studies. Can anthropological analysis, for example, help us understand the kinship structure implied in the patriarchal stories? If so, maybe we will learn more about the people who wrote them. Can sociological analysis help us to understand the socio-economic system that is assumed in the patriarchal stories? (Pastoral nomadism? Barter or coin systems? How is wealth accumulated and transferred?) If so, we may even gain further clues in helping us date the time of the writing of these stories. Finally, can the new forms of literary criticism help us to understand more about the structure of these stories, and how we as readers respond to the way in which they are written? If so, then we gain new appreciation for the writers, and their message.

To begin their study, students should have an English translation that is recent and accurate. No text before the 1950s is acceptable (if for no other reason than the fact that the Dead Sea Scrolls were discovered in 1948). It is preferable to use a New American Bible (NAB) or a New Revised Standard Version (NRSV) or (the text I prefer) the New Jerusalem Bible Study Edition. The New International Version is also good, but beginning students should avoid any and all paraphrases of the Bible such as the Phillips, the 'Living Bible', the 'Good News Bible', and so on.

When reading over a passage, students should make careful use of Bible dictionaries, to make certain that a biblical term has the same meaning as a modern reader assumes. After all terms are identified, places located on maps, it is important to begin analysis of the passage. This will involve careful use of a variety of modern commentaries to various books of the Bible. Students will find that in these commentaries there are a variety of methods that scholars have developed for the analysis of a passage, each one asking slightly different questions of the text. With patience, these questions and forms of analysis will become both fascinating and rewarding. This raises one final point in our introduction to the Hebrew Bible, namely the relationship of the Hebrew Bible to modern religious life.

Faith and the Hebrew Bible

The final question to be considered is the relationship between issues of historical and critical commentary on the various books, and the significance of the Hebrew Bible for modern faith. This is by no means an easy question, as thoughtful readers will have already realized that textual study can be engaged in with no particular religious commitment or orientation at all. From a position of faith, however, these same methods can be helpful in the construction of modern theology. The ability to deal with difficult questions raised by critical analysis is a mark of a mature belief in God, even if it means living with open questions or difficult problems. It is not necessary, for example, to believe in a historical person named Abraham in order to have a deep and abiding faith that God continues to communicate to us by means of the stories about Abraham. That is why study of the text remains so important.

A genuinely Christian theology cannot be constructed apart from listening closely to these writings. The Hebrew Bible remains a primary source for modern faith, and modern Christians do well to begin constructing their own theology by taking seriously the God who liberates slaves, unseats kings, speaks through radical prophets, and acts within history.

Finally, since it is true that serious biblical analysis will change the nature of any serious student's faith, perhaps this is the most compelling reason of all to begin biblical study in a serious way. The effort may result in the realization that these words will not leave us alone, and with the prophet Jeremiah, we will confess:

> I would say to myself, 'I will not think about Him;
> I will not speak in his name anymore.'
> But then there seemed to be a fire burning in my heart,
> imprisoned in my bones.
> The effort to restrain it wearied me ... (Jer 20).

Study questions
1. How did the location of Canaan/Palestine influence the development of religion in the Hebrew Bible?
2. What do we mean when we say that the Hebrew Bible is more *religious* than *historical?* How does this influence our faith?
3. How do the prophets Amos and Hosea compare and contrast with each other?
4. What are some of the main pieces of evidence that support the documentary hypothesis?

Chapter 5

The Canon of the Old Testament

J.H. Hayes

The Old Testament or Hebrew Bible, considered sacred by Jews
and Christians, exists in three major canonical forms. These are
the Jewish, Roman Catholic (and Orthodox), and Protestant
canons. The Roman Catholic Church accepts forty-six books as the
canonical Old Testament. Protestantism possesses a canon of
thirty-nine books. The Jewish canon consists of twenty-four books,
which are identical with the thirty-nine of Protestants although in
a different enumeration and arrangement.

   The Jewish canon contains the following books separated into
three divisions:

   I.   *Torah* **(Pentateuch)**
   1. Genesis (*Bereshith*)
   2.. Exodus (*Shemoth*)
   3. Leviticus (*Wayiqra*)
   4. Numbers (*Bemidbar*)
   5. Deuteronomy (*Debarim*)

  II.   *Nebiim* **(Prophets)**
        Former
   6. Joshua (*Yehoshua*)
   7. Judges (*Shofetim*)
   8. Samuel (*Shemuel*)
   9. Kings (*Melakim*)
        Latter
   10. Isaiah (*Yeshayahu*)
   11. Jeremiah (*Yirmeyahu*)
   12. Ezekiel (*Yehezqel*)
   13. Book of the Twelve (*Tere Asar*)

III.   *Kethubim* (Writings)
14. Psalms (*Tehillim*)
15. Job (*Iyyob*)
16. Proverbs (*Mishle*)
17. Ruth
18. Song of Songs (*Shir Hashirim*)
19. Ecclesiastes (*Qoheleth*)
20. Lamentations (*Ekah*)
21. Esther
22. Daniel
23. Ezra-Nehemiah (*Ezra-nehemyah*)
24. Chronicles (*Dibre Hayamim*)

The books in the Roman Catholic canon which are not found in the Jewish Bible and Protestant Old Testament are Tobit, Judith, Wisdom of Solomon, Ecclesiasticus (or Wisdom of Ben Sirach), Baruch (including the so-called 'Epistle of Jeremiah'), I Maccabees, and II Maccabees. In addition, Esther and Daniel in the Catholic canon contain material not found in the Protestant and Jewish canons. Six additions, comprising 107 verses, appear in the larger version of the book of Esther. The longer form of Daniel incorporates the Prayer of Azariah and the song of the Three Young men (68 verses), the Story of Susanna (64 verses), and the Story of Bel and the Dragon (42 verses). The Greek Orthodox canon is identical with that of Roman Catholicism except for the book of Baruch, which is excluded from the Orthodox canon.

Some of the twenty-four books of the Jewish canon are divided in the following way to produce the thirty-nine books in the Protestant canon: Samuel, Kings, Chronicles, and Ezra-Nehemiah are divided into eight books; and the Book of the Twelve is divided into twelve separate works (the prophets from Hosea to Malachi). In the Christian canons, many of the works found in the third section of the Jewish canon have been distributed to fit into a four-fold pattern of law, historical books, poetry and wisdom, and prophetical writings. Ruth, Chronicles, Ezra-Nehemiah, and Esther are placed with the historical works. Lamentations and Daniel are placed with the prophets. In addition, several of the poetical and wisdom books appear in the Christian canons in a slightly different order than in the Jewish canon. In the Catholic canon, Tobit and Judith follow Nehemiah, Wisdom of Solomon and Ecclesiasticus follow the Song of Solomon, Baruch follows Lamentations, and I and II Maccabees come after Malachi.

How did these different canons of the Hebrew scriptures or the Old Testament develop? Why are they so different? Is it possible to determine when and how the ancient Jewish and Christian communities established and recognized a sacred collection of canonical Old Testament writings? What was the relationship between the early Jewish and Christian canons of the Old Testament? Throughout history, these questions have been matters of discussion and debate. In recent years, new interest in canonical studies and new approaches to the problems involved in the history of the canon have developed and become a central concern in biblical studies (see especially Sanders and Sundberg).

Before discussing the origin and nature of the three Old Testament canons, a few preliminary factors should be noted. First, the term 'canon', which derives from a Semitic word meaning 'reed' and then 'rod', 'rule', and 'norm', was first applied to a collection of sacred writings by Church Fathers in the fourth century AD. Prior to this time, the biblical materials were referred to as 'scripture(s)', 'sacred scriptures', or books that 'defile the hands.' The last expression meant that the writings were so holy that the holiness must be washed away from the hands after handling them. Second, the concept of canon implies the existence of a collection of writings which are accepted as authoritative, as unchangeable, and as normative for religious faith and practice. Thus a canon of scripture has both positive and negative connotations. Positively, a canon denotes certain works that are included in the category of sacred and authoritative. Negatively, a canon excludes certain works which are not accepted as authoritative. A canon exists only when both the exclusive and inclusive factors are consciously functioning in the concerns of the religious community. Third the creation of biblical canons in both Judaism and Christianity was a final stage in a long process. The Bible certainly does not represent all the literature produced in ancient Israel. The scriptures themselves refer to extinct writings such as 'book of the wars of Yahweh' (Num 21:14), the 'book of Jashar' (Josh 10:13; II Sam 1:18), and the 'book of the acts of Solomon' (I Kings 11:41) and so on. In the course of Israel's history many such works were lost, destroyed, or perhaps partially incorporated into biblical works. In addition to now lost works, numerous writings which have survived never possessed or were gradually excluded from any widespread usage in the process which produced closed canons of scripture. Behind the works which became canonical lies a long process in which their contents were shaped and fashioned. The study of this process has been called 'canonical criticism' (see Sanders, especially 1976). Both internal and external concerns contributed to this shaping and fashioning process. The community or parts thereof responded to new crises and new modes of life so as to preserve its identity while adapting to new conditions. In this chapter, we are concerned primarily with the final phases of the process, that is, with the inclusion-exclusion operation.

A. Early references to a developing canon

The first available evidence suggesting the existence of sacred and authoritative writings identical to portions of the Old Testament comes from the second century BC. In his hymn praising famous men, Jesus ben Sirach provides a roll call of the heroes of the faith (see Ecclesiasticus 44-49). References to these men follow the order in which they appear in the Hebrew scriptures. The names included are drawn from the Torah (Enoch, Noah, Abraham, Isaac, Jacob, Moses, Aaron, Phinehas), the Prophets (Joshua, Caleb, Samuel, Nathan, David, Solomon, Rehoboam, Jeroboam, Elijah, Elisha, Hezekiah, Isaiah, Josiah, Jeremiah, Ezekiel, the Twelve Prophets), and perhaps the Writings (Zerubbabel, Joshua, the high priest Nehemiah). References to Zerubbabel and Joshua could have been influenced by the prophetical books of Haggai and Zechariah. Written in Hebrew about 180 BC, this work demonstrates that Jesus ben Sirach possessed knowledge of the main figures in the scriptures. This implies some collection of writings or at least a standardized version of history. If Ben Sirach's list of Israelite heroes follows a collection of texts, then it reflects the following order: the Torah, followed by Joshua, Judges, Samuel, Kings, Isaiah, Jeremiah, Ezekiel, and the Twelve. In addition, Ben Sirach seems to have been familiar with and used other works which later became part of the canon. His writing does not reflect the use of Ruth, Song of Songs, Esther, Daniel, and perhaps Job (see Leiman, 29).

When Ben Sirach's grandson translated his grandfather's Hebrew work into Greek sometime after 132 BC, he provided the translation with a short explanatory prologue. In this foreword to the work, the grandson comments on his ancestor's reasons for writing:

> Whereas many great teachings have been given to us through the law and the prophets and the others that followed them, on account of which we should praise Israel for instruction and wisdom; and since it is necessary not only that the readers themselves should acquire understanding but also that those who love learning should be able

to help the outsiders by both speaking and writing, my grandfather
Jesus, after devoting himself especially to the reading of the law and
the prophets and the other books of our fathers, and after acquiring
considerable proficiency in them, was himself also led to write something pertaining to instruction and wisdom, in order that, by
becoming conversant with this also, those who love learning should
make even greater progress in living according to the law.
You are urged therefore to read with good will and attention, and to
be indulgent in cases where, despite our diligent labour in translating, we may seem to have rendered some phrases imperfectly. For
what was originally expressed in Hebrew does not have exactly the
same sense when translated into another language. Not only this
work, but even the law itself, the prophecies, and the rest of the
books differ not a little as originally expressed.

A number of elements in this passage are significant for an understanding of this historical development of the canon:

1. The grandson of Ben Sirach refers in three places to what
    appears to be two clearly defined collections of sacred writings:
    the Law (*Torah*) and the Prophets (*Nebiim*).
2. A third group of texts is noted and designated 'the others that
    followed them,' 'the other books of the fathers,' and 'the rest
    of the books.'
3. No single term or descriptive phrase is used to refer to this
    third body of writings.
4. The grandson makes claims for Ben Sirach's work which seem
    to place it on a level with the other books and he describes his
    grandfather's work as a *biblion*, a term he used in denoting the
    non-*Torah* and non-prophetic works.
5. Reference is made to the existence of Greek translations of the
    law, the prophecies, and the rest of the books.

The evidence of Ben Sirach's work and his grandson's prologue
leads to the following conclusions about the development of a
sacred collection of texts which would eventually constitute an
authoritative canon:

1. During the second century BC, certain circles in Judaism
    possessed and utilized two collections of texts, the Law and the
    Prophets (see also II Macc 15:9).
2   The extent of these collections may have coincided with the
    later first two parts of the Jewish canon, the *Torah* and the
    Nebiim, although this is an inference drawn from Ben Sirach's

enumeration of famous men rather than from any list of works.
3. Other works were utilized in these communities, probably in the sense of scripture or edifying literature, but the exact number and content of these writings cannot be determined.
4. No concept of a canon as closed, unalterable collection is directly referred to or indirectly alluded to.

Further texts relevant to the development of a canon are found in the books of Maccabees, which were probably written late in the second century BC. II Maccabees opens with two letters; the second in 1:10–2:15 purports to have been written during the days of Judas Maccabeus. Quite likely, however, II Macc 1:18-2:15 was written by the composer of the book who was summarizing a five-volume history written by an otherwise unknown Jason of Cyrene (see Momigliano). This section contains a number of legends about Nehemiah and Jeremiah which are not attested in the Old Testament although reference is made to works where these are reported (see II Macc 2:1,4,13). These writings (*graphé*) or records (*apographais*) probably refer to such works as those of the Jewish historian Eupolemus (see I Macc 8:17; II Macc 4:11), who wrote sometime after the Maccabean revolt and reported some of these apocryphal tales (see Wacholder, 38–40, 237–42). Further, Nehemiah is said to have 'founded a library and collected books about the kings and prophets, and the writings of David, and letters of kings about votive offerings' (II Macc 2:13). This text seems to be arguing that Nehemiah was responsible for the establishment of a Jerusalem library and for collecting a major portion of the sacred writings. 'Books about the kings and prophets' probably refers to those works now found in the second section of the Hebrew canon, i.e., Joshua to II Kings and Isaiah to Malachi, although this and the subsequent references to the various books could refer totally to nonbiblical works. Chronicles, of course, could be classified as a book about the kings and may also have been included in this reference. 'The writings of David' may refer to the book of Psalms. 'Letters of kings about votive offerings' could denote the material in or the book of Ezra, which contains the edicts of Persian kings concerning Jewish worship and the return from exile.

Several conclusions may be drawn from these statements about Nehemiah.

1. The statements reflect the beliefs of the author about how some of the sacred books were collected; that is, it reflects a

current opinion from the late second century and not necessarily the way things actually happened.

2. The writer probably assumes, although he does not mention,
    the supposition that Ezra brought back the Torah from
    Babylon (see II Macc 2:2). Thus Ezra and Nehemiah were
    considered responsible for collecting, authenticating, and
    making available the Law and the Prophets.

3. Additional books – 'the writings of David and letters of kings
    about votive offerings' – were in existence and were held in
    high esteem.

4. These additional works do not yet include all of the books
    which later went to make up the third section of the Hebrew
    canon.

5. The library assembled in Jerusalem, at least in the author's own
    day, may have possessed such works as those designated
    records or writings in II Macc 2:1,4,13.

After describing the activity of Nehemiah, II Maccabees proceeds
to attribute a similar endeavour to Judas Maccabeus: 'In the same
way Judas also collected all the books that had been lost on
account of the war which had come upon us, and they are in our
possession. So if you have need of them, send people to get them
for you' (II Macc 2:14–15). This text does imply his establishment
of some type of library. The book of I Maccabees notes that Judas
and his followers rescued the Law from the hands of the Gentiles
(I Macc 1:56; 2:48). Leiman (29–30) has suggested that the
Maccabeans, shortly after the death of Antiochus IV in 164 BC,
completed the Jewish canon by closing the third section, the
Writings (*Ketubim*), as a response to the Seleucid attempt to
destroy the scriptures.

There is no evidence that the Maccabeans closed the Jewish
canon. II Maccabees only presents Judas and his followers as rescu-
ing the Law from the Gentiles. However, there is internal evidence
in the Hebrew scriptures that suggests that a rather extensive revision was made in the chronological references to the Torah and
the Former Prophets (Joshua–II Kings) during the early
Maccabean period. As is well known, different chronologies are
found in the Hebrew, Greek, and Samaritan versions of the
genealogies in Genesis 5 and 11:10–32 and in such passages as
Exodus 12:40. Also the Greek and Hebrew texts often differ in the
chronological references in the books of Kings. The following
dates, calculated in years from creation, illustrate the differences:

	Hebrew	Greek	Samaritan
Birth of Abraham	1946	3312	2247
Jacob's Descent into Egypt	2236	3602	2537
Date of the Exodus	2666	3817	2752

According to the chronological reference in the Hebrew of I Kings 6:1, Solomon began work on the temple in his fourth year, which was 480 years after the exodus (the Greek reads 440 years). The figure clashes with other references found in Judges-II Samuel. Chronological data for the period of the judges totals 490 years. To this must be added the 40 years in the wilderness; the time for the careers of Joshua, Samuel, and Saul; and the first four years of Solomon. Nonetheless, according to the Hebrew reference in I Kings 6:1, the construction of the temple would have begun in the year 3146 after creation. The total years for the reigns of Judean kings from the beginning of temple construction to the exile number 430, which gives a date of 3576 for the end of the Jerusalem temple. Calculating 50 years for the exile, the new altar in Jerusalem was dedicated 480 years after construction began on the first temple (see II Chron 36:22) or in the year 3626. The Maccabean rededication of the temple in Jerusalem (I Macc 4:36–59) took place in about 164 BC or 374 years later. The Maccabean rededication of the temple took place in the year 4000 after creation.

The above chronological issues strongly suggest that the Hebrew text of the Torah and Former Prophets was edited during the early Maccabean period as propaganda on behalf of the Maccabeans and their work in rededicating the temple. A date for this event in the year 4000 after creation, in light of the Greek and Samaritan divergencies, is too coincidental to be accidental. Although II Macc 2:14 only suggests that Judas collected the books that were endangered during his days, it also seems that editorial revision, especially in chronological references, also took place. If the text of the Law and the Former Prophets was revised by the early Maccabeans, this would not mean that these works did not possess authoritative status. Such a revision would simply suggest that the text had not acquired a status which prohibited any alteration.

Sometime during the second century and probably no later than 150 BC, a new sect developed in Judaism. Part of this group settled in Qumran on the western shores of the Dead Sea. Discoveries of texts and scriptures of this community have been made in caves in the Qumran region, beginning in 1947. The Qumran community seems to have accepted the Law and the Prophets as sacred scripture. In at least two passages, the Dead Sea Scrolls refer to the Torah and the Prophets as the Books of the Law and the Books of the Prophets (for the references, see Vermes, 86, 104). In addition to this, other writings were used by the community and no doubt were considered authoritative. In this second category – the non-Torah and non-prophetic books – belong not only the remaining works that made their way into the Hebrew canon with the exception of Esther but also works such as Ecclesiasticus and Tobit, numerous writings from the so-called Pseudepigrapha, and sacred writings unique to the community (see Vermes). The evidence from Qumran would suggest that the writings which now comprise the first two divisions of the Jewish canon probably had achieved an authoritative status (as in the prologue to Ecclesiasticus) but that in addition to these two divisions, a wide range of writings functioned as 'scriptures'. The evidence also suggests that certain works which became a part of the third division had not yet acquired a set and uniform content. This is best illustrated by the book of Psalms (see Sanders, 1968). Numerous fragmentary copies of the Psalter have been found at Qumran. The most famous of these is the major psalms scroll from cave eleven which contains parts or all of forty-one biblical psalms in addition to eight texts not now found in the biblical version of this book. The forty-one psalms, however, do not appear in the order of the biblical Psalter and at places vary considerably from the biblical text. This suggests that the Psalter had not yet reached a final form or a defined content when the Qumran community split off from the Jerusalem community.

Two versions of the Torah – the Samaritan and the Greek – were in existence by the second century BC and demonstrate that at least the Torah had what might be called canonical authority for a variety of Jewish communities. The Samaritans accepted only the Pentateuch as authoritative and copied this in an archaic script. When the Samaritan Pentateuch came into being and when this Jewish group finally broke with the Jerusalem community are disputed matters. No doubt both of these had occurred by the end of the second century BC (see Purvis). When the first Greek translation of the Torah was made can no longer be determined. *The Letter of Aristeas*, probably written in the second century BC, claims divine authority and inspiration for a Greek translation of the Torah (the so-called *Septuagint*) which was supposed to have been an official translation produced in Egypt (see Orlinsky, 1975). At the moment, the historical character of the letter's contents are not of concern. The point is that the letter demonstrates the

authoritative status of the Torah (even in Greek translation!) in
Egypt in the second century BC.

In summary, what may be said about the second century BC
developments leading toward a canon of sacred scripture?

1. No concept of a canon which implied a list of included books
    over against excluded books existed.
2. The *Torah* was accepted as authoritative, sacred, and inspired
    by Judaism as a whole.
3. The existence of two authoritative collections (*Torah* and
    Nebiim) is attested in Ecclesiasticus and the Dead Sea Scrolls,
    but it is impossible to determine the works in the second
    collection except indirectly (see Eccl 44–49).
4. Other writings were in circulation and utilized as 'sacred scrip-
    ture'. These writings, however, were not equivalent to what
    became the third division of the Hebrew canon.
5. Some works which later became part of the canon had not yet
    reached their final form. This is most clearly illustrated by the
    book of Psalms at Qumran.

B. The close of the Jewish canon

The next references which illuminate the history and development
of a canon come from the first century AD. Philo Judaeus (about
20 BC–50 AD) of Alexandria was a prolific writer on a variety of
subjects. Unfortunately he offers no discussion of the books which
the Jewish community of his day accepted as authoritative. In
discussing the Jewish sect known as the Therapeutae (in his *De Vita
Contemplativa* 25), he refers to its use of 'laws and oracles delivered
through the mouth of prophets, and psalms and other books by
which knowledge and piety may be increased and perfected'. This
statement suggests that he was not familiar with a tripartite division
of the sacred writings or with any concept of a closed canon. This
same situation is reflected in the New Testament where references
to the 'law and prophets' or 'Moses and the prophets' occur (Matt
22:40; Luke 16:16; 24:27; Acts 13:15). The only New Testament
reference to a tripartite division of texts is found in Luke 24:44,
which speaks of the 'law of Moses, and the prophets, and the
psalms'; but such a reference cannot denote the later Jewish
canon.

The fullest statement from the first century AD on the canon is
that by Josephus (about 37–100 AD) written about 90–95 AD. In

comparing the sacred Jewish writings with those of the Greeks, he wrote:

> It therefore naturally, or rather necessarily, follows (seeing that with us it is not open to everyone to write the records, and that there is no discrepancy in what is written; seeing that, on the contrary, the prophets alone had this privilege, obtaining their knowledge of the most remote and ancient history through the inspiration which they owed to God, and committing to writing a clear account of the events of their time just as they occurred) – it follows, I say, that we do not possess myriads of inconsistent books, conflicting with each other. Our books, those which are justly accredited, are but two and twenty, and contain the record of all time.
>
> Of these, five are the books of Moses, comprising the laws and the traditional history from the birth of man down to the death of the lawgiver. This period falls only a little short of three thousand years. From the death of Moses until Artaxerxes, who succeeded Xerxes as king of Persia, the prophets subsequent to Moses wrote the history of the events of their own times in thirteen books. The remaining four books contain hymns to God and precepts for the conduct of human life.
>
> From Artaxerxes to our own time the complete history has been written, but has not been deemed worthy of equal credit with the earlier records, because of the failure of the exact succession of the prophets.
>
> We have given practical proof of our reverence for our own Scriptures. For, although such long ages have now passed, no one has ventured either to add, or to remove, or to alter a syllable; and it is an instinct with every Jew, from the day of his birth, to regard them as the decrees of God, to abide by them, and, if need be, cheerfully to die for them. Time and again ere now the sight has been witnessed of prisoners enduring tortures and death in every form in the theatres, rather than utter a single word against the laws and the allied documents. (*Contra Apionem* I 37–43)

Josephus' statement contains a number of important considerations concerning the canon:

1. The sacred writings were believed to have been composed by inspired men and cover history from the creation to the time of Artaxerxes.
2. Works describing the history after Artaxerxes exist but do not possess an inspired character since the succession of the prophets ended the Persian period.
3. The sacred books are limited in number; namely, twenty-two.

4. The contents of the books are consistent and without discrepancies.
5. The scriptures are the object of great reverence and their wording and contents are sacrosanct.
6. The scriptures are separated into three divisions.

This quote from Josephus also raises a number of problems. First, his division of the books (five books of Moses, thirteen books in the prophets, and four remaining books) parallels no known ancient collection of the Hebrew scriptures. Is Josephus here merely giving his own preferential ordering of the books which reflects his strong historical interests? Or is he drawing upon some arrangement and tradition whose origin and location can no longer be determined? Josephus had contacts with practically all elements in Palestinian Judaism; he claims to have received from the Romans the sacred writings from the temple (*Life* 418) and he was associated with both Alexandria and Rome. Was his ordering of the books derived from the tradition of one of these centres or does it perhaps reflect the priestly tradition from the Jerusalem temple? This cannot be determined, but Josephus' testimony suggests that the ordering of the material which was to become the second and third parts of the Jewish canon was still fluid in his day.

Second, Josephus reports that 'our books, those which are justly accredited, are but two and twenty'. Does this imply that at the time of his writing, even the exact contents of the second and third divisions of sacred scripture were still uncertain? Many scholars have assumed that Josephus' twenty-two are actually equivalent to the later twenty-four books (see Leiman, 32-34 and references cited there). This position argues that Josephus counted Ruth as part of Judges and Lamentations as part of Jeremiah. Evidence to support such a view is the following:

a. In the *Talmud,* Judges and Ruth are ascribed to a common author (Samuel) and Jeremiah is considered the author of Lamentations.
b. A number of late Christian writers (but never Jewish) refer to the twenty-two books which make up the Hebrew canon and in some cases Ruth-Judges and Jeremiah-Lamentations are explicitly treated as units (for the references, see Leiman, 37–50).

A minority of scholars assume that when Jospehus referred to twenty-two books his total was lacking two books which ultimately came to be included in the third division of the canon (see Zeitlin,

Contemporary Catholic Theology – a Reader

172–78; Orlinsky, 1974, 272–77). Evidence to support such a view is the following:

a. Josephus' statement is quite clear and should be taken literally.
b. Evidence from later Judaism suggests that some works – perhaps Ecclesiastes and Esther – were included in the third division after the time of Josephus.

The *Mishnah* reports that there was discussion near the end of the first century AD about the sacredness of some works:

> All the holy writings defile the hands [are sacred]. Song of Songs and Ecclesiastes defile the hands. Rabbi Judah said, 'Song of Songs defiles the hands, but Ecclesiastes was in dispute.' ... But Rabbi Akiba said, 'God forbid! No one in Israel disputed the fact that Song of Songs defiles the hands, for the entire world does not compare with the day that Song of Songs was given to Israel. All the writings are holy, but Song of Songs is holiest of all. If there was a dispute, it was only about Ecclesiastes.' *(Yadaim 3:5)*

This text suggests that the inclusion of Ecclesiastes was probably a debatable issue, no doubt because of the radical skepticism of the work. In addition to Song of Songs and Ecclesiastes, the book of Esther was also a debated inclusion (see Zeitlin, 175-78). The evidence that Esther was included late is as follows:

a. The festival of Purim, which is advocated in Esther, is given as a semi-holiday by the *Megillat Taanit*, which lists the days when fasting is prohibited but which are not noted in the biblical text. This suggests that Esther was not yet accepted as scripture when *Megillat Taanit* was drawn up (late first century AD?) otherwise there would have been no reason to mention Purim.
b. Later rabbis appealed to *Megillat Taanit* to support the celebration of Purim rather than the book of Esther.
c. The *Talmud* notes that 'Esther does not defile the hands' (Rabbi Samuel, 3rd century), that the book 'was composed by divine inspiration to be read but not to be written down', and that 'Esther petitioned the sage "Record me for posterity".' *(Megillah 7a)*.
d. Several Christian writers, of whom the most important witness is Melito, bishop of Sardis (about 170 AD), did not list Esther among the works that the Jewish community considered canonical.

The above considerations suggest that at the time of Josephus the status of Ecclesiastes and Esther was unsettled. Esther was probably not accepted as a 'writing which defiles the hands' until the second century AD and then due to the pressure of public opinion and the influence of its use in Purim (so Zeitlin, 176).

The oldest reference to a Jewish canon composed of twenty-four books is found in II Esdras 14, a work whose first edition probably appeared during the first half of the second century AD. In this account, Ezra is divinely commanded to take five scribes and writing materials, to go apart into a field, to drink a liquid that looked like water with the colour of fire, and to dictate to the scribes who would write without knowledge of the characters they were recording.

> So during the forty days ninety-four books were written. And when the forty days were ended, the Most High spoke to me, saying, 'Make public the twenty-four books that you wrote first and let the worthy and the unworthy read them; but keep the seventy that were written last, in order to give them to the wise among your people. For in them is the spring of understanding, the fountain of wisdom, and the river of knowledge.' And I did so. *(II Esdras* 14:4448*)*

This text clearly assumes a twenty-four book canon. However, to stress this point is not the central emphasis of the passage. First, the text is really arguing for the continued use of the books – the 'seventy' – which did not make it into the canon. Second, an inspiration and divine dictation are claimed for these as for the twenty-four. Third, the text advocates the use of these books by the wise who can understand their great wisdom while the canonical works are to be available to and used by all. The question of the use of these noncanonical books was debated as the following statement from the *Mishnah* illustrates:

> The following have no share in the world to come; he who maintains that the resurrection is not intimated in the Torah, or that the Torah was not divinely revealed, and an Epicurean [a byword for one of deviant belief]. Rabbi Akiba (died in 135 AD) adds: one who reads the outside books [the noncanonical works]... *(Sanhedrin* 10:1*)*

The use of the 'outside books' continued to be a topic of discussion within Judaism for some time and such works as Ecclesiasticus continued to be widely quoted (see Leiman, 86–102).

In summary, what can be said about the final stages of the canonization process in Judaism?

1. In the second century AD, the Torah was accorded an authoritative and sacred status even in its Greek translation.
2. The Prophets were no doubt considered as inspired writings, but the exact titles and number of the books in this group cannot be determined.
3. The third division of the Hebrew canon or what was to comprise this group was very fluid during the last century BC and the first century AD. Various sacred writings were utilized as venerated texts perhaps varying from group to group in Judaism.
4. By the time of Josephus' writing (about 90 AD), Judaism had moved toward a canon that provided a list of authoritative works
5. The development of a final, closed canon of scripture was the work of Pharisaic and rabbinical Judaism which came to prominence after the fall of Jerusalem in 70 AD.
6. Various criteria were used to determine canonicity (most already reflected in Josephus):

    a. books had to be written during the age of prophecy which ended during the Persian period;
    b. the books were inspired by God and were written by prophets; and
    c. the books could not be inconsistent. The criterion of widespread acceptance no doubt was important even if unstated.

7. Works were excluded when they failed to meet the above criteria or where their contents or legal practices openly contradicted Jewish faith and practices as understood in Pharisaic Judaism (see Orlinsky, 1974, 277-86).
8. The period from 70 (the date of the temple's destruction) until about 100 AD was a decisive stage in canonical development. The exact manner in which developments took place during the period, however, cannot be determined and one should avoid speaking of the authoritative actions of councils such as has been assumed for the so-called Council of Jamnia/Jabneh in 90 AD (see Lewis).
9. The final tripartite Jewish canon, including Esther and with the *Talmudic* distribution of the works among the three divisions, was a product of the second century AD.

C. The Old Testament in the early Church

When we turn to the Old Testament canon in the Christian Church, several general factors should be kept in mind. First, the early Church did not inherit a closed canon of normative scriptures from Judaism. Second, the Church did receive from Judaism the Law (the five books of Moses) as authoritative and normative and probably also those works which Judaism designated the Prophets. In addition to these, Christianity was heir to numerous other sacred writings, many of revered and widespread usage. Third, the early Church, due to its rapid orientation to the Greco-Roman world, utilized the scriptures in Greek translations as had some Jewish communities for some time. Fourth, the early Church developed its own Old Testament, which was more inclusive than the Hebrew canon and was characterized by a different order for many of the writings.

The early Church utilized and quoted as scripture a larger group of writings than that which came to be accepted as canonical in Judaism. Quotations from and reliance upon various extracanonical works have been seen in the New Testament. The extent of these will vary from scholar to scholar since none of these works are quoted by name (compare Sundberg, 1964, 54–55; Oepke, 988-92; Leiman, 40–41). The clearest use of extracanonical works by a New Testament writer is found in the book of Jude. The author of this work alludes to an episode (v. 9) known from the *Assumption of Moses* and refers to a prophecy by Enoch (vv. 14–15; from 1 *Enoch* 1:9).

The fact that Christianity went its own way apart from, but not completely out of touch with, Judaism in regard to the canon is supported by a number of considerations. First, many Christians were aware that the collection of scriptures which they used differed from the Jewish canon. Melito, bishop of Sardis (about 170 AD), wrote to his brother Onesimus providing him with a list of books in the Hebrew canon. Onesimus desired 'to know the accurate facts about the ancient writings, how many they are in number, and what is their order ....' According to Eusebius' account (Church History IV. xxvi. 13), Melito claimed to have travelled to the East and explored the issue. His list of twenty-two books, which omits Esther and Lamentations, the latter probably assumed to be part of Jeremiah, and Onesimus' inquiry indicate 'the unsettled state of the Old Testament canon of the Christian Church in the second century AD' (Leiman, 48). Over thirty such lists as Melito provides are known prior to the sixth century and tend to vary in content and sequence of books.

Origen, early in the third century, shows quite clearly that he recognized the differences between Christian and Jewish scriptures by referring to 'their scriptures' and 'our scriptures'. He notes that Jews did not use Tobit and Judith although the Churches did (*Ad Africanum XIII*). Origen also knew that the Greek translation often contained textual readings not found in the Hebrew and vice versa.

> And I make it my endeavour not to be ignorant of their various readings, lest in my controversies with the Jews I should quote them what is not found in their copies and that I may make some use of what is found there, even though it should not be in our scriptures. *(Ad Africanum V)*

He even accused the Jewish leaders of taking 'away from the people every passage which might bring discredit among the people' (i.e., some passages and terms in the Greek text that were interpreted in a Christian sense were not found in the Hebrew text; see *Ad Africanum IX*). Origen carried on correspondence with Africanus concerning the validity and authenticity of some of the additions to Daniel found in the Greek, a further sign of the knowledge that Jewish and Christian collections differed.

Second, Christian writers quoted as scripture many of the writings which were not included in the Hebrew canon. Tobit, Sirach, Wisdom of Solomon, and other works are quoted by the Church Fathers and introduced by phrases as 'it is written' and 'scripture says'.

Third, some texts which never became part of the Christian Old Testament were sometimes quoted as scripture. This is best illustrated by the book of Enoch. Tertullian (about 160–220 AD) defended the authoritative status of the work and wrote:

> I am aware that the Scripture of Enoch ... is not received by some, because it is not admitted into the Jewish canon either. I suppose they did not think that, having been published before the deluge, it could have safely survived that worldwide calamity, the abolisher of all things. If that is the reason (for rejecting it) let them recall to their memory that Noah, the survivor of the deluge, was the grandson of Enoch himself. If he had not this (conservative power) by so short a route, there would still be this (consideration) to warrant our assertion of (the genuineness of) this Scripture: he could equally have received it, under the Spirit's inspiration, after it had been destroyed by the violence of the deluge, as, after the destruction of Jerusalem by the Babylonian storming of it, every document of the Jewish litera-

ture is generally agreed to have been restored through Ezra.

But since Enoch in the same Scripture has preached likewise concerning the Lord, nothing at all must be rejected by us which pertains to us .... By the Jews it may now seem to have been rejected for that (very) reason, just like all the other (portions) which tell of Christ .... To these considerations is added the fact that Enoch possessed a testimony in the Apostle Jude. *(On Apparel of Women I* 3; quoted from Sundberg, 1964, pp. 164–65)

Tertullian here advances four arguments to support the acceptance of Enoch as scripture:

a. its great antiquity;
b. its possible renewal by divine inspiration;
c. its prophecies concerning Christ; and
d. its utilization by the apostle Jude.

Origen wrote that 'the books which bear the name Enoch do not at all circulate in the Churches as divine' (*Contra Celsum V* 54) although in *De Principiis* IV 35, he refers to Enoch as a prophet and quotes two passages from *I Enoch* 17 as grounds out of scripture for understanding a particular subject.

The use of Enoch materials as scripture, although infrequent in the early Church, suggests that early Christians did not work with a closed canon.

Fourth, the great Christian uncial manuscripts from the fourth century testify to the generally unsettled state of the Old Testament in the early Church (see the charts in Sundberg, 1964, 58–59). Among the Old Testament writings, *Codex Vaticanus* contains Wisdom of Solomon, Sirach, Judith, Tobit, Baruch, and the Epistle of Jeremiah. *Codex Sinaiticus* contains Tobit, Judith, I–II Maccabees, Wisdom of Solomon, and Sirach. *Codes Alandrinus*, which dates perhaps from the next century, contains Baruch, Epistle of Jeremiah, Tobit, Judith, I–IV Maccabees, Wisdom of Solomon, Sirach, and Psalms of Solomon. This manuscript evidence demonstrates the fluidity in both contents and the sequential arrangement of books in the early Church's Old Testament.

During the latter half of the fourth century and the first quarter of the fifth century, the early Church moved toward the establishment of a specific Old Testament canon although not without differences of opinion and controversy. Scholars and the Church in the East tended to support an Old Testament limited by the Jewish canon while the Church and theologians in the West tended to support a more inclusive collection.

In the East, the Council of Laodicea (about 360 AD?) opposed the use of noncanonical books in the Church and spelled out the contents of the Old Testament. The list of the canonical books given by the council followed 'the Jewish canon but according to the Greek recension, Jeremiah including Lamentations, Baruch, and the Epistle of Jeremy, two books of Ezra, and we should probably understand Daniel and Esther in their expanded forms' (Sundberg, 1964, 148).

Athanasius (295–373), bishop of Alexandria, was strongly influenced by the Jewish tradition in his enumeration of the canonical books of the Old Testament although he places the Writings before the Prophets; includes II Esdras, combines Baruch, Lamentations, and the Epistle of Jeremiah (Jeremy) with the book of Jeremiah; and omits Esther (see his *Letters on the Paschal Festival XXXIX*). He enumerates the books which he places in the category of noncanonical or apocryphal writings: Wisdom of Solomon, Sirach, Esther(!), Judith and Tobit.

Jerome (about 347–419), after his settlement in Bethlehem, was a strong supporter of the Hebrew canon and among the early Christian scholars had the closest contact with the Jews of his day. He was familiar with the tripartite division of the Jewish canon: Torah (Genesis, Exodus, Leviticus, Numbers, and Deuteronomy), Prophets (Joshua, Judges with Ruth, Samuel, Kings, Isaiah, Jeremiah with Lamentations, Ezekiel, and the Book of the Twelve); and the Writings (Job, Psalms, Proverbs, Ecclesiastes, Song of Songs, Daniel, Chronicles, Ezra with Nehemiah, and Esther). He was also aware of a division in which Ruth and Lamentations were placed among the Writings (see his *Preface to the Books of Samuel and Kings*, quoted in Leiman, 45–47). Jerome concluded his discussion of the contents of the canon by saying:

> This preface to the Scriptures may serve as a 'helmeted' introduction to all the books which we turn from Hebrew into Latin, so that we may be assured that what is not found in our list must be placed among the apocrypha. Wisdom, therefore, which generally bears the name of Solomon, and the book of Jesus, the Son of Sirach, and Judith, and Tobit ... are not in the canon. The first book of Maccabees I have found to be in Hebrew, the second is Greek, as can be proved from the very style.

Jerome argued that while the uncanonical books might be read in the Churches they should be used solely 'for edifying the people, not for the corroboration of ecclesiastical doctrines' (*Preface to*

Solomon's Books). For Jerome, the writings of the Hebrew canon constituted the works used and quoted by Jesus and the early Church and thus whose usage had an apostolic authority.

Not all the Fathers in the East agreed with Athanasius and Jerome and even the latter two scholars frequently quoted from the works they had designated 'apocrypha' as if they were scripture (see Sundberg, 1964, 58, 138–42).

In the western Church, the view espoused by Augustine, among others, came to prevail. Augustine (354–430) argued for an inclusive canon of forty-four books (i.e., the books contained in the Hebrew canon, combining Ruth with Judges and Lamentations with Jeremiah, plus Tobit, Judith, I–II Maccabees, I–II Esdras, Wisdom of Solomon, and Ecclesiasticus; *On Christian Doctrine II*.viii.13). He appealed to the tradition and practice of the Church as authority for his position.

> In order to know what are the canonical Scriptures, you must follow the authority of the greatest possible number of catholic Churches, especially of those which were founded by apostles and merited receiving epistles. Those received by all the Churches will, therefore, be preferred to those received only by some. Of these latter, those will be preferred which are received by the greatest number and by the most important Churches, to those which are received only by the fewest and smallest Churches. If we were to find some held by the majority while others were held by the most important, although it would not be possible to decide easily, however, I would reckon them as having equal authority. *(On Christian Doctrine II.viii.12)*

Augustine offered arguments for the exclusion of some works from the canon although these had circulated in the Church.

> If I may recall far more ancient times, our patriarch Noah was certainly even before that great deluge, and I might not undeservedly call him a prophet, forasmuch as the ark he made, in which he escaped with his family, was itself a prophecy of our times. What of Enoch, the seventh from Adam? Does not the canonical epistle of the Apostle Jude declare that he prophesied? But the writings of these men could not be held as authoritative either among the Jews or us, on account of their too great antiquity, which made it seem needful to regard them with suspicion, lest false things should be set forth instead of truth. For some writings which are said to be theirs are quoted by those who, according to their own humor, loosely believe what they please. But the purity of the canon has not admitted these writings, not because the authority of these men who pleased God is

rejected, but because they are not believed to be theirs. Nor ought it to appear strange if writings for which so great antiquity is claimed are held in suspicion, seeing that in the very history of the kings of Judah and Israel containing their acts, which we believe to belong to the canonical Scripture, very many things are mentioned which are not explained there, but are said to be found in other books which the prophets wrote, the very names of these prophets being sometimes given, and yet they are not found in the canon which the people of God received. Now I confess the reason for this is hidden from me; only I think that even those men, to whom certainly the Holy Spirit revealed those things which ought to be held as of religious authority, might write some things as men by historical diligence, and others as prophets by divine inspiration; and these things were so distinct, that it was judged that the former should be ascribed to themselves, but the latter to God speaking through them: and so one pertained to the abundance of knowledge, the other to the authority of religion. In that authority the canon is guarded. So that, if any writings outside of it are now brought forward under the name of ancient prophets, they cannot serve even as an aid to knowledge, because it is uncertain whether they are genuine; and on this account they are not trusted, especially those of them in which some things are found that are even contrary to the truth of the canonical books, so that it is quite apparent they do not belong to them. *(City of God XVIII 38)*

For Augustine, the appropriate and inspired version of the Old Testament for the Church was that based on the Greek version. However, he claimed that the Hebrew text had been given through inspiration and did not accuse the Jews of having altered the text. Augustine argued that the persons who had produced the writings and translations found in the Greek version of the *Septuagint* were as equally inspired as the original prophets.

> If anything is in the Hebrew copies and not in the version of the *Septuagint*, the Spirit of God did not choose to say it through them [i.e., the *Septuagint* writers and translators], but only through the prophets. But whatever is in the *Septuagint* and not in the Hebrew copies, the same Spirit chose rather to say through the latter, thus showing that both were prophets. *(City of God XVIII 43)*

The inclusive canon of the Old Testament, supported by arguments such as those of Augustine, was accepted and espoused by local Church councils in the late fourth and early fifth centuries; Hippo in 393 and Carthage in 397 and 419.

D. Protestants and the Hebrew canon

The acceptance and usage of the inclusive canon of the Old Testament were almost universal in the medieval Church. Jerome's position, which argued for an Old Testament canon limited to the books in the Hebrew Bible, however, continued to have limited influence. Jerome's view was adopted in the Wycliffe Bible in the early fourteenth century. The revival of Christian interest in the study of Hebrew in the fifteenth century made the Church more aware of the difference between the Hebrew and Christian canons. Johannes Reuchlin (1455–1522), a Catholic German humanist, was very competent in Hebrew and advocated that only those scriptures found in the Hebrew canon should be considered as the Old Testament of the Church.

The issue of the canon became a matter of great controversy as a result of the Protestant Reformation. Martin Luther and his followers, especially Andreas Bodenstein of Karlstadt, argued that the text of the Bible was to be accepted over the authority of the Church and its traditions. In his debates with Johann Maier of Eck, held at Leipzig in June and July 1519, Luther opposed the doctrine of purgatory. Eck argued that such a doctrine was biblical and confronted Luther with the teaching of II Macc 12:46. Luther then advocated that the canon of the Old Testament should be limited to those works found in the Hebrew scriptures and appealed to Jerome's authority and the latter's argument that the Jewish canon was the scripture used by Jesus and the early Church. In Luther's first complete German translation of the Bible in 1534, he included Judith, Wisdom of Solomon, Tobit, Ecclesiasticus, Baruch, Epistle of Jeremiah, I-II Maccabees, the Additions to Daniel and Esther, and the Prayer of Manasseh at the end of the translation with the heading: 'Apocrypha, that is books which are not held to be equal to holy scripture and yet are profitable and good to read.'

Protestantism, as a rule, followed the example of Luther and relegated those books not found in the Hebrew canon to separate appendices in editions of the Bible or else dropped them entirely. In both cases they were no longer assigned any authoritative status. The Church of England, in article six of the Thirty-nine Articles (1562), followed Jerome and said of the 'apocryphal' works that 'the Church doth read them for example of life and instructions of manners; but yet it doth not apply them to establish any doctrine.' The Westminster Confession of 1648 went much further: 'The books commonly called Apocrypha, not being of divine inspiration, are no part of the canon of Scripture; and therefore of no authority to the Church of God, nor to be otherwise approved, or made use of, than any other human writings' (I 3).

The Catholic Church, in reaction to the Protestant Reformation and Luther's position on these writings, engaged in serious discussion over the content of the Old Testament canon. Even at the Council of Trent in March, 1546, various options were debated. The council finally decided to declare all the works in the Latin *Vulgate* (the inclusive canon) as canonical, authoritative, and inspired although I and II Esdras and the Prayer of Manasseh were placed in an appendix following the New Testament. The Eastern Orthodox Church established its canon at the synod of Jerusalem in 1672.

E. The canon and contemporary studies

Subsequent reflection and scholarly research on the origin of the canon have led to a number of positions and practices within the Church and scholarship in general.

1. Catholic scholars and writers tend to refer to canonical and deutero-canonical books. The former designates those works contained in the Hebrew canon and about which there has never been any major controversy in the Church. The latter term refers to those works which Protestants designate the Apocrypha.
2. The view, advocated in rabbinic Judaism and adopted in most of Protestantism, that the Hebrew canon was closed in the time of Ezra has been generally abandoned. The recognition that some works, such as Daniel, were produced after the time of Ezra raised insurmountable obstacles for this view.
3. The belief that the *Septuagint,* or Greek version of the Old Testament, represented the canon of Alexandrian Judaism while the Hebrew canon represented the canon of Palestinian Judaism can no longer be substantiated (see Sundberg, 1964). No normative Alexandrian canon ever existed in Judaism.
4. The *Septuagint,* or inclusive Old Testament canon, was the creation of the early Church. The Church did not inherit a closed canon of scripture from Judaism.
5. A renewed interest in the apocrypha or deutero-canonical writings has become characteristic of Protestantism. Many modern editions of the Bible have restored these works. A recent

edition of the *Oxford Annotated Bible*, for example, contains not only the deutero-canonical books but also III and IV Maccabees.

6. Some Protestant scholars are calling for a reconsideration of the Church's attitude towards the Apocrypha. The fact that the apocryphal writings were considered as scripture by much of the Church for centuries raises the question of what does constitute the Christian canon. Sundberg, for example, has written:

> Any Protestant doctrine of canonization that takes seriously the question of Christian usage and historical and spiritual heritage will lead ultimately to the Christian OT as defined in the Western Church at the end of the fourth and the beginning of the fifth centuries .... It is evident that both in content and doctrine, Protestantism, in its view of OT canon, has broken away from its historical heritage. The basis for this rupture has mistakenly been thought to be that the earliest Christian OT usages, that of Jesus, the apostles, and the NT writers, paralleled the Jewish canon. Since that basis no longer obtains, it remains for Protestant Christians either to return to the historical heritage from which Protestantism sprang or to develop a new apologetic for its OT canon. *(1966, 202–3)*

Bibliography

Campenhausen, H. F. von *The Formation of the Christian Bible* (Philadelphia: Fortress Press, 1972).

Leiman, S. Z. *The Canonization of Hebrew Scripture: The Talmudic and Midrashic Evidence* (Hamden, CT: Anchon Books, 1976).

Lewis, J. P. 'What Do We mean by Jabneh?' *JBR* XXXII (1964) pp. 125–32 = *CHMB*, pp. 254–61.

Meyer, R. 'The Canon and Apocrypha in Judaism,' *TDNT* III (1966) pp. 978–87.

Momigliano, A. 'The Second Book of Maccabees,' *CP* LXX (1975) pp. 81–91.

Oepke, A. '*Biblio apokryphoi* in Christianity,' *TDNT* III (1966) pp. 987–1000.

Orlinsky, H. M. 'The Canonization of the Hebrew Bible and the Exclusion of the Apocrypha,' in his *Essays in Biblical Culture and Bible Translation* (New York: KTAV, 1974) pp. 257–86.

Idem, 'The Septuagint as Holy Writ and the Philosophy of the Translators,' *HUCA* XLVI (1975) pp. 89–114.

Purvis, J. D. *The Samaritan Pentateuch and the Origin of the Samaritan Sect* (Cambridge: Harvard University Press, 1968).

Sanders, J. A. 'Cave 11 Surprises and the Question of Canon,' *MQ* XXI
    (1968) pp. 284–98 = *CMHB*, pp. 37–51.
idem, Torah and Canon (Philadelphia: Fortress Press, 1972).
idem, 'Adaptable for Life: The Nature and Function of Canon,' *MD*, pp.
    531–60.
Sundberg, Jr., A. C. 'The Old Testament in the Early Church: A Study in
    Canon,' *HTR* LI (1958) pp. 205–26.
idem, The Old Testament of the Early Church (Cambridge: Harvard University
    Press, 1964).
idem, 'The Protestant Old Testament Canon: Should It Be Re-examined?'
    CBQ XXVIII (1966) pp. 194–203.
idem, 'The "Old Testament": A Christian Canon,' *CBQ* XXX (1968) pp.
    143–55 = *CMHB*, pp. 99–111.
idem, 'The Bible Canon and the Christian Doctrine of Inspiration,' *Int*
    XXIX (1975) pp. 352–71.
Vermes, G. *The Dead Sea Scrolls in English* (Hammondsworth/Baltimore:
    Penguin Books, 1962, [2]1975).
Wacholder, B. Z. *Eupolemus: A Study of Judaeo-Greek Literature* (Cincinnati:
    Hebrew Union College, 1974).
Zeitlin, S. 'An Historical Study of the Canonization of the Hebrew
    Scriptures,' *PAAJR* III (1931–32) pp. 121–58 = *CMHB* pp. 164–201.

Chapter 6

What is a Prophet?

Jean-Pierre Prévost

Introduction

'A virgin most pure, as the prophets do tell, hath brought forth a baby, as it hath befel ...' These words from a traditional Christmas carol largely represent the view that has long prevailed among Christians about the biblical prophets. They are credited above all, if not exclusively, with having announced the one who is at the heart of our faith, Jesus the Christ. At the same time, the prophets become the heralds of the Messiah, and there is interest in them to the degree that they predicted and prepared for his coming.

This view of the prophets is confirmed and to some degree perpetuated by the lectionary of the Roman liturgy, in which the texts of the prophets, and principally that of Isaiah, have a privileged place in the seasons on Advent and Christmas: the biblical prophets become the bards *par excellence* of the Christian hope.

However, little is known about the prophets themselves and their specific message. To all intents and purposes, all that is remembered of Hosea, Micah, Isaiah, Jeremiah and the rest is that they spoke of the Messiah, and there is no thought of the specific historical context of each prophet and the particular colouring which he gave to his message. When announcements are made in Church like 'A reading from the Book of Amos' or 'A reading from the Book of Habakkuk', or 'A reading from the Book of Zephaniah', I get the impression that many people switch off. Very often they do not have the least idea of the time and place in which these prophets lived. Did they live in the eighth century before Jesus Christ or in the sixth? In a period of peace or prosperity? In

Judah or Israel? In the reign of a just king or that of an oppressor? Were they countrymen or townsfolk? Were they courtiers or commoners? Were they regional heroes or major figures on the national and international scene?

Even more serious is the fact that liturgical custom necessitates a selection of quite brief passages which do not in themselves make it possible to grasp the complexity and totality of the message of a prophet.

Basically, as far as the prophets are concerned, even now we are still in the position of the Ethiopian eunuch who, as the Acts of the Apostles tells us, was reading the scroll of Isaiah, more specifically one of the Servant Songs. 'And the eunuch said to Philip, "About whom, pray, does the prophet say this, about himself or about someone else?" Then Philip opened his mouth, and beginning with the scripture he told him the good news of Jesus' (8:.34–35).

Prophets in freedom

The question has often been asked in our day: 'What does one have to do to be a prophet?' In other words, is there a foreseeable way by which one comes to adopt the role of a prophet? Are there techniques that can be learned? Or even a profile and an itinerary to follow?

If we look at the profile and the itinerary of the biblical prophets, we soon see that there is no laid down model, stereotype or fixed itinerary leading infallibly to prophecy. The biblical prophets had very different religious careers. Not only did they come from all kinds of backgrounds, but their spheres of life and their training, their religious experiences, their manner of communication and their style of speaking varied greatly. Reading their writings and those of their disciples, one could say that 'all roads lead to prophecy', since the prophets show so much originality and freedom.

Let's look at the profiles of some of them in order to get a better idea of this amazing diversity in the ways that lead to prophecy.

Isaiah

He is a married man, a court diplomat. He is in the thick of the action where decisions are taken. At the time when his vocation as a prophet emerges, he seems to be in full possession of himself, sure of himself: 'Send me, Lord!' (Isa 6:8). He is a man of great decisions and great political and religious debates. He is also one of the greatest poets of the Bible.

Jeremiah

He is young. He has all the enthusiasm and the verve of youth. He will soon become fascinated by the promises of Josiah's religious reform. But he remains fearful and vulnerable. In a way he is very 'human'. He will come to experience the disappointments of an abortive religious reform, the disquiet of times of war and exile, the weight of a solitary life – he receives the order to remain celibate (Jer 16:1) – and he will know persecution by his compatriots, in particular by the religious authorities of Jerusalem. He, too, is a poet of towering genius, but he does not have Isaiah's assurance, and no prophet has 'confessed' better than he the way in which the mission with which he has been entrusted tears him apart. 'Why is my pain unceasing, my wound incurable, refusing to be healed? Truly you have become to me like a deceitful brook, like waters that fail' (Jer 15:18).

Ezekiel

He is a member of the priestly class which was so severely affected by the capture and destruction of the temple. But this priest is not purely a cultic official. He can identify at great depth the sense of trial inflicted on his people and communicate it with powerful imagery and unusual symbols. Though his work sometimes seems to us confused and takes on the aspect of a fantastic epic which is difficult to decipher, he has the merit of leaving the well-trodden ways and addressing his contemporaries vividly. A contemporary of Jeremiah, he differs from him particularly by his marital status, since he was a happily married man before he had the tragic experience of mourning a wife whom he cherished as 'the joy of (his) eyes' (Ezek 24:16). He also differs from Jeremiah by virtue of the mission conferred on him to proclaim the word of God in the land of exile, as one of those deported to Babylon.

Hosea

He has experienced a difficult and tormented marriage. God himself invited him to take in marriage 'a woman who is a prostitute' (Hos 1:2). That is not what one would normally expect of a prophet of God! But it is precisely through the difficulties, the misfortunes and the 'impossibilities' of his experience as a husband and father that the prophet is to discover the tenderness and faithfulness of God.

Amos

He is a countryman with intense and colourful language, has nothing about him which indicated the prophet. Furthermore, he claims that he did not seek this role: 'I am no prophet nor a prophet's son; but I am a herdsman and dresser of sycamore trees' (Amos 7:14). In a sense, nothing prepared him for his mission. However, this man, who came late to prophecy, was able to find a clear and firm language in which to denounce the nonsense of triumphalist liturgies which easily adjusted to the unjust and oppressive treatment reserved for the very poorest (5:21–24).

Jonah

And what are we to say of the recalcitrant Jonah, a prophet 'despite himself'? He did not carry much conviction, poor thing! At least he had his little ideas on salvation, and he kept to them. He did all he could to escape his mission. But even against his will, prophecy asserted itself, and the people of Nineveh understood and accepted his message. However, despite the resounding success of his brief intervention in the streets of Nineveh and the sudden conversion of the whole city, Jonah was still not content and prayed to die. Hardly edifying for a man of God who should rather have been rejoicing at witnessing such prodigal demonstrations of mercy!

So there is no predetermined course to follow, nor are there barriers which could get in the way of being a prophet. Among the prophets of the Bible we find both men and women; young men (Samuel and Jeremiah) and old men (Samuel in his old age and the aged Simeon), or people of a mature age; fully active men (Amos, Hosea, Isaiah, Ezekiel), 'career' prophets living among other prophets, like Elisha; and 'surprise prophets' like Eldad and Medad (Num 11:26–27) or Amos; people deeply rooted in their milieu (Hosea, Isaiah, Ezekiel) and 'uprooted' people, working outside their original sphere (Balaam, Amos, Jonah). The prophets came from different social classes: Amos is a countryman and a cultivator; Isaiah is a diplomat who has access to the royal court and from whom the city of Jerusalem has no secrets; Ezekiel is a priest, as is Jeremiah, at least by descent; and Deborah is a judge, fighting and involved in the resistance.

Thus the Bible presents us with a rich mosaic of prophecy and no one can *a priori* be excluded from this vocation which is so important for the life of believing communities.

What is a Prophet?

This is a question which does not interest us in a purely biographical or psychological sense, but in a literary and theological sense. We want to get to know the texts and what they set out to say from the perspective of faith.

The prophets in the Bible

In this chapter, the first question to arise is this. What do we mean by 'the prophets' in an expression like 'How to Read the Prophets'? What will be the object of our study?

Here the Bible has surprises in store for us. The biblical definition of prophets, and more specifically of prophetic books, does not necessarily coincide with ours. The Hebrew Bible, which contains thirty-nine books [forty-six books when the 'Deutero-Canonical' Books: Wisdom, Tobit, Judith, 1 & 2 Maccabees, and Baruch are included – editors], adopted a tripartite division which is different from the arrangement in the 'Old Testament' with which Christians are familiar: the Law (the Pentateuch = the first five books), the prophets and the Writings. So there are an impressive number of books (thirty-four of them) which the Jewish tradition put either with the Prophets or with the Writings. Of this number the Jewish tradition kept twenty-one to form this second part of the Bible, which it denotes by the general title 'the Prophets'. In speaking here of 'prophets' or 'the prophetic literature' we shall be referring to all these twenty-one books of the Hebrew Bible.

The most amazing thing about this classification, as far as we are concerned, comes right at the beginning of the collection. There we find six books which beyond question we would not tend to define as prophetic: the books of Joshua, Judges, (I and II) Samuel and (I and II) Kings. A first reading might incline us to put them in the third section with, for example, the books of Chronicles or those of Ezra and Nehemiah. How could they stand comparison with the majestic poetry and incisive oracles of prophets like Amos, Isaiah or Jeremiah?

The prophets in history

	Prophet	Ministry (BC)
1.	Amos	750
2.	Hosea	750
3.	Isaiah	740–700
4.	Micah	740
5.	Nahum	660
6.	Zephaniah	630
7.	Jeremiah	626–587
8.	Habakkuk	600
9.	Ezekiel	593–570
10.	Obadiah	580
11.	Haggai	520
12.	Zechariah	520
13.	Joel	??? (between 600 and 200!)
14.	[Jonah]	a fictitious story presenting an eighth-century prophet
15.	Malachi	400

Some important dates for placing the prophets

Chronology (BC)	Events
1200–1000	Period of the Judges and Samuel
1000	David, king of Judah and Israel
970	Solomon, king of Judah and Israel
933	Division into two kingdoms Israel = northern kingdom Judah = southern kingdom
722–721	Capture of Samaria and end of northern kingdom
597	Capture of Jerusalem by Nebuchadnezzar and first deportation to Babylon
587	Destruction of the temple by Nebuchadnezzar and second deportation to Babylon
538	Edict of Cyprus, end of exile and return to Jerusalem.

However, we can understand how these books came to be associated with the prophetic tradition. On the one hand, despite its title, I and II Kings, which comprises forty-seven chapters in all, is just as much the history of the prophets as it is of the kings, with the famous interventions of Elijah, Elisha, Isaiah and Nathan, to mention only the leading figures. In fact, at least half of these forty-seven chapters introduce one or more prophets. Similarly, the two books of Samuel give a prime place to two great figures of early prophecy, Samuel and Nathan. On the other hand, on a deeper level, we discover that in these six books history is constantly read and reread in a prophetic manner. Here the prophets intervene precisely in order to invite another reading, a theological reading, of the history lived out by the kings and the people of Israel and Judah.

There remain the other fifteen books. Isaiah, Jeremiah and Ezekiel are no surprises; they have always been recognized as the great classics of biblical prophecy. On the other hand, from a Catholic perspective it is surprising not to find the name of Daniel on an equal level as a fourth prophet. However, his book is later than those of the other prophets and belongs more with wisdom and apocalyptic writings.

Then come the Twelve, often referred to as minor prophets, not because their message is less important but more prosaically because of the brevity of their individual writings.

'What makes the prophets prophets?' Can we draw up an 'identity card' for them which allows us to distinguish true prophecy from false, and give a better definition of what should be understood today by prophet or prophecy?

The meaning of terms

The etymology of the English word 'prophet' is very instructive. It is a composite word derived from the Greek, formed from a preposition (*pro*) and the name of an agent (*phetes*), the latter derived from a root which means 'say'. So prophesying has something to do with 'saying'. It is essentially a verbal activity.

But how are we to interpret the preposition *pro*? In Greek, it has three main meanings:

1. temporal, 'before';
2. spatial, 'in front of';
3. vicarious or representative, 'in place of' (as, for example in 'pro-cathedral', 'pro-proctor').

In the case of the word prophet and its derivatives in English, Christian tradition has clearly favoured the first sense, the temporal sense, thus giving it the meaning of 'predict' and 'prediction'. The prophets thus become those who spoke in advance, who predicted events to come, and, in a quite particular way, the coming of the Messiah and the different aspects of his mission. However, present-day biblical research links biblical prophecy more with the two other senses of the preposition *pro*. On the one hand, the spatial sense would denote the vital link between the prophet and the community, the prophet and the people. The prophet is the one who speaks *before* the community, who addresses a community. He is the one who adopts a position in relation to the people, who puts himself in front of them in order to confront them with the demands of the covenant.

On the other hand, the 'representative' sense indicates that the prophet is not acting on his own initiative or on his own authority. He has been sent by God and must speak in God's name. The prophet speaks in the name of another, as a spokesman (or spokeswoman).

But there is more than vocabulary. A wider study of the whole of the writing prophets and other prophetic figures that we find in the prophetic literature leads us to perceive a certain number of constants or characteristics which define prophecy. So now let's try to trace the profile of the biblical prophets.

Men of the Word

This first characteristic is the one that best defines the mission of the prophets. They are not scribes, but men of the word. They are people who have spoken, who have come forward, and whose ministry has been devoted to the service of the word. Nowadays we would say that they were 'professionals of the word'.

'Of the word', written with a lower case w. Amos, Hosea, Micah, Jeremiah and Ezekiel take up the word in turn and express it each according to his style and his convictions, and with his own distinctive genius.

But their words seek to be first and foremost an echo of the Word (with a capital W). For the prophets claim to speak in the name of an Other.

Ten of the fifteen books of the writing prophets have the expression 'Words of X' or 'Word of the Lord to X for Y' in their titles. Furthermore, his general title is confirmed in the majority of the individual sayings of the prophets, which are usually introduced or concluded with one of the three following formulae:

- The word of the Lord came to X ... (around 110 times)
- Thus says the Lord (436 times)
- Oracle of the Lord (more than 200 times; usually translated in English versions as 'says the Lord')

The prophets bring the Word of another. They are messengers, spokesmen. So their hearers are invited to receive their words as an expression of the Word of God: 'Hear the word of the Lord' (Jer 2:4).

Furthermore, it could be said that the Word is their sole passion, in both senses of the word. That is, the Word is what brings them alive, animates them and leads them to commit themselves to transforming the word and changing the future of their people. But it is also their passion in the sense that it is the Word that makes them suffer. It is because of the Word that they are persecuted and rejected.

No one has expressed better than Jeremiah this paradox of the Word which brings both happiness and suffering to the prophets:

> When I found your words,
> I devoured them.
> Your words became a joy to me,
> and made me deeply happy.
> Your name has been proclaimed over me,
> Lord, God of hosts.
>
> I did not sit in the company of merry-makers,
> nor did I rejoice.
> I sat alone, constrained by your hand,
> for you filled me with indignation.
>
> Why is my pain unceasing,
> my wound incurable,
> refusing to be healed?
> Truly you have become for me like a deceitful brook,
> like waters that fail (Jer 15:16–18)

His contemporary Ezekiel expresses the same conviction in the form of an image. The Word is a book on which the prophet has to feed (Ezek 3:1–3) and which tastes sweet (the sweetness of honey) and bitter in turn. That is how the word of all the biblical prophets is presented: essentially good news of God proclaimed to the poor, it nevertheless remains terribly demanding for all.

Men of the present

Men of the Word, the prophets are also men of the present. People have tried to make them diviners, proclaiming the 'great adventure', those who knew the course of events in advance and predicted it. But that is not the case.

The prophetic books do not devote themselves to an interpretation of the map of heaven or to wise calculations which would make it possible to read the future. On the contrary, they apply themselves to deciphering the present. In this connection it is instructive to re-read the headings of the books of the writing prophets. The editors have taken trouble to put in these the chronological frameworks in which the prophets worked.

Thus, for example, for Hosea, 'The word of the Lord was addressed to Hosea the son of Beeri, in the days of Uzziah, Jotham, Ahaz, and Hezekiah, kings of Judah, and in the days of Jeroboam the son of Joash, king of Israel' (1:1); or for Isaiah, 'The vision of Isaiah the son of Amoz, which he saw concerning Judah and Jerusalem, in the days of Uzziah, Jotham, Ahaz, and Hezekiah, kings of Judah' (1:1); or, much later, for Ezekiel, 'In the thirtieth year, in the fourth month, on the fifth day of the month, as I was among the exiles by the river Chebar, the heavens were opened, and I saw visions of God. On the fifth day of the month (it was the fifth year of the exile of King Jehoiachin), the word of the Lord came to Ezekiel the priest, the son of Buzi, in the land of the Chaldaeans by the river Chebar' (1:1–3).

These chronological references are absolutely indispensable for understanding what follows. The Word of God is not timeless and should not be detached from the history which gave it birth. So it is important to read prophecy in the present; before even wanting to apply it to our times, or to Christianize it, we must first listen to it in its original context.

The prophets are not diviners. The *Septuagint*, the Greek translation of the Hebrew Bible, understood this when it preferred the term *prophetes* to *mantis* (as in cheiromancy) to translate the Hebrew *nabi*. The Greek *mantis* has the connotation of 'diviner'. On the other hand, if we read all the prophetic oracles we see that in fact not much space is given over to prediction; so little, indeed, that one could well not notice it. It is very rare that we hear a prophet venturing to date the fulfilment of his oracles. On the contrary, these oracles are usually introduced with a very flexible formula which in no way presumes a real calendar of events: 'In those days', or 'In that day', or 'Days will come …'

The prophets are not futurologists. They are interested first and foremost in the present, their own present and that of their audience. What interests them is not divining the future but changing the present. The prime concern of their oracles is the present history of their people.

That does not mean that the prophets are confined to the horizon of their own history. They are equally passionate about the future, but this is a future with which they have contact. They reject a determinist reading of history, and they believe that the future is connected with the initiative of God and the response of human freedom.

If the word of the prophets had eternal value, one prophet would have been enough: as an extreme, one could have been content with the words of Moses, or Elijah or Isaiah. But precisely because the prophetic word arises for a given era and in response to precise needs, there have been a great variety of spokesmen: Amos, Hosea, Micah, Isaiah, Joel, Jeremiah, Ezekiel, Jonah, Malachi, and so on: 'In many and various ways God spoke of old to our fathers by the prophets; but in these last days he has spoken to us by a Son ...' (Heb 1:1–2). 'In many and various ways.' Not all spoke at the same time and in the same way. Just as we have the gospel of Jesus Christ in four different versions, so the treasure of biblical prophecy has been handed on to us by a multitude of witnesses and literary forms.

It is also interesting to note how biblical prophecy has come down through time and marked the major stages of the history of salvation. Israel had the good fortune to have prophets for the major transitional periods of its history. First, of course, there was *the* prophet, Moses, and his sister Miriam, a prophetess, at the time of the liberation from Egypt and the journey in the wilderness. There was also Deborah in the time of the Judges, the only judge who is said also to have been a prophetess, who led the history of Israel for forty years. When the time came for Israel to give itself a king, it was the prophet Samuel who guided the destiny of the people. The period of the monarchy, from David to Jehoiachin, i.e. until the exile to Babylon, was the period of prophecy *par excellence.* There were great prophets at the time of the exile and at its heart (Jeremiah, Ezekiel) as there also were for the return (Deutero-Isaiah, Haggai, Malachi, Zechariah). Certainly prophecy died out in the course of the three last centuries before Jesus Christ, but the expectation of a great prophet was no less lively.

So we have to say that the prophetic movement is an extremely lively one. Misunderstood and persecuted, nevertheless the prophets had a following. Circles of disciples received their sayings and re-read them in the light of the new situations which they were called on to live out. Prophecy engenders prophecy. It is not enough to repeat the oracles of the prophets of the past. These oracles require to be meditated on, assimilated and then adapted to meet the needs of the moment.

Men of vision

If for the prophets the word has priority, we must not neglect another dimension of their experience and their activity. For the prophets are also seers, or better, visionaries. Furthermore it is by this title of seer (Hebrew *ro'eh*) that the prophet was first known in Israel: 'Formerly in Israel, when a man went to inquire of God, he said, "Come, let us go to the seer"; for he who is now called a prophet was formerly called a seer' (I Sam 9:9). We should note in this passage the distance in time between the 'now' of the final redactor of I Samuel and the 'formerly' of the time of Saul. In this passage, prophecy does not seem yet to have been freed from divinatory practices.

But it is not in this sense that the prophets are finally to assert themselves as seers. Their 'visions' are of quite a different order from that of divination.

You may be surprised to learn that the book of the great prophet Isaiah is entitled 'Vision of Isaiah' and not 'Words of Isaiah' or 'Word of the Lord which came to Isaiah'. And in a way which is strangely similar, the heading of the book of Amos has 'Words of Amos ... words which he saw ...' In fact chapters 7 to 9 of Amos report to us a series of five visions which support his final plea for the conversion of Israel.

Even the calling of Jeremiah is based on a visionary experience and an interpretation of which the prophet sees:

> And the word of the Lord came to me, saying, 'Jeremiah, what do you see?' And I said, 'I see an almond branch.' Then the Lord said to me, 'You have seen well, for I am watching over my word to perform it.'
> The word of the Lord came to me a second time, saying, 'What do you see?' And I said, 'I see a boiling pot, facing away from the north' (Jer 1:11–13).

Of all the prophets, Ezekiel is certainly the most powerful visionary. The opening of his book sets the tone: 'The heavens were opened, and I saw visions of God' (Ezek 1:1). If the Lord calls on him to listen, he also calls on him to look and to interpret his vision.

Finally, the little book of Obadiah is also presented to us as a vision.

So the prophet is a visionary. In other words, he learns to read events and see them in God's way. He is, as was once said of Balaam, 'the man with the penetrating gaze'. Where others have a complacent or disillusioned view, the prophet presents a view which is both critical and refreshing. This is the sense in which we must re-read the enigmatic passage in Isaiah in which the prophet is compared to a watchman:

> One is calling to me from Seir,
> 'Watchman, what of the night?
> Watchman, what of the night?'
> The watchman says,
> 'Morning comes, and also the night.
> If you will inquire, inquire;
> come back again' (Isa 21:11–12)

Men of the spirit?

Perhaps you will be amazed at the question mark here. After all, doesn't the expression 'man of the spirit' occur quite literally in Hosea 9:7, specifically in parallel with the word 'prophet'? Isn't it customary to speak of the prophetic spirit? However, a careful reply must be given to the question raised.

First of all we must note the extreme reserve of the classical prophets (those who have been included in the canon of scripture) in this connection. Of all the writing prophets, only Ezekiel makes explicit reference to the spirit in giving an account of his prophetic mission. There is complete silence in the others, including Isaiah and Jeremiah. Certainly, it will be said that the spirit was at work in them, but they did not describe their own prophetic experience as an experience of the spirit. And on the few occasions when they allude to the Spirit, it is always in a polemical or ironical context, when they are reacting to the ecstatic or divinatory techniques of those whom they regard as false prophets (Hos 9:7–9; Micah 2:6–11; 3:5–8; Jer 5:10–17).

Does that mean that the spirit is not significant in the experience of the biblical prophets and therefore we must abandon the term 'prophetic spirit'? Certainly not, for there is also a biblical tradition in which the spirit plays a major role in prophecy. One might think above all of the beginnings, with the spirit which is imparted to Moses and then to the elders (Num 11:25), then of the transmission of the prophetic authority from Elijah to Elisha (II Kings 2:15) and above all to Ezekiel, who acts directly under the influence of the Spirit: 'a spirit came upon me ...' (Ezek 2:2; 3:12, 24; 11:5). The link between the spirit and prophecy will be even clearer in the New Testament, with the reading which Peter makes of Joel 3:1–5 on the day of Pentecost: 'And in the last days it shall be, God declares, that I will pour out my spirit upon all flesh, and your sons and your daughters shall prophesy, and your young men shall see visions, and your old men shall dream dreams; yes, and on my menservants and my maidservants in those days I will pour out my spirit; and they shall prophesy' (Acts 2:17–18).

But at any rate let us remember that the spirit who inspired the prophets does not seem to have been offended by the fact that they spoke so little of him in giving an account of their call to the prophetic ministry.

Witnesses and signs for the people

To make the Word of God understandable to their contemporaries, the prophets did more than speak. They performed actions and translated the word by their lives.

If it was above all their oracles and their oral preaching which were remembered, some of their gestures and symbolic actions struck the popular imagination all the more. The prophets had the gift of performing actions which shook, aroused, intrigued and provoked the people to change.

Isaiah certainly made the population of Judah think when he appeared in public, at the time of the Syro-Ephraimite crisis (around 730), with his son Shear-yashub (Isa 7), whose name means 'A remnant will return'. So for him the situation was not desperate. However, shortly afterwards he was to announce a contrary situation, this time bringing with him his son Maher-shalal-has-baz, whose name can be translated 'Prompt-prey-near-spoil' (Isa 8); hope now gives place to disquiet. Then, later in his career, we are told that he walked around Jerusalem naked and without shoes for three years (Isa 20).

Jeremiah also performed a certain number of symbolic actions. He hid a waistcloth that was going rotten in the cleft of a rock to symbolize the present corruption and the lamentable state of the people (Jer 13). He watched with the greatest interest the potter at work in his workshop and understood the care which God takes to form the human creature with his own hands. This also led him to become aware of the fragility of the work which emerges from the hands of the potter and of the divine wrath which was on the point of bursting out against Judah. But also, at the height of the exile, Jeremiah acquired a field in Anathoth, his home village, to show that there was no need for despair and that normal life would soon resume its course (Jer 32). However, it was Ezekiel who proved the champion of symbolic actions. He has an undeniable talent for mime in performing a whole series of actions announcing the rigours of the imminent exile: he shuts himself up in his house, depicts a city under siege, lies only on his left side, prepares his bread in wretched conditions and shaves himself with a drawn sword (Ezek 4,5). He also goes out, in the full sight of all, with the typical bundle of clothes carried by those who are deported (Ezek 12).

But there are not only outward symbolic actions. There are also those which are deeply rooted in life, in the very existence of the prophet. We might think, for example, of the difficult loves, marriage and remarriage of Hosea (Hos 1–3), or of the weight of loneliness which Jeremiah feels when God calls on him to renounce marriage, at least for a time, because of the misfortune which will soon fall upon the house of Judah (Jer 16). And his contemporary Ezekiel has to mourn his wife with extreme detachment (Ezek 24), again because of the gravity of the tragedy which strikes his people.

So one is not a prophet at the level of lip service, but in one's flesh and one's tears, one's loves and failures, in all that makes up a human life. The biblical prophets are of this race, the race of those who have suffered and struggled in solidarity with a people who are deeply afflicted.

Disturbing people

As we know, the prophets never had an easy life. That is not surprising, since they had been chosen always to be in the front line. Contestants by nature, they were necessarily engaged in conflict, with their fellow prophets, or with the kings whom they denounced, or the temple authorities, or finally the people themselves. In a way Ahab was right when he accused Elijah of being 'the troublemaker of Israel' (I Kings 18:17).

No sphere of the collective history of Israel escapes the challenge of the prophets.

In foreign policy, the prophets denounce the alliances with the neighbouring powers, like Egypt or Assyria:

'Woe to the rebellious children', says the Lord,
'who carry out a plan, but not mine;
and who make a league, but not of my spirit,
that they may add sin to sin;
who set out to go down to Egypt,
without asking for my counsel,
to take refuge in the protection of Pharaoh,
and to seek shelter in the shadow of Egypt.
Therefore shall the protection of Pharaoh turn to
    your shame,
and the shelter in the shadow of Egypt to your
    humiliation.
Already your leaders are at Tanis,
the envoys have reached Hanes.
They will all be deceived
by a people that cannot profit them,
that brings neither help nor profit,
but shame and disgrace' (Isa 30:1–5).

Called to intervene on the political scene, the prophets were never afraid to point out the falsity of this kind of alliance sought by the kings of Israel and Judah. On the other hand, Jeremiah, alone against the rest, called for submission to the king of Babylon (Jer 27).

Critical of power, the prophets attacked constantly and systematically all that they considered an abuse of power and injustice:

Your princes are rebels
and companions of thieves.
Every one loves a bribe
and runs after gifts.
They do not defend the fatherless,
and the widow's cause does not come to them
(Isa 1:23).

Run to and fro through the streets of Jerusalem,
look and take note!
Search her squares to see
if you can find a man,
one who does justice
and seeks truth (Jer 5:1).

Gilead is a city of evildoers,
tracked with blood (Hos 6:8).

Assemble yourselves upon the mountains of
    Samaria,
and see the great tumults within her,

and the oppressions in her midst.
'They do not know how to do right', says the
    Lord,
those who store up violence and robbery in their
    strongholds (Amos 3:9-10).

Hear, you heads of Jacob
and rulers of the house of Israel!
Is it not for you to know justice? -
You who hate the good and love the evil,
who tear the skin from off my people,
and the flesh from off their bones (Micah 3:1–2).

Religion, too, attracts extremely severe criticism from the prophets. Not because they are against the religion of their time or right on its periphery, but because they see all its lying aspects. What they denounce is the formalism and triumphalism of a worship which is contradicted by a life of injustice and infidelity:

When you spread forth your hands,
I will hide my eyes from you;
though you make many prayers,
I will not listen;
your hands are full of blood (Isa 1:15).

This people honours me with its lips,
but its heart is far from me (Isa 29:13).

I hate, I despise your feasts,
and I take no delight in your solemn assemblies
(Amos 5:22).

They utter mere words;
with empty oaths they make covenants;
so judgment springs up like poisonous weeds
in the furrows of the field (Hos 10:4).

But it is not only the political and religious leaders who are the cause of this. What the prophets deplore is the faithlessness of a whole people and the widespread failure to know the covenant and its demands. In the face of this situation, the prophets even speak of God putting his people on trial.

Hear the word of the Lord, O people of Israel;
for the Lord has a controversy with the inhabitants
    of the land.
There is no faithfulness or kindness,
and no knowledge of God in the land (Hos 4:1).

Ah, sinful nation,
a people laden with iniquity,
offspring of evildoers,
sons who deal corruptly.
They have forsaken the Lord,
they have despised the Holy One of Israel,
they are utterly estranged.
Why will you still be smitten,
that you continue to rebel?
The whole head is sick,
and the whole heart faint (Isa 1:4–5).

Around the exile, the portrait will be hardly any better, when Jeremiah gives the surname 'apostasy' to Israel (Jer 3:6), while Ezekiel is warned that he will have to deal with a 'rebellious house'.

Men of unconditional hope

Serious though the infidelities of the people may be, the prophets are not the kind of people who accept them and believe that all is now lost. The severity of their denunciations and their threats is aimed at rousing the people in order to lead them back to the truth and help them to rediscover happiness. If the prophets have chosen to speak, it is certainly not to 'quench the smoking flax' (Isa 42:3). They have an unconditional hope. This is not a naïve and tolerant hope, but a bold and demanding one.

The theme of conversion remains one of the leitmotifs of prophetic preaching: 'Return, apostate Israel, says the Lord, I will not look upon you with anger' (Jer 3:11); 'Return, O Israel, to the Lord your God, because your fault has made you stumble' (Hos 14:2); 'On that day you shall not be put to shame because of the deeds by which you have rebelled against me' (Zeph 3:11). It could be said that even an outspoken prophet like Amos was the 'prophet of the eleventh hour'. For all the prophets, in fact, a conversion of the people is always possible. Otherwise, it stands to reason, why prophesy? A prophet as recalcitrant as Jonah must end up by accepting this; even the wicked Nineveh is not destroyed.

However, this is only one side of the coin, that of the conversion of the people. There is another even more important one, that of the future which God is preparing for his people. The prophets constantly proclaim the restoration of the people and a salvation for all nations. In connection with this we can profitably re-read the conclusions of the books of the writing prophets. Eleven books out of the fifteen end with grandiose perspectives of salvation: the people is gathered together, healed, consolidated and saved, and the nations ascend to Jerusalem to form the vast people of the saved.

Do the prophets have an unconditional hope? This was certainly thought to be the case by Ben Sirach, some two centuries before Jesus Christ:

> May the bones of the twelve prophets
> revive from where they lie,
> for they comforted the people of Jacob,
> and delivered them with confident hope
> > (Sirach 49:10)

Prophecy in the feminine

The twenty-one books which form the central section of the Hebrew Bible called 'the Prophets' have made us familiar with the great masculine figures of prophecy: Amos, Hosea, Isaiah, Jeremiah, Ezekiel and so on. The headings of individual books, which serve as signatures, in all probability contain no feminine name. This is a fact which can be deeply deplored today, but it is hardly surprising in the religious and institutional context in which the Hebrew Bible was formed.

That having been said, even for the Hebrew Bible prophecy is by no means the exclusive prerogative of men. Women prophesied and were recognized within their communities as prophetesses. What wouldn't we give today to rediscover just one of their writings! In them we would certainly find one more proof of the remarkable freedom of the breath of prophecy.

But who are these prophetesses? In the Old Testament we find a total of five of them: Miriam, Deborah, Isaiah's wife, Huldah and Noadiah.

Let's examine the role of each of these briefly.

Miriam is known to us as the sister of Aaron and Moses, and we can understand how the biblical tradition has favoured her two brothers, one of whom was to remain the greatest charismatic figure in the history of Israel and the other of whom is the great ancestor of priestly power. However, given the stature of these two spiritual leaders of the chosen people, the role given by the texts of the book of Exodus to Miriam seems all the more important.

First – and this was not the case with her two famous brothers – Miriam is introduced by a title which indicates her role within the community, 'prophetess'. What we are in fact told in Ex 15:20, the first explicit mention of Miriam, is this: 'then Miriam, the prophetess, the sister of Aaron, took a timbrel in her hand; and all the women went out after her with timbrels and dancing. And Miriam sang to them: "Sing to the Lord, for he has triumphed gloriously; the horse and his rider he has thrown into the sea."'

Here is a significant and calm recognition of the status of Miriam within the community; it seems to be taken for granted. Note also in the passage the solidarity of Miriam with 'all the women' and the fact that they sing together the first couplet of the famous 'Song of Moses' which he sang 'with the people of Israel' (Ex 15:1).

In another episode during the course of the journey in the desert, Miriam will be involved in a controversy over the privileged authority of her brother Moses (Num 12:1–16). Along with Aaron, she openly criticizes Moses' conduct in his marriage with a Nubian woman and challenges the exclusiveness of his charisma: 'Has the Lord indeed spoken only through Moses? Has he not spoken through us also?' (v. 2). This criticism did not succeed in pleasing the Lord, whose 'anger was kindled against them, and he departed; and when the cloud removed from over the tent, behold, Miriam was leprous …' (vv. 9,10). It is strange that of the two challengers, only Miriam is punished. But at the same time, as the Jewish tradition has stressed, Miriam seems to enjoy a special status. Though she cannot in any way lay claim to the privileged status of Moses, the man in whom the Lord trusts and who 'sees the form of the Lord', while Miriam and the other prophets have access to God only through a 'vision' or a 'dream', i.e. in 'hidden language', the fact remains that the journey of the people in the wilderness could not be continued 'till Miriam was brought in again' (v. 16)!

Deborah (Judg 4–5) has nothing to fear from the plethora of judges of greater or lesser fame whose memory is celebrated in the book of Judges. First of all as a judge: she can boast of having succeeded in what seems to represent the ideal of success for a judge, namely to have brought peace to the country for a period of forty years (Judg 3:11, 30; 5:31; 8:28). Then, of all the judges who ruled over the country (Judg 1–21), she is the only one to have combined the functions of judge and prophet: 'Now Deborah, a prophetess, the wife of Lappidoth, was judging Israel at that time. She used to sit under the palm of Deborah between Ramah and Bethel in the hill country of Ephraim; and the people of Israel came up to her for judgment' (Judg 4:5). Finally, of all the judges, she is also the only one to whom a song has been attributed (Judg

...dest poems in the Bible, which has some
... of victory sung by Moses (Ex 15). And like
... does not sing it alone: 'Then sang Deborah
... Abinoam on that day ...' (Judg 5:1). In
... and Miriam, and Moses took the initiative.
... of the masculine and feminine roles is to
... ed; we have Deborah and Barak, but it is mani-
... takes the initiative.

... **wife of Isaiah**, the only 'prophetess' whose
... know. With Noadiah, she is also the one about
... career we know least. She effaces herself
... and her husband Isaiah, the giant of prophecy, and
... of the shadows when mention is made of another
... to the couple: 'And I went to the prophetess, and
... d and bore a son' (Isa 8:3). From such effacement
... ose who conclude that the feminine noun prophetess
... *biah*) has the more restricted sense here of 'wife of the
... This is not completely impossible, but it would be some-
... rising and would be a unique instance. It is hard to see
why here too the noun should not have its functional sense rather
than the more restricted relational sense of 'wife of the prophet'.

Then, at the time of King Josiah and what has been called the
'Deuteronomic reform' around 625, we must surely emphasize the
exceptional role played by the prophetess **Huldah** in the discovery
of the Book of the Law (II Kings 22). When the king could very well
have appealed to the prophet Jeremiah, the officers of the temple,
whom he had sent to 'consult the Lord', chose rather to resort to
the services of 'Huldah the prophetess, the wife of Shallum the son
of Tikvah, son of Harhas', who 'dwelt in Jerusalem in the New
Quarter' (II Kings 22:14). Her particulars are given in the way
customary in the headings of the prophetic books. Furthermore she
is the only woman in the whole of the Old Testament to whom
formal oracles are attributed with the traditional introduction,
'Thus says the Lord, the God of Israel ...' (II Kings 22:15, 16, 18),
and the classical conclusion, 'Says the Lord' (II Kings 22:20). It was
from her instructions that the great reform undertaken by Josiah
was to stem (II Kings 23). It is also interesting to note that some
chapters later the author of II Kings refers again to the prophecies
of Huldah with the general formula 'according to the word of the
Lord which he spoke by his servants the prophets' (II Kings 24:2).

Noadiah is mentioned in the prayer of Nehemiah: 'Remember
Tobiah and Sanballat, O my God, according to these things that
they did, and also the prophetess Noadiah and the rest of the

prophets who wanted to make me afraid' (Neh 6:14). Here 'remember' takes on a double meaning: while in the case of the other prophets it denotes a negative retribution, it keeps its usual sense of benevolent and protective concern in the case of Tobiah, Sanballat and Noadiah.

To these five women we should also add the name of the prophetess Anna who, although she is mentioned in the writings of the New Testament (Luke 2:36–38), by her age ('she had reached the age of eighty-four') and attachment to the temple ('she did not depart from the temple, worshipping with fasting and prayer night and day') belongs to the period that we call the Old Testament. If the evangelist Luke does not record her words, as he does those of Simeon, he nevertheless gives her an important role in the announcement of Jesus 'to all who were looking for the redemption of Jerusalem'.

That is the portrait of prophecy in the feminine which can be derived from the Old Testament. We are still far from a full blossoming and a full participation, but there are happy glimpses of a new time when women and men will be able to prophesy equally: 'And it shall come to pass afterward, that I will pour out my spirit on all flesh; your sons and your daughters shall prophesy, your old men shall dream dreams, and your young men shall see visions. Even upon the menservants and maidservants in those days, I will pour out my spirit' (Joel 3:1).

Chapter 7

Introduction to the Study of the New Testament

Jeffrey S. Siker

The writings of the New Testament express the faith commitments of the earliest Christian communities. The writings themselves tell us a great deal about how and why Christian communities came into being, about the ups and downs experienced by the first few generations of Christians, and about the character of early Christian faith and practice. These writings are united by the attempts of the various authors to articulate their belief that Jesus of Nazareth is the Christ, the Messiah, the Son of God, whom God had sent to bring about salvation to God's people. The unity of the various New Testament writings revolves around this experience, faith, and understanding of Jesus as the culmination and paradigm of human existence within the context of first century Judaism.

Although in general these writings share a common vision regarding the centrality and significance of Jesus, they also have very different views about the identity of Jesus and the meaning of Christian faith. As a whole the New Testament can be seen almost as a collage, with overlapping and yet distinct images. Thus, like the Jewish Scriptures, the New Testament is best understood as a collection of various 'books' rather than a single book, even though these writings do have an overarching interest in the significance of believing Jesus to be the Christ, the Son of God. In short, it is crucial to remember that the books of the New Testament were written by different people at different times to widely divergent situations in the life of the early Church.

The books of the New Testament

We can begin with an overview of the New Testament as a whole. Before reading any further, please get out your Bible and turn to the beginning of the New Testament. If you are not already familiar with the different books of the New Testament, and even if you are, I think you will find it helpful to flip through the various writings as we briefly touch on them here. The New Testament contains twenty-seven different 'books'. In general, these writings fall into one of three categories: gospels, letters, and other.

Gospels

There are four Gospels: Matthew, Mark, Luke, and John. The first three Gospels (Matthew, Mark, and Luke) are often referred to as 'the synoptic gospels'. The term 'synoptic' comes from a Greek word meaning to see or look together, to see things the same way. And these three Gospels are very similar in many ways. They overlap to a remarkable degree, containing many of the same sayings of Jesus and stories about Jesus, often with exactly the same wording. As we will see, the striking similarities among these three Gospels points to a close literary relationship.

    The Gospel of John is the Fourth Gospel; it is quite different from the Synoptic Gospels. The Gospel of John has very few of the sayings and stories that we find in the Synoptic Gospels. Indeed, in John's Gospel we get a quite different picture of Jesus.

Letters

There are twenty-one letters, or epistles, in the New Testament, although some read more like letters than others. The letters can be divided into two general groups:

1. the letters of Paul; and
2. the other letters, often referred to as the 'Catholic Epistles', with the exception of Hebrews.

Pauline letters

Thirteen letters are attributed to Paul. However, most scholars agree that Paul did not actually write all of these letters, and that several of them were written in Paul's name after Paul had died. Thus, some letters are 'undisputed' (almost everyone agrees Paul *did* write them), and others are 'disputed' (a large number of scholars agree that Paul *did not* write them).

There are seven undisputed letters: Romans, 1 and 2 Corinthians, Galatians, Philippians, 1 Thessalonians, and Philemon. These are the primary letters used to understand Paul's life and theological perspectives.

There are six disputed letters: Ephesians and Colossians (usually considered together), 1 and 2 Timothy and Titus (these three are known as the 'Pastoral Epistles' and are also usually considered together), and 2 Thessalonians. The primary reasons for the dispute about Pauline authorship of these letters have to do with their significantly different vocabulary, style, and especially theological views when compared to the undisputed letters of Paul. Most scholars tend to use these letters for understanding developments in early Christianity after Paul had died. To dispute the Pauline authorship of these letters is not necessarily to dispute the authority of these letters in their own right within the New Testament.

Hebrews

At first, many early Christians attributed this writing to Paul, in part because of its ending. But fairly early on it became clear that Paul did not write Hebrews, since it is so very different from anything we have from Paul. Hebrews is also not quite a letter (although it has a letter ending), but is more appropriately classified as a written homily intended to encourage some Christians who were growing tired in their faith.

The Catholic Epistles

The term 'catholic' here means 'universal', or 'general'. In comparison to the other letters in the New Testament, the Catholic Epistles are relatively brief. There are seven of them: James, 1 and 2 Peter, 1, 2 and 3 John, and Jude. We know relatively little about who wrote these letters, or when, or where. Most scholars consider James, 1 Peter, and 1 John to be the most significant of the Catholic Epistles.

Other writings

The two remaining documents fit neither the category of Gospel nor letter. They are the Acts of the Apostles and Revelation. The Acts of the apostles has often been viewed as the first Church history ever written, since it picks up the story of the early Church after the resurrection and ascension of Jesus. Indeed, it is no accident that the early Church placed the book of Acts immediately after the Gospels. The Acts of the Apostles was written by the same author who wrote the Gospel of Luke. If you compare the beginning of Luke with the beginning of Acts you will see that both are addressed to a certain 'Theophilus,' and that Acts refers back to the Gospel of Luke as the 'first book'. The title 'Acts of the Apostles' is somewhat misleading, as Acts relates more speeches than other activities, and it focuses almost exclusively on Peter and especially Paul, rather than on other apostles. Peter is pictured as taking the gospel message to the Jews in Acts 1–5 and as inaugurating the mission to the Gentiles in Acts 10–11. Paul, who can be seen as Luke's hero in the book of Acts, is commissioned in Acts 9 to preach to the Gentiles; Luke then follows Paul's missionary travels in Acts 13–28.

Finally, the book of Revelation fits the genre of 'apocalypse' rather than gospel or letter. An apocalypse was a style of writing about a revelation of God's heavenly mysteries, often in the form of dramatic visions complete with incredible heavenly and hellish characters. Apocalyptic writings often flourished during times of intense persecution, when the faithful wondered how they could continue to endure before God prevailed. Apocalypses tried to encourage the faithful with heavenly visions that promised God's ultimate victory over evil powers and assured believers that this victory would take place soon. Although the book of Revelation is the only 'apocalypse' in the New Testament, many of the New Testament writings have apocalyptic features, for example Mark 13 and 1 Thessalonians 4.

Formation of the New Testament canon

Now that we have some idea about what the New Testament contains we might well ask why the New Testament looks like it does. Why four gospels? Why thirteen letters attributed to Paul? Why the Acts of the Apostles, the Book of Revelation, the other letters? How did this particular collection of writings come to be? Although this is a complicated topic, the formation of the New Testament canon took place in basically four stages.

First, an author wrote a document and a relatively small group of people read it. For example, Paul wrote what we call 1 Thessalonians to the Christians in the city of Thessalonica; they read his letter and kept it. Indeed, in 1 Thessalonians 5:27 Paul writes: 'I adjure you by the Lord that this letter be read to all the brethren.'

Second, the document would be copied and circulated. Since there were no copying machines or printing presses, this process could take some time. So it is conceivable that some individuals in Thessalonica copied Paul's letter, perhaps after he had died, and took it to some Christians in the city of Corinth, in order to share what Paul had written to them. In turn some Christians in Corinth may have shared copies of Paul's letters to the Corinthians. The same process took place for the Gospels and the other writings of the New Testament.

Third, various individuals and Christian communities began to make collections and selections among the many Christian writings that were being copied and circulated. It appears that between AD 150-200, about a hundred years after most of the New Testament documents were written, a collection of four gospels emerged, and most of Paul's letters had been gathered into a collection of letters. Along with these writings other influential documents were also often included. For example, the letters of Barnabas and 1 Clement enjoyed considerable popularity in the second century, along with a host of other writings.

How then to decide which writings were authoritative for Christian faith and practice? A need was felt to have a common collection of writings that all Christians could use. How to select? As best we can tell, several criteria were used. One criterion was 'apostolicity', namely, was the document written by one of the apostles, someone who was part of the very earliest Christian movement? Thus, for example, the Gospel of Matthew was considered to have authority because of the tradition that Matthew was one of the twelve disciples, one of the apostles. The Gospel of Mark derived its authority from the tradition that Mark was Peter's scribe, that Mark wrote down what Peter told him to write.

Although Paul was not one of the twelve disciples and had probably never met Jesus, he was considered to be an apostle because of the report that he had had a vision of the risen Jesus. Another criterion for selecting from among the documents was a rather practical one: use. Was the document widely used? Still another criterion, and a somewhat slippery one, had to do with whether the writing seemed to strengthen and promote the community of faith and whether it appeared genuinely to express the faith of the community. Although other factors contributed to the selection process, these criteria were among the most important.

The fourth and final stage was that various collections of New
Testament writings received official stamps of approval from
Church leaders and from early Church councils. It may come as a
surprise, but the very first time we find an official list of what
belongs in the New Testament that exactly matches our New
Testament of today was not until AD 367, when an important
fourth-century bishop by the name of Athanasius decreed, in an
Easter letter to his Churches, that only these writings were to be
considered as authoritative sacred Scripture. Even after this time
there continued to be disagreement in different regions of
Christianity about whether some writings belonged in the New
Testament or not, especially about the book of Revelation,
Hebrews, 2 Peter, 2 and 3 John, and Jude. Thus, although the New
Testament documents themselves were written over a relatively
brief period of time, it took several centuries before there was
widespread agreement about exactly which writings belonged in
the New Testament.

History of tradition

Part of studying the New Testament means being aware in a
general way of how each writing took shape. Did Matthew just sit
down and write his Gospel out? Or did he use sources? What's
going on in Mark when Jesus says, 'Whoever divorces his wife and
marries another commits adultery against her' (Mark 10:11), while
in Matthew Jesus says, 'Whoever divorces his wife, *except for
unchastity*, and marries another, commits adultery' (Matt 19:9)?
Which one did Jesus say? Or did he say both? Or has Matthew
added the clause about unchastity, and if so why?

   Having an understanding of the different stages and layers in the
transmission of the earliest Christian traditions can provide a
tremendous help in answering many questions about the New
Testament, and especially about the Gospels. There are basically
six stages in the history of tradition, and various analytical tools
have been developed to address each stage on its own terms. As a
whole these tools are often referred to collectively as the discipline
or methodology of 'historical criticism', because these tools focus
on the history of the traditions in the New Testament. We will look
at each stage and each critical tool in turn.

Map No. 3

Historical event/historical criticism

The first thing that happens is an event. Jesus, Paul, somebody, says
something or does something. Although the term 'historical criticism' is used to describe the analytical tools collectively, it also
describes one of the particular tools. Simply put, in its more
specific meaning, historical criticism refers to the attempt of scholars to determine as best they can what really happened. For
example, in the Gospel of John the 'cleansing of the temple',
where Jesus drives out those doing business in the temple court-
yard, is one of the first things Jesus does in his public ministry
(John 2:13–17). But in the Synoptic Gospels the 'cleansing of the
temple' is one of the very last events of Jesus' public ministry (Matt
21:10–17; Mark 11:15–17; Luke 19:45–46). Which is it? Thus, the
goal of historical criticism is to get as clear a picture as possible of
the event(s) in question.

One of the most debated issues has to do with who the 'historical Jesus' really was. If we had a videotape of Jesus' life, what would
it look like? To what extent do the Gospels really tell us about the
Jesus of history, especially since the Gospels were written to
proclaim the belief that Jesus is the Son of God who died and has
been raised from the dead? Can a critical historian take the Gospel
accounts at face value? What historical information do the Gospels
convey and how is one to evaluate their accuracy? One thing most
scholars do agree on is that the proclamation of the kingdom of
God was central to the ministry of the historical Jesus (and to the
Jesus portrayed in the Gospels; e.g., Matt 4:17; 13:24–33; Mark
1:14–15), although there is much debate about what Jesus meant
by the kingdom of God. Thus, scholars use historical criticism in an
attempt to reconstruct historical events, especially as they relate to
the life of Jesus.

The discipline of historical criticism also pays particular attention to the historical, social, and religious contexts in which the
various New Testament documents were written. A brief review of
some of these contexts is in order here. Almost all of the New
Testament documents were written during the first century AD, a
time when the Roman Empire was near the height of its power.
This was also a time of great tension between the Jews in Palestine
and the Romans, who had recently conquered the territory and
ruled it firmly. These tensions erupted in a Jewish revolt against
the Romans in AD 66, a war that reached its climax in AD 70 with
the Roman capture of Jerusalem and the destruction of the Jewish
temple, the symbolic heart of Jewish identity. Since the earliest

Christians saw themselves, and were seen by others, primarily as a subgroup (some would say sect) of Judaism, the events in first century Jewish history also had a significant impact on the development of Christianity. All of the first Christians were Jewish. Indeed, we need to remind ourselves that Jesus was Jewish, and not a Christian at all!

Two central factors contributed to the separation of Christianity from Judaism. First, the Christian claim that Jesus was the Messiah, the Christ, was scandalous to most Jews. The Jewish expectation was that the Christ would deliver the Jewish people from Roman rule and usher in God's kingdom. But Jesus did not meet these expectations. Not only did he *not* defeat the Romans, but the Romans put him to death instead! And not only did he die, but he died a shameful death on the cross. How could one believe in a crucified Messiah? And then the early Christians said that God had raised this same failed Messiah from the dead, and that Jesus was God's son who had died for others. From a Jewish perspective these were blasphemous and ridiculous claims.

Second, fairly early on, the Christian movement spread to Gentiles as well, to non-Jews. The crucial question that caused a major split in earliest Christianity was whether or not Gentile Christians also had to observe the Jewish law that God had revealed in the Jewish scriptures, including the dietary restrictions, the sabbath observance, and especially circumcision. Simply put, did one have to become a Jew in order to become a Christian? You can see some of the intense debate about this issue in Acts 15 and in Galatians 1–2. Although many Christians continued to observe Jewish ritual practice, the decision was that Gentiles did *not* have to be circumcised in order to become Christians – the most hotly debated question (see Paul's remark in Galatians 5:11–12!).

This decision compounded the tensions between Jews and Christians, especially with the destruction of the Jewish temple. Just when Christians were moving away from observance of Jewish law, the Jews were placing much more emphasis on observance of the law in an effort to re-establish Jewish identity in the aftermath of the destruction of the temple. The sharp tensions between formative Christianity and formative rabbinic Judaism can be seen throughout the New Testament, especially in the writings of Paul and in the Gospels of Matthew and John. This ends our brief sketch of what historical criticism has helped to show. Historical criticism, then, is concerned with historical events and their significance for our understanding of the New Testament writings.

Oral tradition/form criticism

After the event, people talk about the event. For example, people related what Jesus said and did when he cleansed the temple in Jerusalem. These reports then get repeated again. But not only do they get repeated, stories get attached to other stories, oral traditions congeal and take on various forms. Thus, just like we have different oral forms – jokes (one liners, ethnic jokes, elephant jokes, etc.), or nursery rhymes (Mother Goose and others) – so in early Christianity the sayings of Jesus and stories about him were repeated and collected in various forms: parables, memorable sayings, miracle stories, and the like. The critical tool designed to identify and analyse these various oral traditions is form criticism. The goal of form criticism is to get behind the written materials we have and to examine how the oral traditions took shape and how they were passed on.

In particular, the discipline of form criticism seeks to nail down the particular historical situations in which oral traditions were circulated, to discover how they were used by early Christian communities. One very clear example of oral tradition can be found in a letter written by Paul, 1 Corinthians 15:3–5. There, in describing the core gospel message, Paul writes: 'For I delivered to you as of first importance what I also received, that Christ died for our sins in accordance with the scriptures, that he was buried, that he was raised on the third day in accordance with the scriptures, and that he appeared to Cephas, then to the twelve...' Notice Paul's introductory formula: 'I delivered ... what I received', referring to an oral tradition about the gospel message.

Written tradition/source criticism

After people talk orally about events, the stories get written down. Jesus' sayings from the Sermon on the Mount (Matt 5–7) were in all likelihood independent oral traditions that were written down together. Not only Matthew knew about these written sayings; so did Luke, as is evident from similar sayings materials that are recorded partly in Luke 6 and elsewhere in Luke's Gospel. But the Gospel of Mark shows no evidence of these written traditions. And so the question arises: how is it that Matthew and Luke have very similar sayings material? What written sources did the Gospels use? The first few lines from the beginning of Luke's Gospel make it quite clear that Luke did use various written sources: 'Inasmuch as many have undertaken to compile a narrative of the things which have been accomplished among us ... it seemed good to me also ... to write an orderly account' (Luke 1:1–3). Luke is aware of various other written sources, and he makes use of these sources in putting together his own Gospel account. It is reasonable to presume that Matthew wrote in a similar way. (Indeed, all of the New Testament writers used the Jewish Scriptures as a written source, and we find many quotations from the Jewish Scriptures in the New Testament writings.)

And so we press the question further. Did the author of John use other written sources? Did Paul make use of written traditions when he wrote his letters? These are the questions addressed by the discipline of source criticism. Scholars use source criticism to determine whether an author used written traditions and, if so, what these written sources may have looked like.

One special problem that poses a question for source criticism is the issue of the literary relationship between the Synoptic Gospels. Why are these three Gospels so similar and yet so different? Today, the large majority of scholars have reached a consensus that Mark was the first Gospel written, and that Mark was used independently as a written source by the authors of Matthew and Luke. Matthew and Luke also used a 'sayings source' that has been labelled 'Q', from the German word 'Quelle', which means 'source' (many of the scholars writing about the New Testament in the nineteenth and early twentieth centuries were German). This consensus is known as the 'two document hypothesis' or the 'two source theory'. The literary relationship between the Synoptic Gospels thus looks like this:

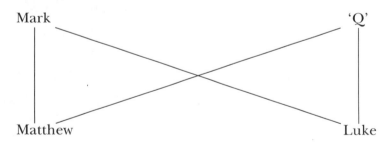

Both Matthew and Luke independently used Mark and 'Q' as written sources for putting together their own Gospels.

Editing the traditions/redaction criticism

After oral and written traditions have been compiled, an editing process takes place in which an author combines the various pieces of tradition (both oral and written) to form a unified and cohesive whole, an extended narrative. The author gives shape to the traditions. Significantly, each author shapes the traditions in order to address a specific group of people with specific concerns in a specific time and place. Thus the theological concerns and biases of each author can be seen in how they edit their sources.

The discipline of redaction criticism seeks to discern how each author has edited the traditions they have used, especially the written traditions. Not only do scholars use redaction criticism to look for special emphases in the editing process, they also use it to discover the author's specific life situation and theological vantage point. One word of caution: redaction criticism works best when we know the sources an author has used. Thus, for example, scholars engaged in redaction analysis of the Synoptic Gospels by and large assume the validity of the two-source hypothesis. This means that redaction analysis of Matthew and Luke stands on relatively firm ground, since most scholars agree that Matthew and Luke used Mark and 'Q'. But redaction criticism becomes much more tricky in the cases of Mark and John, since there is still much debate over exactly what written sources they used.

A good example of how redaction criticism works can be seen from a consideration of the story about Jesus' triumphal entry into Jerusalem, recorded in Matthew 21:1–9, Mark 11:1–10, and Luke 19:28–40. The three texts are printed in parallel columns on pages 121 and 122.

When we compare Matthew's version with Mark's version, several features stand out. First, notice that in Mark 11:2 Jesus tells the disciples that they will find 'a colt tied, on which no one has ever sat; untie it and bring it'. By contrast in Matthew 21:2 Jesus tells the disciples that they 'will find an ass tied, *and* a colt with her; untie *them* and bring *them* to me'. Whereas Mark talks about one animal, Matthew mentions two. Look next at Mark 11:7, where we read: 'And they brought the colt to Jesus, and threw their garments on it; and he sat upon it.' Compare this to Matthew's version in 21:7, 'they brought the ass *and* the colt, and put their garments on *them*, and he sat thereon'. How many animals is Jesus riding in Mark? One. How many animals is Jesus riding in Matthew? Two! Imagine what that must have looked like!

Matthew 21:1–9

¹And when they drew near to Jerusalem and came to Bethphage, to the Mount of Olives, then Jesus sent two disciples, ²saying to them, 'Go into the village opposite you, and immediately you will find an ass tied, and a colt with her;

untie them and bring them to me. ³If any one says anything to you, you shall say, "The Lord has need of them," and he will send them immediately.'

⁴This took place to fulfill what was spoken by the prophet, saying, ⁵"Tell the daughter of Zion, Behold, your king is coming to you, humble, and mounted on an ass, and on a colt, the foal of an ass.'

Mark 11:1–10

¹And when they drew near to Jerusalem, to Bethphage and Bethany, at the Mount of Olives, he sent two of his disciples, ²and said to them, 'Go into the village opposite you, and immediately as you enter it you will find a colt tied, on which no one has ever sat; untie it and bring it.

³If any one says to you, "Why are you doing this," say, "the Lord has need of it and will send it back here immediately."

Luke 19:28–40

²⁸And when he had said this, he went on ahead, going up to Jerusalem. ²⁹When he drew near to Bethphage and Bethany, at the Mount that is called Olives, he sent two of his disciples, ³⁰saying, 'Go into the village opposite, where on entering you will find a colt tied, on which no one has ever yet sat; untie it and bring it here.

³¹If any one asks you, "Why are you untying it?" you shall say this, "The Lord has need of it."

⁶The disciples went and did as Jesus had directed them;

⁷they brought the ass and the colt and put their garments on them, and he sat thereon. ⁸Most of the crowd spread their garments on the road, and others cut branches from the trees and spread them on the road. ⁹And the crowds that went before him shouted,

"Hosanna to the Son of David! Blessed is he who comes in the name of the Lord!

Hosanna in the highest!"

---

⁴And they went away, and found a colt tied at the door out in the open street; and they untied it. ⁵And those who stood there said to them, 'What are you doing, untying the colt?' ⁶And they told them what Jesus had said; and they let them go. ⁷And they brought the colt to Jesus, and threw their garments on it; and he sat upon it. ⁸ And many spread their garments on the road, and others spread leafy branches which they had cut from the fields.
⁹And those who went before and those who followed cried out,

"Hosanna!
Blessed is he who comes in the name of the Lord! ¹⁰ Blessed is the kingdom of our father David that is coming!

Hosanna in the highest!"

---

³²So those who were sent went away and found it as he had told them. ³³And as they were untying the colt, its owners said to them, "Why are you untying the colt?" ³⁴And they said, "The Lord has need of it."

³⁵And they brought it to Jesus, and throwing their garments on the colt they set Jesus upon it. ³⁶And as he rode along, they spread their garments on the road. ³⁷As he was now drawing near, at the descent of the Mount of Olives, the whole multitude of the disciples began to rejoice and praise God with a loud voice for all the mighty works they had seen, ³⁸saying, "Blessed is the King who comes in the name of the Lord!

Peace in heaven
and glory in the highest!'

Assuming the two-source theory, the question is, why did Matthew change Mark's version and add an extra animal for Jesus to ride on? The answer can be found in a second striking difference between Matthew and Mark. Notice that Matthew 21:4-5 has no parallel in either Mark's or Luke's versions. Matthew has added sayings from the Jewish Scriptures, from the prophets Isaiah and Zechariah, to his version of the story. If you look carefully at this quotation you will see that Matthew 21:5 reads: 'Behold, your king is coming to you, humble, and mounted on *an ass, and on a colt*, the foal of an ass.' From Matthew's perspective, Jesus' entry into Jerusalem fulfills the prophecy in Jewish Scriptures regarding the coming of a kingly figure. For Matthew, Jesus is that figure, and he adds the citation from the Jewish scriptures to make his point. Even more, he changes the story he gets from Mark so that Jesus is riding two animals and not one, in order that the exact fulfillment of scripture is all the more striking. However, Matthew used the Greek translation of the Jewish scriptures (known as the *Septuagint*), which in this case misses a common Hebrew technique of Hebrew parallelism, in which a clause often gets restated in a slightly different way, so that in the Hebrew version it is clear that only one animal is intended.

Redaction criticism thus reveals Matthew's theological concern to show that Jesus literally fulfills Jewish scriptures. We can also see in this story Matthew's emphasis on Jesus' Jewish roots, as the addition in Matthew 21:9 makes clear: 'Hosanna to the Son of David!' – while Mark 11:9 has only 'Hosanna!' Redaction criticism can sometimes be painstaking, but it is a valuable tool for highlighting the theological interests and the historical situation of the authors and communities behind the New Testament writings.

Final literary form/literary criticism

After the editing process the document reaches its final literary form. The goal of literary criticism is to understand the final form of the document. In order to understand each writing on its own terms it is important to pay particular attention to the structure of each document. How does the writing move? Where does it speed up and slow down? How does the plot of the writing work? Who are the characters and how are they portrayed? Is there a climax and if so how does the author communicate it? How do the various pieces of the document interrelate? What are the immediate and larger literary contexts of each part of the whole? Very simply, literary criticism asks literary questions about each writing. It depends on some of the results of historical, form, source, and redaction criticism, but its real focus is on the final literary shape of each document. One example from Luke 4:16-30 will illustrate how this way of approaching the text works. Begin by reading this passage before going any further.

As you can see, Luke 4:16–30 presents Jesus at the beginning of his public ministry. This is really Jesus' first public appearance in his ministry, so it has particular importance. Look first how Luke sets the scene up. Jesus is in his home town of Nazareth at the town synagogue on the sabbath. Jesus then stands up to read from the prophet Isaiah. Notice how Luke dramatically slows down the action here. Jesus stands up to read, he is given the book, he opens the book and then gives the reading. Afterwards he closes the book, gives the book back, and sits down. Luke has carefully created a parallel structure here that initially serves to emphasize the reading. It can be pictured as follows:

```
he stood up to read ─────────────────────────────────┐
   there was given to him the book ──────────────────┐│
      he opened the book ──────────────────────────┐ ││
                                  Isaiah reading    │ ││
      he closed the book ────────────────────────┘ ││
   he gave the book back to the attendant ──────────┘│
he sat down ─────────────────────────────────────────┘
```

The Isaiah reading stands at the centre of the parallelism. At the end of 4:20 Luke pauses once again to tell us that 'the eyes of all in the synagogue were fixed on him'. This comment creates a sense of anticipation and suspense. What will Jesus say? Then come the familiar words: 'Today this scripture has been fulfilled in your hearing.' We are then told that the crowd was favourably impressed in 4:22. But the story takes an odd twist after this. In 4:23–24 Jesus presses the congregation and tells them that 'no prophet is acceptable in his own country'. (Luke clearly sees Jesus as a prophetic figure here, a motif that recurs in his Gospel.) And in 4:25–27 Jesus refers to two ancient stories from the prophets to give his interpretation of the Isaiah reading regarding the proclamation of good news to the poor and release to the captives.

Both of the stories refer to Jewish prophets who had brought healing to non-Jews: Elijah to the widow in Zarephath (he heals her son), and Elisha to Naaman the Syrian (who is cleansed of leprosy). The emphasis then falls on the good news going not to Israel, but to the Gentiles; not to the hometown folks, but to the outcasts. The reaction of the crowd then shifts dramatically from 4:22, and in 4:28–30 the crowd is enraged and seeks to throw Jesus off a cliff! Notice the irony. Here Jesus comes at the beginning of his ministry into a very Jewish setting: his Jewish home town of Nazareth, in a Jewish synagogue, on the Jewish sabbath, reading from Jewish Scriptures. And what does Luke have Jesus do with all of this? Here, exactly in this very Jewish setting, Luke has Jesus proclaiming the inclusion of the outcast and Gentiles, a theme which recurs throughout Luke–Acts.

Thus from a literary perspective we can see how Luke uses the context, structure and flow of the story to communicate something about his understanding of the significance of Jesus.

Multiple copies of final literary form/textual criticism

Finally, after a document reached its final literary form it would be copied and recopied, and copies would be made from still other copies. Aside from producing hundreds of copies, this process also produced both major and minor differences between the various copies. Indeed, of all the copies we have of the New Testament, both complete and fragmentary, no two copies are exactly alike. When we are talking about the text of the New Testament, then, the first question that arises is, 'Which text?'

The discipline of textual criticism seeks to establish the text, the earliest and most reliable version of each document. Until agreement can be reached on what the text actually says, it is difficult to discuss the final literary form, or redaction, sources, forms, and the underlying events. Textual criticism, then, is a fairly technical discipline in which scholars compare the thousands of different handwritten copies of the New Testament documents, and seek to arrive at a consensus text. One thing you should know is that the New Testaments we use today are composite texts. This means that scholars, drawing on a large number of manuscripts, produce a working text that is not identical to any single manuscript. Rather, it is a composite text.

The following two examples show how textual criticism works. The first comes from Luke 22. In the New Revised Standard Version of the New Testament, Luke 22:43–44 appears in brackets in the text. At the bottom of the page one finds a note that states, 'Other ancient authorities lack verses 43 and 44.' This note tells us that many ancient manuscripts simply do not have these lines, and that there is some debate about whether they should be included in the New Testament. The second example is more significant; it comes from Mark 16. After Mark 16:8 most New Testaments have a note regarding various endings to Mark's Gospel. Some of the oldest and best manuscripts of Mark's Gospel simply end with 16:8, with the women fleeing the empty tomb. Other manuscripts have a slightly expanded ending, with the report that the women told Peter what they had experienced and that 'Jesus himself sent out through them, from east to west, the sacred and imperishable proclamation of eternal salvation' (NRSV). Still other manuscripts have an even longer ending, adding 16:9–20, complete with appearances of the risen Jesus (lacking in the 16:8 ending). Most scholars agree that Mark's Gospel originally ended with 16:8, with the empty tomb and with no reports about the appearances of the risen Jesus. Depending upon which ending you read, the Gospel of Mark reads in rather different ways. Thus, textual criticism is an important tool that establishes the texts we use.

To summarize this extended discussion of tradition history the following chart may be helpful. It shows the various stages of tradition we have reviewed along with the various tools that scholars use to investigate each layer.

Multiple copies of texts   –   textual criticism
↑
final form of text   –   literary criticism
↑
editing the traditions   –   redaction criticism
↑
written traditions   –   source criticism
↑
oral traditions   –   form criticism
↑
the event   –   historical criticism

Every New Testament document has these layers of tradition and transmission, although redaction and source criticism often apply more to the Gospels than to the letters. We move now to a consideration of the Gospels and the letters of Paul.

The Gospels and Paul: distinctive aspects

The Gospels

The Synoptic Gospels:
Although the Synoptic Gospels are very similar to one another,

there are also some significant differences between them. What follows is a thumbnail sketch of some of the distinctive characteristics of each Synoptic Gospel.

Mark: Begin by reading chapters 1–3 and 11–16 in Mark. As we noted above in the section on written tradition/source criticism, most scholars agree that Mark is the earliest of the Synoptic Gospels, probably written sometime in the late 60s or early 70s of the first century. What stands out in Mark's portrait of Jesus is the dual emphasis on power and suffering. The power and authority of Jesus can be seen in the first three chapters. Here Jesus performs several healings: a man with an unclean spirit (1:21–28), Peter's mother-in-law (1:29–31), a leper (1:40–45), a paralytic (2:1–12), a man with a withered hand (3:1–6), and a man with a demon (3:20–27). Not only does Mark portray Jesus as having authority over illness, he also has authority over sin (2:10) and the sabbath law (2:28). In addition he teaches with great power and wins arguments with the Pharisees and scribes (2:1–12, 23—28).

But Mark places even greater emphasis on Jesus as God's suffering servant. This can be seen clearly in chapters 8–10. The turning point in Mark is 8:27–33. In 8:27–30 Jesus asks his disciples who they say he is, and Peter responds, 'You are the Christ.' Peter seems to understand Jesus' identity. But then immediately following Peter's confession, Mark introduces the first of three 'passion predictions', where Jesus teaches the disciples 'that the Son of man must suffer many things, and be rejected by the elders and the chief priests and scribes, and be killed, and after three days rise again' (8:31). Although Peter had seemed to understand Jesus' identity, Peter rebukes Jesus, which in turn leads to Jesus' rebuke of Peter: 'Get behind me, Satan! For you are not on the side of God, but of people' (8:33). This section (8:27–33) is crucial, because here Mark indicates that the true power of Jesus is seen foremost in his suffering and death.

Mark has Jesus repeat the passion predictions twice more, in 9:30–32 and in 10:32–34, each time surrounded by the failure of the disciples to understand. The climax then comes in the suffering and death of Jesus, culminating in the confession of the centurion at the foot of the cross (15:39): 'Truly this man was the Son of God!' Notice the irony here. A centurion, the symbol of Roman power, confesses that this crucified Jesus – who couldn't be more powerless on the cross – is the Son of God. Mark stresses, then, that true power is expressed in embracing suffering, as Jesus did on the cross, and that discipleship means identifying with Jesus in a ministry of expressing God's power and love by embracing human suffering.

Matthew: Begin by reading Matthew 5–7. While Matthew takes over much of Mark's material and also plays up the significance of Jesus' suffering, Matthew's Gospel has more of a focus on Jesus as the new Moses, the teacher of the new Law, who is concerned with an individual's inward disposition more than with external actions. This concern can be clearly seen in the Sermon on the Mount (5–7). This is the first 'sermon' by Jesus in Matthew, and so it has been given a prominent place in the Gospel. Notice the emphasis on an individual's inner motivation, one's attitude: 'blessed are the poor in spirit' (5:3), 'blessed are those who hunger and thirst for righteousness' (5:6). Or again in 5:21–22: 'You have heard that it was said to the men of old, "You shall not kill; and whoever kills shall be liable to judgment." But I say to you that every one who is angry with his brother shall be liable to judgment'; and again in 5:27-28: 'You have heard that it was said, "You shall not commit adultery." But I say to you that every one who looks at a woman lustfully has already committed adultery with her in his heart.' Strong language. For Matthew's Jesus, God judges not only one's actions, but also one's dispositions, one's heart.

The centrality of Jesus as teacher can also be seen from other extended blocks of teaching in Matthew: chapter 10 (on mission), chapter 13 (parables of the kingdom), chapter 18 (on Church order), and chapters 24–25 (on the coming end times and judgment).

Another feature of Matthew is the very Jewish character of the Gospel. This can be seen already in the very first chapter, with the genealogy of Jesus (1:1–17). Matthew emphasizes that Jesus' lineage goes back to David (the ideal King for Israel) and Abraham (the founding figure of Judaism with whom God established the covenant, sealed with the sign of circumcision). The Jewish Law is still very important for Matthew, as is clear from 5:17–18: 'Think not that I have come to abolish the law and the prophets; I have come not to abolish them but to fulfill them. For truly, I say to you, till heaven and earth pass away, not an iota, not a dot, will pass from the law until all is accomplished.'

Luke: Begin by reading Luke 4–7. The last of the Synoptic Gospels is Luke. Luke also takes over much of the material from Mark, although much less than Matthew does. In fact, Luke has the most unique materials among the Synoptic Gospels, stories that are not found elsewhere among the Gospels, e.g., the parables of the Good Samaritan (10:25–37) and the Prodigal Son (15:11–32). Luke's Gospel, along with Luke's Acts of the Apostles, emphasizes God's inclusion of the outcasts. Luke's Jesus has a special ministry to tax collectors, considered to be notorious figures in first century Palestine (3:12; 5:27–30; 7:29; 18:9–14; 19:1–10), to women (7:11–17, 36–50; 8:2-3; 10:38–42; 13:10–17; 15:8–10; 18:1–8; 23:27–31), and to those who are physically poor (4:18; 6:20; 7:22; 14:13; 16:16–31; 18:22). Luke also has a special critique of the wealthy that is not found so much in the other Gospels (6:24–25; 12:16–21; 16:16–31). And, as we have seen before, Luke's Gospel is concerned to show that in Jesus the Gentiles are included in God's covenant promises (2:32; 4:16–30; 24:47).

Luke also tends to downplay Jesus' suffering and death, and at the same time gives more attention to the resurrection and appearances of the risen Jesus. For example, in the passion narrative, Luke shows a calm, controlled Jesus. In the scene at the garden of Gethsemane, Jesus prays only once that God remove this cup from him (22:39–46), and not three times as in Mark (14:32–42) and in Matthew (26:36–46). Only in Luke does Jesus promise one of the criminals being crucified with him that he will be with Jesus in Paradise today (Luke 23:43). Only in Luke does Jesus pray that God might forgive the crowd, 'for they know not what they do' (23:34). Only Luke eliminates the crown of thorns. Only in Luke does Jesus *not* cry out asking why God has abandoned him – something he does in both Mark (15:34) and in Matthew (27:46). And only in Luke do we find the extended appearance story of Jesus to the two disciples on the road to Emmaus (24:13–35). In Luke Jesus comes across as a righteous and innocent prophetic martyr who has come to bring good news to the outcast.

John: Begin by reading John 1–3 and 9. The first question in turning to John's Gospel is its relationship to the Synoptic Gospels. Most scholars agree that John probably did not know any of the Synoptic gospels in their written form, but that John may well have been familiar with many of the same oral traditions about Jesus, especially the passion materials. This accounts in part for why John is so very different from the Synoptic Gospels.

The Gospel of John probably relied on a written source that contained many of what John calls Jesus' 'signs' (2:11; 4:54; 12:37; 20:30–31). These signs were intended to bring about an initial belief in Jesus' identity as one whom God had sent (cf. 2:11; 4:54). But Jesus' identity has been transformed by John's Gospel so that not only is Jesus the Christ and God's Son; Jesus also participates in God's divinity and even in the creation of the universe as God's *logos*, the Word, the divine principle of order (1:1–5). Jesus' special identity is made very clear in the very first chapter of John's Gospel. John has Jesus go on to make his divine identity even clearer by using 'I am' (*ego eimi*) statements throughout the Gospel. These 'I am' statements are especially significant because the phrase 'I am' is the name God used to refer to God's self in the story of Moses and the burning bush in Exodus 3. This connection was not lost on John's audience, probably Jewish Christians at the end of the first century.

By saying that 'I am the bread of life' (6:35, 48, 51), or 'I am the light of the world' (8:12), or 'I am the good shepherd' (10:11, 14), or 'I am the resurrection and the life' (11:25, 14:6), or 'I am the true vine' (15:1) John has Jesus identify himself with the very source of life. And in 8:58 Jesus says 'before Abraham was I am', a clear indication of Jesus' pre-existence. In John, then, Jesus functions as God's presence: 'No one comes to the Father but by me' (14:6); 'He who has seen me has seen the Father' (14:9).

In John's Gospel Jesus comes across as an otherworldly figure who has descended from the heavens to bring about new life through his own death and resurrection. John's Gospel went through various editions at the hands of a Jewish Christian community engaged in heated debate with Jewish leadership (cf. 8:44; 9:22; 16:2).

The Letters of Paul:

We turn, finally, to look in a general way at the letters of Paul, with special attention to the undisputed letters. Begin by reading 1 Thessalonians, Philemon, 1 Corinthians 4–7, and Romans 1–4 and 9–11.

Paul was a missionary apostle who established various Churches throughout the Greco-Roman world, especially in Greece (Corinth, Philippi, Thessalonica) and in Asia Minor (Ephesus, Galatia; roughly the same territory as modern day Turkey). He tells us very little about himself, but from what he says in Galatians 1–2 it is clear that he had been a fervent persecutor of the Christians before becoming a Christian himself. He had been a Pharisee (cf. Phil 3:5) and says that he experienced a revelation of Jesus (Gal 1:12; cf. Acts 9). Paul relates almost nothing about the public ministry of Jesus. Rather, he concentrates on the significance of Jesus' death and resurrection, which lies at the core of his theology (cf. Rom 3, 6; 1

Cor 15). As a result of his revelation experience Paul felt called to proclaim the Gospel. Paul's missionary activity was directed especially to Gentiles (cf. Gal 2:9), and he had much success in establishing congregations, although not without tremendous struggles and fights along the way. In the letters Paul wrote we hear one side of a conversation, Paul's. We have to reconstruct as best we can the situation that elicited Paul's letters and what was going on in the communities he addressed. His letters address serious problems in various communities, especially in Corinth and in Galatia.

To begin getting handles on Paul's letters, it is helpful to be aware of letter structure. Turn to 1 Thessalonians, which illustrates how the letter structure works. Each letter begins with an address, sender to recipient: 'Paul, Silvanus, and Timothy, to the Church of the Thessalonians ...' (1 Thess 1:1). This includes a greeting, 'Grace to you and peace' (1 Thess 1:1). Then comes the 'thanksgiving section' of the letter, in which the author gives thanks to God for those who are addressed (1 Thess 1:2–10). The thanksgiving section can often tip the author's hand, and give clues as to the issues to be addressed. Then comes the body of the letter (1 Thess 2:1–5:11), where the central concerns of the letter are raised. This is often followed by a 'paraenesis section' in which the author gives ethical admonitions to the recipients of the letter: do this, don't do this. 1 Thessalonians 5:12–22 is a good illustration of such admonitions. Finally, each letter has a closing section (cf. 1 Thess 5:23–28).

Each letter addresses a different situation with different concerns. Paul sought to speak to these contingent, changing situations from his coherent understanding of the Gospel message. First Corinthians gives us a good taste of the kinds of issues Paul faced in working with a Gentile Christian community. He tells the Corinthians (who are experiencing problems of division and of immorality) to be united in Christ (1 Cor 1–4) and to behave in light of their faith in Christ, not by condoning those who sue one another in court or visit prostitutes (1 Cor 5–6). Paul also answers various questions about which they have written to him (1 Cor 7:1), regarding marriage relations (1 Cor 7), eating meat that had been offered to idols (1 Cor 8, 10), spiritual gifts (1 Cor 12–14), and a financial offering Paul is collecting (1 Cor 16).

Map No. 4

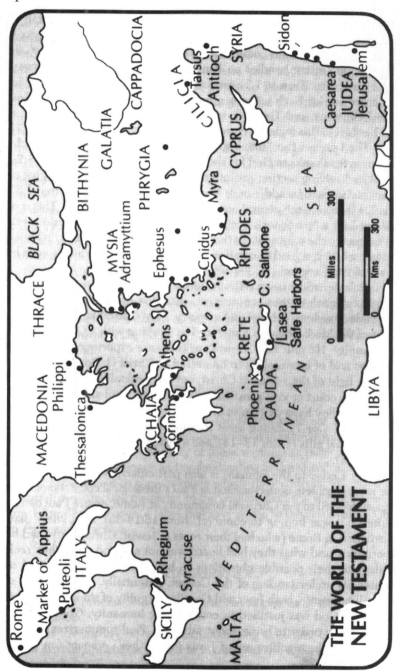

THE WORLD OF THE NEW TESTAMENT

Paul's Letter to the Romans is also particularly helpful, for it gives us the most complete understanding of Paul's theological convictions. Romans was addressed to the Christian community at Rome, where Paul had never visited but was hoping to come (cf. Rom 15:14–33). Paul knew that the Christians in Rome (who had their roots in Jewish Christianity) had heard about him, and what they had heard was not all good. Paul thus seeks to anticipate their possible objections to him before he arrives, and so he relates his understanding of the Gospel. Essentially, Paul seeks to show how all humanity, both Jews and Gentiles, is guilty of sinning against God. Although God was justified in condemning humanity, God instead sent God's Son in order to bring about salvation. Paul summarizes this understanding of the significance of Jesus in a rather compact few verses in Romans 3:21–26.

For Paul, Jesus is an expression of God's covenant faithfulness to God's promises to Israel of old. Part of God's covenant included the extension of God's blessing to the Gentiles, which God has brought about through Jesus. The problem is that most of the Jews have not believed. Does that mean the Jews are rejected? As Paul puts it in Romans 11:1 and 11, 'By no means!' How does Paul explain the paradox that the Jews have not believed but the Gentiles have? 'I want you to understand this mystery, brethren: a hardening has come upon part of Israel, until the full number of the Gentiles come in' (Rom 11:25). For Paul, it is in part a mystery. But Paul is confident that God will extend God's mercy to all people, as he says to the Gentile Christians in Rome (Rom 11:30–32): 'Just as you were once disobedient to God but now have received mercy because of their disobedience, so they have now been disobedient in order that by the mercy shown to you they also may receive mercy. For God has consigned all people to disobedience, that God may have mercy upon all!' In Romans 11:33-36 Paul returns again to the motif of God's mystery. What stands out in his discussion, however, is a rather striking notion. Although the Gentiles and the Jews have been enemies (Rom 11:28), each is saved by God through the other. God has worked it so that one finds salvation, ironically, through one's enemy: Gentiles through the disbelief of the Jews, and the Jews through the belief of the Gentiles. God's covenant promises hold good for all.

Conclusions

We have now touched on many of the New Testament writings. We can see again that there is a tremendous amount of diversity and even tension expressed in the overall unity of these writings as their authors seek to articulate their experience and understanding of the significance of Jesus and how these relate to the Churches which they address. We have emphasized the distinctive character of the various writings, for together they show the multiple images of Jesus that gave shape to the rise of early Christian faith and practice.

Study questions
1. Outline the process which led to the development of the New Testament canon.
2. What is the history of traditions underlying the New Testament, and what are the critical tools used to investigate the different layers of the tradition?
3. Name two distinctive aspects of each of the Gospels.
4. What are some of the central aspects of Paul's understanding of the Gospel?

Chapter 8

The Gospel Stories

Gideon Goosen and Margaret Tomlinson

Mark – a Gospel in a hurry

Author

We do not know who wrote the Gospel which bears the name of Mark. Early Church tradition, based on the somewhat unreliable historian Papias, thought it was the John Mark of Acts, the disciple of Peter (1 P 5:13), but internal evidence does not support this view. In fact, the differences in the background and situation of John Mark, when compared with the impressions the Gospel gives us of its author, are too marked for an identification of Mark the evangelist with John Mark of Acts (cf. Brown & Meier, 1982:191–197, and Doohan, 1986:10–11). The most we can say is that Mark was writing for a community that may have known the influence of Peter until his martyrdom sometime between AD 64 and 67.

Date

Internal evidence suggests that the Gospel was probably written between 65–70, after the death of Peter and towards or at the end of the four-year war between Israel and Rome which resulted in the destruction of Jerusalem in 70. Mark 13 has echoes of this struggle and of the destruction of Jerusalem, as well as mentioning earthquakes (there were three in Nero's reign, which came to an end in 68) and famine (the collapse of Jerusalem was accompanied by famine).

Place

According to tradition, the Gospel was written in Rome. Some scholars have been puzzled by the lack of urban imagery in the Gospel (compared with the Gospel of Matthew, for example) and have suggested a more rural location to the north of Palestine. However, given the internal evidence of the gospel, Rome is still the most favored location.

Intended community

On internal evidence, it is clear that Mark was writing for a predominantly Gentile community (i.e. Christians of non-Jewish origins). There is little concern to show connections with the Old Testament. Mark explains Jewish customs (cf. 7:3–4; 14:12; 15:42), and translates Aramaic words (cf. 3:17; 5:41; 7:11; 10:46). There are more Latinisms in Mark's Gospel than in any other, and it would seem that he is writing for people who knew and used Latin.

Background of the Community

The atmosphere was one of conflict for a community constantly under threat of persecution by the erratic Roman emperors, especially Nero, who had already killed two of their leaders in Rome by 67. The community would have been distressed by the news of the impending destruction, or final destruction in 70, of Jerusalem and its Temple – the place where Christianity had its roots. No doubt some people were asking: is this the end of time? The final event leading to the *Parousia*? (In Mk 13:5-6 and 21–22, there are indications that Mark was reacting against '*parousia* pretenders' – men actually claiming to be the risen Christ returning at the end of time.)

Sources

Before Mark wrote his Gospel, the words and actions of Jesus had been reflected on, in some instances grouped together, and used as the basis of preaching or teaching for over thirty years. Mark seems to have chosen from among the traditions circulating in his community:

1. Probably an early *passion narrative* (arrest, trial, death of Jesus).
    This narrative was filled with Old Testament references (as is

Mark 15) to help believers understand that Jesus went to his cross 'in accordance with the scripture', and to help Jewish converts (grounded in the Jewish scriptures) to believe in a crucified Messiah.

2. An *account of the Lord's Supper* (Paul also used a similar account when writing earlier to the Corinthians: 1 Cor 11:23–26).
3. A cycle of *miracle stories* (chapters 5 and 7).
4. *Controversy stories*. Mark carefully frames these between miracle stories of cures and paralysis.
5. A collection of *parables* (Mark 4).
6. Apocalyptic writing (Mark 13) – a style of writing that belonged to the late Old Testament period (e.g. Daniel) and to earliest Christianity.

The author of the Gospel of Mark brought these materials together, imposing a geographical and chronological framework on the 'Good News about Jesus Christ' – a framework followed by both Matthew and Luke (but not by John). This framework is more theological than historical, presenting a view of the ministry of Jesus from a particular post-resurrection perspective influenced by his (Mark's) own and his community's faith experience.

Structure

Preparation for Public Ministry 1:1–13
The Galilean Ministry 1:1–7:23
Journeys outside Galilee 7:24–10:52
The Jerusalem Ministry 11:1–13:37
The Passion Narrative 14:1–15:47
The Resurrection Narrative 16:1–8; (16:9–20 later addition)

The structure of the Gospel is inverted parallelism or chiasm in which the first section of the Gospel parallels with the last, and the second with the fourth, with the journey to Jerusalem as the centre or hinge of the chiasm:

a. Preparatory events
b. Ministry: Galilee
c. Journey to Jerusalem
b. Ministry: Jerusalem
a. Concluding events: burial

Style

Mark's Gospel has been called 'a Gospel in a hurry'. It is sprinkled with expressions such as 'straightaway' Jesus did this and 'at once' he did that (there are forty such expressions). Mark is an accomplished storyteller, with an eye to detail and a directness which has emotional impact and draws the reader into the experience. Mark's Jesus is a vivid, human Jesus.

Mark does not use the polished Greek of Luke, but rather everyday, colloquial Greek. As has been said, he translates Aramaic words and uses more Latinisms than any other gospel. His Gospel has only two speeches or discourses (4:2–34; 13:5–36). He repeats particular words or phrases within an episode to emphasize the point (e.g. forgiveness of sin 2:5, 7, 9, 10).

Mark also uses a repetition pattern of three: three commissioning stories (1:16–20; 3:13–19; 6:7–13), three passion-resurrection predictions (8:31; 9:31; 10:33–34), three episodes of Jesus at prayer (1:35; 6:46; 14:32–42), three episodes on the mountain (3:13; 6:46; 9:2). He uses parallelism, too, including inverted parallelism or chiasm (e.g. the arrangement of the five controversy stories 2:1 to 3:6).

Theological slant and concerns

Past, present and future all flow together in the Gospel of Mark: the past of the ministry of Jesus of Galilee, outside Galilee, and going to Jerusalem; the present of the ministry of Jesus in and through his Church; the future of the ministry Jesus will exercise when he comes soon as Son of Man. The writer thinks in terms of a drama that began in the past, continues in the present which the community is experiencing, and will reach a climax in the near future with the imminent coming of the end. Thus past, present and future tend to merge in his story.

Mark is concerned for *Gentiles*, e.g. 13:10; 13:27; 14:9. There are references to Gentiles in the miracle stories in Mark 5 and 7 (the Gerasenes are Gentiles). The centurion in 15:39 is a Gentile; he confesses Jesus as Son of God.

Mark uses *geography* for theological purposes. Galilee is a key place for Jesus' preaching and becomes the point of departure for going to Tyre and Sidon to meet the Gentiles. Ultimately, after the Resurrection (16:7), Galilee becomes the gateway for spreading the good news. Conversely, Jerusalem is a city shut in on itself that rejects Jesus and puts him to death. In Mark's story, the lake, mountains and wilderness take on rich theological symbolism that goes beyond traditional Jewish understandings of the significance of these places.

The overall image of Jesus is that of the Anointed One, the *messiah* – a suffering Messiah. The Gospel is of sufficiently early date to reflect the difficulty the Church encountered in its preaching of a suffering rather than a triumphant Messiah. Mark is reminding his readers, constantly faced with the possibility of persecution, that to be a disciple of Jesus means sharing in suffering and rejection before sharing in glory. It is only after the Resurrection that the disciples know who Jesus really is and what discipleship means.

From its very beginning the Gospel moves toward the culminating point of the *Passion*. Mark immediately introduces John the Baptist (1:4), then records his arrest (1:14) and later links Jesus with John the Baptist (6:14ff.), subtly indicating that what happened to John will happen to Jesus. Mark includes a number of controversy stories of conflicts that centre around Jewish structures and practices: the Sabbath, cleaning, fasting, almsgiving – the boundaries by which the Jews identified themselves. From Mark 8 onwards, there are indications that Jesus was convinced that his ministry would end in death (8:32–33; 9:30–32; 10:35–45; 14:34).

Mark presents the Passion as the culminating point in Jesus' experience of rejection and abandonment. It is also the point where, in response to the High Priest's question, 'Are you the Christ, the Son of the Blessed One?', Jesus answers 'I am' (14:61–62) – thus turning the trial, says Doohan (1986:87) into 'an epiphany of the Lord to the worshipping community'.

At the beginning of the Gospel, Mark introduces Jesus as the *man from Nazareth* (1:9). Jesus of Nazareth is the man who goes to the cross. From beginning to end, Mark's story is of a very human Jesus with strong emotions.

Mark is quite explicit about the meaning of *discipleship* (8:34–35). Some have suggested that one of the primary purposes behind the writing of this Gospel was a clarification of discipleship (cf. Doohan, 1986:93), no doubt prompted by the situation of the Christians in Rome, whose world was collapsing around them. Mark often focuses on the uncertainty and fear that Jesus' disciples experienced, at the same time addressing the need of his community to understand the nature and the challenge of discipleship. It is significant that Mark has Jesus present his main teaching on discipleship on the way to Jerusalem (to his death) and that this teaching is framed between two stories of Jesus curing the blind (8

22-26; 10:46–52). He is gradually opening their eyes to see who he is and to understand the true nature of his Messiaship.

The *community of disciples* gathered around Jesus constitutes the Church for Mark. He does not use the word 'Church' and is not preoccupied with its organization and structure. He uses simple images to express his understanding of the Christian community, such as boat (3:9; 4:1), flock (6:34, 14:27), temple – the new temple of God which replaces the old (14:58; 15:29).

Mark has Jesus begin his ministry with the words 'The kingdom of God is close at hand' (1:15). His Gospel has been called a history of the *Kingdom*: he speaks of requirements for entry (10:13–31) and membership (4:1–34).

The nature of the reign of God and human responses to it are presented in the parable of the sower and instruction on its meaning (4:1–34).

Matthew – Jesus As the New Moses

Author

It is generally accepted that the author is not the apostle Matthew. The reasons for this are that an eyewitness would not have relied so heavily on Mark, and secondly, by AD 85–90, the apostle Matthew would probably have been dead. A third reason for rejecting the Apostle Matthew as author, is that the concerns of this Gospel are of second generation Christians. It could be of course, that the Apostle Matthew was associated with the community in which the Gospel arose. This would explain why the tax collector Levi in Mark 2:14 becomes the tax collector Matthew in Matt 9 and 10:3.

The author was probably a Jewish convert who was familiar with the Law, prophets, Jewish traditions and messianic expectations.

Date

It seems clear from internal evidence that this Gospel was written after the destruction of Jerusalem, which is seen as an event in the past (22:7; 21:41). There is also an allusion to the destruction of Jerusalem in the parable of the Great Supper. Ignatius of Antioch (d. 110) in his letters seemingly refers to the Gospel of Matthew a number of times. Within this framework a date of 85-90 is likely.

Place

One cannot be certain but Antioch in Syria is suggested by a number of scholars.

Intended community

His frequent reference to the Jewish scriptures and traditions suggests that his readers were predominantly converts from Judaism. However he also has a missionary outlook and openness towards Gentiles which argues for a Gentile audience as well. This audience is quite likely an urban community. Matthew uses the word for 'city' (Greek *polis*) twenty-six times and the word for 'village' only three times. Mark by comparison uses these words eight and seven times respectively.

There is some internal evidence to suggest that the Matthean community was relatively wealthy. Whereas Mark and Luke tend to refer to small change or lesser denominations ("copper coins', Mark 6:8 or 'minas/pounds', Luke 19:11–27), Matthew frequently uses terms such as gold, silver and talents in his Gospel. A talent, for example, was worth about fifty times the value of a 'minas/pound'.

Background of the community

Matthew reflects a period of consolidation for the early Christian communities. The *Parousia*, seen as imminent in Mark, is not so pressing in Matthew. The threat of immediate and total persecution has passed, although tensions between Christians and their Jewish and Gentile neighbours are real. Matthew speaks of disciples being 'handed over to tribulation' hated by all, and even put to death (10:18, 22; 13:21; 24:9). Jewish Christians were clearly separate from other Jews, however, as can be seen by Matthew's reference to 'their' synagogues and his refusal to say anything good about the Scribes and Pharisees.

The time at which Matthew wrote was one of settling down for the Church while attempting to articulate its life and mission. Questions of order, discipline and authority arise. There are also echoes of the Church's liturgy, for example, 'Go, therefore, and make disciples of all the nations; baptise them in the name of the Father and of the Son and of the Holy Spirit ...' (28:19) gives us the first trinitarian formula in the New Testament which was most likely used in baptism in Matthew's community.

Sources

1. Mark: Of Mark's 661 verses, Matthew reproduces some 606 verses.
2. Q: Matthew and Luke have 200 common verses not found in Mark.
3. M: This source provides material not found in Mark or Q.

This source could have been oral or written. The Infancy Narrative comes from this source.

Structure

The Infancy Narrative 1:1–2: 23
Preparation for Public Ministry 3:1 to 4:11
The Galilean Ministry 4:12 to 13:58
Retirement from Galilee 14:1 to 18:35
The Journey to Jerusalem 19:1 to 20:34
The Jerusalem Ministry 21:11 to 25:46
The Passion Narrative 26:1 to 27:66
The Resurrection Narrative 28:1–20

Matthew can also be arranged into five books, possibly to parallel the five books of the Torah. In each book the discourse is introduced by a narrative section:

Prologue: 1:1 to 2:23
Book one: The Proclamation of the Reign 3:1 to 7:29
Book two: Ministry in Galilee 8:1 to 11:1
Book three: Controversy and Parables 11:2 to 13:52
Book four: The Formation of the Disciples 13:53 to 18:35
Book five: Judea and Jerusalem 19:1 to 25:46
The Passion Narrative: 26:1 to 27:66
The Resurrection Narrative: 28:1–20

Style

Matthew uses better Greek and a richer vocabulary than Mark, whom he often abbreviates. He improves upon Mark whenever he can. In keeping with his Jewish background, he uses the rabbinical styles of composition known as Midrash, Halakah (e.g. 17:24–27) and Haggadah (cf. Infancy Narrative).

Whereas Mark's is a Gospel in a hurry, Matthew's is slower in pace, more reflective, and concerned with the teachings of Jesus rather than his actions. He is a highly skilled writer with an eye to symmetry. There are three divisions in his genealogy, three temptations, three duties (6:1–18), three sets of three miracles (8-9), three signs, three parables of judgment and three challenges to the Scribes (22). There are seven parables of the Kingdom (13), seven woes, and seven parables of warning (23:13–33; 24:32 to 25:46). He plans the whole Gospel around five discourses arranged in inverted parallelism (chiasm) with the first and fifth dealing with blessings or woes, the second and fourth with aspects of the life of the new community, and the central third speech dealing with the Kingdom.

Theological slant and concern

Matthew is a very *Jewish Gospel*. This is firstly shown by the vocabulary used. Matthew refers to the Kingdom of *Heaven*, rather than the Kingdom of God. Other typically Jewish words such as 'righteousness', 'almsgiving', 'prayer', 'fasting', 'sons of God', 'the consummation of the age', and 'the day of judgment' are frequently used. Matthew constantly cites scripture – over 130 times. He often uses the rabbinical style of question (17:24, 25; 18 12; 22:17, 42; 26:66) and counter question (12:5; 21:16; 22:31). Jesus in Matthew's Gospel is initially and primarily concerned with the salvation of Israel (15:21–28). Matthew is also concerned with the *Law* and how Jesus fulfills it.

Although Matthew's is a Jewish Gospel, he can be anti-Jewish on occasions (12:6; 21:28–32; 27:25). At other times he expresses both pro-Gentile bias (2:1–12; 4:14-16; 12:21; 28:19) and anti-Gentile prejudice (10:5). Matthew is very harsh on the *Scribes* and *Pharisees*, referring to them as a brood of vipers (3:7–12), as people who cannot read the signs of the times (16:3), and as murderers of prophets (21:31). Chapter 23 is likewise very strident in its condemnation of them. This attitude is seen to reflect the strong feelings and tensions between the Jewish Christians and the Orthodox Scribes and Pharisees in the local community in which the Gospel arose.

Another concern of Matthew's is that of the *Church*. He is the only evangelist to use the word *ekklesia* which appears three times (16:18; 18:17). It translates the Hebrew '*qahal*', meaning 'gathering of the brethren', which is also Matthew's understanding of the local Church. The Church is a community of the people of God and the disciples of Jesus. Within this community there are 'prophets' (some false prophets) and 'teachers'.

This community had by AD 85 developed an organizational structure for governing its life. Peter, for example, receives 'the keys of the Kingdom of Heaven' (16:19) as first among the disciples. The power of 'binding and loosing' (18:18) is given to all the disciples and enables them collectively to regulate the difference of doctrine or discipline that may occur in the community. Yet within the group Peter clearly holds a position of special prominence as leader: 'Thou art Peter and upon this rock I will build my Church' (16:18).

Matthew's *theology of salvation* is that the Good News, which was initially directed at the Jews, has been rejected by them and is now to be offered to the Gentiles. Matthew indicates that salvation is initially for the Jews by using geographical boundaries. Jesus' ministry is confined within the borders of Israel (15:24; 10:5–6). Matthew has the Canaanite woman 'coming out' of the region of Tyre and Sidon so that it is in Israel that Jesus grants his favor (15:21–28). (Mark has no such qualms about Jesus performing miracles in pagan territory.) Jesus, in Matthew's Gospel, starts his ministry in Galilee, and after his Resurrection he meets his disciples again in Galilee, from whence he sends them out to the whole world (28:19). The movement is clearly from Jewish territory out to the pagan world.

Jesus is seen as the new *Moses*, the *Teacher* and *Law-Giver*, in Matthew's Gospel. Not surprisingly, therefore, much of the Gospel focuses on the teachings of Jesus (as opposed to the actions of Jesus in Mark).

Like Moses on Sinai, Jesus preaches the Beatitudes (the new Law) from the Mount. He is transfigured on a mountain and he meets the eleven disciples, after the Resurrection, on a mountain in Galilee (28:16). The physical setting of a mountain is thus used to emphasize the image of Jesus as the new Moses, the new Law-Giver on Mount Sinai.

In a way, the end of Matthew's Gospel sums up the author's and his community's understanding of their *mission*. Chapter 28:16–20 relates how Jesus, after his Resurrection, met with his disciples in Galilee and commissioned them to go out into the world and preach the Good News. In this account a number of significant points indicate how the new religion (to be known later as Christianity) has made a break with the religion from which it sprang (Judaism): Jesus meets with them on a mountain (like Moses on Sinai) and gives them a new Law; he claims 'all authority on heaven and earth' (allowed only to Yahweh by traditional Jews); he commands them to go and make disciples of all nations (a new missionary perspective for Jews); they are to baptize followers into the new faith, which rite replaces that of circumcision; Jesus replaces the Torah as teacher, as the one who is to be obeyed; and finally the promise he makes is to be with them always, until the end of time (cf. Moloney, 1986:118–122).

Luke – The Compassionate Saviour

Author

According to Fitzmyer and other scholars, the author of this Gospel is quite likely a Syrian of Antioch, a physician (Col 4:14) and collaborator of Paul, named Luke. He travelled with Paul from Troas to Philippi in Greece. He was also in Caesarea and later in Rome. According to one tradition he subsequently worked in Achaia (Greece). Early Christian writers such as Irenaeus (AD 178), Eusebius and Jerome, all refer to the Evangelist Luke and suggest he lived in Antioch in Syria. Another tradition according to which Luke was a painter originates from the fourteenth century and is thus less reliable.

Date

It is dated later than 70 because it separates the destruction of Jerusalem from the end of the world. Furthermore it no longer sees the Kingdom as imminent as Mark does. Scholars suggest a date around 80–90.

Place

Possibly Greece or Asia Minor.

Intended community

The author is clearly writing for Gentile Christians. The internal evidence for this is convincing. Luke dedicates Luke–Acts to a person bearing a Greek name, Theophilus (Luke 1:3; Acts 1:1). He relates the promised salvation to Gentiles or non-Jews. He seldom quotes the Old Testament and eliminates predominantly Jewish preoccupations from Mark or Q sources, e.g. the Sermon on the Plain omits the discussion on the fulfillment of the Law that Matthew has (Matt 5:17–48); Luke also leaves out the section from

Mark (7:1–23) which deals with the details of the clean/unclean controversy of the Jewish ritual for purity.

Background of the community

Luke is writing in a period of expansion for Christians. The *Parousia* is no longer seen as imminent and hence Luke prays for bread 'each day' and exhorts followers to take up their crosses 'daily'. The disciples are settling down to a lifetime of work and prayer. In the meantime the Church will expand and grow under the guidance of the Spirit.

Sources

1) Mark: Luke has 350 verses of Mark's 661 (55%). By and large he follows Mark's sequence.
2) Q: He has 230 verses from this source also found in Matthew.
3) L: This is Luke's own source, which could come from Johannine circles as he shares some motifs with John such as the Temple and Jerusalem. Most of the Infancy narrative also comes from this L Source.

Structure

Prologue 1: 1–4
The Infancy narrative 1: 5 to 2: 52.
Preparation for Public Ministry 3:1 to 3: 13
The Galilean Ministry 3:14 to 9:50
The Journey to Jerusalem 9:51 to 19:27.
The Jerusalem Ministry 19:28 to 21:38.
The Passion Narrative 22:1 to 23:56
The Resurrection Narrative 24:1–53.

Style

The author has a varied style. He writes in good, polished Greek. He is very observant of human behaviour, recording the manner-isms of people in his stories as well as giving psychological insight. In 9:43 Luke comments that Jesus gave the cured epileptic boy 'back to his father' (cf. Mark 9:27); in 18:1 he speaks about the 'need to pray continually and never lose heart'; at other times he is able to give insight into the feelings of the crowd – 'a feeling of expectancy had grown among the people' (3:15) and later 'they imagined that the Kingdom of God was going to show itself then and there' (19:11). (Cf. Also 4:14f; 11:1, 29; 13:1; 17:20.)

Theological slant and concerns

Luke is concerned with projecting Jesus as a prophet. Luke uses this title more than Mark (cf. 4:24; 7:16; 9:19).

Luke is concerned for the *Gentiles.* He omits Semitic words like *Boanerges, abba, Iscariot, hosanna, Gethsemane, ephphatha,* which his audience would not understand. Instead of 'rabbi' he uses *didaskale* (teacher); instead of *golgotha* he uses *kranion* (skull), and instead of 'amen' he uses 'truly'. He writes for people who do not know Palestine. Hence he explains, 'a city called Bethsaida' or 'the feast of unleavened Bread which is called the Passover'.

Luke cares for the *poor.* In the Infancy Narrative, the poor and lowly are chosen for the greatest privileges. In the Beatitudes it is 'happy are you poor' (not 'poor in spirit', as in Matthew). Luke alone has the Isaiahan text about the poor when Jesus appears in the synagogue in Nazareth (4:18) and refers to it again later (7:22). The Story of the Rich Man and Lazarus is exclusive to Luke (16:19–31) as well as the material in Luke 12:13–21 relating to the poor. With the poor go the marginalized in society such as the *Samaritans* to whom Luke also gives particular attention (cf. 9:51–56; 10:29–37).

The *Holy Spirit* and *Prayer* are also emphasized in Luke. He first mentions the Holy Spirit in 1:15. John the Baptist from his mother's womb, is 'filled with the Holy Spirit'. Thereafter Luke frequently mentions the Holy Spirit (cf. 1:35, 41, 67, 80; 2:25, 26, 27; 4:1, 14, 18; 10:21). The Acts of the Apostles, also written by Luke, continues this emphasis on the Holy Spirit. *Prayer* is likewise highlighted with mention made of it before all the important steps in the ministry of Jesus; i.e. at his baptism (3:21), before the choice of the Twelve (6:12), before Peter's confession of faith (9:18), at the transfiguration (9:28), before teaching the 'Our Father' (11:1), and in the Garden of Gethsemane (22:41). Jesus insists that his disciples be people of prayer too (cf. 6:28; 10:2; 11:1–13; 18:1–8; 21:36).

We can also say that Luke's Gospel is one of *messianic* joy. The words used by Luke abound in joyous response to the wonder of what has taken place (our salvation). His disciples are to consider themselves fortunate and blessed. Luke's Gospel has been called the Gospel of *mercy* or *Great Pardons.* The theme of compassion and forgiveness pervades the whole Gospel. One thinks of the stories of the lost sheep, lost coin and lost son (chapter 15), the sinful woman (7:36-58), the story of Zacchaeus (19:1–10). Jesus also forgives his executioners (23:34). Luke has the injunction 'Be compassionate (not 'perfect' as in Matthew) as your heavenly Father' (6:36). This compassion and pardon is *universal* in Luke. His genealogical table (3:23–38) goes back to Adam showing thus how we are all one human family with one Saviour.

Stewardship of wealth is another Lucan theme. Parables such as the Rich Fool, the Dishonest Steward and the Rich Man and Lazarus illustrate the point that the goods of this life are ours to look after and share.

Luke gives greater prominence to *women* than do the other evangelists. In addition to incidents where women play a prominent role which Matthew or Luke have taken from Mark, Luke has his own stories of women and gives them an importance peculiar to his Gospel. It is obvious that Mary plays a central role in Luke's Infancy Narrative (as opposed to Matthew's). In Jesus' public ministry a group of women (Mary Magdalene, Joanna, Susanna and several others, 8:2) journey with him in his travels and are also present at his Crucifixion (while the disciples flee), at his burial and at the tomb on Easter Day. They become the first preachers of the Easter Message (24:9). Luke seems to make the point that women are the first to come to Easter faith and the first to proclaim it (Moloney, 1984:61).

In addition Luke has the story of Martha and Mary (10:38–42), the Widow of Nain (7:11–17), the sinful woman who washed Jesus' feet (7:36–50), the cure of the crippled woman (13:10–17), the lost coin (15:8–10) and the importunate widow (18:1–8). From Luke's projection of women in his Gospel, scholars have concluded that women played a significant role in Lucan communities.

We also note in Luke that the *ministry of Jesus parallels the mission of the Church in Acts*. Jesus is baptized by the Spirit in Luke 3:21ff. Likewise the Church (Acts 2:1ff) is 'baptized' by the Spirit at Pentecost. Other parallels concern the preaching about the Spirit (Luke 4:16–19; Acts 2:17); theme of rejection (Luke 4:19; Acts 7:58; 13:50); cure of the multitudes (Luke 4:40ff.; Acts 2:43; 5:16) and glorification (Luke 9:28-36; Acts 1:9–11).

Infancy narratives

Having discussed the three Synoptic Gospels and before we go on to John's Gospel, let us take up in some detail the question of the Infancy Narratives.

The categories used in form criticism were worked out from the public ministry accounts in the Gospels. The Infancy Narratives (found only in Matthew and Luke) do not belong to the Public Ministry section of the Gospels, and thus are not strictly speaking a form. However, like Passion Narratives and Resurrection Narratives, they can be seen as a sub-genre of the Gospels.

In terms of development of the Gospel structure over a period of time, the Infancy Narrative came last. The Passion Narrative came first as the basic kerygma. Then the Public Ministry accounts (*didache* = the teachings of Jesus as seen in what he did and said) were prefixed to the Passion Narrative. Finally the Resurrection Narrative was appended to the developing Gospel, and in the cases of Matthew and Luke, an Infancy Narrative placed before the public Ministry. Diagrammatically, the stages or building blocks of the developing Gospel could be presented thus:

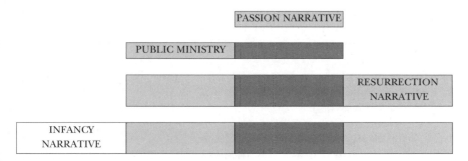

If you look at Mark (without the appendix 16:9–20, which many manuscripts do not have), it consists basically of the Passion Narrative and the Public Ministry. (The Resurrection is briefly mentioned in 16:1–8). It does not have the Resurrection or Infancy Narrative. (Compare Acts 10:36–41 which, in a way, is a miniature Gospel, a summary of Jesus' career.)

The biographical concerns about the birth and early childhood of Jesus were bound to be expressed sooner or later. However, these concerns as expressed in the Infancy Narratives must not be understood in terms of modern historical biography. As Fitzmyer says,

> Early tradition tended to take to itself folklore, astrology and the
> interpretation of the Old Testament. These are known features in
> much ancient tracing of origins, where the sophisticated modern
> use of genealogical and historical records was unknown *(1981: 305)*.

As regards sources, there is no evidence that Matthew used Luke or
vice versa. They both seem to rely on traditions in their respective
communities that existed prior to their writing. In short, we do not
know the sources of these two different Infancy Narratives.
Looking at Luke's account, some commentators suppose two
sources:

a. a Jewish-Christian source for the canticles (Magnificat,
    Benedictus, Nunc Dimittis and probably the section, 'Jesus
    among the doctors of the Law'); and
b. an early Baptist source for the announcement story of John the
    Baptist, and the story of his birth, circumcision and manifesta-
    tion.

The term 'announcement story' as used above requires some
explanation. It is a literary form found mainly in the Old
Testament and is used when some important announcement such
as the annunciation of the birth of a child, is made to a believer.
The usual elements of this particular literary form are as follows:

1. Appearance of an angel (or the Lord himself)
2. Fear response of person
3. The divine message:
     – person addressed by name
     – qualifying phrase describing person
     – person urged not to be afraid
     – woman is to have a child
     – name by which child is to be called
     – phrase interpreting the name
     – future accomplishment of the child
4. Objection of the person
5. A sign to reassure the person

The elements are not always found in this order, nor do individual
stories always have all the elements.

   If we compare Matthew's and Luke's Infancy Narratives we
notice that Luke is less obviously structured than Matthew
(Fitzmyer). Luke emphasizes the parallel between John the Baptist

and Jesus, both of whom are introduced as agents of God's salvation history. John the Baptist is also presented as the precursor of Jesus (as he is the Gospel proper) and plays a transitional role, being part of the Period of Israel. (Luke–Acts can be said to have three stages: Period of Israel, Period of Jesus, Period of the Church/Spirit.) Luke also imitates Old Testament motifs; for example, his reference to David and his lineage (Luke 1:26–33) recalls the childhood of Samuel in the Old Testament (1 Sam:1–3).

Matthew on the other hand structures his Infancy Narrative around five episodes.

Matthew too seems to have used the birth of Moses as a model for his account (compare Ex 4:19 with Matt 2:19f.). (This fits in well with Matthew's portrait of Jesus as the new Moses in the rest of his Gospel.) Some scholars have pointed out elements of midrash in Matthew's account: he uses Old Testament texts as central and then weaves a story around these.

Matthew commences his narrative with a genealogy. Luke places one later on (3:23–38). Matthew is seen to show how Jesus is connected with Abraham and David, the recipients of the messianic promises. Luke goes back to Adam, since his concern is more universal, in keeping with the rest of his Gospel.

Both lists of names are artificial in parts. Matthew has three sets of fourteen (2×7) names (which means leaving out some names). Luke sometimes chooses not to follow the line of the kings of Judah. Both, on occasions when biblical records fail, have to improvise.

Matthew has four women in his genealogy of Jesus: Tamar, who deceived her father-in-law into an incestuous union (Gen 38); Rahab, the prostitute of Jericho who sheltered spies and was admitted to the Israelite community (Jos 2); Ruth, the Moabite who joined the Israelite community (Ruth); and Bathsheba, the wife of Uriah and partner of David's adultery (2 Sam: 11 and 12).

It is difficult to guess Matthew's interest here. Various opinions have been expressed. Jerome regarded all four women as sinners and their inclusion as a foreshadowing of the fact that Jesus had come to save all sinful humankind. However, it is not at all clear that all these women were sinners, and in fact in Jewish piety at the time of Jesus, they were highly esteemed. Another opinion holds that the women were regarded as foreigners and were included by Matthew to show that Jesus was related by ancestry to the Gentiles. There is doubt, however, about Tamar and Bathsheba being foreigners, as well as other reasons for rejecting this opinion.

A third approach, favoured by Brown (1977), is that which identifies common elements the four Old Testament women share with Mary:

a. there is something irregular or extraordinary in their union with their partners – a union which even though scandalous to outsiders, continued the lineage of the Messiah; and
b. they showed initiative or played an important role in God's plan.

It is a combination of these two ideas that possibly best explains Matthew's choice of these women in his genealogy.

Overall, when reading the Infancy Narratives, one should bear in mind that both evangelists use them as overtures to their Gospels, that is, they introduce themes that will be repeated over and over again in the Gospel proper. (In this way they are similar to the function of the Prologue in John's Gospel.) In Matthew's Infancy Narrative we have the themes of the identity of Jesus (raised by the titles used of Jesus), continuity and discontinuity with the Old Testament salvation history, and conflict and rejection. In Luke's narrative, in addition to the theme of Jesus' identify as an agent of God's salvation history, we have the following themes: the journey; universal salvation; the simple and poor; Mary the first believer; missionary discipleship; and Jesus and the Temple.

John – On Eagle's Wings

Author

The identity of the author remains a mystery. Irenaeus, writing at the end of the second century, identified the apostle John with the evangelist John, and others have speculated that the Gospel was written by disciples of John the Apostle who was the Beloved Disciple.

Today the identification of John the Apostle with the Beloved Disciple is seriously questioned (cf. Brown, 1978:33–34; Ellis, 1984: 3; Kysar, 1976:20). Many think that somewhere behind the Gospel is the unnamed 'other disciple' or 'beloved disciple' referred to in the Gospel; a disciple of Jesus but not one of the Twelve, and the leader in the community that gathered around him. It is thought that a Johannine school or group of scholars developed in this community, who interpreted and expanded the Beloved Disciple's teaching as the years went by until someone wrote the Gospel in the form in which we now have it. The same group is also thought to be responsible for the Epistles of John.

The Gospel shows an insider's familiarity with the Old Testament and with Jewish cultic life, so that we may conclude that whoever was behind the Gospel was of Jewish background. However, there are also indications that he may not have been from mainstream Judaism.

Date

Internal evidence indicates that the Gospel was written after AD 85, and probably around 90.

In the 80s, Jewish leaders met at Jamnia to re-establish Jewish identity after the devastating fall of Jerusalem and the confusion caused by the strange doctrines of the followers of Jesus of Nazareth. Probably after 85, another benediction was added to the eighteen benedictions which had to be recited publicly at the daily synagogue morning prayer. This benediction asked that the Nazarenes (Christians) and heretics might suddenly perish (cf. Perrin, 1974:230; Moloney, 1986:163), thus placing the Jewish Christians in a dilemma, since they were banned from the synagogue if they did not recite the benediction. There is clear evidence in the Gospel of the Johannine community's conflict with the synagogue leaders (e.g. in John 9). Moreover, the Gospel of John is the only book in the New Testament that uses the technical Greek term for excommunication from the Synagogue: *aposunagogos* (9:22; 12:42, 16:2).

Given this evidence, it seems reasonable to date the final writing of the Gospel around 90 when the results of the expulsion order would have been most felt in the Mediterranean area.

Place

There is an ancient tradition which says that the Gospel in its final form was written at Ephesus. There does not appear to be any internal evidence either to support or deny this tradition.

Intended community

John's primary audience seems to have been a group of Jewish Christians who were in a situation of increasing tension with the Jewish Synagogue (cf., for example, John 9 and the aftermath of the healing of the blind man). They were torn between their alle-

giance to the Jewish Synagogue and their Jewish roots on the one
hand and the Christian community on the other, and their faith in
Jesus may have been wavering as a result of conflict and persecution (cf. 20:31).

Background to the community

Brown's study of the Johannine community (cf. 1979:25-58; 166-7)
suggests that it was made up of several layers or groups, each of
which, over the years, exercised its influence, which was carried
through into the Gospel's final written form:

1. The originating group of Jews in or near Palestine, which
    included followers of John the Baptist. The group also included
    the Beloved Disciple, who had known Jesus during his ministry.
2. Jews who may not have belonged to mainstream Judaism: they
    were hostile towards official Judaism, had an anti-Temple bias,
    and understood Jesus against a Mosaic background rather than
    the more usual Davidic background (as in the Synoptic
    Gospels). They made converts in Samaria. (It has been
    suggested that this group was associated with Stephen in
    Jerusalem and fled after his martyrdom into Samaria and
    thence further north [cf. Schillebeeckx, 1980: 315]. Under the
    influence of this group, a 'high', pre-existence Christology
    developed. This was particularly upsetting to the Jews because
    it seemed to establish Jesus as a second God. (There are indi-
    cations that it may also have upset some Jewish Christians in the
    community.) The Jews would eventually have the Johannine
    Christians expelled from the synagogues. These Christians
    would have understood very well a Jesus who is portrayed as
    rejected by his fellow Jews.
3. Gentiles – Greek converts who came into the community after
    it moved from the Palestine area, and who were seen as fulfill-
    ing God's plan in place of 'the Jews', who were blind.
       Given the Greek background of some of the community, John
    cannot assume that all his readers will understand Hebrew, so
    he sometimes translates Hebrew words (1:38 and 1:42), and
    uses universal symbols, such as the vine and bread.

Sources

The question of whether John knew the Synoptic Gospels, or any
one of them, has long been discussed, and to date there is no

conclusive answer. While some of the events in John have parallels in the Synoptics (most notably Mark) and the Passion Narratives have much in common, there are obvious differences in style, presentation and order of events as well as in the chronological framework of the Gospel.

The Gospel consists of narrative material (some of it in common with the Synoptics) combined with long discourses which have no parallel in the other Gospels. There are no parables in John, and his use of miracles ('signs') is different from the Synoptics. Some suggest that John may have used a 'signs source' that contained some but not all of the Synoptic miracles and sayings, and that the discourse were developed out of these, or perhaps were based on fragments of homilies by the Beloved Disciple (cf. Ellis, 1984:3–4).

If John were indeed using some early oral or written source(s) in common with the Synoptics, he has so made it his own that it is impossible to identify distinct sources.

Though John draws primarily on Jewish thought and Old Testament themes, it seems that his background may not have been mainstream Judaism but a branch of Judaism that has been influenced by non-Jewish religious and philosophical thought, especially Hellenism. Note must also be made of the similarities between the themes and language of John and of the Scrolls of the non-mainstream Essene sect at Qumran. Brown (1979:30–31) believes that the connection is explained by the presence in John's community in its early stages of some Jews, perhaps followers of John the Baptist, who held the kind of ideas expressed in the Qumran Scrolls, rather than by the Johannine writer's use of the Scrolls themselves. Others suggest that John was influenced by 'a broad type of Judaism which embraced a great variety of forms and expressions' (Kysar, 1976:19).

Structure

1:1–1:18	Prologue
1:19–12:50	The Book of Signs (Public Ministry)
13:1–20:31	The Book of Glory (Last Supper, Passion, Resurrection)
21:1–25	Epilogue (regarded by most scholars as a last minute addition)

Sometimes the structure of John's Gospel is seen in terms of the Jewish feasts:

Prologue: 1:1–19
The First Passover: 1:19–3: 21
Journeys in Samaria and Galilee: 3:22–4:54
The Second Feast at Jerusalem: 5:1–5:47
Another Passover: 6:1–6:71
The Feast of Tabernacles: 7:1–10:21
The Feast of Dedication: 10:22–11:54
The Last Passover: 11:55–17:26
The Passion Narrative: 18:1–19:42
The Resurrection Narrative: 20:1–24:25

Style

The Gospel uses simple, everyday Greek terms whose meaning is never exhausted. In Moloney's words: 'It is written in one of the simplest forms of Greek in the New Testament, and yet it carries one of its profoundest theologies' (1986:168). The writer uses words, images and concepts that a non-Jewish Hellenist would understand ('the way', 'living water', 'new life'); at the same time, he writes with an insider's knowledge of the Hebrew scriptures. He typically begins with everyday realities – water, bread, light – and then leads the reader in a reflective way into their symbolism on many levels.

By comparison with the Synoptics, the Gospel has only a small amount of narrative material combined with large blocks of discourse material. The Book of Signs consists of short stories and seven signs, out of which a long discourse or dialogue grows, leading the listener deeper into the meaning of the event and ultimately of his/her relationship with God (e.g., John 3: Nicodemus and the discussion about being born again; John 6: feeding the multitude and the discourse on the bread of life).

From the very beginning of the Gospel we are struck by John's constant use of dualistic symbols or pairs of opposites (e.g. light/darkness, above/below) which seem basic to the expression of his thought. Other characteristics of John's style are: his use of double-meaning words (words that have one meaning for Jesus and another for Jesus' audience, e.g. 2:19–22, 3:3-4, 4:10–12); explanatory comments (which correct misunderstandings or explain symbolism – e.g. 2:21, 18:9, or remind the reader of something that has already happened – e.g. 11:2); inclusions (what is said at the beginning is repeated at the end, thus serving as a frame for the whole, e.g. 2:1–12, 20:1–18; note the repetition of key words such as names of people and/or places). Inclusions indicate the natural divisions of the Gospel; the present division of the Gospel into twenty-one chapters dates only from the thirteenth century and does not always respect John's inclusions (cf. Ellis 1984:8–10). John (like other Old and New Testament writers) also uses chiasm (e.g. 2:1–12).

Theological slant and concerns

John leaves us in no doubt as to his purpose in writing his Gospel: 'These things are recorded so that you may believe that *Jesus is the Christ, the Son of God,* and *that believing this you may have life through his name*' (20:31). While he may well have been writing for those who had not yet come to believe in Jesus, he was addressing more explicitly his community which, as has already been noted, was engaged in a traumatic debate with the local Jewish Synagogue.

John's primary intention was to strengthen the community as synagogue opposition grew and they were being cut off from their Jewish roots. Through narrative and theological discourse, John develops his theme of faith. Behind the Gospel is the central question: 'What kind of faith is needed to commit oneself totally to all that Jesus has come to reveal?' (Moloney, 1986:176). The reactions/responses of people in the Gospel to Jesus embody various levels of faith, from rejection of Jesus (the 'Jews', that is, the Jewish synagogue leaders who opposed the Johannine community, e.g. 5:15–16; 6:41; 8:59; 10:31ff.), to complete acceptance of him (e.g. Mary, 2:1-11, or the royal official, 4:46–54). Moloney speaks of a journey from no faith to true faith (cf. 1986:175–7).

The signs evoke various responses and decisions – for Jesus or against him. The Book of Glory was written specifically for those who have accepted Jesus as the one sent from God and who can therefore be led further into his revelation of God in his 'hour'.

Not only does John show Jesus leading Nicodemus or the Samaritan woman or the royal official on this journey of faith. At the same time, the reader, whether in the Johannine community then or the Christian community today, is being nurtured and challenged on the same journey: 'These things are recorded so that *you* may believe …'

More urgently than any other Gospel, that of John asks the question: 'Who is Jesus?' John's attempt to explore the question of *Jesus' identity* is expressed in terms, concepts and symbols that are often quite different from the Synoptics – his thought shaped both by the living faith experience of Jesus in his community and by the opposition encountered in the local Synagogue with its accusation that Christians worshipped two Gods. John's response is to state that Jesus Christ is the Messiah, is divine, but is not a second God. The attempt to hold these two truths in tension accounts for the paradox in some of his writing.

Writing for a community that was being cut off from its Jewish roots, John takes four major Jewish feasts, situates Jesus' ministry within the framework of these feasts (cf. 5:9ff., 6:4ff., 7:2ff., 10: 2ff.), and 'develops a Christology that indicates that *the presence of the living God once celebrated in the feasts has now been incarnated in the person of Jesus*' (Moloney 1986:178). Likewise, John shows that the presence of God in the Temple is being replaced by God's presence in Jesus.

John's view of Jesus has been called 'high' Christology. Emphasis is placed on the person of Jesus who comes 'from above', is the pre-existent *Logos*, the unique human presence and revelation of God, one with the Father in being (e.g. 3:35; 4:34; 14:28).

The Prologue to the Gospel uses the term *Logos*, translated as 'Word', to express something of John's understanding of the identity of Jesus Christ – a term used nowhere else in the New Testament. *Logos* had its roots in a number of religious and philosophical systems, and John may well have been influenced by the Stoic and/or gnostic concepts of his time. But the Prologue is also written out of the ancient Hebrew tradition of the Word of God which brought all things into being, and of the tradition of Wisdom literature. However, for John the *Logos* is not a merely abstract philosophical or religious concept – it is a living, historical person who is both (paradoxically) identical with God and yet distinct from God.

John returns to this paradox of identity and individuality again and again through his exploration of the *Father/Son* analogy. Whoever believes in and responds to Jesus (the Son) believes in and responds to God (the Father) (cf. 5:23, also 12:44–50 which is central to Johannine theology). For John the answer to the question 'Who is Jesus?' is not a purely speculative one, but a practical one. Beyond the paradox and the struggle to express the Son/Father Jesus/God relationship is the simple reality lived out in the community's experience that to respond to Jesus is to respond to the Father.

John's view of the *Church* is different from that of the Synoptic Gospels. He does not use the word 'church', nor is he interested in its institutional structure or authority, as was Matthew. But he does emphasize the community aspect of Church, e.g. in the allegory of the Good Shepherd and the Door (10:1–18) and the True Vine (15:1-10). And in Chapters 15–17 he stresses the oneness of Christians – for whom the relationship between Father and Son and between Jesus and the believer is the model. The community is the 'locus of the manifestation of God' *now* (Kysar, 1976:100).

There is no mention of 'apostle' or 'the twelve' in John's Gospel. The writer uses the word 'disciple' – and seems to include in this any believer. We note the prominence given to 'the Beloved Disciple', a prominence based on the fact that he loved Jesus and was loved by him (13:23; 20:2; 21:7, 20). John is presenting in the Beloved Disciple a model of the true believer and is suggesting that any disciple can be the 'Beloved disciple'.

John's interest in the *Spirit* is different from Luke's. He emphasizes the presence of the Spirit-Paraclete in the experience of the Christian community, and is the only New Testament writer to use the word 'Paraclete' for the Spirit (cf. John 14–16, where he talks of the role of the Spirit). Why the use of this unusual and multi-faceted term? Kysar (1976:93–98) suggests that, locked as they were in a tense situation with the leaders of the local Synagogue, the Johannine community needed to speak of the presence of God among them in a distinctive way. Again, there was the problem posed by the delay of the *Parousia*. Christ had not returned in the way they had expected he would, but is present in the community in the form of the Paraclete. The return of Christ is not an event in the future, but is the experience of the Paraclete in the community now.

The Gospels at a glance
The following pages offer a summary sheet of the four Gospels

	Mark	Matthew	Luke	John
Author	Unknown	Unknown, but very likely a Jewish Christian convert who knew Jewish traditions.	Possibly the 'beloved physician' who accompanied Paul to Philippi (Col 4:14). He was a Gentile, a Syrian of Antioch.	Unknown
Date	AD 65–70	AD 85–90	AD 80–90	± AD 90
Place	Rome (?)	Antioch in Syria (?)	Greece or Asia Minor (?)	Ephesus (?)
Intended Community	Gentiles, i.e. non-Palestinian Christians	Predominantly Jewish Christians	Christian Gentiles	Christian-Jews and Jews in Diaspora
Background of the Community	Constant threat of *persecution* under Nero; shocked by the impending or final destruction of Jerusalem, AD 70. End of time, Parousia, thought to be imminent.	Period of *consolidation*; conflict with the official Judaism. Period of second generation Christians. Questions of order, discipline and authority.	Period of *expansion.* Parousia not imminent. Time of expansion under guidance of the Spirit.	Period of *conflict* with official Judaism and reflection on meaning of Christian discipleship.

	Mark	Matthew	Luke	John
Sources	1. An early Passion Narrative 2. An account of the Lord's Supper 3. Parables 4. Controversy stories 5. Apocalyptic writings	1. Mark 2. Q 3. M	1. Mark 2. Q 3. L	John presupposes Synoptics. He may have shared a common oral tradition with Mark. Some association with the Lucan tradition is also possible. However John is quite distinctive and most of his Gospel has little in common with the Synoptics.
Structure	Preparation for Public Ministry 1:1–13. The Galilean Ministry 1:4–7:23. Journey outside Galilee 7:24–10:52. The Jerusalem Ministry 11:1–13:37.	The Infancy Narrative 1:2–2:23. Preparation for Public Ministry 3:1–4:11. The Galilean Ministry 4:12–13:58. Retirement from Galilee. The Journey to Jerusalem 19:1–20:34. The Jerusalem Ministry 21:11–25:46.	Prologue 1:1–4. The Infancy Narrative 1:5–2:52. Preparation for Public Ministry 3:1–4:11. The Galilean Ministry 3:14–9:50. The Journey to Jerusalem 9:51–19:27. The Jerusalem Ministry 19:2–21:38.	Prologue 1:1–18. The Book of Signs 1:19–12:50. The Book of Glory 13:1–20:31. Epilogue 21:1 24:25.

	Mark	Matthew	Luke	John
	The Passion Narrative 14:1–15:47. The Resurrection Narrative 16:1-8 (16:9–20 later addition)	The Passion Narrative 26:1–27:66. The Resurrection Narrative 28:1–20.	The Passion Narrative 22:1–23:56. The Resurrection Narrative 24:1–53.	
Style	Good storyteller with an eye for detail. Quick moving accounts – a Gospel in a hurry. Not familiar with Palestinian geography. Use of Latinisms.	Slower and more reflective than Mark. Rearranges his material. Writes in good Greek but also manifests Aramaic and Semitic influences. More interested in teaching than actions. Contrived approach.	Good polished Greek. Observant of mannerisms of people and full of psychological insights.	Profound and theological. Use of allegories, symbolism and technical vocabulary. Develops themes, e.g. truth, light, life, glory, worker, rather than give series of events. Many discourses.
Theological Slant and Concerns	Jesus seen as a suffering Messiah.	Jesus seen as the Teacher, the new Moses, the Law-giver, the Messiah-King.	Jesus seen as a prophet, the saviour of the oppressed.	Jesus seen as the incarnate Word, the Son of Man, the Light of the World. The Way, the Truth, the Life.

Mark	Matthew	Luke	John
Passion and Resurrection is the key to understanding Jesus.	Frequent use of scripture and its fulfillment.	Parallels Jesus' ministry with Church in Acts.	Emphasizes community.
Uses geography with a message.	Jesus has come to fulfill the Law, not destroy it.	Has concern for the Gentiles and marginalized people.	Sacramental approach of signs and symbols used.
Gives a very human portrait of Jesus and the disciples.	Scribes and Pharisees are strongly criticized.	Prominence given to the Holy Spirit, prayer and messianic joy.	'Eternal life' possible for believers here and now.
	Highlights 'Church' and Peter's role.	Emphasizes proper stewardship of wealth.	A theological Gospel that shows period of reflection on Jesus' message.
	Galilee important for Jesus' ministry and after Resurrection is gateway to the world.	Greater prominence given to women than other evangelists.	
		A Gospel of compassion/mercy (or Great Pardons) and universal salvation.	

164   Contemporary Catholic Theology – a Reader

Bibliography

Brown, R. (1977), *The Birth of the Messiah*, London: Geoffrey Chapman.
Brown, R. (1966), *The Gospel According to John* (2 Vols), Anchor Bible, London: Geoffrey Chapman.
Brown, R. (1979), *The Community of the Beloved Disciple*, New York: Paulist Press.
Brown, R. and Meier, J. (1983), *Antioch and Rome*, New York: Paulist Press.
Charpentier, E. (1981), *How to Read the New Testament*, London: SCM.
Dodd, C.H. (1953), *The Interpretation of the Fourth Gospel*, C.U.P.
Doohan, L. (1985), *Matthew: Spirituality for the 80s and 90s*, Santa Fe: Bear & Co.
Doohan, L. (1985), *Luke: The Perennial Spirituality*, Santa Fe: Bear & Co.
Doohan, L. (1986), *Mark: Visionary of Early Christianity*, Santa Fe: Bear & Co.
Doohan, L. (1988), *John: Gospel for a New Age*, Santa Fe: Bear & Co.
Edwards, O. (1981), *Luke's Story of Jesus*, Philadelphia: Fortress Press.
Ellis, P.F. (1984), *The Genius of John: a Composition Critical Commentary on the Fourth Gospel*, Collegeville: Liturgical Press.
Fallon, M. (1981), *The Four Gospels*, Sydney: Catholic Adult Education Centre.
Fiorenza, E. Schüssler (1983), *In Memory of Her*, London: SCM.
Fitmyer, J. (1981), *The Gospel According to Luke I–IX*, New York: Doubleday.
Hendricks, H. (1984), *The Infancy Narratives*, London: Chapman.
Kelber, W. (1979), *Mark's Story of Jesus*, Philadelphia: Fortress Press.
Kingsbury, J.D. (1986), *Matthew as Story*, Philadelphia: Fortress Press.
Kysar, R. (1984), *John's Story of Jesus*, Philadelphia: Fortress Press.
Kysar, R. (1976), *John: the Maverick Gospel*, Atlanta: John Knox Press.
Mack, B. (1988), *A Myth of Innocence: Mark and Christian Origins*, Philadelphia: Fortress Press.
McKenzie, J. (1968), 'The Gospel According to Matthew', *Jerome Biblical Commentary*, New Jersey: Prentice-Hall.
Moloney, F. (1984), *Woman, First Among the Faithful*, Blackburn: Collins Dove.
Moloney, F. (1986), *The Living Voice of the Gospel*, Blackburn: Collins Dove.
Perkins, P. (1978), *Reading the New Testament: An Introduction*, New York: Paulist Press.
Perrin, N. (1974), *The New Testament*, New York: Harcourt Brace.
Rhoads, D. and Michie, D. (1982), *Mark as Story*, Philadelphia: Fortress Press.
Spivey, R. and Smith, D. (1982), *Anatomy of the New Testament*, New York: Macmillan.
Stuhlmueller, C. (1968), 'The Gospel According to Luke', *Jerome Biblical Commentary*, New Jersey: Prentice-Hall.
Taylor, M. (1983), *John: The Different Gospel—A Reflective Commentary*, New York: Alba House.

Chapter 9

The Spiritual Journey of
Paul the Apostle

Joseph A. Fitzmyer SJ

How did Saul of Tarsus become Paul the Apostle? So we might describe the spiritual journey in the life of Paul the Apostle. But it is not a question merely about the change of name for the Apostle of the Gentiles that is recorded in the New Testament. The question is rather asked about how Saul the Pharisee became Paul the Apostle, how Paul the Jew became Paul the Christian.

Before we try, however, to answer the question about Paul's spiritual journey from Pharisaism to Christianity, it might be well to spell out a bit the significance of the names that he bears in the New Testament.

1. Paul's name

In his own letters Paul never calls himself Saul, but rather *Paulos*, the name that is used of him also in 2 Pet 3:15, and in the Acts of the Apostles from 13:9 on. Prior to that in Acts his name is *Saulos* (7:58; 8:1, 3; 9:1, 8, 11, 22, 24: 11:25, 30; 12:25; 13:1,2,7), the grecized form of *Saoul*, 'Saul'. The latter Greek spelling is found only in the conversion accounts, when the risen Christ accosts Paul on the road to Damascus (9:4; 22:7; 26:14) and when Ananias restores his sight (9:17; 22:13). *Saoul* is a Greek transliteration of the Hebrew name of the first king of ancient Israel, *Šā'ûl*, 'Saul', as in 1 Sam 9:2, 17.[1] This

---

[1] Cf. Acts 13:21. See further H. Dessau, 'Der Name des Apostels Paulus,' *Hermes* 45 (1910) 347–68; G. H. Harrer, 'Saul Who Is Also Called Paul,' HTR 33 (1940) 19–33.

name means 'asked' (of God *or* of Yahweh), signifying that the mother had asked of God a child, and the one so named was God's response. Thus Paul's spiritual journey begins even with the Hebrew name given to him by his mother at birth, for he himself recognized that God had set him apart before he was born and called him through his grace (Gal 1:15). Named after Saul, the great king of Israel, Paul had a native background that recalled a rich Jewish heritage. It reveals that Paul's spiritual journey was thus foreseen and destined by God even from his birth.

However, the name that he himself used was *Paulos*, the Greek form of a well-known Roman cognomen (or family name), *Paul(l)us*, used by the Aemilian gens, the Vettenii, and the Sergii.[2] One can only speculate about how Paul got such a Roman name. It is the only thing in his letters that suggests his connection with a Roman background, even if he says nothing in them about his Roman citizenship, of which the Lucan Paul boasts (Acts 22:27–28).[3] Though *paulus* in Latin means 'small, little', it really says nothing about Paul's stature or modesty, as is sometimes claimed. It does relate him, however, to a number of famous Roman families.

[2] See 'Paulus,' *Der kleine Pauly: Lexikon der Antike* (5 vols.; ed. K. Ziegler and W. Sontheimer; Munich: A. Druckenmüller, (1964–75) 4. 562–68; *The Oxford Classical Dictionary* (2d ed.; ed. N. G. L. Hammond and N. H. Scullard; Oxford: Clarendon, 1976) 791–92.

[3] See also Acts 16:37–38, and the indirect references in Acts 25:9–12; 26:31–32; 28:17–19. Though W. Stegemann ('War der Apostel Paulus ein römischer Bürger?' *ZNW* 78 [1987] 200–29) feels that a consideration of what is known of the socio-historical conditions of Tarsus and of the granting of citizenship to people in the Roman empire of the time, and especially to Jews, makes it unlikely that Paul would have been a Roman citizen, the last word has not been written on this topic. After all, there is no reason that Paul should mention his Roman citizenship in any of his letters, not even in the Letter to the Romans. What he writes of there has no real relationship to himself being a citizen of the Roman empire, not even what he says of the Christian relations to governing authorities in Rom 13:1–7. That may reflect the fact that he is writing to the Christians of the capital of the empire, as some commentators hold, but it says nothing about Paul's own personal relationship to that empire. See further H. Rosin, 'Civis Romanus sum', *NedTTs* 3 (1948–49) 16–27; H. J. Cadbury, *The Book of Acts in History* (London: Black, 1955) 58–85; E. Brewer, 'Roman Citizenship and Its Bearing on the Book of Acts,' *ResQ* 4 (1960) 205–19; A. N. Sherwin-White, *Roman Society and Roman Law in the New Testament* (Sarum Lectures 1960–1961; Oxford: Clarendon, 1969) 144–71; G. Kehnscherper, 'Der Apostel Paulus als römischer Bürger', *SE II* (TU 87), 411–40; C. Burchard, *Der dreizehnte Zeuge: Traditions- und kompositions- geschichtliche Untersuchungen zu Lukas' Darstellung der Frühzeit des Paulus* (FRLANT 103; Göttingen: Vandenhoeck & Ruprecht, 1970) 37–39.

In the Lucan story the Apostle is at first called Saul, but Acts 13:9 marks the transition, *Saulos de, ho kai Paulos*, 'Saul, also known as Paul'. From that point on in the Lucan story he is called Paul. This change of names takes place several chapters after the first account of Paul's conversion (Acts 9); so the change had nothing to do with his spiritual conversion.

Moreover, it is sheer coincidence that Saul begins to be called Paul in the episode where the Roman proconsul Sergius Paulus is converted (13:7–12), though some patristic writers have so explained the change of names,[4] suggesting that Paul assumed the name of this illustrious Roman convert from Cyprus.[5]

It is likely, however, that the Apostle was called *Paulos* from birth and that *Saoul* was the 'signum' or 'supernomen' (added name) used in Jewish circles of the time.[6] For many Jews of the period had two names, one Semitic (like Saul) and the other Greek or Roman (like Paul).[7] The names were often chosen for the similarity of sound.

2. Paul's Jewish heritage

The Apostle was keenly aware of himself as a Jew and boasted of his Jewish background, tracing it to descent from Abraham and to the tribe of Benjamin: 'I am an Israelite, a descendant of Abraham, a member of the tribe of Benjamin' (Rom 11:1; cf. Phil 3:5; 2 Cor 11:22). As an 'Israelite', Paul recognized his privileged status as a member of God's chosen people, 'to whom belong the sonship, the glory, the covenants, the giving of the law, the cult, the promises, and the patriarchs', the seven prerogatives that he lists in the paragraph of Romans in which he expresses his sorrow about the condition of his former coreligionists (9:4–5). As a 'descendant of Abraham', Paul recognized the value of the status of rectitude in God's sight as a result of the promises made to Abraham and all his offspring (Rom 4:13). As a member of 'the tribe of Benjamin', he belonged to the tribe named after the

---

[4] E.g., Jerome, *In Ep. Ad Philem.* 1 (PL 26. 640).

[5] R. Abba writes, 'When Saul of Tarsus enters upon his missionary vocation in the Gentile world, his name is appropriately changed from the Hebrew form, Saul, to the Roman, Paul (Acts 13:9)' ('Name', *IDB* 3. 506). But this is an oversimplified way of presenting the matter.

[6] See M. Lambertz, 'Zur Ausbreitung des Supernomen oder Signum in römischen Reiche', *Glotta* 4 (1913) 78–143.

[7] Compare Joseph Barnabas Justus (Acts 1:23; cf. 4:36); Simeon Niger (Acts 13:1).

youngest son of Jacob, beloved by his father, and the smallest among all the tribes. It was the tribe from which came Saul, the first king of Israel (1 Sam 9:1, 4), after whom the Apostle was named, and from which came Jeremiah, the prophet from Anathoth (Jer 1:1; 32:8).

Paul also boasted of his Pharisaic background: 'as to the law a Pharisee' (Phil 3:6), one 'extremely zealous for the traditions of my fathers' and one who excelled his peers 'in Judaism' (Gal 1:14). The name 'Pharisee' probably means 'one cut off, set apart' (from Aramaic pĕrîsāy), a member of the sect of Palestinian Jews that differed from other Jews and laid great stress on oral tradition or the 'oral tŏrāh' (tŏrāh sĕ-bĕ-ʿal-pēh). It was the Jewish sect that considered itself 'set apart' from the rest of the Jews (Sadducees, Essenes, and 'this rabble that knows not the law' [John 7:49]) because of its strict interpretation of the Mosaic law. Its principle is expressed in the opening paragraph of the Mishnaic tractate Pirqe Aboth, 'Sayings of the Fathers':

> Moses received the law from Sinai and entrusted it to Joshua, and Joshua to the elders, and the elders to the prophets; and the prophets entrusted it to the men of the Great Synagogue. They said three things: Be deliberate in judgment, raise up many disciples, and make a fence around the law.[8]

To be 'deliberate in judgment' meant to interpret the law of Moses strictly; to 'raise up many disciples' meant to proselytize; and to 'build a fence around the law' meant to guard the written tŏrāh with the oral interpretation inherited from the traditions of the Fathers. This was the sect of Jews, then, that was influenced by the Hellenistic ideal of virtue as aretē, 'excellence', and believed that it could produce a holy and virtuous people by instruction and education in the Mosaic tŏrāh.

This Pharisaic background may well explain what Paul meant when he says of himself in Romans that he was 'set apart for God's Gospel' (1:1). In other words, he may have been playing on the name 'Pharisee' and looking on his Pharisaic background, his training as 'one set apart,' as divinely ordained. For it prepared him to become a preacher of God's gospel. Yet it is ironic that that gospel should turn out to be, not a proclamation of strict observance of 'the deeds of the law' (Rom 3:20) in the Pharisaic sense, but of justification by grace through faith 'apart from deeds of the

[8] See H. Danby, The Mishnah (Oxford: Oxford University, 1933, repr., 1964) p. 446.

law' (Rom 3:28), apart from that which meant so much to the Pharisee of his day.

There is a paradox in all of this, since many of the items that seem so characteristically Jewish in his letters and even sloganlike, echoing what seem like typical phrases that one would tend to ascribe to his Pharisaic background, are now known to be associated more with Essene tenets than with Pharisaic.

Apart from such a Pharisaic or other Jewish background to the spirituality of Paul, however, one otherwise notes that Paul lives in the world of the Judaism of the Old Testament. His God is the God of his fathers, the God of 'the old dispensation' (2 Cor 3:14), who spoke through the prophets, and indeed, who announced his gospel beforehand in the prophets (Rom 1:2).

Paul thinks and expresses himself in Old Testament categories and makes abundant use of Old Testament images, quotations, and allusions. He cites the Old Testament more than 90 times.[9] Though he usually quotes the Old Testament according to the Greek Septuagint, his use of it is similar to that of the authors of contemporary Jewish writings or other intertestamental literature.[10] Even his introductory clauses or phrases, when he cites the Old Testament explicitly, are consonant with Jewish practice, even if they are closer to those of Qumran writings than to the Mishnaic.[11]

Paul does not quote Scripture as one would in the twentieth century, but his mode is close to that of contemporary Jewish writers. He may accommodate the Old Testament or give it new meaning (e.g., when he announces his theme about salvation by faith and quotes Hab 2:4 in Rom 1:17 or Gal 3:11); he may allegorize it (e.g., when he makes use of the story of Sarah and Hagar and quotes Gen 16:15 or 17:16 in Gal 4:21–25); or he may wrest it from its original context (e.g., when he quotes Deut 25:5 about not muzzling the ox that treads the threshing floor and applies it to Christian preachers in 1 Cor 9:9). In such use he is no different from contemporary Jewish writers.

Yet he does quote the Old Testament to stress the unity of God's action in both dispensations. He looks upon the Old Testament as God's way of preparing for the gospel or preparing for Christ himself (Gal 3:24). Even if he contrasts the 'letter [of the law] and

---

[9] Yet, curiously enough, never in 1 Thessalonians, Philippians, or Philemon. There may be allusions to the Old Testament in these letters, but there are no explicit quotations of it.

[10] See J.A. Fitzmyer, *According to Paul: Studies in the Theology of Paul*, New York: Paulist Press, 1993, pp. 64–65.

[11] See Fitzmyer, *According to Paul*, pp. 29–31.

the Spirit' (2 Cor 3:6), the Old Testament is still for him the means whereby God speaks to humanity, as he recognizes in Rom 4:23–24, when he acknowledges that what was written about Abraham is still relevant to Christians; cf. Rom 15:4. Indeed, most of Paul's teaching about God, his *theology*, is clearly derived from his Jewish background, echoing in many respects the Old Testament itself.

Yet he is also a Jew of the first century, influenced by *various* currents of Jewish thinking that are now evident from the post-Old Testament world. In any case, we see that Paul's spiritual journey is rooted in his native Judaism.

3. Paul's cultural heritage

The spiritual journey of Paul has to take into consideration not only Paul's Jewish background, but also his cultural heritage. For he was not a Jew of Palestine. Though Luke makes Paul assert that he was brought up in Jerusalem and educated at the feet of Gamaliel (Acts 22:3), his letters never give an indication of the influence of Palestinian Judaism. Indeed, part of the paradox is just how the Pharisaic and other Jewish influence, rooted in Palestine, came to affect so markedly a Jew of the diaspora.

Paul's Roman name, his quotation of the Old Testament in Greek and usually according to the LXX, his composition of his letters in Greek reveal his diaspora background, for he was also a child of the Greco-Roman world. His call and conversion were an experience that took place outside of Judea, near Damascus, an important town in Hellenized Syria. If the Lucan tradition is correct that he was a Jew of Tarsus, 'a citizen of no mean town' (Acts 21:39), its cultural heritage too would have rubbed off on him. For Tarsus was a city in the ancient world famed for its intellectual and pedagogic tradition. It was accorded the status of a free city in the Roman empire by Mark Antony in 66 BC, when it was made the capital of the province of Cilicia. In the first century BC it had become the seat of a famous school of philosophy.

Paul called himself 'a Hebrew' (Phil 3:5), by which he probably meant that he was a Greek-speaking Jew who also spoke Aramaic.[12] That language, however, was widely used in his day throughout Syria and Asia Minor, so that it does not really speak against influence from the Hellenistic world in which Paul would have spent his

---

[12] See C. F. D. Moule, 'Once More, Who Were the Hellenists?' *ExpTim* 70 (1958–59) pp. 100–102.

youth. His writings reveal that he had been liberally educated in the Hellenistic tradition of the time.

Even if Paul had not been trained as a Greek *rhētōr*, his mode of composition and expression often reveals the influence of Greek rhetoric and Greek education. Traces of the Cynic-Stoic mode of argumentation called *diatribē* are found in his letters: a mode of discourse conducted in familiar, conversational style and developed by lively debate with an imaginary interlocutor; its sentence structure is often short, and questions are interjected; antitheses and parallel phrases often punctuate the development (see Rom 2:1–20; 3:1–9; 1 Cor 9).[13]

Even more, his style and his mode of composing letters have been analysed. They reveal that many of the contemporary modes of Greek rhetorical argument are found in them, especially in his letters to the Galatians and to the Romans.[14] The rhetorical elements are important indications of the careful argumentation that Paul has made use of in order to present his gospel and his understanding of Christ and his significance for humanity.

Whereas Jesus' illustrations often reflect the agrarian life of Galilee, Paul frequently uses images derived from urban culture and Hellenistic ambiance. He uses Greek political terminology (Phil 1:17; 3:20), alludes to Greek games (Phil 2:16; 1 Cor 9:24–27), employs Greek commercial terms (Phlm 18) or legal terminology (Gal 3:15; 4:1–2; Rom 7:1), and refers to Hellenistic slave trade (1 Cor 7:22; Rom 7:14) or Hellenistic celebrations in honour of a visiting emperor (1 Thess 2:19). He employs the Hellenistic ideas of *eleutheria*, 'freedom' (Gal 5:1,13), *syneidēsis*, 'conscience' (1 Cor 8:7, 10, 12; 10:25–29; 2 Cor 5:11; Rom 2:15), and the Stoic ideas of *autarkeia*, 'sufficiency, contentment' (2 Cor 9:8), or *physis*, 'nature' (Rom 2:14).

This Greek cultural background eventually enabled Paul, the diaspora Jew, to cope with the problems and difficulties of carrying the Christian Gospel from its Palestinian Jewish matrix into the world of the Roman empire. But his experience in that world too as the Apostle of the Gentiles also contributed to his spiritual journey. For he not only carried the Gospel to the eastern

---

[13] See S. K. Stowers, *Diatribe and Paul's Letter to the Romans* (SBLDS 57; Chico, CA: Scholars, 1981), and the literature cited there.

[14] See H. D. Betz, 'The Literary Composition and Function of Paul's Letter to the Galatians,' *NTS* 21 (1974–75) 353–79; *Galatians: A Commentary on Paul's Letter to the Churches in Galatia* (Hermeneia; Philadelphia, PA: Fortress, 1979) 14–25. For Romans, see J.-N. Aletti, *Comment Dieu est-il juste? Clefs pour interpréter l'épître aux Romains* (Paris: Editions du Seuil, 1991).

Mediterranean world of his day, but also founded Churches and Christian communities in this Hellenistic milieu. His practical experience and concrete contacts with diaspora Jews and Gentiles of that area had a significant impact on his view of Christianity. Would Paul have written about justification as he did, if he had not coped with the problem of Jewish converts to Christianity in the diaspora trying to insist with Gentile converts that they too had to observe the Mosaic law to be saved. The universal scope of Christian salvation undoubtedly dawned on Paul as he worked continually with Jews who failed to accept his Gospel and with Gentiles who did heed his message. Though from his earliest letters he reveals an awareness of the privileged position of his fellow Jews in God's plan of salvation (1 Thess 2:13–14; cf. Rom 1:16; 2:9–10), he eventually had to wrestle explicitly with that problem (Romans 9–11). He admits that he has been 'indebted to Greeks and to Barbarians' (Rom 1:14).

Moreover, the Church as 'the body of Christ' (1 Cor 12:27–28) is almost certainly the result of his understanding of the Christian *ekklēsia* in the light of the contemporary Greco-Roman idea of the state as the body politic.[15] This notion would, then, have come to him, not as a result of his experience on the road to Damascus, but rather as a result of his missionary experience in the eastern Mediterranean world of the time.

Such were the Hellenistic influences on Paul of Tarsus, a diaspora Jew called by God to announce his Gospel to the Gentiles.

4. Paul's call to be an apostle

The most important element in the spiritual journey of Paul was the experience that he had on the road to Damascus. That experience was a revelation made to him about Christ Jesus, and his faith in the risen Christ developed from that experience. It was not merely a psychological 'conversion' that could be explained in terms of Paul's Jewish background, or even in terms of what he writes in Romans 7. That chapter has often been interpreted as an autobiographical description of Paul himself, as a young Jewish boy reaching puberty and coming to an awareness of what the law would mean in his life; hence, crushed by the law's demands, he would have been freed by conversion to Christ. Such an interpre-

---

[15] See Aristotle, *Politics* 5.2.7 (1302b.35–38); part of Stoic philosophy, Cicero, Or. *Philip.* 8.5.15; Seneca, *Ep. mor.* 95.52; Plutarch, *Coriolanus* 6.3–4; *Moralia* 426A.

tation of Romans 7, however, does not do justice to the obvious universal situation of humanity confronted by law that is depicted there. For even as a Christian, Paul was able to look back on his Pharisaic past and say of it that 'as to righteousness under the law' he had been 'blameless' (Phil 3:6). He did not look back, even as a Christian, at his Jewish past as one of failure to cope with the demands of the Mosaic law, under which he lived.

Paul himself speaks of that experience near Damascus as a revelation of the Son accorded to him by the Father (Gal 1:16); in it he 'saw Jesus the Lord' (1 Cor 9:1; cf. 1 Cor 15:8). That revelation of the crucified 'Lord of glory' (1 Cor 2:8) not only summoned Paul the Pharisee to become an apostle, but made of him the first Christian theologian. The only difference between that appearance of the risen Christ to him (1 Cor 15:8) and those to the official witnesses of the resurrection (1 Cor 15:5–7) was that his experience occurred much later, and to him as an individual. But it did put him on an equal footing with the Twelve and others to whom the risen Christ had appeared. In defending his right to be recognized as an 'apostle', which was apparently contested in the early Church by those who knew that he had not witnessed the earthly ministry of Jesus, he exclaimed, 'Am I not an apostle? Have I not seen Jesus our Lord?' (1 Cor 9:1). Paul spoke of his call as an event in which he had been 'seized' by Christ Jesus (Phil 3:12), and as a 'necessity' (or compulsion), which had been laid upon him to preach the Gospel to the Gentiles (1 Cor 9:16; cf. Gal 1:16b). He compared that experience to God's initial creation of light: 'For God who said, "Let light shine out of darkness", has shone in our hearts to give us the light of the knowledge of God's glory on the face of Christ' (2 Cor 4:6).

Thus the compulsion of divine grace pressed Paul into the service of Christ and his gospel. His response to that call was one of vivid faith, in which he confessed with the early Church that 'Jesus is Lord' (1 Cor 12:3; cf. Rom 10:9; Phil 2:11). In a creative act, God illumined the mind of Paul and gave him an insight into what a later disciple of Paul would call 'the mystery of Christ' (Eph 3:4).

We can sum up the effects of that experience on Paul in three ways: First, that 'revelation' (Gal 1:12,16) impressed Paul with the unity of divine action for the salvation of all humanity, which is manifest in both the Old and the New Dispensations. As a result of that encounter with the risen Christ, Paul did not become a Marcionite, rejecting the Old Testament. The Father who revealed his Son to Paul was the same God that Paul the Pharisee had always worshipped and served. He was the creator, the lord of history, the God who continually saved his people Israel, and who proved to be a faithful lord of the covenant despite Israel's infidelities. The experience near Damascus did not alter Paul's basic commitment to the 'one God'.

Second, that vision instructed Paul in the soteriological value of the death and resurrection of Jesus the Messiah in God's salvific plan. If Paul's basic *theology* did not change, his *Christology* did. As a Jew, Paul shared the messianic expectations of his people (see Dan 9:25; cf. 1QS 9:11, where Palestinian Jews were said to be awaiting the coming of a prophet [like Moses, Deut 18:15–18] and Messiahs of Aaron and Israel). He had looked forward to the coming of a messiah (of some sort). But the vision accorded to him near Damascus taught him that God's Anointed One had already come, that he was 'Jesus our Lord, who was handed over (to death) for our offenses and raised for our justification' (Rom 4:25). Before his experience near Damascus, Paul certainly knew that Jesus of Nazareth had been crucified, 'hung on a tree' and hence 'cursed' by the very law that Paul himself had so zealously observed (Gal 3:13; cf. 1:14). But that revelation impressed on him the messianic, soteriological, and vicarious value of the death of Jesus in a way that he never suspected before. With a logic that only a Pharisee could appreciate, Paul saw Christ Jesus taking upon himself the law's curse and transforming it into its opposite, so that Christ became the means of freeing humanity from malediction. The cross, which had been the stumbling block to Jews, became in his eyes 'the power and the wisdom of God' (1 Cor 1:24). Henceforth, Paul would understand that crucified 'Lord of glory' (1 Cor 2:8) as his exalted Messiah.

Third, that revelation also impressed Paul with a new vision of salvation history. Before the encounter with the Lord, Paul saw human history divided into great periods:

a.   from Adam to Moses (the period without the law [Rom 5:14a]);
b.   from Moses to the Messiah (the period of the law [Rom 5:14b];
c.   the messianic age (the period when the law would be perfected, fulfilled, or even done away with).

The experience near Damascus, however, instructed Paul that the messianic age had already begun; it thus introduced a new perspective into salvation history. The *eschaton*, 'endtime', so anxiously awaited before, had already been started; the ages had met (1 Cor 10:11), although a definite stage of the last age or newly inaugurated *eschaton* was still to be realized (as was hoped, not too far in the future). The Messiah had come, but not yet in glory. Paul realized that he (with all Christians) thus found himself in a double situation: one in which he looked back upon the death and resurrection of Jesus as the inauguration of the new age, and another in which he still looked forward to Christ's coming in glory, to his parousia.

Thus, far more than Paul's Pharisaic background, or even his Hellenistic cultural roots, the revelation of Christ on the road to Damascus gave Paul an ineffable insight into 'the mystery of Christ'. It enabled him to fashion his 'gospel', to preach the fundamental good news of salvation in a form that was distinctively his own. But Paul did not immediately understand all the implications of the vision granted to him. It provided only a basic insight that was to colour all that he was to learn about Jesus and his mission among human beings, not only from the early Church's tradition that preceded him, but also from his own apostolic activity in preaching 'Christ crucified' (1 Cor 1:23).

Thus that experience on the road to Damascus was a turning-point in Paul's spiritual journey. It made of him not only an 'apostle of the Gentiles' (Rom 11:13), but a founder of Christian communities, an interpreter of the Christ-event, and the first Christian theologian whose interpretation we have inherited. It was a turning-point because Paul's career did not end with that experience. Thereafter, as a result of his preaching, his founding of Churches, and his writing of letters to the Churches in various places, he continued to grow in the knowledge of Christ Jesus. He learned to interpret the effects of what Christ Jesus had done for humanity in his passion, death, resurrection, exaltation, and heavenly intercession. In other words, he learned to interpret the various effects of the Christ-event.

5. The effects of the Christ-event as seen by the mature Apostle

When Paul looked back at the Christ-event, he saw it as a complex unit, something like a ten-sided solid figure. When he gazed at a panel of it from one direction, he said that Christ 'justified' us; when he gazed at it from another, he said that Christ 'saved' us; or from another, Christ 'transformed' us, and so on. In other words, Paul made use of images drawn from his Jewish or Hellenistic background to describe what was really indescribable. In doing so, he made use of ten different images or figures:

1. *Justification.* Christ Jesus 'justified' us; he brought it about that all sinful human beings might stand before God's tribunal

acquitted or vindicated, that they might stand before him as righteous persons. Thus Paul drew upon his Jewish background (Deut 25:1; Ps 7:9–12) and derived from it the image of justification as an effect of the Christ-event. What Jews of old sought to achieve in God's sight by observing the deeds of the law, Christ Jesus by his death and resurrection brought about for all sinners, Jews and Greeks alike. In his experience near Damascus Paul realized the truth that all human beings have sinned and have failed to attain the share of divine glory destined for them, but also that that share was now achievable through what Christ Jesus had obtained for them vicariously (Rom 3:21–26). Thus, Paul realized that the righteousness that he and other Christians have is not their own; it is a 'righteousness from God' (Phil 3:9; cf. Rom 10:3), a gift freely bestowed by God because of what Christ Jesus has done for humanity. God thus became for Paul the source of life 'in Christ Jesus', because God had made him 'our righteousness' (1 Cor 1:30), the means whereby Paul himself became upright or righteous.

2. *Salvation.* Christ Jesus 'saved' us; he has delivered us from evil (from physical harm, psychic harm, cataclysmic evil and moral evil); he has restored us to a status of wholeness in the sight of God. Thus Christians 'are being saved' by the cross of Christ (1 Cor 1:18,21). Salvation as an effect of the Christ-event has not yet been wholly achieved, for it still has an eschatological aspect (1 Thess 2:16; 5:8–9; 1 Cor 3:15; Rom 5:9–10). That is why Paul tells the Philippians, 'work out your own salvation in fear and trembling' (2:12), adding, however, immediately, 'for God is the one working in you, both to will and to work for his good pleasure' (2:13), lest anyone think that salvation can be achieved without God's grace. Thus Paul realized that his own salvation depended on what God by his grace had wrought in him because of the death and crucifixion of Christ Jesus.

3. *Reconciliation.* Christ Jesus has 'reconciled' us with the Father; he has altered our relationship with God, changing our status from one of hatred, enmity, and hostility to one of love, friendship, and intimacy. Again, the initiative lies in God himself, for through Christ he has drawn us from alienation to peace and intimacy with himself. Thus, Christ has made us *to be at one* with God; he has atoned us (Rom 5:10–11). Moreover, this effect of the Christ-event also has its cosmic effect, because 'God was in Christ, reconciling the world (the *kosmos*) to himself' (2 Cor 5:18–19). Thus Paul makes use of a social-politic image drawn

from his Hellenistic background to express yet another effect of the Christ-event. Moreover, he applies it not only in an anthropological sense, but also in a cosmic sense. He sensed that his own spiritual journey had been advanced by this Christic reconciliation and atonement.

4. *Expiation.* Christ Jesus has 'expiated' our sins; he has wiped away the sins of humanity. For through the death of his son and the shedding of his blood, the Father has publicly displayed Christ Jesus as the new Mercy-Seat. What the sprinkling of the ark of the covenant with the blood of animals by the high priest each year on *Yôm Kippûr* symbolized for Israel (Lev 16:14–20), that Christ Jesus has obtained for all humanity by his own blood and by his death (Rom 3:25). Thus, Paul has again derived from his Jewish background yet another image to explain an effect of the Christ-event. He thus became aware of the significance of the death of Jesus in the expiation of his own sins and how that death contributed to his own progress in his dedication of his life to the service of God and his Gospel.

5. *Redemption.* Christ Jesus has 'redeemed' us; he has ransomed us from bondage to evil and enslavement to sin. For Christ has become 'our redemption' (1 Cor 1:30). Again, Paul sees this effect of the Christ-event as also having eschatological and cosmic aspects, for 'through the redemption which is in Christ Jesus' (Rom 3:24), Christians 'await the redemption of the body' (Rom 8:23), and all (physical) 'creation' is groaning in expectation of that event (Rom 8:19–22). It is not easy to determine whence Paul has derived this image; it may be drawn from his Hellenistic background, the Greco-Roman world in which slavery and emancipation were commonly practiced. But it may also be drawn from the Old Testament idea of Yahweh as *gô'ēl*, 'redeemer', acquiring his people as he freed them from Egyptian bondage (Isa 41:14; 43:14; 44:6; 47:4; Ps 19:15; 78:35). Paul himself recognized that in his spiritual journey he too had enjoyed this emancipation brought about by God through Christ Jesus.

6. *Freedom.* Christ Jesus has 'freed' us; he has given Christians the rights of citizens in a free city; he has made them citizens of heaven: 'our commonwealth is in heaven' (Phil 3:20), i.e. the real Christian homeland, a stake in the life that the risen Christ himself enjoys in the glorious presence of the Father. Again, this image is derived from Paul's Hellenistic background, from the world that knew of cities and states and that enjoyed 'freedom' in the Roman empire. Paul not only exhorted the

Galatians to 'stand fast in that freedom with which Christ has made you free' (Gal 5:1), but he knew that his own spiritual journey shared in this liberated status, 'Am I not free?' (1 Cor 9:1).

7. *Sanctification.* Christ Jesus has 'sanctified' us; he has dedicated us to the awesome service of God, thus marking off Christians from the profane and the secular to engage them in the awesome worship and praise of the heavenly Father. So Christ has become 'our sanctification' (1 Cor 1:30; cf. 1 Thess 4:7), i.e. the means whereby human beings may be so dedicated. This image Paul has derived from his Jewish background, which spoke of the sanctification of persons and objects, dedicating them to the service of Yahweh in his Temple (Isa 48:2; 64:10; Exod 19:14; Lev 19:2). Paul personally was aware of such service, for he compared his own preaching of the gospel to the liturgical or cultic act of the priests who served in the Jerusalem Temple (Rom 1:9). Thus his own spiritual journey included the evangelization of the Gentiles and the priestly offering of them to God as 'sanctified by the Spirit' (Rom 15:16).

8. *Transformation.* Christ Jesus has 'transformed' us; he has gradually reshaped those human beings 'who turn to the Lord' so that they behold the glory of the Lord and are 'transformed into a likeness of him from one degree of glory to another' (2 Cor 3:18). Paul explains how the face of the risen Christ has become a mirror reflecting the glory coming from the creator God: 'It is the God who said, "Let light shine out of darkness", who has shone in our hearts to give us the light of the knowledge of God's glory on the face of Christ' (2 Cor 4:6). This is the most sublime of the effects of the Christ-event that Paul has sketched for us. He has not hesitated to derive from his Hellenistic background an image used in Greek mythology, because even such a rich image could aptly express what for Paul was the magnificent calling of the Christian. As the caterpillar is transformed into the butterfly, Paul himself was transformed; from the Pharisaic Jew he became the Christian apostle of the Gentiles. Greek patristic writers often used this Pauline idea in developing their teaching about the *theosis*, 'divinization', of the Christian.[16]

9. *New Creation.* Christ Jesus has 'created' us 'anew'; what God did at the beginning of all things, that Christ Jesus has done again in a new way (Gal 6:15; 2 Cor 5:17). He has given us 'newness

[16] See Fitzmyer, *According to Paul*, pp. 64–79.

of life' (Rom 6:4), and because Christ has given us a share in his risen life, he has become 'the last Adam' (1 Cor 15:45), i.e., the Adam of the *eschaton*, the Adam of the endtime, the head of a new humanity. Again, Paul has derived this idea from the Old Testament teaching about the creator God. He realized that in his spiritual journey he too had become part of this new humanity. His Adamic existence had become a Christic existence.

10. *Glorification.* Christ Jesus has 'glorified' us; he has made it possible to attain 'the glory of God', of which all sinful human beings had fallen short (Rom 3:23). 'Those whom he [God] predestined he also called; and those whom he called he also justified; and those whom he justified he also glorified' (Rom 8:30). Here Paul has taken another image from the Old Testament, the 'glory' (Greek *doxa*, Hebrew *kābôd*) as the sign of the presence of God to his people or his world. He now sees Christ Jesus obtaining for Christians access to the glorious presence of the Father that he already enjoys as of his resurrection. For the destiny of the Christian is 'to be always with the Lord' (1 Thess 4:17), i.e. to share in the risen Lord's own life and existence in the Father's presence. Paul debated with himself, as he lay in prison, whether it would be better for him to be freed to continue his evangelization or to die and 'be with Christ' (Phil 1:23): 'For to me to live is Christ, to die is gain' (1:21). Thus he envisaged the goal of his spiritual journey, to share in the glory of the risen Christ, the goal for which the Father had predestined him.[17]

So Paul summed up in a striking way the effects of the Christ-event and their bearing on his own spiritual journey. He has thereby made us understand the heights that he himself attained in his journey. In his attempt to formulate for Christians of all generations what Christ Jesus has achieved for them, he has revealed the road that he himself had travelled.

We can do no better than terminate this discussion of Paul's spiritual journey than to quote his own reaction to it all:

Would that you would bear with me a little foolishness! Do bear with me! I feel a divine jealousy for you, for I betrothed you to Christ to present you as a pure bride to her one husband. But I am afraid that, as the serpent deceived Eve by his cunning, your thoughts will be led astray from a sincere and pure devotion to Christ. For if some one

[17] See further *PAHT* PT §67–80.

comes and preaches another Jesus than the one we preached, or if
you receive a different spirit from the one you received, or if you
accept a different gospel from the one you accepted, you submit to
it readily enough. I think that I am not in the least inferior to those
superlative apostles. Yet even if I am unskilled in speaking, I am not
in knowledge; in every way we have made this plain to you. (2 Cor
11:1–6)

Paul himself realized that the spiritual journey that he had made
in his life and ministry of preaching Christ crucified resulted in a
'knowledge' that was not inferior to that of those whom some
people regarded as 'apostles' superior to himself. Paul again
battled with those who refused to recognize him as their equal, as
one on par with the Twelve. He had not been a member of the
Twelve, for he had not witnessed the ministry of Jesus himself. Yet
he turned out to be a superior proclaimer of Christ crucified. For,
as he says,

I must boast; there is nothing to be gained by it, but I will go on to
visions and revelations of the Lord. I know a man in Christ who fourteen years ago was caught up to the third heaven – whether in the
body or out of it I do not know, God knows. And I know that this
man was caught up into Paradise – whether in the body or out of the
body I do not know, God knows – and he heard things that cannot
be told, which no one may utter. On behalf of this man will I boast;
but on my own behalf I will not boast, except of my weaknesses ....
But God said to me, 'My grace is sufficient for you, for my power is
made perfect in weakness'. (2 Cor 12:1–9)

This, then, is the height to which the Apostle Paul travelled in his
spiritual journey. He was made perfect by Christ's grace, despite
the weaknesses that he himself experienced in his ministry of
preaching Christ crucified. He had journeyed far ('from Jerusalem
all the way around to Illyricum', Rom 15:19) and laboured hard to
become not only 'the Apostle of the Gentiles' (Rom 11:13), but an
'ambassador for Christ' (2 Cor 5:20), led in triumph by Christ, who
has spread the fragrance of the knowledge of God everywhere (2
Cor 2:14).

Section II
Theology

Chapter 10

The Present State of Christology

John F. O'Grady

Biblical studies

Discussions about the Old Testament and its meaning cause little reaction among Christians. Anyone can question any aspect of history or archeology or linguistics or theology and make applications and draw conclusions with immunity. Most Christians view what happened to the Jews and the record of their relationship with God as not as important as what happened to Jesus. If there are mistakes or errors or misunderstandings in the Old Testament brought to light by contemporary studies, such findings have little effect on Christianity. This attitude, especially in Roman Catholic circles, has created a situation that encouraged for many years the scientific study of the Old Testament but remained wary of a similar approach to the New Testament.

In 1943 Pius XII published his encyclical *Divino Afflante Spiritu*[1] and for the first time Roman Catholic scholars were encouraged to use a scientific method in the study of the Bible. The green light was given, however, mainly for the Old Testament, not for the New. It was not until the 'Declaration on the Truth of the Gospels' in 1964[2] that Roman Catholic scholars could feel free to use the methods of contemporary scholarship in regard to the New Testament. Since that time the interest in biblical studies has profoundly altered the understanding of Christianity and has

---

[1] See *Rome and the Study of Scripture* (St Meinrad: Grail, 1962).

[2] See *The Pope Speaks,* vol. 10 (1964–65), 86–90. Also published in R. Brown, *Crisis Facing the Church* (New York: Paulist, 1975). For a review of American biblical study see Gerald Fogarty, 'American Catholic Biblical Scholarship: A Review', *Theological Studies*, Vol. 50 (1989) pp. 219–43.

implications for the Church of the next century. In the past thirty years biblical scholarship has flourished in the United States among Roman Catholics. Even weekly news magazines find it interesting enough to make comment. The results of this scholarship have clearly affected the understanding of Jesus. As a result of the new atmosphere in the Church after the Second Vatican Council, believers are continually faced with new understandings of Jesus and the Jesus tradition as recorded in the New Testament.

In the past ten years, however, some caution seems to have arisen again in the Roman Catholic Church with regard to the study of the New Testament and to the meaning of Jesus. As much as some might wish to return to a different period in Church history, most Christians are aware of what some theologians are saying about Jesus even if sometimes they are confused by the publicity involved. Different approaches exist among the various Christian denominations and even within the Roman Catholic tradition. The present state of Christology contains various hues and no one approach or understanding captures the fullness of the reality just as no one colour can capture the fullness of colour. Various approaches have characterized theology over the centuries. Each one has made a contribution. Christians can always gain by studying what has preceded as well as by examining certain of the ideas that are prevalent today.

Images of the Church

Theologians have also studied the Church, seeking to understand how personal images of the Church might influence attitudes and behaviour.[3] Today people seem to have become accustomed to the different ways in which many respond to the Church. The image of an institutional and hierarchical Church with detailed ritual and organization and lines of authority suits well some members of the Church but not all. Even the increase of the use of the Tridentine liturgy can be helpful for some people's piety provided this is not used as a means to deny the reality of the Second Vatican Council. Latin liturgies can prove helpful to faith. Moreover, a folksy home liturgy with people sitting on the floor and singing folk music can do much to create the image of the Church as a community of people on pilgrimage. Such an approach is helpful to others in the

---

[3] Avery Dulles, *Models of the Church* (New York: Doubleday, 1974). Richard McBrien, *The Remaking of the Church* (New York: Harper & Row, 1973).

faith community. The result has been a healthier attitude toward
the divergent opinions that can exist within the Church without
doing harm to its basic meaning. The same should be true with
regard to Jesus.

> Institution and Hierarchical
> Mystical Communion
> Sacrament
> Herald and prophet
> Servant
> Community of Disciples
> People of God

Church concerns

At the outset, however, a certain resistance might be expected.
When a scientific methodology is applied to the New Testament,
and to Jesus, more traditional-minded individuals are apt to react
negatively or at least cautiously. The same might be true if some
begin to entertain the thought that divergent views on Christology
can well be admitted within the Church. But not everyone has to
have the same approach to Jesus. Nor can any one approach fully
manifest the truth of Jesus as the revelation of the Word of God
and the veritable Son of God.

In 1972 the Congregation for the Doctrine of the Faith
published a declaration entitled 'Safeguarding Basic Christian
Beliefs'.[4] In this document the Congregation saw the need to reit-
erate certain traditional Roman Catholic teachings with regard to
Jesus and the Trinity. Concern existed in Rome. Some of the teachings of the Christian faith were being undermined by certain
contemporary theologians, and thus the Church would have to
react to affirm the traditional approach to Christology and to the
Trinity.

Much of the concern seems to have arisen because of the new
terminology in christology as well as the efforts to encounter again
what has been the Christian heritage on Jesus through the study of
the New Testament. Any effort to re-examine such teachings as the
meaning of pre-existence, how in Jesus there exists the one divine
person, and the presence of the human person in Jesus is
presented in the declaration as contrary to true belief in Christ.[5]

---

[4] See *The Pope Speaks*, vol. 17 (1972–73), pp. 64–68.
[5] *Ibid.* p. 65.

After the declaration was published, Pope Paul VI called attention to the statement in his usual Sunday audience and explained why such a statement was necessary. He said that recently the teachings on Jesus had not been properly interpreted.[6] The pope continued that such statements had spread even among 'us believers'. Therefore, the Congregation responded. The conclusion of the declaration, however, should not be overlooked. In spite of their anxiety, the authors of the statement admit the need for updating traditional dogmatic formulations.[7] More recently, the decision by the Congregation for the Doctrine of the Faith to investigate and censure certain European and Latin American theologians may be read as continual signs of anxiety with regard to the contemporary research on the meaning of Jesus.

In June of this past year [1992] Pope John Paul II reaffirmed the belief that Mary was physically a virgin before, during and after giving birth to Jesus. 'The Church feels the need to recall the reality of the virginal conception of Christ.'[8] The gospel accounts of Luke and Matthew 'cannot be reduced to simple stories to give a solid reason for the faithful to believe in the divinity of Christ. Rather, they go beyond the literary style adopted by Matthew and Luke and express a biblical tradition of apostolic origin.'[9] The pope seems to imply that certain questions from the New Testament and others concerning Jesus are out of bounds for further research.

Raymond Brown, a well-known American New Testament theologian, has stated: 'The scientifically controllable biblical evidence leaves the question of the virginal conception unresolved.'[10] He also acknowledges that for Roman Catholics the long-standing Church tradition supplies a different answer from what can be gained in the study of the New Testament.

During the same year that the pope made his statement on the virginal conception of Jesus, John Meier, another American Roman Catholic biblical scholar, wrote in *The Catholic Biblical Quarterly*: 'A historian prescinding from what is held by faith and later Church teaching and working solely with the historical and philological data available would most likely come to the conclu-

---

[6] *Ibid.* p. 69.
[7] *Ibid.* p. 67.
[8] *The Evangelist*, June 18, 1992, p. 8.
[9] *Ibid.*
[10] See *The Virginal Conception and Bodily Resurrection of Jesus* (New York: Paulist, 1973), p. 66.

sion that the brothers and sisters of Jesus were his true physical brothers and sisters.'[11] Meier goes on to say that the whole question of the perpetual virginity of Mary 'is so obscure and ambiguous that it enjoys at best a remote and unclear relation to the foundation of Christian faith and the foundational truths that flow from it'.[12]

Scholarly activity

The research continues. The recent publication of *The Marginal Jew* by J. Meier[13] and *The Historical Jesus* by D. Crossan[14] amply exemplifies that Roman Catholic New Testament scholars have not ceased in their study of Jesus. Nor have they written books that merely support the general tendencies of official Church documents. The publication of *God's Beloved* by B. Cooke[15] and *Christ is Community* by J. Neyrey[16] and *Jesus Before Christianity* by A. Nolan[17] and *A Christological Catechism* by J. Fitzmyer[18] also demonstrates that contemporary Roman Catholic scholars continue to examine every aspect of the Jesus tradition in Christianity. No one seems to have abated in efforts to further understand the meaning of Jesus.

If theology is faith seeking understanding, growth in an appreciation of Jesus and his Gospel will continue. No one generation can claim to speak the last word or disclose the final expression. Each generation must examine the insights of the past in order to offer new generations of believers an understanding of Jesus that will be intelligible to the contemporary spirit. Often enough, in the contemporary research on Jesus, scholars are not concerned with faith as much as past interpretations of faith. For a theologian to re-examine some of the fundamental tenets of Christian belief does not imply a doubt of those beliefs. With the passage of time, words change in meaning, or at least in nuance. To be faithful to its task, theology will always demand a study of what words have

[11] 'The Brothers and Sisters of Jesus in Ecumenical Perspective', Vol. 54 (1992), p. 27.
[12] *Ibid.* pp. 27-28.
[13] John Meier, *A Marginal Jew* (New York: Doubleday, 1991).
[14] Dominic Crossan, *The Historical Jesus: The Life of a Mediterranean Jewish Peasant* (San Francisco: Harper, 1991).
[15] Bernard Cooke, *God's Beloved: Jesus' Experience of the Transcendent* (Philadelphia: Trinity Press, 1992).
[16] Jerome Neyrey, S.J., *Christ Is Community* (Collegeville: Liturgical Press, 1990).
[17] Albert Nolan, O.P., *Jesus Before Christianity* (Maryknoll: Orbis, 1992).
[18] Joseph Fitzmyer, S.J., *A Christological Catechism* (New York: Paulist, 1982).

meant in the past and what they might mean today. The theologian is conscious of the common Christian heritage, but also of the responsibility to reinterpret that heritage.

If Christian theology in general continually needs updating, this is certainly true of the heart of Christian theology, the study of Jesus. When the Church encouraged the scientific investigation of the New Testament, it was also commending the careful methodological approach to Jesus as advocated by most contemporary theologians. Further insights into the origin and development and theology of the various books of the New Testament must of necessity bring about changes in the understanding of Jesus.

In a speech prior to the Second Vatican Council, Pope John XXIII was most careful to distinguish the content of faith from its expression:

> The deposit of faith is one thing; the way that it is presented is another. For the truths preserved in our sacred doctrine can retain the same substance under different forms of expression.[19]

Problems seem to arise when theologians actually try to fulfill their function in the Church and begin to use new terminology which is either not understood by the Church hierarchy or does not meet with approval among the majority of believers. The problem is compounded when popular news magazines take learned articles and digest them into one-page religion sections with startling headlines announcing that theologians question the divinity of Jesus or hold that Jesus was not born of a virgin or do not believe in the physical resurrection of the Lord. When other theologians write of Jesus the liberator, emphasizing his humanity, and de-emphasizing the divinity, oppressed people might find such an image helpful but others find in liberation Christology the loss of the true Jesus Christ.

Scholastic philosophers often remarked that whatever is perceived is perceived according to the mode of the perceiver. In contemporary language: 'People hear what they want to hear.' Surely that is true with regard to the present state of christology, whether the listeners are pope or cardinals or bishops or clergy or religious or laity or even theologians, liberal, centrist or conservative.

[19] *Acta Apostolicae Sedis*, 54 (1962), p. 792.

Many images of Christ

For those who have been nurtured on a 'docetic' or a totally spiritual or divine Christ, anything that seems to emphasize the humanity of Jesus will be suspect. For someone who has viewed Christ as the suffering servant going to his death meek and humble, any effort to make him a social reformer is simply out of order and contradicts the gospel. For a Roman Catholic who has grown up with a formal liturgy, any effort to make Jesus the source of enthusiastic singing of 'Jesus my Saviour' must be not only suspect but even a bit 'mad'.

Many regard Jesus as the all-knowing God in human form. Then how can some of the attitudes of Jesus in the Gospels be explained?[20] How could he ask questions when he knew everything? If Jesus is the all-knowing God, then the only explanation based on the previous premise would be that Jesus, like Socrates, questions as a pedagogical technique. But such a response does not satisfy many careful readers of the New Testament.

Someone who sees Jesus as a good man, an individual who could identify with the human condition and could rise above that condition, would consider any attempt to deny that he lived a human life (by making him out to be God) as tantamount to the destruction of the meaning of Jesus.[21] Anyone who sees the need to reform the social order on the basis of the Gospel will not be content to adhere in belief to a God-man who is content to live under any social system, even an unjust one.[22]

In reality history has many images of Jesus. 'Who do you say that I am?' (Mark 8:27). Not everyone has given the same answer. History offers as many answers as people who choose to respond. Even those who refuse to respond often have their unspoken answer. People still hear what they want to hear. If a person adheres in faith to a Jesus who is the second person of the Blessed Trinity, then everything about Jesus is judged in that light. If someone else sees only the good man who suffered and died unjustly, no amount of rhetoric will persuade that person to see Jesus as the all-knowing, pre-existent Son of God.

---

[20] In Mark 13:32, Jesus remarks that not even the Son knows the day of judgment. Theologians have developed a host of responses in attempting to explain this lack of knowledge, instead of taking the words at their face value.

[21] See John F. O'Grady, *Jesus, Lord and Christ* (New York: Paulist, 1972), chapter 8.

[22] See J. Sobrino, *Christology at the Crossroads* (Maryknoll: Orbis, 1978).

Models of the Church

The Roman Catholic tradition has accepted for some time many models of the Church. Some see the Church as a visible institution, others as a mystical communion, as a sacrament, as a herald or as a servant, or as a gathering of disciples. Each model offers some insight into the meaning of the Church; each offers some understanding. But if viewed exclusively, each model breaks down and fails in its ability to represent the true reality in any complete or final fashion. The Church lives as more than any one approach or one person's or one group's understanding.

People who read A. Dulles' book *Models of the Church* usually can quickly identify with one or the other of the models. This colours not only their reaction to opinions about the Church, but also their lived actions as members of the Church. The scholastics also had an axiom: Action follows being. What a person is will determine the activity; actions follow being. If a person accepts the institutional model as the only model or as the primary model, then a person's activity will follow suit. Whatever will lessen the institutional aspect of the Church in any way must be countered. If a person's primary model is the Church as sacrament or as servant, then often what we would call the visible structure of the Church presents little interest with little regard for such things as hierarchy and official teaching.

Gradually the notion that the use of models provides a good approach seems to have penetrated within the body of the Church, affecting hierarchy and laity alike. Individuals can now acknowledge their opinions of the Church and not feel afraid of professing one model, since they know that it is only one of several and should not be accepted as the exclusive model without some consideration of other opinions. Even when people choose a primary model, they know that complementary or even opposing opinions have a right to be heard. In parishes this seems to have become commonplace as even liturgy is expressed differently to respond to the particular approach or needs of the members and various groups within the congregation.

Jesus and models

At this point in the history of Christianity people find it acceptable to maintain different models of the Church without detriment to the unity of belief. Believers should also be able to accept a similar position with regard to Jesus. In the past some felt that such a proposal may well lead to the sacrificing of the clarity that has been part of the Christian tradition for centuries. Many felt that there should not be many models of Jesus, but only one model. The one approach has been expressed in the official teaching of the Church in the course of its development, in particular through the ecumenical councils.

No doubt, the Church did have clarity in the past with regard to christology. The Council of Chalcedon made its declaration and purported to have settled the question for all times:

> ... one the same Christ, the Son, the Lord, only begotten, in two natures unconfused, unchangeable, undivided, inseparable. The difference of natures will never be abolished by their being united but rather the properties of each remain unimpaired, both coming together in one person and substance, not parted or divided among two persons but in one and the same only begotten Son, the divine Word, the Lord Jesus.[23]

But how much of these statements is understood today? Do the words have the same meaning? Does this declaration respond to the needs of the Church in the twenty-first century? Was there ever agreement, or unanimity, in the understanding of Jesus in the early Church or even in the conciliar period?

On the fifteen-hundredth anniversary of the Council of Chalcedon, a group of German scholars published a series of articles. Karl Rahner's contribution was entitled 'Chalcedon, Beginning or End?'[24] For this renowned theologian, the Council of Chalcedon did not represent the end of theological speculation, nor the end of the debate within the Christian community as to the meaning of Jesus, but a beginning. The council was a starting point that would allow further development and refinement, and continual updating. The clarity of the conciliar definition has often been paid for with the loss of continual rethinking. Continuing to examine the meaning of Jesus is essential. Only then may Christianity make sense of the central mystery of the faith to all generations.

Fortunately, while the councils have made efforts to clarify and control, they have also consistently pointed out that in the end we

---

[23] *Teachings of the Catholic Church*, ed. K. Rahner (Staten Island: Alba House, 1967), p. 154.

[24] Karl Rahner, 'Chalkedon-Ende oder Anfan', *Das Konzil von Chalkedon*, ed. A. Grillmeier and H. Bacht, vol. 3 (Wurzburg, 1954), pp. 3-49.

are dealing with mystery.[25] Such an impetus, far from discouraging continued thought, discussion and debate, actually promotes it.

Mystery

The term 'mystery' has been used in many ways in the Bible as well as in the history of theology. History provides a starting point for the continual quest that challenges the theologian. In scripture the word 'mystery' does not mean something that no one can ever know, but rather the plan of God that brings salvation to all through the coming of Jesus of Nazareth. In Jesus 'the manifold wisdom of God is made known' (Eph 3:8); 'in him dwells the fullness of divinity' (Col 3:9). In him the mystery that God has preserved for all times has been revealed: 'To unite all things in him, things in heaven and things on earth' (Eph 1:10).

> Mystery: Is a primordial aspect, essential and permanent, of total reality, in that reality as a whole (that is infinite) is present for the finite, created, spirit in the latter's intrinsic openness to the infinite. Spirit, as this openness to the infinite, is the capacity to accept the incomprehensible as such, i.e. as permanent mystery.[26]

This great mystery concerns not so much God as God, nor even Jesus in himself, but rather the relationship between God and creation. The mystery involves a plan to unite all things in heaven and on earth, a destiny for all creatures to share in the unity of God and realize the perfection inherent in creation. Paul writes in Romans:

> We know that the whole of creation has been groaning in travail, together until now, and not only the creation but we ourselves who have the first fruits of the Spirit groan inwardly as we await for adoption as sons, the redemption of our bodies (Rom 8:22–23).

God the Father has involved himself in creation through Jesus, and his plan is to accomplish the unity of all reality through Christ.

[25] See Karl Rahner, 'The Concept of Mystery in Catholic Theology', *Theological Investigations*, vol. 4 (Baltimore: Helicon, 1966), pp. 36–73. Raymond Brown, 'The Semitic Background of the New Testament *Mysterion*,' *Biblica*, 39 (1958) pp. 42–48; 40 (1959), pp. 70–87.
[26] K. Rahner and Herbert Vorgrimler, *Theological Dictionary* (New York: Herder and Herder, 1965), pp. 300–301.

In the course of centuries people of faith have always sought to understand this mystery. As a result people found themselves brought into a greater awareness of the meaning of God and the plan of salvation. No one person could ever reach the point of a full understanding or complete appreciation of this mystery. Even the collective experience of the Church has not exhausted the reality that was the meaning of Jesus and his salvation. At the outset of this study all face mystery, inexhaustible intelligibility as they try to encounter, in a personal way, the meaning of Jesus the Christ.[27] This richness cannot be captured in any one model nor in any one period of time nor by any one individual.

Jesus can be known and experienced more fully and immediately than he can be explained and expressed. A connaturality exists between believer and the believed. In the presence of such an intimate relationship all attempts at analysis, at the moving from the non-conceptual to the conceptual, and then to the verbal in oral or written form, are doomed to frustration. People who live and are involved with the mystery of Jesus never can objectify its meaning. A certain intersubjectivity, the very basis of faith in the first place, precludes a complete categorical expression. People of faith live that faith and depend on that faith prescinding from any efforts at formulation found in official documents or in theology textbooks.

The Church Fathers of the Second Vatican Council were well aware of the continual need to grow in understanding of this mystery. They related the mystery of Jesus to that of the Church and saw all as part of the divine plan to unite all things in Jesus.[28] The concept of mystery not only places certain limitations on the content of this study, it also affects methodology. Theologians cannot easily extrapolate from clear, unequivocal concepts or definitions to others. They cannot simply take the pronouncement of a council and maintain that these concepts and words express the final and irrevocable approach to the understanding of Jesus. Neither can theologians simply apply the concepts abstracted from personal experience to the mystery of God nor to the mystery of Jesus. Everyone may know something of the meaning of personhood, since all have the experience of being persons, but to presume to extend this interpretation to the mystery of God should cause hesitation. People also have some concepts of the meaning of being human, not just through personal experience, but also by

---

[27] Rahner, *op. cit.*, pp. 41–43.
[28] 'Lumen Gentium', *Documents of Vatican II*, ed. Walter Abbott (New York: America Press, 1966).

means of human history. But to delineate what it means to be divine should stop all people in their tracks. Learned concepts do not directly apply to the mystery of God uniting all things. They tell something but far from everything.

As a result, some people just give up the quest. Believers can become quietists if they so choose and ignore the theological endeavour. Since no one will ever have all the answers and since even what approximates an answer is provisional, why should the Christian engage in any theological speculation? Prayer and the efforts to live a good life suffice.

Evidently, however, God has chosen to communicate through Jesus. Some value must exist in struggling with the interaction of the divine and human, even if the final outcome remains in shadow. Furthermore to retreat and remain silent about the meaning of God in Jesus denies the gift of the human spirit to always seek truth and to live for the inquiring. Besides, people have engaged in theological discourse for centuries and the proliferation of books shows no sign of abating.

Images of Jesus in art

The history of Christianity contains various images of Jesus. Nowhere is this more evident than in various portrayals of Jesus in Christian art. A comparative study through the ages would find a clear relationship between popular piety (another form of images) and the artistic depictions of the Lord. The statue of Jesus at the portal of the Cathedral of Chartres commands with power. He holds a book. The statue is entitled 'The Teaching Lord'. The artist had a clear image of Jesus as one who commands respect and teaches with authority. At the same time, the facial expression is kind and gentle. Jesus' eyes are soft and warm, his lips curved slightly in a smile.

Compare this image from the twelfth century with the figure on many of the holy cards of the twentieth century associated with devotion to the Sacred Heart. The features are usually weak and ethereal with little power, often with a sadness that does not tend to inspire.

The history of theology also has its images, models, symbols, or paradigms. These approaches or images or models have a long history in the learned traditions of Christianity as well as in the ordinary heritage of believers. The basis for such diverse images can be found in the New Testament itself.

Jesus in the New Testament

In the Gospels and the other writings of the early Church we find myriad images of Jesus which formed various foundations for speculation about his meaning. Jesus is the Lamb of God, the Word, the prophet, the messiah, the almighty Lord of heaven and earth; he is the servant who assumes humble tasks and who suffers unjustly. Jesus is the teacher who teaches with power; he is the miracle worker who performs prodigies as the healer. Jesus is also the vine, the shepherd, the door, the gate, the light. Each of these images of Jesus captures some aspect of his person. No one image can claim the exclusive portrayal of the meaning of the Lord. Each one contributes to an overall picture. The New Testament teems over with images. As the record of the experience of the early Church, the writers of the New Testament present in their collective consciousness and individual writings the many faces of Jesus.

```
TITLES
Lamb of God
Word
Prophet
Messiah/Christ
Lord of All
Son of Man
Servant
Teacher
Miracle Worker and Healer
Shepherd
Suffering Servant
Perfect Greek Gentleman
All-knowing Son of God
```

The study of the history of Christology also shows the use of many images and approaches or models. For some early believers he was a divine man (*theios aner*). Some heretics saw him as a gnostic redeemer come to gather together the various sparks of light that had been scattered in the human race. Later theology would see him as the second person of the Blessed Trinity. Certain contemporary theologians see him as the man for others; still others regard Jesus as the great liberator.

Signs and symbols

All of the above images, whether from the New Testament, or from the history of theology, from Christian art or common piety, reveal psychological and existential aspects of people who believe in Jesus. They are signs and they are symbols.[29] They reach down into the very depth of the reality of Jesus and bring up some aspect of his person that appeals to the human psyche and to faith. How much of the reality is actually made present depends upon the particular choice of image or symbol. Some symbols communicate through evoking a response. The face of Jesus from Chartres, for example, evokes a sense of trust and confidence. The image of holy cards might also help some to accept a tender and compassionate Jesus. Other images appeal more to the conceptual side of human nature. Symbols of Jesus can transform a person's attitude toward life; they can integrate perceptions, change value systems, reorient loyalties and create a sense of commitment and attachment far stronger than abstract concepts. Good symbols have more than just an intellectual appeal and more than just an aesthetic appeal. They are involved with the whole person – with all of the facets that create a human being in concrete human existence. When symbols make the reality known, more than an academic exercise results. The symbol actually contains the reality it expresses and thus can engage the person and focus the human experience in a definite way.

Any group of people that hopes to remain bound together in some sense of unity will depend on symbols to help them accomplish that task. All are familiar from the history of Christianity with the symbol of the fish used by early believers to remind them of Jesus. The five Greek letters for fish were an acronym for: Jesus Christ, Son of God, Saviour. Recent secular history used the swastika which helped unite people in a fanatic commitment to a dictator and still causes anxiety whenever seen. People in the 1960s and 1970s used a peace symbol. The clenched fist still is used to symbolize power, especially for those who have no power. The Olympic torch and five rings finds recognition throughout the world. Good symbols arouse courage, peace, authority, love and even hatred.

When examining the many images of Jesus they suggest attitudes, feelings, course of action and devotion. They help to unite

---

[29] See Karl Rahner, 'The Theology of the Symbol', *Theological Investigations*, vol. IV (Baltimore: Helicon, 1966), pp. 221–52.

people in a common bond of affection and commitment. But always, as images, they are incomplete and should not be seen as perfect in themselves. The images express the reality toward which they lead but for which they cannot substitute.[30]

For an image to gain acceptance it must conform to the experience of people and faith. At the same time the images help to shape that faith. The community must learn from the experience of its individual members with regard to images and at the same time must help inspire images for edification. To be effective the image or symbol must be deeply rooted in the experience of the community of believers. One person's approach never suffices. The Church depends not upon an image that is short-lived or based upon the experience of a limited few nor of a particular period in the history of faith. True symbols will eventually rise to the surface, even in the midst of a period of confusion and a multiplicity of inadequate and unworthy images. But even the best images have limited value precisely because the believer always faces mystery, inexhaustible intelligibility. They help, but should never perdure as absolutes.

Crisis of images

The present period of Church history seems to be experiencing a crisis of images. The crisis persists and is not limited to the religious sphere, for the previous relatively stable culture suddenly seems no longer firmly established. The rapid change in the western arena has caused a breakdown in some of the most common symbols and images of human life. Kings rise and fall; presidents who are supposed to epitomize the best of American traditions misuse power and become symbols of the worst. The stability of great universities as symbols of longevity and learning and integrity is compromised by involvement with government or business control and a lack of ethics. Schools are torn in many directions, with student and faculty crises. Banks, considered to be the foundation of economic stability, actually close their doors. Even the Soviet Union no longer exists. For more than forty years that particular political system symbolized for many westerners the power of evil. The Berlin wall fell and with it the mighty dominant communist system shook and disintegrated. People may have been united by opposition to a particular regime, but now the symbol of

[30] *Ibid.*

that regime lies broken. If the symbols that help to unite disparate elements of society, even if they unite in opposition, begin to crumble, no wonder that people are afraid and confused.

With regard to the Church, perhaps rather than a crisis of faith, believers face a crisis of images. The Roman Catholic Church used to convey stability; the rock of Peter was truly a rock. Religious men and women portrayed a sense of commitment and symbolized this commitment in action and even in dress. Now the images have been altered and people feel insecure. Church leaders resign in disgrace, acknowledging their sins. Laity and members of the hierarchy openly profess differing views where once all walked to the same rhythm. Dissent has become commonplace.

The crisis concerns, of course, more than just the understanding of the Church. The entire Christian message is based upon images. These images, however, are often taken from pastoral scenes in first century Palestine and never from the twentieth century technological society. Most people have little contact with lambs and shepherds, or even with vines and grapes. Servants, where they exist, are not in the same social category as in the time of Jesus. Even the developments in the later writings of the New Testament involve some urban society but still fall short of the global village society of today.

People need to examine the images of the past and to supplement these images with others, more in conformity with the faith community that has been reforming itself for the past four hundred years. The development of the new images will continue wherever the faith lives a vibrant and exciting vision. The Church has already decided to make many changes in its outward appearance, in consonance with changes that have taken place in the secular culture. The images of Jesus also need to relate to the experience of the larger community. Religious language has become impoverished with regard to imagery because there seems to be so little in experience that bears the stamp of the numinous. Mundane and this-world-centred-life needs to experience an awareness of the transcendent present in life. ''Tis ye, 'tis your estranged faces that miss the many splendour'd thing.'[31]

---

[31] Francis Thompson, 'In No Strange Land', *The Oxford Book of English Verse* (New York: Oxford University Press, 1940).

New images of Jesus

Examples of creative theological thinking do exist. J.A.T. Robinson derived his image of Jesus as the human face of God[32] from the theology of the later Karl Barth;[33] Dietrich Bonhoeffer was the first to speak of Jesus as the man for others.[34] Edward Schillebeeckx coined the phrase 'Jesus as the sacrament of encounter' to explain his sacramental theology.[35] Karl Rahner sees Jesus in relationship to the evolution of humanity and thus the image is that of a perfected human person.[36] Bernard Cooke views Jesus as the compassion of God.[37] Each of these images must encounter a *kairos*, the right time. The religious community must be psychologically set for the image. Paul Tillich made all aware that images are not created or destroyed by human effort; they are born to die. They often acquire a mysterious power that seems beyond human control or even beyond human comprehension.[38]

All know the importance of images in human life and how essential they are for the life of the believer. People live and die with images and by images. In the efforts to communicate faith, believers must constantly try to find new images that can convey something of that faith. When St. Patrick stumbled upon the shamrock as the image of Trinity, he was being faithful to the human need to express concretely an abstract notion. The archdiocese of Miami chose to use a logo of people gathered together with uplifted hands to symbolize the archdiocese as a community of people praising God together. This logo appears on all the official stationery of the archdiocese and helps to raise people's awareness of the meaning of Church.

Images and analysis

Theology also depends upon images and symbols. For a true

[32] J.A.T. Robinson, *The Human Face of God* (Philadelphia, Westminster, 1967).
[33] Karl Barth, *The Humanity of God* (Richmond: John Knox, 1960).
[34] D. Bonhoeffer, *Letters and Papers from Prison* (New York: Macmillan, 1967).
[35] Edward Schillebeeckx, *Christ the Sacrament of Encounter With God* (New York: Herder and Herder, 1963). See also *Jesus: An Experiment in Christology* (New York: Seabury, 1979).
[36] Karl Rahner, *Foundations of Christian Faith* (New York: Seabury, 1978), chapter VI.
[37] See B. Cooke *God's Beloved: Jesus' Experience of the Transcendent* (Philadelphia: Trinity Press International, 1992).
[38] Quoted in Dulles, *Models of the Church*, p.20.

theology, however, along with the symbol comes analysis. The Church cannot settle for the shamrock for the symbol of the Trinity without analysis. What meets the needs on the level of cate-chetics does not always reach the level of theology. Nor must the theologian limit interest to those images that are current. Studying the symbols of the past proves worthwhile, even if they have lost some of their power. They once vitalized the Church and maybe today believers can uncover some of that vitality that can be used again. People should also examine some of the current symbols and see what value they are actually conveying. The theologian is not always the preacher, and so the person who proclaims Jesus to the ordinary believer must be careful to choose images that convey some sense of understanding, just as the theologian must be aware of what is actually being preached. The theologian always studies and analyzes symbols. In a *kairos*, the person devoted to the study of Jesus may actually help to form a symbol that is acceptable to the collective spirit of the faith community.

When a theologian uses a particular image in theology, the primary interest lies in gaining some insight into the under-standing of faith. The theologian knows the usefulness of the images, but also the limitations. No symbol contains the fullness of the reality, and thus no one particular image can be erected into an absolute, nor can it ever be construed as a substitute for the reality itself. The good theologian will use images reflectively and with sobriety. As someone dedicated to the careful study of the faith, the theologian carefully and critically evaluates the images of the past as well as the images of the present. The result distinguishes the valid expression of some aspect of the mystery of faith from that which is inadequate, invalid or even prejudicial to faith.

An image used theologically, reflectively and ontically deepens the theoretical understanding of a reality, and becomes a model. Some models are also images; that is, they can be imagined easily. Other models are more abstract. With regard to Jesus, the New Testament models him as a shepherd, or as a preacher or a prophet. To model him as the second person of the Blessed Trinity or the Word of God, however, does not connote the idea of an image, since the ideas are more abstract.

Models in science and theology

The physical sciences and the social sciences have used models extensively in the past. Only recently have models been used in theology. Avery Dulles titled his book on the Church *Models of the Church*. I.T. Ramsey also demonstrates how the use of models can be helpful in theology.[39] There are obvious similarities and differences between the way the various sciences used models and the way theology uses them. In science the use of models is effective if the model allows for deductions as well as verification: 'In any scientific understanding a model is better, the more prolific it is in generating deductions which are then open to experimental verification and falsification.'[40] A model that fails to respond to some of the questions to be answered is by that fact limited in its usefulness. A model that does not allow for experimentation is also of limited value, since the researcher cannot verify the truth purported to be represented.

With certain restrictions, theologians have applied these notions to theology, even though developed primarily in other fields. E. Cousins explains clearly the use of models in theology:

> Theology is concerned with the ultimate level of religious mystery which is even less accessible than the mystery of the physical universe. Hence our religious language and symbols should be looked upon as models because even more than the concepts of science, they only approximate the object they are reflecting.[41]

The symbol, however, can never become an absolute. Cousins is convinced that the use of a model prevents this possibility:

> ...to use the concept of model in theology, then, breaks the illusion that we are actually encompassing the infinite within our finite structures and language. It prevents concepts and symbols from becoming idols and opens theology to variety and development just as the model method has done for science. Yet there is a danger that

---

[39] I.T. Ramsey, *Models and Mysteries* (New York: Oxford, 1964).

[40] *Ibid.* 4. See also Max Black, *Models and Metaphors* (Ithaca: Cornell University Press, 1962).

[41] E. Cousins, 'Models and the Future of Ministry', *Continuum* 7 (1969), pp. 78-91. John McIntyre, in *The Shape of Christology* (London: SCM Press, 1966), is the first theologian, as far as I can establish, to attempt to use the approach of models in christology. His particular theological stance differs considerably from mine, but I have profited by his attempts and acknowledge this debt.

it will not go far enough for it may not take sufficiently into account the level of religious experience.[42]

The last comment of Cousins merits study. Certain disadvantages arise from using a methodology from the physical sciences. Religious experience involves more than the intellectual; it encompasses the entire person. No one can compare religious faith with the analysis of the universe in any complete fashion. Analysis can be used, but in all analogies the differences predominate. Faith concerns more than can be contained in any model. Recognizing this deficiency, however, models can help the theologian not only in efforts to explain faith, but in exploring faith.

On the level of explanation, models tend to synthesize what people have already experienced or have come to believe in a faith experience. Just as a good scientific model will synthesize and respond to many facets and problems and questions, so the theological model will synthesize the biblical experience as well as the experience of centuries of lived faith in the history of Christianity.

The gospel models of Jesus as a shepherd, or the Lamb of God, or one of the prophets convey certain aspects of the meaning of Jesus, and the Church has accepted them. He is the one who provides for and protects; he is the one who offers himself without hesitation to God his Father; he is the one who fulfills the aspirations of the Old Testament and points out the religious dimension present or absent in human life. Each model points out one specific aspect of Jesus and his ministry, but each has its obvious limits. No model above takes into account the specific relationship between Jesus and God his Father. Nor do they deal with an appreciation of Jesus as the one like his brethren 'in all things but sin' (Heb 4:15). Thus, other models must be used to supplement these models taken from scripture. In the history of theology, Jesus has been explained as the second person of the Blessed Trinity. More recently, Jesus is the man for others, the sacrament of God, the human face of God, the great liberator, and the ground of being.

Using models

In the use of models, the more applications the models have, the better they suggest a true relationship between the reality of Jesus and the image that is used to convey the reality. No complete har-

---

[42] *Ibid.*

mony is possible, since the symbol is forever limited in expressing the reality it contains. The exploratory use of models involves the specific theological task of breaking new ground and offering a means for the theologian to fulfill the task as one who is seeking understanding. Such a responsibility demands much and involves many pitfalls. Somehow the theologian must steer a course between the Scylla of exploration for its own sake and the Charybdis of theological stagnation in long-outdated ideas. Christian theology has a norm in the Gospel of Jesus as experienced and expressed in the early Church. Thus in some sense every exploration further enunciates the reality of Jesus always present in the Church. The ongoing sense of revelation as the unfolding of the offer of a relationship with God demands Jesus living among his people now, continuing to offer himself in ways that are meaningful to people of every age. Exploring the present experience of Jesus by the faithful also forms part of the theological enterprise. A true development in theology and not just the unfolding of what was always known does exist. The present experience of the Church is in a certain sense unique, and that experience itself will bring new insights into the meaning of faith.

The present pope, John Paul II, has learned from personal experience the role of the Church in a Marxist regime. That has given him an understanding of Jesus that would not be possible at any other moment in history. The experience of faith in Latin America or in the emerging nations of Africa and Asia has developed new insights into the meaning of Jesus. In the Second Vatican Council the specifically American experience of faith gave birth to the decree on religious liberty. In each period of history, theological reflection has nourished insights that grew out of the interchange of human experience and Christian faith. The result has raised the consciousness of the entire Church to appreciate another aspect of the inexhaustible meaning of Jesus of Nazareth.

Verification

A further problem in the exploratory use of models in christology involves verification. Dealing with the mystery of God and humankind precludes any easily deduced conclusions. Nor can any empirical tests be used to see if the model is actually helpful or harmful to Christian faith.

The model of Jesus as the great liberator causes some to suspect that this must imply the approval of violence and thus cannot be valid. This may not be the case. The model need not automatically entail the sanctioning of violence, thus contradicting the fundamentally non-violent stance of Christianity. Clearly, empirical tests cannot be used for verification of this model, since statistics in themselves cannot tell what is right or wrong in the struggle for justice. The number of people espousing liberation theology in Latin America and in other parts of the world is not a criterion for rightness, nor is the number of people opposed to liberation theology a sign that the model is wrong. Even the presence of some people in the movement who advocate violence does not, in itself, vitiate the value of the model.

Discernment

Just as the discernment of spirits is necessary in the spiritual life, so too a process of discernment is crucial in the realm of theology. Ignatius Loyola saw the need to seek guidance to discover the significant values in the life of faith. This concept can be applied here as well. K. Rahner faces the question of authority in the Church and speaks of a certain 'feel' for the rightness of a position. He speaks of a sense of peace that will be the sign that the person is on the right track:

> That serene, joyous, harmonious lucidity in which there can alone be any hope of finding the correct solution in individually important affairs may also be the fruit of the spirit.[43]

A corporate discernment of spirits can be most helpful in coming to some judgment with regard to the use of models for Jesus:

> As this life of Christ is deepened in us by the Holy Spirit there is created in the Christian a 'sense of Christ', a taste and instinctual judgment for the things of God, a deeper perception of God's truth, an increased understanding of God's dispositions and love toward us. This is what Christians must strive to attain individually and corporately; theologians call it Christian connaturality. It is like a nature instinct or intuition but it is not natural, since it results from the supernatural reality of the divine indwelling and the impulses of grace.[44]

This feel for what is right or wrong, valid or invalid, is important

[43] Karl Rahner, *The Dynamic Element in the Church* (New York: Herder and Herder, 1964), p. 168.
[44] John Powell, *The Mystery of the Church* (Milwaukee: Bruce, 1967), p. 8.

in the evaluation of any model. Jesus had the same idea when he remarked, 'By their fruits you shall know them' (Matt 7:20). The Christian community will recognize a model truly helpful for faith, even though this may take time and involve opposition. Where the model results in anger or discord or the destruction of individuals in any way, then the Spirit is not at work. The models may be evaluated by the effect they have on the Church, the worldwide community of believers who profess the gospel on which every model must ultimately be based.

Faith is not just a theoretical engagement of the mind. Faith is lived. Theory and practice are not separate realities. Faith in Jesus exists in people and in history, neither divorced from them nor isolated from their historical experiences. The continual interplay between the individual believer working out of personal history in conjunction with other believers brings faith to birth. When these realities are in balance, one can confidently judge the validity of a model of Jesus.

Jesus as ruler

An example from the history of theology should help to clarify this method of discernment. In medieval times the model of Jesus as the ultimate ruler of all gave birth to a sense of judgment and control that produced an authoritarian Church in the late middle ages. If Jesus controlled all people and if the Church shared in this power, then the Church had an obligation to rule over everyone in an absolute manner. Consequently the Church could forbid anyone to think differently from the official teaching.

Church leaders also saw themselves empowered to dethrone kings and force infidels to submit to baptism. The model was taken not from the role of Jesus in the gospels, but from the experience of secular, civil authority. Turning Jesus into a secular potentate and then using that model to control the society from which it arose demonstrates how questionable that particular model was from the outset.

All models used in theology are incomplete. They illuminate certain aspects of Jesus and obscure others. Certainly the model of Jesus as ruler has some foundation in the New Testament. The Father has given to *him* power and judgment (John 5:22; Matt 28:18) but this should not be interpreted by the understanding of rulers in secular society.

Paradigm

The study of Jesus discloses many models. Some will have outlived their usefulness based upon the continual growth and perception of the reality of Jesus as still present in his community. Images and models have always proliferated in the history of Christianity. With such a multiplicity, often enough the human mind will want to limit the plurality and search for one model that will be the summation or epitome of all. Can one model unify the data of scripture and that of the two thousand years of Christian experience? At various times in the history of theology, people have tried to offer such a model. In the terminology used in this book, that model would then become a paradigm. When a model successfully solves a great many questions and problems and allows for the greatest number of deductions and further invites a variety of personal understandings, then such is a paradigm as expressed. Paradigms are 'concrete puzzle solutions which, employed as models or examples, can replace explicit rules as a basis for the solution of the remaining puzzles of normal science'.[45]

In the past, the chief paradigm for Jesus was the second person of the Blessed Trinity. This formed the basis for scholastic christology and has been part of the official teaching of the Church for the past fifteen hundred years. In recent years the Church has chosen to use other models, at least in unofficial documents, but the paradigm has remained the same. The eternal only-begotten-Son-second-person-of-the-Blessed-Trinity is the model that responds to the most questions and problems and allows for the greatest expression of the reality.

Is this the paradigm that the Church wants to use in the twentieth or twenty-first century? Are followers of Jesus and members of the Church expected to maintain and hold to this model as a paradigm, or can they use it as one model and turn to some other paradigm? Must this model be a paradigm for preaching and religious education, or may it give way to other paradigms while maintaining its position in speculative theology?

Whatever one's personal position, the transition from one paradigm to another creates problems. Each model brings its strengths and weaknesses. When one model becomes a paradigm, the weaknesses are often forgotten and the strengths are emphasized. When paradigms shift, people who have grown accustomed to the

[45] T. S. Kuhn, *The Structure of Scientific Revolutions* (Chicago: University Press, 1970), p. 175.

strengths of one and have never been aware of its weaknesses will react sharply against the introduction of a new paradigm. Not only are theologians threatened who have worked out their own positions in terms of the previously reigning paradigm, but ordinary people are affected at the level of their beliefs and practices. Piety suffers.

No one should be surprised, then, to find polarization with regard to Jesus and his image in the contemporary Church. Theologians often seem unable to communicate and the Church officials fall back on a reaffirmation of more traditional models. In times of controversy the usual tendency is to solidify and reaffirm a previously held tradition. Such is the situation of the Church at the end of the twentieth century; theologians and others must learn not only to live with that fact, but also to gain insights from it. If no one paradigm provides the final answer, then it seems that an acceptance of many models within a dominant paradigm is the rational and responsible approach. Only further confusion will result from an effort to convert a single model into a final and eschatological one.

Instead of seeking one absolute paradigm, since each one captures only part of the reality, the Christian community might choose to recognize the plurality and celebrate the complementarity of the models. A model may also be erected into a paradigm, but only for a time, and only with the realization that it must accommodate other models.

In the history of Christology the beginning is always the New Testament. From there, the Church has developed its various approaches to Jesus. To be all-inclusive is impossible. Certain models will always deserve their place. Theologians usually adopt a model or a combination of models. They commit themselves to a particular stance in systematic and practical theology. Believers do the same thing. Action follows being.

Study topics and questions
1. Why do people bother to study the Bible?
2. Critically analyzing the New Testament can cause problems. Why do theologians insist on doing it?
3. The Church must have concerns when people start rethinking fundamental doctrines.
4. Why are contemporary scholars so interested in the historical Jesus?
5. All approaches to Jesus are equally good.
6. The idea of 'mystery' as inexhaustible intelligibility makes sense.

7. Is there a crisis of faith today? Is there a crisis of images?
8. What new images of Jesus appeal to you? What is your own image of Jesus?
9. Do models and paradigms help or hinder in understanding Jesus and the Church?
10. Make a list of as many images of Jesus as you can recall. Put them in order of personal preference.

Chapter 11

The Doctrine of the Incarnation: Human and Cosmic Considerations

Dermot A. Lane

The doctrine of the Incarnation: human and cosmic considerations

The doctrine of the Incarnation stands at the centre of Christian faith and is the bedrock for our understanding of the major truths of Christianity: the Trinity, the Church, the sacraments, grace, and eschatology. In broad terms the Incarnation is the doctrine about Jesus of Nazareth as the Son of God made human. Biblically speaking, it is summed up in the statement that the eternal word of God was made flesh and dwelt among us (John 1:14). This is usually expressed in the story of God coming down from heaven and entering fully into the human condition in the life and death of Jesus. The Incarnation has tended to be associated with the infancy narratives of the New Testament and is understood to have been inaugurated at the time of the annunciation.

Theologically speaking the biblical account of the Incarnation is usually expressed in the technical language of the two nature-one person model formulated at the Council of Chalcedon (451). Jesus possesses a fully human nature and a fully divine nature which exist in one single person who is the Logos of God. Jesus is presented as true God and true man; he is the eternal son of God made flesh; he is the personal presence of God in the world.

The classical presentation of these basic truths of the Incarnation has been shaped by the Councils of Nicea (325), Ephesus (431) and especially Chalcedon (451). The Council of Chalcedon provided the philosophical framework which has successfully held together the christological dogma of the Incarnation for the last sixteen hundred years. The Chalcedonian framework is hallmarked by the complex philosophical categories of substance, nature and person.

In recent times, however, the classical presentation of Chalcedon has come in for serious criticism. It is pointed out that the technical language of substance, nature and person no longer communicates today what it did at the time of the great christological councils. Further, it is complained that these technical terms have been understood in an overly static and essentialist manner. Most of all, it is argued that the Chalcedonian framework bears little or no visible relationship to the historical life, death and resurrection of Jesus as understood by modern exegesis. It should be noted that these observations are directed not against the truth of the Incarnation as expressed at the Council of Chalcedon but rather at the language and the non-historical terms of that Council's declaration.

Vatican II, conscious of the changes that have taken place in this century, pointed out:

> The human race has passed from a static concept of reality to a more dynamic, evolutionary one. In consequence there has arisen a new series of problems, a series as important as can be, calling for new efforts of analysis and synthesis.[1]

The doctrine of the Incarnation is one of those areas in theology which at present calls for a new synthesis as a result of the shift from a static view of reality to a more dynamic, evolutionary position. The classical understanding of the Incarnation has been cast in a closed, static and unhistorical framework. Given the emergence of historical consciousness and philosophical pluralism today, it has become increasingly difficult to communicate the truth of the Incarnation in the technical language of Chalcedon without being misunderstood. Consequently, it has become necessary to move beyond the classical framework and language in a manner that seeks at the same time to safeguard the underlying doctrinal truth of Chalcedon. In setting out to do this we should remember the principle enunciated by Pope John XXIII and adopted by Vatican II: 'For the deposit of faith or revealed truths are one thing; the manner in which they are formulated without violence to their meaning and significance is another.'[2]

Faithful to its own principles, Vatican II does in fact talk about

[1]   *Gaudium et Spes,* a. 5; see also a. 4, 36, and 62.
[2]   *Gaudium et Spes,* a. 62.

the Incarnation in a language and framework that goes beyond Chalcedon. The Council points out that:

> The faith is that only in the mystery of the Incarnate word does the mystery of man take on light ... Christ, the final Adam, by the revelation of the mystery of the Father and his love, fully reveals man to man himself and makes his supreme calling clear... For by his incarnation the Son of God has united himself in some fashion with every man. He worked with human hands, he thought with a human mind, acted by human choice, and loved with a human heart.[3]

Clearly the focus here is on the human, anthropological significance of the Incarnation. The mystery of the Incarnation reveals the Son of God to the world, but it also reveals the dignity and destiny of every human being. Jesus Christ as the Word Incarnate is the key to a proper understanding of what it means to be fully human. Clearly the anthropological aspects of the Incarnation are to the fore here at Vatican II.

A more recent statement of the doctrine of the Incarnation by Pope John Paul II takes up the emphasis of Vatican II and adds significantly to it:

> The Incarnation of God the Son signifies the taking up into unity with God not only human nature, but in this human nature, in a sense, of everything that is flesh ... The Incarnation then, also has a cosmic significance, a cosmic dimension: the 'first born of creation' unites himself in some way with the entire reality of man, within the whole of creation.[4]

According to this statement there are two fundamental truths contained in the mystery of the Incarnation. Firstly, the Incarnation is about God taking up human nature into the self of God. Secondly, the Incarnation also embraces the whole of creation as part of the new and special relationship that now obtains between God and humanity; this latter point is referred to as the cosmic aspect of the Incarnation.

There are, therefore, at least two aspects to the mystery of the Incarnation that are worth exploring. These are the anthropological and the cosmological. The anthropological concerns the ontological relationship that exists between God and humanity exemplified in the historical life, death and resurrection of Jesus as

---

[3] *Gaudium et Spes*, a. 22.
[4] *Dominum et Vivificatum* (On the Holy Spirit in the life of the Church and the World), Vatican City: 1986, a. 50.

the Word made flesh; this relationship between God and humanity has special significance for the way we understand the human condition. The cosmological aspect concerns the relationship between God and the cosmos disclosed in the mystery of Jesus Christ. It is surely important today to keep together both the anthropological and the cosmological aspects of the Incarnation, given the damaging ecological consequences of separating the human from the cosmic in recent times. The purpose of this chapter will seek to explore the anthropological and cosmological significance of the Incarnation.

The image of God and the human person in classical Christology

In going beyond Chalcedon it is, of course, necessary to be aware of some of the difficulties inherent in the classical presentation of christology. These difficulties circle around the image of God and the image of the human person associated with the Chalcedonian dogma.

The image of God coming down from heaven and earth at the time of the Incarnation seems to imply unwittingly the introduction of a previously absent divine presence into the world. Little or no account is taken of the general presence of God in the created world and among the people of God in the history of Israel. If anything, the Incarnation seems to take place in separation from God's all-pervasive presence in the world. As a result the Incarnation comes across as a 'bolt out of the blue', giving the impression that it is more of an isolated exception than a definitive disclosure of God's presence of the world.[5] The Incarnation therefore is in danger of coming across as something of an interruption of the normal processes of God's presence in the world, appearing as a temporary divine intrusion which is terminated with the ascension of Christ. The imagery of God coming down and going up is contrary to the real meaning of the Incarnation which can be summed up in the language of Emmanuel, that is, God permanently with us.

A similar problem arises when we look at the understanding of the human person involved in the classical account of the Incarnation. When we say God became flesh in Jesus, the impres-

---

[5] J.A.T. Robinson, 'Need Jesus have been Perfect?', *Christ, Faith and History*, S.W. Sykes and J.P. Clayton (eds.), London: Cambridge University Press, 1972, p. 39.

sion is often given that God takes over the human person Jesus and that the humanity of Jesus from the moment of his birth onwards is somehow divinely predetermined. The freedom of the man Jesus seems to be eliminated and this in turn negates the existence of human responsibility, merit or value attaching to anything Jesus does throughout his mission and ministry. The man Jesus appears to be a purely passive recipient in the mystery of the Incarnation.

The source of these impressions is the static and non-historical framework in which the divine-human drama of the Incarnation is expressed by the Council of Chalcedon. If we are to do justice to the historical interplay that takes place between God and humanity in Jesus, then more attention will have to be given to the freedom of the man Jesus. In fact one of the most effective criteria for safeguarding the historical character of the Incarnation is that of paying particular attention to the freedom of Jesus.[6]

A further difficulty in the classical framework of the Incarnation is the suggestion that the identity and vocation of Jesus are somehow fixed and determined at birth. Yet we know in the light of modern psychology that self-identity is not something determined solely at birth. The human person is not born into the world with a fixed identity. On the contrary, authentic self-identity is that which emerges historically out of a complex series of experiences and relationships in freedom with others in the world. In reality, the emergence of human self-identity is something that becomes fixed and final at death and not at birth. Self-identity, therefore, is a developing historical reality which is permanently in a process of becoming. This does not mean that the development of self-identity is an independent, free-floating affair in the life of the individual. Rather, personal identity is shaped by the environment of one's life from birth onwards; it results from the interplay between individual freedom and human destiny. The self is constituted through a series of personal experiences and free relationships with the world and other selves. The self-in-becoming is an historical outcome rather than a predetermined given at birth.

The need for a new perspective

It should be clear from these brief observations on the images of God and the human person implicit in the traditional framework

---

[6] See D. Gray, 'The Divine and Human in Jesus', *Proceedings of the Catholic Theological Society of America*, vol. 31 (1976), pp. 21–39.

of the Incarnation that there is a need for a change in perspective. This change is best summed up in what Bernard Lonergan called the shift from a classical culture to the rise of historical consciousness.[7] Broadly speaking there has been a move, especially in this century, away from the perception of cultural forms as fixed and closed to an understanding of culture that is thoroughly historical and open-ended. The world as we experience it is no longer understood as something determined and immutable; instead it is experienced as an unfinished project which is still under construction. In particular, this shift in consciousness has affected our understanding of the place of the individual in the world. The human person is no longer studied as an 'object' out there in a given position but as a 'subject' who is personally responsible for the shaping of his or her destiny. We look at the individual from 'the inside out' and not from 'the outside in'.[8] The human person is a subject, a radically relational subject, who develops historically through relationships with other subjects.

Further, not only the human person but also the world around the person is understood to be radically relational, processive, and interdependent. The world in which we live is a vast network of web-like relationships, dynamic processes and organic interconnections. A fundamental unity is perceived to exist between spirit and matter, self and world, subject and object – a unity that has been significantly enlarged and enriched by the findings of postmodern cosmologies which we will take up more explicitly when dealing with the cosmic dimensions of the Incarnation.

Before applying this changed historical and relational perspective to the mystery of the Incarnation we need to say something, by way of introduction, about the overall relationship that exists between God and the world. In some respects the question about the meaning of the Incarnation today is as much a question about the general presence of God in the world as it is a question about the particular presence of God in Jesus of Nazareth. The Incarnation of God in Jesus took place in a particular historical and religious context. Some understanding of this context is necessary if we are to make sense out of the Christian claim that God was

[7]   B. Lonergan, 'Theology in its New Context', *The Theology of Renewal*, vol. 1, L.K. Shook (ed.), New York: Herder and Herder, 1968, pp. 34–46; 'The Transition from a Classicist Worldview to a Historical-Mindedness', *A Second Collection*, W. Ryan and B. Tyrell (eds.), London: Darton, Longman and Todd, 1974, pp. 1–9.

[8]   B. Lonergan, 'The Subject', *A Second Collection*, London: Darton, Longman and Todd, 1974, pp. 69–86.

personally present in Jesus of Nazareth. Without some reference to this context, the Incarnation may well appear as an anomalous exception to the general presence of God in the world before and after the Christ-event.

Situated in this larger context, the Incarnation will begin to be seen as the personalisation and crystalisation of God's overall presence in the world. How then are we to understand God's general relationship to the world and history as context for the particular Incarnation of God in Jesus?

The God of the Hebrew scriptures is a God who exists in sharp contrast to the immutable, detached, unmoved mover of Greek philosophy. The God of the people of Israel is a personally active, dynamic and involved God made known to the Israelites through their experience of history:

> The Lord said 'I have seen the affliction of my people who are in Egypt, and have heard their cry because of their taskmaster; I know their sufferings, and I have come to deliver them out of the land of the Egyptians, and to bring them out of that land ... and now behold the cry of the people has come to me, and I have seen the oppression with which the Egyptians oppress them. Come I will send you to Pharaoh ... ' (Ex 3:7–10)

The unfolding of Hebrew history is the unfolding of a God who journeys faithfully with the people of Israel.[9] The God of Israelite experience is equally the God of the liberating exodus and painful exile. This strong sense of God's constant presence is formulated in Israel's faith in God as creator portrayed in the creation narratives of the Book of Genesis, in many psalms, and in the Wisdom literature. God who is active in history is the same God who in the beginning created the heavens and the earth (Gen 1:1) who fills the whole world and ... holds all things together (Ws 1:7). It is the same personal God of Jewish history and creation from the beginning who is the subject of the Incarnation.

Before taking up the doctrine of Incarnation, reference must be made to the story of humanity's faith response to God's presence in history and creation as a backdrop to the Christ-event. Here we should remember that the personal act of faith is always a free act. The presence of God in the world does not coerce the individual into belief. To the contrary, the divine presence in history and creation is experienced as a gracious invitation and a persuasive

---

[9]   This theme is most helpfully developed by D. Carroll in *A Pilgrim God for a Pilgrim People*, Dublin: Gill and Macmillan, 1988, especially in chapter 3.

calling to the free act of personal trust and self-surrender. The individual lives out his or her life within the ambit of a disarming, gracious presence.

In broad terms every human person experiences himself or herself as a self-transcending being, a being who reaches out beyond the self towards some unifying centre of communication, a being who experiences an unrestricted desire to know and to love, a being who is restless in virtue of his or her awareness of human incompleteness. The goal of this searching self-transcendence is the elusive mystery we call God. At the same time the individual discovers within this experience that he or she is nonetheless estranged from this goal of self-transcendence. The human self experiences at the same time a real sense of both belongingness to and separation from the holy mystery we call God. It is this common human experience of God that lies behind the colourful story of Israel's faith in Yahweh. It is, in particular, this story of God's gracious self-communication to the individual and the community in history and creation and at the same time the individual's and community's incomplete response to this invitation that sets the stage for the historical process of the Incarnation.

The historical drama of the Incarnation

We have seen, in broad strokes, that God communicates God's self through creation and history and that the individual person, through the experience of a searching self-transcendence, responds in faith to this divine presence. It is in the light of this structure of God's gracious self-giving and the individual's fragile response in faith that we can now turn explicitly to the divine-human and human-divine exchange that took place historically in Jesus of Nazareth. The story of God's gracious self-communication in history and humanity's restless self-transcendence comes to a unique point of contact in the historical life, death and resurrection of Jesus. God and the human person come together in perfect unity in Jesus; the divinity of Jesus is co-present/active in and through the sacred humanity of Jesus. A real unity, a hypostatic unity as the Council of Ephesus called it, is established between the divine and the human, between infinite self-giving and human receiving in freedom, between heaven and earth, once and for all in the life of Jesus.

When we look at the life of Jesus we discover that the activity of God's gracious self-communication is at work in a particular and even more intense manner. God's personal outreach to human nature in the person of Jesus is deeper than heretofore in the history of Israel. The divine self-giving to humanity is on the one hand continuous with the previous activity of God in creation and history. On the other hand, it is important to stress that there is a qualitative difference in the divine outreach given in Jesus. This difference in the quality of the divine self-giving is expressed and symbolised in the biblical narratives surrounding the birth, the baptism, the transfiguration and the death of Jesus.

This new divine initiative is personally addressed to the man Jesus throughout his life. As in the case of every divine invitation, the one addressed is free to accept or to reject the call. Examples of the challenging character of the divine call can be seen in the temptations of Jesus in the desert, in the garden of Gethsemane, and on the cross. On the other hand, moments like the baptism at the Jordan, the reading of the prophet Isaiah in the synagogue at Nazareth, the journey up to Jerusalem, the cleansing of the temple, are indications of Jesus' consistent openness, receptivity and faithfulness to the divine call. Clearly, the horizon of the life of Jesus is shaped and influenced from beginning to end by his unique awareness of this divine call and his continuous experience of the co-presence of God in his life. In particular, it was Jesus' experience of God as *Abba* that informed his mission and ministry. The experience of God as Father is the basis of his self-understanding as the Son of God and the source of his understanding of the coming Reign of God. It is these historical realities in the ministry of Jesus, namely the experience of God as Father, the strong sense of a filial relationship with the Father, the unfolding awareness of the nearness of the Reign of God, the consciousness of being sent by God to represent God and to do the work of God that provide the key to the divine identity of Jesus.

As noted earlier, self-identity is something that unfolds historically in and through different experiences and relationships in life. We do not come into the world with a pre-determined identity. Rather we leave the world at death with a historically achieved self-identity. To be sure, the circumstances of our entry into the world play an important role in the achievement of identity, as they most surely did in the case of Jesus. At the same time the circumstances of entry into life have to be worked out historically through the exercise of personal freedom. A delicate relationship exists between the interplay of destiny and freedom, identity and history in the life of Jesus.

In the case of Jesus, we can say that the identity of Jesus is influenced historically by the quality and character of his free response to God's unique call. The whole life of Jesus is God-shaped and kingdom-centred, so much so that the subjectivity of Jesus is intimately connected with the subjectivity of God the Father which is permanently present to Jesus. It is in and through the multiplicity of these continuous experiences and relationships that the true identity of Jesus as the eternal Word of God incarnate emerges.

The interaction that takes place between God's gracious outreach and the obedient response in faith to this divine outreach is such that Jesus is historically revealed as the Word made flesh, the eternal son of God incarnate. The personal identity of Jesus, therefore, may be said to be co-constituted by the activity of God reaching deep down into the heart of human nature and that human nature freely accepting the divine summons in the life of Jesus. The Christ-event is that which is effected historically from the perfect union between God and the human Jesus. As a result of this unity between God and humanity, Jesus is personally God in human form, the eternal Word of God made flesh.

An example of what is involved in the historical constitution of Jesus' divine identity may be taken from the domain of interpersonal relationships. The reciprocal love that exists between a husband and wife is such that historically over a period of time the husband may incorporate into his own self-identity certain aspects and dimensions of the beloved's personality and vice versa. The encounter between the two subjectivities shapes the development of a new self-identity in the husband or the wife as the case may be. A similar process can occur in the experiences and the relationships that take place between a father and his son or a mother and her daughter. The son realises his own self-identity through a series of different experiences in life. A formative factor within these identity-shaping experiences will be the experience he has of his own father and the particular regard the son has for the father. If there is a close bond between the father and the son, then there is a sense in which the son will incorporate the characteristics of his father into his own personality.

In an analogous manner we can say that Jesus, through a process of permanent openness to the Spirit of God the Father, is the perfect expression of the Father as Son. This process of divine-human and human-divine activity is instituted before the birth of Jesus. From his conception onwards Jesus is uniquely destined to be the Son of God Incarnate. The divine destiny of Jesus, however, has to be worked out historically in and through the free exercise of trust and love. While it is necessary to emphasise the particular initiative of God in the Incarnation from the conception of Jesus onwards, it is equally important to focus on the freedom of the man Jesus in responding to this divine initiative. To this extent we must say that the Incarnation was a historical process instituted by God at the conception of Jesus, which was subsequently sustained and perfected by the loving response in freedom of Jesus. A balance must be maintained between the divine risk of predestining the man Jesus to be the Son of God incarnate and the human freedom of Jesus in successfully living out that divine destiny.

It is this historical perspective that the so-called New Testament adoptionist texts were trying to communicate. In his introduction to the Letter to the Romans, Paul points out that God 'designated Jesus son of God in power according to the spirit of holiness by his resurrection from the dead' (Rom 1:3-4).[10] The author of the Letter to the Hebrews reminds us that Jesus 'learnt obedience through what he suffered and being made perfect, he became the source of eternal salvation' (Heb 5:8-9). Further, St Luke tells his audience that the Jesus whom they crucified, 'God has made him both Lord and Christ' (Acts 2:36). In each instance there is a strong sense of the historical and processive character of the Incarnation.

Traces of this understanding of the mystery of the Incarnation can be found among contemporary christologists. Two examples will suffice here. Walter Kasper, in his book *Jesus the Christ*, notes how the indeterminate and open aspect that belongs to the human person is determined definitively by the unity of the person with the Logos. As a result of this unity of Jesus' human person with the eternal Logos, human personality comes to its absolute unique fulfilment.[11] In other words the encounter between the personality of Jesus and the eternal Logos effects the fulfilment of human personality. This encounter does not diminish the human personality but rather brings it to completion and perfection.

A second example worth mentioning here is that of John Cobb who wrote an article entitled 'A Whiteheadian Christology' in 1971 and later developed this into a book entitled *Christ in a Pluralistic*

---

[10] A legitimate alternative translation for 'designated', according to the RSV, is 'constituted'.

[11] W. Kasper, *Jesus the Christ*, London: Burns & Oates, 1976, p. 248. Echoes of the same kind of thinking can be found in K. Rahner, 'Current Problems in Christology', *Theological Investigations*, vol. 1, London: DLT, 1961, pp. 183–184; E. Schillebeeckx, *Jesus: An Experiment in Christology*, London: Collins, 1979, p. 656. A helpful and more elaborate account of the complex issues involved here can be found in A. Baxter, 'Chalcedon and the Subject in Christ', *The Downside Review*, January 1989, pp. 1–21.

Age.[12] According to Cobb the presence of the Logos in the world constitutes the selfhood of Jesus. During his life Jesus chose freely to constitute his selfhood as one with the presence of God and by doing this he was the fullest Incarnation of the Logos in the universe. This view likewise resembles in broad outline the basic perspective being proposed here for a historical and processive understanding of the Incarnation. In noting this broad agreement with Cobb's christology we would want however to question his apparent neglect to bring out clearly enough the special and qualitatively new initiative taken by God in instituting this process in Jesus.

In search of the cosmic dimension of the Incarnation

Having explored some of the aspects involved in 'the taking up into unity with God ... of human nature' we can now attempt to seek out 'the cosmic dimension of the Incarnation'. In trying to talk about the cosmic dimension of the Incarnation we are really asking questions about the relationship of Christ to the whole of the universe: does the mystery of Christ have anything to say to our present understanding of the world in which we live? Does the significance of the Incarnation extend beyond the salvation of human beings and their history?

Discussions about the cosmic Christ have not been to the fore in the christological renaissance of the last thirty years, nor indeed in the Christology of the last two to three hundred years.[13] Jaroslav Pelikan is surely right when he says the main reason for this neglect is that the 'enlightenment philosophy deposed the cosmic Christ'.[14] The philosophy of enlightenment, inspired by the discovery of the scientific method in the seventeenth century gave rise to cosmologies that were inimical to Christology. The separation of faith and reason had the effect of putting Christology on the sideline of the dialogue with developments in science. Further, the

[12] J. Cobb, 'A Whiteheadian Christology', *Process Philosophy in Christian Thought*, D. Browne, R.E. James, and G. Reeves (eds), Indianapolis: Bobbs-Merrill Company, Inc., 1971, pp. 382–398; *Christ in a Pluralist Age*, Philadelphia: Westminster Press, 1975.

[13] There are some notable exceptions to this statement. The most outstanding is Teilhard de Chardin who had much to say about the cosmic Christ in his diaries and published works. See J. Lyons, *The Cosmic Christ in Origen and Teilhard de Chardin: A Comparative Study*, Oxford: Oxford University Press, 1982.

[14] J. Pelikan, *Jesus Through the Centuries: His Place in the History of Culture*, Newhaven and London: Yale University Press, 1985, p. 182.

situation was compounded by the existence of changing cosmologies. For example, the shift from a geocentric universe to the heliocentric universe of Copernicus and the move from Newtonian mechanism to Einstein's theory of relativity and quantum physics did not encourage contact between Christology and cosmology. In addition, the persistent presence during this period of a dualism between nature and grace pre-empted any kind of critical correlation between the theology of Incarnation and a 'scientific' understanding of the world. As a result there is little or no theology of the cosmic Christ in modern Christology, even though there is the presence of a cosmic Christology in the Synoptics, St Paul, St John and the Greek Fathers as we shall see presently.

In contrast to this lacuna in Christology, there is at present a new quest of the cosmic Christ in train which is comparable to the quest of the historical Jesus that took place in the 1950s and 1960s.[15] This quest of the cosmic Christ has been brought to the fore by the emergence of a new cosmic consciousness concerning the immensity and antiquity of the universe we live in. This in turn has resulted in a series of significant developments in the last decade or so which raise questions either explicitly or implicitly about the relationship of Christ to the cosmos. These developments include the emergence of creation-centred theologies,[16] the promotion of a new dialogue between science and religion,[17] the rediscovery of the importance of cosmology,[18] and the recognition of an ecological crisis.[19] What is the relationship of the

[15] The emerging literature on cosmic Christology would include the works of T. de Chardin; J.A. Lyons, *The Cosmic Christ in Origen and Teilhard de Chardin: A Comparative Study*, Oxford: Oxford University Press, 1982; J. Pelikan, 'The Cosmic Christ', *Jesus Through the Centuries*, pp. 57-70.; G. Strachan, *Christ and the Cosmos*, Dunbar, 1985; I. Bergeron and A. Ernst, *Le Christ universel et l'évolution selon T. de Chardin*, Paris. 1986.

[16] See D. Carroll, *Towards a Story of the Earth*, Dublin: Dominican Publications, 1988; G. Daly, *Creation and Redemption*, Dublin: Gill and Macmillan, 1988.

[17] H. Rolston, *Science and Religion: A Critical Survey*, Philadelphia: Temple University Press, 1987; J. Haught, *The Cosmic Adventure: Science, Religion and the Quest for Purpose*, New York: Paulist Press, 1984; R.J. Russell, W.R. Stoeger, and G.Y. Coyne (eds.), *Physics, Philosophy and Theology: A Common Quest for Understanding*, Vatican City State, 1988.

[18] S. Toulmin, *The Return to Cosmology: Post-Modern Science and the Theology of Nature*, Berkeley: University of California Press, 1982; D. Griffin (ed.), *The Re-enchantment of Science: Post-Modern Proposals*, New York: Suny Press, 1988; D. Griffin, *God and Religion in the Post-Modern World: Essays in Post-Modern Theology*, New York: Suny Press, 1989.

[19] S. McDonagh, *To Care for the Earth*, London: Chapman, 1986; T. Berry, *The Dream of the Earth*, San Francisco: Sierra Book Club, 1988.

Incarnation to creation? Can Christian faith engage in a mean-ingful dialogue with the new stirrings in science? Is the care of the earth a purely practical expedient or a Christian responsibil-ity rooted in the Incarnation?

These theological shifts have resulted in a new appreciation of the importance of cosmology. Cosmological assumptions concern-ing origins of the universe and the structure of the world as a whole do have a bearing on the way we understand theology and, in particular, on how we see the place of Christ in relation to creation. Indeed the credibility of Christology in the future will depend to a large degree on its ability to enter into a meaningful conversation with the emerging post-modern cosmologies. Of course, part of the problem here is that cosmologies have come and gone at considerable speed in the last few centuries. However this must not become an excuse for refusing the dialogue, espe-cially from a religion whose centre of gravity is the Word of God becoming flesh and entering into a new communion with human nature and with the world in which that human nature exists.

Initiating a conversation between cosmology and Christology

How then can we initiate this dialogue between cosmology and Christology with a view to rediscovering the cosmic Christ? How can we move towards some appreciation of the cosmic significance of the Incarnation? What is the relationship of the Incarnation to creation?

The first point to note here is that such a dialogue is by no means something new to Christianity, even though the dialogue may have broken down in a practical way over the last three centuries. A dialogue between Christology and cosmology did in fact take place in the early centuries of Christianity, especially through the Wisdom Christology present in the Pauline corpus and the Synoptics, the *Logos* Christology of St John, and the theol-ogy of the Greek Fathers. Indeed, it was partly the ability of Christianity, especially in the first few centuries of its existence, to enter into a meaningful dialogue with the cosmology of the day, that enabled it to move from being a religion of particularity to being a religion of universal significance. The key to this growth, through the dialogue of early Christianity with the surrounding culture, was the doctrine of the eternal Word/*Logos* of God incar-nate in Jesus of Nazareth. The Word that was made flesh historically in Jesus was understood to be the definitive revelation of the same creative Word that made heaven and earth in the Book of Genesis and that was active in the history of Israel.

Among the Greek philosophers there was the recognition of a principle of reason/order/meaning/intelligibility which was understood to pervade the universe and this recognition existed since at least the fifth century BC. In the second century AD, some would argue the first century AD, an important dialogue was initiated concerning the relationship of the incarnate *Logos* of John's Gospel and the *logos* of Greek philosophy. This dialogue, over a period of several centuries, gave rise to a clear recognition of Jesus as the personification of the Logos of Judaism and the *logos* of Greek cosmologies from Plato to middle Platonism and Stoicism. This recognition was registered formally at the Council of Nicea which defined Jesus 'of one being (*homoousios*) with God the Father' and which then went on to say that 'through the one Lord Jesus, the son of God, all things were made'. In effect, Jesus as the Word made flesh is the key to the meaning of history in Israel and the structured intelligibility of the universe in Greek philosophy.[20] Jaroslav Pelikan sums up this colourful period of dialogue between Christianity and Greek philosophy in the following way:

> For by applying this title (*Logos*) to Jesus, the Christian philosophers of the 4th and 5th centuries who were trying to give an account of who he was and what he had done were enabled to interpret him as the divine clue to the structure of reality (metaphysics) and, within metaphysics, to the riddle of being (ontology) – in a word, as the cosmic Christ.[21]

The foundation for this breakthrough was laid by the resurrection (Acts 1:10–11, Acts 2:32-36) and Wisdom (Ph 2:6–11; Rom 8:19–23; Ep 1:3–14; Col 1:15–20) christologies of the infant Church. This breakthrough that occurred in early Christianity via dialogue with the different cosmologies is an important precedent and model for the conversation that should take place today between cosmology and Christology.

Care must be taken not to set up false expectations or hopes concerning the outcome of the conversation between Christology, and cosmology. It would be theologically naïve to expect contemporary cosmologies to be able to add new light to our

---

[20] For some further details of this coming together of Greek philosophy and early Christianity see D. Lane, *The Reality of Jesus: An Essay in Christology*, Dublin: Veritas Publications, 1975, chapter 7, esp. pp. 95–100.

[21] *Jesus through the Centuries, op. cit.* p. 58.

understanding of Christology just as it would be scientifically *simpliste* to think that Christology could contribute new information to the search of cosmology for a better understanding of the universe as a whole. Pushing the origins of the universe back some fifteen billion years does not alter substantially the questions about origins that theology has to face, though it must be admitted that the larger context does provoke a new kind of awe and wonder which are essential elements in any adequate theological response to these questions. The uneasy relationship between science and religion during the period of the enlightenment has at least taught important lessons in humility to both Jerusalem and Athens. At the same time it must be said that an open conversation between cosmology and christology could have a mutually enriching effect on their respective modes of understanding and praxis. It could also enable both disciplines to retrieve what may have been lost or forgotten within respective traditions. It could also help to moderate the claims of both areas by providing more inclusive points of reference.

Further, it must be noted that the proposed dialogue between Christology and cosmology will not be achieved by making simple correlations between the past and the present. Recognition must be given to the cultural distance between early Christianity and twentieth-century cosmologies. For example, the ancient cosmologies with which early Christianity entered into dialogue are significantly different from the changing cosmologies of the twentieth century. The ancient cosmologies were by and large static, fixed and closed, whereas late twentieth-century cosmologies are dynamic, processive and open-ended.

Historians of cosmology now broadly distinguish three great eras in the history of cosmology: pre-modern, modern, and post-modern cosmologies. Pre-modern cosmologies, lasting up to the seventeenth century, were hierarchical, organic, patriarchal, static, fixed and respectful in their relationship towards nature. Modern cosmologies, from the seventeenth century to the middle of the twentieth century, have been mechanistic, materialistic, reductionist, atomistic and dominating in their relationship with nature. The third great era in cosmology, at present struggling to come to birth, is commonly called, for want of a better name, the post-modern era of cosmology.[22] The precise details of this post-modern cosmology have not yet been worked out in any

[22] Post-modern cosmologies are championed by such diverse authors as S. Toulmin, T. Berry, and D. Griffin whose works have already been mentioned in footnotes 18 and 19 above.

coherent and consistent manner. If anything, post-modern cosmologies are more aware of what they stand for in terms of their reaction to, dissatisfaction with, and unease towards the modern cosmologies. As one post-modern cosmologist puts it:

> We no longer live in the modern world. The 'modern' world is now a thing of the past ... Natural science is no longer modern science. Instead it (natural science) is rapidly becoming a post-modern science ... The world has not yet discovered how it is to define itself in terms of what it is, but only in terms of what it has ceased to be.[23]

Yet, it is possible to say that the basic qualities of this emerging post-modern cosmology are organic, processive, inclusive, non-patriarchal, holistic and radically relational.

It is this newly emerging post-modern cosmology that we propose should become a conversation partner with Christology in any attempt to rediscover the cosmic dimensions of the Incarnation. For that reason it is perhaps necessary to say something more about the shape, however tentative and provisional, of this post-modern cosmology.

A new cosmic story

One particular expression of the post-modern cosmology can be found in the writings of Tom Berry, who synthesises what is best in Teilhard de Chardin and the findings of contemporary science into what he calls a New Story.[24] According to Berry we need to remember that the vast universe as we know it through astronomy and astrophysics came into being some fifteen thousand million years ago. Some scientists talk about the origins of the universe in terms of 'the big bang theory' or 'the story of a cosmic explosion'. More significant is the suggestion that out of this extraordinary beginning, however this may be symbolised, there emerged over hundreds of millions of years the vast system of galaxies. These in turn gave rise to the earth, which in turn gave birth to the plants, animals and human life. Within this New Story a strong emphasis is placed on the fundamental unity that obtains between the galaxies, the earth, life forms and the emergence of human existence. Human existence is perceived as the earth in a particular mode of

---

[23] S. Toulmin, *The Recovery of Cosmology*, *op. cit.* p. 254.
[24] See T. Berry, 'A New Story' in *The Dream of the Earth*, 1988. This 'New Story' was originally published by T. Berry in *Teilhard Studies*, New York, Winter 1978.

self-consciousness. The human person embodies the earth in a new condition of self-awareness and freedom. As Berry points out: 'We bear the universe in our beings as the universe bears us in its being.'[25]

This arresting line of Berry's puts one in mind immediately of strikingly similar lines from Gerard Manley Hopkins:

> And what is earth's eye, tongue or heart else, where
> Else, but in dear and dogged man.[26]

What is significant about this New Story of the cosmos is the extraordinary unity that exists between the original 'fireball' and the galaxies, the solar system, the earth, and different life systems. According to the scientists we live in 'a finely tuned universe' which developed the particular way it did, in contrast to the many other possible outcomes, because it knew, as it were, that human beings were coming.[27]

A delicate balance of support and nurture exists between the universe, the earth and human existence, which at present is in danger of being seriously disrupted through ecological collapse. This balance is imaged in terms of 'a symphony of life' or 'a cosmic dance'. Within this New Story there is 'a growing awareness of the physical/psychic dimension of reality'[28], of the 'withinness' and 'withoutness' of matter, the subjectivity and objectivity of the physical world which comes to full expression in the self-consciousness of the human person.

It is within the context of this New Story of cosmology that a new dialogue with Christology might take place with a view to rediscovering the cosmic Christ. To be sure the New Story is quite incomplete and there are considerable differences when it comes to particular details. Yet there is sufficient agreement on the broad outlines of the new cosmic story to challenge and enrich Christology. According to one physicist, Brian Swimme:

> For the first time in human existence, we have a cosmic story that is not tied to one cultural tradition, or to political ideology, but instead gathers every human group into its meaning … Islamic

[25] T. Berry, *op.cit*, p. 132.

[26] G. Manley Hopkins, 'Ribblesdale', *The Major Poems*, W. Davies (ed.), London: J.M. Dent, 1979, p. 88.

[27] See D. Nicholl, 'At Home in the Universe', *The Tablet*, 23 April 1988, pp. 463-465. See also J. Barrow and F. Tipler, *The Anthropic Cosmological Principle*, Oxford: Oxford University Press, 1986.

[28] T. Berry, *The Dream of the Earth, op. cit.* p. 133.

people, Hopi people, Christian people, Marxist people and Hindu people can all agree in a basic sense on the birth of the sun, the development of the earth, the species of life, and human cultures.[29]

Dialogue from the side of Christology

When we turn to the New Testament Christology, we are struck immediately by the fact that one of the major points of reference, if not the major one, for understanding and interpreting Jesus is creation. The New Testament abounds with references to principalities and powers, heaven and earth, angels and spirits, stars and clouds, above and below – all of which are symbols of one kind or another referring to the cosmic context of the Christ-event. According to E. Schillebeeckx belief in creation is 'the all-supporting basis for the Jewish Christian *Kerygma*'.[30] One of the principal horizons of New Testament Christology is creational and as such exists in stark contrast to the horizon of christological thinking from the seventeenth century to the twentieth century, during which it might be argued that our Christology became too anthropocentric and too ecclesiological. The missing link in modern Christology has been the absence of a living cosmology. The emergence of a new cosmic story today is a challenge and an opportunity to redress this imbalance, not at the expense of a necessary anthropological and ecclesiological emphasis but to their mutual benefit.

A brief review of the titles of Jesus in New Testament Christology reveals that many of them contain a direct connection with creation as their primary point of reference. We will confine ourselves here to three of these titles: Jesus as the Wisdom of God, Jesus as Lord and Jesus as the eternal *Logos*.

Most commentators agree that one of the earliest Christologies in the New Testament is that of Wisdom Christology and that the identification of Jesus with Wisdom in the Gospels and the Pauline corpus enabled Christianity to assume cosmic significance early on.[31] The figure of Wisdom in the Hebrew and deuterocanonical

[29] B. Swimme, 'The Cosmic Creation Story', *The Reenchantment of Science: Post Modern Proposals*, D. Griffin (ed.) New York: Suny Press, 1988, p. 52.
[30] E. Schillebeeckx, *Christ*, London: SCM Press, 1980, p. 529.
[31] See the helpful and important article by E.A. Johnson, 'Jesus, the Wisdom: A Biblical Basis for Non-anthrocentric Christology', in *Ephemerides Theologicae Lovanienses*, LXI (1985) 116–135; J. Dunne, *Christology in the Making: An Enquiry into the Origins of the Doctrine of the Incarnation*, London: SCM Press, 1980, chapter 6.

scriptures is personal, female, and cosmic, having a functional equivalence with the activity of Yahweh in the self-understanding of Israel.[32] One clear reference to Jesus as the Wisdom of God is found in the First Letter of St Paul to the Corinthians:

> For the Jews demand signs and the Greeks seek wisdom, but we preach Christ crucified, a stumbling block to Jews and folly to the gentiles, but to those who are called, both Jew and gentile, Christ the power of God and the wisdom of God (1 Cor 1:22-24).

For Paul, Jesus is the Wisdom of God and this identification of Jesus with the Wisdom of God links Jesus with the cosmic role of Wisdom in the Hebrew scriptures which is one of creating, caring and ordering the world and the affairs of history. Further on in the same Letter to the Corinthians Paul attributes explicitly some of the basic cosmic qualities of Wisdom from the Hebrew scriptures to Jesus:

> For us there is one God, the Father, from whom are all things and for whom we exist, and one Lord Jesus Christ through whom we exist (1 Cor 8:6).

The second half of this verse echoes many of the attributes of Wisdom contained in the Book of Proverbs and the Book of Wisdom.

An even greater concentration on the cosmic character of Jesus as the Wisdom of God can be found in Colossians 1:15–18:

> He is the image of the invisible God, the first born of all creation; for in him all things were created, in heaven and on earth, visible and invisible, whether thrones or dominions or principalities or authorities, all things were created through him and for him. He is before all things, and in him all things hold together.

Clearly the symbols in these verses are cosmic and much of the language parallels the language of the biblical Wisdom literature. What is instructive about this early Wisdom Christology of the New Testament is the insistent reference to creation as the primary context for understanding the universal significance of the Christ-event.

Another equally important Christology derives from the confession of Jesus as Lord (Rom 10:9, Acts 2:36). This title 'Lord' is both

---

[32] E.A. Johnson, *op. cit.*, pp. 263–276.

personal and cosmic in significance. Though it derives in origin from the social realm where someone who possesses authority and power over others is called 'Lord', it very quickly takes on cosmic significance in the light of the resurrection. Jesus is declared Lord in virtue of his exaltation which raises him up above the earth, sitting at the right hand of God the Father, giving him power over the whole of creation. Thus Jesus as Lord is divine ruler over the universe, taking on a kind of cosmic lordship. This is brought out in the christological hymn of Philippians which, significantly, is structured in the cosmology of the day that sees the world according to the threefold categories of heaven, earth and under the earth:

> And being found in human form he humbled himself ... Therefore God has highly exalted him and bestowed upon him the name which is above every name, that at the name of Jesus every knee shall bow, in heaven and on earth and under the earth, and every tongue confess that Jesus Christ is Lord to the glory of God the Father
> (Phil 2:8–11).

The third example of a Christology that takes creation as its primary point of reference is the *Logos* christology. The basic expression of a *Logos* Christology is found in John's prologue, verses 1 to 16. In the Hebrew scriptures, 'the Word of God is God's utterance ... God's effective power ... God's rational energy reaching out into the world'.[33] The opening lines of John's prologue 'In the beginning was the Word ... ' are intended to recall the opening words of the Book of Genesis: 'In the beginning God created the heavens and the earth'. The context, namely that of creation in the beginning, is the setting for the rest of John's prologue. The same creative Word of God that is active in the beginning is now the same creative Word that was made flesh in Jesus. The transition from creation to the historical event of Jesus is dramatic and the link between creation and Jesus is quickly established. The christology in the prologue of John's Gospel is creational and creation is itself christological. These New Testament Christologies, situated in the context of creation, are a challenge to modern Christology to rediscover its lost cosmic moorings.

A second aspect arising out of the conversation between cosmology and Christology is the need to widen the terms of reference in the dialogue. Christological references to creation, in both the

---

[33] J. Dunne, *Christology in the Making*, p. 248.

New Testament and subsequent theology, will have to begin to include not only the earth inhabited by human beings but also the whole of the universe. Given the indisputable linkage between human existence, the earth and the universe coming from the new cosmic story and the impossibility of understanding one without the other, it becomes necessary, for example, that discussions about the meaning of the Incarnation be seen to embrace not only the significance of the Incarnation for human existence but also for our understanding of the earth and the universe. Can we not say that the eternal Wisdom/*Logos* of God that became personally incarnate in Jesus, is the same divine Wisdom and *Logos* that is present nurturing and ordering life on the earth (see Gen 1, Pr 3:19; 8:22–31; Ws 7:22–8:1) and, equally, the same eternal Wisdom/*Logos* that nurtured, ordered and continues to hold together the cosmic process that began some fifteen billion years ago? Within this scheme of things we can begin to see a profound unity between the general involvement of God in the universe-earth-human process and the particular involvement of God in creation and Incarnation. The Incarnation of Wisdom/Logos in Jesus is the coming into full glow of a cosmic process of divine self-communication set in motion millions upon millions of years ago. The Incarnation, therefore, is not some isolated divine intrusion that took place at one moment two thousand years ago but is rather the culmination and crystallisation of a divine cosmic process initiated at the dawn of time. The Incarnation was 'first' in God's intention – but not in time. Thus it becomes possible to say that from the beginning God was present in the universe-earth-human process and that the universe-earth-human process was present in God without however identifying God with the cosmos or the cosmos with God in a pantheistic way. Instead, we can adopt what some call a pan-en-theistic vision of God's presence in the organic reality of the universe, earth and human existence. This pan-en-theistic vision of God's presence in the world would seem to be implicit in a cosmic understanding of the Incarnation. A fundamental unity exists between the whole of creation and Incarnation; the Mystery of Christ can be seen as a microcosm of what is taking place in the macrocosm of creation. A modern version of this can be found in Brian Swimme who suggests that, 'The human face is there in the structure of a fireball.'[34] The symbolic face present

---

[34] B. Swimme, 'Science: A Partner in Creating the Vision', *T. Berry and the New Cosmology*, A. Lonergan and C. Richards (eds.), Connecticut: Twenty-Third Publications, 1987, p. 88.

genetically as it were at the dawn of creation is the presence of divine Wisdom and the eternal *Logos*, that is the cosmic Christ, within the evolutionary process.

A third and final dimension emerging in the dialogue between cosmology and Christology concerns the presence of the cosmic Christ in the world today. So far we have been looking backwards from the Incarnation to creation. It is also possible, indeed necessary, to look forward from the Incarnation to the presence of Christ in the universe today. Taking the perception of the person coming from the New Story as the earth in a state of self-consciousness, could we not say that when the eternal *Logos* of God personally adopted human nature in Jesus, the *Logos* of God also adopted the earth and the universe in so far as these are actually embodied in the man Jesus. This would mean, in effect, that the *Logos* of God was and is personally present in the earth and in the universe. In the light of the Incarnation, therefore, the earth and the universe today assume special divine significance, analogous to the divine dignity of the person, deserving similar respect and reverence. There is something 'sacred', indeed sacramental, about the earth and the universe and their mutual processes in virtue of the Incarnation. Through the Incarnation God has taken 'matter' unto God's self. It is this awesome and sacramental quality of the earth and the universe at large that was lost since the time of the Enlightenment due to the absence of a living cosmology. The new dialogue between cosmology and Christology should be able to restore a numinous, even a mystical quality to the whole of the living world as we know it today: human existence, the earth and the universe. David Tracy is surely pointing us in the right direction when he suggests that what is needed in theology today in the growing situation of a global pluralism is a rediscovery of the place of nature in history, a relocation of redemption in the context of creation and a recovery of the meaning of 'God' and 'self' in relation to the cosmos.[35]

A number of important theological consequences begin to flow from this initial conversation between cosmology and Christology. These can only be mentioned in summary form here.

1. If we can begin to see the Wisdom and *Logos* of God that became incarnate in Jesus as something that was and is contin-

[35] D. Tracy, 'Practical Theology in the Situation of Global Pluralism', *Formation and Reflection: The Promise of Practical Theology*, L.S. Mudge and J.N. Poling (eds.), Philadelphia: Fortress Press, 1987, pp. 146–152.

ually co-present in different degrees in the entire cosmic process, then the universe begins to appear a little more benign and friendly as a place to live in. In modern times, due to the demise of a living cosmology, the outer reaches of the universe appeared to many as cold, indifferent and even hostile. A dialogue between cosmology and Christology which makes room for the involvement of the cosmic Christ from the beginning of time could reduce to some extent that sense of cosmic isolation and loneliness which arises from seeing the universe simply as a place without a purpose.

2. If, as a result of our conversation between cosmology and Christology, we can begin to see the earth not as a machine but as a living organism which must be respected and revered, especially in virtue of the Incarnation, then there is some hope for the ecological movement. A rediscovery of the sacramental character of creation is a first step in the development of an appropriate theology of ecology. Humanity must not understand itself as existing objectively over and against the earth but rather as an integral part of the earth. This relocation of human identity within and not aloof from the living world of nature is an important step towards the preservation of the earth for the future. If a new alliance between humanity and the sacramentality of the earth can be established, then a new relationship between history and nature will begin to emerge. History and the so-called progress of history is not the right framework for cultivating the earth; instead the earth is an important part of a new framework for developing the history of humanity.[36]

3. If a cosmic Christology helps us to rediscover the 'sacred' and therefore the sacramental character of the earth, then we have a richer context for a theology of the individual sacraments. Our disconnectedness from the earth, caused to a large degree by modern cosmologies, is partly responsible for the blunting of our appreciation of the sacramental system. If, according to modern cosmologies, the world of matter is lifeless, then it becomes difficult to see how the matter of water and oil, bread and wine can become living symbols of God's saving and sacramental presence in Christ.

4. If our dialogue between cosmology and Christology brings us back to cosmic origins, giving us a new sense of the unity of the

[36] J. Moltmann, *God in Creation: A New Theology of Creation and the Spirit of God*, London: SCM Press, 1985, p. 56.

universe, the earth and human existence, then it also propels us into the future towards conclusions. There is a growing awareness that origins and endings, though distinct, are nonetheless closely related. Equally there is an increasing awareness that the destiny of the individual is bound up with the destiny of the universe. More and more it is becoming clear that individual eschatology must be complemented by a cosmic eschatology. The conversation between cosmology and Christology which points towards the cosmic Christ also points us in the direction of a cosmic eschatology.

To sum up, the Incarnation stands at the centre between creation and the consummation of creation in the eschaton. There is a fundamental unity between creation, Incarnation, and consummation. The ultimate 'centripetal force' of that unity is the crucified and risen Christ who is the Incarnation of the creative Wisdom/*Logos* of God holding all things together – past, present and to come. It is hardly surprising that it was a cosmologist, A.N. Whitehead, who with his keen sense of the presence of God pervading the cosmic processes, could write, 'The world lives by its incarnation of God in itself.'[37]

Another way of capturing much of what we have been stammering to say concerning the human and cosmic dimensions of the Incarnation is given to us in the words of Elizabeth Barrett Browning:

> Earth's crammed with heaven,
> And every common bush afire with God:
> But only he who sees
> Takes off his shoes.[38]

The final word, however, must be reserved for T.S. Eliot who captures and encapsulates the spirit of our reflections.

> These are only hints and guesses.
> Hints followed by guesses; and the rest
> Is prayer, observance, discipline, thought and action.
> The hint half guessed, the gift half understood, is Incarnation.[39]

---

[37] A.N. Whitehead, *Religion in the Making*, New York, 1926, p. 151.
[38] 'Auror Leigh', *Poetical Works of Elizabeth Barrett Browning*, New York: 1897, p. 466.
[39] T.S. Eliot, 'The Dry Salvages', *Four Quartets*.

Chapter 12

Jesus, Saviour and Son of God

Monika Hellwig

Probably the most fundamental belief of Christians about Jesus of Nazareth is that he has come to the rescue in a hopeless situation. Christian faith begins with the experience that Jesus makes a difference. He makes the decisive difference in what we are able to hope for the world at large and for each of us in particular, both in the course of our lives and beyond death. He also makes the decisive difference in what we are able to be collectively as human community and individually as human persons.

Christian tradition gives us a rather stylized picture of who Jesus is and how and why he makes such a difference. For most of us the experience of Jesus as Saviour and Son of God (Christ and Lord) is first an experience of the Church that gives testimony of him, then a quest for the elusive 'real' Jesus, and finally an engagement with 'the Christ of faith'. This process is a little like a journey through the Gospels of the New Testament. First the Gospels present us with an interpretive account of Jesus full of allusions to the Hebrew Scriptures and to Jewish expectations. Then they confront us with the brutal fact of his death by crucifixion in a Roman execution carefully documented as to time, place, circumstance and agents. Finally they call on our faith and allegiance with the resurrection accounts.

The original Christian experience, of course, was not in that sequence. Sometimes the meaning of the Christian proclamation of Jesus as Christ and Lord really does not mean very much to people in later centuries until there is an opportunity to share in imagination the original experiences and responses out of which the official proclamations about Jesus grew. The original experience began with groups of apparently very ordinary people who became attracted in various ways and for various reasons to a wandering preacher who spoke wherever he could find people and call them together in towns, villages or the countryside. The thrust of his message seems to have been to recall them to the hope that their religious traditions in Israel gave them and to recall them to fidelity to trust and confidence in God. He spoke in ordinary language and conveyed the sense of God's presence and caring by his own human presence and caring for others and by his own human way of living his life, establishing values and priorities, praying and relating to others. He had a rousing, vivifying impact on the downtrodden poor of Roman Palestine whom he had found as listless and hopeless as the dry bones lying around on the plain in Ezekiel's vision (Ezek 37). In him – in what he was, in the way he lived and in what he said and did for them – people tended to find new life, hope, challenge, purpose in life, and healing.

For these people Jesus was so closely identified with his message that we have no record of how he looked, dressed, walked, how tall he was and so on. Of his personal habits and mannerisms, his likes and dislikes, we know only what pertains immediately to his message. From the scant evidence we have, it seems that Jesus identified himself wholeheartedly, passionately with his message, with the task that 'the Father' had given him. For us western Christians of the twentieth century there is a certain cultural gap between ourselves and Jesus of Nazareth, a first-century Jew in the land of Israel where everything had religious meaning, where the language of everyday business, farming and craft was resonant with God's revelations, where every city, village, mountain, rock and stream carried memories and promises of God's saving power, and where the daily burden of Roman domination, brutality and contempt offered a constant reminder of the great need that people had of those memories, those promises, that saving power. There is a cultural gap between our situation and that of Jesus which makes it difficult for us to catch the full impact of his preaching as his first listeners were able to catch it.

The message of Jesus had to do first of all with the powerful and compassionate fidelity of God. Living among people who were harshly oppressed, bewildered and discouraged, Jesus became for many of them the joyful discovery that God never forgets or abandons his creatures, that God is infinitely compassionate and powerful to implement his compassion in ways beyond human ingenuity and understanding. The evangelists present this message variously as the good news of the coming of God's reign or kingdom, the intimate revelation of God as self-giving Father, the uncovering of the continuing and personal providence of the Creator, and so forth. What seems to be common under these various themes is the person of Jesus himself. If Jesus preaches that 'the hour of salvation' has arrived, it is because he offers himself as the turning point in human history. He offers himself, not only his words, to the people as the definitive compassion of God. He offers himself as the saving power of God which is so different from anything that we usually think of as power.

The Gospels tell us of this in the way they describe the public ministry and preaching of Jesus. They tell of his utterly generous availability to the people, particularly to their spiritual needs – their need for inspiration, hope, encouragement, guidance, challenge, correction, appreciation and attention and warm friendship – but also to their physical needs for healing and sustenance. They tell us of the circumstances, manner and content of his preaching. He preached in the open air, by the lake, on the hillsides, informally, to the ordinary poor peasant people who seem to have been despised both by the Romans and by the Jewish leadership of the time. He preached whenever people were gathered and he had the opportunity. We know that the content and manner of his preaching were very simple, appealing to the unlearned, appealing to their experience of nature and of everyday life and work. The manner and content of his preaching invited the people to become aware of God's presence and power and loving care everywhere in all things and at all times.

If the message of Jesus had to do first of all with the powerful and compassionate fidelity of God, it had to do secondly but just as essentially with the human response in which the compassionate power of God could become fruitful for the redemption of the people from the bitterness and despair of needless suffering caused by the prevailing conditions of sin. There was a transforming consolation in the preaching and presence of Jesus precisely because there was a far-reaching exigence in it. It expressed the exigence of the all-holy God on creatures whose very existence only makes sense and yields happiness and fulfillment if they direct all that they are and do and have in service, praise and gratitude to that God. This was the message of Jesus that was expressed in his person and in his life and activity. All that he said in his preaching was simply formulated in words to help others understand the simple truth of his own experience.

No doubt it was this directness and spontaneity and this self-validating quality in the preaching of Jesus that made people aware that the spirit of God was being breathed forth among them again, and that made them say of him that he taught with power. No doubt it was this also that made him a figure of contradiction. The challenge in his person called for an unconditional self-surrender. Those who would not respond to that challenge by a radical turning around of their lives, a fundamental change of consciousness and goals, could only grow to fear and hate him. Especially those whose unjust privileges and worldly pretensions were most obviously and publicly threatened could only cast about in their minds and seek counsel how to silence him effectively. Because of the way we understand power in our sinful history, the way to silence a prophet always seems to be simply to kill him. But because our sinful understanding of power is quite incorrect, this never works out as it is expected to do. The blood of martyrs is always a loud and clear witness for their cause.

Looking back after the events, the followers of Jesus began to see the difference he made, his self-definition and who and what the was in relation to God and in relation to themselves, mainly in terms of his death. They looked at the interplay of forces that brought him to his death and saw that he himself had gone to it willingly, discerning it as ultimately the only uncompromising response and self-gift to the Father and to the people, given the intractable complexity of the sinful situation and the hold that fear had over those involved. In the indescribable experience that they had of his risen presence among them and of the new life burgeoning forth in their community, everything fitted together and they began to see him at the centre of history and at the heart of the mystery of God's presence in the human community. They saw him as Redeemer or Saviour of the whole human situation. In his own existence Lucifer's 'I will not serve' had been completely and definitively reversed in that stance of total service, the ultimate self-gift in which, paradoxically, the true image of God is dazzlingly realized and revealed (Phil 2:6–11). But the fact that Jesus brought about this reversal of the human tragedy in his own life and person has definitively changed the human situation for the rest of us, because he has conquered the old enemy, fear (Heb 2:10–18), and because he has made a new beginning for us (1 Cor 15:45–49).

It is probably the train of thought just presented here that led the early Christian communities to add introductions to three of the Gospels which were not part of the original compositions. A quick comparison of the four Gospels of the New Testament (also known as the canonical Gospels to distinguish them from other gospels circulating in the early Church which did not become official) will show an important difference. The Gospel according to

Mark begins with the public preaching ministry of Jesus that led eventually to his arrest, trial and execution and culminated in his resurrection and the challenge to the disciples to carry on his work. The Gospels according to Matthew and Luke have the same pattern, but each is prefaced by an introductory section consisting of the first two chapters. These are known today as the 'Infancy Narratives.' At first they seem simply to give some family details about the origins, birth and childhood of Jesus. More careful study by scripture scholars has shown that they give rather a kind of theological statement of who Jesus is – a kind of theological statement that is quite different in style and method from the way we would do it today.

The Infancy Narratives tell us who Jesus is by way of story. It is a story that links him to creation and to human history, both the history of sin and the history of God's promises of redemption. The genealogies (Matt 1:1–17 and Luke 3:23–38) seem at first very dull reading, but when one fills in the stories behind the names one finds that the genealogies have much to say about who Jesus is. All these figures stand in line of God's promises of redemption and are part of the process of tradition of the revelation, the hope and the response. Jesus comes as the fulfillment of it all, and this is expressed even by the symmetry of the arrangement in generations (which is artificial). A further important part of the statement made by the genealogies emerges from the fact that not all the persons mentioned in them are wholly admirable people or wholly in the orthodox line of descent. Jesus is presented as the fulfillment but not as the predictable or merited outcome of this history. Jesus is the gift of God that is beyond the merits of the ancestors; he is the gift of God who is not bound by the limits and rules of the law because his very nature is to show compassion where it is neither earned nor imagined.

An important component of what the earliest community wanted to say about Jesus in these Infancy Narratives has to do with the stylized figures of Zechariah and Elizabeth, Anna and Simeon, Mary and Joseph. We never really find out what kinds of people they are. They are in the story to tell us how Jesus fits into Israel's history and expectations. Zechariah appears in the Gospel of Luke as a priest of Israel in the course of his temple ministry to receive the message that John the Baptist is to be the preacher of the great authentic movement of repentance in Israel that is to prepare the Lord's way. Elizabeth is shown as elderly and barren, reminiscent of Sarah the wife of Abraham. Story is laid upon story here. The child, John, is not born in the ordinary course of Israel's history but as the special grace of God beyond the expectations or deserts of that history, and this child is the one who is shown later in the Gospels (Matt 3:11–17; Luke 3:15–18) as the one who sums up Hebrew piety pointing to Jesus as the coming one sent by God.

In a splendid tableau (Luke 1:39–56) the third Gospel juxtaposes the two highly stylized figures of Elizabeth and Mary, both pregnant with the hope and expectation of a people in the sight of God – the hope of Israel typified by Elizabeth bearing John, the one who summons to repentance and points to Jesus, and the hope of the Christian Church typified by Mary bearing Jesus, to bring him forth as Saviour in vindication of the oppressed and lowly, the poor who trust in the power of God alone.

This is followed by the scenes presenting Joseph as the typical 'just man' of Israel – Joseph whose dreams and whose Egyptian flight and exile are reminiscent of the story of Joseph the son of Jacob in the Hebrew stories of the patriarchs. The new Joseph of the Gospels is confronted with the pregnant Mary who represents the Church claiming to bring Jesus, Saviour-Messiah, into the world. Joseph (just Israel) must face the problem that Mary's child, as Messiah-Saviour, hope of Israel and fulfillment of the promises, is a paradox and a sign of contradiction. Israel has clearly not 'fathered' him, endorsed him, authenticated his messiahship. He is a Messiah-Saviour illegitimately conceived. He poses a severe problem to just Israel, to the faithful who look to God for their salvation and the fulfillment of all their hopes. In response to Joseph's anguish, Mary the Church is silent because there is nothing that she can say except to bring forth Jesus into the world as Christ, showing him as he really is, the Saviour 'anointed' by God, coming to Israel and the world as the wonderful gift of God beyond the merits of the ancestors and preparation of the ages and the discernment of the leaders of Israel.

What the angel, the heavenly messenger or divine revelation, shows Joseph in the story is that Jesus does not need to be endorsed or authenticated ('fathered') as Messiah-Christ-Saviour by Israel or its leaders. His credentials are established in heaven. The transcendent God himself has silently and mightily fathered him. His features are the living image of the invisible God. His voice is the sounding forth of the silence of God. His self-gift is recognizable as the creativity of God, and the weakness of his death becomes self-validating as the saving power of God's compassion.

Clearly, the stories themselves, as given in the Gospels of Matthew and Luke in the opening chapters, remain resolutely stories and do not launch forth into explanations such as the above. But for readers who know how to relish and meditate stories, and who are familiar with the stories of the Hebrew scriptures, these particular simple stories and tableaux open vistas of association, analogy, application and reflection, and through the centuries Christian piety has indeed used and meditated the stories in this way. What is said here about the birth and the encounters that preceded the birth gives a language and a frame of reference in which to discuss what Jesus the crucified, the risen Christ, the Lord of history and coming One means to his believers and followers. When the liturgy in the cycle of the year uses these texts, it trains our eyes to look to the future to see God and be able to interpret our position and task in the present in relation to God. It does this on the old Hebrew principle of meditating on the wonderful works of God in the past in symbolism and categories which make it easier for us to understand and appropriate God's revelation to us, so that we can begin to see the focus of God's promises in the future and discern God's action in our present.

The Christmas story itself carries much more interpretation and theological reflection than our modern eyes readily discern. It is set within a situation of bitter oppression of the poor of the world by the context that is sketched in of the taxation, the unseasonable and compulsory journey, and the lack of accommodation and provision for the poor and powerless people thus herded about the country. We are told that it is from these powerless and oppressed people that Jesus springs and that it is in these circumstances of powerless human frustration that he emerges in the world and into our history. The evangelists (Matt 2:1–12; Luke 2:1–20) then juxtapose for us the derelict and outcast circumstances of the birth with the proclamation of it by star and angel song. They contrast the quest for Jesus by the wise from afar who come to do him honour with the quest for Jesus by the power that concretely and politically holds sway over his life and that seeks to crush and discredit him. They set the unconcern of the world for the momentous event side by side with the homage and recognition of the shepherds, the poorest of the poor in that culture, who alone were able to hear and understand the angelic announcement. They show Jesus as the great paradox of human history – the healing power of God foreordained as the centre of history and its turning point, anonymous and despised if not hated. They also portray him as the Son of God in power but truly human in utter weakness.

All of this is a reflection on the identity and meaning of Jesus as it has emerged for the early community not only in his birth and childhood but also in the totality of his adult life, his death, his resurrection and his impact on his followers and on the world. All of this therefore leads naturally enough to the scenes that reflect on the relation of Jesus to the history of Israel, to its temple worship (the presentation scene) and to its wisdom and teaching (the scene of the finding in the temple). It is also summed up, so to speak, in the tableau that shows us Jesus emerging from ordinariness to assume his redemptive task in the accounts of the baptism by John in the Jordan.

In the Infancy Narratives of the Gospels according to Matthew and Luke, Jesus is shown to us as human in his vulnerability, his Jewish inheritance, his poverty and his humble place in society. He is also shown surrounded by an aura of divinity. Clearly, the Christian community quite early had to come to terms with what they meant when they gave Jesus titles of divinity, when they prayed to him, and when they put their whole and unconditional faith in him in a way that is really only appropriate to God. The introduction to the Gospel according to John, usually known as the Prologue, which may have been an ancient Christian hymn, reflects a further step in the question and answer about the identity of Jesus.

John 1:1–5, 9–14 and 16—18 begins by identifying Jesus with the Word of God that was with God from the beginning and through which all creatures received their being and life and light. This is an allusion to a theme of the Hebrew scriptures. In Genesis 1 creation is by the saying, the speech or utterance, that is, the Word of God. But this Word of God is not really a separate being but *is* God speaking. What the Prologue seems to say, then, is that the man Jesus whom the first Christians had known, seen, touched and heard came to be recognized by them as the Word or utterance of God. He is the very speaking of God in the world, the same speaking by which God has given being and life and light to creatures from the beginning. In him that Word that God is speaking has become a vulnerable, palpable human being so that God is no longer dark, silent, transcendent and terrible, but is known through Jesus as a light shining quietly in the world making God's presence known in graciousness and fidelity. Jesus is recognized as the image or reflection that gives the invisible God a face in the world. He is recognized as the Son who uniquely embodies the nature and being of the heavenly Father.

This identification of Jesus as the Word of God that was being spoken from the beginning links him with other texts of the Hebrew scriptures, such as those which personify Wisdom and speak of it (her) as being with God from the beginning, even before the creation (for instance, Prov 8:22-31). Such expressions in Hebrew thought suggest a polarity in God, a certain diversity and possibility of relationship, of action and of interaction even while Jews always stoutly maintained that God was absolutely and unambiguously One. When the Johannine Prologue makes this connection between Jesus and personified Wisdom, it casts an aura of mystery and of divinity over the person of Jesus. It also suggests that as the Word of God Jesus existed before his earthly, human life, and indeed beyond the boundaries of time 'before the beginning of the world'.

Obviously, Christians could not leave this assertion in the realm of the poetic, in the language of hints and suggestive comparisons and allusions. Very soon in the Greek thought-world of the early Church questions came pounding on the Christian consciousness and understanding about the meaning of these allusions. They were questions that were hard to answer. Some have thought both then and ever since that they were questions best left unasked because there has always been a tension between the language of faith and the language of philosophy. This tension in language reflects accurately the tension between assent to something as true because it has been revealed to us in our experience and assent to something as true because it can be logically, rationally proven.

St Thomas Aquinas in the thirteenth century was still wrestling with that tension, as are theologians today. Aquinas was aware, and makes his readers aware, that the struggle to understand one's faith is not easily separable from philosophy but must be conducted with a proper humility. This humility consists in the first place of realizing that the truth about God and about God's dealings with us is much greater than anything we can ever hope to understand. Therefore, while there are some steps toward knowing about God which we can take on the basis of our own reasoning from observation of nature and history they could certainly never carry us very far. But we have in fact been offered (by revelation) further knowledge of two kinds – knowledge that we might have attained by reason if our reason were not distorted by sin, and knowledge we could never have attained by reason but which offers a sure foundation for faith and understanding because it is given to us by God who shares his own wisdom and thereby offers us 'first principle' or foundations on which to build a coherent and systematic human understanding.

This, of course, makes good sense to anyone in proportion to that person's faith. Without faith it sounds evasive, obscurantist and even magical in its appeal. It is largely for this reason that it is always easy to ridicule and 'disprove' what Christians have believed about the meaning and identity of Jesus. There is no escaping the fact that the heart of Christian faith is in a paradox, an apparent contradiction that enshrines precious elements of Christian experience. These elements of Christian experience will not be surrendered in response to logical analysis or philosophical argument. In a sane person or a sane community deeply rooted personal experience does not yield to academic arguments that try to undermine it. But the possibility remains of exploring the truth that is received in experience in intellectual efforts to gain a deeper understanding or to integrate the apprehension of that truth in the wider sweep of one's total understanding of reality.

From early times Christians have attempted to do just this. In the earliest centuries they were very tolerant of alternate approaches used side by side. Attention focused on dealing with particular proposals that seemed to endanger Christian life and faith. St Ignatius of Antioch in the early second century was concerned with a tendency that still affects us today – the tendency to see everything about Jesus as very ethereal and remote and not happening to a real man. In the letters he wrote on his way to Rome to be martyred, and especially in his letter to the local Church at Ephesus, he addresses Christians, none of whom are old enough to have known Jesus in the flesh, and insists on the solid humanity of Jesus, a man of flesh, born of Mary, subject to suffering, and one who died. It is this flesh and blood, tangible, feeling, suffering, dying man who comes to us as a 'loud scream out of the silence of God', and (in more conventional language used in the letter to the Magnesians) it is this flesh and blood man in all things pleasing to God by whom he was sent, who is the Son of the Father and the Word that goes forth from silence, in whom the Father is shown forth as a saving God.

The great Church Father, Irenaeus of Lyon, by the end of the second century was dealing with the problem of Gnosticism. This was the heresy that saw such total and irreconcilable disunity between body and spirit, between the tangible world of our corporeal, historical and social experience and the inner world of our consciousness. Clearly, the Incarnation of the divine Word in the historical man Jesus could make no sense in a Gnostic context. Irenaeus, of course, insists on the Incarnation, that is, the realization of the divine Word in history in the flesh and blood man, Jesus, but he goes further than that. He introduces what is known as the 'recapitulation' theme, which happens to be particularly helpful to us in our times that are so attuned to psychology and the perceptions of the social sciences.

Irenaeus recalls that by sin, that is, by disobedience or turning away from God, human persons have lost their likeness to God, and thereby the unity of the human race and indeed of the whole creation is disrupted. The despair and sense of meaninglessness that underlie Gnosticism are precisely the reflection of this disruption or disintegration in which matter and spirit seem to go in contrary directions and the historical, social project of the human race is nothing but vexation doomed to ultimate frustration. In this context of a sinful history, Irenaeus points to Jesus as the new head (the recapitulation) of the human community and the human project. He re-establishes God's image and likeness and he reintegrates all dimensions of creation, physical and spiritual, in his person in such depth and totality that he is able to draw other persons into his own unity, undoing the destruction of original sin.

But all this for Irenaeus is clearly by divine initiative, because the human race and the human project were too irrevocably lost to be salvaged by the freedom given to the human person in creation. The Word of God has become a man to accomplish the restoration by descending all the way into the sinful human situation even to death. In Jesus, the Word of God becomes what we are so as to make us what he is. He does this by being among us and instructing us. But the sublime revelation of God is realized precisely in the palpable bodily life and death of Jesus. It is only by living according to the law and example of Jesus that one comes to experience the unity which is the true answer to Gnosticism.

After Irenaeus, later reflection on Jesus as both human and divine tends to focus on much more specialized and culturally limited questions. There tended to be an interest in *how* the unity of divine and human could have come about, which is not so helpful to Christians in their own efforts to live as followers of Jesus. Attention began to focus not only on the question as to how the man Jesus can be identified with the Word of God (the *Logos*, in Greek) but also on the question as to how the *Logos* or Word is related to the Father. One favorite answer to this latter question was that given by Tertullian, a North African who wrote in Latin at the beginning of the third Christian century. The Word, or eternal divine Son, is related to the Father as the ray of sunlight is related to the sun. This image was repeated and extended – the Son is to the Father as the shining is to the light, as the outreach is to the source, in other words. It is an image that still appears in the Creed of Nicea and Constantinople which is recited at the Sunday Eucharist in Catholic Churches. It is a good image. It implies unity as well as distinctness. It also implies that there never was a 'before' when the Word was not.

Tertullian had apparently accepted the formulation that the Son of God became man, so he had to explain how this could be without his ceasing to be divine. He answered that this becoming involved a double manner of being in which the two 'substances' of the divine and the human remain intact because they are not 'poured together' or blended into one third substance but are joined so that Jesus does things that are proper to divinity such as miracles and signs and suffers things proper to being human like hunger and thirst and weeping and death. But all is done by one person, one single subject. It is perhaps unfortunate for later generations who depended rather heavily on Tertullian's vocabulary and formula that he assigns such a purely passive role to the human, rather than a cooperative role in which human freedom and creative initiative come into play. It seems to lead Tertullian himself to see the whole mystery of the Incarnation as a matter of bringing into existence a Jesus who can be made to suffer and die. Even our contemporary piety is sometimes liable to take this one-sided and rather negative view.

Clement of Alexandria, on the other hand, who wrote about the same time in Greek, is convinced that the Incarnation is the expression of the overwhelming love of God who wanted to communicate himself in human form so as to gather human persons to himself in greater intimacy by teaching them that intimacy. Clement's disciple, Origen, developed these ideas in ways that were to cause difficult debates in the Church for two centuries after his death. His thought is subtle. In trying to understand what can be humanly understood of the mystery of God, Origen emphasized the spiritual, conscious, free character of the union of the Son with the Father who expresses himself in the Son or Word and that same spiritual, conscious, free character of the union of the human Jesus with the Word. Origen and his school were later accused both of making Jesus somewhat less than human, somewhat too ethereal, and of making the Word somewhat less than divine. His concern, however, was to show Jesus as a model of union with God for other human persons. In response to problems that some saw in the way this thought was developed, the fourth-century writers of the school of Antioch tried to reaffirm the fully human, historical Jesus within the teaching on the union of human and divine.

The writings of these Church Fathers of the first four centuries are full of inspiration for contemporary Christians in the following of Jesus and in prayer to Jesus, but they can also be quite confusing or misleading to contemporary Christians because they wrote in an era in which the Church had not yet agreed on a clear vocabulary or a normative set of analogies or conceptual patterns in which to speak or write about Christology. Consequently, they seem sometimes to contradict one another or even themselves and they can sometimes be badly misunderstood by the modern reader. Beginning in the year 325 at the Council of Nicea, the assembled representatives of the local Churches scattered through the ancient world took up some of the questions that were troubling the faithful at that time. From a believer's point of view, this council and those which followed to the mid-fifth century were a triumph of the Spirit and the grace of God in the Church. The moving human force behind their assembling was in fact the imperial interest of Constantine and his followers, and there is plenty of evidence that they had not assimilated the teaching of the Christian Gospel in any great depth but did find the Churches and their leaders a useful tool for government and administration. The teachings of these councils are not inspirational in themselves, and one could not really get an adequate picture or account of Jesus Christ from them. What they do is only to set certain ground rules or to give a frame of reference for discussion of Christology.

The Council of Nicea gave us the formulation we still have (as streamlined at Constantinople) in our Sunday Eucharist creed: we believe 'in one Lord Jesus Christ, the Son of God, only begotten, born from the Father, that is, from the substance of the Father, God from God, light from light, true God from true God, begotten not made, of one nature with the Father, through whom were made all things in heaven and earth, who for us men and our salvation came down, was incarnate and made man and suffered, and rose again on the third day'. The Council Fathers of that time were concerned about the teaching of a priest of Alexandria, Arius, and his followers who seemed to be denying the divinity of Jesus, saying there was a time when he was not, that is, before he was brought forth he was not, that he came into existence out of nothing, was different in nature from the Father, being a creature and subject to change.

Quite probably Arius was misunderstood. Much of the contemporary conflict and tension in which learned and holy theologians are being accused of heresy moves in similar patterns over familiar ground. Usually the theologian is trying to make the traditional faith and teaching meaningful and spiritually relevant to the contemporary Christian struggling to live coherently as a believer and a follower of Christ. Usually the censors who call the theologian to task are mainly concerned that the ancient formulae of words remain intact and in place. Sometimes non-theologians become quite distressed and scandalized when precisely those writers who most inspire the laity with new understanding and new motivation for discipleship and service of Jesus Christ are those constantly censored, while the theology that seems to be regarded officially as safe appears to be quite unrelated to the living of a Christian life. History is helpful. It shows that some of this tension is inevitable and even healthy. However, what is probably most helpful of all is to remember that we are in the realm of mystery where there are no formulae entirely safe from misunderstanding because there are no words and expressions that are strictly appropriate. We are always in the realm of poetic imagery.

In the decades after the Council of Nicea people seem to have felt very strongly that all their real inspiration was being ruthlessly swept away, and the following of Arius seems rather to have increased in protest than diminished in acceptance of the council. The great bishop of Alexandria, St Athanasius, seems to have contributed significantly to the solution of this by reintroducing the very inspirational thought of Irenaeus of the second century. However, another kind of problem arose (one which also still plagues us today). A bishop by the name of Apollinaris tried to resolve the paradox of the Christian belief about Jesus by making him not quite human. It seemed to him that Jesus was simply the Word animating a human body. There is a danger of this sometimes in contemporary piety among people who think of themselves as conservative and strictly orthodox. They find it repugnant to think of Jesus as having to find things out by trial and error, having to struggle to come to a decision; the thinking and deciding seem to be divine activities, and only physical movements and physical suffering seem to be properly human. What is so bad about this is that it seems to imply that the only way that the followers of Jesus can imitate him is in passivity, not in shouldering responsibility for what goes on in the world. Apollinaris in teaching this, however, certainly did not mean to turn people away from the imitation of Jesus. He wanted to assure them that they were really saved because it was really the Word of God that had come among them and died for them. The Council of Constantinople in 381, nevertheless, ruled out this position.

The issues from previous centuries returned in the fifth century. A bishop named Nestorius had taught that the faithful should not refer to Mary as the Mother of God, but only as the mother of Jesus

Christ, the man. There was a new round of efforts at a precision that was not then and will not ever be possible, but under the rubric 'Mary is the Mother of God' the Council of Ephesus in 431 reasserted that we are speaking of one single subject, one single person, Jesus, the man, the divine Word. To relate to him is to enjoy a human relationship with him who is human, born of Mary, and it is also to be in immediate relationship with God present and acting in our world. Therefore, it is not inappropriate to say of Jesus Christ what may be said of the divine: we are to pay honour to Jesus Christ and place our faith in him in an unconditional way that is appropriate to the divine. Modern Christians may feel a certain impatience with the endless quibbling over words and the use of words, but the issue behind them is important. It is the issue of our way of seeking and finding salvation.

This was not the end of the matter yet. Oddly enough, the persistent temptation for Christians through the centuries seems to have been to resolve the essential paradox not by denying that Jesus could be divine but by denying that he was truly human. Under the name of Eutyches and of the so-called Monophysite (one-nature) heresy, it was proposed to think and speak of Jesus as a man who had been so absorbed into the divine that although one might speak of both the divine and the human before, after the union the human is quite swallowed up and ceases to have any significance. The Council of Chalcedon in 451, to which reference is so frequently made in our times in questions of orthodoxy in Christology, gave a resounding answer to this. Reaffirming earlier teaching of the previous councils, a letter of St Cyril of Alexandria which had been written to Nestorius, and a letter of Leo the Great of Rome which had been written just two years before to Flavian of Constantinople, this council confesses that Jesus is perfect (complete) in divinity and perfect in humanity (that is, fully divine and fully human), truly God and truly man with a human soul and body, one in nature with the Father according to the divinity and one in nature with us according to the humanity, indeed like us in all but sin, eternally begotten of the Father and born in the time of Mary, one therefore in two natures (or modes of being) and not divided into two persons nor losing the properties of the two modes of being.

Again, much of this vocabulary, even when it has been summarized, translated, and expressed in as contemporary a manner as possible, is quite irksome to the contemporary believer. What is truly important, however, in Chalcedon is its insistence on the full, complete, tangible, sensitive, intelligent, responsible humanity of

Jesus. This was the special agenda of Chalcedon. As such, it was a council that foreshadowed the constant concern of New Testament scholars and theologians and preachers of our own times to make Jesus credible to believers as a man in the midst of the human community and the human situation who has indeed redeemed us and who draws us to imitate him and become one with his project in human history precisely because he is one of us and therefore can bring us into full communion with him.

Strangely, in the centuries since Chalcedon this council and its definition have often been cited as though their primary concern had been to insist further on the divinity of Jesus. In fact, sometimes Chalcedon has been quoted and used as though it intended to insist on the divinity of Jesus at the expense of the full humanity. Sometimes, therefore, in contemporary debates about 'Chalcedonian orthodoxy' it seems that the position being maintained is not so much that of the council which became normative for the Christian Churches but rather that of the Monophysites against whom the council was assembled in the first place. When all is said and done, the concern of the ordinary believer, who need not be troubled by theological technicalities, is simply that in Jesus we have one who is the Saviour of all, a man as human as we are but sinlessly, flawlessly focused on the heavenly Father so as to be able to gather us all into that focus, a man to whom we can turn with the trust and self-surrender that is due to God, knowing that we shall not be deceived.

Related Material

A good account of Jesus as we can know him from scripture is offered by Bruce Vawter, *This Man Jesus* (Doubleday). Vincent Zamoyta, *Theology of Christ: Sources* (Bruce), gives a selection of texts written at various times in Christian history and showing the development of thought about Christ and its formulation. For more detail on the development of Christology in the early centuries as it looks to a contemporary scholar, one might turn to Aloys Grillmeier, *Christ in Christian Tradition, from the Apostolic Age to Chalcedon (451)* (Sheed & Ward). A standard Catholic contemporary interpretation of the Catholic Christian tradition in Christology can be found in Walter Kasper, *Jesus the Christ* (Paulist Press). More provocative accounts which try to resolve some of the difficulties and unanswered questions of the contemporary believer confronted with traditional formulations of Christology are to be found, for instance, in Piet Schoonenberg, *The Christ* (Herder/Seabury), Jon Sobrino, *Christology at the Crossroads* (Orbis), which is written specifically from the point of view of socio-critical questions about salvation, and, for those prepared for extensive and heavy reading. Edward Schillebeeckx, *Jesus* and *Christ* (Seabury).

Chapter 13

His Own Person or Divine Puppet?

Enda Lyons

It is one thing to *say* that Jesus was 'truly human'. It is another to be convinced of this and really mean it. It is not at the level of creed that our reluctance to think of Jesus as a real human being is likely to manifest itself today – at this level there is 'a profound orthodoxy'. It begins to emerge, rather, only when the details of our picture of Jesus begin to become clear. If we are to be sure that we really do see Jesus as a human being, we need to reflect on his life in some detailed way. This section on *The Ordinariness of Jesus* will focus on certain features of human life and will emphasise that these were in fact characteristics of his life too. The features chosen are ones which, in my experience, people do not usually associate with Jesus, and which, in fact, they are often afraid to associate with him. Any ambivalence which might still be lurking in the reader's mind regarding Jesus *really* being a real human being should in this way be uncovered.

Jesus' attitude before God

The first point on which it is important to reflect, it seems to me, is how Jesus saw himself in relation to God. Did this human being, the carpenter from Nazareth, stand before God in an attitude of creatureliness before his Creator or in some other relationship?

The answer which immediately occurs to the Christian is that Jesus stood before God as the Son in whom the Father is well pleased, to use the language of the baptism and transfiguration stories. And this, of course, is the correct Christian answer. Christians, believing as they do that Jesus was uniquely the Son of

God, naturally believe that he stood before God in this unique relationship.

But while the man, Jesus, stood before God as the Son in whom
the Father was well pleased, it is of the greatest importance to
remember that the Jesus who stood before God in this way, was
nonetheless a human being, a carpenter from Nazareth. As such,
he stood before God 'in utter creatureliness'. To say otherwise
would surely be equivalent to saying that he was not really a human
being at all: human beings are, after all, creatures.

It was because Jesus stood before God in a creaturely way that the
scriptures, including the Gospels, can present him as acting as only
a creature can before God.

It is why they can present him as, for example, *praying to God*.
Here the agony scene immediately comes to mind (Mark 14:32ff.;
Matt 26:36; Luke 22:39ff.). But there is also the passage in Mark
which says: 'In the morning, long before dawn, he got up and left
the house, and went off to a lonely place and prayed there' (1: 35;
Luke 4:42). There is the passage in Luke which says 'he spent the
whole night in prayer to God' (6:12). And there is the passage
where Matthew says: 'After sending the crowds away he went up
into the hills by himself to pray' (14:23). There are also, of course,
the many occasions on which it is said that 'he gave thanks' (e.g.
Matt 15:36; Luke 22:19).

It is because of his creatureliness that Jesus could also have *felt
abandoned by God*, and so could be presented as crying out on the
cross the line from Psalm 22: 'My God, my God, why have you
deserted me?' (Mark 15:34; Matt 27:46).

It is the fact of his sense of creatureliness before God that alone
explains *his attitude towards the Father's will*. We will notice that
whenever in the gospels he is confronted with the Father's will (as
in the agony scene), he is presented as experiencing it as authoritative, making demands on him, and as something which he ought
to obey (Mark 14:32ff.; Matt 26:36; Luke 22:39ff.). The reason is
that though it was the will of the One he called 'Father', it was,
nonetheless, the will of the One who gave him his being in the first
place and who continued to give it to him – it was the will of his
Creator.

Jesus: free before God

In trying to think of Jesus as a real human being it can be helpful
also to reflect further on the fact that Jesus was *free* before God. To

say that Jesus was not really free would, of course, be the same as saying that he was not really human. So it was that when, in the seventh century, Sergius I, Patriarch of Constantinople, said that the human will of Jesus was absorbed by and was lost in the divine will, the Sixth Council of Constantinople declared that Jesus, being truly human, had his own human will.

It is not necessary here to discuss in any detailed way the notion of human 'freedom'. Being one of the basic characteristics of the human creature, it is not a simple matter. In the present context it will help to draw attention to just two characteristics of earthly freedom and their implications for understanding Jesus.

Jesus: author of his own script

There is nobody today of whom I know who sets out to deny, in so many words, that Jesus was free before God. There are, however, many who, perhaps without being fully aware of this, actually think of him as not being really free. For there are many who see Jesus as one who, throughout his life, followed, almost blindly, a course of action laid out for him by God. They recall many passages from the gospels which say 'as it was written' or 'this was to fulfil the prophecy', and they interpret these passages as though they were referring to a script written by God for Jesus' life, and in the writing of which Jesus himself had no part. They altogether forget, or ignore, the 'hindsight' perspective from which the Gospels were written and the dramatic way in which the Jesus-story is related. They do not see Jesus, then, as being a free man, but rather as that 'puppet on strings' of which Karl Rahner speaks.

It is true, of course, that, for all of us, the direction of our lives is to some extent shaped by forces outside our control. It is shaped, for example, by the time in history, and the place in the world in which we are born, by who our parents were, by our gender, our genes, our upbringing, and so on. But, allowing for all this, we still have, to some extent at least, the shaping of our destinies in our own hands. The fact is that all through our lives we find ourselves standing, in freedom, before various possible courses of action, and choosing between these: we choose, for example, what career to follow, whether to marry or not to marry, whether to marry this person or another. According as we make these free choices, we determine, to that extent, what course our life takes from there. In that way we ourselves make and shape the person we become and so we are, at least in that sense of the phrase, 'self-made' people. In so far as we do all this freely, we are responsible for who and what we are. It is we ourselves, then, who, within the limits referred to above, freely write our own script for our own lives.

As regards Jesus, Christians obviously are convinced that God was deeply and intimately involved with his life, from its inception to its passing on to newness of life in the resurrection. However, once we say that Jesus was 'truly human', then we may not think of God's involvement in his life as in any way taking away from his freedom. How we might explain this is another matter – it is a matter which will arise later in the broader context of the relation between the divine and human in Jesus. But, however we might explain it, we must acknowledge it to be a fact.

Because the divine presence and action in Jesus did not remove his freedom, the pattern of his life was basically the same as ours. Jesus, just as much as we, was frequently faced with various possible course of action. He, just as much as we, was frequently choosing freely between the possibilities which lay before him, whether it was a matter of what career to follow, or, later, of how best and most effectively to exercise his ministry – whether, for example, to accept the offer to be made king or to chose the more lonely road of the prophet, or, later still, of whether or not to avoid confrontation. Jesus had, then, the making of himself and the shaping of his destiny in his own hands in the same general way that we all have. Accordingly, it was *he himself* who was responsible for the course which his life took and for the person he became. It was *he himself* who decided freely to leave carpentry and become a preacher or rabbi; it was *he himself* who freely chose to opt particularly for the poor and the outcast; it was *he himself* who freely decided to reject the offer to become king; it was *he himself* who freely chose to confront the religious authorities; it was *he himself* who chose to accept the chalice of death and suffering. Since Jesus wrote his own script for his life, at least as much as we write our script for our lives, he was far from being a divine 'puppet'; he was, indeed, very much 'his own person'.

Jesus and temptation

The second implication of Jesus' freedom which is worth thinking about here is that Jesus could be, and was, tempted. Theologically speaking, to be tempted means to be attracted to chose what one knows in one's heart would not be the right thing to choose – generally, when we talk about temptation we seem to talk about temptation to do wrong rather than to do right. To be tempted is, then, to be attracted to make an immoral choice – it is to be attracted to be immoral. And it is to be really attracted to this, for if there is no real attraction, there is no real temptation.

It is interesting that the Gospels, though written after Jesus was recognised to be Son and Lord, make no bones whatsoever about presenting him as being open to temptation.

The accounts of the temptations after forty days in the wilderness immediately come to mind. It is not our task here to deal in a detailed way with these accounts except to suggest, with scholars, that they are perhaps best understood as representing, in a dramatic and symbolic way, the temptations to which Jesus was subjected throughout his whole life. What concerns us here is not the precise nature of these temptations, but the fact that three of the Gospels, Mark, Matthew and Luke, do not hesitate to present Jesus as being, from the very outset of his ministry, one who was open to temptation.

Of course it is not only in these stories that the gospels present Jesus as being subjected to temptation. Peter too is presented as tempting him by trying to dissuade him from going up to Jerusalem, a journey which would involve that fatal confrontation with the religious authorities. The strength of this temptation comes out in the reply attributed to Jesus: 'Get behind me, Satan!' (Mark 8:33; cf. Matt 16:23).

In the Gospel according to Mark, temptation seems also to have come to Jesus even from his own family: these, it would appear, had serious reservations and doubts about his activities: 'He went home again, and once more such a crowd collected that they could not even have a meal. When his relatives heard of this, they set out to take charge of him, convinced he was out of his mind' (3: 20-21).

With regard to being subjected to temptation, the Letter to the Hebrews does not hesitate to put Jesus on the very same level as the rest of us when it says: 'For it is not as if we had a high priest who was incapable of feeling our weaknesses with us; but we have one who has been tempted in every way that we are, though he is without sin' (4:15).

'... though he is without sin'

The purpose of this chapter is not to deal with the uniqueness of Jesus: its aim is rather to emphasise that, however unique he was, he was a humble human being. However, the phrase 'without sin' used in the above passage from Hebrews, though it does refer to the uniqueness of Jesus, requires some comment at this point. This is because, in my experience, this phrase can actually be an obstacle to people thinking of Jesus as being really human: 'After all', it has often been said to me, 'to err is human, and so, to sin is human. If Jesus did not sin, he was not really human at all'.

The problem here is a mistaken idea of what 'without sin' means. Ultimately, of course, it is a mistaken idea of what 'sin' means.

We might begin by saying what sin is not. Sin is not the same as the experience of human weakness – thus the Gospels of Mark and Matthew can present Jesus as saying 'the flesh is weak' (Mark 14:38; Matt 26:42).

Nor is sin the same as the immaturity of the child. Maturity means ripeness. But growing to ripeness or maturity, especially to moral ripeness and maturity, is a normal and natural part of the process of human growth. So Luke does not hesitate to speak of Jesus as growing, not just physically, but (in a reference to Samuel of old), 'to maturity' (2:40). He even speaks of Jesus as increasing 'in wisdom, in stature, and in favour with God and people' (2:52). I find it interesting that though this is a text with which most people are familiar, the idea of Jesus growing in favour with God often seems somehow new to many.

Sin, we should remember, is a very specific concept. It has to do with moral living – or, rather, with the absence of this. It occurs when, and only when, a person freely chooses what he or she knows should not, in this situation, be chosen. Sin, then, involves free choice and knowledge.

To say that Jesus was 'without sin' cannot, then, be the same as saying that he was never young and never experienced the immaturity that necessarily goes with being young. Nor is it even necessarily the same as saying that he never, throughout his whole life, erred or made a mistake. Strictly speaking, it is to say only that he never *freely* chose what he *knew* to be contrary to the Father's will and, so, that he was never immoral.

To err, then, may be human. But to sin is not the same as to err. To sin, properly understood, is to decide, knowingly and freely, to go off-target in human living – as the Greek word *hamartia* ('missing the mark'), one of the main biblical words for sin, suggests. Far, then, from being a humanizing factor in life, sin is, in fact, a de-humanizing factor. So, contrary to what seems to be often thought, to say that Jesus was 'without sin' is not at all to imply that he was not human. Rather, it is to say that, being always and consistently a moral person, he was, therefore, always and consistently *authentically* human. Once we understand sin in this way, we will immediately understand why Christians, believing as they do that in Jesus God was present in human history in a definitive way, believe that Jesus was actually 'without sin', and why they even believe that it would have been altogether inconceivable for him to have sinned. A point worth mentioning, if only in passing here, is that his 'sinlessness' did not at all separate Jesus from sinners. The opposite, rather was the case: judging by the way Jesus is presented in the Gospels, and in Christian preaching generally, as the friend of sinners, even dining with them, his 'sinlessness' drew him towards sinners and sinners towards him. What this says about the God who Christians believe was present in Jesus offers food for considerable thought and reflection.

Talking about the 'sinlessness' of Jesus is, then, really only a rather negative way of talking about his consistently moral and virtuous living. We should not think of the 'sinlessness' of Jesus as being merely the innocence of the child. Virtue and childlike innocence, I find, are often confused with each other – so much so, indeed, that the innocent child is sometimes put forward as the model of virtue. Innocence has to do with 'guilelessness' or 'ignorance of evil' (in its literal sense, the word suggests simply 'harmlessness'). Innocence is a characteristic of every infant and is, therefore, something in which knowledge and free choice do not necessarily play any part at all. In itself, therefore, it does not at all constitute truly moral living. In virtue, however, knowledge and free choice are essential elements, for virtue has to do with moral living. The 'sinlessness' of Jesus, then, is not at all the same as the nice ready-made innocence of the child: it is not, in John Macquarrie's phrase, 'a merely negative "dreaming innocence"'. 'Sinlessness' refers rather to the rugged, hard-won virtue of the mature moral person.

Since the question of the 'sinlessness' of Jesus arises here only in passing, it is not our task to try to explain this unique aspect of Jesus. However we explain the fact of Jesus being 'without sin', and even the inconceivability of his sinning, it would seem to me at least that we may not do so by saying that Jesus was not free to sin or to act immorally. To say that Jesus was not free to be immoral would seem to me to be the equivalent of saying that he was not moral at all. In this earthly situation at least, one can be moral only through freely choosing to do what one knows to be right. And one can freely choose what one knows to be right, only if one can also freely choose not to do it – that is, only if one can freely choose to do what one knows to be wrong. To say that Jesus was not free to be immoral would seem to me, then, really to amount to saying that he was not free to be moral. But if he was not free to be moral was he actually moral at all? He might, in that situation, be said to be 'innocent', but he could hardly be said to be moral.

* * *

There is far more to professing that Jesus was 'truly human' than often meets the eye. In professing this, if we take seriously the Christian community's insistence that Jesus had human freedom, we must also be saying, with Karl Rahner, that Jesus 'possesses a genuine spontaneous, free, spiritual active centre, a human self-consciousness' which, as creaturely, faces God 'in a genuinely human attitude of adoration, obedience, a most radical sense of creaturehood' (*Theological Investigations*, vol. 1, p. 158).

We are saying, in the words of Luke, that Jesus too had to grow 'in stature and in favour with God and people' (2:52).

* * *

Note

The question as to whether or not Jesus was a creature arose in the Arian controversy in the fourth century. But the context in which it then arose was different from the present one. The question in that controversy concerned whether the 'Word' who 'was made flesh' in Jesus was God or a creature. Arius, as is well known, said the 'Word' is not really God but a creature, a position which was, of course, rejected by the Council of Nicea in 325. In our present context the question is not whether the 'Word' is a creature – in the words of the prologue of the Gospel according to John, 'the Word was God' – but, rather, whether Jesus, the one in whom the divine 'Word' became flesh, faced God with a sense of creatureliness.

Chapter 14

The Church and the Council

Thomas P. Rausch SJ

When Pope Pius XII died in 1958, the Catholic Church was, to all casual observers, in excellent shape. In the first half of the twentieth century the Church had been led by a number of strong popes, particularly Pius XII himself, who had guided the Church through the Second World War and focused its energies against the postwar threat of Communism. The Church was continuing to grow in both numbers and influence. Seminaries, convents, and monasteries were filled to the bursting point. New religious houses were being built throughout the United States and in many other countries. Catholic theology, if not very creative, was very orthodox; there was almost no dissent, no public disagreement. Catholics knew who they were; they were proud of their Church and had a clear sense of their own identity.

Pre-Vatican II Catholicism

But there was a shadow side to this picture. The Catholic Church in the middle of the twentieth century considered itself very much a Church under siege. Deeply suspicious of the modern world, the Church was on the defensive. Catholic scholarship had been crippled by the atmosphere of suspicion and distrust that followed the Modernist crisis at the beginning of the twentieth century. Books by Catholic authors were rarely published without a review by ecclesiastical authorities; they had to obtain an *imprimatur* from the bishop or a *nihil obstat* from an official censor of books. The only really acceptable model for theology was that of the dogmatic manuals of the Roman schools, a textbook theology that relied on an abstract and ahistorical neoscholasticism. Rather than asking new questions and investigating biblical and historical sources, this textbook theology demonstrated traditional positions by citing biblical proof texts and numbers from Denzinger's *Enchiridion Symbolorum,* a compendium of papal and conciliar teachings.

When Pius XII died at the end of the 1950s, a number of progressive Catholic scholars like Karl Rahner, Yves Congar, Henri de Lubac, Marie-Dominique Chenu, Teilhard de Chardin, and the American Jesuit John Courtney Murray had been either silenced, forbidden to write on certain topics, or disciplined. The threat of having their books placed on the Index of Forbidden Books hung over them. Seminary professors were required to take an oath against Modernism each year. In the United States, where Catholic scholarship was particularly undistinguished, Msgr John Tracy Ellis and Thomas O'Dea had just asked in two important books why the American Church and its universities had contributed so little to the intellectual life of the country.[1]

The Catholic Church officially was not interested in ecumenism, the movement aimed at restoring unity to the divided Christian Churches. What became the modern ecumenical movement resulted from a gathering of Protestant Christians at the World Missionary Conference at Edinburgh, Scotland, in 1910. From that came the Faith and Order Conference, which met for the first time at Lausanne, Switzerland, in 1928. Shortly afterward Pope Pius XI issued his encyclical *Mortalium animos,* forbidding Catholics to participate in ecumenical meetings of non-Catholics. The Catholic approach to Christian unity was quite clear: 'There is only one way in which the unity of Christians may be fostered, and that is by promoting the return to the one true Church of Christ of those who are separated form it.'[2] This 'one true Church' approach was characteristic of Catholic thinking for the first half of the twentieth century. Catholics looked upon Christians in other Churches as good but misguided people. Though the Holy Office published a letter in 1949 allowing Catholic participation in the ecumenical movement under certain very strict conditions, in the years immediately before Vatican II most Catholics were warned not to attend a Protestant service or even to send a child to a Protestant summer camp.

A genuine theology of the laity was only beginning to emerge. The lay movement known as 'Catholic Action' began in Italy in

---

[1] John Tracy Ellis, *American Catholics and the Intellectual Life* (Chicago: Heritage Foundation, 1956); Thomas O'Dea, *American Catholic Dilemma: An Inquiry into the Intellectual Life* (New York: Sheed & Ward, 1958).

[2] *Acta apostolicae sedis* 20 (1928) and 14.

1930. Particularly through its Belgian and French expressions, it was to give a new energy to the Church in Latin America, laying the ground for what would be known in the late sixties as the theology of liberation. But the official Church seemed unable to recognize that lay men and women had a real share in the mission of the Church. In Church documents the 'lay apostolate' was defined as 'the collaboration of the laity in the apostolate of the hierarchy'.[3] Ministry was the prerogative of the clergy.

Liturgically, although a liturgical movement had been growing in the Church since late in the nineteenth century, at the time of Pius XII's death Rome was trying to discourage the 'Dialogue Mass', which had people praying and responding to a leader in English while the priest at the altar prayed quietly in Latin. In many Catholic colleges and universities Catholic college students were required to read a popular book called *The Thirteenth: Greatest of Centuries*.[4] The sense that the Catholic Church had its attention fixed firmly on the past rather than on the future could not have been more clearly illustrated.

How had the Catholic Church become so stuck? In a very real sense the Church had never completely recovered from the shock of the Reformation in the sixteenth century. As a result of the Reformation, within a period of some forty years half of Europe had become Protestant. But there were other causes for the Church's distrust of the modern world as well. The scientific revolution and the rationalism of the Enlightenment, or Age of Reason, in the seventeenth and eighteenth centuries with the accompanying assaults on Church doctrine, authority, and ritual left the Church on the defensive; both movements presupposed an autonomous human reason that left no room for revelation or the transcendent. Then came the revolutions of the late eighteenth and nineteenth centuries, including the French Revolution. The latter sought to change the nature of Church government by forcing the clergy to obey a civil constitution that stripped the pope of any juridical authority over the Church in France. Finally, it attempted to restrict the practice of the faith itself.

In 1863 Pope Pius IX, considered quite liberal in the early days of his pontificate, published his *Syllabus of Errors*, a list of eighty concepts and movements that he considered typical of modern civilization. Among the errors condemned was the proposition that

---

[3] 'Allocution to Italian Catholic Action', *Acta apostolicae sedis* 32 (1940) 362.
[4] James J. Walsh, *The Thirteenth: Greatest of Centuries* (1907; reprint, New York: Fordham Univ. Press, 1952).

'the Roman Pontiff can and should reconcile himself and reach agreement with "progress", Liberalism and recent departures in civil society' (DS 2980). Even the territory the Church considered its own was under attack. In 1870 Garibaldi seized the Papal States for what was to be the newly united Italian state. The loss of this vast area of central Italy ruled by the popes for more than a thousand years was traumatic.

Modernism

The Modernist crisis at the beginning of the twentieth century left the official Church even more fearful of the new scholarship.[5] The movement designated by the term 'Modernism' was never really a coherent theological system; what it represented was an attempt by some Catholic scholars to enter into a dialogue with modernity by using modern methods of biblical and historical investigation. These 'critical' methods, developed largely by Protestant scholars in Germany, opened up a rich new world of biblical scholarship that gave new insight not just into the texts themselves but also into the way that God's revelation emerged out of the history of God's people.

Unfortunately, many who used those methods, both Protestant and Catholic, inherited to a considerable degree the rationalistic presuppositions stemming from the Enlightenment. In too many cases they relativized doctrines, rationalized whatever could not be explained scientifically, and reduced the content of revelation to subjective human experience. Doctrines became symbols without any propositional truth, miracles were explained away, and Christian revelation was reinterpreted as something devoid of any supernatural influence, a particular expression of a general religious experience available to all. Thus, in a number of ways, 'Modernism' can be seen as a Catholic version of Liberal Protestantism.

Characteristic of all of these thinkers was a concern to bring history and subjectivity into the work of theology. Alfred Loisy (1857-1940) was a French biblical scholar whose book, *The Gospel and the Church*, published in 1902, attempted to show how the Church resulted from a necessary institutionalization of Jesus' preaching of the kingdom of God. George Tyrell (1861-1909), an English Jesuit and convert to Catholicism, was a philosopher of

---

[5] See Gabriel Daly, *Transcendence and Immanence: A Study of Catholic Modernism and Integralism* (Oxford: Clarendon, 1980).

religion. His main interest was in revelation as an inner religious experience, something that could be expressed symbolically but could never be understood simply as a group of propositions. Friedrich von Hügel (1852–1925), a theologian and spiritual teacher, interpreted Christianity in terms of its institutional, intellectual, and mystical elements. Though not considered a Modernist himself, he was in frequent contact with Modernist thinkers and is often associated with them.

The Catholic Church reacted strongly to what it perceived as a threat to its faith. In 1907 two documents were published condemning Modernism, Pius X's encyclical *Pascendi* and a decree of the Holy Office, *Lamentabili*. The encyclical pointed out some real errors in what it understood as Modernism, though scholars today are not in agreement about the extent to which those errors were actually present in the thought of the scholars against whom the encyclical was directed. Loisy and Tyrell were excommunicated; von Hügel escaped condemnation.

Over the next fifty years Catholic scholarship was to pay a heavy price for the measures enacted to excise the Modernist threat from the Church. *Pascendi* had encouraged strict censorship, the setting up of diocesan vigilance committees to watch over Catholic teaching, and the turning in of the names of those suspected of Modernist ideas to the Holy Office. With the pope's approval a secret society known as the *Sodalitium Pianum* was set up to keep under surveillance even members of the hierarchy suspected of Modernist tendencies.[6]

What followed was a long period of suspicion and repression. Bishops and seminary professors were required to take annually the oath against Modernism, mentioned earlier. Any teaching that did not conform to the theology of the Roman manuals was suspect; scholars were not infrequently dismissed from their positions, and others had their books placed on the Index. The congregations of the Roman Curia, the Vatican bureaucracy that was to assist the pope in his leadership of the Church, became even more powerful. The members of these curial congregations and commissions, for the most part Italian clerics, watched over doctrine and morals, decided what positions were to be held and taught by Catholic professors, disciplined dissenters, kept a close eye on seminaries, appointed bishops and set up new dioceses. They dispatched apostolic nuncios and delegates to represent Rome in national Churches, supervised

---

[6] Carlo Falconi, *The Popes in the Twentieth Century* (London: Weidenfeld & Nicolson, 1967) pp. 54–55.

religious orders and congregations, particularly those of women, and regulated the sacramental and liturgical life of the Church.

Currents of renewal

The picture was not completely a bleak one. The brightest side of the period from 1920 to 1960 has been described by the French word *ressourcement*, 'return', understood as a return to the sources of Catholicism in scripture, the Fathers of the Church, the liturgy, and philosophy.[7] This return to the sources gave rise to or supported a number of currents of renewal that were ultimately to play a major role in reshaping the face of Catholicism at the Second Vatican Council. Furthermore, in the period after the Second World War the world itself was changing. After the horrors of Nazism the Christian Churches experienced a resurgence of faith. There was a new optimism and a new sense of freedom. We need to consider briefly those currents of renewal.

The Modern Biblical Movement

The modern biblical movement was made possible by the development in the largely secular German universities of various critical, historical, and literary methods of investigating biblical texts (historical criticism, form criticism, redaction criticism, source criticism, textual criticism). Fearing that it was tainted by the Modernist spirit, the new biblical criticism was for a long time resisted by the Church. The Pontifical Biblical Commission issued a number of decisions between 1905 and 1915 that required Catholic biblical scholars to hold positions critical scholarship was beginning to call into question, among them the substantial Mosaic authorship of the Pentateuch, the historical nature of the first chapters of Genesis, the view that the Book of Isaiah was the work of a single author, that Matthew was the first Gospel to be written, and so on.[8]

The turning point came with the 1943 encyclical of Pope Pius XII, *Divino Afflante Spiritu*, a document that has often been referred to as the Magna Carta of Catholic biblical scholarship. In

[7] See Stephen Happel and David Tracy, *A Catholic Vision* (Philadelphia: Fortress, 1984) pp. 134–36.
[8] See Raymond E. Brown, *Biblical Reflections on Crises Facing the Church* (New York: Paulist, 1975) pp. 6–10.

it the pope gave Catholic scholars the freedom to use the methods of historical-critical scholarship that had previously been denied them. Catholic biblical scholarship, which had previously lagged behind that of Protestants, began to flourish as Catholic scholars instructed in the new methods began teaching in seminaries and universities. Subsequent decrees from the Pontifical Biblical Commission confirmed this new direction, even reversing previous directives when in 1955 the secretary of the commission gave Catholic scholars complete freedom in regard to those earlier restrictive decisions of 1905–1915 except where faith or morals were involved.

The Liturgical Movement

The liturgical movement represents a second current of renewal, which began long before the Second Vatican Council. If today some people at times associate the liturgical movement with guitars and folk songs, with liturgical drama, dance, and banners in Church, it actually describes an attempt to recover the symbolic and communal riches of traditional Christian worship, thus giving new life to the official prayer and worship of the Church. Its roots are to be found in the Benedictine monasteries of Germany, Switzerland, and France, which in the nineteenth century began to popularize the use of Gregorian chant and to encourage a more active participation in the liturgy on the part of the laity. Dom Prosper Guéranger (1805-1875) of Solesmes in France, with his writings on the liturgical year, is often considered the founder of the movement. In Belgium Dom Lambert Beauduin (1873-1960) stressed that the liturgy was a profound way to deepen the life of faith, that it was an action not just of the priest but of the gathered faithful.

The liturgical movement in the United States is most often asso- ciated with St John's Abbey in Collegeville, Minnesota, and with the name of Virgil Michel (1890–1938), a monk of the abbey. Father Michel became familiar with the liturgical movement during his studies in Europe. When he returned to the United States in 1925, he dedicated himself to promoting liturgical renewal as well as to addressing the social ills that were the product of an increasingly industrialized society. He began publishing a monthly liturgical review, *Orate Fratres*, and founded The Liturgical Press. Through these publishing efforts several generations of North Americans were to become familiar with the liturgical move- ment. After Michel's death in 1938 one of his former students, Fr

Godfrey Dickmann, took over the review. He was to edit it for twenty-five years, changing its name in 1951 to *Worship*. Collegeville, with its abbey, university, and press, has remained a centre of the liturgical movement in the United States.

For many years prior to the council those interested in liturgy would withdraw to various progressive monasteries to make retreats, to take part in the monastic liturgy, and to learn Gregorian chant. In 1940 the Benedictines in the United States began sponsoring The Liturgical Week, a series of seminars, or congresses, on the liturgy. The first of a number of international congresses of liturgical scholars convened in 1951 at Maria Laach in Germany. The great body of scholarship produced by the liturgical movement was to bear fruit in the council's Constitution on the Sacred Liturgy.

The New Theology

For too long the Catholic theology favoured in Rome had been confined to the categories of the Scholastic philosophy and theology inherited from the great universities of the Middle Ages. Particularly influential was the work of the Dominican Thomas Aquinas. Indeed, Leo XIII in his encyclical *Aeterni Patris* (1879) had attempted to impose Thomism on the entire Church, while Pius X made Thomas' *Summa Theologiae* the textbook to be used in all pontifical institutions.[9] The Modernist 'crisis' at the turn of the century was occasioned by one attempt to break out of this narrow approach and to enter into dialogue with contemporary thought. The so-called *nouvelle théologie* ("new theology'), a term used to describe the work of some scholars in France and Germany in the two decades before the council, represented another.

The term *nouvelle théologie* was apparently used for the first time by the Holy Office's Msgr Pietro Parente in February 1942 in *Osservatore Romano,* the official Vatican newspaper, and it was used pejoratively. But, like Modernism, the new theology was not really a system. It was an attempt by a wide range of scholars – Yves Congar, Henri de Lubac, Jean Daniélou, and Marie-Dominique Chenu in France; Karl Rahner and Otto Semmelroth in Germany; Hans Urs von Balthasar in Switzerland – to return to the biblical, patristic and liturgical sources that had so enriched the self-understanding of the Church of the first millennium. Ecclesiology was a

---

[9] See Avery Dulles, *The Craft of Theology: From Symbol to System* (New York: Crossroad, 1992) p. 120.

key issue for these theologians. Other topics included the development of doctrine, creation, evolution, original sin, grace, and the Eucharist.

Because the approach of these scholars was biblical and historical rather than neo-Thomist, they were attacked by the Scholastic representatives of the Roman orthodoxy, who saw their work as a new kind of Modernism. This seems to have been the concern of Pius XII in his 1950 encyclical *Humani Generis*. The encyclical called for a return to a Thomistic approach in both philosophy and theology; it also argued that the proper task of theologians was to show how those things taught by the magisterium of the Church are found in scripture and tradition (DS 3886). A number of those associated with the new theology were disciplined; they 'were removed from their professorial chairs, prevented from upholding their views in lectures or writings, condemned to silence and inactivity'.[10]

In 1954 in what has been described as a 'raid on the Dominicans,' three French Dominican provincials were removed from office, and a number of Dominican scholars, among them Chenu and Congar, were disciplined at the insistence of the Holy Office, fearful of what were considered to be dangerous innovations in their teaching. Chenu, a distinguished medieval theologian, had been comparing changes in thirteenth-century society and Church to those in the twentieth. Congar's writings took up issues such as the organic nature of tradition, Church reform, the theology of the laity, and ecumenism. Both were dismissed from their teaching positions. Nevertheless, both attended the Second Vatican Council, where their work was to help shape a number of the council's documents.[11]

Pius XII

Humani Generis was not a progressive encyclical. It has frequently been used as evidence that Pius XII was not a reformer. But contemporary scholars are coming to a new appreciation of the extent to which this austere, patrician pope prepared the way for Vatican II. His encyclical *Divino Afflante Spiritu* (1943) brought modern biblical criticism into the Church, even if the officials in the Roman Curia continued to snipe at those who used it. As late

[10] Falconi, *The Popes in the Twentieth Century*, p. 283.
[11] Thomas O'Meara, '"Raid on the Dominicans": The Repression of 1954', *America* 170 (1994) pp. 8–16.

as 1962 these officials launched several attacks on the Jesuit-run Biblical Institute in Rome and sought to have two of its professors removed from the faculty.

Another important encyclical of Pope Pius XII was *Mystici Corporis* (1943), with its sacramental vision of the Church as the body of Christ. It was followed in 1947 by *Mediator Dei*, the pope's great encyclical on the liturgy. Though the latter warned against the excesses of some liturgical reformers, it encouraged the liturgical movement and commended the Dialogue Mass.

John XXIII

Then, in 1958, Pius XII died. His death marked the end of an era. Few suspected that a new one in the life of the Church was about to begin. When the cardinals gathered in the Sistine Chapel to elect a successor, the expectation was that nothing would change. Most of those assembled wanted someone who would continue Pius XII's strong, conservative leadership. But the conclave deadlocked; none of the front runners was able to receive sufficient votes to be elected. Finally a compromise was reached. The cardinals turned to a seventy-six-year-old by the name of Angelo Roncalli (1881—1963). He was to be a transitional pope. The general sense was that he was too old to do any damage.

Roncalli, or John XXIII, as he is known to history, was a round, thick-set Italian with a face like something out of a Michelangelo painting. He came of solid peasant stock, farmers from northern Italy. But in spite of his appearance, Roncalli was a shrewd and sophisticated churchman. Ordained in 1904, he served in his early years as a seminary professor at Bergamo, as a chaplain during the First World War, and as a counsellor to university students. Most of his career had been spent outside of Rome in the papal diplomatic service. He had represented the Vatican in Bulgaria and Turkey, gaining in the process a deep appreciation for Orthodox Christianity as well as a familiarity with the languages and problems of eastern Europe. In 1944 he was appointed apostolic nuncio to France, where he was exposed to the theological and pastoral renewal taking place there. During this time he befriended an ecumenical group of Protestants trying to live a monastic life in a little village in Burgundy called Taizé. But in spite of all his accomplishments, his heart was first of all a heart of a pastor. Finally, in 1953 he was made patriarch of Venice, where he could give full expression to his pastoral concerns.

Shortly after his election to the papacy the new pope, talking to his secretary of state about the problems facing the world and the Church, told him that he was going to call a council. Pope John's council was to radically change his Church.

The Second Vatican Council: 1962–1965

On January 25, 1959, Pope John and seventeen cardinals, many of them from the Roman Curia, met at the Basilica of Saint Paul-Outside-the-Walls for a pontifical vesper service to conclude the octave of prayer for Christian unity. In a brief address the pope announced that he intended to summon an ecumenical council, adding at the end a prayer for 'a renewed invitation to the faithful of the separated communities that they also may follow us amiably in the search of unity and grace, to which so many souls aspire in all parts of the earth'.[12] The cardinals greeted his announcement with a stunned silence. Why couldn't the new pope leave well enough alone? The last thing the leaders of the Roman Curia wanted was to bring together all the bishops of the Church, particularly some of the more progressive bishops of France, Germany, Austria, Belgium, and Holland.

The preparatory phase

In convening a council, to be called the Second Vatican Council, or Vatican II, the pope made clear that it was to be an ecumenical council for the whole Church. In the months that followed he clarified his goals for the council. First, he wanted it to be an *aggiornamento*, a renewal or, more accurately, a 'bringing up to date' of the Catholic Church. The story is often told that the pope once described what he wanted the council to accomplish by going to the nearest window and opening it up to let in some fresh air.

Second, Christian unity was to be a primary aim of the council; indeed it had been his purpose from the beginning. To promote his ecumenical intentions Pope John took a number of concrete steps, each of them highly symbolic. First, he asked that official observers be delegated by the Orthodox and Protestant Churches. Second, he arranged to have them seated in a place of honor in the front of the Basilica of St Peter close to the section reserved for the cardinals. Finally, he established a new Vatican congregation, the

---

[12] 'Pope John's Announcement of Ecumenical Council', *Council Daybook*, Sessions 1–2 (Washington: National Catholic Welfare Conference, 1965) p. 2.

Secretariat for Promoting Christian Unity, charged with bringing the Catholic Church into the ecumenical movement, and placed its resources at the service of the observers.

When it became clear that the pope was not to be dissuaded from having a council, the Curia leaders adopted the strategy of stage managing it so that it would remain firmly under their control. The ten commissions and two secretariats set up to prepare the council were stacked with officials from the corresponding curial congregations. These bodies prepared seventy schemata, or drafts, on various dogmatic and disciplinary issues to be considered by the bishops when they gathered in Rome. The plan, obviously, was to overload the council, making the work of the Curia indispensable.

But in two important addresses the pope made clear to the bishops assembling for the council that its work was to be their own. In a radio address on September 11, 1962, he spoke of the need for the Church to address issues of peace, the equality and rights of all peoples, the problems of under-developed countries, and the miseries faced by so many, and he suggested that the Church be presented as 'the Church of all, and *especially of the poor*'.[13] None of these topics had been raised by the preparatory commissions.

Then, on October 11, in his address officially opening the council, he called on the twenty-five hundred bishops gathered from all over the world at a solemn liturgy in the Basilica of St. Peter to look not at the past but to the future. Disassociating himself from 'those prophets of gloom who are always forecasting disaster', meaning his critics in the Curia, he said that the council was not to be a discussion of this or that fundamental doctrine, but rather 'a step forward toward a doctrinal penetration and a formation of consciousness' faithful to the Church's authentic doctrine, but one that 'should be studied and expounded through the methods of research and through the literary forms of modern thought'. Most often quoted was his affirmation of the renewal of the Church's theological language: 'The substance of the ancient doctrine of the deposit of faith is one thing, and the way in which it is presented is another.'[14]

[13] Cited by Peter Hebblethwaite, 'John XXIII', in Adrian Hastings, ed., *Modern Catholicism: Vatican II and After* (New York: Oxford Univ. Press 1991) p. 30.
[14] The text of his address is in Walter M. Abbott, ed., *The Documents of Vatican II* (New York: Herder & Herder, 1966) 710–19; see pp. 712, 715.

The work of the council

At the first working session of the council on October 13 the agenda called for the election of members for the council's ten commissions, which were to present the schemata to the council fathers and consider whatever amendments they might propose. The Curia hoped that those members who had served on the preparatory commissions would simply be reelected; to help the fathers, a list of their names was handed out. But in an important intervention Cardinal Liènart, Archbishop of Lille, suggested a delay so that before so important a step was taken, the bishops could consult in their national or regional conferences about those they wanted to elect. His proposal was endorsed by Cardinal Frings of Cologne, and both interventions were greeted with loud applause from the council fathers. With such a strong show of support, the motion to delay the election was approved. The bishops had begun to assume control of the council.

The council met in three sessions. The debating and voting on the various documents took place on the floor of the Basilica of St Peter, where the council fathers, the twenty-five hundred bishops and heads of the religious orders of men, were seated. But much of the real business of the council took place less formally in the conference rooms, restaurants, and coffee bars of Rome, where innumerable conversations took place among the different groups gathered for the council – bishops meeting with one another, with their *periti* or theological advisors, with scholars and journalists, and with the observers from the Protestant, Anglican, and Orthodox Churches.

Inviting official observers from the other Christian Churches gave an ecumenical flavour to the council from the beginning. There were some forty observers present when the council opened on October 11, 1962; by the time it closed, their number had risen to eighty. In spite of the secrecy that the Curia tried to preserve in regard to the deliberations of the council, the observers received advance copies of the drafts of the councils' documents. Treated as honoured guests they were able to be present for all the daily sessions in the basilica and to attend some of the meetings of the commissions. A translation service was also set up for them.

After Cardinal Suenens observed that no women were present for the council's deliberations, some were added as 'auditors'. By the end of the council there were twenty-two women present, among them Sr Luke Tobin, superior of the Sisters of Loretto in the United States.

The council generated an enormous amount of interest. In occasionally reversing previously held positions, even positions taught by popes, the council illustrated the dynamic character of Catholicism. Two of the documents drafted by the conservative Theological Commission, the schema on the Church and the one on divine revelation, were sent by the council fathers back to the commission to be rewritten. The sixteen documents that emerged from its deliberations established the guidelines for Church renewal, still unfinished, in a number of areas.[15]

The Church

The Dogmatic Constitution on the Church (*Lumen Gentium*) represents an attempt to articulate a contemporary self-understanding of the Church that stands in marked contrast to the clerical and monarchical ecclesiology of nineteenth- and early twentieth-century Catholicism, often symbolized by a pyramid in which all authority descends from the top down. Particularly significant is its stress on the Church as the people of God, its doctrine of episcopal collegiality, and its theology of the laity.

Chapter 1 introduces the Church as a 'sacrament of intimate union with God, and of the unity of all mankind' (LG 1). Treating the nature and mission of the Church, it touches on the relation between the Catholic Church and other Churches. In speaking of 'the unique Church of Christ,' the constitution states: 'This Church, constituted and organized in the world as a society, *subsists in* the Catholic Church' (LG 8). The earlier 1963 draft had read 'This Church ... *is* the Catholic Church.'[16] This small change of 'is' to 'subsists in', made by the Theological Commission after the second session, was immensely significant ecumenically; it meant that the Catholic Church was no longer proclaiming an exclusive identity or strict equation between the Church of Christ and itself. Even though the council understands the Catholic Church as a realization of the Church of Christ in its essential completeness or fullness (LG 14), it implies that the Church of Christ is also present in various ways in other Churches and ecclesial communities (LG 8).

Rather than beginning with the hierarchy, chapter 2 describes

[15] Two of the documents, those on the Church and on divine revelation, were dogmatic constitutions; the document on the liturgy was a constitution, the one on the Church in the modern world a pastoral constitution, and the rest were decrees or declarations.
[16] Italics added.

the whole Church as the people of God, the ruling image in the council's ecclesiology. Reference to the diverse 'charismatic gifts' (LG 12), elsewhere described as 'both hierarchical and charismatic' (LG 4), is evidence of a recovery of the rich theology of the charismata that play such an important role in 1 Corinthians 11-14. The distinction between the 'ministerial' or 'hierarchical priesthood' and the 'common priesthood' (priesthood of all believers) underlines the share of all the faithful in the priesthood of Christ (LG 10).

Chapter 3 developed a collegial understanding of the episcopal office. The battle over collegiality was one of the most important of the council; it implied a return to the ancient understanding of the Church and its government. Together with the pope, the bishops have supreme authority over the universal Church (LG 22) and share in its infallible teaching office (LG 25). Bishops are thus not to be understood as vicars of the pope but as heads of local Churches (LG 27). The Church itself becomes a communion of Churches, as it understood itself in the first millennium, rather than a single, monolithic institution. By making clear that the bishops share in the Church's charism of infallibility, the council provided a new context for the interpretation of the teaching of the First Vatican Council (1870) on papal infallibility.

Chapter 4 turned to a theology of the laity, stressing that through their baptism and confirmation lay men and women share in the mission of the Church (LG 33) and in the threefold office of Christ as prophet, priest, and king (LG 31). From this emphasis was to come the multiplicity of lay ministries in the postconciliar Church, a recognition of the obligation of competent lay people to express their opinion for the good of the Church (LG 37), and a new involvement of lay men and women in the Church's task of theological reflection (cf. GS 62). The constitution envisions lay men and women as living out their vocation precisely 'by engaging in temporal affairs', working 'for the sanctification of the world from within, in the manner of leaven' (LG 31).

Chapter 5 is on the call of the whole Church to holiness, chapter 6 on religious, and chapter 7 on the union of the Church on earth with the heavenly Church, the saints in heaven, and the souls in purgatory. Its description of the Church as a 'pilgrim Church' moves away from the notion of the Church as a 'perfect society', dominant in Catholic ecclesiology since the time of Robert Bellarmine. The final chapter is on the role of the Blessed Virgin Mary in the mystery of Christ and the Church.

Revelation

The council's Dogmatic Constitution on Divine Revelation (*Dei Verbum*) takes a personalist rather than a propositional approach. Revelation is not something 'contained' in sources, even though the first chapter of the Theological Commission's rejected original draft was entitled the 'Two Sources of Revelation'. The council defined revelation as God's self-communication in history, which reaches its fullness in the person of Jesus, and through life in the Spirit offers men and women a share in God's own divine nature (DV 2). In the council's understanding, then, revelation is personal rather than propositional, it is Trinitarian in form, Christological in realization, and historical in its mediation.

Chapter 2 discusses the transmission of God's revelation in scripture and tradition. Chapter 3 reflects the influence of the modern biblical movement in its discussion of the interpretation of scripture. Echoing Pius XII's *Divino Afflante Spiritu*, it stresses the importance of searching out the biblical author's intention and identifying the text's literary form. The final chapter outlines measures to restore the Word of God to its central place in the life of the Church and particularly in its liturgy (DV 21); it calls for new translations from the original texts, encourages biblical scholars in their work, and points to the central place of scripture in theology. Priests, deacons, and catechists are exhorted to share the Word of God with those entrusted to them and the faithful urged to read the Bible frequently and to use it for their prayer. Thus the Constitution on Divine Revelation ended the benign neglect of the Bible, which characterized the Catholic Church since the Reformation, and emphasized the central role of the Word of God in the liturgy.

The liturgy

The Constitution on the Sacred Liturgy (*Sacrosanctum Concilium*) initiated a thorough renewal of the Church's official prayer and worship. It encouraged greater participation in the liturgy on the part of the laity (SC 14) and mandated the revision of liturgical texts and rites to make the liturgy more fruitful in the life of the Church (SC 21). Its most obvious reform, reflecting its emphasis on the importance of the Word, was its provision for the celebration of the liturgy in the language of the people (SC 36). Many of its suggestions and tentative steps toward renewal have in the years since the council become commonplace: the liturgical homily, the prayers of the faithful or universal prayers of the Church, the kiss of peace, Communion under both species, concelebration, congregational singing, and a multiplicity of new liturgical ministries for lay men and women.

Ecumenism

Moving beyond the Church's earlier suspicion of the ecumenical movement, Vatican II firmly committed the Catholic Church to the search for Christian unity. The Decree on Ecumenism (*Unitatis Redintegratio*) recognizes that Christians from different Churches and ecclesial communities are already in an imperfect communion with one another through baptism (UR 3). They are already sharing to some degree in the life of grace. It stresses that all ecumenism begins with conversion of heart and in the name of the Catholic Church officially begs pardon of God and of other Christians for its own sins against unity (UR 7). Then it outlines the principles for Roman Catholic ecumenical involvement. It recommends joint prayer services, though it is more cautious about common worship (UR 8). Ecumenical dialogue is encouraged, and those engaged in dialogue are reminded that 'there exists an order of "hierarchy" of truths'. In other words, not all doctrines are of equal importance, since 'they vary in their relationship to the foundation of Christian faith' (UR 11).

Religious freedom

The greatest battle at the council took place over the Declaration on Religious Freedom. The schema was bitterly contested by those who followed the traditional argument that 'error has no rights' and who therefore wanted the Church to continue maintaining that in predominantly Catholic countries it should in principle be able to prohibit the practice or spread of religions that it considered false. Other faiths, including other Christian faiths, might be tolerated for political reasons, but they had no intrinsic right to equality of treatment. According to John Courtney Murray, the principle author of the decree, the council was clearing up a longstanding ambiguity: 'The Church does not deal with the secular order in terms of a double standard – freedom for the Church when Catholics are a minority, privilege for the Church and intolerance for others when Catholics are a majority.'[17]

[17] John Courtney Murray, introduction to 'Religious Freedom', *The Documents of Vatican II*, ed. Walter M. Abbott, p. 673.

In the heated debates over religious freedom, the experience of the bishops from the United States played an important role. On Wednesday, September 23, 1964, three American cardinals spoke in favour of the document. It was finally approved, though by the narrowest margin of any vote of the council (1,114-1,074). Reversing the teaching of Pius IX and Leo XIII, *Dignitatis Humanae* proclaimed that human beings have a right to religious freedom, to worship freely according to the dictates of their consciences, rooted in their dignity as human persons (DH 2).

Non-Christian religions

Moving beyond the traditional axiom 'no salvation outside of the Church', the council acknowledged that those who sincerely seek God and open themselves to God's grace can be saved even if they have no explicit knowledge of Christ (LG 16). According to the Declaration on the Relationship of the Church to Non-Christian Religions (*Nostra Aetate*), the Catholic Church looks upon the great world religions with respect, recognizing that their teachings often reflect a ray of divine truth (NA 2).

The Church and the modern world

Perhaps the most significant shift represented by the council was the turn toward the world and especially toward the poor. From its opening sentence, the Pastoral Constitution on the Church in the Modern World (*Gaudium et Spes*), the longest of the council documents, calls attention to the plight of the poor and the afflicted: 'The joys and the hopes, the griefs and the anxieties of the men of this age, especially those who are poor or in any way afflicted, these too are the joys and hopes, the griefs and anxieties of the followers of Christ. Indeed, nothing genuinely human fails to raise an echo in their hearts' (GS 1). In addition to stressing that great efforts must be made to satisfy the demands of justice and equity (GS 66) and to its calling Christians to a new level of concern for the poor (GS 69), the constitution devotes chapters to the subjects of marriage and the family, including the concept of responsible parenthood, the development of culture, socioeconomic principles, the right of all to participate in political life, and the question of war and the arms race. *Gaudium et Spes* was to help inspire a host of contemporary socially conscious religious movements, among them, Latin American liberation theology, indigenous theologies in Africa and Asia, the pastoral letters of the American bishops on peace and economic justice, and feminist theology.

Conclusion

The documents of the Second Vatican Council reflect the divided nature of the council itself. Some of them seem schizophrenic, juxtaposing side by side traditional and progressive views. For example, the Dogmatic Constitution on the Church balances almost every statement on episcopal collegiality with a reaffirmation of traditional papal prerogatives.

But the council was enormously successful in unleashing the currents of renewal in the Church. Within relatively few years Catholicism experienced sweeping changes in its liturgy and worship, its theology, its understanding of authority and ministry, its religious communities, its parish life, even its popular culture. Not all the changes have been beneficial for the Church, and for many Catholics there has been and remains considerable confusion.

The situation of the Church at the end of the twentieth century cannot be attributed only to the council. The second half of this century has seen a number of movements – among them an increasing secularization, a widespread crisis of authority and of social institutions, the so-called sexual revolution, national liberation movements, feminism, and a growing concern for social justice – that would have brought about massive changes in the Church and in Catholic life even without the council, just as they have in society at large. But the council brought to the Church a new vitality, and by calling the Church to the renewal of its structures, theology, and life, has enabled it to play a conscious role in its own change and transformation.

One of the most useful concepts to appear at the time of the council was that of a 'non-historical orthodoxy', developed by Michael Novak in his book *The Open Church*.[18] 'Non-historical orthodoxy' describes a belief that, over time, has mistakenly assumed the certainty of a doctrine held to be orthodox, a matter of faith, even though it represented at best a theological position that had no real biblical or historical foundation. Catholics in the period prior to Vatican II grew up and took for granted a host of 'Catholic' positions – on papal infallibility, the nature of the

---

[18] *The Open Church: Vatican II, Act II* (New York: Macmillan, 1964); see especially chapter 5, 'The School of Fear'.

Church, the source or sources of revelation, the sacral nature of
the priesthood, the existence of limbo, and so on – all of which
could be considered examples of non-historical orthodoxy.

It is also true that positions taught by the ordinary magisterium
and held – in some cases for centuries – as Catholic doctrine have
ultimately been changed as a result of theological critique and a
lack of reception by the faithful. Examples from Church history
include teachings on the temporal power of the popes; the denial
of salvation outside the Church; the conciliarist teaching of the
Council of Constance; the Church's acquiescence in the practice
of slavery, sanctioned by four ecumenical councils; and the justification and authorization of the use of torture for obtaining an
admission of guilt.[19] Examples of more recent papal teachings
modified or rejected by Vatican II include Pius IX's inability to find
any truth or goodness in non-Christian religions, his condemnation of the proposition that Church and state should be separated,
his denial of religious freedom as an objective right, and Pius XII's
exclusive identification of the Catholic Church with the mystical
body of Christ.[20]

The council not only began a renewal of Catholic life; it also
changed the way Catholics understood themselves and their
Church.

[19] See Luis M. Bermejo, *Infallibility on Trial: Church, Conciliarity and Communion*
(Westminster: Christian Classics, 1992).
[20] J. Robert Dionne, *The Papacy and the Church: A Study of Praxis and Reception in
Ecumenical Perspective* (New York: Philosophical Library, 1987).

Chapter 15

The Church (*Lumen Gentium*)

Richard P. McBrien

History and content

The Second Vatican Council was concerned primarily with the nature and mission of the Church. Its explicit theological focus, therefore, was ecclesiological rather than christological, eschatological, or anthropological. Two of the council's sixteen documents served as the twin pillars of its ecclesiology: the Dogmatic Constitution on the Church (*Lumen Gentium*) and the Pastoral Constitution on the Church in the Modern World (*Gaudium et Spes*). This essay is concerned exclusively with the former document, although in the beginning both were intended to be part of a single document on the Church (*De Ecclesia*).

The first draft of *Lumen Gentium* (more precisely: *De Ecclesia*) was prepared by the council's Theological Commission (*De Doctrina fidei et morum*), headed by Cardinal Alfredo Ottaviani, Prefect of the Holy Office (now the Sacred Congregation for the Doctrine of the Faith). The Commission's secretary was Father Sebastian Tromp SJ, formerly professor of ecclesiology at the Pontifical Gregorian University in Rome and the principal author of Pope Pius XII's encyclical *Mystici Corporis* (1943), on the Church as the Mystical Body of Christ.

The first draft of what was to become *Lumen Gentium* consisted of eleven chapters and an appendix:

1. The nature of the Church militant
2. The members of the Church and the necessity of the Church for salvation
3. The episcopate as the highest grade of the sacrament of

orders; the priesthood
4. Residential bishops
5. The state of evangelical perfection
6. The laity
7. The teaching office of the Church
8. Authority and obedience in the Church
9. Relationships between Church and state and religious tolerance
10. The necessity of proclaiming the Gospel to all peoples and in the whole world
11. Ecumenism
Appendix: Virgin Mary, Mother of God and Mother of Men

This initial draft was discussed in six separate meetings during the final week of the council's first session (1–7 December 1962). Although there was some praise for the Theological Commission's work, the most significant comments called attention to the deficiencies of the first draft. Several bishops found the draft 'too juridical' in tone and too little concerned with the Church as mystery, faulted its lack of structural coherence (a point raised explicitly by Milan's Cardinal Montini), complained that it portrayed the laity too much as mere appendages of the hierarchy, expressed concern that the document was insufficiently sensitive to the legitimate role of the state alongside that of the Church, deplored the absence of any genuine ecumenical dimension, and criticized its lack of attention to the works of the Eastern fathers of the Church and to various biblical images of the Church, especially that of people of God. Bishop Emile de Smedt of Bruges (Belgium) synthesized these criticisms in a ringing, three-pronged attack on the first draft. He challenged its 'triumphalism', its 'clericalism', and its 'juridicism'.

Cardinal Suenens insisted that this central conciliar text should speak first of the Church's inner life (*Ecclesia ad intra*) and then of its outward life in the world (*Ecclesia ad extra*). The second part was later separated off from the first in a document known as 'Schema 13' (still later as *Gaudium et Spes*). Cardinal Suenens also suggested the title *Lumen Gentium*, noting, however, that Christ alone is the real 'Light of the Gentiles'.

A central commission was appointed to direct and co-ordinate the work of the various conciliar commissions (including that of the Theological Commission) during the nine-months' recess between the first and second sessions. Six norms were laid down by the council secretariat to guide the work of the central commission. The second norm is of particular interest, given the kind of criticisms directed against the first draft of *Lumen Gentium*: 'The stress is on the pastoral, rather than doctrinal or juridical, nature of the council.' The norms explicitly referred to Pope John XXIII's speech on the council's opening day (11 October 1962), in which he insisted that this council had not been called for doctrinal but for pastoral purposes.

A second draft was prepared by the Theological Commission and presented to the council fathers at the beginning of the second session in September 1963. It contained only four chapters:

1. The Mystery of the Church
2. The hierarchical constitution of the Church and the episcopate in particular
3. The People of God and the laity in particular
4. The call to holiness in the Church

This revised draft elicited a more positive reception, although the discussion still revealed a basic (but far from equal) division between the bishops on their approach to the document as a whole. In the first chapter the Church was no longer spoken of as the Church militant but as a mystery, a community still on pilgrimage rather than already finished and perfected. Nevertheless, Cardinal Raul Silva Henriquez of Santiago (Chile) felt it necessary to suggest an additional chapter on the People of God.

Chapter two caused the greatest controversy: it was concerned with the question of collegiality. Conservative Italian and Spanish bishops expressed grave caution about this concept, preferring a more juridical understanding of the episcopate – one in which each individual bishop is related vertically and subordinately to the pope, without horizontal relationships with the other bishops. Opposition to collegiality was rooted in the concern that collegiality might compromise the primacy of the pope (and perhaps also the 'sovereignty' of the bishop in his own diocese). The overwhelming majority of the council fathers, however, including Pope Paul VI, did not regard this as a serious danger, and so the discussion and the voting moved inexorably forward in support of the doctrine of collegiality, based on appeals to the New Testament, the liturgy of episcopal consecration, and the theology and practice of the East.

As the discussion moved to the third chapter of the second draft, it was clear that the fathers wanted the chapter divided and the material on the people of God moved to a position immediately following chapter one, and before the chapter on the hierarchy. It was also clear that, in spite of some residual clericalism in the text, the bishops were generally enthusiastic about the portrayal of the laity as full partners in the life and mission of the Church. Most of the pastoral application, however, would be reserved for a separate document: the Pastoral Constitution on the Church in the Modern World (*Gaudium et Spes*).

The discussion of the second draft focused finally on Mary, about whom a separate schema had been prepared, 'The Blessed Virgin, Mother of the Church'. Again, there was division within the council. One side favoured the idea of a separate schema, while the other wanted it made a part of the constitution itself. On 25 October 1963 the council moderators asked the council fathers to come to a decision, one way or the other. A debate was arranged, for and against the incorporation of the chapter on Mary into the general schema on the Church. Cardinal Franz König of Vienna spoke on behalf of incorporation, and Cardinal Rufino Santos of Manila spoke on behalf of separation. Cardinal Santos insisted that Mary's role in our redemption transcended her place and function within the Church. But Cardinal König's argument prevailed, if only by a slim margin (1,114 to 1,074); namely, that Mary is a type of the Church and is herself its pre-eminent member. For theological, pastoral and ecumenical reasons alike, she should not be isolated from the unity of the economy of salvation nor from the central ecclesiological focus of the council itself.

Between the second and third sessions of the council the Theological Commission tried to bring the text into line with various criticisms and suggestions. Pope Paul VI, in his turn, worked tirelessly to win the widest possible support for the emerging document. In his opening address to the third session (14 September 1964), he linked the work of the Second Vatican Council with that of the First Vatican Council (1869-70). Vatican I had provided formal declarations concerning the primacy and infallibility of the pope, but it did not have time to complete its teaching on the hierarchical structure of the Church. Specifically, Vatican I left no doctrine of the episcopate. For Pope Paul VI this constituted 'the weightiest and most delicate' subject still facing Vatican II. This Council would have 'as its principal objective the task of describing and honouring the prerogatives of the episcopate'. Otherwise, the pope feared, the false impression would persist that Vatican I had 'limited the authority of bishops' and had 'rendered superfluous ... the convocation of a subsequent ecumenical council'.

The four chapters of the document on the Church were expanded to six, and two new chapters were added to bring the total number to eight: one on eschatology and another on Mary. A section was added in chapter one to show the subordination of the Church to the Kingdom of God (LG 5); the relationship between the Church of Christ and the Roman Church was carefully nuanced to leave room in the Body of Christ for the non-Catholic Churches (LG 8 and 18); a separate chapter was added on the people of God to bring out the historical nature of the Church and the fundamental equality of its members (chapter two); another chapter was added on the laity, underscoring their participation in the prophetic, priestly, and kingly ministries of Jesus (chapter four); a separate chapter on religious was approved (chapter six), and so, too, was the new chapter on the eschatological nature of the Church (chapter seven); and, after much discussion, the council fathers approved the new chapter on Mary, carefully formulated to avoid both Marian maximalism and Marian minimalism (chapter eight).

The major debate over this penultimate draft, however, had to do with the doctrine of the episcopate in chapter three. The drafters were caught between two forces: the one jealous of papal prerogatives and fearful of any undermining of papal primacy, the other suspicious of papal absolutism and supportive of collegiality. The text bent over backwards to reassure the former group. If it succeeded in satisfying some of the more conservative western bishops, it weakened the text in the eyes of the easterners, who insisted on the divine institution of the episcopacy. When the final votes were taken, however, more than two-thirds approved, even though about 500 voted *placet juxta modum* (yes, with reservations). Accordingly, a *nota explicativa* ('explanatory note', also known as a *nota praevia* because it 'came before' the Theological Commission's comments on various last-minute *modi*) was hastily added as an appendix to the constitution to meet the minority's persistent concerns about papal primacy (16 November 1964). The *nota* insisted that the word 'college' was not to be taken in a juridical sense, that the college does not even exist without its head whose function as 'Vicar of Christ and pastor of the universal Church' is left 'intact', and that the pope, 'as supreme pastor of the Church, may exercise his power at any time, as he sees fit, by reason of the demands of his office'. Not surprisingly, the council majority was exceedingly displeased, and the third session ended in an atmosphere marked by considerable tension. Nevertheless, the entire document was approved with near unanimity on 19 November 1964, followed by a final solemn vote on 21 November.

The final version of *Lumen Gentium* thus has eight chapters:

I.   The Mystery of the Church: the Church's sacramental nature, the Trinitarian framework for the mystery of the Church; various biblical images of the Church, especially that of body of Christ

II.   The People of God: the Church as on pilgrimage through history; the Church and Christ's threefold mission as prophet, priest and king; the Church and the sacraments; the Church and non-Catholic Christians and non-Christians

III. The Hierarchical Structure of the Church, with Special Reference to the Episcopate: the New Testament basis for the episcopate; the relationship between the episcopate and the papacy; collegiality; the local Church; priests and deacons

IV.   The Laity: the fundamental equality of the laity with clergy and religious; the place of the laity in both the Church and the temporal world

V.   The Call of the Whole Church to Holiness: the holiness of groupings within the Church: bishops, clergy, religious, laity; the holiness of the Church itself

VI.   Religious: the nature and import of consecration and religious profession and of the observance of the evangelical counsels

VII. The Eschatological Nature of the Pilgrim Church and her Union with the Heavenly Church: the Church and the kingdom of God; death and the resurrection of the body; the communion of saints

VIII. The Role of the Blessed Virgin Mary, Mother of God, in the Mystery of Christ and the Church: The role of the Blessed Virgin in the economy of salvation; the Blessed Virgin and the Church; devotion to the Blessed Virgin in the Church; Mary as a sign of sure hope and of solace for God's people on pilgrimage

Prefatory Note of Explanation (*nota praevia*, or *nota explicativa*): a 'theological qualification' of the doctrine of collegiality adopted in chapter three, to safeguard the primacy and pastoral independence of the pope.

Implementation and structure

The authority of an official teaching of the Church is not deter-mined solely by its source, in this case an ecumenical council, but also by the way in which the teaching has actually transformed the self-understanding and pastoral practice of the Church as a whole. This is what is meant by 'reception'. The principle of reception also guides and shapes what follows in this second major section of the entry.

(a) Methodological principles

The first and methodologically most significant point to be made about *Lumen Gentium* is that it begins with a chapter on the 'mystery' of the Church, unlike the traditional textbooks and cate-chisms which began with the Church as 'hierarchical' institution. The Church is indeed, first and foremost, a mystery, that is to say, 'a reality imbued with the hidden presence of God' (Pope Paul VI, 29 September 1963). This is more than an editorial move. It reflects a fundamental shift in the way we understand the reality of the Church. Thus, when we confess that 'we believe in the Church', the act of faith is centered on the presence of God who is in the Church, and not on the hierarchy or on the Church simply as a religious institution or ecclesiastical organization.

Second, the mystery of the Church in *Lumen Gentium* is placed in a 'trinitarian' framework (LG 2–4), thereby situating the Church in the context of salvation history (elected and called by the Father) and also underscoring its communitarian dimension (enlivened by the Holy Spirit). The Church is no longer conceived in Christomonistic terms, as if it were related only to Christ as the 'prolongation of the Incarnation'.

Third, *Lumen Gentium*, portrays the Church according to many different biblical images, not just as the Mystical Body of Christ, which had been interpreted in the past in a highly juridical manner. If there is, for the constitution, a single dominant biblical image of the Church, it is indeed that of people of God, to which an entire chapter is devoted.

Fourth, the sacraments are also presented in *Lumen Gentium* as an integral part of the mystery of the Church rather than as a kind of appendage to Christology (LG 10–11). Indeed, the Church itself is presented as a fundamental sacrament of Christ, just as Christ is the fundamental, or primordial, sacrament of God (article 1).

Fifth, the fact that the chapter on the hierarchical structure of the Church follows the chapter on the People of God is also highly significant. This reverses the priorities and modifies the perspective of pre-Vatican II Catholic ecclesiology. The Church is primarily a people in whom God is present and through whom God acts on behalf of all humanity. The Church is not primarily a hierarchical institution, nor can it speak and act as if it were.

A final methodological principle concerns the place of Mary in the document. Like the sacraments, Mary is no longer considered separately from the mystery of the Church and the economy of salvation. Neither is Mariology any longer an appendage to christology. Mary is instead a type or model of the Church. Thus, the Church is a community seen, like Mary, as ever open to the Word of God, obedient to the Word in faith, and serving always the mission of Jesus Christ.

(b) General ecclesiological principles

First, *Lumen Gentium* presents the Church as itself a sacrament, 'a sign and instrument, that is, of communion with God and of unity among all men' (LG 1). This is clearly one of the most significant emphases in the entire constitution, and indeed in the whole of the council itself. The sacramental character of the Church has extremely important practical consequences; specifically, it means that the Church must signify what it is. If the Church is the Body of Christ, it must look and act like the Body of Christ. If the Church is the People of God, it must look and act like the people of God. If the Church is the temple of the Holy Spirit, it must look and act like the temple of the Holy Spirit. Church renewal and reform are a direct theological consequence of the sacramentality of the Church, and the strong emphasis on both since Vatican II is a direct result of this teaching.

Second, the Church is not only a sacrament of our union with God and with one another; it is also 'for each and everyone the visible sacrament of this saving unity' (LG 9). This principle must be seen in the context of one of the most important developments in contemporary Catholic theology, linked especially with the work of the late Karl Rahner SJ; namely, the shift away from an Augustinian pessimism about salvation to a more hopeful, universalistic outlook, as reflected in this and other documents of the council. The human race is no longer seen as a *massa damnata* from whom a few are saved to manifest the glory and mercy of God, but as an essentially saved community from whom a few may, by the exercise of their own free will, be lost.

Third, the Church of *Lumen Gentium* is also an eschatological reality, which means that we cannot understand the nature and mission of the Church except in relationship to the Kingdom of God. The Church and the Kingdom of God are inseparable and yet not the same. To identify the Church and the Kingdom of God, as was done so often in the years before Vatican II, is equivalent to ecclesiastical triumphalism (to which Bishop de Smedt had referred). LG 5 makes it clear that the Church is 'the seed and the beginning of that kingdom' rather than the Kingdom of God itself.

Fourth, in a principle that is reminiscent of the Reformation itself, *Lumen Gentium* acknowledges that, since the Church is not yet the Kingdom of God, it is at the same time holy and sinful (LG 8). Therefore, although the Church is the very Body of Christ and the temple of the Holy Spirit, it 'follows constantly the path of penance and renewal'.

Fifth, without prejudice to the universality of the Church, particular and local Churches retain their own importance and dignity in *Lumen Gentium* (LG 13, 23, and 26). LG 23 is especially important because it acknowledges that the unity and faith and the divine constitution of the universal Church are not undermined by diversity in discipline, liturgy, theology and spirituality. On the contrary, 'This multiplicity of local Churches, unified in a common effort, shows all the more resplendently the catholicity of the undivided Church.' This assurance was borne out in the immediate post-conciliar period. LG 26 is also exceedingly important because it expresses very succinctly the principle of local Church that underlies this diversity:

> This Church of Christ is really present in all legitimately organized local groups of the faithful, which, in so far as they are united to their pastors, are also quite appropriately called Churches, in the New Testament. For these are in fact, in their own localities, the new people called by God, in the power of the Holy Spirit and as the result of full conviction (cf. 1 Thess 1:5). In them the faithful are gathered together through the preaching of the Gospel of Christ, and the mystery of the Lord's Supper is celebrated.

This renewed emphasis on the doctrine of the local Church has also reinforced the council's positive estimation of pastoral diversity and led to a new appreciation for the pastoral practicality of the principle of subsidiarity, heretofore found only in the Church's social teachings. If the local Church is a true expression of the Body of Christ in a particular place, its own unique experience and pastoral wisdom must not be suppressed in an effort to impose uniformity on the universal Church. The development of national episcopal conferences since Vatican II has been one ecclesiological implication of this.

Sixth, indeed, the interaction of the universal Church and the network of local Churches that constitutes the universal Church is at the core of the doctrine of collegiality. It should allow the Catholic Church, in its self-understanding and pastoral practice, to transcend its former attachment to papal absolutism. This is one of the major areas of Vatican II ecclesiology which poses great pastoral challenges to the Church in our own time. Unfortunately, the principle of collegiality has encountered stubborn resistance as it is being assimilated into the life, structure and mission of the Church. Many of the Church's present pastoral leaders continue to prefer a more centralized structure of authority and jurisdiction and make every effort to circumvent the pastoral prerogatives of bishops and faithful at the level of the local Church.

Seventh, this tendency to administer the Church as if it were in fact a monarchical institution also ignores the crucial principle articulated at the beginning of chapter four: 'Everything that has been said of the People of God [in chapter two] is addressed equally to laity, religious and clergy.' All have 'a common dignity ... deriving from their rebirth in Christ' (article 32). This principle of communal equality applies especially to the threefold mission of the Church, which is, in turn, participation in the threefold mission of Jesus Christ, as prophet, priest and king. The principle has been embodied since Vatican II in such pastoral developments as parish and diocesan councils and in the increasing involvement of the laity in theology, religious education, liturgy, spiritual direction, and even parochial and diocesan administration.

Eighth, the whole Church, therefore, is also called to holiness, and not just the ordained and religiously professed (chapter five). This emphasis on the universal call to holiness is at least partially responsible for the 'democratization' of Catholic spirituality since the council. It is no longer a matter of concern for priests, nuns and brothers alone.

Ninth, *Lumen Gentium* also significantly recasts our understanding, and eventually our practice, concerning the relationship between the Catholic Church and the various other Christian Churches and non-Christian religions. 'This Church, constituted and organized as a society in the present world, subsists in the Catholic Church, which is governed by the successor of Peter and by the bishops in communion with him' (LG 8). The council explicitly avoided making the kind of identification of Body of

Christ and Catholic Church that we find in Pope Pius XII's encyclical, *Humani Generis* (1950). On the contrary, we have a fundamental Christian bond with all other Christians. We honour and are nourished by the same sacred scriptures; we believe in the Trinity; we are consecrated by the same baptism; and we recognize and receive many of the same sacraments. We are even united with some other Christians in the place we accord to the episcopate, the Eucharist, and the Blessed Virgin Mary. We also share with our non-Catholic brothers and sisters a common experience of prayer and other spiritual benefits (LG 15). Furthermore, because we all come from the same creative hand of the one God, we are spiritually related as well to non-Christians, especially Jews and Moslems (LG 16).

Tenth, although the Church of *Lumen Gentium* is clearly a Church that offers the salvation of God in Christ, *Lumen Gentium* recognizes that salvation is possible even apart from explicit faith in Christ, or even apart from any religious faith at all: 'Nor shall divine providence deny the assistance necessary for salvation to those who, without any fault of theirs, have not yet arrived at an explicit knowledge of God, and who, not without grace, strive to lead a good life' (LG 16).

(c) Ecclesiological corollaries

First, the Church must be a Church of poverty, following 'the same path' as Christ who 'carried out the work of redemption in poverty and oppression' (LG 8). This is a corollary of the fundamental principle concerning the sacramentality of the Church. As *Lumen Gentium* declares: 'Likewise, the Church, although she needs human resources to carry out her mission, is not set up to seek earthly glory, but to proclaim, and this by her own example, humility and self-denial' (LG 8).

Second, by way of a corollary of the principle that the Church is the whole people of God, *Lumen Gentium* teaches that all the faithful share in the one priesthood of Christ: 'the common priesthood of the faithful and the ministerial or hierarchical priesthood are none the less ordered one to another; each in its own proper way shares in the one priesthood of Christ' (LG 10). The ordained priesthood ministers to this general, or common, priesthood of the whole Church, recognizing the latter's 'contributions and charisms' and moving the faithful 'with one mind [to] co-operate in the common task' (LG 30).

Third, these charisms are available to all the faithful 'of every rank' (LG 12). This is a corollary of the principle that the whole Church is called to holiness, and not just the ordained or the religiously professed minority.

Fouth, membership in the Catholic Church is not sufficient to guarantee salvation, nor is it something we merit and, therefore, can take pride in. 'Even though incorporated into the Church, one who does not however persevere in charity is not saved … all children of the Church should nevertheless remember that their exalted condition results, not from their own merits, but from the grace of Christ' (LG 14). *Lumen Gentium* tilts consistently against triumphalism. This is a corollary of the principle that the Church is not itself the Kingdom of God, but that salvation is available to the many, not just to the few.

Fifth, the episcopal office of sanctifying, teaching and governing is transmitted by ordination, not by the granting of jurisdiction (LG 21). *Lumen Gentium* explicitly rejects the popular, but misguided, view that bishops are simply 'vicars of the Roman Pontiff'. On the contrary, they are 'vicars and legates of Christ' and their pastoral power, which 'they exercise personally in the name of Christ', is 'proper, ordinary and immediate' (LG 27). This is a corollary of the wider principle of collegiality.

Sixth, there is no inequality in the Church based on race, nationality, social or economic condition, or sex (LG 32). This, too, is a corollary of a larger principle which understands the Church as the People of God wherein all are equal in dignity: laity, religious and clergy alike. This corollary also raises some controversial questions about access to ministry and to pastoral influence in the Church.

Seventh, as another obvious corollary of the principle that the Church is the whole people of God, *Lumen Gentium* teaches that the lay apostolate is a direct participation in the mission of the Church, and is not simply a participation in the mission of the hierarchy: 'The apostolate of the laity is a sharing in the salvific mission of the Church. Through Baptism and Confirmation all are appointed to this apostolate by the Lord himself' (LG 33). Therefore, the laity has something also to contribute to the life of the Church and not simply to the transformation of the world in the so-called temporal order: 'By reason of the knowledge, competence or pre-eminence which they have the laity are empowered – indeed sometimes obliged – to manifest their opinion on those things which pertain to the good of the Church' (LG 37). The traditional division of labour – clergy in the 'sacristy' and laity in the world – is artificial and even false.

Finally, holiness is a principal sign of the credibility of the Church: 'God shows to men, in a vivid way, his presence and his face in the lives of those companions of ours in the human condition who are more perfectly transformed into the image of Christ' (LG 50). This stands as a corollary of other principles; namely, that the whole Church is called to holiness, and that the Church is itself a sacrament, called to practise what it preaches. The witness and example of the Church as a community is always a matter of highest missionary significance. Renewed attention to Church reform since Vatican II is a direct consequence of this ecclesiological insight.

(d) Deficiencies

Although one of the great achievements of the Second Vatican Council, *Lumen Gentium* is not without deficiencies. Two are offered here by way of example.

To be sure, Vatican II was an ecclesiological council, but ecclesiology itself presupposes Christology, among other fundamental theological areas. Unfortunately, the council's christology remains always implicit, and it is not a Christology that reflects the rich biblical and theological developments of the last twenty-five years. 'While this may be understandable from a historical point of view, theologically it is not the healthiest of situations', Edward Schillebeeckx OP has written. 'However, a Church which proclaims more of Jesus as the Christ and less of itself would delight a great many Christians' (Schillebeeckx, 1981, p. 103).

In general, chapter three of *Lumen Gentium* is unaffected by even the main lines of New Testament scholarship regarding the early Church. The chapter assumes, for example, that Jesus gave the company of his original disciples a kind of ecclesiastical blueprint from which they were to build an entire structure. Thus, the chapter assumes that the apostles and the Twelve were one and the same group and that each local Church was governed by a bishop from the beginning. Furthermore, there is a constant preoccupation with papal authority, but without the nuancing we find in such ecumenical studies as *Peter and the New Testament*, a 'collaborative assessment by Protestant and Roman Catholic scholars' in the United States (Brown *et al.*, eds., 1973). The prefatory note of explanation for chapter three (*nota praevia*, or *nota explicativa*) only accentuates this stress on the papal office and its prerogatives, at the expense of a genuinely collegial understanding of the Church.

Conclusion

On balance, *Lumen Gentium* has stimulated an extraordinarily rich and fruitful change in Catholic self-understanding and pastoral practice (what we mean by 'reception'). One can only reflect on the document, some twenty-five years later, with a full measure of admiration and gratitude. The achievement of Vatican II should call us, however, not to some new form of progressive triumphalism (a counterpart perhaps to the triumphalism generated by the council of Trent), but to a higher sense of our own responsibility, individually and corporately, to live up to the ideals of the Church that *Lumen Gentium* so compellingly articulated.

Bibliography

Baraúna, G., ed. (1966) *L'Eglise de Vatican II*, 3 vols. *Unam Sanctam*, no. 51a,b,c. Paris, Cerf.

Brown, R. *et al.*, eds. (1973) *Peter and the New Testament.* New York, Paulist Press.

Dulles, A. R. (1982) *A Church to Believe In.* New York, Crossroad.

Dulles, A. R. (1985) *The Catholicity of the Church.* Oxford, Clarendon Press.

Fagin, G. M., ed. (1984) *Vatican II: Open Questions and New Horizons.* Wilmington, Delaware, Michael Glazier.

Grootaers, J. (1986) *Primauté et Collégialité.* Le dossier de Gérard Philips sur la Nota Explicativa Praevia (*Lumen Gentium* ch. III). Leuven, Leuven University Press

Holstein, H. (1970) *Hiérarchie et Peuple de Dieu d'après 'Lumen Gentium'.* Paris, Beauchesne.

Kloppenburg, B. (1974) *The Ecclesiology of Vatican II*, trans. M. J. O'Connell. Chicago, Franciscan Herald Press.

Lindbeck, G. (1970) *The Future of Roman Catholic Theology.* Philadelphia, Fortress Press.

McBrien, R. P. (1980) *Catholicism.* Minneapolis, Winston, chapters 17–24.

Miller, J. H., ed. (1966) *Vatican II: An Interfaith Appraisal.* Notre Dame, Indiana, University of Notre Dame.

O'Donaghue, N. D. (1983) 'Vatican II: The Hidden Questions', *Doctrine and Life*, vol. 33 pp. 41–7.

Rahner, K. (1963, 1966, 1969, 1973, 1974, 1976, 1981) *Theological Investigations*, vols. 2, 5, 6, 10, 12, 14, 17, and 20. New York, Crossroad; London, Darton, Longman and Todd.

Rahner, K. (1974) *The Church after the Council.* New York, Seabury Press.

Richard, L., Harrington, D.J., and O'Malley, J.W. (1987) *Vatican II: The Unfinished Agenda. A Look to the Future.* New York, Paulist Press.

Rikhof, H. (1981) *The Concept of the Church.* London, Sheed & Ward.

Schillebeeckx, E. (1981) *Interim Report on the Books Jesus and Christ.* New York, Crossroad.

Tillard, J. M. R. (1981) 'The Church of God is a Communion: The

Ecclesiological Perspective of Vatican II', *One in Christ*, vol. 17, pp. 117-31.

Van Eijk, A. H. C. (1987) 'The Church as Sacrament. A Contribution to Ecumenical Understanding', *Bijdragen*, vol. 48, pp. 234–58.

Vorgrimler, H., ed. (1967) *Commentary on the Documents of Vatican II*, vol. I. New York, Herder & Herder.

Willebrands, J. (1987) 'Vatican II's Ecclesiology of Communion', *One in Christ*, vol. 23, pp. 179–91.

Chapter 16

The Church in the Modern World
(Gaudium et Spes)

Enda McDonagh

When the Pastoral Constitution, *The Church in the Modern World* (*De Ecclesia in Mundo Hujus Temporis*; but better known by its opening words, '*Gaudium et spes* ...' ('The joys and the hopes ...'), was approved overwhelmingly by the fathers of Vatican II and Paul VI added his signature, the council endorsed a document unprecedented in conciliar history and quite radical in Church history. Its unprecedented character derived from the pastoral concerns of the council as originally conceived by John XXIII. Its openness to the world of its time built on social and other encyclicals, various episcopal and lay initiatives and on the pioneering theological work of Chenu, Congar, Rahner and many others. In face of the flat rejection of the 'modern world' by Pius IX in the Syllabus of Errors just a century before and its continuing influence to the very eve of the council, the council's shift in perspective may well be described as revolutionary. It was certainly profoundly liberating.

Nevertheless, such adjectival evaluation offers little direct insight into the document and may easily become a source of futile controversy. Radical or conservative in a document is as radical or conservative interprets. More significant may be the document's sense of incompleteness. This is obviously true in the discussion on marriage and the family (GS 50) in regard to the means of family planning. It is also clearly true in regard to some of the other 'urgent questions' as pastoral reflection and teaching continue to develop through papal documents like *Populorum Progressio*, *Laborem Exercens* and *Sollicitudo Rei Socialis*; through documents of the Synods of Bishops and through pastoral statements by particular conferences of bishops such as those of the American bishops on peace and war and on the economy. Subsequent theological movements such as Latin American liberation theology, feminist theology, the beginnings of African and Asian theologies and of theologies of the environment reveal the limitations of history and geography in this and other conciliar documents. Church and world continue to change. Vatican II was well aware of this fact and of its inability to stop the world in order to get off (a tendency evident in much of the previous century). In this Constitution (and in other documents) it saw the Church as a dynamic, pilgrim people within the historically developing human community. The openness that became so quickly characteristic of the council found its fullest expression in Schema 13, as this Constitution was known for so long, but so did the incomplete, unfinished nature of the council's business. *The Church in the Modern World* is not a tidy, closed statement of principle, requiring no more than dutiful application to new circumstances.

Origins and history

The remoter origins of this Constitution in Church teaching, theology and practice may be found, as indicated above, in the development of the Church's social teaching from Leo XIII. No less important were the recovery of confidence in biblical studies with Pius XII's encyclical *Divino Afflante Spiritu*, the renewal in patristic studies, the emergence of '*la nouvelle théologie*' despite the setback associated with *Humani Generis*, and a host of practical missionary and pastoral initiatives in the first half of the century. John XXIII's convocation of the council (25 January 1959), and particularly his opening address, emphasized the pastoral thrust of his intentions. Yet there was no hint of any major pastoral document in the preparatory documents. After Cardinal Suenens's intervention on 4 December 1962 outlining a programme for the council both *ad intra* and *ad extra*, endorsed the following day by Cardinal Montini, proposals for such a document began to take shape, first as Schema 17 and later, and for most of the remaining period of the council, as Schema 13.

Social issues had been considered by the Theological Commission and the Commission for the Lay Apostolate. From these commissions came the mixed commission that was to develop the schema. The consultations over almost three years (January 1963 to December 1965) in Rome, Malines, Zürich, Ariccia and in-between times and places were complex and protracted. In method, structure and content the document changed course many times. How far it should be doctrinal or pastoral, general or particular, evangelical or philosophical exercised consultants and fathers of the council right up to the end. The treatment of particular questions (part II of the final document), for example, remained for long a series of appendices to the earlier 'doctrinal' statement. And the particular questions themselves, especially those of marriage and the family and of peace and war, were in doubt and debate up to the very end.

Papal activities, independently of the council, influenced the development of Schema 13 quite significantly. Pope John's encyclical *Pacem in Terris*, issued shortly before he died in 1953, seemed to some council fathers to make the work on Schema 13 redundant. In fact, it headed them in the right direction and proved a valuable resource in method and content, although there was some modification in the council's document of the encyclical's very strongly worded teaching on war. The establishment of a papal commission on birth regulation and Paul's explicit instructions precluded full treatment of this aspect of marriage in the council document. His visit and address to the United Nations during the council's final session, while it was debating this constitution, reinforced the value and validity of its subject for many fathers.

Method and style

As there was no proper precedent, questions of approach, method and style figured prominently in the discussions of commissions and in debates in the Aula. Encyclicals on social issues were perhaps the closest model in approach and concern. They had, prior to John XXIII, adopted a largely natural law approach to social, economic and political questions. In the background, and sometimes in the foreground, lay the conceptual analysis of two distinct 'perfect societies', Church and state. The power of this approach was still evident in manuals of public ecclesiastical law on which Cardinal Ottaviani, Prefect of the Holy Office, was a notable authority. However, its appeal was waning. As the Church recovered more biblical richness in self-understanding, natural law categories (for all their continuing validity in so many areas) seemed less appropriate to those charged with discussing the Church in the world.

'World' itself was a world away from state, particularly state as 'perfect society'. The ambiguity, indeed multiguity, of the word caused much difficulty for drafters and debaters. The biblical difficulty of a world that God so loved (John: 3.16) and a world that Jesus' disciples must be in but not of (John: 17.16) had been greatly exacerbated in the history of the Church and of theology. The world as created and viewed as good was inextricably entangled with the world as sinful and destructive. But this was also a world redeemed in Jesus Christ. Under the influence of his redeeming grace, the world of the whole human community could be approached as positive partner by the community of explicit believers in Christ. In adopting this approach, the Constitution sought release from the suspicion and fear which certainly characterized the Church in Europe for so much of the previous hundred years.

This approach was basically evangelical, founded in the biblical goodness of creation and new creation with their universal thrust. Difficulties about describing the world, about the categories and the language to be used, found their resolution within this evangelical evaluation. The two-tier nature and grace terminology, as well as the older dualism of sin (world) and grace (Church), yielded to a descriptive language about human achievements and failures which could then be analysed in the light of the Gospel of Jesus Christ. Technical theological language was as far as possible avoided in favour of a language shared by Christians and others. So the wider human audience which was also addressed could be engaged and perhaps opened up to the further Christian reflection central to the document. The 'signs of the times', a concept crucial both to this Constitution and to the council as a whole, must of course be recognizable before they could be usefully scrutinized and analysed in Christian terms.

This approach and language were reinforced by the pastoral tone of the document. 'Pastoral', in the sense of loving care, first of all for Church members, but then for all Christians and all humanity, was a key word of the whole council. It is sometimes contrasted with 'doctrinal' and 'juridical' in so far as they involve more explicit attention to exposition of truth and disciplinary regulation. Truth and discipline have their 'pastoral' loving-care dimensions. The Pastoral Constitution was very aware of this and doctrine, expressed in a caring mode of course, was central to its development. Indeed, for many at the council and subsequent commentators, the main contribution of the document was seen to be a Christian doctrine of humanity or a Christian anthropology. Its emergence involved a pastoral sensitivity, a loving awareness of humanity in its actual condition and a loving sense of responsibility to it. Such care and commitment are also a source of understanding and knowledge, and not just derived from them.

The Constitution deliberately avoided condemnations. The one exception, on indiscriminate nuclear warfare (GS 80), maintained despite criticism, helped to prove the rule. Beyond that the language was one of encouragement rather than juridical imposition. The combination of evangelical approach, non-technical language and evident loving concern suggest that in the Constitution a new style of Church teaching was emerging, if not always successfully. Clarity occasionally was lost as the language or ideas were insufficiently developed. The chapter on culture (GS 53–62) is one illustration. The attempts to achieve clarity by sheer repetition throughout the document are seldom successful. These are the hazards of innovative work and of committee work. One must finally marvel at the achievement, given its scope, innovative character and the continuing pressures of time and diversity of personnel at Commission and council levels.

Structure

The structure of a document like this is always closely related to method and style. As method and style were clarified for the Constitution, so was the structure. That of the final text responded quite faithfully to the original inspiration, although it had undergone several crises in the meantime. The integration of the particular questions and the addition of an introductory statement were the latest major changes which gave the text that unity, substance and relevance for which it received a final massive endorsement.

After a Preface signalling the basis and intent of the document, comes the Introductory Statement on 'The Situation of Humanity in the Modern World'. This is a general descriptive statement in language acceptable to Christians and others. The two main parts that follow are designated 'The Church and the Human Calling' (Part one) and 'Some Problems of Special Urgency' (Part two). It should be noted here that the translations from the 1960s, which are still in vogue, were not yet sensitive to risks of sexist language. So instead of 'Human Condition' one finds 'Man's Condition'; instead of 'Human Calling' 'Man's Calling', and so on. This commentary will endeavour as far as possible to avoid such language without, one hopes, offence to the original sense.

Part one, 'The Church and the Human Calling', is divided into four chapters: 1. The Dignity of the Human Person (GS 12–22); 2. The Community of Humankind (GS 23–32); 3. Human Activity

Throughout the World (GS 33–9); 4. The Role of the Church in the Modern World (GS 40–5). Part two, 'Some Problems of Special Urgency', is divided into five chapters: 1. Fostering the Nobility of Marriage and the Family (GS 47–52); 2. The Proper Development of Culture (GS 53–62); 3. Socio-Economic Life (GS 63–72); 4. The Life of the Political Community (GS 73–6); 5. The Fostering of Peace and the Promotion of a Community of Nations (GS 77–90).

The logic of the overall structure is quite clear. The Introductory Statement sets the contemporary scene. Basic or general considerations in Part one on human person, community and activity in the context of the Gospel are completed by examining the overall role of the Church in the modern world. All this should provide the proper preparation for discussing the more specific issue of Part two. Yet, as frequently happens in such exercises, the discussion in Part two, while consistent with that in Part one, might well have gone on independently of the first part. This is no doubt partly due to the more developed state of discussion on many of these specific issues, with the exception of culture, and partly to the truly innovative aspects of Part one. They were not entirely ripe for integration into some of the more mature discussions in Part two.

With Part two itself there is a certain lack of coherent development. 'Some Urgent Problems' cannot be expected to form a neat logical package, so the chapter on 'Marriage and the Family', while overlapping with other problems, for example, demography and poverty, stays uneasily within a (healthy) tradition of personal values while the others are concerned with more social values. Here the order is not entirely clear, with some clear issues of economics appearing in the discussion of the international community in chapter five and so separated from the discussion in chapter three. Similarly, with political issues in chapter four and chapter five. The chapter on 'Culture', while in point of fact unsatisfactory and less mature than the other discussions, could well in theory have formed the overall matrix for Part two. Certainly it would have been a more coherent starting-point than 'Marriage and the Family'.

Bishops and experts alike were conscious of some of these deficiencies. However, they rightly decided that time was running out and it was better to have something than nothing, so they approved the present document as the best available in the circumstances and time available.

Title

The final official title, *De Ecclesia in Mundo Hujus Temporis*, literally, 'The Church in the World of this Time', aptly caught the intentions of its promoters. Despite earlier variations, it became a firm choice for the majority in the final debates. Difficulties about both major terms 'Church' and 'world' have already been noted and will arise again.

A different difficulty arises about the word 'modern' in English translation, which as indicated is not an absolutely literal translation of the Latin (*hujus temporis*, of this time). My preferred translation in Abbott, unfortunately uses 'The Church Today' as a running head, missing the great word 'world'. French and German translations, by contrast, are literal, such as *L'Eglise dans le Monde de ce Temps* and *Die Kirche in der Welt von Heute*. In cultural and political debates, with which the Constitution is directly concerned, 'modern' is often used to cover the last two centuries – history since the American and French revolutions. With this usage the Constitution and its authors could well feel comfortable. For many Catholics and others, Vatican II – and particularly this Constitution – meant the final acceptance of the democratic revolutions. Their rejection by popes and Church leaders in the nineteenth century had been definitively overcome.

In other respects too, 'modern' could be a useful term to those who accept the Constitution. The Industrial Revolution, urbanization and the further implication of developing technology are addressed honestly and fairly. The achievements of science are no longer seen as a threat. Galileo has become an embarrassment. The hope is for dialogue and partnership between science and religion. The values of the Enlightenment, so long the bogey of Church authorities, are being critically integrated into Catholic thinking and teaching.

The Constitution is also regularly referred to by the first three Latin words of the text, *Gaudium et Spes*. This traditional form of reference for Church documents captures very well the spirit of the document as a whole.

Finally, it was termed a 'Pastoral' Constitution. While the title 'Constitution' adds weight to its teaching beyond that of 'decree' and places it beside the documents on the Church, Revelation and the Liturgy, 'Pastoral' sets it on its own against the 'Dogmatic' Constitutions on the Church and Revelation. The word may be interpreted diversely. On the one side, it might be used to diminish the weight of its teaching – it is *merely* pastoral. On the other, it can be said that Pope John declared his intention to call a *pastoral* council so that *Gaudium et Spes* as its one and only *pastoral* Constitution represents the central purpose of Pope John better than anything else and thus has, in a way, the greatest authority. It may well be claimed that this document does express better than any other what was finally most characteristic of Vatican II.

Preface and introductory statement

Gaudium et Spes are in fact the first words of the Preface. The distinction between preface and the subsequent 'Introductory Statement' may be worth noting. The Preface (GS 1–3) stresses the intimate connection between Church and world as the Church makes its own the joys and hopes, the griefs and anxieties of all humanity. It addresses not only all Catholics and Christians but all of humanity in order to be of service. The engagement, openness and desire to be of service are far removed from the triumphalism and exclusivism that have characterized Church statements at other times.

Following this up, the Introductory Statement (GS 4–10) attempts to discern (that is, discover in difficult circumstances) 'the signs of the times' by surveying, fairly briefly at this point, the current human situation. The language and categories are accessible to people beyond the Church. The preliminary and selective nature of the description opens up the deeper and more detailed reflection without trying the substance of the Constitution's reflections to the necessarily limited and perhaps transient features mentioned here.

The profound and rapid changes evident in the contemporary world affect every dimension of human living. Many listed here receive fuller treatment in the main text. However, it is worth remarking on the further reference to 'socialization' and its relation to 'personalization'. Socialization first appeared in John XXIII's encyclical *Mater et Magistra* (1960) and met with some sharp criticism in the United States of America and elsewhere. Its reappearance here and the balance attempted later between person and community (GS 12–32) in human living and in the light of the gospel, offers an important contribution to human and Christian anthropology. Under the heading 'The Broader Desires of Humankind', reference is made to women's claims to 'equity with men before the law and in fact'. But there is no sign of foreseeing the immense impact the women's movement was about to make on society, Church or theology. A final section on 'Deeper Questions' arising from this sketch indicates the document's fuller strategy. Such questions may open one up to what Jesus Christ has to offer, to what God has achieved in Jesus Christ for humanity's self-understanding and fulfilment. We have here the beginnings of a christology formulated precisely 'to illuminate the mystery of man'.

Part I: The Church and the Human Calling

The introduction and the four chapters of this part outline a Christian anthropology for our times. The first two chapters on 'The Dignity of the Human Person' and 'The Community of Humankind' seek to integrate the irreducible personal quality of each human being as created in the image of God with the equally constitutive social dimension of the human in relationship and structure. Despite the best efforts of these chapters and the document as a whole, the integration is not complete. The individual person remains dominant, with the social essential perhaps but subordinate. The influence of personalism was a dominant and in many ways a welcome influence at the council. Its grounding in the image of God and final relation to Christ gave the person a power and role congenial to the council fathers. That community was equally rooted in God's image and Christ's body did not have quite the same impact. 'Socialization' remained to some extent the poor relation of 'personalization', as the emphasis on the person as centre and goal of society and society's functions indicated.

A more complete Christian anthropology would have recognized that the person may only be person as person-in-relationships-in-structures, as person-in-community, and as in an immediate dialectic with a community-of-persons. Only by such hyphenated expressions may we hope to break the hold of a personalism that in practice readily becomes individualism, without falling victim to the collectivism against which the council rightly warns.

In the discussion of a Christian anthropology, sin enters immediately after the paragraph on creation in God's image (GS 13). It is a brief reference and fits into the document's overall positive affirmation of humanity and world. Even with later references to human death and to the suffering and danger to which humanity is exposed in poverty, hunger and war, there seems to be insufficient awareness of the tragic dimensions of human life. This is surprising as the dominant theologians and fathers of the council had experienced at first hand the awful tragedies of war in Europe and the horrors of the Holocaust. It is very much a reflection of the optimism of the 1960s, in which war and Holocaust seemed, temporarily, almost forgotten.

The paragraphs on conscience and freedom (GS 16–17), as essential aspects of human dignity, relate clearly to the council's Declaration on Religious Liberty (*Dignitatis Humanae*). The subsequent paragraphs on atheism (GS 19–21) embody a long and difficult discussion in Commission and council. Relationship to God enters into human dignity. The council makes this dimension very clear. Yet it displays considerable sensitivity in differentiating between the various forms of atheism, theoretical and practical, systematic and personal. It does not ignore possible personal culpability, but is also conscious of Christian responsibility for others' lack of belief. And it shows itself willing to work with all in the cause of human dignity. Despite strong pressure, explicit condemnations of Marxism, communism or other systems were avoided.

The return to Christology – Christ, the new human being, the final Adam – at the end of chapter one (GS 22) confirms the council's strategy: humanity can only be finally understood and explained in terms of Jesus Christ. In him we are revealed properly to ourselves.

The Community of Humankind in chapter two is presented as part of God's plan (GS 24). The 'Interdependence of Person and Society' (GS 25) and 'Promoting the Common Good' (GS 26) emphasize the further intimate connection of the personal and social. The primacy of the person reasserts itself in GS 27, although the attempt to maintain the intimate connection continues in GS 30 on the limitations of an individualistic ethic. Chapter two finds its inevitable completion in Christ, with 'The Incarnate Word and Human Solidarity' (GS 32).

'Human Activity Throughout the World', the concern of chapter three (GS 33–9), gives a positive and helpful account of human creativity and work. 'The Rightful Independence of Earthly Affairs' (GS 35) is another effort to recognize certain 'secular' implications of creation/incarnation and the demand that the Church be servant not Lord. The Christ-fulfilment of human work anticipated in the Eucharist (GS 38) reaches its completion in 'A New Earth and a New Heaven' (GS 39). The eschatological character of Christian faith, Church and world, strongly insisted on by one group of consultors and fathers, receives explicit if brief treatment here. The values of the 'Green Movement' are no more anticipated in chapter three than are those of feminism in earlier sections, yet some basis is offered for current environmental discussion. More apocalyptic views of eschatology are also largely ignored.

Chapter four, 'The Role of the Church in the Modern World', moves from Christian anthropology to active ecclesiology or missiology, but the relationship between the Church and world is seen to be a two-way one, of mutual interaction: 'The Church knows how richly she has profited by the history and development of humanity' (GS 44) – that may well be one of the council's most significant admissions.

The bonds uniting Church and world (GS 40) prompt the Church to help individuals and society. The dignity and freedom of the individual, human rights, are given final foundation in the Church's teaching and – it is claimed – helped to effective implementation in the Church's practice. Again, although she has 'no proper mission in the political, economic or social order' (GS 42), the Church's religious mission supports society and recognizes the value of movements towards unity and socialization.

The paragraph on the Church's help to society is hesitant and tentative in comparison with later or even earlier Church documents. The council is clearly feeling its way. The earlier paragraph on helping the individual is much stronger and clearer, confirming perhaps the stronger sense of the individual in this anthropology. Church help to human activity (GS 43) is mainly concerned with the duties of lay Christians. It forthrightly rejects any false opposition between worship and one's professional social activities. 'Secular duties and activities belong properly although not exclusively to lay people.' The duty of bishops and clergy is primarily to see that these activities of the laity 'are bathed in the light of the gospel'. This general view of the council may be insisting on too sharp a distinction between clergy and laity. However, it did help to cope with two traditional difficulties, the tendency of bishops and clergy to interfere improperly in political and social affairs and the tendency of the laity to separate sharply their Sunday worship and their work lives.

GS 44 endorses once again the mutual relationship sought by the council. The help that the Church receives from the modern world includes the progress of the sciences and the wisdom of the philosophers, the leadership of politicians, even the actions of critics and persecutors. It is an exciting passage: 'With the help of the Spirit, it is the task of the entire People of God, especially pastors and theologians, to hear and interpret the many voices of our age ... in this way revealed truth can be better understood.'

The spirit, methodology and purpose of the council were here exceptionally well expressed.

This chapter, like each of those in part one, ends christologically. If these four paragraphs (GS 22, 32, 39 and 45) are put together, they present a quite exciting doctrine of Christ and a partial response to the complaint that the council concentrated to much on ecclesiology and too little on Christology.

Part II: Some Problems of Special Urgency

Marriage and the family

Chapter one, 'On Fostering the Nobility of Marriage and the Family', was inevitably one of the most sharply debated chapters of the Constitution. After adverting to the state of marriage and the family in the modern world (GS 47), the Constitution develops a theology of marriage that is scriptural, sacramental and deeply human. A community of love open to life established in covenant between free and equal partners and founded in the covenant relationship between Christ and his Church might fairly summarize the council's teaching. Juridical and contractual language is avoided. So too is the discussion of (or distinction between) primary and secondary ends. Children are the fruit of conjugal love and are to be welcomed accordingly. The loving family is life-giving beyond its own boundaries to society as a whole.

This is an excellent expression of a theology of marriage that had been developing in the Church since the 1940s. It has by and large stood the test of time since.

The discussion of responsible transmission of life (GS 50 and 51) is sensitive to the pressures on families to limit or postpone further children without violating the objective moral law. Indeed, here for the first time the Church positively stressed the concept and practice of 'responsible parenthood': that it is morally right for the married to decide when and how many children they should have: 'Parents themselves should ultimately make the judgment in the sight of God.' This constituted a major step forward in the field of Catholic marital teaching. The question as to which means can rightly be used must seem secondary in comparison. In practice, they were, of course, vital. The increasingly common use of the contraceptive pill and worldwide fears of the consequences of a population explosion, linked with a falling death-rate, made a reconsideration of the morality of artificial contraception urgent. Its earlier rejection by other Churches, including the Anglican Communion, had already been reversed and the pressure to reconsider the teaching of Pius XI and Pius XII in this area coming both from lay people and many pastors was immense. Conciliar discussion of contraception was, however, forbidden by the pope, who insisted that it be further investigated by a special papal commission and then left to him to decide. The council accepted this and merely declared, without specifying which, that those methods of regulating procreation found wrong by the Church's teaching authority should not be practised by Catholics.

Footnote 14 of the Latin text, with its references to Pius XI's *Casti Connubii* and some allocutions of Pius XII at the direction of Paul VI, made the state of play clear but was not meant to foreclose further discussion. Reference to the Papal Commission was to explain why the council could not complete the work itself. The footnote's terms have been claimed to be ambiguous depending, according to some commentators, on where you put a comma. After mentioning the work of the Commission, the footnote concludes; '*Sic stante doctrina Magisterii, S. synodus solutiones concretas immediate proponere non intendit*' ('With the doctrine of the magisterium in this state, this holy Synod does not intend to propose immediate concrete solutions'; Abbot, p. 256. Placing the comma after *sic* to make it read *Sic, stante doctrina magisterii …* could translate as: 'So, with the doctrine of the magisterium still intact, etc.', but this is a highly implausible interpretation which does not fit the context of the footnote.) The accepted punctuation and translation in fact suggest that the Church did not regard the issue as a closed one despite the teaching of earlier popes. The way was left open for a papal decision in either direction. The judgement of *Humanae Vitae* three years later was not necessarily implicit within what the council was permitted to say.

Many people regretted then and since that the council was not free to complete the discussion on birth control. There were, undoubtedly, great practical difficulties in the way, not least the pressure of time. If these could have been overcome and the council had reached some conclusion, whatever it might have been, it would probably have received much more widespread support than *Humanae Vitae* did subsequently. A reaffirmation of the traditional position by the council in 1965 would never have produced the crisis that it did when coming from the pope three years later.

The proper development of culture

This, the subject of chapter two, was by far the most novel of the special questions considered, and Cardinal Lercaro spoke of it as being at the heart of the Constitution.

The Introduction (GS 53) displays a proper openness to attempts to define, or rather describe, culture. It adverts to attempts by the more empirical sciences to categorize cultures as total ways of life of particular peoples at particular times, a series of human creations. Acceptance of a plurality of cultures and the categorization of religion with cultural schemes indicate the free spirit of the document. The freedom of spirit was, however, also a source of weakness owing to vagueness of language and concept, and it came in for some criticism both within and without the Aula. The lack of maturity, remarked on earlier, affects the chapter as a whole. Yet it breaks important new ground. There are some valuable insights and it must be regretted that so little theological attention has subsequently been paid to it.

Two crucial features of human culture for Christians emerge. It is in and through culture that divine as well as human creativity is revealed. To discern God's activity in the world, to read the divine signs of the times, the Church must be in dialogue with and so understand the language of particular cultures. This applies to the Bible as expression of a particular culture. All divine communication is mediated through human culture. Moving in the other direction, the Church must seek to translate its message and liturgy from one culture to another. The Word of God must take flesh in cultures outside traditional Western ones (GS 58). The Constitution does not develop such points. The language and repetition tend to obscure them, and they still await more serious theological exploration and practical implementation.

The logic of creation and incarnation that has just been applied to faith and culture also involves respect for the autonomy of culture, of human creative activities, in science and the arts, in politics and economics. The Church's acceptance of scientific progress and its respect for scientific method is stressed once again. This is part of a wider respect for the search for truth, for artistic freedom and for the integrity and freedom of intellectual enquiry. All this must be understood, worked with and applied by Christians and theologians in the search for fuller truth and deeper harmony between gospel and culture.

Despite a certain vagueness in this chapter as a whole, its final article (GS 62) is precise enough, and one of the most important

of any council text, applying as it does the spirit of the Declaration
on Religious Freedom to the Church's own intellectual life:

> Furthermore it is to be hoped that many lay people will receive an
> appropriate formation in the sacred sciences, and that some will
> develop and deepen these studies by their own labours. In order
> that such persons may fulfil their proper function, let it be recog-
> nized that all the faithful, clerical and lay, possess a lawful freedom
> of enquiry and of thought, and the freedom to express their minds
> humbly and courageously (*in humilitate et fortitudine*) about those
> matters in which they enjoy competence.

Some of the bishops objected to 'courageously' (*in fortitudine*), but
the council accepted it. It is not a text to be forgotten.

Economics and politics

Chapters three and four, and chapter five, section two (GS 83-90),
deal with economic and political issues in ways that owe a good
deal to the encyclicals of John XXIII and have been developed
since Paul VI, John Paul II, the Synod of Bishops and particular
bishops' conferences. Again, brief commentary on the more
important points must suffice.

Chapter three, 'Socio-Economic Life', is a look at the current
economic scene with its achievements and failures, leading to a
series of important if conventional points about the primacy of
human beings over economics, which is to be at the service and in
the control of human beings. Reducing human beings to
economic units in a collectivist or free-market economy offends
against this basic human and Christian vision. So do the huge
differences in people's share in economic power and in the goods
of the world (GS 63–6). In seeking principles for proper economic
development, the Constitution expresses the primacy of the
human by the primacy of labour over profits as the person's way of
providing a living for self and family. Freedom to organize as
workers, to withdraw labour, to participate in its fruits and in deci-
sion-making about it are reaffirmed.

As for the goods of the earth and their ownership, the
Constitution remains consistent with its entire understanding of
humanity in creation. The goods of the earth belong first to the
whole human community (GS 69). This reversal of the usual order
in discussing ownership makes theological sense and recalls the
reversal effected in the Constitution on the Church where the
People of God are discussed prior to structures and hierarchy.

Private ownership is subsequently justified as a safeguard of personal freedom, but it is subsequent and secondary. The obligation to provide everybody with a basic income, the social obligations of all private property, respect for communal ownership as it has traditionally existed, the rights of a person in extreme necessity – all these emphasize that the world's goods belong primarily to the whole human community. A just economic system must recognize this primacy. So must Christians in seeking first the Kingdom of God (GS 72). Some further international implications of this are taken up in chapter five, section two.

Chapter four, 'The Life of the Political Community', opens with a description of modern political society stressing appreciatively the world-wide pursuit of personal rights, minority rights and civil liberties as ways to realizing the 'common good'. It is striking how a traditional Catholic political preoccupation with the primacy of the common good and natural law is here expressed and given concrete shape in modern liberal, democratic terms. It is on the basis of the organization of people to pursue 'a dynamically conceived common good' (GS 74) with respect for rights and the possibility of democratic participation that the council endorses the 'evolution' of modern politics. While there is nothing new or surprising in all this, the council's clear-cut and positive endorsement does finally bring to an end the century-old quarrel between Church authorities and democracy.

The role of the Church in political life is handled circumspectly but hardly brilliantly. Its witness to and protection 'of the transcendence of the human person' is primary. 'In their proper spheres, the political community and the Church are mutually independent and self-governing.' However, in promoting justice, charity and other social virtues, the Church contributes significantly to the common good.

Sentences like 'the Church herself employs the things of time to the degree that her own proper mission demands' make little sense, implying as they do that the Church is not only in part external to the state, but also basically outside time and society. Here as elsewhere an underlying inadequacy in a theology of the world and the Church in the world surfaced to produce a certain confusion.

To complete the discussion of economics and politics, it is helpful to consider the second section of chapter five before the discussion of peace and war in section one. Chapter five as a whole is entitled 'The Fostering of Peace and the Promotion of the Community of Nations'; section two bears the title 'Building up the International Community' (GS 83–90).

As mentioned earlier, the final debates on this Constitution occurred during and after Pope Paul VI's visit to the United Nations in New York. There is a natural tendency within the Catholic Church to favour mechanisms for international co-operation and organization (the Hapsburg empire in the past, the United Nations today). John XXIII's *Pacem in Terris* had strongly taken up the need and met with world-wide acclaim: it was part of its appeal. The United Nations Declaration on Human Rights in 1948 has become increasingly integrated with Christian and Catholic social theology. Cardinal Roncalli's presence in Paris as Papal Nuncio during the years leading up to the Declaration has been claimed as significant both for the Declaration and for subsequent Church teaching. It is in this spirit that this section of the Constitution promotes the cause of international solidarity and unity.

There is a keen awareness of the social and personal reasons for disunity and discord, from economic and political oppression to personal jealousy and ambition. International political co-operation is essential, requiring effective organizations and a reformed international economic order. The obligations of developing and advanced nations and of the international community to create such a reformed economic order for the fulfilment of all is spelled out.

The difficult problem of high population growth is also faced (GS 87). The need for regulation, and the responsibilities of the political authorities are recognized within, however, the limits of the moral law and with final respect for the rights of parents in deciding on size of family. Consistency with the chapter on the family and with John XXIII's teaching in *Pacem in Terris* ensures that the matter was here ignored, and few of the council fathers would have been willing to go as far as they did prior to Vatican II. The duties of Christians in all this is related to the international presence of the Church as support, guide and inspiration in the development of a truly just and peaceful political and economic order. As earnest of this commitment, it is proposed that an international Catholic Church agency be established 'for the world-wide promotion of justice for the poor' (GS 90). This practical suggestion, implemented in the Secretariat for Justice and Peace, was proposed by one of the few outsiders to address the council, American lay Catholic, James J. Norris. That it should be Catholic rather than ecumenical was criticized, but defended on the grounds that for ecumenical co-operation there must first of all be a Catholic institution. It is certainly the outstanding institutional consequence of the Constitution.

Peace and war

Section one of chapter five bears the title 'The Avoidance of War' (*De Bello Vitando*). Its first significant discussion is of the nature of peace (GS 78). This paragraph refuses to accept peace as a mere absence of war or simply a balance of forces. Following again *Pacem in Terris*, it attempts a far more positive description of peace as an 'enterprise of justice' and as related to the gift and intention of the Divine Creator and founder of society.

The real concern of the section, however, does remain the avoidance of war. This is understandable enough in the light of the international tensions of the times and the possibilities of total nuclear destruction. These debates probably generated the most interest and certainly the most heat of any in the Constitution. While the final text emphatically condemned the indiscriminate destruction of cities or other extensive populated areas as 'a crime against God and man' (GS 81) – by far the strongest condemnation made anywhere by the council – it drew back from Pope John's wider condemnation in his final legacy to the world, *Pacem in Terris*, of modern war in any circumstances, and also from one of the multiplications of weapons as a deterrent. While the resultant text remains strong in striking rhetorical phrases ('the arms race is an utterly treacherous trap for humanity') its teaching upon war remains ambiguous and open to a range of interpretations.

The condemnation of total war and the arms race had not gone undisputed, especially by some United States bishops, and various stratagems were suggested to avoid what seemed to some a 'pacifist' bias. However, the wider condemnation of the consequent misuse of resources badly needed for the hungry and deprived could hardly be faulted, any more than could the urgency of the ultimate goal – the abolition of war (analogous it would seem to the abolition of slavery). For that, it was agreed, a new international authority is needed.

The condemnation of total war, the rejection of the arms race as a safe way to peace and the acceptance of the right to conscientious objection, were very considerable steps beyond the traditional just war theory and its understanding in the 1950s. The overall position of the Constitution did not, nevertheless, outlaw wars of defence or undermine the authority of those responsible for them. On paper, at least, some balance was struck.

If the Constitution made little, in the strategy for peace, of conscientious objection, it did not even advert to the power of peace movements like those of Gandhi and Martin Luther King as expressing the spirit of the Gospel and of *shalom*. Again, a brief reference to opposition to injustice within the state (GS 74) is quite inadequate as a commentary upon gross oppression, and is seen by some as a failure to address the issue of revolution. Here, as in many other matters, Pope Paul was to advance in *Populorum Progressio* far beyond the viewpoint of *Gaudium et Spes*.

The concluding paragraphs of the Constitution constitute an appeal to everyone, whether or not one even explicitly believes in God, to help the vast programme the council has tried to sketch in this document to 'fashion the world more to man's surpassing dignity, search for a brotherhood which is universal ... meet the urgencies of our age ...' Whether or not the Constitution in its many sections adequately spelt out the intricate problems of culture, marriage, politics and economics, the programme of this worldly renewal is in its extent an exciting and moving one. It might be hard to claim that the text of *Gaudium et Spes* has in many of its parts greatly influenced the subsequent life of the Church, but it seems undeniable that the overall emphasis of this vast document – so much longer than anything else the council produced – has done so. Its influence has depended not on its precise analysis of formulations, but on the direction of concern it so clearly indicated.

Affirmation and reservation

The text remains. Twenty-five years on it is still an inspiring and powerful document. Yet its splendid achievement should not obscure its limitations. A few will be discussed here, but not in any ungrateful or ungracious spirit.

The first, most obvious and perhaps most superficial limitation is the Constitution's European or first world character. This criticism might be applied to all the council's documents, it is more obvious and more telling in a document purporting to deal with the world as it is in the light of the gospel. The attention to third-world or second-world situations is, apart from the chapter on economics, merely occasional.

The second limitation must be the absence of the cross from the gospel reflections: social sin, mass oppression, a sheer conspiracy of evil needed to explain so much of human history, all that is largely absent. The world it portrays is one needing development rather than liberation. It is one whose problems seem rather easily resolvable with a bit of goodwill and a renewal of Christian idealism. And this from a dominantly European-American gathering whose members had been through two world wars in this century and still had to live with the responsibility of the Holocaust. The sense of the tragic is largely missing from its world-view as the cross is from its theology.

There are limitations and confusions too in its understanding of the way Christ related to the world, because it concentrates on the mediating symbol of the Church and largely ignores that of the Kingdom. Any attempt to discuss the Church in the world without spelling out the Church's role in discerning, promoting and realizing the Kingdom in the world is bound to be limited and frustrated. And the world proves very difficult to focus without a clearer vision of the relation between creation and new creation and the emergence of the Kingdom in myriad ways beyond but not unrelated to visible Church. Effectively, Christians looking for authoritative guidance in almost any field touched upon by *Gaudium et Spes* are likely to find it better in subsequent documents, from Paul VI's *Populorum Progressio* to John Paul II's *Sollicitudo Rei Socialis*, but to understand the emergence of the vast movement that has led to the Catholic pursuit throughout the world of justice and peace, liberation and brotherhood, the impact of *Gaudium et Spes* remains decisive.

Bibliography

Commentaries

Baum, G., and Campion, D. (1967) *Pastoral Constitution on the Church in the Modern World of Vatican II*. New York, Paulist Press.
Falconer, A., *et al.* (1985) *Freedom to Hope, Documents of Vatican II*. Dublin, Columba Press.
Rahner, K., *et al.* (1967) *Gaudium et Spes, l'Eglise dans le Monde de ce Temps*. Paris, du Cerf.

Theology since the council

Rahner, Schillebeeckx, Congar *et al.* have in their personal writings and through such publications as *Concilium* taken the programme of Vatican II and particularly the first half of the Constitution on *The Church in the Modern World* on to further and fuller development. Their writings in the late 1960s and 1970s are very important.
Rahner, K. (1974) *Theological Investigations*, vol. XI. London, Darton, Longman and Todd.

Contemporary Catholic Theology – a Reader

Rahner, K. (1976) *Theological Investigations*, vol. XIV. London, Darton, Longman and Todd.
Schillebeeckx, E. (1968) *God and Man*. London, Sheed & Ward.
Schillebeeckx, E. (1971) *World and Church*. London, Sheed & Ward.
Schoonenberg, P. (1964) *God's World in the Making*. Dublin, Gill and Macmillan.

A somewhat different line has been opened up by J.B. Metz and others with the development of 'Political Theology'. Where the Constitution had sought to integrate critically so much of the liberal and secular tradition of the previous two centuries, Political Theology pursued more explicitly the dialogue with socialism. It also sought to take account of the interruption of the Holocaust as crucial to future Christian theology.
Metz, J.B. (1968) *The Church in the World*. London, SCM.
Metz, J.B. (1981) *The Emergent Church*. London, SCM.

With Latin American liberation theology, a more radical turn was taken. Gutierrez, G. (1973) *A Theology of Liberation*, London, SCM, remains the classical work, but a great many other significant works have appeared including:
Boff, L. (1988) *Trinity and Society*. New York, Orbis.
Bonino, (1983) *Towards a Christian Political Ethics*. London, SCM.
Segundo, (1977) *The Liberation of Theology*. Maryknoll, NY, Orbis.
Sobrino, J. (1978) *Christology at the Crossroads*. London, SCM.

English language theologians in Britain and Ireland have been more eclectic, drawing on very different traditions, as they sought to develop some of the themes and the spirit of *The Church in the Modern World*. A short list is provided:
Davis, C. (1980) *Theology and Political Society*. Cambridge University Press.
Dorr, D. (1982) *Option for the Poor*. Dublin, Gill and Macmillan.
Lane, D. (1977) *Liberation Theology, An Irish Dialogue*. Dublin, Gill and Macmillan.
Lash, N. (1981) *A Matter of Hope*. London, Darton, Longman and Todd
Mackey, J.P. (1987) *Modern Theology*. Oxford University Press.
McDonagh, E. (1980) *The Demands of Simple Justice*. Dublin, Gill and Macmillan.
McDonagh, E. (1989) *The Gracing of Society*. Dublin, Gill and Macmillan.

The United States and Canada have also supplied a rich if eclectic pattern, in addition to feminist and black theologies. The foundational work of David Tracy is pre-eminent here, but people like John Coleman and Gregory Baum have been combining social analysis with theological reflection in very illuminating ways.
Baum, G. (1982) *The Priority of Labour*. New York, Paulist Press.
Baum, G. (1988) *Theology and Society*, New York, Paulist Press. An outstanding review of twenty-five years of Catholic social teaching.

Coleman, J. (1982) *An American Strategic Theology.*

Lamb, M. (1982) *Solidarity with the Victims.* New York, Crossroad.

McCann, D. (1982) *Liberation Theology and Christian Realism.* New York, Orbis.

Tracy, D. (1981) *The Analogical Imagination.* London. SCM.

Tracy, D. (1987) *Plurality and Ambiguity.* London, SCM.

While a good deal of writing has occurred on special issues in marriage and sexuality, the overall vision of *Gaudium et Spes* is still valid and valuable. Among the more useful books are:

Cahill, L.S. (1985) *Between the Sexes.* Philadelphia, Fortress.

Dominian, J. (1981) *Marriage, Faith and Love.* London, Darton, Longman and Todd.

Genovesi, V.J. (1987) *In Pursuit of Love.* Wilmington, DE, Michael Glazier.

Guindon, A. (1976) *The Sexual Language: An Essay in Moral Theology.* Ottowa, University Press.

Keane, P.S. (1976) *Sexual Morality: A Catholic Perspective.* Dublin, Gill and Macmillan.

Chapter 17

The Church We Believe In

Francis Sullivan SJ

Practically all Christians, however divided in other respects, are united in professing their faith in 'one, holy, catholic and apostolic Church'. This fourfold description of the Church is part of the solemn profession of faith which was promulgated by the First council of Constantinople (AD 381),[1] and which subsequently became the common creed of the Christian Churches of both East and West. It is this creed, commonly know as Nicene,[2] which Catholics, Orthodox, and a great many other Christians use when they profess their faith together in the course of their Sunday worship.

While it is generally recognized that differences in ecclesiology are the ones that constitute the most stubborn obstacles to Christian reunion, there are good grounds for hope in the fact that most Christians do agree in professing their faith in 'one, holy, catholic and apostolic Church'. Indeed, honest facing up to the contradiction between our common faith in the 'one Church', and the divided state of Christianity, is a prime motive for the ecumenical movement.

It is true of course, that the mere fact that Christians use the same words in professing their faith about Church does not eliminate their deep differences in ecclesiology. Profoundly divergent answers will be given when one asks: What do you mean when you say 'the Church'? and How do you understand it to be one, holy, catholic and apostolic? Ecumenical progress, then, calls for the

[1] For further information about this council and the sources of its creed, see F. Sullivan SJ, *The Church We Believe In*, Gill and Macmillan, 1988, chapter 10.

[2] The reason why this creed is called 'Nicene' is explained in Sullivan, *The Church We Believe In*, chapter 10.

effort to reach a common understanding of the faith we profess. Theology has an important role to play here, because theology is defined as 'faith seeking understanding'. Ecumenical dialogue is most fruitful when it is a concerted effort, on the part of people coming from different theological traditions, to seek a deeper understanding of the creed in which they already profess a common faith, in the hopes that such a deeper understanding will get beneath their differences to the common ground where they are at one.

An essential step in this process is for Christians to seek to deepen and clarify their understanding of the faith in the light of their own respective traditions. What we are seeking here is an understanding of our profession of faith concerning the Church, in the light of the Roman Catholic tradition. In doing this, we shall be paying special attention to the teaching of the Second Vatican Council, especially in its Dogmatic Constitution on the Church *Lumen Gentium,* and in its Decree on Ecumenism *Unitatis Redintegratio.* We shall be seeking a deeper understanding of our Catholic faith concerning the Church, and its oneness, holiness, catholicity and apostolicity.

It is not our purpose to develop the apologetic argument by which, in the past, the effort was made to prove that only the Catholic Church satisfied the requirements of these four 'notes of the Church', so that it alone had the right to consider itself the one true Church of Christ. One of the many drawbacks of that approach was that it restricted consideration of these 'notes' of the Church to their visible or empirical aspects. The supposition of such an apologetic (and often polemical) approach was that the four 'notes' were more visible and easily verified than the Church itself, and hence could serve to identify the true Church.[3] But there is much more to the oneness, holiness, catholicity and apostolicity of the Church than what we can see of them. We shall be looking at them not merely as visible 'marks' or 'notes', but in their full reality as attributes or properties of the Church, in all their aspects, whether empirically verifiable, or knowable only by faith. Indeed, as we shall see, just as the Church itself must be recognized to be a 'mystery of faith', so each of these four properties shares in its nature as 'mystery'. That is why a truly theological approach is needed: starting with what we believe, and seeking a deeper understanding of our faith.

---

[3] Cf. G. Thils, *Les notes d l'Eglise dans l'apologétique catholique depuis la réforme,* Gembloux, 1937.

We shall begin with some reflections on the significance of the fact that in the creed, after professing our faith in God the Father, in our Lord Jesus Christ, and in the Holy Spirit, we go on to profess faith in the Church. Can we believe in the Church in the same way that we believe in God? What right does the Church have to be included in the creed as an object of our faith? What does it mean to say that the Church, along with such mysteries as the incarnation and the redemption, is also a 'mystery of faith'? These are some of the questions to which we shall now turn our attention.

In what sense do we 'believe in' the Church?

In the English translation of the creed with which Catholics profess their faith during Sunday Mass, after saying: 'We believe in one God the Father ... We believe in one Lord Jesus Christ ... We believe in the Holy Spirit' we also say: 'We believe in one holy catholic and apostolic Church.' This translation does not bring out the difference between 'believing in' God and 'believing in' the Church: a difference which the official Latin version of the creed expresses by using the term: 'believe in' only with reference to the Divine Persons. The Latin text does not say, as the English does: 'We believe *in* the Church.'[4]

Since we do not follow the Latin in its restriction of the term 'believe in' to refer to belief in God, it is all the more important for us to understand the difference between 'believing in' God and 'believing in' something other than God. When we say we believe in God, what we mean is that we *put our faith* in God: we commit ourselves to God as the ground of our very being, as the ultimate motive of our faith, as the one in whom we place our trust, in whom we put our hope for salvation and eternal life. It is not a question of merely believing that God exists, or believing certain things about him. It is a question of a commitment that we make of ourselves to him, in faith, hope and trust. We cannot make such an act of faith in any creature; we cannot 'believe in' any created reality in the same unique way in which we believe in God.[5]

In what sense, then, do we 'believe in' the Church? To answer this question, let us look at the creed again. When we have said 'We believe in God the Father', we go on to profess our belief in what

[4] The Latin creed says: 'Credo *in* unum Deum ... et *in* unum Dominum Iesum Christum ... et *in* Spiritum sanctum' but not *in* Ecclesiam: 'Et unam sanctam catholicam et apostolicam Ecclesiam.'
[5] Cf. St Thomas Aquinas, *Summa Theologiae* IIa IIae, q.1, a.9, ad 5; 1.2, a.2.

he has revealed to us about his work of creation; when we have said 'We believe in one Lord Jesus Christ' we go on to express our belief in his incarnation, death, resurrection and future coming in glory; when we have said 'We believe in the Holy Spirit' we go on to express our belief in the Church, baptism, resurrection of the dead, life everlasting. The difference, with regard to our faith, is between God himself and the created works that God has accomplished and revealed to us. It is the very nature of these works of God on our behalf, that even after they have been revealed, they still far surpass our capacity fully to grasp or understand them. In that sense they are rightly called 'mysteries' of our faith. While they are not identical with God, they are so associated with him who is the ultimate mystery that, even when revealed to us, they must remain, at least in this life, objects of faith rather than of complete understanding. As we have said above, theology is defined as 'faith that seeks understanding'; but since the object of faith is 'mystery', the understanding that theology can reach will always fall short of a total grasp of the reality.

What that means, then, is that when in the creed we say 'We believe in the Church', we are acknowledging the fact that the Church, like the incarnation of the Son of God and his death and resurrection for our redemption, is a 'mystery of our faith': an element in the whole 'economy of salvation' which God has accomplished and revealed to us. We are accepting the Church as part of the total object of our Christian faith. We are professing our faith that the Church is not a purely human institution, but is a work of God, a part of God's plan for the salvation of the world.

This follows, in the first place, from the very fact of the inclusion of the Church among those things about which Christians profess their faith in the creed. It is surely significant that we find mention of the Church in the baptismal creed that was in use in Rome around the end of the second century. It would be useful to recall here what we know about the development of the early Christian creeds.

The formulation of 'creeds' had its origin in the practice of requiring that converts should make a profession of Christian faith as they were being baptized. In the early Church, baptism was a real bath, in which the candidate was totally immersed three times in the baptismal pool. Prior to each immersion, the candidate was asked to profess his faith: the first time in God the Father, the second time in the Lord Jesus Christ, and the third time in the Holy Spirit. The earliest baptismal creeds that have come down to us are in the form of three questions, to which the candidate would reply: 'I do believe.' (We still use this form of profession of faith when we renew our baptismal vows at the Easter vigil.) It seems almost certain that in the most primitive form, the third question would have been simply: 'Do you believe in the Holy Spirit?' But we know, from the *Apostolic Tradition* of Hippolytus, written about the year 215, that by the end of the second century, the third question asked of the one being baptized in the Church of Rome was: 'Do you believe in the Holy Spirit in the holy Church?'[6]

From the third century on, every baptismal creed that has come down to us, whether in the earlier question-and-answer form, or in the later declaratory form (such as we have in the so-called Apostles' Creed, which is still our baptismal creed), mentions the 'holy Church' after the Holy Spirit.[7] Actually, the Church never appears in a baptismal creed without the adjective 'holy'; the Apostles' Creed adds 'catholic' and, as we have already seen, it was the creed of the council of Constantinople in 381 that definitively settled on the four attributes that were already being mentioned in the baptismal creeds of some Eastern Christian Churches.

If one asks what prompted the second century Church to begin to require that candidates for baptism profess their faith in the 'holy Church', the most likely answer is the one suggested by J.N.D. Kelly, a foremost authority on the history of the creeds.[8] He suggests that it was because about this time, as we know from the writings of St Irenaeus, the gnostic heretics, who posed the most serious threat to the true faith, despised the people who belonged to the Churches over which the bishops presided. The gnostics prided themselves on having a higher, more perfect knowledge of revelation than was being taught by the bishops, so they gathered in their own private meetings, despising the Christian Churches and their leaders. Against the gnostics, St Irenaeus insisted that it was only in the holy Church that the Holy Spirit could be found and his gifts received.[9] In this atmosphere it is understandable why those seeking baptism should be asked to profess their faith 'in the Holy Spirit in the holy Church'.

6 Hippolytus, *The Apostolic Tradition*, 21; tr. Gregory Dix, London, 1937, p. 37. See also J.N.D. Kelly, *Early Christian Creeds*, 3 New York, 1972, p. 91 and p. 114.
7 What we know as the 'Apostles' Creed' is the more developed form of the early baptismal creed of the church of Rome. The popular attribution of this creed to the twelve apostles is without historical foundation.
8 *Early Christian Creeds*, pp. 159-160.
9 *Adversus haereses* III, 24, 1; PG 7, 966; Harvey II, 131.

The Church as a mystery of faith

We have said that in seeking a deeper understanding of what Catholics believe about the Church we shall be paying special attention to the teaching of the Second Vatican council. It is appropriate, then, that in considering the reasons that justify the description of the Church as a mystery of faith, we should begin by examining the first chapter of *Lumen Gentium*, which is entitled 'The Mystery of the Church'. When the theological commission presented this text to the council, they explained their use of the term 'mystery' here in the following way: 'The word "mystery" does not mean merely something unknowable or obscure, but, as is now generally recognized, it signifies a reality which is divine, transcendent and salvific, and which is also revealed and manifested in some visible way. Hence this term, which is thoroughly biblical, seems altogether appropriate for designating the Church.'[10]

This last phrase makes it clear that it is the Church itself that is being described as a 'mystery'. As a reality which is 'divine', the Church is no merely human institution; as 'transcendent', it will always surpass our efforts fully to grasp it; as 'salvific,' it forms part of God's plan of salvation for humanity. At the same time, it is not something invisible; it has been revealed and manifested to us in a visible way.

The commission also noted that 'mystery' is a thoroughly biblical term. It is true that the Bible does not explicitly describe the Church as a mystery; the closest approach to this is the text in Ephesians (5:31ff.) where the 'becoming one flesh' of man and wife is described as a 'great mystery' in its application to Christ and the Church. But the 'mystery' which is one of the major themes of Colossians and Ephesians is intimately associated with the Church: it is God's design to include the Gentiles in his plan of salvation, and thus to bring the whole world under Christ as its head (cf. Col 1:26f; 2:2; Eph 1:9f; 3:1-6).

Chapter one of *Lumen Gentium* proceeds to offer a number of considerations that justify seeing the Church as a mystery. The first of these is the suggestion that the Church can be looked on as a 'kind of sacrament'.

---

[10] AS III/1, 170. Our reference here is to the report *(relatio)* given to the bishops at the council by the theological commission responsible for the text. These reports, which are all published in the *Acta Synodalia*, provide valuable help for interpreting the conciliar documents.

The Church as a 'kind of sacrament'

The opening words of the Constitution on the Church *Lumen Gentium*, 'the light of the nations', refer not to the Church but to Christ. But the next sentence introduces the Church as 'in Christ a kind of sacrament: that is, a sign and instrument of intimate union with God and the unity of all humanity.' It is striking that the very first description of the Church in this document involves applying to the Church itself the notion of 'sacrament' – an idea that most Catholics had been accustomed to think of only with reference to one or another of the seven sacraments. In fact it was only quite recently that theologians had begun to speak of Christ as the 'primordial sacrament', and of the Church as 'sacrament of salvation'. What does such use of the idea of 'sacrament' contribute to our understanding of Christ and his Church?

First of all, it is important to note that to speak of the Church as 'a kind of sacrament' is already to suggest that it belongs to the category of 'mystery', because *sacramentum* was one of the words that the early Latin Christians used to translate the Greek word *musterion*: mystery. Just above we have referred to the passages in Colossians and Ephesians which speak of 'the great mystery' of God's plan of universal redemption in Christ. In each of these key passages, the Latin New Testament translated *musterion* as *sacramentum*. Hence, we can be sure that when the Latin Fathers described something as *sacramentum*, they had very much in mind its nature as 'mystery'.

A good example of this is St Augustine's description of the origin of the Church: 'it was from the side of Christ as he slept on the cross that there came forth the wondrous sacrament which is the whole Church.'[11] This one sentence suggests some of the reasons that prompted St. Augustine to describe the Church as *sacramentum*, where the word clearly means 'mystery'. First of all, he sees the Church as the fruit of Christ's passion and death, thus having its origin not in a mere act of institution, but in the redemptive work accomplished by Christ on the cross. He sees the Church as symbolized by the blood and water that flowed out from the side of Christ: no doubt because this blood and water were identified with the sacraments of baptism and eucharist, the most fundamental elements in the life of the Church. Finally, the reference to Christ 'sleeping the sleep of death' presents Christ as the 'new Adam' from whose side the Church came forth as the 'new Eve', thus

[11] *Enarr. In Ps.* 138, 2; CCL 40, 1991.

suggesting that as the first Eve was drawn from Adam's side to be his bride and 'helper' (Gen 2:18), so the Church is the bride of Christ who has a helping role to play in Christ's ongoing work for the salvation of humanity. The richness and depth of the ideas about the origin, nature and function of the Church suggested in this one sentence of St. Augustine offer a striking illustration of the fact that when the Latin Fathers used the term *sacramentum* of the Church, they had in mind its nature as a mystery of Christian faith. No merely human institution could be described in terms such as these. It is to be noted, too, that the nature of the Church as 'mystery' is rooted in its intimate association with Christ and the mystery of our redemption.

Association with Christ is also seen as the basis of the description of the Church as 'sacrament' when the council speaks of the Church as being 'in Christ a kind of sacrament: that is, a sign and instrument of intimate union with God and of the unity of all humanity' (LG 1). Here the term 'sacrament' is being used not only with its original meaning as 'mystery', but with a further, specific meaning which the term acquired in the course of its Christian usage through its application to such 'mysteries' as baptism and eucharist. For the council explains that it is applying the term 'sacrament' to the Church insofar as the Church, like the seven sacraments, is a 'sign and instrument' of divine grace. Over the centuries, the term 'sacrament' had become identified with those acts of liturgical worship which are understood both to signify and instrumentally to effect the sanctifying of the person who receives them. While these are rather simple acts, performed with ordinary things like water, bread and wine, by quite human ministers, they are accepted in Christian faith to be genuine 'mysteries', since they not only signify but really contain and effect the divine realities of grace which they symbolize.

It is in this sense that the council describes the Church as 'in Christ a kind of sacrament', explaining that this is because the Church is 'a sign and instrument of intimate union with God and the unity of all humanity.' What this means is that the Church, like the seven sacraments, is an 'efficacious sign of grace': a visible, historical institution which contains and effects a hidden, divine reality. The council specifies a twofold grace of which the Church is 'sign and instrument': namely, 'intimate union with God' (the vertical dimension) and the 'unity of all humanity' (the horizontal dimension). Intimate union with God involves the reconciliation of sinners with God, the enjoyment of friendship with him in this life, and the intimacy of the beatific vision in the life to come. The 'unity of all humanity' describes the universal peace and harmony that would prevail from the recognition of God as the one Father of all peoples and nations, and the practical living out of the love which all owe to one another as children of God and members of his family. The role of the Church: to be a sign and instrumental cause of such realities as these, is surely grounds for recognizing the Church as a 'mystery,' containing and effecting results that go far beyond what any merely human institution could accomplish. Of course it is only 'in Christ', that is, as his instrument, that the Church can have such a role. As the council says in a later passage, it is Jesus who is the 'author of salvation and the source of unity and peace', while God has established the Church to be 'a visible sacrament of this saving unity' (LG 9).

The Church as the work of the Trinity

As the triune God: Father, Son and Holy Spirit, is the ultimate mystery of Christian faith, so the nature of the Church as mystery is rooted in its relationship with the mystery of the Trinity. After the initial article which presents the Church as a 'kind of sacrament' ,the following three articles of *Lumen Gentium* explain how the Church is related to each of the Divine Persons. Here again our purpose is simply to point out the basis for including the Church among the mysteries of faith to be confessed in the creed.

In LG 2 the Church is seen as part of the Father's plan to share divine life with mankind. The Church is thus seen to have a history that extends far beyond merely human calculations, being foreshadowed from the beginning of the world, prepared through the old covenant with the people of Israel, and directed toward the gathering of all the just in the universal Church of the world to come.

Article three of the text goes on to explain how the Church is the fruit of Christ's redemptive work on earth. Carrying out the Father's plan, Christ inaugurated a new phase of God's reign on earth, and the Church is seen as the presence of God's kingdom 'in mystery'. Here again the Church is seen as the fruit of Christ's passion and death, stressing its origin in the mystery of redemption and its role in the ongoing work of redemption by the celebration of the eucharistic sacrifice. Thus the focus is on the Church as an integral element in the mystery of our salvation.

In the creed the mention of the Church always comes in the

third article, in association with the Holy Spirit. *Lumen Gentium* 4 suggests some of the many reasons why this is so fitting. It is the role of the Spirit to sanctify the Church, to dwell in her as in a temple, to guide her into all truth, to maintain her unity, to furnish her with gifts for ministry, to renew her and lead her to final union with Christ. The article concludes with a quotation from St Cyprian, describing the Church as 'a people made one with the unity of the Father, the Son and the Holy Spirit'.[12] One can also conclude that the Church is truly a mystery, by reason of its unique relationship with each of these Divine Persons.

The Church and the kingdom of God

In LG 5 the council develops the idea of the Church as mystery in virtue of its role with regard to the present reign of Christ and the future kingdom of God. As Christ came to inaugurate a new phase of God's reign over the world, and manifested the presence of this reign by his works of power over the forces of evil, so the Church has the mission to proclaim and promote the reign of Christ as Lord, and to be on earth 'the initial budding forth of his kingdom', while ever looking forward to the final coming of the kingdom of God. While the Church on earth cannot be identified with the present reign of Christ (which surely extends beyond the limits of the Church), still it is the function of the Church both to manifest the presence of his gracious reign and to promote it among men, so that, while the text does not use the term in this way, the Church can be seen as the sacrament: that is, the sign and instrument of Christ's reign in this age, pointing to and preparing people for entry into God's future kingdom. Here again we see solid reasons for recognizing the Church as a mystery, deeply engaged as it is in the working out of God's plan for the coming of his kingdom.

Biblical images of the Church

One consequence of the nature of the Church as 'mystery' is that it cannot be adequately defined or even described by any one simple concept. This is brought out by the variety of images which the scriptures have used with reference to the Church, suggesting

[12] *De oratione dominica* 23, PL 4, 553.

that one can approach a description of this mystery only by trying to see it in the light which each of these many images can cast on it. This is the approach which is suggested in LG 6, which mentions a number of biblical images, such as those associated with shep-herding, with agriculture, and with building. For our present purpose it will suffice to dwell briefly on just the last one mentioned, namely, that of the Church as bride of Christ. This image was developed most fully by St Paul in Ephesians 5:21-33, where he presents the love of Christ for the Church as the model for the love which husbands should have for their wives. In this passage, St Paul explicitly terms the union between Christ and his bride the Church a 'great mystery'. It was out of love for the Church that Christ gave up his life, so as to purify her and prepare her for marriage with himself; and now that she is united with him he nourishes and cherishes her as his own body. It hardly needs to be said that such a relationship as this surely justifies the descrip-tion of the Church as a 'mystery'.

The Church as the body of Christ

After presenting a variety of biblical images of the Church in article six, the constitution devotes the whole of the following article to the distinctively Pauline notion of the Church as the body of Christ, thus emphasizing the particular importance of this idea for the theme of this chapter: the mystery of the Church. Because of this importance, it will also be appropriate for us to analyze this section at somewhat greater length.

After a brief introductory paragraph, article seven consists of two parts: the first based on the teaching of St Paul in his major epis-tles: 1 Corinthians and Romans, and the second on the later epistles, especially Colossians and Ephesians.

In the introductory paragraph, the key sentence reads: 'By communicating his Spirit to his brothers, called together from all peoples, Christ made them mystically into his own body.' Equally important is the beginning of the second paragraph: 'In that body the life of Christ is poured into the believers...' Here we see the reason why the idea of the Church as 'body of Christ' is not a mere image: it is a way of expressing the fact that the members of the Church are living a supernatural life by virtue of the same divine life, the same Holy Spirit, of which the sacred humanity of Christ enjoys the fullness. Christ in glory shares his own life with his disci-ples by communicating his 'life-giving Spirit' to them. As the text says, he thus makes them 'mystically' into his own body. It is important to understand the force of the word 'mystically'; its root is the same as that of the word 'mystery'. The word 'mystically' here, and 'mystical' in the expression 'mystical body', really mean that there is a mystery involved in the sharing of the same divine life between Christ and his Church. This sharing of the same life is the reason why the Church is Christ's 'body' in a way that is much more than a mere figure of speech.

The following paragraph shows how St Paul's idea of the Church as Christ's body is firmly based on his insight into the effects of the sacraments of baptism and the Eucharist. It is through baptism that believers receive the fruits of Christ's death and resurrection, namely, his life-giving Spirit; and when they eat the eucharistic body of Christ, their life in one body with him and with one another receives a new dimension of reality.

The second part of article seven develops further aspects of this doctrine, found mainly in Colossians and Ephesians. In these letters St Paul introduced an idea he had not used in the earlier letters, namely, that of Christ as head of his body the Church. Paul developed this idea along two lines: first, applying to Christ the attributes associated with the notion of 'head' as the one having priority over the members of his body, and, second, seeing the 'head' as the model for all the other members to follow and imitate.

There follows a paragraph on the role of the Holy Spirit, the gift by which Christ shares his life with the members of his body. Here the text introduces a new insight from the writings of the Fathers of the Church: namely, that the Holy Spirit is like the soul of the Church, since it is the source of the body's life, unity and vital activities.

The final paragraph invokes the passage of Ephesians 5:22–28 where St Paul applies to Christ and his Church the idea from Genesis 2:24 that a man and his wife become 'one flesh'. So also, the Church is both Christ's bride and his body, which he loves, nourishes and cherishes, and fills with divine gifts.

While St Paul did not use the term 'mystical' body, it is certainly appropriate, provided one keeps in mind that what this word tells us is that we are dealing with a mystery. On the other hand it would be a grave mistake to give the adjective 'mystical' a meaning that would practically eliminate the concreteness which the noun 'body' had for St Paul.

The Church as 'one complex reality'

With article eight we arrive at what is generally recognized to be the most profoundly theological article of the whole constitution on the Church. As we know from the commentary given by the theological commission when it presented this text to the council, the primary intention of this article was to dispel any impression that the 'mystery' which had been described in the preceding seven articles was something of the ideal order: something which could be the object of an act of faith, but which was not the same thing as the 'institutional Church' of everyday experience.

The concern of the commission to counteract such an impression was certainly not without foundation. The idea that the 'mystical body' was a purely spiritual reality, an invisible 'sphere of divine grace', quite different from the visible Church, was not only a popular error, it was a point of view that had been advocated by not a few Catholic theologians. In fact, the first draft of the constitution on the Church at the First Vatican council in 1870, which began with the presentation of the Church as the mystical body, was strongly criticized on the grounds that the Church was not something mystical, but was rather a visible, hierarchical society.[13] This reflected the fact that in the theological schools, the notion of the mystical body was generally treated as an aspect of the theology of grace, whereas ecclesiology had to do with the Church as a 'perfect society'. The treatment of the mystical body in the treatise on grace easily led to the conclusion that 'being in the state of grace' was the criterion of membership in this body. This involved a very real difference between the mystical body and the Church, since on the one hand many non-Christians might be in the state of grace, whereas membership in the Church did not necessarily require this. In any case, a mystical body composed only of people in the state of grace would be visible only to God, since only God would know who belonged to it. It would clearly be something other than the visible Church.

Twenty years before the Second Vatican council Pope Pius XII issued his encyclical *Mystici Corporis* in which one of his main purposes was precisely to show that authentic Catholic tradition did not support such a separation between 'mystical body' and 'visible Church'. Indeed, the pope insisted that the mystical body and the visible Church are one and the same reality.[14]

[13] Mansi 51, 751–763.
[14] AAS 35 (1943) 199.

Unfortunately, what made his teaching difficult for many to accept was that he not only identified the mystical body with the Church, but he identified it in an exclusive way with the Roman Catholic Church, with the consequence that other Christians, even in the state of grace, could not be considered to be really (*reapse*) members of Christ's mystical body.[15] Since quite a few Catholic theologians did not see how such people could be excluded from the mystical body, they continued to maintain a real difference between the mystical body and the Church, with the result that Pope Pius returned to this question in his encyclical *Humani Generis* in 1950, and again insisted that Catholics must hold that the mystical body of Christ and the Roman Catholic Church are one and the same thing.[16] However, even this second statement of Pius XII did not really eliminate the impression that, at least in popular thinking, the mystical body was purely a spiritual reality, something that could hardly be identified with the visible, hierarchical Church.

This was one aspect of the problem which the theological commission at Vatican II intended to confront. Another aspect was the fact that, on the one hand, practically all Christians accepted the 'one, holy, catholic and apostolic Church' in their profession of faith, but many could not recognize any existing Church as corresponding to the one described in the creed. This led to the idea that the Church of the creed must be seen as an object not only of faith but also of hope: an ideal Church which will be realized only when the presently divided Churches are again reunited, or when the future kingdom of God has come. The result, again, is a dichotomy between the Church of faith and the Church of experience: between the mystical body and the institutional Church.

It was this dichotomy that the theological commission wished to confront in the final article of their chapter on the 'mystery of the Church'. Their approach was to recognize that some aspects of the Church can only be grasped by faith, while others are a matter of experience; that the factors that constitute the Church as a 'spiritual communion' are different from the factors that constitute it as a 'hierarchical society' – and nonetheless, the spiritual community and the hierarchical society are not two different realities. On the contrary, there is but one Church: a *complex reality*, which is, under different aspects, *both* a 'community of faith, hope and charity' and a 'visible society'; both mystical body and hierarchically structured

[15] AAS 35 (1943) 202; D-S 3802.
[16] AAS 42 (1950) 571.

Church; both visible assembly and spiritual community. While these terms bring out very different facets of the Church, it is one and the same Church that all of them describe.

The complex nature of the Church is even more strikingly brought out when the text goes on to describe it as composed of both human and divine elements. While it does not give specific examples of such elements, it is useful to suggest some examples here. Under the heading of human elements, one would no doubt include, besides the men and women who make up the people of God, all those factors in the life of the Church that make it an appropriate subject for research by such human sciences as history, sociology, social psychology, and the like. While these sciences cannot reach the depths of the mystery of the Church, there is still a great deal in the make-up of the Church as a human institution which these sciences can analyze, and concerning which they can make pertinent observations.

What did the theological commission have in mind when it spoke of 'divine elements' in the Church? We have already mentioned the idea, familiar to St Augustine and other Fathers of the Church, that the Holy Spirit is like the soul of the Church. Does this justify speaking of the Holy Spirit as the divine element in the composition of the Church? There are problems with such a proposal. If one sees the Church as a complex reality, made up of divine and human elements, then whatever the divine elements are, they would seem to be really a part of the whole. But one cannot really think of the Holy Spirit, a Divine Person, as being really a part of something. For this reason, the Constitution is careful not to describe the Holy Spirit in a way that would suggest that the Spirit is literally the soul of the mystical body. It said, rather, that 'his work could be compared by the holy Fathers with the functions which the soul fulfills in the human body' (LG 7).

If not the Holy spirit, then, what are the 'divine elements' that enter into the composite reality which is the Church? I suggest that the term 'divine' here is best understood in the sense in which we are accustomed to speak of created grace as 'divine grace', refer- ring to its source in God, and to its effect of raising those who receive it into union with God. In this hypothesis, the divine elements in the make-up of the Church would consist of all those gifts of divine grace with which the Holy Spirit endows the Church. These include not only the various gifts by which individual members of the Church are made holy, but even more importantly those grace-gifts which enter into the very structure of the Church. *Lumen Gentium* speaks of such gifts in n. 4: 'The Spirit furnishes

and directs her with various gifts, both hierarchical and charismatic, and adorns her with the fruits of his grace.' In another
context it speaks of 'the charism of infallibility of the Church
herself' (LG 25). What this means is that the hierarchical structure
of the Church is also composed of human and divine elements,
since the 'various hierarchical and charismatic gifts' of the Holy
Spirit are essential to that very structure. One cannot therefore
think of the 'institutional Church' as a purely human organization.
Even precisely as 'institutional', it is a complex reality, composed
of both human and divine elements. Without the Spirit's 'hierarchical and charismatic gifts', it would perhaps be an institution,
but it would no longer be the institutional *Church*.

If we identify the 'divine element' in the Church not with the
Holy Spirit but with his created gifts of grace, how then should we
understand the relationship between the Holy Spirit and the
Church? The conciliar text answers this question by proposing that
this relationship is something like the relationship between the
humanity of Christ and the Divine Word. It might help to identify
the several elements in this analogy. The individual humanity of
Jesus is compared with the social humanity of the Church. The
humanity of Jesus is inseparably united with the Divine Word; the
Church is vivified by the Holy Spirit. The humanity of Jesus serves
the Divine Word as a living instrument of our salvation; the Church
serves the Holy Spirit as his instrument for the building up of the
body of Christ (and thus for the ongoing work of salvation).

Of course we have to remember that we are dealing here with an
analogy, which means that two things are somewhat, but not
perfectly, alike. The union between Jesus as man and the Divine
Word is such that there is really only one person there. Jesus is not
added as a fourth person to the Trinity: he is truly the Second
Person incarnate. The Church, on the other hand, as the people of
God, is made up of a great number of persons who do not lose
their individual personhood by being members of the Church. If
one speaks of Christ and his Church as being 'one mystical
person', this is for the same reason that we speak of the Church as
Christ's 'mystical body' – namely, because he shares his divine life
with his Church. And this divine life is the fruit of the Holy Spirit's
indwelling in the Church. But there is not the kind of 'hypostatic
union' between the Holy Spirit and the Church that would mean
that the Holy Spirit is the 'divine personality' of the Church, in the
way that the Divine Word is the one Person in Christ. Because of
the hypostatic union, everything that Jesus did was really attribut-
able to the Divine Person; it is certainly not the case that everything

the Church does can be attributed to the Holy Spirit. We cannot blame the Holy Spirit for the many mistakes and failures that have marred the Church's history. On the other hand, everything the Church has accomplished for the salvation of men and women and for the promotion of Christ's reign on earth, it has been able to do only through the power of the Holy Spirit working through it as his instrument. While the union between the Church and the Holy Spirit is not 'hypostatic', it is an inseparable dynamic union, and is an essential aspect of the mystery of the Church. Any notion of the Church that would overlook the role of the Holy Spirit in it would be sadly deficient.

There is another corollary to the analogy between the Church and the mystery of the Incarnate Word that can help us to understand how the Church can be both a visible institution and a mystery of faith at the same time. The fact that Jesus walked among his disciples as a man whom they could see and touch did not make him any the less a mystery to be grasped only by faith. When Peter confessed Jesus as 'the Christ, the Son of the living God' (Matt 16:16), Jesus reminded him that it was his Father in heaven who had revealed this to him. When Thomas cried out: 'My Lord and my God,' he was acknowledging that the Jesus who stood before him in tangible form was a mystery far beyond his capacity to understand. Likewise, the opening sentence of the first letter of John declares that what the disciples of Jesus had heard, had seen with their eyes, and touched with their hands, was in reality 'the Word of life which had been from the beginning with the Father' (1 Jn 1:1–2).

In other words, for his own disciples, Jesus was both a man like themselves and a mystery for their faith. In fact, the deepest aspect of the mystery was precisely the union of human and divine in the same person. God as pure spirit is indeed a mystery; but God incarnate in the man of Nazareth is the mystery of mysteries. In the light of the analogy between the Church and the Incarnate Word, we can see that there is no contradiction involved when we say that the visible, institutional Church is also a mystery for our faith. There is no reason to imagine that there are two Churches: one that we can believe in as the 'mystical body', the 'bride of Christ', the 'temple of the Holy Spirit', and the other the empirical institution that confronts us in our daily life. The mystery is that there is really but one Church which is both object of our (sometimes painful) experience and object of our confession of faith, just as for the disciples there was but one Jesus, whom they could see to be a man like themselves, but whom they also came to believe in as their Lord and their God.

Where is the Church to be found today?

We arrive now at the paragraph which has received more comment than probably any other in the documents of Vatican II. It begins: 'This is the unique Church of Christ which in the creed we avow as one, holy, catholic and apostolic.' The initial word 'This' clearly refers back to the 'complex reality' described in the previous paragraph: that Church which is both 'mystical body' and 'hierarchically structured society'. To describe this as 'the unique Church of Christ' is to insist that there is and can be only one Church of Christ, just as it would be absurd to think of Christ having more than one mystical body or more than one mystical bride. This unique Church, then, is the 'one, holy, catholic and apostolic Church' in which practically all Christians profess their faith in the creed.

But can this mystery of faith be concretely identified with any historical Christian Church? The first answer to this question is: yes, it is none other than the Church of the New Testament, the Church which Christ, after his resurrection, entrusted to Peter (John 21:17), commissioning him and the other apostles to be its pastors and teachers (Matt 28:18f). It is noteworthy that this answer focuses on the risen Christ as founder of the Church. In a later passage, *Lumen Gentium* points to the sending of the Holy Spirit by the glorified Christ as the act by which he 'has established his body, the Church, as the universal sacrament of salvation' (LG 48). In this context of faith, the theological commission is not dealing with questions that can be raised about the intention of Jesus, during his public ministry, to lay the foundation for his future Church. It is sufficient to recognize the New Testament Church, the Church of Acts and the letters of St Paul, as the one which Christians acknowledge to be the Church of Jesus Christ, the Church of their profession of faith.

But now comes the crucial question, the one on which believing Christians are so deeply divided: is the Church of the New Testament, the Church of their faith, to be found concretely existing in any Christian Church today?

The answer of the *final text* of *Lumen Gentium* is as follows: 'This Church, constituted and organized in the world as a society, subsists in the Catholic Church, which is governed by the successor of Peter and by the bishops in union with that successor, although many elements of sanctification and of truth can be found outside of her visible structure. These elements, however, as gifts properly belonging to the Church of Christ, possess an inner dynamism toward Catholic unity' (LG 8).

The words 'final text' have been emphasized, because there is a very significant difference between what the council finally said at this point and previous drafts of the Constitution (and, indeed, previous official statements of Roman Pontiffs). We shall conclude this chapter on 'the Church as a mystery of faith' by simply quoting the explanation which the theological commission gave of the passage of *Lumen Gentium* we have just cited. 'The intention is to show that the Church, whose inner, hidden nature has been described ... is to be found concretely existing in this world, in the Catholic Church.'[17] 'The mystery of the Church is not something imaginary, ideal or unreal: it exists in the concrete Catholic society which is governed by the successor of Peter and the bishops in communion with him.'[18] The burden of this chapter has been to insist that while the Church is a 'mystery', it is not something of the ideal order; something altogether different and distinct from the 'institutional Church.'

[17] AS III/1, 176.
[18] AS III/1, 180.

Chapter 18

Evaluation and Interpretation
of the Documents of Vatican II

Francis Sullivan SJ

This chapter will focus on Vatican II. It will consider three issues: first, the factors that contributed to the uniqueness of Vatican II, second, the criteria by which the doctrinal weight of its statements should be evaluated, and third, principles to be followed in the interpretation of its texts.

The uniqueness of Vatican II

The primary reason for the uniqueness of Vatican II is the direction that was given to it by John XXIII, the pope who summoned it. Ecumenical councils of the past had been summoned by emperors and popes to meet crises facing the Church. These crises in most cases were caused by erroneous doctrines that endangered the unity and purity of the faith. Hence the major work of ecumenical councils had been to condemn such errors, and to define as dogmas the truths which had been under attack.

In the speech which he gave on the opening day of Vatican II, October 11, 1962, Pope John XXIII made it clear that he had summoned this council for a different purpose. He recognized the fact that there was 'no lack of fallacious teaching, opinions, and dangerous concepts to be guarded against and dissipated'. But, he added, 'The Church has always opposed these errors. Frequently she has condemned them with the greatest severity. Nowadays, however, the spouse of Christ prefers to make use of the medicine of mercy rather than that of severity. She considers that she meets the needs of the present day by demonstrating the validity of her teaching rather than by condemnations.'[1]

So this council was not to condemn the erring with sentences of *anathema*. But there was to be a further difference from previous councils: namely, in the way it would present the Church's beliefs to the world. Here, Pope John insisted that 'the authentic doctrine … should be studied and expounded through the methods of research and through the literary forms of modern thought. The substance of the ancient doctrine of the deposit of the faith is one thing, and the way in which it is presented is another. And it is the latter that must be taken into great consideration with patience if necessary, everything being measured in the forms and proportions of a magisterium which is predominantly pastoral in character.'[2]

It was these last few words that set the tone and agenda of the council. Its exercise of teaching authority was to be predominantly pastoral in character.

But what did this mean? While most agreed that it meant there would be no *anathemas*, it soon appeared that there were very different notions of what was meant by a 'pastoral magisterium'. This difference of opinion became most obvious when the council came to express its mind on such questions as the sacramental nature of episcopal ordination and the collegiality of the episcopate. Those opposed to the decisions which were taken by the council on these issues belittled their significance, on the grounds that, being purely 'pastoral' in character, they had no truly doctrinal value, and therefore those who disagreed were free to maintain their own opinion. Others maintained that the pastoral nature of the council's teaching did not exclude the binding quality of its authoritative decisions on questions of doctrine. It became obvious that an official stand had to be taken on this basic issue. This was done in the form of an announcement made by the secretary general of the council at the general congregation of November 16, 1964 (just a few days before the promulgation of the Dogmatic Constitution on the Church). He said:

The question has been raised what ought to be the *theological quali-*

[1] Walter M. Abbott, *The Documents of Vatican II*, p. 716.
[2] *Ibid.*, p. 715. The English version of Pope John's opening speech published by Abbott is an accurate translation of the original Italian text, which was published in *L'Osservatore Romano*, Oct. 12, 1962, p. 3, and in *La Civiltà Cattolica* n. 2697 (Nov. 3, 1962) 209–17, here 214. However, the same issue of *L'Osservatore Romano*, pp. 1–2, gives the official Latin text of the Pope's address, which has an expanded version of the sentence that begins with the words: 'The substance'. This could be translated: 'For the deposit of faith, or the truths which are contained in our venerable doctrine, are one thing, and the way they are expressed is another, with, however, the same sense and same meaning' (p. 2, col. 5).

fication of the doctrine which is set forth in the schema *De Ecclesia* and is being voted on.

The theological commission gave the answer to this question when it evaluated the *modi* pertaining to chapter three *De Ecclesia* in these words: 'As is self-evident, a conciliar text must always be interpreted according to the general rules known by all.'

On that occasion the theological commission referred to its own *Declaration* of March 6, 1964. We repeat that text here:

In view of conciliar practice and the pastoral purpose of the present council, this sacred synod defines matters of faith or morals as binding on the Church only when the synod itself openly declares so.

Other matters which the sacred synod proposes as the doctrine of the supreme teaching authority of the Church, each and every member of the faithful is obliged to accept and embrace according to the mind of the sacred synod itself, which becomes known either from the subject matter or from the language employed, according to the norms of theological interpretation.[3]

There was nothing new in the first sentence. The norm already laid down in canon law would apply: no doctrine was to be understood as infallibly defined unless the council clearly expressed its intention to define it. The second sentence was clearly aimed at those who claimed that the doctrine of a 'pastoral' council would have no binding force. It reminded them that an ecumenical council had the supreme teaching authority of the Church. However, the 'mind of the council' with regard to the binding force of any specific element of its teaching was to be determined 'according to the norms of theological interpretation.' One would think that this clear announcement would have settled the issue. However, it became apparent, from the articles and commentaries that appeared after the close of Vatican II, that there was still a wide spectrum of views as to the binding character of the doctrine of this 'pastoral' council. This leads to our second point.

The evaluation of the documents of Vatican II

Three schools of thought can be distinguished on this issue: one can label them 'minimizers', 'maximizers,' and 'moderates'.

The 'minimizers' were those who continued to oppose the decisions taken by the council on such issues as the sacramentality of

---

[3]   In the editions of the documents of Vatican II, this is found immediately following the text of *Lumen Gentium*. In the Abbott edition it is on pp. 97-98.

the episcopate and the collegial nature of the Church's hierarchical structure. In articles published in Italian journals,[4] G. Hering, H. Lattanzi and A. Gutierrez argued that the pastoral character of the teaching of Vatican II deprived its doctrine of the binding force which conciliar decisions would normally have. Carlo Colombo, known to have been Pope Paul's most trusted theological advisor during the council, wrote a strong letter, criticizing the editor of one of those Italian journals for printing such an article, on the grounds that it contradicted the expressed mind of the pope. In fact, in the address which he gave at the opening of the third session of the council, Paul VI had said: 'It is the role of the council to settle some difficult theological controversies ... to explain to the faithful of the Catholic Church, and to the brethren separated from it, the true notion of the orders of the sacred hierarchy...and to do this with its certain authority, which may not be called into doubt.'[5]

Among Italian theologians one also finds a 'maximizer' on this issue: Umberto Betti, who contributed an article on the theological qualification of *Lumen Gentium* to a volume of studies on the council's Dogmatic Constitution on the Church.[6] In J. Ratzinger's judgment, 'Betti takes a view that raises most of the council's declarations practically (though not technically) to the status of dogmas.'[7] Among Betti's statements which tend to justify Ratzinger's comment are the following:

> The chapters of the constitution have the same value as the doctrinal chapters of the other ecumenical councils, in particular, the Councils of Trent and Vatican I.[8] The only difference between the doctrine of Vatican I and that of Vatican II consists in the fact that the latter is not the equivalent of a definition in the technical sense of the word; that is why its denial would not involve *ipso facto* the exclusion from ecclesial communion which is attached to the profession of heresy. But even if its infallibility, and hence its irreformability, lack explicit declaration, one must not think that on that account it does not exist.[9] These brief considerations lead to the following conclusion, which it seems cannot be evaded: the

---

[4] *Palestro del Clero* 44 (1965) pp. 577–92; *Divinitas* 9 (1965) pp. 393–414, 421–46.
[5] AAS 56 (1964) 809.
[6] 'Qualification théologique de la Constitution', in G. Barauna, ed., *L'Eglise de Vatican II*, (Unam Sanctam 51b) Paris: Cerf, 1967, vol. 2, pp. 211–218.
[7] *Commentary on the Documents of Vatican II*, New York: Herder & Herder, 1967, I:299.
[8] 'Qualification théologique', p. 214.
[9] *Ibid.*, p. 217.

doctrine set forth in the constitution, taken *en bloc*, is irrevocable.[10]

Among the 'moderates' on this issue, I would mention Joseph Ratzinger and Yves Congar, who have both expressed their opinion on this question in their contributions to the same collection of studies that contains Betti's article.

Ratzinger raised this question at the end of his article, which dealt with the sections of chapter three of *Lumen Gentium* that treat of the episcopate.[11] He first notes that while the teaching of the council on the sacramentality of the episcopate is the one that comes closest to being a dogmatic definition, it still falls short of what that requires. Hence there is no new dogma. On the other hand, the doctrine as a whole is the expression of the supreme magisterium of the Church, and that implies a certain measure of obligation to accept it. Consideration of the nature of doctrines taught, the intensive discussion that led to the decisions, and the role of the pope in the whole conciliar process brought Ratzinger to the following conclusion:

> The conciliar text by far surpasses the ordinary declarations of papal magisterium, including the encyclicals, regarding the nature of the theological obligation which it entails. It is a document produced by the most intense work over many years, and it expresses the sense of its faith at which the whole Church assembled in council has arrived. It has formulated this document as a profession of its Credo ... The conclusion is that it has an importance of the first rank among modern doctrinal texts, in the sense that it is a sort of central interpretation.[12]

Yves Congar has discussed the doctrinal weight of the teaching of Vatican II in the conclusion which he wrote for the same volume of studies on the council's doctrine on the Church.[13]

> The only passage of the Dogmatic Constitution on the Church that could be considered a truly dogmatic declaration is the one that concerns the sacramentality of the episcopate (LG III, n. 21): in fact, it settles a question that until now had been freely disputed by theologians. At the same time it is proposed as a teaching on the same level as the others, without the use of the emphatic, repeated

[10] *Ibid.*, p. 218.
[11] 'La collégialité épiscopale, développement théologique', in Barauna, vol. 3, pp. 763–90.
[12] *Ibid.*, pp. 789–90.
[13] 'En guise de conclusion', vol. 3, pp. 1365–73.

and solemn formulas that normally introduce a 'definition'. ... The manner of expressing it is not that of a dogmatic definition, but the matter is so important, the place it occupies in the doctrine of the episcopate so decisive, that one can hardly see how on this point the council has not issued a definitive judgment. But this is without doubt the only case of this kind. On so many other points ... one might dare to say that by a unanimous act of the extraordinary magisterium the council has proposed the common doctrine of the ordinary, universal magisterium. This is not the same as a 'definition', but it does suffice for the doctrine thus proposed to be binding as teaching on which the Catholic magisterium is in unanimous agreement.[14]

I would offer a comment on Congar's phrase: 'unanimous act of the extraordinary magisterium'. He is clearly using the term 'extraordinary magisterium' here to refer to the exercise of teaching authority by an ecumenical council. An ecumenical council is an extraordinary event, and on many accounts its magisterium is also extraordinary. On the other hand, there are good reasons for using the term 'extraordinary magisterium' as a technical term to refer to what the First Vatican Council called 'solemn judgments', i.e. dogmatic definitions, as contrasted with the 'ordinary' exercise of magisterium, which would include everything except solemn definitions.[15] Using the terms in this latter sense (which I think is preferable) one would say that, since Vatican II nowhere expressed its intention to define a dogma, its exercise of magisterium belongs in the category of 'ordinary,' that is to say, non-defining magisterium.

The fact that the teaching of Vatican II, while it represents the almost unanimous consensus of the whole Catholic episcopate, including its head the pope, still remains in the category of 'ordinary magisterium' is a unique feature of this council. Joseph Ratzinger has raised one of the questions which this suggests: How does the conciliar exercise of ordinary magisterium compare with the one with which we are more familiar: namely, that of the popes in their encyclicals? As we have seen above, his reply is: 'The conciliar text by far surpasses the ordinary declarations of papal magisterium, including the encyclicals, regarding the nature of the theological obligation which it entails.' While Ratzinger was referring to a specific conciliar text, namely that concerning episcopal collegiality, his judgment would seem applicable to a number of

[14] *Ibid.*, pp. 1366–67.
[15] See DS 3011; ND 121.

other texts in which Vatican II has taken a position that differs from what previous popes had taught in their encyclicals.[16] There can be no doubt that the teaching of the council on such issues as religious liberty, the ecclesial status of other Christian Churches, and the significance of non-Christian religions prevails over what had been the official position of the Catholic Church put forth by the ordinary papal magisterium prior to Vatican II.

Does Ratzinger's opinion that some texts of Vatican II surpass papal encyclicals regarding the nature of the theological obligation which they entail mean that the teaching authority of an ecumenical council is greater than that of the pope alone? The answer to this question calls for a distinction between teaching authority as such, and the various ways in which that authority can be exercised. In the light of the First Vatican Council's definition regarding papal magisterium, one must say that the pope has the same supreme teaching authority that the whole episcopal college has. Rahner explains this by saying that the pope, as head of the college, can exercise the supreme authority which resides in the whole college as its one subject. Others would distinguish between the pope and the college (with the pope as its head) as two inadequately distinct subjects of supreme authority. In either theory, one must hold that the pope's authority is equal to that of the whole episcopal college.

On the other hand, when we compare a text of Vatican II with a papal encyclical, we are comparing two examples of the exercise of magisterium, in which those possessing supreme teaching authority have chosen not to use their authority in its supreme degree, but have rather chosen to teach in a non-definitive way. In other words, we are here comparing two examples of the exercise of *ordinary* magisterium. As we have seen, it is the distinctive characteristic of ordinary magisterium that it admits of varying degrees of authoritativeness. Thus, while the pope's teaching authority as such is always supreme, one rightly attributes greater authority to some documents of his ordinary magisterium than to others. Similarly, when Ratzinger attributes greater authority to a text of Vatican II than to papal encyclicals, he is comparing, not the teaching authority of the council with that of the pope, but two examples of the exercise of ordinary magisterium. As we have seen above, he argues from the fact that the Vatican document was

---

[16] J. Robert Dionne has made a thorough study of five doctrines which had been taught in papal encyclicals, on which Vatican II has taken quite a different stand. See his book: *The Papacy and the Church. A Study of Praxis and Reception in Ecumenical Perspective*, New York: Philosophical Library, 1987.

produced by the most intense work over many years, and that it expresses the sense of its faith at which the whole Church assembled in council had arrived. One could also argue that there is less chance of error in a document produced and scrutinized over many months by several thousand bishops, with the help of theologians from all over the world, than in a document produced by the pope and his advisors alone. One's confidence in a conciliar document will thus be greater, and this gives it a stronger motive of credibility and hence more doctrinal authority. Reasons such as these are appropriate for evaluating the relative doctrinal weight of different examples of the ordinary exercise of teaching authority; they do not imply that papal teaching authority as such is inferior to conciliar authority.

The fact that the ordinary exercise of magisterium admits of varying degrees of authoritativeness means that it will be important to distinguish among the various levels of authority exercised by the Second Vatican Council. While all the conciliar documents, in a global way, have the teaching authority proper to decrees of an ecumenical council, it was clearly not the intention of the council to exercise the same degree of authority in all its documents, or in all the statements made in them.

Evaluating the varying levels of authority exercised by Vatican II

The council's intention to attribute different levels of authority to its documents is manifest in the titles which it gave to them. Two are 'dogmatic constitutions',[17] one is a 'pastoral constitution',[18] one is simply a 'constitution',[19] nine are 'decrees'[20] and three are 'declarations'.[21] It is true that the council never explained the significance which these titles have with regard to the degree of authority exercised in the respective documents. However, one incident shows that for the members of the theological commis-

[17] 'On the Church' and 'On Divine Revelation'.
[18] 'On the Church in the Modern World'.
[19] 'On the Sacred Liturgy'.
[20] 'On the Instruments of Social Communication,' 'On Ecumenism,', 'On Eastern Catholic Churches', 'On the Bishops' Pastoral Office in the Church', 'On Priestly Formation', 'On the Appropriate Renewal of Religious Life', 'On the Apostolate of the Laity', 'On the Ministry and Life of Priests', and 'On the Church's Missionary Activity'.
[21] 'On Christian Education', 'On the Relationship of the Church to Non-Christian Religions' and 'On Religious Freedom'.

sion, the titles were not insignificant. At one point during the council, when a new revision of the schema on the Church was printed for distribution to the bishops, most of the members of the commission were surprised to see that its title had been reduced from 'Dogmatic Constitution on the Church' to 'Constitution on the Church'. At the next meeting of the commission the majority insisted that the term 'Dogmatic' be restored to the title. Of course, as we have seen, this does not mean that in the two 'dogmatic constitutions' some new dogmas have been defined. But it does indicate the intention of the council to exercise its teaching authority in those two documents on matters of *doctrine*, to a *degree* that justified distinguishing them by this title from the other documents. On the other hand, it would be a mistake to conclude that it was only in those two 'dogmatic constitutions' that the council has spoken authoritatively on matters of doctrine. It certainly did so in a number of other documents, including the one it called 'pastoral constitution'. This suggests that to evaluate the level of authority exercised by Vatican II in any instance, more important than the title of the document will be the factors that indicate the 'mind of the council' with regard to the authority it intended to exercise in any particular statement. As the theological commission said in its *Declaration* on this issue, this can be known from the subject matter or from the language employed, 'according to the norms of theological interpretation'.

One of the 'norms of theological interpretation' is that very often considerable light can be shed on the intentions of a council from the study of its *acta*. In the case of Vatican II, the interpreter has available the thirty volumes of the *Acta Synodalia Sacrosancti Concilii Oecumenici Vaticani Secundi*, in which to follow the progress of any text through the council. One factor that must be taken into account in weighing the level of authority exercised in any text is the degree to which the decision expressed in it was a major focus of discussion and deliberation during the council. This factor clearly entered into the judgment expressed by Congar concerning the authoritativeness of the decision taken by the council on the question of the sacramentality of the episcopate. As we have seen above, the 'intensive discussion that led to the decisions' was likewise a key element in Ratzinger's estimate of the doctrinal weight of the conciliar decision on episcopal collegiality. Study of the *Acta Synodalia* will show that, in the course of the council, certain issues stand out as having been the object of the most intense discussion and deliberation, in not a few cases involving an intervention of the pope himself in the proceedings. It is reasonable to conclude that decisions reached by the council on issues like these will have a degree of doctrinal weight that is proportionate to the seriousness of the deliberations by which they were reached. In some instances of this kind (though by no means all) the council expressed its intention to make a particularly important doctrinal statement by introducing it with the phrase: 'This sacred synod teaches'.[22] Another way in which the council added a certain solemnity to some of its statements was by the use of the term: 'We believe', where this was clearly an expression of Catholic belief, and not of mere opinion.[23]

The evaluation of the Council's 'pastoral' statements

In his recent book *Theology and Church*, Walter Kasper has observed that while everything Vatican II said was meant pastorally, 'there are also pastoral statements in the narrower and more specialized sense. We find these particularly in *Gaudium et Spes*, which bears the name 'Pastoral Constitution.'[24] In what follows, it is clear that by 'pastoral statements in the more specialized sense', Kasper is referring to those which deal with matters of practical morality, that is, the application of moral principles to specific situations. He notes that where practical morality is concerned, general principles are not enough. Clear directives are necessary, and such directives presuppose an evaluation of the particular situation into which the general principles have to be translated. Kasper concludes that in evaluating the bind force of this kind of conciliar teaching, the following special considerations should be kept in mind.

---

[22] Examples of this are the following: 'Basing itself upon sacred scripture and tradition, it [this sacred synod] teaches that the church now sojourning on earth as an exile, is necessary for salvation' (LG 14). 'Therefore this sacred synod teaches that by divine institution bishops have succeeded to the pace of the apostles as shepherds of the church' (LG 20). 'This sacred synod teaches that by episcopal consecration is conferred the fullness of the sacrament of orders' (LG 21).

[23] Two examples of this are found in the Decree on Ecumenism: 'It was to the apostolic college alone, of which Peter is the head, that we believe our Lord entrusted all the blessings of the New Covenant...' (UR 3 d), and 'This unity, we believe, dwells in the Catholic Church as something she can never lose...' (UR 4 c).

[24] Walter Kasper, *Theology and Church*, New York: Crossroad, 1989, p. 173.

In these pastoral statements a clear distinction has to be made between the different levels of a statement and their varying degrees of obligation. To be more precise, a distinction has to be made between the generally binding doctrinal foundation, the description of the situation, and the application of the general principles to the pastoral situation described. In the description of the situation, the council had to fall back on recognitions of a secular kind, for which it possessed no special ecclesiastical teaching authority. The binding nature of these situational decisions is therefore dependent on the validity of the arguments which are brought into play. Their authority is therefore essentially different and, above all, less than the authority of the doctrinal statements themselves. This in its turn has consequences for the application of generally binding statements about faith and morals to the specific situation. The obedience required here cannot be simply the obedience of faith, in the sense of *fides divina et catholica*. And yet this does not by any means relegate such statements to the sector of what is not obligatory at all, and a matter of pure choice. Nor are they solely disciplinary. Catholics are required to enter into such statements with a religiously motivated inner assent, and to go along with them. But this assent and response includes co-responsibility, spiritually and morally. The possibility that here the individual Christian, after a mature examination of conscience, may arrive at a different judgment from that of the Church's magisterium is in line with the best theological tradition.[25]

Interpretation of the texts of Vatican II

In the same section of his book, Walter Kasper has observed that besides the usual principles for interpretation of conciliar texts, given the unique features of Vatican II 'there are also a number of particular principles for the hermeneutics of this council's doctrinal statements'. He suggests four such principles.

1. The texts of Vatican II must be understood as a whole; it will not do to stress certain statements in isolation.
2. The letter and the spirit of the council must be understood as a

---

[25] *Ibid.*, pp. 174–75. Since writing these lines, Walter Kasper has become Bishop of the diocese of Rottenburg-Stuttgart. An instance of the application of the principle he expressed here can be seen in the joint pastoral letter which he, along with Archbishop Oskar Saier and Bishop Karl Lehmann, published on the pastoral care of divorced and remarried Catholics. See *Origins* 23/38 (March 10, 1994) pp. 670–73.

unity. Every individual statement can only be understood in the light of the spirit of the whole. The spirit of the whole, and hence the meaning of an individual text, can only be discovered by pursuing the textual history in detail, and from this extracting the council's intention. This intention was the renewal of *the whole* tradition, and that means the renewal, for our time, of the whole of what is Catholic.

3. Vatican II must be understood in the light of the wider tradition of the Church. It belongs within the tradition of all previous councils, and it is this tradition which it wished to renew. The council must therefore be interpreted in the context of this tradition, particularly the trinitarian and christological confessions of the ancient Church.

4. The continuity of what is Catholic is understood by the last council as a unity between tradition and a living, relevant interpretation in the light of the current situation. This principle was already at work in previous councils (even if only implicitly), when these councils lent tradition a precise, articulated form, in the light of some specific error. But what then took place in particular cases, was thought about explicitly by the last council, and was given universal reference: for the council talks about a relation to the 'signs of the time'.[26]

Hermann Pottmeyer, another prominent German Catholic theologian, has written a very perceptive article about the special problems involved in the interpretation of the documents of Vatican II.[27] Surveying the previous twenty years of interpretation of the council, he finds that two interpretative approaches are in conflict: one looks exclusively to the new beginnings promoted by the majority, the other looks exclusively to statements that reflect pre-conciliar theology. The two approaches share the same method of selective interpretation. They fail to recognize the transitional nature of the council, which strove to achieve renewal of the Church while remaining faithful to its tradition.

As Pottmeyer sees it, what gives rise to selective interpretation is the fact that the council did not achieve a synthesis of the two factors, but rather used the method of juxtaposition. Alongside a doctrine couched in preconciliar language is set a doctrine that formulates some aspect of the renewal sought by the majority. While such juxtaposition represents a compromise, Pottmeyer

---

[26] *Ibid.*, pp. 172–73.

[27] 'A New Phase in the Reception of Vatican II: Twenty Years of Interpretation of the Council', in G. Alberigo, J-P. Jossua and J.A. Komonchak, ed., *The Reception of Vatican II*, Washington: The Catholic University of America Press, 1987, pp. 27–43.

insists that this was necessary for the achieving of consensus, and in any case the council probably could not have succeeded in going beyond juxtaposition to a new synthesis.

Some have criticized the council's method of juxtaposition for what they judge to be internal contradiction, but Pottmeyer replies that this reproach can be leveled not so much at the council itself as at the post-conciliar use of selective interpretation that seizes upon one thesis without attending to the complementary thesis.

Pottmeyer calls for the abandonment of selective interpretation, and the application of a hermeneutic that reflects fidelity to the council, its intention, its procedure, and its transitional character. Such a hermeneutic pays careful attention to the history of the texts, in both the pre-conciliar and the conciliar phase.[28]

> An appropriate hermeneutic requires, therefore, that the texts be interpreted in the light of the evolution both of the council and its texts, and of the tendency manifested therein. When dealing with the juxtaposition of two theses, we must take into account the council's will to continuity as well as its will to move in a new direction.
>
> 'Progressive' interpretations have occasionally forgotten that the council retracted nothing in the dogmas of Trent and Vatican I. It did indeed relativize these dogmas in the sense that it no longer regarded their formulations as the absolutely final stage of development in the understanding of the faith, but instead located them within the whole tradition of faith. 'Conservative' interpretations have occasionally forgotten that despite their will to continuity the council fathers attached differing values to the theses in question. The theses defended by the minority do not represent the will of the council to the same degree as the theses that passed by an overwhelming majority.[29]

Pottmeyer then calls attention to a danger that in his view 'progressive' interpretations of the council have not always avoided: of a hermeneutical misunderstanding that attempts to separate the 'spirit' of the council from its letter, and then leaves the letter behind. He insists that this does not represent fidelity to the council. The 'spirit' of the council makes itself known from the direction given in the texts; on the other hand, it is only in this 'spirit' that the texts are properly understood.[30]

[28] An extremely valuable instrument for following the history of the Dogmatic Constitution *Lumen Gentium* from the first draft to its final text is provided by the volume *Constitutionis Dogmaticae 'Lumen Gentium' Synopsis Historica* edited by G. Alberigo and F. Magistratti, Bologna: Ist. Sc. Relig., 1975.

[29] *Ibid.*, p. 40.

[30] *Ibid.*, p. 42.

The final paragraph of Pottmeyer's article seems a fitting conclusion to this chapter.

> In fact, the reception of Vatican II is not yet complete. All attempts
> to break off the process of reception – whether through overly
> restrictive legislation or through a 'progressive' interpretation – are
> incompatible with a professed fidelity to the council. A new phase in
> the process of reception is certainly due, one that will end the
> conflict of selective interpretations and explain the letter of the
> conciliar text in accordance with the 'spirit' of the council, aided by
> a hermeneutic that does justice to the character of Vatican II as a
> transitional council.[31]

---

[31] *Ibid.*, p. 43.

Chapter 19

Ecumenism

Christopher Butler

Constantly, since New Testament times, it has been a Christian conviction that outward unity among believers is a normal consequence of redemption, and that schism between Christians is a result of sin. There was, throughout antiquity and up to the time of the Reformation, a consensus that the Church on earth not only ought to be, but is, visibly one, and that this unity is permanently guaranteed by divine assistance. Faced with the existence of other Christian bodies from which his own was separated, the Christian held that these other bodies were 'outside the Church'; and he would be swift to mention that 'outside the Church there is no salvation'.

Such was the view held within the Great Church of the third and fourth centuries, from which all our existing forms of Christianity can trace their descent. The Great Church, it was held, was the one ark of salvation, the only refuge from the deluge of divine judgment. But it was also the view normally held in the ancient 'schismatical' bodies – Novatianists, Donatists, what you will – which have since died out. They, too, held that visible unity was the *esse* of the Church; but, of course, they believed that their own body was the Church, and that the Great Church was a false pretender. All would have echoed Origen's cry: 'My desire is to be truly ecclesiastical' – i.e. a genuine son of the Church, with which Origen identified the Great Church.

The suggestion has recently been made that St Augustine wavered on this cardinal point of ancient ecclesiology, or at least that he made theoretical concessions which were inconsistent with it. A hundred and fifty years earlier, St Cyprian, objecting to the practice of reconciling to the Church those baptised in schism without 're-baptising' them, had argued: Where there are valid sacraments, there the Church is; but schismatics are outside the Church; therefore, sacraments administered by schismatics are invalid. St Augustine, in his dispute with the Donatists (who denied the validity of the sacraments of the Great Church) found himself at odds with Cyprian, and maintained that schismatics could administer valid sacraments. But Augustine did not draw the conclusion that therefore schismatical bodies form (separated) parts of the Church; he agreed with Cyprian and virtually all Christian antiquity that the Church does not subsist in a number of separate communions. It remains true that the admission, which has become general in western Christendom, that valid sacraments can be found in more than one communion sets a problem for theological developments which have become overdue.

The nature of the Church on earth was not originally at the centre of the Reformation disputes. Their consequences, however, included the fragmentation of western Christendom, and this, in turn, gave rise to new theories about the Church, including – in some quarters – a denial that the Church is necessarily a visible unity, and sometimes to a denial that she is a visible entity at all. On the Catholic side of the Reformation controversies there was a reaction towards a rigidity if possible even more narrow than before. Meanwhile, the Orthodox Churches, not directly affected by the Protestant Reformation, simply maintained their old position: the Orthodox communion is the true Church of Christ, from which both Catholics and Protestants are divided by schism.

In modern times, the whole world position of Christianity has been changing from that inherited from the Middle Ages. Medieval Christendom was a solid geographical and human block, surrounded by Islam and barbarism. The medieval synthesis of religion, politics and culture made it easy to identify being Christian with being fully human – a supposition which at first seemed to be confirmed when discovery opened up America, Africa, and Asia, disclosing what was taken to be a low state of culture among the non-Christian inhabitants of these regions, who were regarded simply as savages. (Jesuit attempts to reconcile Christianity with the great cultures of China and India were eventually frustrated by the action of Rome.) The conquistadores opened the way for the missionaries, and the latter brought with them not only the Gospel but a western culture which had been more or less inadvertently regarded as a necessary part of a package deal.

The breakdown of 'colonialism', together with a juster appreciation of cultures other than that of Europe, has made Christians more aware alike of the distinction between 'the faith' and 'Europe' and of their own minority situation in face of the total experience and population of the world. Despite their doctrinal and other differences among themselves, they are acquiring a sense of sharing with one another a common conviction and a common faith peculiar to themselves. This sense has, of course, been enormously intensified by the major historical phenomenon of anti-religious Communism, and, in the last few years, by the growing clamour of irreligious humanism.

Already before the first world war, the problems raised by rival Christian missions in non-European countries had given birth first to practical difficulties and then to a sense of guilt, and thus the Ecumenical Movement was born. After nearly forty years, at Amsterdam in 1948, the World Council of Churches came into existence, giving a new institutional expression to ecumenical aspirations. The membership of the World Council includes most of the great Protestant bodies, the Anglican communion, and some of the eastern Orthodox Churches. But a number of the more extreme evangelical bodies stand aloof, and the Catholic Church has never sought membership.

In fact, the Catholic Church was for many years very reserved in its official attitude to the Ecumenical Movement as a whole. A general suspicion that the movement entailed a measure of doctrinal indifferentism or at least compromise combined, to cause this reserve, with a particular notion that the movement was in some way implicitly committed to the view that no existing Christian body could claim simply and exclusively to be the Church founded by Christ – and this represents a claim which the Catholic Church had traditionally made for itself. However, it should be noted that, although eastern Orthodoxy makes a similar claim for its own communion, some of the eastern Orthodox Churches have for a long time succeeded in combining this claim with vocal membership of the World Council of Churches. And for more than ten years the World Council itself has made it clear that it neither stands for nor excludes any particular ecclesiology and does not require any member-Church to renounce any of her own claims.

The first signs of a thaw in Rome's attitude came with a very cautious Instruction issued by the Holy Office a few years after the last world war. Soon after that there came into existence an unofficial but permitted international conference of Catholic theologians interested in the ecumenical problem. And at length, before the opening of the Second Vatican Council, John XXIII set up at Rome, but outside the framework of the curia, the Secretariat for forwarding the Unity of Christians, with Cardinal Bea at its head. This Secretariat assumed a unique position in Vatican II itself. It was not created as a conciliar commission, and its original membership was of the Pope's own choosing; yet it functioned as an extremely influential commission of the council. It had been made responsible for inviting, and entertaining, official observers from other Churches. But after the withdrawal of the abortive draft document on the Sources of Revelation, it made its influence felt, mainly through Cardinal Bea, in the early drafting of *De Divina Revelatione.*

It is beyond my scope here to recount the long and chequered story leading up to the acceptance and promulgation, on 21 November 1964, of the Decree of Ecumenism. Nor need I summarise its contents.

The importance of ecclesiology in the Ecumenical Movement, and the difficulties which can flow from a rigidly determined ecclesiology are obvious. Professor Greenslade, writing from personal experience of ecumenical dialogue, says of the question of the nature of the Church: 'Participation in the movement forces precisely this consideration almost daily upon one, with an urgency and in a manner not perhaps familiar to members of the Roman Catholic Church.' And he adds, with reference to a Catholic critic of his own ecclesiology: 'I am bound to conclude that there are facts which he is not facing, facts of the utmost importance since they consist in what – as we believe – Christ has done and is doing through his Holy Spirit.'[1] Replying to the same Catholic critic, Bishop Tomkins argues that 'schism *within* the Church does not preclude the idea of schism *from* the Church, nor necessarily imply … a purely "invisible" Church'. These quotations may introduce our examination of Vatican II's ecclesiology so far as it relates to ecumenism. But first, I remark that the Decree on Ecumenism explicitly sees in the movement the operation of the Holy Spirit, something therefore that 'Christ is doing through his Holy Spirit'; something, in other words, of the utmost importance.

Both *Lumen Gentium* and our Decree restate, as was to be expected, the Roman Catholic Church's peculiar claim for itself, which has been the theme of treatises on the Church ever since the Reformation. The Catholic position is based on two convictions: first, that visible unity, or full communion between all its parts and members, is of the *esse*, not merely of the *bene esse*, of the Church as established by Christ; second, that this unity is centered in the

---

[1] *Schism in the Early Church*, 2nd edition, p. xv.

apostolic and episcopal 'college' with the successor of St Peter (the bishop of Rome) at its head. The early history of the principle that, as the Council of Aquileia (AD 381) puts it, 'the rights of communion derive from Rome' or from the bishop of Rome may be studied in the history books; it may be remarked that the dispute between modern Catholics and Orthodox concerns the question whether this center of communion is of divine origin or is merely an ecclesiastical or canonical creation.

The problem, and it is not an easy one, is, granted this unchanged and unchangeable Catholic position, how to make Catholic participation in the Ecumenical Movement not just an exercise in Christian courtesy but a positive and constructive contribution. No one, it is true, on engaging in ecumenism is expected to begin by denying or sacrificing his own basic convictions; though he must not insist on these as the starting-point of dialogue. But these specific Roman Catholic convictions are certainly an obstacle to easy dialogue. Can the Catholic ecclesiology be enriched and qualified without being surrendered?

We may approach this problem by asking, in the light of the council documents: Who, when we consider men individually, belongs to the Church?; and again: What can we say of the non-Catholic Christian Churches as Churches or Christian communions; is there any sense in which they also 'belong to the Church' as collectivities?[2]

The chapter on the People of God in *Lumen Gentium* develops its thought between two complementary ideas. It begins by stating, in biblical language, that 'whoever fears God and does what is right is acceptable with him' (n. 9; cf. Acts 10:35). This is a principle of the widest application, and a later reference to those who, through no fault of their own, have not yet come to an expressed acknowledgment of God (n. 16) suggests that it can take within its scope, professed atheists who 'strive to attain to a (morally) good life' (*ibid.*); in doing which, the council points out, they are in fact – though they do not recognise it – helped by divine grace. The other governing idea of the chapter follows immediately: 'It has pleased God to sanctify and save men, not singly and without any mutual connection, but by constituting them as a people which should acknowledge him in truth and serve him with holiness' (n. 9).

Thus human salvation moves between, involves, two poles. Subjectively, it requires – of adult human beings – that 'they fear

---

2 I have examined these questions at greater length in 'Les Chrétiens non-catholiques et l'Église', in *L'Église de Vatican II*, Vol. 2, ed. G. Baraúna, pp. 651–68.

God and do what is right'. They must be men who rule their lives by their conscience; and, as moral theology points out, a genuine conscience is always to be obeyed, even if, inculpably, it is misinformed – there are those who judge themselves conscientiously required to profess atheism. But there is an *objective* aspect of salvation.[3] Man cannot save himself; salvation is a gift from God, and God was free to give it the form and content which seemed good to him. He chose, in fact, a social form, and the chosen content is summed up in Christ and his new covenant. Salvation has thus been incorporated into and entrusted to the Christian People of God, the Church; and we have already seen that the council teaches that the Church 'subsists in the Catholic Church, governed by Peter's successor and the bishops in communion with him' (*ibid.*, n. 8). Hence we are told (n. 14) that 'those could not be saved, who though they were not unaware that the Catholic Church was founded through Jesus Christ as necessary, yet refused to enter it or persevere in it.'

It may be relevant here to point out that there is a strong vein of intransigence running through the Bible. The people of Israel is contrasted with 'the Gentiles that know not God' and, in fact, is addressed by God through the words of his prophet: 'You only have I known of all the people of the earth.' Doubtless God is the creator of nature and of man, and is the Lord of all history. But, for this 'intransigent' vein of thought, it would hardly be too much to say with the ancient Rabbis that the whole divine purpose in creation and history reaches its end in Israel, to the welfare and destiny of which all else is subordinate and contributory. This intransigence is carried over into the New Testament. Jesus is the Messiah promised to Israel, and his Church is the spiritual (true) Israel. 'There is no other name under heaven given among men by which we must be saved except the name of Jesus Christ of Nazareth (Acts 4:12); and it is as a Christian speaking to Christians that the author of the first Epistle of St John can say: 'We know that we are of God, and the whole world is in the power of the evil one' (5:19).

There is, it is true, another line of thought to be found in both Old and New Testaments, a line which may be called universalistic. But it is based on intransigence. Israel – in the New Testament the

---

[3] That salvation has an objective aspect is common ground among Christians. 'For us men and for our salvation' the Son of God was incarnate, died, and was raised from the dead. This aspect is already adumbrated in deutero-Isaiah's teaching that Israel has a divine mission to the Gentiles. It has priority over the subjective aspect, inasmuch as it was 'when we were yet sinners' – i.e. before we 'feared God' – that Christ died for us.

Christian Church – has a mission to bring light, indeed salvation, to all mankind. But it is the light and redemptive grace of the God of Israel, of Jesus Christ: 'God was in Christ reconciling the world to himself, not counting their trespasses against them, and entrusting to us the message of reconciliation' (2 Cor 5:19). Because God's whole purpose of man's salvation is summed up in Christ, the function of the Church is indispensable: 'Everyone who calls upon the name of the Lord will be saved. But how are men to call upon him in whom they have not believed? And how are they to believe in him of whom they have not heard? And how are they to hear without a preacher?' (Rom 10:13f). And once a man has believed he still has to be baptised: 'Repent, and be baptised every one of you in the name of Jesus Christ for the forgiveness of your sins; and you shall receive the gift of the Holy Spirit' (Acts 2:38).

Thus, on the supposition that the Roman Catholic Church is the unique Church of Jesus Christ, the historical embodiment of his messianic and eschatological people, the 'intransigent' vein in the *De Ecclesia* is fully justified. But it has to be theologically reconciled with the 'universalistic' implications of the affirmation that whoever 'fears God and does what is right' is acceptable with God.

We may begin by considering a particularly interesting group of unbaptised persons, bearing in mind that *Lumen Gentium* teaches that 'Christ alone is the mediator and way of salvation, and becomes present to us in his body, which is the Church. He himself by emphasising the necessity of faith and baptism in express words (cf. Mark 16:16, John 3:5), has thereby confirmed that necessity of the Church, into which men enter through baptism as through a door' (n. 14). The group we have to consider is constituted by the catechumens, those who have been moved by the Holy Spirit, and by an express act of will seek to be incorporated in the Church, and are, in fact, being prepared for baptism. Catechumens were a familiar feature of the ancient Christian scene, as they still are in missionary countries. Of them the constitution says that 'already Mother Church encompasses them as her own with love and solicitude' (*ibid.*). The language is rather vague, but still we have here a group of unbaptised persons whom the Church recognises as 'her own'. Implicitly, I suggest, the council accepts the very ancient and uncontradicted conviction that catechumens, though actually not yet baptised, are yet in such manner related to the Church 'the instrument of the redemption of all' (n. 9) that, if they die before baptism, they are held to be saved. As a group (for no one can judge the interior dispositions of any individual) they are thus regarded as men in

whom salvation, that is to say Christ, is already present and efficaciously operative. Externally, they have not yet passed through
the 'door' of baptism; but in reality they are already, in some
sense, 'inside' the ark of salvation. In them the Church already
transcends its own visible limits; in them baptism, not yet externally received, is already operative. They are a privileged case,
because they already have an explicit desire for baptism and so
for incorporation in the Church; but they are a decisive case,
since they show that lack of material or external incorporation
into the Church does not prove that one is not, in the vitally
important sense that determines salvation, already 'within' it.

In n. 16 the constitution considers the situation of a large mass
of other unbaptised persons, who, however, differ from catechumens because, unlike them, they lack any explicit desire to be
baptised. Such are non-Christian Jews, Moslems, followers of other
religions, and, as already noted, professed atheists or agnostics. All
are classified here as 'those who have not yet accepted the Gospel',
and they are said to be in various ways related to God's people. And
it is said, in general, of all who are in inculpable ignorance of
Christ's gospel and Church, but who 'seek God with a sincere
heart' and seek to fulfil in act his will, which they recognise
through the imperative of their conscience, that they can attain
eternal salvation. This implies a notable, but not novel, extension
of the theological notion utilised in the case of catechumens.
Theology is, of course, familiar with the idea that a desire of receiving a sacrament may do duty for actual reception, in cases where
the latter is physically or morally impossible. Indeed, in the
instance of the sacrament of penance, it is acknowledged that
contrition brings immediate remission of sin, while leaving intact
the obligation of actual sacramental confession when a suitable
occasion offers. There is thus no special difficulty about catechumens with their explicit desire for baptism. Where, however, this
explicit desire is absent, either through ordinary ignorance of the
traditional Christian faith, or through a conscientious non-recep-
tion of its teaching, we have to fall back on what is known as an
'implicit desire' of the sacramental means. A person who genuinely
'fears God and does what is right' would obviously wish to become
a Christian if he recognised this as God's will; it *is* God's will, and
he wishes to do God's will; hence, he may be said to desire implicitly what he rejects explicitly. He is like a man who fails, through no
fault of his own, to recognise the friend whom he genuinely loves.
The implication of the council's positive attitude to all these
groups of non-Christians is, that in them also Christ is (anony-

mously) at work, and that in them also the Church, *extra quam nulla salus*, is transcending her own visible limits.

Obviously, then, the constitution had to take a still more positive line about non-Catholic Christians; about those who 'being baptised, are honoured with the name of Christian, but do not profess the complete faith or do not maintain the unity of communion under Peter's successor' (n. 15).[4] There are many links which unite the Church to these: not only baptism, important as it is because it actually incorporates into Christ (and the Church is Christ's body), but the Bible as the norm of belief and life, and – not to speak of Christian zeal and devotion – there may be other sacraments, too; and in general there is a 'certain communion in prayers and other spiritual benefits, nay a union in the Holy Spirit' (n. 15).

The question of non-Catholic Christians is, we may say, posed in this passage of *Lumen Gentium*. It is here given only a very vague and exiguous answer. More, however, can be gleaned from the Decree on Ecumenism. Schism – a word which the decree avoids, as it does the word 'heresy' – is, in itself a sin; it is a sin against the charity which binds Christians internally and externally with all their fellows. But the decree states explicitly that, while there may have been sin on both sides at the origin of our modern divisions, those who are today *born* in separated Christian bodies are not to be accused of this sin of division; in fact, the Catholic Church embraces our separated brethren with reverence and love. 'For those who believe in Christ and have duly received baptism are established in a certain *communion* with the Catholic Church, albeit not a perfect communion' (n. 3).

The notion of communion, and the distinction between perfect and imperfect communion, may be said to be fundamental to this decree. It is a notion firmly embodied in the New Testament: 'That which we have seen and heard we proclaim also to you, so that you may have fellowship (*koinonia*, communion) with us; and *our fellowship is with the Father* and with his Son Jesus Christ' (1 John 1:3). It appears to signify that kind of association which is involved in common possessions.[5] In this general sense, we may say that the

---

4 Explicit mention is not made of, e.g. Quakers, who do not include sacraments in their idea of 'essential Christianity'. Obviously, they are to be 'classified' somewhere between catechumens and those who 'do not know of the Gospel'. Their faith in Christ would lead them to baptism, if they understood that it is the 'necessary' door to the Church, and the way in which Christ wishes us to be incorporated in his mystical body.

5 The Greeks had a saying, which puts the thing in reverse perspective: The possessions of friends are common to each.

common land of a medieval village was a material reality, shared as a possession by each of the families, and constituting a link between the personal lives of all the villagers. To possess something is to be *constituted in relationship with* everyone to whom that thing is a reality, and *especially* to everyone who, like you, possesses it. Thus there is born the reality and idea of a commonwealth.

A primitive expression of the idea of Christianity as communion was the pooling of material possessions in the early Church in Jerusalem: 'The company of those who believed were of one heart and soul, and no one said that any of the things which he possessed was his own, but they had everything in common' (Acts 4:32). The experiment seems to have been abortive, though it has been continued or re-enacted in the 'religious communities' of later Christianity. But the 'goods' which believers possess in common are, of course, above all spiritual 'goods' which Christ communicated to the apostles (*De Divina Revelatione*, n. 7). They are summed up in the gift of the Holy Spirit, whereby Christ himself, God's supreme 'gift' to man, is made sacramentally present in and through the Church. The common possession of these spiritual goods sets up a communion between believers. And, by a natural development of linguistic usage, the Church herself comes to be called a 'communion' (St Augustine speaks of *communio sacramentorum*, a phrase which emphasises that the sacraments, as signs conveying what they signify, are the visible means of communion); and again the eucharistic meal is called 'Holy Communion', since in it we become 'one body', the body of Christ.

Within this general notion of 'communion' the decree makes a distinction between 'perfect' and 'imperfect' communion. By perfect communion it means the total sharing of the whole sacramental reality of Christianity by those who are 'fully incorporated into the society of the Church', those, that is to say, 'who having the Spirit of Christ, accept its complete structure and all the means of salvation established in it, and are in its visible organism (*compage*), joined with Christ who rules it through the supreme pontiff and the bishops – joined in him by the bonds of the profession of faith, the sacraments, ecclesiastical government and communion (*De Ecclesia*, n. 14).[6]

---

[6] It should be obvious that the term 'perfect communion' does not involve a claim that the Catholic Church, as she existentially exists, is morally perfect – such a claim would, of course, be absurd. The term is an improvement on the familiar term 'perfect society', used to describe a society with its *sui iuris* for all purposes involved in its intrinsic *raison d'être*. A nation-state is a perfect society in this sense; a trade union is not, because it is subject to the overriding law of the state within which it exists.

Before discussing imperfect, or incomplete, communion, it is well to emphasise the unique feature of perfect or complete communion: it involves a common experience made tangible not only in friendly sympathy, external good works, and common witness to the Gospel, not only in a positive mystical relationship to Christ the head of the Church, but in actual worship and shared community life, above all in the sharing of a common eucharistic table. Every Christian knows by experience that his links with the other members of his own 'communion' are unique, as compared with those that bind him to other Christians, even though in the sphere of theology and in apostolic concern he may be closer to the latter than the former. This uniqueness has a doctrinal depth. The Bible teaches that it is by sharing in 'one bread' that we become one body; this sharing is diminished where there is not complete communion. The ancient Church branded schism as the setting up of 'altar against altar'. One of the profoundest motives of the ecumenical movement is the wish to recover this full eucharistic communion of all with each and each with all. Imperfect communion, as we shall now proceed to say, is real and valuable. But the measure of its reality is the ache at its heart for full communion.

Such being 'perfect communion', it is obvious that Christian communion can be imperfectly realised in a number of modes. Unbaptised believers, for example Quakers, are united to those baptised by their common faith in Christ, their common veneration of the Bible, and their common inherence in the Christian tradition as a reality of the historical order. At the other extreme we have, for example, the Christians of eastern Orthodoxy, who are united to Catholics in the apostolic succession, the Eucharist and the other sacraments; thus they 'are joined with us in the closest relationship' (*De Ecumenismo*, n. 15). Between these limits, there are all those who by baptism are united with each other and with Catholics through the sacrament of 'incorporation into Christ' and are therefore properly acknowledged by 'the sons of the Catholic Church' as their 'brothers in the Lord' (n. 3). Besides faith and baptism, there are also, of course, many other 'common goods' which deepen communion and enrich it both as reality and as idea.

It must be observed that such common possession of authentic elements of the total Christian treasure does not merely unite various groups among themselves; it unites the members of each group with those of all the other groups, including the group called the Roman Catholic Church. Perfect communion, in other words, has a real extension in imperfect communion, and once again we see how the Church transcends her own visible limits; once again we appreciate the cautious statement: 'The Church *subsists in* the Roman Catholic Church' – which falls short of a sheer material identification of Church and Catholic Church.

From consideration of the relation to the visible Church of individuals who are in 'imperfect communion' with her, it is possible to pass on to consider the situation of the separated Christian bodies as such. Any failure on the part of the decree to do so would have had most unfortunate results, since the ecumenical movement has taken the form of a convergence of Christian groups, not merely of individual Christians. The step had not been taken in *Lumen Gentium*, but is taken in the decree: 'the separated Churches and communities, though we believe that they suffer from deficiencies, are by no means destitute of significance and importance in the mystery of salvation. The Spirit of Christ does not refuse to use them as means of salvation, means whose effectiveness is derived from that fullness of grace and truth which has been entrusted to the Catholic Church' (n. 3). This statement, I think, has no parallel in previous official pronouncements of the Catholic Church, and it deserves to be carefully scrutinised.

Christianity is a mystery of communion. Every authentic Christian 'element' is, in its measure, a 'unifying' factor, a factor which produces communion, fellowship, between those who alike acknowledge and live by it. The separated Christian bodies are therefore – from the Catholic point of view – to be seen as ambivalent. As 'separated' they may be said to exist in virtue of a rejection of some element of the total gift of God in Christ to his Church. But as 'Christian bodies' they are, in fact, built upon Christian elements, and are alike cause and effect of the acceptance of such elements by their own adherents. A secular nation-state, however 'Christian' its laws and *mores*, is 'built' on natural foundations. But a Christian Church is built upon 'supernatural' elements, elements accepted as deriving from the Gospel. They must therefore be considered to be themselves – doubtless in varying degrees – supernatural. And as such they play a positive part in the divine design of man's supernatural redemption and salvation, *as that design takes concrete shape amid the sins and imperfections of mankind*. In an ideal order there would be no separated Christian bodies, but only one visible universal Church, and towards this ideal the Ecumenical Movement may be said to be moving. But in the actual historical order, where sin and error have intervened, the actual salvation of actual men is being promoted by the Holy Spirit both in and by the

Catholic Church and in and by other bodies.[7] Hence the decree, while firmly maintaining that the Catholic Church is 'the general aid of salvation' in which 'all the fullness of the means of salvation can be attained', boldly speaks of the separated bodies (without distinction) as 'used by the Holy Spirit as means of salvation'.

At this point a Catholic might wonder whether the council was not in danger of slipping into the 'branch theory' of the Church. If there are numerous Christian bodies, each divided from the others, but all genuine Christian communions, means of salvation – and some of them, at least, besides the Catholic Church, entitled to be called 'Churches' – then is not the one Church to be conceived as the sum of these bodies? But the council had no intention of countenancing this theory, long ago denounced as an error. The theory is excluded by the council's explicit teaching. In *Lumen Gentium* we learn that the Church has been given, in perpetuity, by Christ a ministerial or hierarchical structural principle; and that this, again by Christ's institution, is expressed in the apostolic-episcopal college, of which the reality is essentially bound up with the full communion of each member with all the others. (A bishop can exercise his sacramentally given functions of teacher and ruler 'only in *hierarchical communion* with the head and members of the college', n. 21; he is 'constituted a member of the episcopal body by virtue of sacramental consecration and hierarchical communion with the head and members of the college' (n.

---

[7] The decree refers to the non-Catholic Christian bodies as Churches and communities. Some have seen an invidious distinction here. The council was in something of a dilemma. Modern non-Catholic practice speaks of 'the Churches' without discrimination. Catholic precedent, however, confined the use of the title 'Church' to the Catholic Church herself (and her dioceses, each a Church within the Church) and to those eastern Christian bodies which, though estranged from Rome for many centuries, have an undoubted continuity of full sacramental and especially eucharistic life, carried on from before communion with the West ceased. By speaking of 'Churches and communities' the decree bore witness to this Catholic precedent, but it did not clearly indicate which bodies it would refer to as Churches and which as 'only' communities. Behind the linguistic distinction there may lurk a theological consideration. The Eucharist is the heart, centre, food, and growing-point of ecclesial communion at its fullest: 'The bread which we break, is it not a participation (*koinonia*) in the body of Christ? Because there is one bread, we who are many are one body, for we all partake of the one bread' (1 Cor 10:16f). Hence, it seems natural to speak of a 'Church' where there exists a Eucharist which we can unconditionally recognise as such. Such *unconditional* recognition can be more easily given to eastern Orthodox Eucharists than to some others. [It is also possible that the drafters had in mind that some Christian bodies prefer not to be called 'Churches'.]

22). This doctrine is presupposed in the Decree on Ecumenism, and is implicit in its teaching that 'perfect communion' is to be found only in the Catholic Church. The 'branch theory' is not constructed to safeguard this truth. Yet it seems inescapable that the decree forces us to acknowledge, outside the visible unity of the Catholic Church, not only 'vestiges' of the Church, not only individuals who, especially if they are baptised, have some communion with the Church and, if incorporated in Christ, are in some degree incorporated in his mystical body which is the Church, but Christian communions of an ecclesial character which, at least if they have 'the genuine and complete substance of the eucharistic mystery' (*De Ecumenismo*, n. 22) (which is the food of the mystical body, and of which the unity of the mystical body is, says St Thomas, the *res*) can truly be called 'Churches'.

There is a field for further theological investigation here. We seem driven to say that the Church, existing in its integral fullness in the Catholic Church, exists also, by self-transcendence, in bodies out of communion with the Catholic Church. We shall mean by 'out of communion' that they do not enjoy 'perfect communion'; but we shall admit that they have with us, and we with them, a communion which is very real, which can increase, and which is ontologically ordered, by the elements which constitute it, towards perfect communion. Our resulting ecclesiology may lack something of the clarity and definiteness of views associated with the name of Bellarmine; but it will have gained in richness and nuance, and in recognition of the mysteriousness of Christianity, not easily framed in precise human language. Perhaps we could say, with a distinguished Orthodox theologian, 'We know where the Church is; it is not for us to judge and say where the Church is not.'[8]

Our examination of the decree has shown that the notion of 'communion', while fully traditional, is yet flexible. In this respect it has a great advantage, for the ecumenical dialogue, over the description of the Church as 'a society'. A society is something whose edges are essentially sharp. You belong to it so long as you recognise and are recognised, in a juridical sense, but its governing authority; otherwise, you do not belong to it. Communion, by contrast, exists wherever there is common possession, whether of material or spiritual riches. There is a primordial communion between all men through their possession of a common specific

---

[8] P. Evdokimov, *L'Orthodoxie*, p. 343.

(and rational) nature.[9] There is a closer communion between men of a single culture or single political system. There is a certain communion between all who recognise the existence of a holy creator God. But there is obviously a much greater 'communion' between all those who acknowledge Jesus Christ as the redeemer of mankind. And this is still more true of Christians who, having been truly baptised, are thereby marked with a common seal of incorporation into Christ – a sealing which we believe to be indelible in this life. On the other hand, since all must agree that Christ gave a total endowment of spiritual means to his Church, there must remain a marked difference between forms of Christian communion based on the common sharing of only part of this totality and a 'perfect communion' in the totality of the Sacred Tradition.[10]

It may be almost superfluous to enlarge upon the value, for ecumenical dialogue, of such an ecclesiology of communion. Its importance is that it approaches the whole question of the Church and her nature as visible on earth, from a basis which does not presuppose, on the part of those taking part in the dialogue, an acceptance of the belief that the perfect communion exists on

[9]   It is often said that this sharing of a common rational nature by all men creates a universal human society. I prefer to avoid this phraseology. There is no universal authority, at the natural human level, that can at present give that cohesion which I think necessary to constitute a society; the 'authority of conscience' is not external but internal, and – since men's conscientious judgments vary – can be divisive. But it seems true to say that the possession of a common human nature makes men potentially a society, and that it is a dynamic factor making for a universal society. However, in the actual historical order it seems doubtful whether this potentiality can be realised except with the help of a universal *supernatural* society – the Church.

[10] F. D. Maurice, in his important work *The Kingdom of Christ*, builds his ecclesiology on 'signs of a spiritual society'. He enumerates various signs: baptism, the creeds, forms of worship, the Eucharist, the ministry and the Bible. And he argues that these signs are all present in the Church of England. Maurice's 'signs' correspond to our 'common spiritual goods'. Like them, they tend towards communion. While a Catholic would say that Maurice did not grasp the whole idea of the structured episcopal college, one can read with admiration his clear sense of the universality of the episcopate: 'The overseers or bishops of the Christian Church have felt themselves to be emphatically the bonds of communication between different parts of the earth. The jurisdiction of each has been confined within a certain district; but, by the very nature of their office, they have held fellowship, and been obliged to hold fellowship, with those who lived in other districts ... This episcopacy has not been merely an accidental addition to, or overgrowth upon other forms of priesthood. In those countries where it has been adopted it has been the root of all other forms, and has been supposed to contain them within it' (*op. cit.*, pp. 98f). The *De Ecclesia* similarly sees the presbyterate as a participation of the priesthood held in fullness by the bishops.

earth – or that it is identical with the Roman Catholic Church. Just as it enables Catholics to recognise other Christian bodies as genuinely Christian communions, linked with the Catholic Church by all that is held in common between them, so it enables non-Catholics to acknowledge the Catholic Church as a Christian communion, closely linked to them by the same constitutive elements. Behind this common agreement, or rather beyond it, there remains, of course, disagreement about the actual existence here and now, or the identification, of the perfect communion. But if ecumenical dialogue is directed towards visible Christian unity, it is implied that a perfect communion either *can* exist on earth, or at least is the ideal which must govern ecumenical endeavour. The Catholic, like the eastern Orthodox, in holding that what can exist does exist, and has a divine guarantee of perpetual existence, can claim that he holds to a 'realised' eschatological conception of the Church. But he can respect and co-operate, in thought and practice, with those who hope from the future for what he believes God has guaranteed in the present.

A view of the Church whose sole recommendation was that it could help the Ecumenical Movement might arouse suspicion. But the ecclesiology of communion is, in fact, intimately related to the general view of the Church inspiring the documents of Vatican II, and particularly *Lumen Gentium*. We have already seen that the Constitution on the Church represents a move away from a rather narrow juridical outlook whereby the nature of the Church is deduced from the nature of the papal primacy. This constitution offers an ecclesiology which seems to be basically sacramental. The mystical body of Christ is given substance in human history by sacramental signs; and the visible Church herself is not only a sign of human unity but a sign and instrument of divine salvation; it makes present and active within history the redemptive incarnation of the Son of God. And the centre and climax of this whole sacramental order is the Eucharist, 'whereby the Church continually lives and grows' (*De Ecclesia*, n. 26). As the Constitution on the Liturgy puts it, it is through offering 'the immaculate Victim', Christ, and with him themselves, to God in the Eucharist that the faithful 'are daily consummated into unity with God and among themselves' (*De Liturgia*, n. 48). Thus the climax of sacrament is also the focal point of communion. When St Thomas, as already mentioned, describes 'the unity of the mystical body' as the *res* or fruit of the Eucharist he is echoing the Christian tradition in its purest form. 'Church' and 'communion' become one thing in the mystery of the Eucharist. Holy Order is itself a sacrament; but it is

a sacrament subservient to the mystery of the Eucharist and therefore to communion. Since communion, in its perfection, takes
shape as the existential common or social life of believers gathered
round the altar, the bishops, in virtue of their sacramental status,
have an authority which has a partial expression in juridical terms.
But this juridical element in the Church, seen in the wider vision
of the ecclesiology of Vatican II, is not creative of the Church. The
Church is daily created or re-created in and by her sacramental
life, and the juridical element in her government is there to
prevent that sacramental life from anarchy and disintegration. In
short, though it is true that *ubi episcopus, ibi ecclesia*, it is still more
deeply true that *ubi Eucharistia, ibi ecclesia*. And this means that the
local Church, centred in the Eucharist – which can only be celebrated as a space-time event – is, as has been said, one of a number
of 'cells, each of which contains the whole living mystery of the one
body of Christ'.[11] The world-wide communion is 'a communion of
communions', not some sort of army in which all power is delegated from above and each platoon has significance only as
bestowed on it through its subordination. It is at the local level of
the eucharistic fellowship that the People of God actually lives and
that Christ is made present through that People.

We have seen that the decree approves the idea that every
Christian – and, we may add, every Christian ecclesial body – finds
communion with the Catholic Church through sharing in the
Gospel blessings. It is proper that this communion should find
external expression. This will come about through genuine frater-
nal charity among Christians, and more specifically through
ecumenical dialogue. But there should be other expressions of the
already existing unity of Christians. As the decree indicates, there
should be mutual respect and a common effort in the witness we
all bear to the Christian faith and hope. And there should be
common Christian co-operation in the broad field of social-
economic and, indeed, cultural action (n. 12). The point is taken
up in one of its aspects in the Constitution on the Church in the
World of Today, where it is said to be desirable that Catholics
should actively and positively co-operate, to play their part in international fellowship, 'both with the separated brethren who, like
them, profess gospel charity, and with all men who thirst for true
peace' (n. 90). A more delicate theological issue arises concerning
'praying together'. The decree acknowledges the value of this on

[11] T. F. Stransky, *The Decree on Ecumenism, a New Translation with a Commentary*, p.
27.

suitable occasions, but speaks with caution of a particular form of it: *'communicatio in sacris'* (n. 8). The term is not defined in the decree. T. F. Stransky, a staff member of the Secretariat for Unity, states that the decree uses it directly to refer to participation in the sacramental life of other Churches, especially in eucharistic services; indirectly, to refer to the sharing of any form of prayer offered by or with members of other Churches.[12] Such common worship, especially if it is liturgical, and above all if it is eucharistic, presents difficulties in ecumenical practice which are now notorious. The liturgy, above all the Eucharist, by its nature 'signifies unity'; it normally expresses, and deepens, a unity already present. In early Christianity as already stated, the existence of *altare contra altare* was seen as the very hallmark of schism; and, on the other hand, even catechumens might be dismissed from Mass before the beginning of the Great Prayer. Thus many have felt, and the feeling is particularly strong among the eastern Orthodox, that it would be something like profanation to hold 'joint Eucharists' before external unity is attained. On the other hand, the grace flowing from the Eucharist is a grace of charity, a grace therefore making directly for unity; so that it could be urged that 'joint Eucharists' would be most effective ways of forwarding ecumenism. The decree therefore states that *'communicatio in sacris'* is not to be considered as a means of indiscriminate application with a view to restoring Christian unity; and leaves the decision in particular cases to the competent authority.

Ecumenism is, in itself, an affair of practice based on theology rather than of pure theology. Are there any theological grounds for hoping that practical ecumenism, inspired by prayer and taking shape especially in dialogue, may, in fact, culminate in Christian unity? It seems that there are. Dialogue, as we have seen, seeks to operate from a basis of shared convictions and to extend the area of such common convictions through a process of clearing up misunderstandings and communicating insights. Behind the dialogue, however, there will usually be divergent convictions, and these may comprise: first, truths held by faith on the one hand, but not accepted by another or other parties to the dialogue; second, tenets which are neither 'of faith' nor necessary corollaries of what is held by faith; and of these tenets some may be erroneously supposed to be 'of faith'. Faith, however, results from a supernatural enlightenment of man's natural powers whereby he is enabled to assent to, and hold by, divine revelation and its content. The

[12] T. F. Stransky, *op. cit.*, p. 41, n. 9.

precise or 'formal' object of faith is truth revealing itself, for which, and for which alone, it has a natural affinity. It would seem to be strictly impossible to give the assent of faith to something which is not actually true and not given or implied in divine revelation; though it is plainly possible to withhold the explicit assent of faith from something which is actually revealed or implied by revelation, while giving a genuinely 'faithful' assent to other aspects or contents of divine revelation. In the latter case, we shall have to speak about 'implicit faith' and we could compare the situation of a man who has no 'implicit' desire for the baptism which he explicitly refuses. Now the ecumenical dialogue is calculated to communicate insights, and thus to bring the participants to a recognition of aspects of divine revelation which they had overlooked, or to which they had given insufficient attention. It is also calculated to clarify the distinction between what we really 'believe' and what we only hold by opinion. It can lead therefore to mutual enrichment in the apprehension of divine revelation and mutual purification of the articulated faith. It sets the participants, in other words, on convergent theological courses. Doubtless, the achievement of Christian unity will be God's work, not men's; but ecumenism can pave the way to it, and 'dispose' us for the reception of this great and hoped-for grace.

The actual practice of the ecumenical dialogue may be helped by a sentence added during the fourth session of the council, which has been described[13] as possibly the most important change made in the text at that stage: Catholic theologians, in comparing doctrines, 'should bear in mind that there is an order of "hierarchy" of the truths of Catholic doctrine, since these truths are variously linked up with the foundation of the Christian faith' (n. 11). This sentence must not be misunderstood. It does not mean that, of the articles of faith, or among defined doctrines, there are some which are unessential; nor that some are only probably true. You cannot be a Catholic on the basis of a selection of Catholic doctrines excluding some which you, or others advising you, think to be 'unimportant' or disputable. All doctrines, in other words, are equally necessary. But they are not equally important. The doctrine of man's redemption by Christ is not more true than the doctrine of indulgences; but it is vastly more important. When doctrines are viewed in their aspect of being equally necessary they are seen, as it were, two-dimensionally. But the world to which they belong is three-dimensional, a world of perspective.

[13] T. Stransky, *op. cit.*, p. 64, n. 30.

The importance of this distinction between truth and varying importance is obvious as regards the ecumenical dialogue, in which it should quickly become apparent that most of the more important truths are held in common. This is only to be expected if the criterion of importance is the closeness of the link between a doctrine and the 'foundation of the Christian faith'.[14] It may be of even greater consequence that the acceptance of the distinction could have profound effect on Catholicism as existentially lived. We have already seen that the council, without in any way denying the 'juridical' element in the Christian totality, has shifted the emphasis from this element to the sacramental aspect of the body of Christ. Such shifts of emphasis can change the quality of a religion as actually lived – and can increase or diminish its existential credibility.

[14] How is the 'foundation' to be designated? The first proclamation of the faith was presumably 'Jesus is risen'. Very early too, were such 'confessions' as 'Jesus is the Christ', 'Jesus is Lord'. The decree wisely abstains from further precision.

Chapter 20

What's 'Special' About
Christian Morality?

Denis F. O'Callaghan

At a recent conference of religion teachers the above question brought to light a very broad spectrum of views. Some claimed that Revelation and the presence of the Spirit to a large extent made the Christian community independent of reason's guidance. The majority held that the history of Christian ethics clearly showed that God by supernatural intervention did not short-circuit human reason but left to Christian persons and community the task of discovering answers to concrete moral questions. Both sides claimed to have authority on their side: 'Loyal internal and external obedience to the teaching authority of the Church obliges not only because of the reasons adduced, but rather because of the light of the Holy Spirit, which is given in a particular way to the pastors of the Church in order that they may illustrate the truth' (*Humanae Vitae*, par. 28). 'In fidelity to conscience, Christians are joined with the rest of men in the search for truth, and for the genuine solution to the numerous problems which arise in the life of individuals and community relations' (*Church in the Modern World*, par. 16).

It appears to me that the *really* unique factor in Christian morality is not any particular ethical value or ethical principle. It is the Christian faith itself. Faith here means that understanding of the meaning of human life which Christ possessed and which he taught to his followers. Two apt quotations come to mind here – one from the Venerable Bede as cited in the *Dutch Catechism*, the other from the American Walter Rauschenbusch, whose *Christianity and Social Crisis* has seen many editions.

> In AD 627 the monk Paulinus visited King Edwin in northern England to persuade him to accept Christianity. He hesitated and

decided to summon his advisers. At the meeting one of them stood up and said: 'Your majesty, when you sit at a table with your lords and vassals, in the winter when the fire burns warm and bright on the hearth and the storm is howling outside, bringing the snow and the rain, it happens of a sudden that a little bird flies into the hall. It comes in at one door and flies out through the other. For the few moments that it is inside the hall it does not feel the cold, but as soon as it leaves your sight, it returns to the dark of winter. It seems to me that the life of man is much the same. We do not know what went before and we do not know what follows. If the new doctrine can speak to us surely of these things, it is well for us to follow it.'

Jesus had learned the greatest and deepest and rarest secret of all – how to live a religious life. When the question of economic wants is solved for the individual and all his outward adjustments are as comfortable as possible he may still be haunted by the horrible emptiness of his life and feel that existence is a meaningless riddle and delusion. If the question of the distribution of wealth were solved for all society and all lived in average comfort and without urgent anxiety, the question would still be: how many would be at peace with their own souls ... Universal prosperity would not be incompatible with universal ennui and *Weltschmerz*.

'Who am I? Where did I come from? Where am I going?' – these questions, familiar legends now on many a school wall-chart, are the most fundamental that one can ask. To these Christ gave the answer – it is from God the Father you come, and it is to him you return; he loves you beyond human comprehension to the extent even of sending his Son to redeem you and bring you to his Kingdom; your fellow man is your brother, enjoying the same dignity of origin, that same destiny and that same love; the created world is your temporary home, in it under God's loving providence by living the good life you should grow in God's image and build up that community which preshadows the Kingdom to come.

This is the Gospel in its simplest terms. It is this good news that gives formal meaning and identity to Christian morality. If a moral system gets force and value from its philosophy of life, from its insight into the meaning of life, it is his supreme understanding of human life which gives Christ his unique warrant as moral teacher and which makes Christian morality special.

Without question this faith context deepens the moral sense of the Christian. It is against this background that he formulates his moral principles. Naturally this Christian emphasis will be more marked on some principles than on others. One area where this appears strongly is that of respect for life. The Christian assesses the value of human life through the eyes of God rather than through those of man and so his norms may differ from those proposed by the humanist.

St Paul summed up the Christian moral life in the immortal phrase, 'Faith working itself out in *agape*'. One may paraphrase this as: 'The understanding of the meaning of life possessed by Christians expressing itself in love of God and love of neighbour'. For St Paul *agape* is not something one is obliged to do by faith – it is the lived reality of faith, the real expression of faith. On this same theme Augustine remarked that charity belongs in the Christian life like weight in a falling stone. With this instinct of the faith the inbuilt dynamic of *agape* moves one to live the Christian life almost by spontaneous impulse. Hence the oft quoted or oft misquoted maxim of St Augustine, *Dilige et quodvis fac*, love and do what you will.

Galatians, chapter 5, from which the text at the beginning of the last paragraph was taken, gives a clear and striking picture of St Paul's concept of the Christian moral life – faith lives itself out in *agape*; *agape* as subjective motive inspires the Christian to live a good life; *agape* as objective value includes all the matter of the commandments; *agape* is diffused in the heart of the Christian by the indwelling Spirit of Christ so that his good actions are fruits of the Spirit. In Paul's mind, then, it is not only the more human understanding behind it that makes Christian morality unique. It is the mystery of Christ and his Spirit that provides its deep inner core of meaning and gives it its most special character. The fact that many Christians are unaware of this presence of the Spirit is not an argument against it. It is an argument for better catechesis.

Christian apologetics would be on the wrong track were it simply to try to isolate some concrete *ethical* principle or other as the special individuating note of Christian morality, thinking that when one had filtered out everything of common denominator with any other ethical system what remained over would constitute the unique factor in Christian morality. It would be a fruitless task. Just *what* would remain over when one had filtered out the theme of love of God and love of neighbour (common with Jewish morality), the theme of love of enemies (common with higher Indian religions), the Golden Rule (common with Greek moral philosophy)? Some ethically distinctive points may well remain, but would they really identify and differentiate the Christian moral system?

If genuine ethical values can be discovered and real ethical principles can be formulated by man reflecting on his human experience by his human reason it should come as no surprise if some sage somewhere succeeds in establishing principles in this or that moral area which bear comparison with those proposed in the Christian tradition. Furthermore, if we believe that God extends his gratuitous saving love to non-Christians should we not admit that this grace can enlighten the heart of a Greek philosopher or of a Hindu mystic? St Clement of Alexandria certainly thought so, and his words have been echoed in Christian theology down the ages.

One risks impoverishing Christian morality when one seeks merely for concrete ethical factors unique to it. But as a moral *system* it is unique – primarily in its faith context as explained above, but also in the manner in which it sets out its priorities and knits so many aspects into a single whole. This perspective of emphases and this synthesis do provide a very definite identity.

First is the close link between religion and behaviour so that moral action is worship and service of God. This is already a familiar theme in the Old Testament (cf. Isa 58). The Jewish historian Josephus in his tract *Against Apion* puts it very well:

> The reason why our lawgiver (Moses) in his legislation far exceeded all other legislators in his usefulness to all, is that he did not make religion a part of virtue, but had the insight to make the various virtues part of religion, I mean justice, fortitude, self-control, and the mutual harmony in all things of the members of the community with one another. All our actions and studies and words have a connection with piety towards God.

Second is the mustering of all the virtues under agape, so that they are practised not for their own sake merely as was the Greek *arete* or moral excellence, but in order to make agape more operative in one's life and behaviour. Stanislas Lyonnet in his *Sin, Redemption and Sacrifice* (Rome 1970, pp. 47–8) makes the following useful comment on St Paul:

> By their content, the Pauline lists differ still more from those of Hellenism. Noteworthy in that respect is the sobriety of the Pauline lists of virtues, with the conspicious absence of the term *arete* (moral excellence). Practically, these virtues are reduced to brotherly love and its obvious manifestations ... Even in the longest list, Gal 5:22-23, the enumeration does little else than expound the first term, *agape*, the one fruit of the spirit, so that taken as a whole, the virtues correspond more or less to the description Paul gave of *agape* in 1 Cor 13:4–7.

Third is the authentic nature of Christian moral norms. There is no 'alienation' because these norms embody values and attitudes which the Christian has made his own or should have made his own. In a well-known text Irenaeus of Lyons says the following:

'The law will no longer say Do not commit adultery to one who does not conceive even a thought of another's wife, or Thou shall not kill to one who has removed from himself all anger and aggressiveness, or Thou shall not covet the field of your neighbour, or his cow or his ass to one who makes no count of earthly things and collects merits for heaven, nor Eye for eye, tooth for tooth to one who does not consider anyone his enemy but everyone his neighbour and so cannot stretch out his hand for revenge (*Exposition of the Apostolic Teaching*, n. 96).

One must take Christian morality all as a piece, the Sermon on the Mount, the parables and addresses of Christ, the moral teaching of the apostolic Church. The whole picture then hits one with that consistency and inner conviction which mark moral truth. No wonder the Jews commented: 'Never did man speak like this man! He teaches with authority.' The opening statement of Vatican II's *Declaration on Religious Freedom* is relevant here: 'The truth cannot impose itself except by virtue of its own truth, and it makes its entrance into the mind at once quietly and with power.'

Chapter 21

Approaching Christian Morality

Vincent MacNamara

One could begin this study by considering the history of morality within our Judaeo-Christian tradition and there might be good reasons for such an approach. But it seems best first to determine in some fashion the particular area of Christianity that concerns us: that of morality. So I propose that we try to isolate the word 'morality' in 'Christian morality' and to reflect on what we mean by it. We all know a fair bit about morality so we should feel reasonably comfortable with the subject. It is not as if we were heading into unknown territory. We feel the call to be moral – fair, just, caring, unselfish, forgiving etc. – and are often unhappy that we are not as good as we might be. We are well aware of making distinctions between acts which we call right or good and the opposite which we call wrong or bad. Our conversations and newspapers witness to such concerns: 'There is no honesty today'/'She is a very upright person'/ 'He will give you a fair deal'/'I find it hard to forgive him the wrong he did me'/ 'He treated her very badly'/ 'Human life is sacred'/ 'Survey shows decline in moral standards'/ 'Irish people are racist'/ 'Ireland responds generously to distress'/ 'There is a right to divorce'.

We think of morality primarily as applying to acts. But a little reflection shows us that we refer it also to intentions, dispositions, desires and character. And we use different forms of moral language: consider the difference between 'Do not steal'/ 'She is a very honourable person'/ 'Honesty is an important virtue today'. We not only make these distinctions between one kind of behaviour and another. We recognise that the statements are not merely factual or neutral statements: they commit us in some way. It is not like saying that something is white or round. When we say that a piece of behaviour is immoral we recognise that it is to be avoided. When we acknowledge that a course of action is right we mean that it is commendable, that its pursuit by ourselves or others is worthy of praise: we recognise some kind of call to live in that way. There is something prescriptive in our understanding of morality, some sense of obligation or claim on us. Whether we will follow what we recognise to be the moral way or not is, of course, another matter altogether.

This, I suppose, is our unreflective experience. It is what we have picked up as we have gone through life. For most of us it is very much part of our tradition and especially of our religion. But however prominent moral considerations might be in our consciousness we may find, if we question ourselves, that we are not too clear about what we mean by this morality talk. We are not clear about where morality comes from, about what it means to call (or why we call) a particular piece of behaviour right or good, and about what we mean by saying that the right ought to be done and the wrong avoided.

Let us spell that out. First, we have trouble about the source of morality, in particular about whether it comes from God – from the Ten Commandments perhaps – and about how our moral conduct relates us to him. Second, we have trouble about our criterion for saying what kind of conduct is acceptable or not. (It may well be that we have never examined our moral positions, that we have a lopsided morality, a Victorian morality or a bourgeois morality, or that what passes for morality in our lives is really parental directives.) It is this problem of determining what is right and wrong that interests people almost exclusively about morality. But we need to go beyond particular issues to ask ourselves why we say and how we know (who tells us) that things are right or wrong. And we need to go beyond that again to ask what we mean by the whole business of calling acts right and wrong. That is, we must ask ourselves not only what is right and wrong but what the words 'right' and 'wrong' mean for us and why we use them. What would you say? You may hold a set of moral principles: murder/abortion/stealing/lying are wrong. What do you mean by the 'wrong' bit? Third, we have trouble with the prescriptive element, with what we might refer to as moral obligation, with *why* we must do right and avoid wrong. We sometimes refer to morality as a law, perhaps as the law of God. Is it from God that morality gets its binding force?

We have trouble, I think, nailing down the moral point of view. That there is such a point of view we have no doubt. We need the language of morality and most of us would regard it as entirely natural to have recourse to the kind of judgment that we label as moral. We cannot say what we want to say about ourselves and others, we cannot describe how life presents itself to us, without its language and concepts. So deeply engrained in us is this dimension of experience that it would be difficult for us to live a day without the whole tissue of language of 'right', 'wrong', 'good', 'bad', 'duty', 'obligation', 'ought', 'praise' and 'blame', as well as much moral language of a softer kind. This is not to say that we are always in the area of morality when we use such words, but we often are. We say 'he ought to be here any minute', 'he should have taken a 7 iron', 'he is a good philosopher'. These we know are not about morality. But compare 'he ought to treat his wife better', 'he should not kill', 'he is a good man'. These are about morality. It is true that there are fuzzy edges around the area of morality, some points at which we are not sure whether we are making moral judgments or perhaps judgments about manners or good taste. But by and large we know when we are talking morality and when we are not. It is an area that has a high degree of determinateness.

In making moral statements we are not merely expressing our tastes: they are not in the same category as statements that a person likes cucumber or the Connemara landscape or tweeds or heavy rock. It is perfectly alright for you to like one thing and for me to like another. Such things do not greatly matter: there is no right and wrong or true and false about them. But there are areas of living in which it matters a great deal what we value and do – issues of one's right to life, or justice, of respect for others, i.e. moral issues. We are not prepared to say that in making these statements we are merely expressing a subjective view of desirable human behaviour and that it is perfectly fine for another to hold and act on the opposite point of view. We believe that there is an objectivity about our statements, like for example, 'torture is wrong'. If we hold this position we do not regard others as rationally justified in holding the opposite: we do not mean that torture is wrong for us but may be right for them. We believe that there is a truth to be discovered here, a truth for living that is as rigorous as truth in any other area and that the judgments we are making are somehow founded in the natures and relations of things. We would expect to be able to give reasons of some kind for our positions, to justify them. Or at least we feel that they are justifiable, that an expert could in some sense demonstrate the reasonableness of them.

If we were asked to give some elementary account of this experience we might come up with a variety of suggestions. There would possibly emerge ideas of fairness, impartiality, respect for self and others, concern for human flourishing, a vision of a good society, a recognition that there is a kind of life that fits our rational nature. They are different but related ideas. They are all in some sense about persons in community. So even at this stage we can mark down that morality is not a series of unexplained and arbitrary commands and prohibitions coming from heaven only knows where. It arises rather as the human community's awareness of the claims and demands of interrelatedness. All of morality in the end is about this. It is the search for the acts, attitudes, dispositions – and more fundamentally perhaps the virtues and institutions – that make for successful being with others.

This moral strand of experience is a powerful and compelling one. It makes insistent demands and while it can be ignored it is only with difficulty that it can be entirely quelled or silenced. There is something deep in us that wants to be moral, that desires goodness, and it is well to remember this. Not to realise this is to fail to understand oneself. We will argue later that listening to the moral thrust is listening to what we most deeply desire. But to call attention to this alone would be to give a false picture. The intriguing thing is that it appears in the midst of much else. We are centres of so much energy and not all of it points unerringly in the moral direction. We do not always listen to the call of morality because we do not want only to be moral beings. We want to be and do and express ourselves in many other ways. We have such a restless urge to create our own identities, our egos, to satisfy fundamental needs and desires, to bond and to be separate, to be loved and to be independent. We experience these drives as powerful forces within us – powerful and also subtle because we seek to achieve the ends or objects of our energy in all kinds of guises and camouflages, even under the guise of virtue, goodness and holiness. So, as each of us knows, there is an energy in us that does not necessarily take account of fairness, impartiality or respect for others. We beg, flatter, threaten, manipulate, love, hate, compete, fight and sometimes kill to satisfy our insistent needs.

There seems to be a conflict between our thrust towards morality and the rest of our energies. Or perhaps it is that we are disjointed, that we have not got our act together. We have not integrated our energies in the service of our deepest and most complete desires, of whole human living. Each of us experiences the problem uniquely because each is the history of how he/she has coped through the years with the demands of these energies: the particular shape and momentum which they have in our lives is the legacy of that history. We are responsible for it only in part. None of us has been invited to choose the terrain of his/her life's struggle. It has been basically staked out by the evolutionary process: we are at the same time vegetative, animal, human – half-beast, half-angel. It has been further determined by our genetic code, our parents, our early experiences. And, as we shall see, it has been affected by how we have lived our lives until now. But one way or another we have to live with ourselves: we have to include all this in our understanding of our (moral) selves and in our efforts to achieve wholeness and harmony.

It would be interesting to discover what kind of image we have of this. We may see ourselves as a jumble of conflicting urges and energies. Many people see a clear duality, a division in themselves, a good and bad self: they plug into St Paul's experience of two laws within him, one the source of good actions and the other apparently urging him towards what is wrong (Rom 7). Others see morality as imposed on them from outside, something foreign to them, to which they consent with their heads but which does not touch their hearts: it enables them to keep their altogether wayward energies in check – but only just. Religious upbringing may have encouraged us to see things in this way. Religion or philosophy does play quite a part. Its basic metaphysic or world-view colours our thinking on such related issues as: am I good; is creation/human nature good; are body, flesh, matter, *eros* good and to be trusted; what is my most fundamental energy; is morality in harmony with my being and desires or is it anti-life; is there evil in me – and in what way; am I split; can I be moral; what if I cannot; do I need 'outside' help; is there evil in the world – a devil 'who wanders around the world seeking the ruin of souls'? Our stance – and it may be unreflective – on such issues shapes our sense of ourselves and our moral lives. Our religious tradition in the main has had a predominant distrust of desire and instinct: they were to be curbed by grace and sacrament; *'agere contra'* was the watchword.

It is well to be realistic about our situation. On the one hand there is no point in suggesting that each of us is a pure and limpid foundation of moral striving. On the other we have to recognise that our instincts and energies are the source of our being and doing: without them we would not survive, create or relate. We might think of ourselves perhaps as trying to fashion or allowing to emerge out of the totality of our energies a personality or character that corresponds to our deepest desires. These, I think, are about some vision of a life of harmonious being-with-others. I think we all have in our hearts a kind of person we would like to be, an ideal self. If we were asked to write our ideal obituary it is very likely that we would include all the noblest and most other-regarding virtues. It is what we want. It is part of us. It is an energy in us. It is important then to recognise that there is a deep desire in us for moral living, for goodness. If our image of ourselves does not include this we have got it wrong and we may go through life with a distorted view of and feel about ourselves.

Two elements

(a) Judgment about good and bad activity

Let us pursue further this business of morality. Two different but related points have emerged already. The first is that we label certain kinds of activity as right or good. The second is that we know that we ought to do what is right and avoid what is wrong: there is within our experience a sense of – of what? Some would say a law or obligation to act in a certain way, others of a tension towards one's potential being, others of the call of a value that is worth pursuing, others of the sense of the fittingness of a way of life, of the flourishing it brings.

What do we mean by referring to activity as right or good? Take the word 'good'. 'This is a good car'/ 'She is a good teacher.' 'Good' talk is a particular kind of talk. It is not as easy as talk about the size or weight or colour of things. It is sometimes referred to as value language – as against fact language. It involves more discussion and seems to have criteria built into it in a way that fact language does not. It is so much easier to say that this car is 3 metres long or that this teacher is 164cm or blonde or slim or French. It is possible to reach agreement on such matters in a way that is not possible with 'good'. It is not easy to agree about a good car or teacher or cook or lawn-mower or sculptor or pianist. People will argue and disagree about such matters. If we seek to resolve the disagreement perhaps the best we can do is to ask ourselves what cars or lawn-mowers or teachers or cooks or artists are meant to do – and we might have trouble with 'meant to'.

We are in the same general area of value-language when we say that someone performed a good act or has a good character, but we have introduced a new dimension. Because we recognise that one can be a good teacher or cook or artist – or an expert on prayer or religion – without being a person of good character. One can be very developed and complete (and perhaps then 'good') at the one level but not at the other. Indeed one may fail at the level of morality precisely in the effort to become good at a different level – it is not uncommon that one develops a talent or profession and in the process neglects his/her family. Of course one may be a good teacher and a bad cook or a good pianist and a hopeless golfer: we all know that and nobody worries about it. Few will criticise a person who neglects the pursuit of excellence in cooking or games. But it is a different matter with good character or good action. The judgment that someone is good as a person or has a good character is one of much deeper significance. Most of us recognise in our better moments that it is this judgment that really matters, and we are alarmed if someone sees no distinction between concern for games or gardening and that for the lives of refugees faced with starvation. The simple searing judgment that one is or is not a good person is not in the same category as judgments about other kinds of achievement. (It is the kind of judgment that one often hears at funerals – 'she was a decent woman' – when other apparently less significant considerations fade into the background.) Of course if people disagree about good lawn-mowers or cooks or artists they will disagree even more profoundly and perhaps more strongly about good living, and much of the history of ethical writing has been about this disagreement and the reasons for it. But they will largely agree that there *is* a judgment of a moral kind to be made, that there is something called moral living and moral character.

This moral awareness is a fact of life and an abiding fact in our history and literature. In all cultures and in all times men and women have recognized this level of assessment. They may differ about what is right and wrong. But they have no doubt that some kinds of act and purposes etc. are right and the opposite wrong. In a particular culture it may be accepted that a man has ten wives. (They stand in a particular relationship to him and he to them and both sides to all others in the society: this establishes norms which have significance in the society, which all are expected to adhere to and the violation of which may bring sanction.)

It is inspiring to find Plato say that it is better to suffer wrong than to cause it. (Many have remarked on the curious asymmetry involved here which reaches its highest point in the teaching of the New Testament that we should even be prepared to lay down our lives for others.) Aristotle puzzles about the fact that the action which we know to be right and fitting for us does not always bring reward. There is the famous statement of Cicero that there is a moral law in us from which neither Senate nor people can dispense us and to deny which is to flee from ourselves and go against our nature. And perhaps the even more famous statement of Sophocles' Antigone that she had a moral responsibility towards her dead brother which no State law or custom could override.

(b) Sense of obligation

But why should we do what we call 'right' or 'good'? How does the prescriptive idea – the sense of obligation, call, or fittingness get into these notions? Why should we do what very often we do not like doing or what does not appear to be our advantage? You will hear people say when some piece of sharp practice is suggested to them, 'I could not do that' when it is obvious at another level that they can do it. There is nothing stopping them from doing it. Well, nothing physical. But is there something? I remember one evening walking through the botanic gardens of a city where I was giving a course on morality: a mother and child came towards me and the mother said to the frolicking child, 'You cannot pick the flowers, everyone would want to pick the flowers.' It was a useful starting point for a lecture next morning: it seemed to me that she was giving expression to moral experience and even revealing her own moral theory. What does 'cannot' or 'could not' signify? What does the language of 'ought' or 'should' mean or where does it come from? It is a useful exercise to ask ourselves such questions: it forces us to sharpen our ideas about morality.

Some Christians collapse the whole of morality into religion. They operate with the idea that it was God who gave us our moral rules. And since morality has come from God, who is creator and Lord of all things, they have a clear notion of moral obligation: God has set out the way of life which we must follow; he has ordered us to obey it; he will reward us with heaven if we do so and punish us in hell if we do not. I find that if you push people a bit about morality or its source they almost invariably refer it back to God – probably to the Ten Commandments. This is a rock bottom for them.

> Mosaic imperatives bang home like rivets;
> God is a foreman with certain definite views
> Who orders life in shifts of work and leisure.
> (Seamus Heaney, *Death of a Naturalist*)

This amounts to saying that God decided some time in the past what is right and wrong, that indeed the very meaning of the word 'wrong' is 'prohibited by God'. Others have some sense that the right/wrong distinction is independent of God and somehow rooted in the natures of things: God has given directives about morality, they say, but it is only to confirm and clarify matters. Still others think of God mainly in terms of the force of morality, of obligation. They say that morality is rooted in the natures of things and may say that we are left by God to work out the details of right and wrong but that we are to do the right and avoid the wrong because God wills this – it is the law of God that we do so. This is what they mean by 'ought' or 'should' in moral contexts: this is *why* we must do the right and avoid the wrong. God, for them, is the source of moral obligation.

It is difficult for Christians to separate their morality from their religion. In a sense they are right: if one is a believer one's morality will be affected in various ways, as we shall see. [MacNamara argues later in his book that we all do morality in some context: Christians do it in theirs – editors.] But the best service we can do to Christian morality may well be to distinguish our moral from our religious experience. There are many who are entirely convinced of the validity of the distinction of right and wrong and who are deeply conscious of the need to abide by it but who do not believe in God. This comes as a surprise to some Christians: you will hear them say, 'they are very good people although they do not go anywhere' (i.e. to any Church). Non-believers are often very sensitively moral people – even to put it like this is to suggest some surprise. There is no reason why they should not be. But we have become so accustomed to experiencing morality in a religious context and to having Churches make statements about it that we behave as if somehow they had ownership of it or a monopoly of it or special insight into it. Not only do unbelievers live well but some of the most important movements for moral progress have been initiated and inspired by those who were not Christian or were even anti-Christian. So too some of the best work in understanding of morality has come from unbelievers. It is important for Christians to advert to that. It looks entirely obvious. But morality has become so subordinated to our religious tradition that the point needs to be made. So I have insisted that we try to make distinctions between faith and morals.

Morality a human institution

This has been leading to the suggestion that we see morality as a human institution, as something that arises spontaneously out of our human situation. It might help to ground it if we referred to it as the moral fact. It is a fact of life that as we become aware of life together in community certain basic directions of action suggest themselves – with regard to the meaning and dignity of the individual, to human welfare, to fairness and impartiality, to the creation of a just society. We come to realise that being true to ourselves as persons involves us in response to such considerations, that our selfhood becomes possible in our relations with others. This recognition of the inescapable claim of such values as truth, life, justice, equality and fraternity has been one of the greatest and most precious insights of the human spirit.

In doing morality, then, (and in trying to teach or defend it) we are concerning ourselves with one of the great questions of the human race, i.e. how is the human person to live? Which is also the question: what does it mean to be a person? It has been a concern of human kind from the beginning. It is not a question that we make so much as a question that we find within ourselves and to which we must attend if we are to be at peace. It makes a claim on us: we cannot manipulate it easily; in a sense it is greater than we are. It is sometimes said that it has a sacred character about it, that it is religious. I take that to mean that it is perceived and experienced as something of utmost importance and dignity, something to which we must attend or pay the price of knowing that we have not been true to ourselves. We cherish and reflect on certain classic statements of it in philosophy and in literature because we find that certain writers have successfully caught and illuminated it for us.

It is important then to recognise this moral experience in ourselves and others. Even for Christians it is a useful starting point. To see it in this perspective may be some relief, indeed, especially for those who teach morality. One sometimes feels burdened by the task of teaching as if somehow the Church had made morality or was responsible for it. It is not Christianity that has made morality, not the Church, not even God, except in the sense that he has made us. It is even more fundamental, more basically human than that. So if we are teachers we should not feel that we are importing morality into the lives of others. It is there already in some sense: what we are trying to do is to help people to understand themselves. Our role is to awaken and encourage their own questions about how the human being is to live. It is a question that is native to all of us, and no one can afford to belittle it or treat it lightly. We can make contact with it even in those who appear to rebel against morality. Because while they may reject particular statements of it they would insist that they be treated rightly. For example, young people in school are quick to sense favouritism: they are sensitive about being bullied or treated harshly; they may even insist that morality should not be rammed down their throats. They are saying in their own fashion that there is a way for people to live together. Perhaps we can build on that.

What I am talking about here, obviously, is the basis or source of morality. The fullest implications of living together are to be worked out. Some of them are easy to come by: there should be respect for truth and life, equality before the law, freedom of conscience, provision for the young and defenceless. Others are more difficult: is violent revolution legitimate in situations of unjust rule; are government cutbacks unfairly affecting the disadvantaged; is the zygote to be treated with the same respect as one's next door neighbour; how is one to act in a situation where mother and child will die if one does nothing? Nobody doubts that there will be differences about such details. But long before that stage is reached there can be some agreement on what morality is all about and on the original source of principles. At this level at least we can be seen to make sense to people.

The autonomy of morality

I am suggesting that morality has a certain autonomy. By this I mean that it makes its own demand: you could say that one should be moral because one should be moral. One does not need to know God before becoming aware of moral distinctions or moral demands: morality does not immediately need religion. It is true that a religious tradition, like any other group, may have arrived at certain conclusions about how one is to be moral, may give support to the whole enterprise of morality, may have its own understanding of the ultimate significance of it. But even if religion is abandoned, a person is still left with the morality question unless being human is also to be abandoned. Morality has been so dominated by religion that young people especially seem to think that because they have given up faith they are entitled to give up morality. This is to misunderstand its origin. You might say that if there were no God there would be no morality because we would not exist. That is true. But God is not the author of the principles of morality. Morality is a human thing. What God asks of us is that we listen to ourselves, listen to the moral call within us.

Neither does morality depend on reward. Many fine moral

people who do not believe in God or in heaven do believe in being moral. For them virtue is its own reward, i.e. the knowledge that they are living in the way in which they believe human beings should live. They are not slow to point out that if they live well it is because they believe in the value and dignity of the other and not simply because someone has told them to do so or because they hope for any reward. Some even accuse Christian morality of being anti-morality because it is so closely linked to reward in the popular consciousness. Christians, they say, are not really interested in morality but only in themselves – in saving their souls. They have a point. Morality makes its own demand: it appeals to us to recognise that there is a truth for doing, that there is a humanising way of living together, that there is a form of genuine society to be created. To collapse morality into religion, to attribute its genesis to a decree of God is to make a true appreciation of it difficult. If someone is led to believe that morality has only to do with being a Christian or that it is something that one accepts if one wishes to ensure future happiness, then it has been devalued. It is easy to have such notions in a religious morality.

Morality therefore is independent of the Churches. It is a human experience and institution which Churches must rather acknowledge. It may be important to the religious life of Churches. They may think they are good at it or know a lot about it or protect it. (There will be those, of course, who will dispute such claims.) They may demand it from their members. But they do not have a monopoly of it. They do not make morality and cannot in any sense make things right or wrong. They have to *find out* what is right or wrong. They can give their opinion on such matters. But as in every other area of life the value of their opinion depends on their competence, their diligence and their honesty. Things are never right or wrong because somebody says so, but because of the way we are in the world. So the fact that a Church makes statements about war or rights or revolution or marriage does not affect the morality of such actions. They are either right or wrong in themselves. Neither can the Churches afford to ignore the fact that there are a great many honourable and intelligent non-Christians who are just as concerned about moral issues as they are. They ought perhaps to see their role as that of sharing with all people of goodwill the struggle to discover what is best for the human community, what is the good society. Their concern for morality should be a passion for the welfare of society and not just a defence of established positions.

The human search for morality

It helps, I think, to see morality as the result of the great search of the human race from the beginning. It is a continuing search: there is room for and need for development through the ages. Society once regarded slavery as acceptable. Plato, Aristotle and probably St Paul would have told you that it was part of the natural law that some are born slaves and some free. It took the human race a long time to break out of that. Society once regarded women as inferior and to some extent it still does: we are only slowly and painfully coming to a realisation of the implications of seeing all as equal. Child labour and *laissez faire* capitalism, especially in international trade, were once thought to be normal but not anymore. My own country has seen a welcome – at least I think it is welcome – development of thinking about our moral obligation to the handicapped, the travellers, homosexuals, those born out of wedlock, prisoners, etc. We once regarded capital punishment as moral. Well, is it? Our society seems to be divided about it. How many more areas do we have to develop? We are now more concerned about ecological ethics and one finds books about animal rights. The frontiers of morality are being pushed out. One could think of the whole of humanity slowly and painfully trying to work out over the ages what it means to live satisfactorily together. In that sense it is true to say that we make our morality. At least we discover it. But 'discovery' here is not like finding something ready-made. We have to work at it, to figure things out.

Who is to say, people often ask. Who is to say whether a particular position is an instance of development or the opposite? You could consult your tradition or your elders. But how do they know? One often gets the reply that the Church will tell us. But official Church authorities make statements only about a few crucial issues. For most of the thousand and one everyday moral situations there is no Church teaching. We have to do the best we can. There is nobody to go to, at least nobody except ourselves and our fellow human beings. Aristotle would have told you to go to the wise person and that surely is good advice. Some find this difficult. They find it difficult to accept that moral knowledge depends on our fallible minds and the idea of change is hard to take. But that is how it is. It is no more likely that we will have certainty about the moral question than about anything else – psychology or philosophy or medicine for example. We do not know the answers to many of the problems in these areas: why should we expect to know them about morality? There are several critical areas of faith in which we might have liked more certainty. We know so little about God – in fact we seem to be less bold in making statements about Him than we were a few decades ago. We go on searching in all the major areas of Christology. We know next to nothing about our future condition, about life after death. And yet we manage. In morality we have to manage as best we can also. We have to find the best answers we can for ourselves and our children. That is all we can hope for.

With regard to this very issue there seems to be a division between those who, while appreciating the value of the past and the need to conserve, still see society as in a continuing state of search and discovery – in the area of morals as in every other area – and those who see morality as something that is settled, that has been decided by God and given to the Churches to promote and defend. For the second group questions about morality are non-questions: all has been determined. Morality is perhaps seen as a matter of loyalty to one's Church and the questioning of it is regarded as at least a carelessness about one's heritage and at worst an undermining of the order of one's Church and society. But morality is about something more fundamental than loyalty. It is about truth, and the truth of living together in love, and that is independent of the Churches. The natural law tradition is the quintessence of this. Essentially it has said that things are right or wrong because of their nature, not because the law of the land says so and not because religion says so. There is an independence to the institution of morality.

Misinterpretations

To concentrate on the inner character of morality in this way is to invite misinterpretation. So I had better say what I do *not* mean. I do not mean that everybody simply makes up his/her own mind without reference to community or tradition. One learns morality in a community as one learns everything else: the moral tradition is part of the total wisdom of the community which is being handed on. I do not mean that one has to wait until a person 'sees' and accepts a moral position interiorly: morality can be taught and at some stage in a child's life perhaps one should insist. Neither do I mean that all are equally good at working out the requirements of morality or equally open to it. We have in the community experts in the science of morality (as in any other science) and experts in living it. Nor do I mean that everything is fine provided you think that what you are doing is right: there is a truth to be discovered here as elsewhere and it is important for the individual and for the community that it be discovered. I therefore do not mean that one solution to a moral question is as good as another or one moral system as good as another. I do not mean that a Christian does or thinks about morality exactly like a humanist: it will be as a Christian and out of the Christian vision of life that he/she will work out the details of morality – just as a Marxist or atheist will do it from his/hers. A Christian will see morality as, in some sense, the law of God. He/she will have religious reasons for being moral that the humanist has not. His/her morality will be significant for a relationship with God. And it may be that a specific content to Christian morality will be found.

I have talked about morality as a general term and have said that it is found in all ages and cultures. But that may be to over-simplify. I have no doubt that there are quite different notions about it. I do not mean only about what is right and wrong but about how things come to be right and wrong and what these terms mean. Ask yourself what would someone in an Eastern culture mean by morality, or someone, say, in an African animist culture, or a person who has always lived in deprived circumstances in the slums of a great city, or an agnostic Oxbridge don. We gather them all under the one umbrella of morality, but it may be that there is only a very general family resemblance between their ideas. It may be that the only thing that morality has in common from one society to another is that rules for living are generally accepted in the society, that they are in some way enforced (at least by public opinion) and that in relation to other rules they are considered to be overriding.

My interest so far has been to establish some preliminary points about the basic meaning and source of morality. I have been trying to winkle out what ideas we have about it. We all have a kind of unreflective morality. To ask ourselves questions is to try to become more aware, more conscious of our processes, and that can only be good. The problem still remains of finding the right answers to the question of how we should live. But my hope is that we would realise that the whole paraphernalia – the whole panoply of values, rules, commandments, as well as the explorations of meta-ethics – is an attempt to understand the experience and spell out its implications. For the individual the task of moral life is to listen to the experience and grow in openness to it, to do the truth in love. For the community the task is to encourage the individual to interpret this experience aright and to be able to respond to it. It is an educative task. It is a worthy vocation.

Chapter 22

The History of Moral Theology

Timothy E. O'Connell

Children have always asked the question: 'Where did I come from?' As they have begun to experience themselves as persons, they have realized that their roots are part of their identity. Of course, the issue of one's roots can be addressed at various levels and in various ways; a child's question is quite different from an adult's. But one way or another, to one degree or another, the question always seems to present itself.

The matter of one's history is also relevant to the transpersonal world of ideas and cultures and institutions. Where did we come from? Where did these ways of understanding, of living and functioning, come from? Why are we the way we are today? And just as the personal question cannot be avoided, neither can this corporate questioning.

At least it can be avoided only at high cost. For to the extent that we do not understand our past, we really do not understand our present, and we are less prepared intelligently to construct our future. So the purpose of this chapter is to sketch the broad outlines of our ethical history. We want to try to understand the historical reasons for the way Catholic moral theology has developed and for the way it expresses itself today. We want to see, at least in a general way, the path by which we have come to the present. We want to recognize that foundation on which, of necessity, our future must somehow be constructed.[1]

---

[1] [In the first edition of *Principles For A Catholic Morality* (1978)] a note at this point explained a major difficulty in composing the chapter: the absence of a book-length history of Catholic moral theology. At that point the available resources consisted of brief historical summaries, not unlike this chapter, and monographs on very narrow questions and specific periods.

Patristic era

The writing on moral topics in the first five hundred years of the Church's history is fascinating, both because it represents the initial understandings of Christian theology and because it bears so many similarities to the reflections of our own time. From the very beginning, a concern with the behavioural implications of the Gospel proclamation manifested itself. The *Didache* (ca. AD 75) begins with a portrayal of the 'two ways', the way of virtue and the way of evil, and challenges the listener to a deep conversion.

But this ethical concern did not result in any comprehensive moral systems, let alone any single, universally accepted system. Indeed, the writing of the period was not even the product of 'theologians' in a professional sense. Rather, it was produced by pastors and monks, by individuals who used it as part of their ministry, either to serve a local Church or as counsel to disciples in the mystical journey. As such, the writing was characterized by a desire to respond to the concrete needs of the community in a way that was still authentic to the core of the Christian faith.

What is more, this dialectic of faith and experience was differently handled by various authors. Clement of Alexandria (d. 216), for example, exhibited a rather optimistic vision of life, a willingness to integrate the Gospel truth with the insights of the pagan world. He viewed pagan wisdom as 'so many seeds strewn by the *Logos*'[2] and thus expected a fundamental continuity between experience and revelation. Clement was not above dealing with concrete issues; at one point he described in detail the typical day of the Christian with its various ethical challenges. But even in such discussions he revealed a humanistic and optimistic perspective. In contrast, Origen (d. 253) was quite negative. It is true that he was an educated man, in touch with pagan knowledge and willing to make use of it. Indeed, it was Origen who first used the classic

---

There was no book-length discussion of this history. The wish was expressed that 'this lacuna will soon be filled'. It is a pleasure to note that a significant step toward the elimination of this difficulty has been taken with the publication of J. Mahoney's *The Making of Moral Theology* Oxford: Clarendon Press, 1987. For a more comprehensive discussion of the evolution of this discipline, the reader is referred to this book. In developing the points that comprise this historical overview, we have primarily followed the lead of Bernard Häring, *Law of Christ* Westminster: Newman, 1961, Vol. 1. pp. 3–33. This has been supplemented by material from articles in the *New Catholic Encyclopedia*, from T. Deman, *Aux origines de la théologie moral*, Montreal: Institut d'Études Médiévales, 1951, F. Murphy, *Moral Teaching in the Primitive Church*, New York: Paulist Press, 1968.

[2] Quoted in Häring, p. 7.

concept of the cardinal virtues in Christian theology. But even so, one discerns in his discussions of sin, of human freedom, and of the meaning of salvation a relatively pessimistic view of human life. As a representative in theology of the burgeoning monastic movement, of the concern for 'white martyrdom,' Origen was much more inclined to dichotomize the life of Christian faith and the life of the world.[3]

A century later, a landmark book was written by Ambrose, the bishop of Milan (d. 397). His *De officiis* followed the lead of Cicero in both title and area of concern. Though contextualizing his reflections with the vision of Christian faith and doctrine, Ambrose addressed himself to the myriad 'duties' of the believer. And he sought to articulate these moral responsibilities in a concrete way that presaged the works of casuistry that would flourish 1,300 years later. Perhaps we might call Ambrose the first of the Christian casuists.

Most notable of the patristic figures, however, is Ambrose's disciple, Augustine of Hippo (d. 430). Augustine is a compelling, and at the same time rather confusing, representative of the early Church. Some have called him one of the greatest moral theologians of all time.[4] Others note the negative influence of his rigorist, perhaps subtly Manichean perspective on later Church teaching.[5] All these points are debated despite the fact that Augustine never attempted to develop a coherent and inclusive system of moral theory. Instead, his style (and it is a characteristic one of his era) was to range far and wide across the spectrum of theological concepts and human concerns. Augustine sketched his personal theological vision in his *Confessions*, he developed his understanding of the world in *City of God*, and he wrote shorter works on such diverse ethical topics as lying, widowhood, and especially sexual ethics.

If Augustine does not demand our attention because of his systematic approach, he does because of the shape of his thought. He addressed himself to the perennial underlying issues of ethics: the relationship of faith and works, of grace and freedom, of sin and virtue. He focused on the centrality of love in the Christian life. He utilized a rather psychological, introspective, and inductive

---

[3] These two figures offer an interesting example of theologian David Tracy's distinction between analogical and dialectical thinking in theology. Cf. his 'Presidential Address'.

[4] For example, Häring, p. 8; G. Regan, *New Trends in Moral Theology*, New York: Newman, 1971, p. 23.

[5] For example, A. Kosnik *et al.*, *Human Sexuality*, New York: Paulist Press, 1977, p. 37.

approach to the development of ethical insight. And in all these ways he revealed himself as a fundamentally modern Christian thinker.[6]

Sixth century

In the history of Christian theology the sixth century marks an important watershed. The Christian faith had emerged from its minority status and had become the commitment of the masses. It had become the officially espoused religion of the state, and its theological vision and pastoral approach had to be appropriately adjusted.

One of the more significant elements of that adjustment was the change in practice as regards the Sacrament of Reconciliation. During the Patristic era this sacrament had been relatively rare. Its use was limited to the confession of truly major sins, lengthy penances were required before absolution, and the penitent was not allowed to return to the sacrament with any frequency. In effect, it functioned as a liturgy of reconciliation with the community, within the context of a Church discipline that included excommunication for those guilty of behaviours that were highly threatening to the community.

During the sixth century, however, this practice changed. Particularly in Ireland and through the ministry of the Celtic monks, the confession of sin became more private and more frequent, a much more comprehensive variety of sins were submitted to the confessor, and penances began to be fulfilled after absolution. In a word, auricular confession, as we know it, entered the life of the Church, and the Sacrament of Reconciliation became much more an ongoing component of the Christian life.

This innovation, however, had immediate implications for moral theology, for it was presumed that the penances should fit the particularities of the sins confessed. Therefore, some systematic

---

[6] In one other particular Augustine stands as significant for modern theology, and that is in his roots in Platonic philosophy. There is no doubt that Platonism is a philosophy that risks dualistic excesses, and some would probably say that Augustine himself is a contributor to such excesses. But in my view it need not be so. Platonism also offers the possibility of grounding a richer, more poetic and mystical approach to theology. Indeed, it seems to have done so in our time. So if it is true that much modern theology is Platonic in the best sense of the word, and if Augustine is a major representative of this theological approach, he is on that account particularly deserving of our attention. Cf. T. O'Connell, 'Old Priest, New Theology: A Dilemma', *American Ecclesiastical Review* 167 (1973), pp. 236–251.

reflection on the nature of sin, its varieties, and on the demands of retributive justice was required. Moreover, at this time the level of clerical education was notably low, with the result that priests could not generally be trusted to make unguided judgments in these matters. As a result, there emerged at this time a series of compendiums known as Penitential Books.

These were not really works of theology. Even less were they descriptions of the ideals to be sought in the Christian life. Rather, they were simply lists of typical sins along with an indication of the appropriate penance in each case. But despite their modest intent, these books exercised a far-reaching influence on the nature of moral theology.

For one thing, the Penitential Books addressed to priest-confessors. Thus began the rather unhealthy identification of moral theology both with the Sacrament of Penance and with priests. This presumption that moral theology is primarily for priests has survived to our own time, and only recently has it been challenged.[7] Second, the very specific purpose of these books inevitably led to the association of moral theology with Christian minimalism. That is, the very existence of lists such as those in the Penitential Books tempted the Christian world to conclude that virtuous and faithful living consisted in the avoidance of the sins mentioned therein and that successful avoidance of these sins justified confidence in one's moral righteousness. There was, or appeared to be, no reason to 'walk the extra mile'. Third, the specific association of penance with sin encouraged an approach to Christian forgiveness that emphasized not mercy but justice. Absolution became more a matter of retribution. And thus the focus on the loving kindness of God, though never lost, was quite overshadowed.

Finally, the Penitential Books contributed to an emphasis on the importance of the individual act, an emphasis that remains today. [Here] it is important to note how this act orientation, the urge to fragment the Christian life into its smallest possible components, developed. And the Penitential Books played a significant role in that development.

Eleventh to thirteenth centuries

Shortly after the passing of the first millennium, the character of

---

7 For example, even the outstanding volumes of Bernard Häring, *The Law of Christ*, carry the subtitle: *Moral Theology for Priests and Laity*, feeling the need to be explicit about the intention to address others than priests.

European culture underwent a significant change, and that change had considerable influence on the progress of moral theology. This was the era of the rise of the great European universities. Centres of learning in widely dispersed locations were founded over an amazingly short period of time. And these were entirely new sorts of learning centres: not monastic schools, not even the educational programmes of the cathedral canons, but relatively autonomous institutions whose utter *raison d'être* was the pursuit and communication of knowledge.

It was still Catholic Europe, of course, and thus the study of God held a central place in these new universities. Thus, for the first time it is appropriate to speak of the *science* of theology in something like the sense we use today. But if theology influenced the academic scene, it is also true that the academic world influenced theology.

Systematic thought was the order of the day; the urge was to integrate, summarize, and articulate logically. This approach became the approach of theology as well. It was the era of the 'Summas', those great constructs of systematic theology, those attempts to proclaim the Gospel in a philosophically consistent and logically compelling manner. And among the thinkers who contributed to this development, two in particular deserve our attention.

One was the Franciscan, Bonaventure (d. 1274), whose fundamental commitment was still to the Platonic tradition that had prevailed in the centuries before. Out of that perspective he developed a brilliant synthesis of Christian theology and morality. For Bonaventure, the central characteristic of people was their will, their power to decide and to act. The intellect, though extremely important, was a tool to be used for action. Indeed, Bonaventure declared that the purpose of all theology was 'not merely to serve contemplation, but also to make us holy. In fact its first purpose is to make us holy'.[8] And even in his discussion of the intellect he emphasized the 'practical intellect' as our highest achievement.

Bonaventure had no separate presentation of moral theology; that was not the style in the age of the *Summas*. But for the reasons mentioned, his theological synthesis was an amiable contribution to later reflections on that reality.

The other figure was Thomas Aquinas (d. 1274). Aquinas, the Dominican, holds unparalleled fame in Catholic theology, and for many wise reasons. In his time the writings of Aristotle were being

---

[8] From his *Prologue to the Commentary on the Book of Sentences*; quoted by Häring, p. 11.

rediscovered, and Aquinas especially demonstrated the aptness of that philosophy for the articulation of Christian theology. For Aquinas, as for Aristotle, humans were preeminently intellectual beings, rational animals. And their highest achievement was precisely that contemplation which Bonaventure played down. Theology was for understanding; it was a pure science in the service of pure truth. It is clear, then, that Aquinas would have no place for a separate science of moral theology. The isolation of behaviour from truth was precisely what he opposed. But to say this is not to say that he was disinterested in ethical questions. By no means.

On the one hand, the method espoused by Aquinas led surely to an attempt to understand the Christian life; our understanding of ourselves and of our behaviour was an important component of our attempt to understand God. And, on the other hand, once the Gospel was heard and understood, it was clear that a responsive lifestyle was demanded. So Aquinas was more than willing to discuss the specifics of that lifestyle. Indeed, the whole *pars secunda* of his *Summa Theologiae* is a sort of treatise on moral theology, dealing first with general concepts (I-II) and then with specific ethical topics (II-II). But for our purposes the important point is that these ethical discussions were incorporated into the overall synthesis of Christian theology and not isolated in any way.

To a certain extent, this integration of dogmatics and ethics characteristic of both Aquinas and Bonaventure is also characteristic of the whole of the High Middle Ages. There was no compartmentalizing of theological components, no isolating of faith and action, no dichotomizing of grace and nature. Reality was viewed holistically, theology was developed holistically. And in writings such as the *Summas*, this integrating perspective yielded a rich and clearly contextualized moral theology.

Fourteenth to sixteenth centuries

Shortly after the deaths of Aquinas and Bonaventure, there began a process of change and development that can hardly be overestimated in its influence on moral theology. The first step in the process was marked by two highly significant changes in the theological situation.

On the one hand, the philosophical context shifted substantially. The high Scholasticism of the thirteenth century devolved, in the fourteenth, into a nominalistic vision of reality. The conviction that the human person was capable of distilling concepts, universal notions that capture and represent the real essence of things, was replaced by a scepticism on this matter. Philosophers such as William of Ockham (d. 1349) became convinced that there were no such essences, that the human person did not achieve universal concepts. Rather, the object of human intellectual attention was the uniqueness of each existing thing. The only way in which one could move beyond the unique existent was by a somewhat arbitrary process of 'collection'. Nominalists willingly conceded that it was common practice to grant various groupings of objects a general and inclusive name. But in their judgment these names were simply that and nothing more. There is no essence or nature 'tree'. We simply group various unique existing things and call them 'trees'. For nominalists, reality is fundamentally discontinuous.

This philosophical development was ethically important because it rendered useless the attempt to discuss the nature of the Christian life and to predict intrinsically good or intrinsically bad acts. Where there is utter uniqueness, there is no tool of predictability. And where that tool is lacking, there can ultimately be no useful objective component to ethical decision making. In fact, the consequence of a nominalist epistemology is complete ethical individualism. My situation is utterly unique, and I am an utterly unique person. Hence only I can judge what I must do; and even I can only judge in the midst of the experience.

If society finds itself threatened by this individualism – as it surely must, since such individualism invites a chaotic narcissism – it has only one alternative: the arbitrary imposition of law. Society cannot attempt to impose demonstrably rational guides for action, for these presume the existence of universals and essences. So it can only have recourse to power, to the naked demand for conformity. Thus, if the immediate consequences of nominalism is individualism with its potential for social chaos, its eventual consequence is tyranny, the imposition of order through dominative power.[9]

The other highly significant change in the theological situation of the time was economic. This was the period in which medieval feudalism was beginning to give way to an emerging structure of middle-class commerce. The exchange of goods and services greatly increased, individual mobility become more common, and

[9] This same line of argument is used by John Courtney Murray to show that the American political vision logically requires a commitment to natural law, to the objectivity and discernibility of value. Cf. *We Hold These Truths*, New York: Sheed & Ward, 1985.

thus a quantity and variety of relationships among strangers became necessary. In this situation, it was no longer sufficient to appeal to the duties of fraternity to justify correct behaviour. Instead, it became necessary to articulate the precise demands of justice, to specify with great accuracy just what was due one. As a result, traditional Christian virtues such as love, fidelity, and piety came to be neglected as justice and equity were emphasized. And a certain moral minimalism was inevitable.

These two developments, the philosophical and the commercial, combined to give fifteenth-century morality a peculiar flavour. Law was celebrated as central to moral thinking and living and was seen as a tool for expressing the necessary minimum, for establishing rights and duties in such a way as to regulate the rapidly multiplying relationships within the European community. There was a pragmatic and utilitarian tone that, though somehow surprising, is in retrospect completely understandable.

Into this situation, then, came one of the most influential figures in the history of Christendom: Martin Luther (1483–1546). Luther the monk, Luther the Christian tortured by personal feelings of inadequacy and sinfulness, Luther the student of St Paul. This Martin Luther entered a Christian situation that was far removed from the Gospel ideal. The situation emphasized justice, and Luther was convinced that no one is just. The situation emphasized the law, and Luther shared Paul's distrust of law. The situation focused on minimums, and Luther felt driven to perfection. The situation cherished good works, and Luther placed his trust in faith.

We are, of course, sketching with a broad brush events that included innumerable subtleties. But for our purposes it may suffice to become conscious of the polarities, for they indicate the shape of the response to Luther. When the Church finally formulated its Counter-Reformation in the Council of Trent (1545–1563), it was faced with a full-scale rebellion. Much of Europe had been lost to the Church, and the first priority was to establish the lines of demarcation with clarity. Unlike many, if not most, of the councils in the history of the Church, the Council of Trent did not have reconciliation as its goal. Rather, its purpose was protection, the isolation of the rebels, the clear delineation of the boundaries of the Church, crisis management of a certain sort. This strategy had many effects, but not the least was the imposition on moral theology of a definition and an approach that have lasted into our own time.

In a situation of such total conflict the council, and the Church, may be forgiven for an overwhelming emphasis on the practicalities of behaviour. This was not the time for leisurely theological or philosophical discussions; like any period of war, it left little time for speculation. Action was required, unanimity and uniformity were necessities, and thus the response of the council had those characteristics.

For one thing, seminaries were established. For the first time in the history of the Church, a clear and formal system for the education of clergy was developed. Clergy were to be isolated from the crises and turbulence of the day, placed in safe, protected environments, in intellectual greenhouses, as it were. (This, after all, is a literal translation of the Latin *seminarium*, from *semen*, seed.) They were to be provided with clear and concise directions for their ministry. They were to be inculcated with loyalty and a willingness to obey.

For another thing, the kind of education provided for seminarians was to emphasize the behaviour necessary for the Catholic. It was important to know what to do, and those areas of theology that indicated the proper action were to be highlighted. And thus, again for the first time in the history of the Church, a separate science of moral theology emerged. No longer was it merely a matter of reflecting on the truths of the faith and, in the course of this reflection, taking note of their behavioural implications. Now it was a matter of an isolated conversation aimed only at a specific and detailed presentation of the requirements of the Christian life.

For a third thing, when this separate moral theology emerged, it took on a specific character. It, too, was expected to emphasize the concrete, the objective, the necessary and required. And thus, as moral theology became separated from its roots in dogmatic theology, it became affiliated with that other science dedicated to these qualities, namely, canon law. The law indicated most clearly what one must do; and so it was completely reasonable to graft moral theology onto law, to give them the intimacy of sister sciences. This integration was done so completely and so successfully that, even to our day, textbooks of Christian ethics have often borne the title *Theologia moralis ad normam juris canonici* (moral theology according to the norm of canon law).[10]

---

[10] It was not only in moral theology that this permutation took place; similar changes can be discerned in liturgical theology. From a science with clearly dogmatic roots and with implications for spirituality, it became a science of the correct, of the valid and licit, of rubrical propriety. Liturgy, too, developed an affiliation with canon law. Again, this was a development that has lasted to our day. Even today the Gregorian University in Rome publishes two journals: *Gregorianum*, a journal of theology, and *Periodica de re morali, canonica et liturgica*, a journal of moral, canonical, and liturgical matters.

Seventeenth and eighteenth centuries

The consolidation of the post-Reformation period did not, of course, bring to an end the questioning that has always characterized moral theology. But it did establish the terms in which that questioning took place. Throughout the centuries after Luther, the issue was predominantly one of the precise meaning of the law. What, exactly, is the right thing to do? What is the minimum expected of the Catholic Christian? How can one permit a certain amount of legitimate Christian freedom while at the same time protecting the supremacy of objective moral demand? What is the proper response to a situation in which the demands of the law are in doubt?

Questions such as these were hotly debated by moralists. At the one extreme, a Jansenist rigorism was proposed; at the other (and partly in reaction to Jansenism), a laxist preoccupation with freedom. And all these debates eventually led to the development of a variety of moral systems for the responsible resolution of ethical doubts. Of these systems, perhaps the best known today is 'probabilism', the system that held that when there is a genuine division of expert opinion on a specific moral issue – and therefore two probable (reasonable) opinions – one may feel free to follow the more lenient opinion. And this even if the lenient opinion is held only by a minority of the experts.

One of the major figures in the debates of the time was Alphonsus Liguori (1696–1787). Alphonsus is notable in the history of moral theology not precisely because he was creative or innovative, but rather because he was a prudent man, able to formulate balanced, reasonable, and humane opinions. In the midst of a morass of disagreements, with zealots on all questions, Alphonsus was a beacon of reason, of common sense, in the eighteenth century. Although he actually supported 'equiprobabilism', a slightly more strict alternative to probabilism, his commitment to prudent moderation made him a model for moral theology up until the very recent past.

Alphonsus is also significant because his moral method, noting the various opinions and then seeking to walk a prudent middle course, modeled an ethical style that has perdured. That style is exemplified in the 'manuals', textbooks that summarize the prudent and reasonable position on the various issues of the time. Manuals were largely designed for the use of seminarians, and they were clearly oriented toward the application of moral theology in the confessional. But although they were in some ways conservative documents, greatly dependent on arguments from authority, they were also somehow pastoral. For given the legalistic premise that prevailed, there was a great tendency to multiply laws to the point of completely eliminating the reality of Christian freedom. In this context, manuals often functioned as voices of reason, guiding the confessor away from the extremes and toward the moderate position. They prevented the priests of the day from arbitrarily imposing unreasonable demands on their people and instead protected a certain gentle and patient spirit in moral theology.

Still, one could hardly celebrate the manuals as paradigms of profound moral theology. They were simply too much creatures of their own philosophical, theological, and cultural milieu to be that. And so eventually a move away from the manuals was to be expected, a fundamental renewal of moral theology was required.

Nineteenth and twentieth centuries

When the renewal of moral theology began, one of its earliest manifestations was at the University of Tübingen, in Germany. Perhaps the first significant figure in the renewal at that school was John Michael Sailer, bishop of Ratisbon (1750–1832). He was soon followed by John Baptist Hirscher (1788–1865). These two men, and the school they represented, were greatly influenced by the revival of scriptural studies in Germany. And in light of those new scriptural insights they began to question not specific moral teachings, but rather the whole style of moral theology. They issued a call for a more kerygmatic moral teaching, with emphasis on the inner realities of conversion and discipleship. They pointed out the essential link between Christian morality and Christian spirituality. They participated in the revival of interest in the Fathers of the Church, and particularly Augustine. Noticing patristic themes that resonated with the science of psychology developing in northern Europe, they called for increased psychological sensitivity in moral theology. Finally, and perhaps most importantly, they demanded a reunification of moral theology and dogmatic theology; they sought to reestablish the truly theological roots of Christian ethics.

This renewal did not achieve hegemony with any speed. Such political realities as the First Vatican Council, the *Syllabus of Errors*, and the mood of suspicion that separated Italians and Germans made this impossible. But it did continue, and at a slow and painful rate it developed. In the early years of this century, theologians continued to develop their ideas of moral theology. Such individuals as Joseph Mausbach (1861–1931) and Theodore Steinbuchel (1888–1949) made significant contributions. And when German theologians Bernard Häring (1912–[1998]) and Josef Fuchs (1912–) assumed their posts at two Roman universities (the Alphonsianum and the Gregorian, respectively), the widespread dissemination of these ideas was assured.[11]

Conclusion

To say this, however, is not to say that the renewal of moral theology has been completed. Quite the contrary – if anything, it has just begun. Perhaps it is because institutions are, by instinct, more conservative about behaviour than about intellectual doctrines. Or maybe it is because a renewed moral theology must depend on (and await) renewals in scriptural and dogmatic studies. But the fact is that Christian ethics continues to lag behind the other theological disciplines in renewal and renovation.

In large part, the fundamental renewal of scriptural sciences took place in the early part of this century. Even the development of dogmatic theology was well advanced before the Second Vatican Council. Indeed, in many ways the council was the ratification and implementation of that development in terms of the theology of revelation, Church, culture, and liturgy. But in the area of moral theology this is not the case. The council said very little about moral theology; and when it did speak, its words had much more the tone of a call for renewal to come than of a ratification of tasks completed. Consider these words that, significantly, appear in the Decree on Priestly Formation:

> Special attention needs to be given to the development of moral theology. Its scientific exposition should be more thoroughly nourished by scriptural teaching. It should show the nobility of the Christian vocation of the faithful, and their obligation to bring forth fruit in charity for the life of the world. (art.16)

[11] The focus on the German sources for twentieth-century renewed moral theology may be influenced by the major roles of Häring and Fuchs. A broader perspective might note the major importance also of renewed theology in nineteenth-century France, the *nouvelle théologie*, with its connections to seminary education through the Sulpicians. It is obvious that the intellectual forces shaping the Second Vatican Council were rooted in the intellectual ferment in both these countries and that recent developments in moral theology are, partly through the council, also notably dependent on them.

Since the close of the Second Vatican Council there has been no fundamental change in the intellectual situation. There has been a major reconsideration of many of the themes of moral theology. Indeed, the possibility of this book [*Principles for a Catholic Morality* – editors], as well as both the possibility and the necessity for a second revised edition, bespeak the ferment of the time. But it remains true that the Church today finds itself 'between the times'. It is clear that the ethical vision of the nineteenth and early twentieth century, with its reliance on unjustified arguments from authority and its tendency toward naïve positivism, is inadequate. There is, by the grace of God, no going back to that perspective. At the same time, no new intellectual synthesis has captured the imagination and satisfied the searchings of the whole Church. Instead, there is a situation of disagreement and, to a certain, unavoidable extent, confusion. A feeling of historic transition prevails.

Hence the moment at which we find ourselves in moral theology, the moment when it is being revised, remains a moment of beginning. It is not the time for complete new systems. Even less is it a time for the repetition of old formulas. It is a time to mine the past for useful and helpful insights. And it is a time to begin to reformulate and rearticulate the perennial truths of the Christian life. It is a time to ask hard questions, and it is a time to attempt tentative but internally coherent answers to those questions.

Chapter 23

Sexual Morality and Social Justice

Thomas Rausch SJ

Christian discipleship should inform both our interpersonal and our social lives. Sexual morality is concerned with the appropriate expression of the drive for intimacy, love, and generativity, which plays such an important role in our interpersonal relationships. Social justice describes what happens when our societies are organized in such a way that each person is respected and all are able to participate in the social, political, and economic life of the community. The issues raised by both of these areas touch us personally. Both have been addressed extensively by the teaching authority of the Church, and both are areas of controversy that generate considerable emotion, concern, and very different reactions to Church authority.

Some Catholics today disagree with Church teaching on questions of birth control, divorce and remarriage, sexual relations outside of marriage and between committed homosexuals, and (to a lesser extent) abortion. Other Catholics, who accept the Church's teachings on these issues, have considerable difficulty accepting its teaching in the areas of social justice, for example, on the right of peoples to immigrate, the question of using nuclear weapons as a deterrent, and the implications of the principle of distributive justice, which affirms the right of all members of a national community to participate equitably in its economic life. Similarly, in the past some Catholics disagreed with the Church's teaching on the right of workers to join unions or with its condemnation of the evil of racism and segregation. In this chapter we need to consider both sexual morality and social justice.

Sexual morality

It is only honest to acknowledge that the Catholic Church has been profoundly ambivalent in its attitude toward human sexuality. On the one hand, it has always recognized sexuality as a good, a gift of God given to our first parents for their mutual love and for bringing new life into the world. This has remained the deepest conviction of the Catholic tradition. On the other hand, the Church has often seemed fearful of sexuality's mysterious power. Echoing Augustine's pessimism, it has too often narrowed the meaning of sexual union to procreation, barely tolerated the pleasure in each other that accompanies it, and developed around it a moral theology that has tended to view sexuality in terms of disembodied acts rather than complex human relationship.

The Catholic view that human sexuality is a divine gift that finds its appropriate genital expression in a loving and exclusive relationship, open to new life, is rooted in scripture. The Book of Genesis teaches that sex is for procreation (1:28) and mutual love (2:18-24). The Song of Songs, a frankly erotic poem, celebrates the physical love of man and woman. Jesus presupposed the divine institution of marriage and affirmed its permanence. By rejecting the provision of the Mosaic Law that allowed a man to divorce his wife but not the reverse, he taught a mutuality in sexual relationships that had not been honoured in the tradition. Paul recognizes marriage as a charism, a gift of grace for the building up of the Church (1 Cor 7:7). The Letter to the Ephesians sees the intimate union of husband and wife as a great mystery (*mysterion*) that images the union of Christ and the Church (Eph 5:31-32), an intuitive understanding of what the later Church would recognize as the sacramentality of marriage.

Lisa Sowle Cahill emphasizes that the Bible sees sexuality not in isolation but always in relation to the community. Still, there are biblical texts condemning certain types of sexual acts that are considered deviant from the general norm of heterosexual, monogamous, permanent marriage. These include:

adultery (Lev 20:10; Gen 39:9; Prov 2:17; Sir 23:16–21; Exod 20:14; Deut 5:18; Mark 7:22; Matt 5:28; 15:19; 1 Cor 6:9); fornication (Sir 42:10; Deut 22:13–21; Lev 19:29; *porneia* or 'sexual immorality' as including fornication, Mark 7:21; Matt 15:19; 1 Cor 5:9–11; 7:2; 2 Cor 12:21; Gal 5:19; Eph 5:3, 5), homosexual acts (Lev 18:22; 20:13; Rom 1:27; 1 Cor 6:9).

Cahill presents these texts not to suggest that the Bible offers a systematic reflection on sexuality but because these acts are seen by the biblical authors as being incompatible with the life of faith in the religious community. Much more important is the nature of the community and the characteristics of the life of its members.[1]

Certainly the expectation is present from the beginning that those who have been baptized into Christ and into the community of his disciples should live in a way that reflects those two fundamental Christian realities. Paul instructs the community at Corinth to excommunicate one of its members who has been living in an incestuous relationship with his stepmother; his concern is not just for the individual but the for the well-being of the community (1 Cor 5:1–13). Similarly, in the case of some Christians who are involved sexually with prostitutes, he argues that a union already exists between each of them and Christ, and therefore, any sexual union should reflect the holiness of this relationship (1 Cor 6:15–20). He is suggesting here a theology of sexual relations.

Development of moral theology

The early Christians, formed in part by the great conflict in Paul's time over circumcision and the Mosaic Law, did not understand their life in Christ in terms of a new moral law. They knew the teaching of Jesus that love of God, inseparably joined to love of neighbour, sums up all the commandments (Mark 12:29–31; Matt 22:37–40). They sought to internalize the Gospel call to conversion. They were conscious of discerning the Spirit's presence in their communities and in their lives. Thus a post-New Testament Christian author, writing about how Christians lived among their neighbours but were different from them, pointed out that they didn't expose their children or share their wives with one another (*Ad Diognetus* 5).

How then did Catholic teaching on sexuality become so legalistic in its expression, so concerned with sin? John Mahoney, in his fine study of the development of Catholic moral theology, points especially to the legacy of Augustine and to the preoccupation with

[1] 'Humanity as Female and Male: The Ethics of Sexuality', *Called to Love: Towards a Contemporary Christian Ethic*, ed. Francis A. Eigo (Villanova Univ. Press, 1985) p 87.

sin that developed in conjunction with the practice of auricular confession.[2]

Few thinkers have had a greater influence on Christian theology in the West than Augustine (354–430), bishop of Hippo. The doctrines of God, Trinity, grace, original sin, Church, sacrament, the Roman primacy – to mention just a few – bear his influence to this day. But as many have observed, there was a dark side to Augustine's thought, a profound pessimism evident in his view of the damage done by original sin to human nature and in his preoccupation with the problem of sin and evil.

This dark side was to mark Catholic theology in at least two significant ways. First, his principle that God does not command the impossible, formulated to stress the sovereign power of grace against Pelagius' emphasis on what human freedom could accomplish on its own, was to impart a rigorist dimension to Catholic moral teaching that has carried down over the centuries. Pius XI appealed to this principle in his condemnation of contraception in *Casti Connubii* (1930),[3] and John Paul II cited it in his 1993 encyclical on the principles of moral theology, *Veritatis Splendor* (no. 103).[4] Some today would see this same rigorist reasoning in the Church's teaching that the only moral option for a person who is homosexual in orientation is a life of celibacy.

Second, no doubt affected by his own long and difficult struggle for chastity, Augustine saw human sexuality after the fall as so dominated by lust that the only moral end of intercourse was procreation. This Augustine doctrine also was to have a long history in Catholic theology. In the Middle Ages theologians following Augustine continued to teach that marital intercourse for pleasure rather than for procreation was sinful – mortally according to the rigorists, or at least venially in the view of the greater number of moral theologians.[5]

Another major factor that contributed to moral theology's preoccupation with sin was the introduction in the sixth century of the practice of auricular confession. Before that, sacramental reconciliation was reserved for apostasy, adultery, and murder; it was a public ritual and could be received only once in a person's lifetime. But the introduction of private confession, a practice

---

[2] *The Making of Moral Theology: A Study of the Roman Catholic Tradition* (Oxford: Clarendon, 1987).

[3] *Ibid.*, pp. 53–54.

[4] *Origins* 23 (October 14, 1993).

[5] John T. Noonan, *Contraception* (Cambridge, Mass.: Harvard Univ. Press, 1965) pp. 251–52.

borrowed from the monastic tradition, led to the development of
the penitentials, books designed as an aid to priest confessors in
discovering and classifying sins and assigning their proper
penances. The first penitentials, simple and unsophisticated theologically, gave way later to more systematic *summas* for confessors,
particularly after the Fourth Lateran Council (1215) mandated
yearly confession and Communion during the Easter season.
These *summas* continued to proliferate – *summas* for confessors,
summas of moral cases (particularly favoured by the Jesuits),
summas of moral theology – down into the mid-twentieth century.
From this tradition a moral theology developed that was designed
for confessors. Unfortunately, it was a moral theology cut off from
dogmatic and spiritual theology. Trent's emphasis on the *judicial*
role of the priest in confession contributed to its legalistic tone. Its
preoccupation with sexual sins was heightened by a seventeenth-
century declaration of the Vatican's Holy Office that 'classified
every transgression on matters of sexuality as an objectively serious
matter constituting mortal sin'.[6]

The traditional teaching on sexuality coming from this moral
theology was presupposed by Catholics – if not always honoured –
down to the time of the Second Vatican Council. But after the
council the credibility of that teaching began to erode. In this
process Church teaching on artificial contraception played a key
role. Many had hoped that the council's reforms would soften the
Church's strict approach to questions regarding sexuality. There
were some encouraging signs. The council, in avoiding the traditional language of the 'primary and secondary ends of marriage',
finally moved away from the subordination of the mutual love of
the spouses to procreation, which had been the Church's position
since at least Augustine's time (GS 48-50).

In 1963 Pope John XXIII appointed an international committee
to investigate the Church's traditional ban on contraception,
particularly in response to the anovulant 'birth control pill' developed by Dr John Rock and others in the late 1950s. But in 1967
Pope Paul VI rejected contraceptive methods in his encyclical
Humanae vitae. Commentators on Catholic theology have made the
point that *Humanae vitae* dealt the teaching authority of the magisterium a blow from which it has yet to recover.[7]

---

[6] Mahoney, *Making of Moral Theology*, p. 33.
[7] See, for example, George Gallup, Jr and Jim Castelli, *The American Catholic
People: Their Beliefs, Practices, and Values* (Garden City, N.Y.: Doubleday, 1987) p.
51.

But there were other factors as well that contributed to a loss of confidence in the Church's sexual doctrine, among them the so-called sexual revolution in the late 1960s and early 1970s, helped by the wide availability of contraceptive pills, the women's movement, and an increasing dissent from the magisterium's sexual doctrine (particularly after *Humanae Vitae*) on the part of Catholic theologians.

In 1976, concerned that even faithful Christians were 'unsettled', the Congregation for the Doctrine of the Faith published a 'Declaration on Certain Questions Concerning Sexual Ethics'.[8] The declaration reaffirmed the Church's traditional teachings in no uncertain terms. These teachings, it argued, are based on certain precepts of the natural law that have 'an absolute and immutable value' (no. 4). According to Christian doctrine, 'every genital act must be within the framework of marriage' (no. 7); thus any sexual acts outside of that context are forbidden. The declaration singled out masturbation, premarital sex, and homosexual acts for special consideration and reaffirmed the tradition that there is no 'parvity of matter' where sex is concerned: 'The moral order of sexuality involves such high values of human life that every direct violation of this order is objectively sinful' (no. 10).[9]

It is not the place in a chapter such as this to enter into an involved discussion of all the questions raised today in regard to the Catholic Church and sexuality. It will have to suffice to present the Church's official teaching and, at the same time, to point out some of the questions that are being raised today by Catholic moral theologians. We will consider birth control, abortion, masturbation, premarital sex, and homosexual relations.

Birth control

Although contraception by any means had been condemned by theologians since at least the fourth century, it did not become a critical question until the end of the nineteenth, when the practice of birth control began to become more common in Europe. After a number of statements against contraception by national hierarchies and a qualified approval of contraceptive methods by the 1930 Lambeth Conference of Anglican bishops, Pope Pius XI condemned any form of contraception in his encyclical on

8   *Origins* 5 (1976) pp. 485–94.
9   For a survey of reactions to the declaration, see Richard A. McCormick, 'Notes on Moral Theology,' *Theological Studies* 38 (1977) pp. 100–14.

marriage, *Casti Connubii* (1930). Pius XII moved Catholic teaching forward a step in 1951 when, in his address to the Italian Society of Catholic Midwives, he approved periodic abstinence during a woman's fertile period for the purpose of avoiding conception, provided there was sufficient reason. This was the so-called rhythm method.

With the appearance of contraceptive pills in the 1950s, the question of artificial contraception was raised with a new intensity. Paul VI did not want the Second Vatican Council to enter into discussion of the question; instead, he expanded to sixty-nine members the international commission set up by John XXIII to study the Church's teaching on contraception.

In 1967 the commission voted sixty-four to four (Archbishop Karol Wojtyla – later Pope John Paul II – did not attend the meeting) in favour of changing the traditional teaching that all use of contraceptives was immoral. Nevertheless, after an agonizing consideration of the issue, Paul VI reaffirmed the traditional ban in his 1968 encyclical, *Humanae Vitae*, arguing that 'each and every marriage act must remain open to the transmission of life' (no. 11) because of the inseparable link between the unitive and procreative meanings of the sexual act (no. 12).

Few questions have been as divisive for contemporary Roman Catholicism as this papal teaching against contraception. The encyclical represents an authoritative but noninfallible exercise of the magisterium, as the Vatican pointed out at the time it was released. Episcopal conferences in as many as thirteen countries showed a tendency to mitigate the papal position in their response.[10] Charles Curran, a moral theologian at that time at The Catholic University of America, authored a statement dissenting from the pope's position; Curran argued that spouses could responsibly decide according to their conscience that artificial contraception in some circumstances is permissible and indeed necessary to preserve and foster the values and sacredness of marriage. Over six hundred theologians, priests and academics, signed this statement. Today many theologians take the position that the unitive and procreative meanings of sexuality need to be kept together in principle, but not necessarily in every act of intercourse.

[10] See Vincent J. Genovesi, *In Pursuit of Love: Catholic Morality and Human Sexuality* (Wilmington: Glazier, 1987) pp. 237–38.

The debate sparked by *Humane Vitae* has continued over the years.[11] At the 1980 Synod of Bishops on the family in Rome, Archbishop John R. Quinn of San Francisco spoke for many – laity, clergy, and no doubt a number of bishops – when he observed that there was widespread opposition among Catholics to the encyclical's teaching on the intrinsic evil of each and every use of contraceptives. He cited a study that indicated that 76.5 percent of American Catholic women were using some form of birth control, and 94 percent of these were using methods condemned by the encyclical. Quinn suggested that the Church try to create a new context for its teachings on contraception emphasizing what the Church has said about responsible parenthood; that it begin a dialogue with theologians on the problems raised by dissent from the teachings of *Humanae Vitae*; and that careful attention be given to the way in which encyclicals are written and communicated.[12]

Abortion

If the traditional teaching of the Church against contraception has not been widely received by the Catholic faithful, the situation in regard to abortion is quite different. Most Catholics today believe that to directly terminate life in the womb is a serious moral evil, even if not all of them are agreed on how best to address the problem of abortion in a pluralistic society such as the United States.

From its earliest days the Catholic tradition has been against abortion.[13] The *Didache*, which dates from the early second century, teaches that 'you shall not kill a child by abortion, nor kill at birth' (2.2). It was only in the second half of the twentieth century that this tradition began to be challenged by an increasingly secular world, giving rise to a number of papal and episcopal statements concerned in part with the relation between law and morality.[14] On January 22, 1973, the U.S. Supreme Court handed down its *Roe v. Wade* decision on abortion, permitting the direct termination of pregnancy up to the end of the third trimester. The Congregation for the Doctrine of the Faith issued its *Declaration on*

[11] For a survey of reactions to the encyclical see Richard A. McCormick, 'Notes on Moral Theology', *Theological Studies* 30 (1969) pp. 635–44; 40 (1979) pp. 80–97.

[12] 'New Context for Contraception Teaching,' *Origins* 10 (1980) pp. 263–67.

[13] See John Connery, *Abortion: The Development of the Roman Catholic Perspective* (Chicago: Loyola Univ. Press, 1977).

[14] Richard A. McCormick, 'Notes on Moral Theology', *Theological Studies* 35 (1974) p. 325.

Procured Abortion in November 1974. The 1983 revised Code of Canon Law states that 'a person who procures a completed abortion incurs an automatic excommunication' (can. 1398). Pope John Paul II's 1995 encyclical *Evangelium Vitae* reaffirmed in the strongest terms the Church's teaching on abortion, stressing that all are called to a greater responsibility to protect innocent human life.

Although the Church has not determined officially when human life actually begins, it has taken the course of maintaining that human life is present from the moment of conception or fertilization. This means that it considers any intervention such as an I.U.D. (intrauterine device) or a 'morning after' pill, which prevents a fertilized ovum from becoming implanted in the wall of the uterus, as an abortifacient.

A number of Catholic theologians such as Richard McCormick, Charles Curran, Bernard Häring, and Karl Rahner suggest that discoveries in reproductive biology make it unlikely that an individual human life can be present until two or three weeks after fertilization. 'Hominization' requires two changes to take place in the early embryo. First, it must pass the stage of 'twinning', the stage during which the embryo can divide into two or more, after which there is the certainty that the individuality of one or more embryos has been established. Second, it must change 'from a cellular form of human life to a form which begins to display the differentiation characteristic of the human organism'.[15] This argument leaves a limited period of fourteen to twenty-one days, a gray area within which, for serious reasons such as rape or incest, an early embryo might be terminated. Others, however, argue that human life is so sacred that even potential human life must be protected. Indeed, it is important to note that Church documents 'generally place the fight against abortion in the larger context of respect for life at all stages and in all areas'.[16]

A therapeutic abortion, removing a fetus for medical reasons such as an embryo that has become lodged in the fallopian tube and thus cannot develop to term (ectopic pregnancy) or in the process of removing a cancerous uterus, is a different question. Such procedures would constitute an indirect abortion; they are permissible and necessary to save the life of the mother.

How can the Church win a greater hearing for its position on the

[15] See Carol A. Tauer, 'The Tradition of Probabilism and the Moral Status of the Early Embryo,' *Theological Studies* 45 (1984) pp. 5–6.

[16] McCormick, 'Notes on Moral Theology', 35 (1974) pp. 490–91.

sanctity of life? In a recent article Todd David Whitmore has made the case that the Church's position would be much stronger if it subsumed the language of 'right to life' under its traditional notion of the 'common good', and if it set abortion in the context of the issue of gender roles in society. Using a survey that lists as the most common reason for having an abortion the inability to continue work or education if the pregnancy were brought to term, he argues that the Church needs to more adequately recognize women's rights to participate in the public realm, so that 'reproductive freedom' is not perceived as the only way to guarantee that right.

At the present time, despite some helpful steps in this direction on the part of the American bishops, the Church continues to treat social roles among gender lines, stressing women's role in the home and family without adequately recognizing their right to participate equally in the public realm. One way to do so would be to teach that men also have responsibilities in the domestic realm, so that the question of child care would be a joint discernment within a family and not merely the responsibility of the woman. In the case of single women, the Catholic community as an eschatological community should be willing to provide support for raising a child that is at least commensurate with the sacrifices it expects of the woman. Since raising a child is an eighteen-year commitment, that means much more than offering one year of support.[17]

Masturbation

Magisterial pronouncements against masturbation occur as early as the eleventh century.[18] The doctrine of no 'parvity of matter' where sexual sins are concerned has contributed to masturbation assuming an inflated importance in Catholic moral theology and probably in the lives of many Catholics as well. Today opinions vary widely on the subject. Many see masturbation as a normal part of adolescent sexual awakening and maturing. In such cases there is often a diminished freedom and thus a lessening of responsibility. A compulsive habit of masturbation suggests that a healthy integration of one's sexuality has not yet taken place; it would seem to have different meanings in an adolescent and an adult, a married person and someone who is single.

Most Catholic moralists are reluctant to take the view that

[17] Todd David Whitmore, 'Notes for a "New, Fresh, Compelling" Statement,' *America* 171 (October 8, 1994) pp. 14–18.

[18] See John P. Dedek, *Contemporary Sexual Morality* (New York: Sheed & Ward, 1971) pp. 51–55.

masturbation is merely a neutral form of sexual release. They point out that phenomenologically it suggests an expression of sexuality that is self-centred, solitary, and hedonistic rather than relational, mutual, and giving and thus is a frustration of the integrative dimension of our sexual nature. To engage in masturbation knowingly and deliberately is to inhibit the integration and personal transformation that is the fruit of life in the Spirit. Vincent Genovesi wisely observes that the fact that many people who experience periods of regular masturbation that alternate with periods of abstinence suggests that these people do not accept masturbation as a good; they see it as a sign of weakness, an embarrassment. 'But a person's very lack of complacency, the unwillingness to grant masturbation a permanent and undisputed place in one's life, argues strongly that in such circumstances masturbation may more inspire a person to humility than be an expression of basic and serious sinfulness.'[19]

Premarital sex

One of the most difficult topics to raise in a homily with undergraduates today is the subject of premarital sex. Instantly one senses a chilling of the atmosphere; heads go down, eyes are averted, the chapel becomes uncomfortably tense. Some of the couples sitting side by side are living together. As they leave the chapel at the end of the liturgy, most will look the other way rather than greet the presider. It is clear that the Church's teaching on premarital sex for many of them is unwelcome; they are not interested and some will say so explicitly.

Nor do they receive very helpful guidance from the colleges and universities they attend. At most, including Catholic ones, responsible administrators and professionals presume that students are sexually active. They are more concerned with respecting the diversity of their students than with giving anything that could be interpreted as narrowly 'confessional'. 'Sexual responsibility' for eighteen- to twenty-two-year-olds means that sex be consensual and safe. As Michael Hunt, a Paulist priest with many years experience as a university campus minister, observes, the message is usually something like this: 'We don't care how you behave sexually as long as you don't force yourself on anyone and you use a condom for safety.'[20]

---

[19] Genovesi, *In Pursuit of Love*, p. 318.
[20] *College Catholics: A New Counterculture* (New York: Paulist, 1993) p. 52.

Catholic theologians 'always and everywhere' have held that premarital intercourse is a grave sin.[21] Yet Catholics have been as much affected by changing societal attitudes toward sex as anyone else. According to Andrew Greeley, 'at the present time only one out of six American Catholics thinks that premarital sex is always wrong'.[22]

The Church's deepest vision in regard to human sexuality is that the unitive and procreative meanings of sexual intercourse are intrinsically related, and thus it sees an inseparable relationship between matrimonial fidelity and sexual expression. Sexual intercourse represents the total gift of each to the other; if it is loving it implies commitment. But if the outward or physical sign is not the manifestation of an inner, spiritual reality that includes an unconditioned love and gift of self, if the union of a couple's bodies is not the symbol of the union of their spirits, their sex easily becomes exploitative. Without this self-gift and faithful commitment of each to the other, there is no community of love into which new life can be received and nurtured. The tragedy of abortion, some 1.5 million every year in the United States, occurs most often because couples enter into a sexual relationship before they are ready to welcome the new life to which it is ordered.

Today many young people use the term 'relationship' to describe an exclusive but nonbinding sexual friendship. Because such relationships are essentially temporary, they are not able to realize either the unitive or the procreative meaning of sexuality. According to Richard McCormick, the Christian view is just the reverse: 'It has been a Christian conviction that it is a relationship lived in the promise of permanency that prevents the collapse of sexual expression into a divisive, alienating, and destructive trivialization.'[23] Or as Greeley has observed, 'sex without public commitment is fraught with dangers of deception, self-deception and exploitation, particularly of women by men'.[24]

Some moralists today distinguish preceremonial from premarital sex, suggesting that once the commitment is there, sexual expression might be in some cases appropriate. But others ask, is the commitment really there if it is not yet able to be made publicly? And isn't it possible that consummating their union before they are ready to make that public commitment is to cut short a process of

[21] Dedek, *Contemporary Sexual Morality*, p. 36.
[22] Sex and the Single Catholic: The Decline of an Ethic,' *America* 167 (1992) p. 345.
[23] McCormick, 'Notes on Moral Theology,' 35 (1974) p. 461.
[24] Greeley, 'Sex and the Single Catholic,' in *Sex: The Catholic Experience*, Chicago: Thomas More, 1994, p. 343.

discernment – the whole point of a period of engagement – as to whether each is able to make that commitment?

One of the reasons so many marriages fail today is that too many couples short-circuit this discernment process. Rather than letting their sexual union be the seal and expression of a love that has grown to the point where they are deeply committed to each other, they begin living together before they have learned how to talk to each other, to share their innermost feelings, to be comfortably quiet in each other's presence, to be intimate with each other in various ways short of genital expression. It is easy to confuse 'good sex' with genuine love, and when the sex is no longer new or exciting, they find out that the love it was supposed to express is not there. Unfortunately, this discovery often comes too late.

A different case is presented by the adult who is neither married nor given the charism of celibacy but who may be in an intimate relationship in which there is sexual expression. Lisa Cahill raises this question; she observes that our traditional framework for evaluating sexual relations is not particularly helpful here and suggests that in such cases the Christian community must take itself as a source of moral insight. Her argument is clearly challenging the tradition. But it is difficult to disagree with her comment that 'responsibility in sexuality is no more an either/or, black-and-white matter than it is in other spheres of human moral existence, such as economics, war and peace, or respect for life. Exercises of sexuality which fulfill or depart from the norm are not all equally good or equally bad.'[25]

Homosexual relations

One of the most difficult questions facing the Christian community today is posed by its official inability to recognize faithful and exclusive relations between those who are 'constitutionally homosexual' or homosexual in orientation as appropriate expressions of intimacy and love.

There are a number of explicit condemnations of homosexual relations in both the Old and New Testaments, but many contemporary commentators and biblical scholars do not see in them a condemnation of homosexual relations as such, as the concept of the constitutional homosexual was unknown until modern times. In their judgment the biblical texts are concerned with participation in idolatrous worship by consorting with male and female

[25] Cahill, 'Humanity as Female and Male,' p. 91.

temple prostitutes (Lev 18:22; 20:13; Deut 23:18; cf. 1 Kgs 14:24; 15:12), a common practice in the ancient Near East, or with violation of the duty of hospitality (Gen 19:4-8), or with pederasty (1 Cor 6:9-10; 1 Tim 1:10). A more difficult text is Romans 1:24–31, where Paul is clearly talking about homosexual relations in themselves; but the fact that he sees those he is condemning, both men and women, as giving up natural relations and choosing homosexual ones is taken as evidence that he did not understand homosexuality as a condition.[26] Other scholars of course do not agree with this interpretation, or they judge it irrelevant to the biblical condemnation.

It is clear today that a person does not choose to be homosexual, even if we are not yet sure just what causes a homosexual orientation. The *Catechism of the Catholic Church* acknowledges that a homosexual orientation is not a matter of choice (2358). Thus the term 'sexual preference' is inaccurate. The Church distinguishes between homosexual orientation and homosexual activity; it is only the latter that is considered immoral. The American Catholic bishops have stated that 'homosexuals, like everyone else, should not suffer from prejudice against their basic human rights. They have a right to respect, friendship and justice. They should have an active role in the Christian community.'[27]

Irresponsible, promiscuous, or violent homosexual acts are as morally evil as heterosexual ones. The moral dilemma facing the Church today is what it might say to gays and lesbians who are in stable, exclusive, and faithful relationships and who want to express their love sexually. The official Church has not been able to move beyond its traditional condemnation of homosexual acts. But many moral theologians are questioning this position today. They ask, why cannot the question be seen in a broader context, so that it includes not just the act, but the quality of the relationship? Is it realistic to insist that the only moral possibility for homosexuals is celibacy, particularly given the recognition that the charism for celibacy is precisely a charism, given to some and not to others? Should not true homosexuals be encouraged to form stable and lasting relationships, even if these relationships may sometimes involve sexual expression? These are difficult questions that will continue to trouble the Christian community.

[26] For a review of this discussion see Genovesi, *In Pursuit of Love*, pp. 262–73. See also Jeffrey S. Siker, *Homosexuality in the Church: Both Sides of the Debate* (Louisville: Westminster/John Knox, 1994).

[27] *To Live in Christ Jesus: A Pastoral Reflection on the Moral Life* (Washington: USCC, 1976) p. 19.

Veritatis Splendor

Recently Pope John Paul II, himself a moral philosopher and former professor of ethics at the Catholic University of Lublin in Poland, intervened in the conversation over fundamental moral theology and its applications. In his encyclical *Veritatis Splendor* (1993) his concern was to reaffirm the traditional teaching of Catholic moral theology that the negative precepts of the natural law are universally valid (no. 52). Showing a remarkable familiarity with the contemporary debate, he specifically rejected teleological, proportionalist, and consequentialist ethical theories for holding 'that it is never possible to formulate an absolute prohibition of particular kinds of behaviour' that would in every case be in conflict with the moral values indicated by reason and revelation (no. 75). Thus he was reaffirming the existence of 'intrinsically evil acts', actions that are always wrong in themselves apart from the circumstances and intention of the one acting (no. 80). He also reaffirmed the traditional concept of mortal sin, maintaining that one's fundamental option or orientation toward God can be radically changed by particular acts (no. 70).

Veritatis Splendor is a powerful restatement of the tradition. It deserves careful consideration, the religious respect, and the obedience (*obsequium religiosum*) that is owed to an authoritative teaching of the ordinary papal magisterium (LG 25). But Catholics and other Christians will probably continue to raise questions of their tradition and the teaching of their Churches as they seek to integrate their personal and sexual lives with the Gospel call to discipleship.

Social justice

Perhaps one of the Second Vatican Council's most significant documents was its Pastoral Constitution on the Church in the Modern World, *Gaudium et Spes*. This document, with its vision of the Church at the service of the world (GS 3) and its call for Christians to come to the relief of the poor (GS 69), was to inspire many Catholics to play an active role in the various liberation movements that have marked the latter part of the twentieth century.

But it is by no means the only example of recent Catholic magisterial teaching on social justice and human rights. The roots of the Church's social teaching are to be found in the prophetic writings of the Hebrew scripture and in a rich tradition of Catholic social thought that includes over the centuries thinkers such as Augustine, Aquinas, Suarez, von Ketteler, Maritain, and John Courtney Murray as well as a tradition of papal social encyclicals reaching back over the last hundred years.

The social encyclicals

The social encyclicals of the popes represent the most recent ecclesial expression of the Church's social teaching. From Leo XIII's *Rerum Novarum* (1891) on the rights of workers, these social encyclicals have expanded in focus to embrace issues of development and economic justice between nations, technology and the arms race, the widening gap between the rich and the poor, and a critique of both communism and capitalism. At the heart of the social teaching and grounding its pro-life stance is Catholicism's profound conviction of the preeminent value of every human person created in the image of God (GS 12). It is, unfortunately, a tradition too little known to most contemporary Catholics.[28] Richard P. McBrien distinguishes three periods in this tradition.[29]

Stage I: 1891—1939. Leo XIII's *Rerum Novarum* (1891) was set in the context of the Industrial Revolution, which in both Europe and the United States allowed the laws of the marketplace to completely dominate the rights of workers. Wages were miserable, child labour was taken for granted, and any attempt of workers to form protective associations was resisted, often with force. *Rerum Novarum* focused on those rights, particularly the right to a just wage that would support the workers' families and the right to join unions. The encyclical affirmed the right of private property but stressed that it must serve the common good; in other words, it was not an absolute right. It stressed that governments should intervene to prevent harm to individuals or to the common good.

According to Donal Dorr, by defending the rights of workers to join associations, including 'workingmen's unions' (no. 36), Leo was moving beyond a call to conversion of the oppressors to address the problem of what would today be called the structural

---

[28] See Michael J. Schultheis, Edward P. De Berri, and Peter J. Henriot, *Our Best Kept Secret: The Rich Heritage of Catholic Social Teaching* (Washington: Centre of Concern, 1987).
[29] See *Catholicism*, rev. ed. (San Francisco: Harper, 1994) pp. 913-14. For the texts, see Michael Walsh and Brian Davies, eds., *Proclaiming Justice and Peace* (Mystic, Conn.: Twenty-Third, 1991); Joseph Gremillion, *The Gospel of Peace and Justice: Catholic Social Teaching Since Pope John* (Maryknoll, N.Y.: Orbis, 1976) covers from 1961 to 1975 and includes the more important documents from Medellín.

level of injustice. Yet the pope's approach was still quite conservative. Suspicious of the emerging trade-union movement because of its secularist and sometimes anti-Catholic character, he encouraged Catholic workers to form their own associations, with the result that the Church was not able to influence or support the labour movement as much as it might have.[30] Nevertheless, in calling attention to the issue of justice in the social order, Leo was raising the voice of the Church on behalf of the poor . His encyclical provided a firm foundation for Catholic social teaching, one that would continue to function as a standard and a point of reference for subsequent popes.

Forty years later Pope Pius XI developed Leo's social teaching in his *Quadragesimo Anno* (1931), formulating for the first time the principle of subsidiarity (nos. 79–80), the idea, based on the priority and rights of the individual and the family, that larger social bodies should not take over the responsibilities of smaller groups or associations. He also introduced the concept of social justice (*iustitia socialis*) as a 'directing principle' or norm for public institutions and the economic order (nos. 88–90).

In 1937 Pius XI issued *Mit Brennender Sorge*, an encyclical sharply critical of the Nazi government for violating the rights of the Catholic Church; it was read from all Catholic pulpits in Germany. In the last year of his life he was preparing an encyclical on the unity of the human race. A major section of the document, reportedly analyzing and condemning anti-Semitism in Germany and racism in the United States, was prepared at the pope's request by the American Jesuit John LaFarge. Unfortunately, someone in Rome thought the document, with its specific condemnation of anti-Semitism, inopportune, given the inflammatory political situation in Europe, and the completed draft was prevented from reaching the pope's desk. Pius XI died in 1939, without publishing what was to be his encyclical on racism.

Stage II: post World War II. The period after the Second World War saw an internationalization of Catholic social teaching. The documents appearing in this period dealt with the organization of the international community, the demands of social justice on the international level, and the moral issues raised by warfare in a nuclear age.

John XXIII's first encyclical, *Mater et Magistra* (1961), called attention to the widening gap between the rich and the poor. The

---

[30] Donal Dorr, *Option for the Poor: A Hundred Years of Vatican Social Teaching* (Maryknoll, N.Y.: Orbis, 1983) pp. 26–27.

encyclical stressed the social function of private property and called for a reconstruction of social relationships. *Pacem in Terris* (1963), his encyclical on peace, was an appeal to all people of good will. The pope called for a ban on nuclear weapons and stressed the responsibility of each individual to protect life: 'If civil authorities legislate for, or allow, anything that is contrary to … the will of God, neither the laws made nor the authorizations granted can be binding on the consciences of the citizens, since "we must obey God rather than men" (no. 51).

The social teachings of the Second Vatican Council were contained in two documents that appeared in 1965. *Gaudium et Spes* (Pastoral Constitution on the Church in the Modern World) treated the practice of social justice as part of the mission of the Church.[31] *Dignitatis Humanae*, the Declaration on Religious Freedom, was one of the most controversial of the council's documents. It was drafted by John Courtney Murray, the American Jesuit who had been silenced by Rome in the 1950s but was invited to the second session of the council at the insistence of Cardinal Francis Spellman of New York.

Pope Paul VI's *Populorum Progressio* appeared in 1967. Besides repeating the traditional teaching that the right to private property is not absolute, the pope addressed the issue of land reform: 'If certain landed estates impede the general prosperity because they are extensive, unused or poorly used, or because they bring hardship to peoples or are detrimental to the interests of the country, the common good sometimes demands their expropriation' (no. 24). He also rejected liberal capitalism as 'a system … which considers profit as the key motive for economic progress, competition as the supreme law of economics, and private ownership of the means of production as an absolute right that has no limits and carries no corresponding social obligation' (no. 26). A nervous *Wall Street Journal* denounced the encyclical as 'warmed-over Marxism.'[32]

Justice in the World (1971), the document of the Third Synod of Bishops, linked evangelization with a commitment to the transformation of the world: 'Action on behalf of justice and participation in the transformation of the world fully appear to us as a constitutive dimension of the preaching of the Gospel, or, in other words, of the Church's mission for the redemption of the human race and its liberation from every oppressive situation' (no. 6).

---

[31] See Timothy G. McCarthy, *The Catholic Tradition: Before and After Vatican II* (Chicago: Loyola Univ. Press, 1994) p. 251.
[32] March 30, 1967.

Stage III: 1971 onwards. The most recent stage of Catholic social teaching has dealt with the widening gap between the rich and the poor, the problems caused by technology, the arms race, torture and oppression, and includes a critique of both communism and capitalism.

Octogesima Adveniens (1971), a letter sent by Paul VI to Cardinal Maurice Roy, president of the Pontifical Council on Justice and Peace, deals with problems stemming from urbanization, including the condition of women, youth, and the new poor. Gregory Baum notes three significant points in the letter. First, it recognizes that socialism was an option for Catholics. Second, it takes a more nuanced approach to Marxism, rejecting it as a complete philosophical system and as a political form of government associated with dictatorship but acknowledging its usefulness as a form of social analysis, though one that must be used with the greatest care. Finally, the encyclical manifests an appreciation of the critical function of 'utopia', a notion borrowed from the revisionist Marxist philosopher Ernst Bloch that is able to provoke a vision of an alternative society.[33]

Pope Paul's apostolic exhortation on evangelization, *Evangelii Nuntiandi* (1975), stresses that evangelization has a social dimension as well as a personal one. The former involves human rights, family life, peace, justice, development, and liberation (no. 29). The pope sees profound links between evangelization and liberation because the person 'who is to be evangelized is not an abstract being but is subject to social and economic questions' (no. 31). He notes that though some base communities are characterized by a bitter criticism of the Church and its hierarchy, others cause the Church to grow and can be a place of evangelization (no. 58).

Evangelization belongs to the very mission of the Church; it is the responsibility of local Churches as well as of the universal Church. All Christians, clergy and laity alike, have an important role to play in evangelization.

Pope John Paul II's first social encyclical, *Laborem Exercens*, appeared in 1981. It has been praised for being a genuine teaching document, one that seeks not just to instruct but to clarify and explain. Stressing the priority of labour over capital and of people over things, it offers an evenhanded critique of both liberal capitalism and Marxism. Developing a spirituality of labour, the pope

---

[33] Gregory Baum, 'Faith and Liberation: Development Since Vatican II', Gerald M. Fagin, ed., *Vatican II: Open Questions and New Horizons* (Wilmington: Glazier, 1984) pp. 90–93.

sees work as necessary for human dignity and for the development of the kingdom.

A key concept for the pope is solidarity (no. 8). Its frequent appearance in the encyclical at the time when the Polish solidarity movement was engaged in its struggle with the country's Communist government 'undoubtedly had the effect of giving a certain discreet aura of Vatican approval to the Polish Workers Movement'.[34]

Sollicitudo Rei Socialis (1987), Pope John Paul II's encyclical on the social concerns of the Church, was designed to celebrate and develop further Pope Paul VI's *Populorum Progressio*. It emphasized the widening gap between the developed countries of the Northern Hemisphere and the underdeveloped countries of the Southern, attributing much of the blame for this situation to the existence of two opposing blocs, liberal capitalism in the West and Marxist collectivism in the East. The Church's social teaching is critical of both systems.

The pope makes it clear that the Church does not have a solution for the problem of underdevelopment, some 'third way' between the two competing systems. Echoing liberation theology, he calls for 'the option or love of preference for the poor', a concern for the poor that must condition 'our daily life as well as our decisions in the political and economic fields' (no. 42). The encyclical represents the pope's strongest challenge to the affluent countries and is noteworthy for calling attention to ecological concerns (no. 39).

Centesimus Annus (1991), marking the centenary of *Rerum Novarum*, was published after the collapse of Communism in Eastern Europe and the Soviet Union. The encyclical is more positive toward capitalism, with its recognition of the positive role of business and its allowance for human creativity in the economy. Yet capitalism has its own inadequacies. It cannot be simply the goal of third World and developing countries, where there is need to circumscribe freedom in the economic sector within a juridical framework that respects a more comprehensive notion of freedom rooted in ethical and religious values (no. 42).

Evangelium Vitae, John Paul II's lengthy encyclical on human life, appeared in 1995. Taking as his point of departure 'the sacred value of human life from its very beginning until its end' (no. 2), the pope calls on all people of good will to affirm 'a new culture of human life' (no. 6). Examples of the contemporary lack of respect

---

[34] Dorr, *Option for the Poor* p. 248; Dorr notes that the pope first analyzed solidarity as a concept in 1969 when he was archbishop of Cracow; see p. 245.

for life include the unjust distribution of resources that leads to poverty, malnutrition, and hunger for so many millions, the violence of wars and the scandalous arms trade, the reckless tampering with the world's ecological balance, the spread of drugs, and the promotion of certain kinds of sexual activity that present grave risks to life (no. 10).

In particular the encyclical concentrates on 'attacks affecting life in its earliest and in its final stages' (no. 11). The encyclical breaks new ground in speaking out so strongly against the death penalty, arguing that today, 'as a result of steady improvements in the organization of the penal system', cases in which the death penalty would be justified in order to protect society 'are very rare if not practically nonexistent' (no. 56).[35] It reaffirms the Church's position that 'abortion willed as an end or as a means, always constitutes a grave moral disorder' (no. 62) and condemns 'the use of human embryos or fetuses as an object of experimentation' (no. 63). Though it rejects euthanasia, suicide, and 'assisted suicide' as contrary to God's law, it respects a patient's decision to forgo 'aggressive medical treatment' that 'would only secure a precarious and burdensome prolongation of life, so long as the normal care due to the sick person in similar cases is not interrupted' (no. 65). In the final chapter the pope calls for the creation of a new culture that respects and protects each human life. Christians should show special concern for the poor and the disadvantaged; their communities should support single mothers, marriage and family counseling agencies, treatment and care programs for those with drug addictions, minors, the mentally ill, persons with AIDS, and the disabled (nos. 87–88).

The Church and the environment

Though *Evangelium Vitae* includes the abuse of the environment among the modern threats to life, the Catholic Church has been late in incorporating a concern for the environment into its official teaching.[36] The bishops at Vatican II did not raise the issue and the council documents reflect what is today called a 'domination theology', one that sees the natural world as existing for the exclusive

---

[35] At the release of the encyclical (March 30, 1995), Cardinal Ratzinger announced that the reservations on the death penalty present in the *Catechism of the Catholic Church* would be reformulated in light of the pope's teaching; see *Origins* 24 (April 6, 1995) p. 690.

[36] Sean McDonagh, *The Greening of the Church* (Maryknoll, N.Y.: Orbis, 1990) p. 175; see 'The Environment in the Modern Catholic Church', pp. 175–203.

use of humankind (cf. GS 34). This theology can be found in Paul VI's 1967 *Populorum Progressio*, which quotes the command in Genesis 1:28 to 'fill the earth and subdue it' (no. 22). The second creation story in Genesis suggests a greater responsibility toward the natural world; according to this account the Lord God 'took the man and settled him in the garden of Eden, to cultivate and care for it' (Gen 2:15). The image here is not domination but stewardship.

Pope Paul's 1971 letter *Octogesima Adveniens* expressed a concern for the environment (no. 21), and Pope John Paul II made several references to the exploitation of the earth in his first encyclical, *Redemptor Hominis* (nos 8, 15, 16). But his report on the 1984 Synod of Bishops on reconciliation, *Reconciliatio et Paenitentia*, missed a great opportunity to include the growing alienation of human beings from the environment that sustains them as among those relationships in need of reconciliation. His 1988 encyclical *Sollicitudo Rei Socialis* was the first to include a strong emphasis on environmental concern. And his January 1, 1990, message for the World Day of Peace, 'Peace with God the Creator, Peace with All Creation', was entirely devoted to the environment.

The World Council of Churches has had environmental concerns on its agenda since at least 1975. In 1983 at its Vancouver Assembly, it broadened a concern for a 'sustainable' society to include a concern for 'justice, peace, and the integrity of creation'.[37] Regrettably, the Catholic Church declined an invitation from the WCC to cosponsor a 1990 world conference on justice, peace, and the integrity of creation held in Korea.

Since the council some national and regional conferences of bishops have produced a number of important documents and pastoral letters on social issues. Even if these documents do not represent an official exercise of the magisterium, they have already played an important role in the development of the social conscience of Catholics.

CELAM

The first postconciliar meeting of the Episcopal Conference of Latin America (CELAM II) took place at Medellín, Colombia, in 1968. The meeting marked a turning point for the Church in Latin

---

[37] According to Sean McDonagh, Pope John Paul II's January 1, 1990 document, mentioned above, is heavily dependent on the WCC JPIC program, though this is not acknowledged in the text; see his *Passion for the Earth* (Maryknoll, N.Y.: Orbis, 1994) p. 106.

America as the bishops began to reflect on the reality of life in their countries in light of the council, the social teaching of the Church, and the new theological reflection taking place in their Churches, which would be known as liberation theology. The sixteen documents of Medellín locate the problems of Latin America not in underdevelopment itself but in 'a situation of injustice that can be called institutional violence'.[38] They call for a solidarity with the poor on the part of the Church, one that will include a redistribution of resources, and for 'conscientization' of the poor so that they will begin to take responsibility for their own lives. The word 'liberation' appears frequently and Jesus is spoken of as a liberator from sin, hunger, oppression, misery and ignorance.[39]

This 'turn toward the poor' was recognized immediately by government officials in the United States. In 1969 Nelson Rockefeller in a report prepared for President Nixon warned that the Catholic Church in Latin America had become 'a force dedicated to change – revolutionary change if necessary', pointing to the Medellín documents as an example. Somewhat condescendingly comparing the new spirit in the Church to youthful idealism, he argued that it was 'vulnerable to subversive penetration'.[40]

CELAM III took place in Puebla, Mexico, in 1979. Reviewing the situation in Latin America, the bishops found that it had worsened; most of their countries faced greater poverty, more foreign debt, a growing urban underclass as the greater percentage of their populations shifted from rural areas to the cities, and an increase in repression.[41]

The conference lacked the unanimity experienced at Medellín; it was more divided between progressives and conservatives. Nevertheless its final document supported the vision that had emerged at Medellín; it called for liberation without violence and for lay participation in the work of evangelization, and it encouraged the movement for Basic Christian Communities. The expression 'preferential option for the poor,' appearing as a

[38] CELAM II, 'Peace', no. 17; the Medellín documents can be found in Gremillion, *The Gospel of Peace and Justice*, pp. 445–84.

[39] See Edward L. Cleary, *Crisis and Change: The Church in Latin America* (Maryknoll, N.Y.: Orbis, 1985).

[40] 'Rockefeller Report on the Quality of Life in the Americas', *The Department of State Bulletin* 61 (December 8, 1969) p. 504. For a fascinating report on the Church's struggle for human rights in Latin America and the conflict with U.S. policy, see Penny Lernoux, *Cry of the People* (New York: Penguin, 1982). Her book was finished shortly before some of the worst periods of violence began.

[41] McCarthy, *The Catholic Tradition*, p. 275.

chapter title in the document, has come more than anything else to symbolize the direction taken by the Latin American Church since Medellín.

CELAM IV, timed to coincide with the 1992 quincentenary of the arrival of Columbus and thus of Christianity in the 'New World', was held in Santo Domingo, Dominican Republic. The spirit at Santo Domingo was even more divided than at Puebla. The majority of the bishops, many of them appointed by Pope John Paul II, were more conservative. A new concern was the number of Catholics in many Latin American countries being lost to prose-lytism by the Evangelical and Pentecostal Churches. Still, the conference reaffirmed the direction taken at CELAM II and III.

U.S. Catholic conference

In the 1980s the U.S. bishops published two pastoral letters to assist Catholics in the formation of their consciences on the issues of peace and the economy. Each letter was the product of a broad consultative process involving conversations with theologians, representatives of business, the defense department, and other government officials. Three separate drafts of each letter were published before a final document was approved by the bishops. The entire process models an exercise of the episcopal teaching office, which allows for input from other important voices in the Church.

The Challenge of Peace (1983) is concerned chiefly with the question of nuclear war.[42] It argues that neither the use of nuclear weapons against population centres, the threat to so use them even as a deterrent, nor the initiation of nuclear war can be justified morally. The bishops give no more than 'a strictly conditioned moral acceptance of the principle of nuclear deterrence' (no. 186); they reject the concept of 'prevailing' in a nuclear war and the quest for nuclear superiority; and they state that nuclear deter-rence should be used as a step toward nuclear disarmament.

Economic Justice for All (1986) is an attempt to apply the principles of Catholic social teaching to the U.S. economy.[43] Its thesis is that the morality of every 'economic decision and institution must be judged in light of whether it protects or undermines the dignity of the human person', regardless of that person's social or economic

---

[42] *The Challenge of Peace: God's Promise and Our Response* (Washington: USCC, 1983)
[43] *Economic Justice for All: Pastoral Letter on Catholic Social Teaching and the U.S. Economy* (Washington: USCC, 1986).

status (no. 13). The bishops are careful to distinguish between the principles they enunciate, having behind them the authority of the Church's social doctrine, and the concrete but admittedly controversial recommendations they offer (no. 22).

Both letters were widely read and much discussed. The letter on peace was more positively received; the one on the economy was more controversial, but it also might be the more prophetic. In 1992 the bishops abandoned an effort to write a letter on women after a number of interventions from the Vatican. Among their other efforts are pastoral letters on African Americans, Hispanics, and persons with disabilities.

Catholic social principles

While Catholic social teaching is built on the principle of the dignity of the human person, its approach is communitarian rather than individualistic. In this way it stands in stark contrast to the individualistic ethos of contemporary American and Western culture. A systematic review of Catholic social teaching would uncover the following basic principles:

1. *The dignity of the human person.* Each human being is created in the image of God, and therefore each human life is sacred and may never be treated as a means. A consequence is that everything in the economic and political realm must be judged in light of whether it protects or undermines human dignity. This is the foundational principle of Catholic social thought.

2. *Priority of community and the common good.* The person is social by nature and must be seen in relationship to the community, which is necessary for the person's full development. Human rights must be protected if individuals are to participate in society. Individual rights have correlative responsibilities and must be exercised with a view toward the common good. The family is the basic unit of society.

3. *Distributive justice.* Of principal concern to the common good is just distribution. Without it the right of each person to have access to what is considered essential to a dignified standard of living cannot be realized. The purpose of the economy is to serve the common good (rather than the maximization of profit).

4. *Priority of labour over capital.* Persons are more important than things. Material goods are not the sole reason for the economic community, for the dignity of persons is primary,

and work must serve this dignity. Work has an inherent dignity, and the person's dignity is inseparable from his or her work. Through work the person becomes more human.

5.   *Right to participation.* All people have a right to participate in the economic life of a society. This includes the right to work, given that work is essential to human dignity. Full employment is a primary goal. Unemployment cannot be allowed as a means to some other goal, for then capital has priority over labour. Work is the primary means to participate in the economic order, and workers should not be denied access. Workers should also be given the opportunity to participate in the day-to-day decisions of the organization. Work is not merely an economic function but also an activity that influences the psychological and spiritual character of the person.

6.   *The principle of subsidiarity.* Whenever possible decisions should be made at local levels rather than by higher bodies, thus giving primacy to individual initiative. Intermediate associations (families, local communities, unions, societies, etc.) should be free to perform operations proper to themselves without interference from the state.

7.   *Limited right to private property.* The right to private property is not absolute; it cannot be separated from one's obligation toward the common good.

8.   *Obligation to the poor.* Both individuals and civil societies have obligations to those most vulnerable. Not everyone has an equal start in economic life, and hence blame for poverty does not lie exclusively with the individual. Regardless of the cause of poverty, the poor have equal dignity with all others.

Conscience and authority

So far in this chapter we have reviewed the Church's teachings in the areas of sexuality and social justice. Now it is time to consider the role of conscience. In the Catholic tradition both conscience and authority have important roles in helping the individual recognize what he or she ought to do in a particular situation. But both conscience and authority can easily be misunderstood.

Conscience

Catholicism values conscience as the person's ultimate guide. The Second Vatican Council described conscience as 'the most secret core and sanctuary' of an individual, where he or she is alone with God (GS 16). The council here was echoing Aquinas, who taught that conscience in its most general meaning was a habit (*synderesis*), an intuitive sense deep within each person to do good and avoid evil. Aquinas understood conscience in the strict sense as the process of searching out what this sense of our obligation to do good and avoid evil means in some particular situation.[44] Since this involves a process of discernment in which the particular good may not be immediately clear, it might involve using natural reason or appealing to the revelation entrusted to the Church.

Today many Catholic moral theologians follow Timothy O'Connell's analysis of the tradition in which conscience refers to our human moral consciousness, which includes

a.   our basic grasp of the moral imperative, to do good and avoid evil;

b.   the process or 'moral science' of discovering the particular good to be done or evil to be avoided; and

c.   the specific judgment made in a particular case.[45]

Since conscience must ultimately terminate in a practical judgment reached after a careful consideration of a situation, it is important not to reduce it to a subjective inner feeling or voice. Nor should it be identified with what Freud called the 'superego', a superimposed censor that represents the 'oughts' of various authority figures in our lives and relies on guilt to bring about compliance. Conscience involves the whole person: intellect, intuition, moral sensitivity, and practical judgment.

Though a person must always follow his or her conscience, that conscience can be in error, either because he or she has not developed the maturity to move beyond self-interest and social conformity in making moral judgments, or through ignorance, or because the person has not made the effort to discover the truth. Thus each person has an obligation to form a correct conscience.

Authority

The Church, which Catholics recognize as both mother and teacher, assists in this process. This is where authority comes in. As the community of the disciples of Jesus, the Church's authority is

[44] *Summa Theologiae* I. 79.12-13.
[45] *Principles for a Catholic Morality* (San Francisco: Harper & Row, 1990) p. 109ff.

expressed in its scripture, its tradition, and in its magisterium, or official teaching office.

Sacred scripture relates for us the story of God and God's holy people. It gives us the Decalogue, the Ten Commandments (Exod 20:2-17), which spell out the parameters of living in covenant relationship with God. That covenant relationship is violated if we worship other gods or dishonour our parents, if we commit murder or adultery, steal, ruin the reputation of our neighbours or covet what belongs to them. From the prophets we are reminded of God's love for justice and constant command to remember the poor and the powerless – 'the resident alien, the orphan, and the widow' (Jer 7:6; cf. Deut 24:21). Through the Gospels we come to know Jesus; as Pope John Paul II said in *Veritatis Splendor*, following Jesus is the essential and primordial foundation of Christian morality (no. 19). The Gospels enable us to become familiar with Jesus' words and teachings, offer us the wisdom contained in his parables, and challenge us to model our lives on his example of faithful service.

The tradition bears the Church's accumulated wisdom, the wisdom that comes from the Christian community's proclamation, celebration, and transmission of its faith through countless generations. The tradition is exemplified in the lives of the martyrs and saints. It includes the Church's conviction that God has infused into each human heart the 'natural law' to do good and avoid evil, as well as the Church's understanding of what the human good is in particular circumstances, based on the biblical revelation and its own reflection on the moral order revealed in creation and in the dignity of the human person.

The magisterium teaches in the name of the Church and so in the name of Christ; through it the authority entrusted by Christ to the apostles and their successors, the bishops, comes to expression. Thus the magisterium not only reminds Catholics of what the Church has taught officially in the past, it also functions as a living teaching office, proclaiming moral principles and applying those principles both to our personal lives and to the social order.

Catholicism has a deep sense that every aspect of human life – personal, sexual, economic, and social – is to be transformed in light of the promise of God's reign in Jesus. Much of the Church's official teaching in the area of sexuality and marriage stands in sharp contrast to the values of popular modern culture. Catholics take this teaching mission of the Church seriously and respect it; perhaps this is why some people think that Catholics are always talking about morality and sexuality. The Church continues to insist on the sanctity of life, the indissolubility of marriage, and the inseparable relationship between matrimonial fidelity and sexual expression. At the same time, in this area of applying principles of Christian morality to everyday life, conscience and authority may occasionally come into conflict.

An informed conscience

How are these conflicts between conscience and authority to be resolved? The principle remains that in the final analysis one must follow one's conscience. But conscience is not autonomous. Since one's conscience can be erroneous, the primacy of conscience can never be used to avoid the responsibility of forming a correct conscience, which includes for Catholics a serious and prayerful effort to incorporate the moral vision emerging from the Catholic tradition, understood in its full sense of scripture, the tradition of the Church, the sense of the faithful, and the teaching magisterium exercised by the pope and the bishops.

In this process of forming conscience, the magisterium has a special role to play. For example, Catholics who say that 'the Church has no right to tell me what I do in my bedroom' or who argue that the Church's social teachings are an unwarranted intrusion into the realm of the political may be acting more out of self-interest or class consciousness than from a genuine desire to discover the truth. In a narcissistic and secularized society like our own we need a moral vision we can live by. It is important that the magisterium continue to perform this prophetic function of assisting Christian people in the formation of their consciences. Yet in the final analysis it remains true that authority can never be a substitute for responsible decisions made in accordance with a well-formed conscience[46]

Conclusion

These issues of sexuality and justice that we have been considering are important because they attempt to express the implications of discipleship and the Christian vision of the kingdom for our personal and social lives. If they are controversial, it is because they touch each of us so personally.

[46] See the helpful little book by Philip S. Kaufman, *Why You Can Disagree and Remain a Faithful Catholic* (Bloomington, Ind.: Meyer-Stone Books, 1989).

Catholic teaching on sexuality is of long standing. That it has changed so little with the times is not necessarily an argument against it. Christian life should be informed by the Gospel, not by the values of a particular culture. However, an ethical vision should never blind one to compassion and a recognition of the uniqueness of the individual. If the Church is uncompromising in its role as teacher, it generally is compassionate in its pastoral practice. There are also other voices in the Church that deserve a hearing.

The social doctrine of the Church is of more recent articulation, but it also has roots deep within the tradition. The Acts of the Apostles presents the Christian community as one in which 'no one claimed that any of his possessions was his own, but they had everything in common' (Acts 4:32). That may represent a vision of the ideal, but perhaps our age needs such a vision.

We live in a world of an ever-increasing gulf between the rich and the poor, not just within nations but globally. At the present time some countries are simply dissolving into anarchy; their economies are no longer functioning, and their cultural, religious, and civil systems of restraint are beginning to collapse. The ensuing chaos in countries where even teenagers have automatic weapons threatens the security of even the most powerful nations. Beyond these economic divisions our natural environment itself is in crisis. The exhaustion of nonrenewable resources, the elimination of the tropical rain forests, the resulting loss of topsoil, the poisoning of the rivers, lakes, and air, the depletion of the ozone layer, the amassing of tons of toxic waste – all this has brought into jeopardy the very ability of the planet to sustain human life.

In a world so much under threat, a communitarian tradition that speaks of the common good, distributive justice, the right of all to participate in the goods of society, and a limited right to private property may be a rich resource. But it is a threatening one because it calls those in prosperous First World countries to reexamine and perhaps to change their way of life.

For Catholics it is a given that God speaks through the Church, though not *only* through the Church. If there are times or situations when a person cannot in conscience accept what the Church teaches, then after sufficient prayer and study that person must follow his or her conscience.

But it is equally necessary today to affirm the right of the Church to teach, and the obligation Catholics have to acknowledge that teaching (cf. LG 25). If magisterial teaching must be received by the faithful in order to be effective in the life of the Church, it is also true that the bishops of the Church who constitute its magisterium have an important prophetic role to play in bringing the light of the Gospel to bear on issues faced by the Church in the contemporary world.

Chapter 24

From Symbol to Sacrament

Tad Guzie

Doctrine takes time to develop. We first tell our lived experiences in story and celebrate them in festivity. Logical analysis and systematic concepts come much later, after much further reflection.

Recall for a moment the [following] scene: a group of people assembled for the eucharist in someone's living room, sometime during the second century. If you were to ask any of those people about their 'sacraments', they would not have known what you meant. They could talk to you about the meaning of baptism or the breaking of the bread, and of course they had names for each of their rituals. But it took centuries before a *generalized* concept like 'sacrament' was developed to cover all such rituals.

The process here is normal enough. We do things long before we generalize about the nature of what we are doing. Scientists in their laboratories observe a phenomenon and spend days or even years isolating it before they can generalize and give it a name. In the sacramental realm, Christians lived their symbols long before they began exploring *how* and *why* outward symbols signify inward things. It is not surprising that the earliest generalized definition of a sacrament, which comes to us from Augustine (+ 430), does little more than state the connection between symbol and the reality signified. A sacrament, he says, is a 'visible form of invisible grace'.

The early Christians knew very well, if they ever wanted to put into words, that their outward rituals signified something spiritual. Augustine's generalization would not have surprised them. Augustine himself did not dream that he was uttering the elements of a definition which was destined to become famous. He was simply explaining in one of his letters how the fruit of a Christian ritual does not depend on the moral character of the minister. The minister, he wrote, deals only with the 'visible form' of the sacrament; God alone is responsible for the 'invisible grace'. Augustine was not engaging in a methodical reflection on the meaning of sacrament. He was simply answering a pastoral question.[1]

But Augustine's writings were an important resource for subsequent centuries, even his correspondence with its comments on occasional questions. In any dispute Augustine came to be considered a weighty authority. As time passed and new questions came up, theologians kept repeating Augustine's 'definition' of sacrament, elaborating on it and working it in with their own theological perspectives. We inherit the definition, filtered through the middle ages, the Council of Trent and post-Tridentine scholastic theology, in the form that is well known to any Catholic: Sacraments are 'outward signs instituted by Christ to give grace'.

The definition as we have inherited it is much more restrictive than Augustine's formula. In his own list of sacraments, Augustine included many actions and things which he considered 'visible forms of invisible grace': the kiss of peace, the font of baptism, the blessed salt, the creed, the Lord's Prayer, the ashes of penance. Augustine's formula defines a *symbol*, not just the particular symbolic actions that we call by the name of sacraments. I will come back to this point later. For the moment all we need to note is this first stage of generalization associated with the word 'sacrament'.

As time passed there was more and more concern with naming those rituals which are at the centre of the Church's life. There are many signs of holy things, many visible forms of invisible grace, but which things and rituals are 'efficacious'? That is, which rituals carry with them the guarantee of God's grace?

This was the question that preoccupied the medieval schoolmen. Along with the refining of a generalized definition of sacrament came an enumeration of those particular rites that could be fittingly included in the list. The number seven was not reached all at once. Hugh of St Victor, who died in 1141, discussed Augustine's definition and put many nuances on it, but he still included a good many 'visible forms of invisible grace' in his list of sacraments: holy water, liturgical vessels, and vestments, the dedication of Churches,

---

[1] *Epist.* 105.3.12 (CSEL 24, 604). In the historical material that follows, I shall not give detailed documentation. The material is well known and is not disputed by scholars. It can be found in any good historical survey of sacramental theology, e.g., B. Leeming, *Principles of Sacramental Theology* (London: Longmans Green, 1956).

and (significantly for Vatican II and the theology of our own time) the incarnation of Jesus and the Church itself as the body of Christ.

Peter Abelard, a contemporary of Hugh, enumerated six sacraments, omitting holy orders. (We shall see later how orders and matrimony are sacraments in a different sense from the other five.) By the time of Peter Lombard, who died just twenty years after Hugh and Abelard (1161), theologians seemed to be agreeing on the list of seven. This agreement was reflected in the canons of local Church councils in the late 1100s and early 1200s.

How was this agreement on the number seven reached? A number of factors seemed to be pulling together at once. Under the influence of the new blossoming of dialects and philosophy after the dark ages, theologians became more and more concerned with accurate generalization and definition of familiar realities. They were reflecting, with new tools for reflection, on the lived experience of their time. With the new or rediscovered tools of logic and philosophy, they were trying to understand the pastoral life of the Church in a coherent way.

A distinction between 'sacraments' and 'sacramentals' did not exist before the twelfth century, but it was inevitable that it should be created. It was clear, then as now, that some visible forms of invisible grace are more important than others. The seven rituals which the schoolmen agreed on as 'sacraments' were in fact rituals that were common to all of the Churches and transcended local differences. Even the Eastern Churches could and did accept this enumeration. Finally, as the scholastics liked to point out, it was 'fitting' that there should be seven sacraments, because seven is a number which symbolizes wholeness.

The New Testament and the practice of the *early* Church had little to do with the numbering of the seven. Baptism and the eucharist are of course amply discussed in the New Testament. But the medievals also tried to find in the pages of the gospels the precise moments when Christ 'instituted' each of the other sacraments. The sacrament of Christian marriage, it was argued, was instituted at the wedding feast of Cana (John 2). Holy orders and the sacrament of penance were instituted when, on Easter eve, Jesus appeared to the disciples, breathed on them (therefore 'ordained' them), and sent them forth with the commission to forgive sins (John 20).

Modern scholarship does not accept this kind of proof-texting because it is now evident that the New Testament writers were addressing different questions from those which the medieval schoolmen were trying to answer. In fact, the early Church's

commentaries on such biblical texts are in accord with the conclusions of modern biblical scholarship. The story of the marriage at
Cana has to do with the banquet of the messianic kingdom and with
Christ's institution of marriage. The appearance to the disciples on
Easter eve has to do with the whole mission of the Church and its
proclamation of God's love and forgiveness – not simply with the
rituals of holy orders or penance as we know them. It is also clear to
us now, as it was not clear to the schoolmen of the middle ages, that
the ritual practices of the early Church were understood and organized in a different way from those of the medieval Church.

Scholastic theologians themselves detected problems here, both
during and after the middle ages, because they discussed distinctions between 'direct' and 'indirect' institution of the sacraments
by Christ. In any case, the numbering of the seven sacraments did
not come out of reflection on biblical data or the life of the early
Church. It came from the actual liturgical practice of the medieval
Church and observation of what was universal in practice, with
some influence from the fitting symbolism of the number seven.

On the eve of the Reformation, two main points of doctrine or
generalization about the sacraments had evolved. First, there was
agreement that certain rituals must be considered 'efficacious'
forms of grace. Even if the minister is sinful, certain rituals are
guaranteed in a special way by God. They 'effect the grace which
they signify', and it is the Lord, not ourselves, who causes this
grace. Second, there was agreement that seven rituals belonged to
this category: baptism, confirmation (now, but not originally, a
separate rite from baptism), the eucharist, penance (now exclusively, but not originally, individual confession), extreme unction
(now a sacrament of the dying, not a sacrament for the sick), matrimony and holy orders (now seen more as rites than as ministries of
ways of living).

Other things and rites which an earlier tradition considered as
sacraments in accord with Augustine's definition (the kiss of
peace, the baptismal font, holy water, vestments, etc.) remained
visible forms of invisible grace. But such 'sacramentals' (a new
term) could not be said to carry the guarantee of grace: they do not
ineluctably effect what they signify.

Although the language surrounding the sacraments had now
become physicalist to an extreme, not all theologians failed to
nuance their way of expressing how the sacraments cause grace.
Aquinas, for example, abandoned the phrase *ex opere operato* in his
last writings (the phrase is a piece of technical Latin jargon which
implies that the sacraments take effect 'automatically', and indeed

it is hard to translate the phrase in any other way). Behind the physicalist language that gave power to the 'things' of the sacraments, there still lay the point which the better theologians of that age were most interested in getting across. The point can be expressed easily enough in less magical, more biblical language: certain rites of the Church should be seen as privileged expressions of the covenant between the Lord and his Church.

The Reformation did not call this principle into question. In the sixteenth century it was the number of sacraments, not the sacramental principle itself, that became the problem. In an age when sacramental practices had become tied up with abuses like indulgences and superstitious guarantees of salvation, the reformers wanted to get back to biblical simplicity and to the norms of the early Church. The medievals had used biblical texts to support their numbering of seven sacraments. The new textual criticism of the Renaissance called many of these arguments into question, and the Bible could no longer be used to validate all of the sacramental practices of the day. What should be done?

In general, the Protestant reformers agreed that the term 'sacrament' should be restricted to those rituals which Christ commanded to be observed, and to which he gave a promise of grace. All agreed that baptism and the eucharist fulfilled this criterion. As to the other five sacraments, opinions differed. Calvin and Zwingli rejected them out of hand as spurious ceremonies. Luther and Melancthon on the other hand were sympathetic toward penance, which they saw related to baptism. Luther also saw spiritual and pastoral value in the rites of confirmation and extreme unction. Though these rites were not commanded by Christ and cannot be called 'sacraments' in the strict sense, they remain useful and even very healing 'ceremonies'.

The Reformation opened in a new phase in the process of doctrinal development concerning the sacraments. Primacy had always been given to baptism and the eucharist, and the schoolmen made distinctions among those sacraments that were 'necessary for salvation' and those that were not. Several medieval theologians had subordinated holy orders and marriage to the other sacraments because, unlike the other five, these two are not for all the faithful. When the reformers insisted on distinguishing between the two biblical sacraments (baptism and eucharist) and other rituals which are not endowed with a specific command of Christ, they exposed questions which theology had not dealt with in any depth. How are the sacraments related to one another? Above all, how is each of the traditional seven related to the life of the *Church*?

Unfortunately, the sixteenth century did not manage to formulate these questions thoroughly and accurately, much less explore them. As the Reformation evolved, most Protestant Churches lost touch with the lived experience of many sacraments. They increasingly abandoned all rites which Jesus had not explicitly commanded in the Gospels. Even the eucharist was less and less frequently celebrated, as reaction to medieval abuses and emphasis on faith and hearing the Word led to a rabid anti-sacramentalism in most Protestant communities.

Catholicism responded to all of this at the Council of Trent by reaffirming the authority and traditions of the Church. This council had to deal with a morass of needed reforms, and it is not surprising that the quality of its work was uneven. Trent's decree on grace and justification is a remarkably balanced piece of theology. On the other hand the decrees on the sacraments, issued in different sessions of the council over a spread of years (1545–1563), dealt more with practical abuses than with the articulation of a cohesive theology.

On theological grounds, Trent did little more than reaffirm the sacramental principle and re-enumerate the sacraments. There are seven efficacious sacraments, said the council, no more and no less. An explicit command of Christ is not required for authenticity; one must not reject a tradition on scriptural grounds alone. Trent reasserted the *fact* of the sacraments without exploring the interrelationship or subordination among them, or the relationship of all the sacraments to the life of the Church.

It was left for the twentieth century to pick up this phase of doctrinal evolution. A very critical development took place in our century as theologians turned to reflection on the nature of the Church. A reflective sense of being Church existed in the early Christian centuries; and it was in this context that rituals and sacraments were understood, namely as expressions of the Church and its life in Christ. But this sense of being Church waned, and by the middle ages the Church had come to be defined in legalistic and institutional terms. Thus, by the time a formal theology of the *sacraments* was elaborated, there was no longer a well-articulated theology of the *Church* to underpin it.

In the sixteenth century neither Catholics nor Protestants possessed the theology that is so familiar to us now, namely that the *Church itself* is the core sacrament, as Christ is himself the sacrament of God. Prior to any other enumeration of the sacraments, Christ and his people are the first 'visible form of invisible grace'. Today the idea of being Church has become the starting point for all sound sacramental theology. In this perspective, our rituals are sacramental because we the Church, with Christ, are the core sacrament, celebrating in many ritual forms the grace and love of God.

Our age has picked up still another question which the past had left unexplored. Theology faithfully maintained that the sacraments are 'outward signs', but it never developed a thorough explanation of the exact meaning of sign or symbolic reality. In fact, a good many Catholic catechisms virtually denied the traditional definition which they asserted. Having stated that the sacraments are outward signs, they went on to explain that the eucharist is not *just* a sign but *really* the body and blood of Christ.

What are symbols for? How are they related to reality? What do symbols mean, and what do they do? For the past thousand years Christian theology answered such questions only in terms of the seven sacraments. In our time, scholars have looked into the larger question of what *any good symbol* means and what it does. The early Christians celebrated going into water, breaking the bread, anointing with oil, laying on hands; they savoured the blessed salt, they exchanged the kiss of peace, they treasured the font of baptism. All of these actions and things were 'visible forms of invisible grace', and when Augustine named them as such, he was doing no more and no less than defining a good *symbol.* Later ages would work other definitions out of Augustine's formula. But the fact is that the sacraments *are* symbols: this is where the theology of the sacraments began, and it is where our own age has had to return.

The problem for us is that the sacraments have become so 'churchy', so separated from the lives we live at home and at work and at play, that we no longer spontaneously relate them to the other symbols that surround and affect us. The middle ages asked: What do sacraments do, and how are they efficacious? We now have to ask a larger question: What do *symbols* do, and how are they efficacious?

Symbols do what abstract thought cannot do. Symbols bring us into touch with realities which are at once familiar and mysterious. We use symbols to bring into our heads and hearts realities which are intimate to us, but which always lie beyond the power of our heads to pigeon-hole and absorb into abstract ideas. Augustine spoke of visible forms of invisible grace. The same idea can be put in a more contemporary way: symbols are tangible, and when we touch them we touch a mystery that is at once familiar and elusive.

The love between a man and his wife is familiar; it is present to them day in and day out. Yet it remains a mystery, because any love defies rational analysis. For some couples wedding rings might be a reminder of an ideal love, a love that never came to be, or a romantic love that has faded. For a couple who possess their present love, the rings are a carrier of something real and present. Worn and felt and noticed at various moments of the day, the rings are symbols of the familiar mystery which the wife and husband are living. Don't such things as rings touch into a familiar mystery?

The covenant between Yahweh and his people was a familiar reality for the Israelites, but like any love it exceeded the mind's ability to abstract and rationalize. On one solemn occasion when the tribes of Israel were called together to renew their commitment to their Lord, Joshua took a great stone and set it up under the oak tree in the sanctuary of the Lord (Josh 24:27). He named that stone as a symbol of the covenant the people had renewed, the familiar mystery they had chosen to live. Afterward, could anyone see or touch that stone without being touched?

Life and fertility, strength and courage, wisdom and gentleness are abstract words for other familiar mysteries. The Indian tribes of North America used animals and birds and fish to symbolize the energies and values that were most central to their existence, their struggles and happiness and hopes. Composed into a totem pole, these different figures are a powerful expression of the identity of an Indian nation, of the familiar mystery that the nation experiences and lives. Why are we touched, quite irrationally, when we see a totem?

Flags and emblems serve the same purpose for modern folk. Our nation's flag symbolizes a reality that is no less familiar and no less mysterious than the forces of nature: people working together to form a society, *e pluribus unum*, with the goal of freedom and justice for all. Why are we moved, again quite irrationally, when our nation's flag is carried in parade?

We use symbols like stones and wedding rings, totems and flags and emblems, precisely because they *work* where logic or a sermon does not. Symbols, not discourses or discussions, do the most effective job of bringing into our awareness the realities of loving and being alive, living and struggling and dying together. The best discussions we have are invariably the ones that bring us closer into touch with these familiar mysteries, the mysteries that are exposed to us by all the symbols of living and struggling and dying that surround us. Any of these familiar mysteries are 'invisible graces' which we spontaneously express to ourselves in visible forms, whether it be rings or stones or flags or the breaking of bread.

Augustine's classic definition of a sacrament thus applies no less to a wedding ring than it does to the water of baptism. This was no problem for Augustine or for any of the early fathers, but it became a problem as later theologians sought more precision about the meaning of the Christian sacraments. As sacramental theory evolved, the sacraments became so thoroughly distinguished *from* other symbols that the very notion of *symbol* no longer did the job of describing what the sacraments were about.

The best illustration of this is the dispute that took place over the eucharist in the eleventh century, which I alluded to earlier and which has reverberated into the catechism of our own day. The two sides argued whether the eucharistic elements were 'only a symbol' or whether they were 'really' the body and blood of Christ. Symbol and reality, symbol and the familiar mystery, were no longer in the kind of harmony I described above. Symbol had come to mean something *other than* the reality which it signified, something vague.

Orthodoxy was forced to insist on the reality of Christ's presence in the eucharist, but it was crippled in two ways. First, as we saw earlier, the whole question was now put in terms of the elements of the eucharist, the things of the sacrament rather than the action, the bread and wine rather than the breaking of the bread and the sharing of the cup. Second, in a climate where the idea of symbol had come to mean a mere reminder of reality, not a 'realizer' of reality, no one investigated the meaning of what a symbol does. In the absence of a philosophy of symbol, the medieval schoolmen turned to the Greek philosophy of substance to affirm the reality of Christ's presence in the eucharistic elements; the reality was affirmed by maintaining that the substance of the bread and wine is changed. It did not occur to anyone to ask whether 'substance' is in fact the most helpful category for understanding symbolic realities like the sacraments.

Any symbol can degenerate into a mere reminder. A flag can become a nostalgic reminder of a glorious past, and wedding rings can become reminders of a sweeter and more romantic love that existed on the day of the wedding. Perhaps some people coming to Shechem a generation after Joshua saw the stone he placed under the oak tree as a mere reminder of a more fervent moment in their history. But when symbols are only reminders, *they are no longer symbols*. A real symbol always brings us into touch not just with a memory but with a living present, and indeed a present which contains a hope for the future and which helps to carry us into the future.

Traditional theology worried that the sacraments, especially the eucharist, should be thought of as 'only symbols'. The question is whether there can be any such thing. Either a thing is *really* a symbol or it is *not really* a symbol. Does the wedding ring signify the covenant that exists between this woman and this man, or doesn't it? Did Joshua's stone signify the renewed covenant or didn't it? Does the flag of this nation signify what this nation is now about, or doesn't it?

The profoundness of a symbol lies in its being just what it is. Giving or receiving a gift, sharing a meal, laying hands on a friend in love or blessing are profound things. A symbol is its own reality, and *in* its own reality it leads us into the profound mystery which it signifies. If a symbol is worth its name, it is so expressive of the familiar mystery which it signifies that it could never be called 'only a symbol'. If there were such a thing, why should we get angry when someone burns our country's flag? If a contractor goes to an Indian community to build houses and a totem stands in his way, why not just cut it down? The wedding rings that my wife and I wear are the same gold bands that my grandparents wore. If they were lost, and if they are 'only symbols', why should we be upset at anything more than the high price of gold?

All true symbols shape our reality. When a symbol is brought forward or enacted, reality is altered for us. *All true symbols are efficacious.* In the very act of signifying a reality, they both make and change our reality.

How then are the sacraments different from other symbols? Only in the reality which they signify, not in their being symbols. The breaking of the bread signifies that we, though many, are one body in Christ. A flag does not signify this mystery. Going into the baptismal water signifies our going into Christ's death with him in order to live a new life. Giving a gift does not signify this mystery.

But at the same time, the familiar mysteries signified by displaying a flag or giving a gift are no less 'mysteries' than those signified by the sacraments. Theology has faithfully maintained that the sacraments confer the grace of God through the merits of Christ, not through our own merits. But this gratuity, this givenness, also applies to the other familiar mysteries that symbols touch. The relationship between ourselves and nature, the care and friendships that exist between people, the visions that bind a nation together are also a given: such things are given by God, not created by our own efforts alone.

Christians have priorities among the great and gratuitous mysteries of life. This means that some symbols will be more precious than others, more central to the venture of living as

Christians. This is precisely why seven sacraments came to be distinguished from the other symbols around us. But today our task is to reintegrate the sacraments into the larger human story. Any catechist or teacher will attest to this. The sacraments simply are not understood when they are put into a category by themselves. On the contrary, appreciation for the riches of the sacraments seems to develop only as people, young and old, are brought back into touch with the other rich symbols and surround them and efficaciously touch their lives.

Chapter 25

Liturgy (*Sacrosanctum Concilium*)

Aidan Kavanagh OSB

The Constitution on the Liturgy, *Sacrosanctum Concilium* promulgated on 4 December 1963, was the first document issued by the Second Vatican Council. This was not because the council fathers assigned *a priori* most importance to this subject, but because *Sacrosanctum Concilium*'s pre-conciliar preparation proved far more satisfactory than that of other comparably important texts. But coming first as it did, *Sacrosanctum Concilium* set the atmosphere for subsequent debates and documents.

Its ecclesiology of the Church as a diversified people of faith gathered in unity round its bishop influenced the Dogmatic Constitution on the Church, *Lumen Gentium* (1964), the Decree on Ecumenism, *Unitatis Redintegratio* (1964), the Pastoral Constitution on the Church in the Modern World, *Gaudium et Spes* (1965), and the Decree on Missions, *Ad Gentes* (1965). Certain of these later documents, moreover, such as *Lumen Gentium* 3–14 and *Ad Gentes* 13, develop certain aspects of *Sacrosanctum Concilium* beyond its own preliminary content; for example, the priority of faith and baptism and on the catechumenate (SC 64–71).

It would not be unfair to characterize *Sacrosanctum Concilium* as a 'Liturgical Movement' document. This does not mean that it represents only late and narrow enthusiasms of liturgical advocates. It means, rather, that it rests on a massive tradition both legislative and scholarly extending back some four centuries and culminating in this century in the movement of pastoral liturgy.

Basic is the historical research that strove from the sixteenth century to recover a clearer picture of what was truly traditional in the welter of western worship materials. This began even before the Council of Trent (1545–63), the liturgical reforms of which were not completed until 1614.

Next comes the large body of liturgical legislation issued by the Holy See, estimated as some 6,000 entries during the first three centuries after Trent, and around 300 during the present century (Megivern, 1978, pp. xiv–xvi).

Third was a second and more sophisticated wave of scholarly research into liturgical origins extending from the seventeenth century to now, represented by scholars of great stature: from Bona and Mabillon in the seventeenth century to Edmund Bishop and J.A. Jungmann in the twentieth.

This long and patient recovery of liturgical sources made possible the fourth body of literature on which *Sacrosanctum Concilium* rests, namely, that of the pastoral and parish-oriented phase, the modern Liturgical Movement, dating from an address by L. Beauduin at the Louvain Conference of 1909, and followed by a half-century of sensitive reflections by thinkers such as Beauduin himself (who died on the eve of the Council), R. Guardini, V. Michel, G. Diekmann, C. Howell, P. Parsch, H.A. Reinhold and others.

At the same time and under comparable influences, the other fundamental modern theological disciplines were evolved – biblical exegesis and theology, historical theology, the history of doctrine, and patristics and finally, the Ecumenical Movement was born. All this influenced liturgics. In addition, the modern social action and liturgical movements were conceived in the same egg, so to speak: *actuosa participatio*, as papal documents on both liturgy and social reform from Leo XIII onward would name it, and the two movements have lived in symbiosis ever since, at least until recently. Particularly during the pontificate of Pius XII, this pastoral phase was enhanced by the encyclical *Mediator Dei* (1947), and affected Catholic worship markedly in the growing use of the vernacular, the practice of the 'dialogue Mass', and most strikingly in the 1951 restoration of the Easter Vigil and the 1955 reform of Holy Week (Megivern, 1978, pp. 128 and 128–40).

The 130 paragraphs of *Sacrosanctum Concilium* are a distillation of this long development into remarkably brief and intense form. The first words of this Constitution were also the first words the Council addressed to the world, and are, in consequence, in a special way programmatic:

> The sacred Council has set out to impart an ever-increasing vigour
> to the Christian life of the faithful; to adapt more closely to the

needs of our age those institutions which are subject to change; to foster whatever can promote union among all who believe in Christ; to strengthen whatever can help to call all mankind into the Church's fold. Accordingly it sees particularly cogent reasons for undertaking the reform and promotion of the liturgy (SC 1).

Remarkable though it may now seem, the Council's primary self-understanding was not framed in terms of peace or social activism, but in terms of 'the reform and promotion of the liturgy'. Indeed, in one of the Council's most categorical statements, the liturgy is the summit toward which the activity of the Church is directed; it is also the fount from which all her power flows (SC 10). This is even more remarkable when one recalls that the vast majority of bishops who voted for the document had not before the council in their own dioceses been involved in, much less in the forefront of, the Liturgical Movement. With few exceptions they had been enforcers of the official liturgical practices and rather cautious followers of papal encyclicals such as Pius XII's *Mediator Dei* (1947). Standard fare in the majority of parishes worldwide was low Mass in Latin, sometimes followed by Benediction of the Blessed Sacrament or, as in some places in Germany and Austria, accompanied by fairly indiscriminate hymn-singing in the vernacular.

While the Mass was greatly revered, much popular piety was just as much shaped and influenced by a spread of para- and non-liturgical devotions to the Sacred Heart, the Mother of God, and the saints. The Breviary (containing the Liturgy of the Hours) was obliged to be read daily by all clerics in major orders; outside religious houses it was rarely celebrated in public, even in part, and almost never in parishes. Although one might hear some choral music in larger Churches, the restoration of 'Gregorian' chant and the polyphonic tradition based on it, commended by Pius IX, Pius X and Pius XII, never really caught on in parishes, despite the labour of love expended on it by many devoted and talented people.

These matters are recalled to illustrate what a contrast *Sacrosanctum Concilium* afforded when it stated the Council's intent to impart new vigour to Christian life, to adapt more closely to the needs of the age, to promote union among believers in Christ, and to strengthen the call of all mankind into the Church's fold by undertaking the reform and promotion of the liturgy. This move put worship squarely at the heart and front of Christian endeavour because worship presumes the presence of God in Christ by the Holy Spirit, from whom the whole of creation, revelation and redemption flow. The most appropriate response to this active presence is not analysis or speculation, but worship in thanksgiving for all that has been gratuitously given our race.

While Christians obviously do more than worship (SC 9), all they do is finally directed towards, and flows forth from, this crucial activity (SC 10-13). So 'Mother Church earnestly desires that all the faithful should be led to that full, conscious, and active participation in liturgical celebrations which is demanded by the very nature of the liturgy, and to which the Christian people, "a chosen race, a royal priesthood, a holy nation, a redeemed people" (1 Pet 2:9, 4–5) have a right and obligation by reason of their baptism' (SC 14).

The document draws many cogent inferences from this (SC 15–46), among which is the basic practical reform policy, revision of the liturgical books as soon as possible (SC 25). Conciliar liturgical reform for the past quarter-century has turned on revision of the Roman Rite's library of liturgical books as on a hinge; the final revision of some is still under way, while some already reformed are being fine-tuned even yet. General norms for this process are given in chapter I (1–46). Specific norms follow for the Eucharist in chapter II (47–58), for the other sacraments and sacramentals in chapter III (59–82), for the Divine Office or Liturgy of the Hours in chapter IV (83–101), for the liturgical year in chapter V (102–11), for sacred music in chapter VI (112–21), and for sacred art and sacred furnishings in chapter VII (122–0). To initiate, oversee and write the reforms for actual use, a special commission, later named 'the *Consilium* for the Implementation of the Constitution on the Sacred Liturgy', was established in 1962 by John XXIII's *motu proprio Sacram Liturgiam* (Flannery 1, pp. 41–4); this body was absorbed in 1969 by the newly reconstituted Sacred Congregation for Divine Worship, which remains the main curial body governing implementation of the reform. Its first secretary, A. Bugnini, had been secretary of Pius XII's Commission for Liturgical Reform and represents the sole example of curial continuity of a reformist kind from the time of Pius to the middle years of Paul VI.

The revision of liturgical books was at its most intense during the reign of Paul VI between the years 1963–73 (Megivern, 1978, pp. xvii–xxi). The pope in 1977 looked back on the course of the reform with basic confidence, but mixed feelings about those who would run too fast and those who would not run at all (Megivern, 1978, pp. 453–7). Left unmentioned were problems caused by the quantity and rapidity in the reforms themselves, problems that reflect perhaps the greatest of all the reform's weaknesses, namely, the almost total absence of any anthropological dimension in the approach to revision of so massive and long-standing a ritual system. For ritual patterns, which have much to do with sustaining identity and the social bond, are for these reasons essentially conservative and normally need to change slowly.

SC 23 cautions that before revisions are made, a careful investigation – theological, historical, and pastoral – should always be made into 'each part of the liturgy which is to be revised'; the anthropological dimension seems never to have crossed anyone's mind. Thus the naivety of SC 31: 'The [revised] rites should be distinguished by a noble simplicity. They should be short, clear, and free from useless repetitions. They should be within the people's powers of comprehension, and normally should not require much explanation.' This is an educationalist outlook, certainly not that of anyone knowing anything about ritual behaviour, which is rarely short, clear, free of repetition and usually transcends the comprehension of the whole congregation, including its officiants. Yet it is this simplistic educationalist sense of rite that has tended to be given prominence in the revisions of the liturgical books, and to have taken root in people's minds, to the detriment of traditional sacred polyphony (repetitions) and to that perhaps greatest of liturgical arts, ceremony. Hence the untranscendental blandness felt by many in their attempts to use the reformed rites, and the rites' often aggressive educationalism when used imprudently.

Anthropological studies by Mary Douglas, Victor Turner and many others could have been helpful here, from Van Gennep's 1909 work on *Rites of Passage* onwards, but recent manuals in liturgics contain little bibliography on the anthropology of ritual behaviour, and the category 'Ritual' does not even appear in their indexes (cf. Jones, Wainwright and Yarnold; Wegman; Cattaneo). This is the more unfortunate since the recent upsurge in calls for inculturation of Christianity, and in particular, liturgy in Africa and the Far East, carries with it anthropological issues not covered by the more usual theological, historical and pastoral approaches. One may anticipate fearsome mistakes being made without some well-learned anthropological lessons being attended to as inculturation proceeds.

Reception of *Sacrosanctum Concilium* and its reforms has been generous and positive. The reforms themselves are mostly of high quality, far more richly traditional in the best sense than those of Trent, given its times, ever could have been. They include several (all of them in fact restorations) that have profoundly changed the way in which the Church thinks of itself and is perceived by others.

Chief among these is surely the move from Latin, the sacred language of the clergy and 'their' liturgy, to the vernaculars of the modern world. Pius XII had already grudgingly noted in 1947 that 'the use of the mother tongue in connection with several of the rites may be of much advantage to the people' (*Mediator Dei* 60). Few could then have imagined that the entire liturgy would be vernacular within thirty years, making both worship and ministry more accessible to non-clergy, thus reflecting deep ecclesiological shifts even yet not wholly assimilated. Abetting this was the restoration of Catholic initiatory practice (SC 66–71), culminating in the reformation of the baptismal rites for infants (1969) and adults (1972), and of confirmation (1971), by which the catechumenate was restored as a permanent structure (SC 64) and evangelization emphasized. Shifts in language and initiation signalled recovery of a less clerical and more egalitarian view of the Church as the baptized people of God, which all but demanded three other restorations: Communion under both kinds for all (SC 55), Eucharistic concelebration by bishops and presbyters (SC 57), and the permanent diaconate (*Lumen Gentium* 29). These restorations of practice and reforms in ritual procedure have left no group – lay, clerical or monastic – unaffected in the deepest manner.

Paul VI was assiduous in implementing these reforms (indeed, he carried them even to translating the Eucharistic prayer into the vernacular, something which few if any council fathers had contemplated or wished to authorize); John Paul II perhaps less so, in his concern to appeal to Lefebvreists by spreading permissions for celebrating the 'Tridentine Mass' and commending celebration of the conciliar reforms in Latin. Although the use of Latin for the post-conciliar rite has always been an option, many view the maintenance of the 'Tridentine Mass' as a mistake that compromises the quality, not to say the deeply traditional Catholicity, of the conciliar reforms themselves. Some would see this as an unwarranted use of the liturgy for short-term ends meant to overcome a minor schism, which could finally not succeed. History will no doubt show Paul VI to have been the pope most intelligently committed to liturgical restoration and reform over the long haul; his instincts and courage were both deep and correct. Despite the problems reform always presents, he knew that once this was embarked on one must persevere and see it through.

But if the liturgical reforms have been qualitatively good on the whole, especially in the area of Christian initiation, the use to which the reforms have been put in many places remains uneven. Their lack of preparation for the reform called for by *Sacrosanctum*

Concilium has hampered English-speaking congregations, especially, from grasping and then enacting much more than the letter
of the reform. The symbolic minimalism that afflicted the liturgy
of such groups prior to the Council is still often in evidence, as is a
certain clericalism which has now spread idiosyncrasies to new
ranks of lay ministers and liturgy committee members. Perhaps
more serious is the increasing speed with which parish liturgy may
become a celebration of middle-class values, creating a narrow new
elitism which tends to exclude the lower classes and alien ethnic
groups (cf. Archer; Douglas; Flanagan). As this happens, not only
is the Church splintered, but the organic sacramentality of the
Church as redeemed humanity standing worshipfully and in unity
before God in Christ by the Holy Spirit falls away. Individualism
flourishes, and the liturgy may almost become the plaything of its
celebrants, in which case it ceases to be a bulwark against individualism and becomes instead a casualty to it. Such a liturgy,
understandably, no longer appears to have any connection with
social *actuosa participatio* by which both Church and world might be
built up by a community of faith, the very given of baptism in
Christ Jesus.

This situation is general enough in some parts of the western
world to contribute to a noticeable decline in Sunday liturgical
attendance, which may be as much as 30 percent in the United
States over the past twenty years. What is needed now is a new
phase of the Liturgical Movement to re-expound in post-conciliar
terms what it is truly all about: in particular

a. the fundamental purpose of liturgy (SC 2, 106);
b. the concept of participation in its theological and ascetical
    aspects, linking it to the sacrificial character of the liturgy,
    especially in the Eucharist, as the basic articulation point for
    a liturgical 'spirituality' (SC 47–48);
c. the concept of sacrament embracing both act and the Church
    that acts (SC 5–8);
d. the intimate relationship between liturgy and the edification
    of the social order in the modern world (SC 9–12; *Gaudium et
    Spes*);
e. the objective normativeness of the liturgical act itself, in all
    the details of its ceremony and iconography, as the Church's
    primary theological and contemplative endeavour.

What is called for is a new and richer '*mystagogy*' that expounds the
liturgy in its own terms from within, and a theology more sensitive

to the nature of the liturgical assembly as a theological corporation in its own right, speaking a theological language of symbol and ceremony soaked in the gospel of Jesus Christ for the life of the world.

Bibliography

Archer, A. (1986) *The Two Catholic Churches: A Study in Oppression.* London, SCM.

Cattaneo, E. (1984) *Il culto Cristiano in occidente.* Rome, C.L.V. Editizioni Liturgiche.

Chupungco, A. (1982) *Cultural Adaptation of the Liturgy.* New York, Paulist Press.

Douglas, M. (1970) *Natural Symbols: Explorations in Cosmology.* New York, Pantheon.

Flanagan, K. (1987) 'Resacralizing the Liturgy', *New Blackfriars*, vol. 68, pp. 64-75.

Flannery OP, A. (1975) *Vatican Council II: The Conciliar and Post-Conciliar Documents,* New York, Costello Publishing Company; Dublin, Dominican Publications.

Grimes, R. (1982) *Beginnings in Ritual Studies.* Washington, University Press of America.

Jones, C., Wainwright, G., and Yarnold, E. (1978) *The Study of Liturgy.* London, SPCK; New York, OUP.

Koenker, E. (1954) *The Liturgical Renaissance in the Roman Catholic Church.* Chicago, University of Chicago Press.

Lévi-Strauss, C. (1963) *Structural Anthropology.* New York, Basic Books.

Megivern, J. (1978) *Worship and Liturgy: Official Catholic Teachings.* Wilmington, N.C., McGrath.

Turner, V. (1969) *The Ritual Process: Structure and Antistructure.* Chicago, Aldine.

Van Gennep, A. (1909, ET 1960) *The Rites of Passage.* Chicago, University of Chicago Press.

Wegman, H. (1985) *Christian Worship.* New York, Pue.

Chapter 26

The Development of the Catholic Sacraments

Joseph Martos

> Properly speaking, a sacrament is something that is a sign of a sacred reality pertaining to men; so that what is properly called a sacrament in the present sense of the word is a sign of a sacred reality that makes men holy. (Thomas Aquinas)

> The holy Roman Church maintains and teaches that there are seven ecclesiastical sacraments. One is baptism, which has already been mentioned. Another is confirmation, which bishops confer through the imposition of hands, anointing those who have been reborn. The others are penance, the Eucharist, the sacrament of orders, matrimony, and the last anointing which is administered to the sick, according to the teaching of St. James. (Second Council of Lyons)

The numbering of the Catholic sacraments as seven dates from the twelfth century. Prior to that time the word *sacramentum* still had a rather broad meaning, and it could be used to designate any number of sacred signs and symbols. By the thirteenth century the meaning of *sacramentum* had become much more restricted, and the word was used only to refer to the ecclesiastical rites listed by the Second Council of Lyons.

The medieval period was a crucial one for the Catholic sacraments in other ways, too. Their rituals became more standardized, their religious meanings became more solidified, and the theological explanations for them became more unified. During the patristic period the forms of some of these rituals had varied considerably, their meanings were sometimes debated, and their theology reflected a variety of regional traditions. In the Middle Ages, however, Christians in the eastern and western parts of the old Roman Empire drifted apart and finally stopped speaking to each other. Byzantine Christianity, the Orthodox tradition, remained rooted in the patristic heritage of liturgy, theology, and regional autonomy; European Christianity, the Catholic tradition, retained its patristic roots but saw its liturgy and theology evolve in new directions under the authority of Rome. The sacraments in the Orthodox Churches therefore tended to keep their diverse ancient forms, while those in the Catholic Church developed a newer, more uniform, more western style.

The first Catholic developments were in the area of sacramental practice; they began in the sixth century and continued almost imperceptibly during the next few hundred years. The rite of confirmation became separated from that of baptism. The eucharistic liturgy became a clerical affair with little lay involvement. The practice of public penance disappeared and was replaced by private confession. The marriage ceremony came to be regarded as a sacramental rite. Ordination to the priesthood developed into a sequence of holy orders. The anointing of the sick became the anointing of the dying. By the twelfth century these sacramental practices had not only achieved a more or less stable form, but were also becoming regarded as the principal sacraments in the Church.

These practical developments were followed in later centuries by theological developments. In the thirteenth century there arose a new style of Catholic theology based on the philosophy of Aristotle. Old theological problems were reexamined and new types of answers were introduced. In time a more or less standard approach to Catholic sacramental theology appeared, and even though there were scholarly disagreements about peripheral matters, there was general agreement on all of the main issues.

It was during the Middle Ages, then, that the sacraments of the Roman Catholic Church emerged in the forms that they would retain until the twentieth century. Their number was fixed at seven, their practice became more uniform, and their general theology was established.

1. Seven liturgical sacraments

The years from the sixth to the eleventh century were hard times for the Catholic Church. The intellectual centres of Italy were in ruins; the provinces in north Africa and the middle east fell under Moslem control; the Greek provinces were isolated both geographically and culturally. The collapse of the Roman empire in the west, the Germanic invasions and subsequent missionary efforts in Europe left little energy for original theological work. Church leaders did what they could to Christianize the continent, and ever so slowly their efforts succeeded. But they were practical men, with little taste for theological speculation. The missionary monks, poorly educated as they often were, brought with them only what they knew: the book of the Gospels, the creed, and the sacramental means of salvation. Those who remained in the monasteries copying ancient manuscripts or producing new psalters were sometimes even illiterate: they knew the shapes of the letters but they could not read them.

It was during this long period that the Catholic sacraments underwent their greatest changes. Instead of being an elaborate initiation ritual, baptism was reduced to a simple rite of water and words. Instead of being a public, once in a lifetime affair, penance became a private, repeatable sacrament. Instead of being a repeated anointing in times of illness, extreme unction became a final anointing at the time of death. And along with these changes in their ritual forms the sacraments underwent changes in their sacred meanings, some only slightly, others more drastically.

During this period, too, the liturgical practices of the Church began to centre around seven major rituals: the baptism of infants and converts, the confirmation of baptism by the bishop, the rite of penitence and forgiveness, the anointing of the dying, the ordaining of priests, the uniting of people in marriage, and the Eucharistic Liturgy or Mass. There were of course many other ritual practices: initiation ceremonies for men and women who entered monasteries, the daily chanting of prayers by monks and nuns, various types of blessings and exorcisms, the veneration of martyrs and relics, pilgrimages to sacred shrines, and other pious devotions. But there were seven which were becoming in practice, if not yet in theory, the primary liturgical sacraments of the Church.

Then in the twelfth century, after the 'barbarians' had been converted and Europe began to experience some relative political peace and economic prosperity, the intellectual task of understanding religion began afresh, first in the monasteries and then in the newly founded schools. For hundreds of years monks had laboriously copied and recopied fragile manuscripts to keep their contents from being lost forever. Now at last there were people who had the leisure to read them and think about what they contained. They were trying to understand for themselves what it meant to be a Christian, to have faith in God, to be a member of the Church; they were trying to find explanations of the mysteries that they had been celebrating for centuries in ritual. And so they turned with renewed interest to the Bible, to the writings of the Church Fathers, and to the statements of the early councils.

It was an enormous undertaking. The monks and schoolmen were looking for a coherent understanding of the Christian religion, but they found themselves confronted with a bewildering variety of texts: sermons and letters, commentaries and treatises, statements of bishops and councils. And the texts did not always agree with one another in matters of theology. So in order to make some headway through this mountain of information, early medieval scholars began making summaries of what they read and collecting quotations on various subjects such as the Incarnation, the Trinity, the Church, and so on. Soon there were 'books of sentences' or collections of opinions on every major theological topic, including sacraments.

Early in the twelfth century there was still little agreement about the exact nature and number of the sacraments in the Church. Most theologians admitted that there were 'sacraments of the Old Law' such as temple sacrifices and other Jewish rituals, as well as 'sacraments of the New Law' such as those found among Christians. Hugh, a monk in the Abbey of St Victor in Paris, thought Augustine's definition of a sacrament as a sign of the sacred was too broad, and he proposed a definition which was narrower in scope; but when it came to treating the things that he considered to be sacraments he discussed not only the familiar seven but also such things as the Incarnation of Christ, the Church, holy water, blessed ashes, the sign of the cross, and vows. Lists of sacraments by various authors ranged from twelve all the way up to thirty. On the more conservative side, a book of sentences compiled before 1150 treated only five ecclesiastical sacraments, and Peter Abelard around the same period enumerated six, leaving out holy orders.

One of the largest collections of sentences was compiled by Peter Lombard in Paris. In his work, he gathered together biblical quotations and patristic texts on every major theological issue of the day, and added his own observations and conclusions about them. Published in four parts, it was both systematic and thorough, and within a short time it came to be adopted as the standard theological source book for all beginning theology students. The last part contained a large section on the seven principal ecclesiastical sacraments as they were practised in the twelfth century. Because of the book's popularity and wide usage, Lombard's enumeration of the Catholic sacraments soon became accepted by theologians and preachers alike, and by the end of the next century it was accepted by synods and councils.

But Peter Lombard's textbook did more than crystallize theological thinking around the liturgical rites of baptism, confirmation, eucharist, penance, extreme unction, matrimony, and orders. It also offered a definition of sacraments which for the first time enabled Catholics to distinguish between these seven and other sacred signs and rituals. He wrote, 'Something is properly called a sacrament because it is a sign of God's grace, and is such an image of invisible grace that it bears its likeness and exists as its cause' (*Sentences* IV, 1, 2). The seven ecclesiastical sacraments were for him causes as well as signs of grace, and this made them different from 'sacramentals' which were signs but not causes of grace. Among the sacramentals were included such things as statues and crucifixes, holy water and oils, blessings and prayers, religious promises and vows, and other Church ceremonies. From that time on, then, many things which could be considered sacraments in a broad sense were no longer given the name *sacramenta*, and Catholic theologians began to use the word almost exclusively in reference to the familiar seven rites.

The decision to restrict the name *sacrament* to just these seven, however, was not a sudden one. For some time there had already been tendencies in this direction. The early medieval theologians recognized that some of the *sacramenta* were believed to have definite spiritual effects. They also observed that some of the *sacramenta* were rituals which 'bore the likeness' or acted out, as it were, the meaning of the effect that they were supposed to cause. And it was these *sacramenta* which presented the greatest challenge in trying to explain just what they were and how they worked. It is understandable, then, that these special *sacramenta* were singled out for special treatment. When theologians argued about sacraments it was usually these sacraments that they had in mind. And so in the course of time it was these sacraments which came to be commonly referred to as the sacraments.

2. Sign and reality

The twelfth and thirteenth centuries were high points of Catholic sacramental theology. Medieval thinkers succeeded in putting together the scriptural data, the patristic contributions, and the sacramental practices of their day into a logically coherent framework that proved satisfactory for centuries. But why were the medievals no longer satisfied with Augustine's broad definition of sacrament as a sign of a sacred reality? Why did they want a 'proper' definition like the one offered by Peter Lombard? And why did the search for such a definition take the route that it eventually did? To begin to answer these questions we must look at an earlier theological problem and see how it was resolved.

Around the middle of the eleventh century, Berengar of Tours attacked the idea that the bread and wine consecrated at Mass became the body and blood of Christ. He believed in the presence of Christ in the eucharist, but he believed that it was a spiritual presence. To him it was obvious that something had to be either a sign or a reality; it could not be both. Smoke is a sign of fire, but it is not fire; a crown is not a king but only a sign that the man who wears it is one. Applying this logic to the eucharist, he argued that the consecrated bread and wine either had to be signs of the body and blood of Christ or else they had to be the real body and blood of Christ. And it was equally obvious to Berengar that the consecrated bread and wine were not the real body and blood of Christ: they looked nothing at all like human flesh and blood, and besides, the real Christ had ascended bodily into heaven. Berengar's conclusion was that the bread and wine were and remained signs; they were not the real thing. And in support of his conclusion he cited Augustine: 'A sacrament is a sign of a sacred reality.' If the eucharist was a sacrament, he argued, it had to be a sign of Christ's body and blood, not his real body and blood.

Berengar's attack did not go unchallenged. A number of his contemporaries argued against him, and in 1059 his ecclesiastical superiors forced him to sign a confession of faith in which he admitted the real presence of Christ in the Eucharist. But the ecclesiastical reaction against Berengar did not explain how Christ became present in the bread and wine; it simply reaffirmed the Church's traditional belief that they were Christ's body and blood despite the fact that they still looked like bread and wine. It took medieval theologians about a hundred years to work out a satisfactory philosophical explanation for this belief.

Berengar had assumed, as did most other theologians of his day, that there were only two elements involved in a sacramental ritual: the ritual itself and the reality that it signified, the *sacramentum* or visible sign and the *res* or real thing that it pointed to. The visible sign in the Eucharist was clear enough: it was the bread and wine, together with the words of consecration, 'This is my body. This is my blood', said over them during the Mass. But what was the reality that the eucharist pointed to? Slowly the medieval theologians came to the conclusion that the ultimate reality signified by the Eucharist was not a physical reality but a spiritual one; the ultimate purpose of consecrating the bread and wine was not to make Christ physically present on the altar but to receive him in communion. And so the ultimate reality, the *res* of the Eucharist, was the spiritual union with Christ. But what, then, was the status of the consecrated bread and wine before they were received? Were they a sacrament or a reality? The answer that was finally worked out was that they were both. Or rather, it was agreed that the bread and wine were in reality the body and blood of Christ, and that these in turn were a sign of union with the real Christ which was achieved in the receiving of communion.

To Catholics of a later age this solution seemed quite natural, and yet it took decades for Catholic theologians to come to it. Why? One reason was the authority of Augustine. Besides his definition of a sacrament as 'a sign of a sacred reality', there was also another which was attributed to him: 'a visible sign of invisible grace.' Both of these definitions indicated that there were only two elements in a sacrament. But if the writings of Augustine were part of the problem, they also suggested a solution. Augustine himself in his polemics against the Donatists had spoken of the seal or character received in baptism as a sacrament. The seal was, so to speak, both a reality and a sign: a reality since it was something really received, and a sign since it marked a person as belonging to Christ. And as these writings of Augustine were rediscovered and reread, the possibility of a parallel solution to the eucharistic problem became clearer.

In the end, medieval theologians developed a three-fold distinction in reference to the sacraments: the *sacramentum tantum* being the element which was 'only a sign', the *sacramentum et res* being the element which was 'both sign and reality', and the *res tantum* being the element which was 'only a reality'. In reference to the Eucharist, the words of consecration and the outward appearance of bread and wine could be considered as only a sign; the body and blood of Christ really present under the appearance of bread and wine could be considered as both a reality in itself and a sign pointing to the spiritual nourishment to be received in communion; and the grace of that union with Christ could be considered as a reality which was not also a sign of something else. In reference to the other sacraments, the symbolic words, gestures, and objects in the rite could be considered as the sacramental sign, the *sacramentum tantum*; a change in the soul of the subject of the rite could be considered as the sacramental reality, the *sacramentum et res* which was received by participating in the symbolic ritual; and the spiritual benefit of receiving the sacrament, God's freely bestowed grace, could be considered as the sacred reality; the *res tantum* which the sign pointed to and helped to cause.

Taking the lead suggested by Augustine, this triple terminology was applied first to baptism and then to the other liturgical sacraments. The baptismal seal on the soul of the recipient was not just a sacrament and it was not just God's grace; it must therefore be, the theologians reasoned, a sacramental reality produced by the rite which made it possible for the baptized person to receive the grace connected with that sacrament. But baptism was not the only sacrament which was believed to have a permanent effect on the recipient. Confirmation and orders could likewise be received only once, and because of this it was argued that they too must bestow an indelible character on the soul. And this character, like the seal of baptism, could be considered a sacramental reality, neither pure sign nor pure grace.

It was not so easy to discover the sacramental reality bestowed by the other three liturgical sacraments of matrimony, penance, and extreme unction, since all of them could be received more than once and so none of them were believed to confer a permanent character. And yet there had to be some sacramental reality given by them, the medieval theologians reasoned, because this element had been found in four of the sacraments, and if all seven were sacraments they should all have the same essential elements. In this respect medieval thought was basically the same as classical Greek thought: it tried to understand the essential nature of things, and one of its working assumptions was that the natures of similar things were essentially similar. If, for example, one could discover the nature of one's own soul, one would possess an understanding of the essential nature of any human soul. Similarly, by understanding of the nature of virtue or sin, of the state or the Church, of animals or angels, one would arrive at an essential understanding of any instance of those things. Believing that they had hit upon an understanding of the essential nature of a sacrament, therefore, medieval Catholic theologians assumed that what was true of some of them had to be true of all of them.

Medieval thought was like Greek thought in another respect, too, in that it strove for logical coherence in its theories. And having found a theory of sacraments which enabled them to give a coherent account of the Eucharist, baptism, confirmation, and orders, the theologians of the Middle Ages sought to bring that same kind of coherence to their explanations of the remaining three sacraments. In matrimony the sacramental reality produced by the rite seemed to most theologians to be the bond of marriage between the husband and wife. Marriage produced a real change in a man and a woman: it made the man a husband and it made the woman a wife. Furthermore, the marriage bond was a sign that they should be united in love the way Christ is united to the Church, and that they would receive the grace they needed to fulfill their marital obligations to each other. It was harder to determine the sacramental realities involved in the remaining two sacraments. Some claimed that the sacramental reality produced by penance was the repentance of the penitent, while others held that it was reconciliation with the Church; in either case the sacrament received would in turn permit the grace of God to effect the forgiveness of sins. Finally, most theologians came to agree that the sacramental reality produced by the rite of extreme unction was the commitment of the dying person to the mercy of God, and that this could have the effect of either physical recovery or spiritual strengthening.

It can be readily seen that the sacramental realities produced by the various sacramental rites were not all of the same order: one was a real change in bread and wine; three were permanent changes in the soul of the subject of the rite; three were less permanent changes. But whatever obscurity there was in the notion of the *sacramentum et res*, it was slight in comparison to the logical clarity that it brought to the medieval attempt to understand the Church's sacramental system. Once the schoolmen adopted the three-fold analysis of the nature of sacraments, they had a conceptual scheme that enabled them to approach an entire range of related theological questions: the nature of the sacramental character itself, the meaning of valid and invalid sacraments, the nature of sacramental causality, and many others. The notion of the sacramental reality thus became a central concept in the whole Catholic theology of sacraments; its importance cannot be overestimated.

Perhaps the most significant result of this development was the fact that the word *sacramentum* was commonly applied to the sacramental reality produced by the rite as well as to the rite itself. Following the example of Augustine and other Church Fathers, the medieval theologians came to speak regularly of 'administering' and 'receiving' the sacraments; but when they did so they were referring to the *sacramentum* which was also a *res*, a thing, a reality which could be given and received. They were referring to the sacramental reality conferred or bestowed by the rite, not to the sacramental rite itself. Thus the entire Catholic theology of the sacraments in the Middle Ages eventually became a theology of the *sacramentum et res*, a philosophical explanation of the sacramental effect that was believed to be produced by each of the Church's seven major liturgical rites.

3. The sacramental character

The theology of the sacramental character had not developed much between the fifth and twelfth centuries, when the medievals picked up where the Fathers had left off. Augustine had settled some basic questions about the baptismal seal: that it was a stamp of Christ impressed on the soul, that it could not be lost, that it could be called a *sacramentum*. Later it was generally believed that confirmation also bestowed an indelible character on the soul, and after a period of hesitation it was decided that ordination conferred such a character as well.

Now, however, in the drive to develop a comprehensive theology of the sacraments, further questions were raised: What was the exact nature of the sacramental character? Was it something real in the soul or was it just a special relationship between the soul and God? If it was something real, what kind of reality was it? Why should it be called a sacrament if it was invisible? Was there a philosophical explanation for the fact that it could not be lost? Was there any difference between the baptismal character and that given by the other sacraments?

The search for the answers to these and similar questions led Catholic thinkers into some of the more esoteric areas of medieval theology. Moreover, neither the answers given nor the reasons behind them were always uniform; they varied from theologian to theologian. Still, in the course of the Middle Ages a general consensus emerged around most of the major issues, and quite often the direction of that agreement can be found in the writings of Thomas Aquinas, not only because of the comprehensiveness of his theology but also because of its influence on later theologians. By focusing mainly on Aquinas, therefore, it is possible to draw a brief but fairly accurate picture of the state of Catholic sacramental theology during this period.

The main development in the theology of the sacraments in the twelfth century had been the introduction of *sacramentum et res* as a workable solution to the problem posed almost a hundred years earlier by Berengar. Both Hugh of St Victor and Peter Lombard had used that terminology in reference to the Eucharist, and it was largely through the influence of the latter's *Sentences* that it gained acceptance among other theologians and began to be applied to other sacraments. In time it became a standard term in the Catholic theological vocabulary, so when Aquinas began his career around the middle of the thirteenth century he could write: 'The sacraments add two things to the soul. One is a sacramental reality like the character or some other adornment of the soul; the other is a reality only, namely grace' (*On Book IV of the Sentences* 1, 1, 4). Catholic thinkers in the thirteenth century, then, understood the character to be *sacramentum et res*, a sacramental reality. But this presented a special problem: How could the character be rightfully called a sacrament?

Sacramentum in earlier times had referred mainly to observable rites and sacred objects; and although Augustine had argued for its applicability to the baptismal seal, he himself often used the word to refer to rituals and the things used in them. In fact, Augustine's definition of a sacrament as a visible sign of invisible grace clearly referred to observable rites and seemed to contradict the idea of the seal's being a sacrament. How could the seal be a sign of anything if it was spiritual and therefore invisible? Some theologians speculated about its being seen by God or the angels, but the more accepted solution was to give a broad interpretation to Augustine's words. *Visible* could mean either visible to the eye or visible to the mind, that is, knowable. And since it was possible to know who had the seal by knowing who had been baptized, theologians reasoned that the seal was in that sense visible. Thus Aquinas argued that the baptismal character could be known because the reception of the sacrament could be seen. And others argued that the character was visible through its observable effects: membership in the Church in the case of baptism, firmness in the faith in the case of confirmation, position in the hierarchy in the case of holy orders.

The solution to this problem led naturally to the solution to the next: Were the characters given by baptism, confirmation, and orders the same or different? As long as the character was considered to be completely invisible there was no way to answer this question. But as soon as it was decided that the character was visible through the sacramental rite and its observable effects, it was clear that the characters for each of the sacraments must be different.

But what of the metaphysical status of the character? How was one to understand it philosophically? Granted it was a spiritual reality, some kind of impression or change wrought in the soul, how was one to understand the metaphorical words *impression, seal, image, character*? The Aristotelian philosophy which the medieval theologians had adopted gave them at least one answer immediately. Whatever the character was, the reason why the Fathers had been right in calling it indelible was because the character had to be received in the human soul, which was immaterial and therefore not subject to decay. A metaphysical alteration in the soul, then, would be permanent, it would last forever, it could not be lost.

Aristotle's philosophy offered a number of categories for thinking about the soul and its abilities: faculty, habit, disposition, power, activity, passion. But Aristotle, having lived before the birth of Christ, never had to deal with questions of Christian theology. Medieval thinkers thus found themselves faced with the task of deciding which of his categories could be used to think about the nature of the character. During the first half of the thirteenth century they tried to adapt one category and then another to their needs, but each of their proposals ran into philosophical difficulties that seemed insurmountable. It was Aquinas who finally developed an acceptable solution by reinterpreting some of Aristotle's categories in a way that made it possible to apply them in one way to the natural order, to human nature which was fallen but not yet redeemed, and in another way to the supernatural order, to the human soul which was enlightened by faith and elevated by grace.

Although the details of Aquinas' theory of the supernaturally elevated soul were sometimes abstruse, the ideas behind it were fairly fundamental to Christianity. Just as in creation God made man in his own image, so now through the sacraments Christ made man anew in his own image. Christ was essentially a mediator between God and man, and in that sense a priest. In the words of the Epistle to the Hebrews, '. . . in Jesus, the Son of God, we have a supreme high priest who has gone through to the highest heaven . . . one who has been tempted in every way that we are, though he was without sin' (Hebrews 4:14–15). So Christ was truly a man, but he alone of all men loved God so perfectly that his whole life was a continual offering to his Father, culminating in his complete self-surrender on the cross. Christ, then, was a redeemer priest; and he brought about man's redemption by transforming and elevating human nature, making it possible for others to be born into a new dimension of existence, that same divine dimension in which he had lived his whole life. The means of entering into and sustaining that new life he had left with his Church, and these were the sacraments.

The sacramental character, therefore, was a transformation of a person's soul, a spiritual conformation to the redemptive, self-sacrificing priesthood of Christ. Augustine had spoken of the seal of baptism as the image of Christ, but for Aquinas it was not as though a person were stamped on the arm with a tattoo; rather it was as though the whole person were cast into a new mould and emerged in a new image, that of Christ, who loved and was obedient to the Father. Still, receiving the gift of new life was one thing; using that gift and living that life was another. This was why those who had been baptized could still sin, why those who had been confirmed could still deny the faith, why those who had been ordained could still live for themselves rather than God. Each sacrament brought with it a slightly different yet more complete participation in Christ's priesthood: all were called to new life, all adults were called to a mature life of faith, some were called to continue Christ's sacramental ministry in the Church.

In the categories of Aristotelian philosophy, the sacramental character was therefore a power, but a supernatural power that could be given only by God. The character of baptism was a liberation from the deformity of original sin, an openness to receiving the other sacraments. The character of confirmation was a power to live a life of active faith, an ability to publicly confess Christ, a capacity to participate fully in the Church's worship. The character of orders was a disposition to service in the Church, a capability of preaching the Gospel, a power to administer the sacraments so that others might enter and grow in the Christian life. The powers conferred by the characters were thus also orientations toward activity, just as the power of sight is oriented toward seeing, as the power of emotion is oriented toward feeling, and as the power of intelligence is oriented toward understanding. And therefore, just as in the natural order one had to open one's eyes to see, one had to open one's heart to feel, and one had to open one's mind to understand, so also in the supernatural order having the supernatural power to participate in the priesthood of Christ did not mean that it would be automatically used.

In fact, there was one important difference between a person's natural powers and the supernatural powers of a Christian. The use of natural powers was an activity of the person who had them; one used one's own power to see, to feel, to understand. But the exercise of supernatural powers was always also an activity of the one who gave them, and they were God-given powers. Thus the use of those powers was always dependent on a person's openness to receiving God's gifts, and their exercise was never a purely human activity but always a cooperation with divine activity, with God acting in one's soul. One who was baptized always had to look upon others who afterward fell into sin and say with Paul, 'There but for the grace of God go I.' A Christian at worship thanked and praised God, yet he was aware that somehow his worship was somehow also the work of God's spirit within him. Receiving a spiritual power through the sacraments, therefore, oriented one toward grace, but it was not the same as cooperating with it.

In summary, during the thirteenth century the sacramental character came to be understood by Aquinas and others as something real, a supernatural power that enabled a person to cooperate with God's grace. It could not be lost or destroyed because it was a power of a human soul, which was immaterial and, according to Catholic teaching, immortal. The character or power could not be seen, and yet it could be known through the sacramental rite in which it was received; and so it could legitimately be called a sign or a *sacramentum*. Finally, since the character was known through the sacramental rite, and since there were three rites, each of which signified something different, there had to be three different sacramental characters. The premises behind these conclusions could be found in scriptural and patristic texts as they were understood in the Middle Ages. The style of reasoning used was that of classical Greek thought. And the conclusions themselves made sense in the light of the sacramental practices of the medieval Church and the religious beliefs and experiences of medieval Christians. But there was more to sacramental theology than the explanation of the character, and to understand it more fully it is necessary to learn more about its background.

4. Aristotle, Aquinas, and the sacraments

If the scriptures and the Fathers gave medieval theologians something to think about, it was the Greek philosopher Aristotle who gave them a way to think about it. His writings were virtually unknown to the Fathers, who preferred the idealism of Plato and the sometimes mystical metaphysics of the neoplatonic philosophers. Many of his works had been preserved in the great libraries of the eastern empire, but in the seventh and eighth centuries the Moslem conquest swept westward across Africa and pushed northward into Asia Minor, and Christian Europe lost all but the names of most of them. Some of his writings did survive in the west, however. They were a collection of works on logic, which began to be studied first in the monastery schools and then in the cathedral schools as the medieval renaissance began. Those who adopted Aristotle's logic developed a style of thinking and reasoning which soon became a trademark of the schools. Those who taught in them were known as schoolmen or *scholastici*, and their method of philosophizing came to be called scholasticism. Berengar of Tours, for example, was an early scholastic who tried to analyze the doctrine of the Eucharist using Aristotelian logic.

In the meanwhile, a number of Moslem theologians had read Aristotle and had chosen him as their philosophical mentor. Then, in the twelfth century, Christian intellectuals near Moorish Spain began to learn about the missing writings of Aristotle which had been translated into Arabic. Wanting to meet Moslem theology on its own grounds, they obtained copies of the missing works and had them translated into Latin. These translations of translations, unclear and erroneous in parts, were then brought to Paris for study, and slowly the main body of Aristotelian writings was introduced to the schools of Europe. Early in the thirteenth century copies of these writings in the original Greek were discovered in Constantinople and translated directly into Latin. And one of the first persons in the west to study these more accurate translations was the Dominican monk Thomas Aquinas.

The effect of Aristotle on the west was incalculable. In his books on psychology and biology, physics and metaphysics, politics and ethics, Christians discovered an encyclopedic knowledge of the world which was completely different from their own. And yet this Greek philosopher, born almost four centuries before Christ, was evidently a master not only of logic, but of all the sciences then known. Some Church leaders feared the influence that a pagan thinker might have on students, and his works were banned from the universities more than once. Nevertheless, through the efforts of Aquinas, his teacher Albert, and others, Aristotle's ideas were gradually accepted as complementing rather than contradicting the knowledge that Christendom called its own. Eventually, Aristotelian science and philosophy were taught in all the schools and incorporated into the medieval view of reality. And Aristotle himself came to be so esteemed that the schoolmen, instead of referring to him by name, called him simply the Philosopher.

The Aristotelian vocabulary was replete with technical terms such as *substance* and *accident, matter* and *form, power* and *activity*, and medieval thinkers did their best to understand their meanings and then use them to develop philosophical explanations of the Christian mysteries. *Transubstantiation*, for example, was basically an Aristotelian way of speaking about the change of bread and wine into the body and blood of Christ: the 'substance' or reality changed, while the 'accidents' or appearances did not. Aquinas and the scholastics also spoke about sacramental rituals, the *sacramentum tantum*, as being 'composed of matter and form' since according to Aristotle everything in this world was composed of matter and form, and rituals were things in this world. What Aristotle meant was that everything in the world around us has, as it were, two basic aspects. On the one hand it is sensible or experienceable in some way: it is seeable, hearable, touchable, tasteable, or smellable. On the other hand it is also intelligible or understandable: it has a meaning, we have an idea or concept of what it is. Now, what we see of something is very often the material it is made of – wood, stone, metal, and so forth; hence, Aristotle referred to the sensible aspect of things as their 'matter'. Likewise, very often the shape of a thing gives us an idea of what it is – we tell a woman from a man or a table from a chair by their shapes; hence, Aristotle referred to the intelligible aspect of things as their 'form.'

Theologians in the Middle Ages not only agreed with Aristotle's analysis, but they also noticed that ecclesiastical rituals had something like a 'matter' and a 'form' to them. On the one hand, there were sensible gestures and objects used in them, and on the other, there was the meaning that the rituals had. Moreover, the meaning of the rituals were often given in words used – the pouring of water was just the pouring of water, without the words 'I baptize thee. . .' So the scholastics used the terms *matter* and *form* as a kind of technical shorthand to talk about the experienceable and understandable aspects of sacramental rituals.

For Aristotle, *science* meant a knowledge of the causes of things, and the scholastics endeavoured to make theology a science in the Aristotelian sense of the word. Now, *cause* was also a technical word in the Aristotelian vocabulary, and broadly speaking a cause was anything on which something else depended. Thus, for example, matter and form were causes in the Aristotelian way of looking at things, since in order to be what it was a thing had to be sensible and have certain meaning. Purposes were also causes: they were the reasons why things were made or done. Causes in the modern sense of the word – like a spark causing a fire – were also causes for Aristotle, but they were only one kind of cause. The important point to realize about the Aristotelian method of analyzing causes, however, is that it worked backward, as it were, from effect to cause.

Aquinas realized this, and he applied this method of causal analysis to the sacraments. Why was this woman a Christian? Because she was baptized. What caused sins to be forgiven? Confession and the absolution of the priest. How is it that Christ is present in the Eucharist? It was caused by the words of consecration spoken over the bread and wine. Sacraments were causes in the Aristotelian sense, therefore, because various aspects of the Christian life depended on them. Moreover, different aspects of the Christian life could be traced back to different sacraments. The reason why priests were different from married people was because they had received different sacraments. The experience of the presence of Christ and a feeling of love for others could be directly related to the reception of communion. The restful resignation (or even the remarkable recovery) of a dying man might be traced back to the fact that he had received the last rites. So it was clear to Aquinas, using this kind of causal analysis, that different effects had different sacramental causes, or to put it the more common way, that different sacraments had different effects.

Some of these effects were sacramental realities such as the character of confirmation or the bond of marriage. These were known by faith, and their cause was the sacramental ritual itself. Thus, for example, Catholics could know by faith that Christ was present in the Eucharist even when they did not experience a sense of his presence. Other effects were graces, sacramental graces: the unselfish love of a husband and wife in marriage, the feeling of spiritual cleansing in confession, a happy and productive ministry in priesthood, the spiritual gifts of wisdom, understanding, fortitude, and piety from confirmation. They were graces because they were God's free gifts; he owed them to no one. But to those who were open to receiving them, he gave them freely.

Almost every aspect of Christian life in a Christian culture such as medieval Europe could be connected in one way or another with one or another of the sacraments. Both the sacramental realities that Aquinas believed in and saw evidenced in the society around him, and the graces that he experienced and saw manifested in others, could therefore be related to sacramental rites as their causes. But Aquinas also insisted that the sacraments were not their ultimate cause. In themselves the rites were only symbolic gestures; the ultimate cause of all sacramental effects was God himself. For the sacramental realities were supernatural powers orienting a person to receive grace, and the sacramental graces were God-given gifts. The sacraments were, so to speak, God's instruments,

vehicles, channels of grace. In Aristotelian terminology the sacraments were instrumental causes, things through which God acted
in people's lives, creating and sustaining the Church, bringing
people to salvation, and making them holy.

But if sacraments were merely instrumental causes of grace, why
did Aquinas claim that they were necessary? Why could God not
bring people to salvation without intermediary symbols and
gestures? In framing his answer, Aquinas once again argued from
effect to cause, only this time the effect considered was the sacramental rituals themselves. Sacraments were necessary, he
reasoned, because signs were a necessary part of human life.
Whenever people communicated, they used signs: sounds in the
air, marks on a page, and so forth. Signs were instrumental causes
of knowledge; through signs people came to know what others
were trying to say to them. In other words, signs were instrumental
causes but they were necessary because they were needed for
communication. In the same way, he argued, sacraments were
instrumental causes but they too were necessary; they were signs of
sacred realities that God wanted to communicate to people for
their own benefit. Without signs such as the sacraments people
would not come to know or experience God's salvation. It was a
conclusion that made a great deal of sense in a world where books
were scarce and few could read; for most Christians the sacramental liturgies were the main form of religious instruction.

Finally, since it was God who acted in and through the sacraments, it was clear to Aquinas – as it had been clear to Augustine
in the case of baptism – that the real effectiveness of sacraments
did not depend on the worthiness of the minister. People knew by
faith that they had received sacramental realities, and they experienced in their lives sacramental graces, regardless of the sanctity of
the person who performed the ritual. Early in the thirteenth
century, theologians had wrestled with this question, and the main
objections to saying that the sacramental effects did not depend at
all on the minister or recipient came from those who envisioned
cases where the rite might be performed in jest or in ignorance.
Suppose, for example, that a child playfully poured water over an
unbaptized friend's head and said the words of baptism; would the
friend be baptized? Or suppose that a priest were teaching a
student how to say the Mass and said the words of consecration
over an unnoticed piece of bread; would it automatically become
the body of Christ? From considering marginal cases such as these
and reflecting on liturgies that were genuinely sacramental, the
scholastics came to acknowledge that intentions did play a role in

sacramental rites: both the minister and the recipient must have the intention of participating in a sacramental rite, or as they would have said it, of doing what the Church does. Without that intention the rite would be an empty ritual, and so there would be no sacramental effect.

Barring such bizarre circumstances, however, the scholastics generally agreed that it was the rite, not the minister, that was the cause of sacramental effects. How otherwise could one explain that most of the fathers considered the sacraments of heretics and schismatics to be valid? How otherwise could one explain the experience of union with Christ after receiving communion from a priest whom one later discovered was living in sin? The scholastics' way of referring to this independence of the rite from the sanctity of orthodoxy of the minister was to say that the effects of the sacraments were caused *ex opere operato*, literally, 'by the work worked', or 'from the doing of the thing done'.

As already said, the twelfth and thirteenth centuries marked a high point in medieval theology. These two centuries saw the rediscovery of the Church's patristic heritage, the organization of theology into major areas of inquiry, and the working out of an intellectual method to deal with theological problems. In the hands of theologians like Aquinas, the scholastic method provided the Catholic Church with logical and coherent explanations for the sacraments and for all the other mysteries of the Christian faith. Catholic thinkers of that age sought to explain as much as they could of their religion, without explaining it away. It was an age of *fides quaerens intellectum*, of faith seeking understanding.

But there were also other tendencies in medieval Christianity, tendencies that were more practical than theoretical. There were those who were more concerned with the proper administration of the sacraments than with the philosophical explanations of them. There were also tendencies that were more analytic than synthetic. Aquinas and the scholastics had woven a theological synthesis, but it was not perfect; and the tendency of later thinkers was to find the flaws in the system. Lastly there were events, political and otherwise, which had nothing directly to do with theology, but which made the medieval synthesis tend to be less and less relevant to what was actually happening in Christendom. It is to those tendencies that we must now turn.

5. Legalism, nominalism, and magic

Peter Lombard's *Sentences* was not the only medieval compendium
that had a great impact on the Catholic sacraments. Around 1140
Francis Gratian published a comprehensive treatise on ecclesiastical or canon law in which he gathered, organized, and edited
materials on almost every aspect of the Church's institutional functions. The original title of the work was *The Agreement of Disagreeing
Canons*, but it was popularly known as Gratian's *Decree*. Like the
Sentences, it was mostly a collection of texts from other sources, but
the texts included in the *Decree* were letters, decrees, and directives
of popes, bishops, and councils. Like the *Sentences*, it cited authorities on both sides of disputed issues, to which Gratian added his
own opinions. Like the *Sentences* it included a large section, the
whole third part, on the sacraments, but the *Decree* was more
concerned with questions of administration (for example, whether
or not lay people may baptize, or who may legally enter into
marriage) than with questions of theology.

Also like the *Sentences*, soon after its appearance the *Decree*
became a primary source book for students of canon law and the
main reference book for those who needed to be informed about
ecclesiastical regulations. Since it contained conflicting rules and
opinions it could never be adopted as an official code of canon law,
but since there was as yet no unified judicial code in the western
Church it continued to influence ecclesiastical decisions for a
number of centuries. In regard to the sacraments, it had the effect
of bringing an additional measure of uniformity to the rites and
the rules surrounding them.

It was only slowly that theology and canon law developed into
separate disciplines, but from the very beginning there were some
important differences between the theological and canonical
approaches to the sacraments. Theologians were primarily
concerned with understanding the sacraments and explaining how
they functioned within the spiritual life of the Christian; canonists
were primarily concerned with regulating the sacraments and
determining how they functioned within the institutional life of
the Church. In theology, for example, the main effect of baptism
was the reception of grace; in canon law, the importance of
baptism was that it made a person a member of the Church with
certain rights and obligations. Also, theologians were primarily
interested in the essential nature of the sacraments; they sought to
understand what they basically were and how they worked when
they were devoutly entered into. Canonists on the other hand were

primarily interested in individual sacramental acts; they sought to specify what each particular rite must contain in order for it to do its spiritual work. Thus in theology the Mass was regarded as a sacramental participation in Christ's offering of himself to the Father; in canon law the mass was treated as a sacramental ritual containing certain basic elements such as prayers, readings, gestures, and the materials for consecration.

As the theological and canonical interpretations of the sacraments were developing, they influenced one another. Initially it was the theology of the sacraments that had the greater impact; later it was the other way around. Until the twelfth century, sacraments had been regarded primarily as signs rather than as causes of spiritual realities; even in the thirteenth century, influential theologians like Bonaventure and Scotus held theories that explained the sacraments as signs rather than as causes of God's grace. But Aquinas insisted that this explanation did not do justice to the writings of the Fathers and the testimony of the saints, and in the long run it was his causal explanation of the sacraments which the canonists accepted. Still, for Aquinas, the sacraments were primarily signs: they were effective because they were signs, and they produced their effects the same way that signs do, as instrumental causes. But for the canonists the crucial point was that they were effective signs: they were causes of sacramental realities and grace in the soul. And for them this meant that great care had to be taken to preserve the signs by administering the sacraments correctly, in order to ensure that they kept their spiritual effectiveness. Put succinctly, Aquinas' insistence on the causal nature of the sacraments led canonists to insist on the proper performance of the rituals.

In time, this emphasis on proper performance led paradoxically to a kind of minimalist attitude toward the sacramental rites. Instead of suggesting that sacramental liturgies should be richly symbolic and personally involving so that people could experience their spiritual effects fully, the idea of sacraments as causal signs suggested that there were certain minimum standards that had to be met if their spiritual effectiveness were not to be lost entirely. Would a baptism be effective if dirty water were used, for instance, or if the words were not properly pronounced? How much of the Mass could be eliminated without affecting the transubstantiation of the bread and wine? What essentials had to be observed if extreme unction were administered in an emergency? Questions of this sort concerned the 'validity' of the sacraments. A valid sacrament was one which met the minimum ritual requirements; if any of these requirements were not met the ritual was considered to be invalid, that is, it was not really a sacrament and it therefore had no sacramental effects.

It was agreed that in order for a ritual to be effective it must have the proper matter and form, be performed by the proper minister, and be done with the proper intention. The terms *matter* and *form* were borrowed from theology, but to the canonists the matter was simply the materials and gestures used in the rite, and the form was the prescribed words that were said. Certain kinds of oil could be used in confirmation, for example, while others could not. Again, if the priest did not make the sign of the cross over the host during Mass, it would still be consecrated. Or again, a confession in which the priest omitted some of the words of absolution could still be valid. The proper minister for most of the sacraments was a priest, but there were exceptions. A lay person could validly baptize if the proper words were said while the water was poured; even a non-Christian could baptize under exceptional circumstances, as long as it was done with the intention of performing a Catholic sacramental act. A bishop was the ordinary minister of confirmation, but he could validly delegate that power to a priest. But a bishop was the only valid minister of holy orders; even if a priest performed the rite with permission it would be invalid. The proper intention was usually the general intent to do what the Church did, but it was particularly important in the case of matrimony. The bride and groom were considered the ministers of the sacrament; the priest was merely an official witness of their union. And so if a couple went through the motions of a wedding ceremony without really intending to be united in Christian marriage, the sacrament would be void and the marriage could be annulled.

What, however, was the effect that a valid sacrament was supposed to have? It was the *sacramentum et res*, the sacramental reality caused by each of the particular sacraments: the seal of baptism, the characters of confirmation and orders, the bond of marriage, reconciliation with the Church, the commitment of the soul to God, the body and blood of Christ. Canonically considered, if the sacramental ritual was validly performed, the sacramental effect occurred *ex opere operato*; that is, by virtue of the performance of the proper ritual, the sacrament caused what it signified.

But what about grace, the second effect of the sacraments? According to theologians after Aquinas, the sacraments always caused grace but it was not always received. As they interpreted Aquinas' theory, sacramental grace was caused not by the observable rite, the *sacramentum tantum*, but by the sacramental reality, the *sacramentum et res*. One could infer the existence of the sacramental reality from the valid performance of the rite; but since grace was a hidden reality, a *res tantum*, freely given by God, one could never be certain whether or not another person had actually received sacramental graces. One could be certain that God offered the graces through the sacramental reality since God always offers his gifts freely, but it was always possible that the person who received the sacrament was not also open to receiving the sacramental gifts.

Thus the graces caused by a sacrament came to be called its 'fruits'. A sacrament was considered fruitful if the one who received it also received the graces appropriate to the sacrament; if in fact no grace was received, it was considered unfruitful. And what were the graces, these fruits? Certainly they could be religious experiences such as having a sense of Christ's presence in the Eucharist or feeling God's mercy in penance; but they could also be other things such as children in marriage, a priest's talent for inspirational sermons, or the strength to live a virtuous life, looked upon as gifts, graces from God.

The most prevalent explanation for why a person might receive a sacrament and yet experience none or few of its graces was that the recipient did not have the proper disposition to receive them. Pride, fear, greed, love of self, or some other such attitude might be a sort of spiritual obstacle blocking his cooperation with the graces that God was offering through the sacrament. Even God respected man's will, the theologians reasoned, and so he would not force his gifts on anyone who was not disposed to receiving them.

This distinction between the sacramental reality and the sacramental graces also helped theologians to explain what they saw as the 'reviviscence' of the sacraments in certain cases. Suppose, for instance, that a married man after a period of infidelity to his wife suddenly realized the anguish he was causing her and renounced his mistress; or less dramatically, suppose that a baptized and confirmed Christian experienced a deeper religious conversion many years after receiving those sacraments. According to the theory of reviviscence, God had been continually offering his grace since the time that the sacrament had been received, but it was only when the obstacle of sin or vice was removed that grace could flow through the sacramental reality into the soul. The sacrament, or rather the effects of the sacrament, had thus revived after a period of dormancy.

The theological distinction between the sacramental reality and sacramental grace was helpful to canon lawyers as well. The sacramental reality could be considered to be unfailingly bestowed by a valid sacramental rite, and therefore who was baptized, married, or ordained could be a matter of public record. But sacramental graces were private affairs, governed by the inner disposition of the soul. No one could be sure, for example, whether the harmony between a husband and wife was a result of their natural abilities or whether it was a supernatural help from God given through the sacrament of marriage. Therefore the canonists could consider a sacrament valid even if it did not bear fruit, that is, even if no graces were received, even if receiving the sacrament made no noticeable difference in a person's life.

The theologians and canon lawyers of the Middle Ages also drew one other important distinction in reference to the sacraments which, like the ones already mentioned, still survives in the Catholic Church's code of canon law. This distinction regarded the 'liceity' or legality of sacramental rites. Briefly, a sacrament was considered licit if it was administered in accordance with all of the regulations stipulated by canon law; it was considered illicit if one or more of those regulations was violated. Thus to change or omit prescribed parts of the Mass would be illicit, and the same would be true for any of the other sacramental rites. Likewise, for a priest to celebrate Mass or administer other sacraments in a diocese without the permission of the local bishop would be canonically illegal. However, in neither of these cases would the sacraments administered be considered invalid, unless the conditions for validity had also been disregarded.

This difference between validity and liceity was important because it meant that sacraments which were illicitly administered were often canonically valid. Thus if a priest from another diocese unlawfully heard a dying person's confession or administered extreme unction, those who went through the sacramental ritual unaware of his legal impediment could still be assured that they had truly received a sacrament. Even more seriously, if a deposed or heretical bishop ordained men to the priesthood, he would do so illicitly but the priests would be validly ordained; and the sacraments that they in turn administered would be likewise valid even though illicit.

Although this approach to the administration of the sacraments became explicit only in the course of the development of canon law itself, the legal and theological principles behind it went back to Augustine and his position in the Donatist controversy. And by accepting the distinction between validity and liceity, Catholics today can regard the sacraments of Orthodox Churches as valid even if not canonically licit. Yet if the distinction has its brighter side in an ecumenical age, it had its darker side in the Middle Ages. At a time when canon law was still in formation and rules for the proper administration of the sacraments were not yet codified, the minimalist rules for the valid administration of the sacraments, instead of being the barest acceptable standards, tended to become the norm. This is not to say that there were no beautifully performed liturgies in the Middle Ages, or that there were no devout and conscientious priests, or that there were no Catholics who reverently participated in the sacramental rites of the day. There were many, especially in the monasteries and in the cathedrals and in the university chapels. But there were also many – the peasants in the countryside, the craftsmen in the cities, and even the slowly growing middle class of merchants and professionals – who little understood the subtleties of canon law. Their acquaintance with the sacraments was all too often an experience of rituals reduced to their bare essentials, and their understanding of the sacraments was all too often a mechanistic idea of sacramental causality. To them, the rite produced what it signified, nothing more and nothing less: the washing away of original sin, people confirmed in the Church, the body and blood of Christ, the forgiving of mortal and venial sins, married people, priests, and spiritual readiness for death.

And there was plenty of death. In the fourteenth century, bubonic and other plagues swept across Europe, killing an estimated twenty-five million people. In some places, two thirds to three quarters of the population died within a few years, though in other places the plague took only a tenth or a fourth. And the plague was indiscriminate: it took young and old, poor and rich, saint and sinner. But those who braved the Black Death to nurse the afflicted or bury the dead took an even greater risk of infection, and they were often the young who had strength, the poor who could not escape to a less pestilent region, and the saintly who cared more for others than for themselves. The plague also made no distinction between artist and labourer, between merchant and farmer, between educated and illiterate, and in the course of that century the medieval renaissance came to an untimely end. Culture declined, trade dwindled, schools closed.

The Black Death put an end to the theological renaissance, too. Aquinas and Bonaventure had both died in 1274, long before the plague years, but there was no one who was able to continue their work, to carry on where they had left off. There might have been, among the monks and scholars of the Dominicans and the

Franciscans, but many monks died tending the sick, and the schools were often vacated for fear of contamination. In addition to commenting on the *Sentences*, beginning theology students now wrote commentaries on the *summas* of the past masters as well, and possibly on the lately recovered writings of Aristotle. It was a tedious introduction to the divine science, but it seemed like the logical thing to do. It had worked well in the previous century, and besides, it was the only theological method that they knew.

But Aquinas' *Summa Theologica* was deceptive. It did not represent what Aquinas did, the way he had worked out his conclusions. It only presented his conclusions already worked out, along with summary reasons for and against them. One of the hallmarks of Aquinas' theological method was that it was largely inductive: he reasoned from the way things were to explanations of why they were that way. Just as Augustine had developed his theology largely by reflecting on the beliefs and practices prevalent in his day, Aquinas often drew his ideas from reflections on his own religious experience, which was that of a saintly monk. And yet his own writings, especially the *Summa*, hardly show this. His method of presenting his ideas was often more deductive in appearance, beginning from more general consideration and working toward more specific questions and applications. In his own mind he reasoned from effect to cause, but in his writings it seemed that he often moved from cause to effect. Thus God, for example, who for Aquinas was the ultimate cause of everything in the universe, was treated at the beginning of the *Summa Theologica*, while the sacraments, around which revolved his life as a priest and a monk, were treated in almost the last section, left unfinished. Aquinas and his better contemporaries knew what they were talking about when they talked about the effects of the sacraments, for they were often talking about their own lives. But they did not write about their lives and their religious experiences; they wrote using the customary categories of their day: matter and form, substance and accidents, nature and grace, and so forth. And those who later read what they wrote tended to think they were talking about entities called matter and form, substances hidden under visible accidents, metaphysical objects called essences, and supernatural influxes called graces.

Thus the later scholastics erected an elaborate intellectual system of theological terms that had little or no reference to the lives that people actually led or to the religious experiences that they actually had. The sacraments that were received were spiritual realities in the soul that were neither experienced nor known except in virtue of the sacramental rites. The sacramental characters were invisible signs impressed on the soul distinguishing Christian from non-Christian, confirmed from unconfirmed, priest from lay person. The powers that the sacraments gave were hidden spiritual powers: baptism prepared the soul to receive the other sacraments, holy orders gave special priestly powers, all of them gave the power to receive sacramental graces. The causal effectiveness of the sacramental rituals was guaranteed by God, who gave the graces, and by Christ through whose merits they were distributed. But the grace that they caused was an unexperienced entity, given to those whose souls were properly disposed, yet hidden and unknown except by faith.

Thus the Aristotelian causal analysis that Aquinas had used was reversed. Now the first cause was God, who through the Incarnation of his Son had established the Church and instituted the seven sacraments. Since the rites were divinely ordained, they worked by the power of God, and they caused their effects automatically as long as they were correctly performed. Their proper performance was guarded by canon law, which gave the conditions for their validity and liceity, enumerated their effects, and indicated their necessity. And now the sacraments were necessary for salvation not because people need signs, but because only the Catholic Church had the sacraments, and 'outside the Church there is no salvation.'

For the twelfth and thirteenth-century theologians, arguments from authority had great weight, not only because their theological training began with the *Sentences*, but also because quoting the scriptures and the Fathers was their way of tying their own work to the ancient Christian tradition. Yet when these theologians developed their own ideas they felt no qualms about choosing one Father over another, or about interpreting a text in favourable light, because in their writings they were talking mainly about what they themselves had worked out, not about what the Fathers had said. But those who followed in the fourteenth century tended to do otherwise. They followed what they believed to be the example of Aquinas and others, and since the great scholastics had always quoted authorities and only rarely referred to their own experience in their written works, they tended to argue more from authority than from experience. Thus, by following the style of the *summas* and being unaware of the style of their authors, the later scholastics tended to write about what Aquinas and the others wrote instead of thinking the way they thought. It was as though they assumed that since the answers in theology had all been worked out, all they had to do was study and comprehend them.

Those who followed this tried and proven *via antiqua*, the old way, formed themselves into schools – not new colleges or universities but schools of thought. The Dominican school followed Aquinas, the Franciscan school followed Bonaventure or Scotus; there were those who followed less well-known scholastics, and there were those who preferred Augustine. But there were also those who rejected this bookish repetition of the past and struck out on what they called the *via moderna*, the modern way. They were skeptical of the metaphysical speculations of the scholastics and the unproductive rivalries between the schools, and they sought a way to cut through both of them. The tool they chose was logic, the logic of Aristotle, used not in the service of theology but in the service for which the ancient Greek had originally intended it, that of critical reasoning. And they interpreted Aristotle's categories not as categories of reality but as categories of thought, referring only to words and the way they were used. Foremost among these new thinkers was William of Ockham, in England.

The label that was eventually given to this new way of thinking was 'nominalism,' since it was a philosophical method that focused on words, *nomina* in Latin. The nominalists insisted that the metaphysical realism of the scholastics was a mistake. To them it was obvious that matter and form, essence and existence, substance and accidents were not real in themselves. The real things in the world were individuals: people and animals, trees and stones, and so forth. The metaphysical terms that the scholastics used were actually just concepts, abstractions, products of the mind. The scholastics had believed, for example, that there were metaphysical principles which could be used to deduce scientific knowledge about the real world, principles such as the notion that every real thing must have a cause. But the nominalists contended that these metaphysical principles were in fact logical principles, rules of thought which helped one to learn about the real world, but which said nothing directly about the real world.

One by one the metaphysical assumptions of scholastic theology came under attack. Ockham denied that it was possible to prove that there was only one God or to know anything definite about him using reason alone, although as a Catholic he still believed that God existed and as a theologian he accepted what had been revealed about him. He also denied that it was possible to prove the existence or immortality of the human soul: the soul was at best a plausible explanation for human life and activity, and immortality could be hoped for but it could not be demonstrated. Again here, though, Ockham was willing to admit that human beings have immortal souls, for this was a truth of faith; what he denied was that it was philosophically provable.

The uncertainty of metaphysics was matched by a similar uncertainty in ethics. Philosophers might use reason to discover ethical principles or formulate moral codes, but these were not strictly provable. They were simply practical guidelines, general rules that should govern human behaviour in society, and philosophical reasoning could never demonstrate that they had to be true. If indeed they were true, it was only because God had willed them to be true. In fact, Ockham claimed, the whole order of creation, including the moral order, depended on the will of God. Things were the way they were because God willed them to be that way; if he had willed otherwise the world would be different, including the laws of nature and the rules of ethical behaviour. If he had wanted to, he could have made a world in which the moon was hot and the sun was cold, in which it was noble to commit adultery and dishonourable to show mercy to the poor. For if God was all powerful and completely free, Christians believed, he could have created a universe that was different from the present one, simply by willing it.

After Ockham the philosophical and theological unity of Christendom was shattered. Nominalism showed that philosophical reasoning could lead to conclusions quite different from those of theology, and it contended that reasoning itself had to deal with words and statements rather than the real world. All that could be known from experience, it claimed, was experience; everything else was metaphysical speculation. Nominalism thus succeeded in diminishing, at least in the minds of many, the credibility of scholasticism, and it opened the way for a variety of philosophical and theological approaches in the schools of fifteenth-century Europe. Some followed Meister Eckhart of Germany, preferring the intuitive truth of mystical experience to the uncertain truth of philosophy. Some continued to follow the *via antiqua*, preferring the achievements of the past to the disagreements of the present. Some developed new philosophies, preferring originality to antiquity. Some went down into skepticism, or preferred *fides sine intellectu*, faith without understanding.

Sacramental theology in the late Middle Ages could no longer depend on philosophy for its explanations, and so it turned to canon law. The words of the canonists were still the words of the great scholastics, but now they had legal rather than theological meanings. Matter and form were the things that were necessary for validity. Validity was what was required to cause the sacramental reality. The sacramental reality gave power in a legal sense: baptism gave the power to receive the other sacraments, matrimony gave the power to have legitimate intercourse, orders gave the power to administer the sacraments, penance gave the power to receive communion and the other sacraments worthily. In the end, a large portion of canon law dealt with the sacraments, and a large measure of sacramental theology was dependent on canon law.

Sacramental practice suffered a worse fate: it became sacramental magic. *Ex opere operato* meant that the rituals worked automatically. The priest poured the water on the infant's head, saying the right words, and the child was saved from hell. The bishop anointed the candidate for confirmation and he received an indelible mark on his soul. Two people recited their marriage vows and they were thereby bonded together for life. The priest said the words of absolution in the confessional and sins were immediately washed away. By the words of consecration the bread and wine were suddenly transformed into the body and blood of Christ. The soul of the person who received the last rites went directly to heaven.

The magical attitude that invaded the Church's liturgical sacraments also pervaded other pious practices. Special prayers to the Blessed Virgin or the saints were certain of being heard. Gazing intently at the host or crucifix could guarantee that a son would be born. Touching relics of martyrs or saints could cause miraculous healings. Chanting the proper holy phrases would keep away temptation. Making a pilgrimage to Rome or a famous shrine would earn merit in heaven. Reciting certain prayers at the proper times would cancel all the punishment one could expect after death. Making a donation to the Church could release a soul from purgatory.

None of this was ever officially sanctioned by the Catholic hierarchy. None of it even entered the manuals of sacred theology or was approved by canon law. But it was going on among the people and it was condoned by the clergy. And it was setting the stage for a revolution.

For further reading
Marshall Baldwin, *The Medieval Church* (Cornell University Press, 1953) is a concise and readable history of Christianity in the Middle Ages.
Christopher Dawson, *Medieval Essays* (Doubleday Image Books, 1959) contains a number of essays on the Church and medieval thought.

For further study

Elizabeth Rogers, *Peter Lombard and the Sacramental System* (New York, 1917) shows the changes that took place in numbering and defining the sacraments in the middle of the twelfth century.

Peter Garland, *The Definition of Sacrament According to Saint Thomas* (University of Ottawa Press, 1959) gives a technical but clear explanation of Aquinas' understanding of sacraments as signs of grace.

John Gallagher, *Significando Causant: A Study of Sacramental Causality* (Fribourg University Press, 1965) is a detailed treatment of how Aquinas and other scholastics have explained that sacraments cause grace.

Bernard Lonergan, *Grace and Freedom in Aquinas* (Herder and Herder, 1971) develops the approach to grace and causality followed in this chapter.

Thomas Aquinas, *On the Truth of the Catholic Faith (Summa Contra Gentiles)* (Doubleday Image Books, 1957) contains a handy summary of his main ideas on the sacraments in Book IV, chapters 56–78.

Robert Hoyt and Stanley Chodrow, *Europe in the Middle Ages* (3rd edition, Harcourt Brace Jovanovich, 1976) is a standard history which gives good attention to medieval Christianity.

Heiko Oberman, *The Harvest of Medieval Theology* (William B. Eerdmans, 1962) gives a more positive view of nominalism than the usual one, presented in this chapter.

Chapter 27

The Sacraments in the History of the Church

Philippe Béguerie and Claude Duchesneau

> What was visible in our Redeemer has thus passed into the sacraments. St Leo

Twenty centuries of Church history, twenty centuries of the presence of the sacraments in this history, is a long time – indeed it is an amazing time!

But at the same time, since this is a history, a life, there is both permanence and change, stability and evolution.

The questions which more or less every Christian asks about the sacraments indicate an interest in a basic part of the life of the Church and Christian existence. In the end of the day, what are the sacraments, where do they come from and what do they represent today?

These questions become even more live ones when in catechesis one has to explain the sacraments to children or initiate them into their first celebration and above all when, in pastoral work, one has to prepare young people for marriage or parents for the baptism of their child.

Not all Christians can be historians or theologians of the sacraments, but knowledge of faith must be supported by a minimum of knowledge, particularly history – and that is even more urgent in the present-day world, which is so technical and so precise. 'Always be ready to give account of the hope that is in you', St Peter said to the first Christians (I Peter 3:15).

That is why, while fully aware of the lack of precision and subtlety that a summary can have, in the following pages we shall try to see how our sacraments have been present in the history of the Church. But the aim of this work will not just be to do history. The real concern of the inquiry will be to understand better what the sacraments are so as to live them out better today.

Questions people ask
- I can see that the sacraments are actions of the Church, but how can they also be actions of Christ?
- Why are there seven sacraments?
- Did Jesus Christ institute all the sacraments?
- Do all the sacraments have the same importance?

When it all began

We shall never become the early Church again. It would even be unhealthy to involve ourselves in nostalgia over beginnings. On the other hand, we know that our Christian life today depends on the time when it all began, and on our faithfulness to what these first beginnings set in place. What can we say about the sacraments?

The situation of the first Christians was this. Most of them had known Jesus and even gone about with him for three years. Now Jesus had just died. He had been crucified. But God raised him: they were witnesses of this (Acts 2:32). Jesus 'disappeared from their sight' (Emmaus, Luke 24:31). But he was alive: God had made him Lord and Christ (Acts 2:36). The first Christians wanted to pursue their relationship with Jesus, to celebrate the God who had not abandoned his Son to the power of death (Acts 2:24) and to proclaim this good news to everyone.

How were they going to do that? By two activities, different but complementary. The first was turned outwards: missionary preaching (see Peter's speech at Pentecost, then the scattering of the Jerusalem community when persecution broke out, Acts 8:4); the other was turned inwards; baptism as a sign of adherence to Christ and involvement in the community (see Pentecost, Acts 2:41) and the communal meal in the course of which 'bread was broken' and shared to make a memorial of the Lord Jesus (see Acts 2:42; 2:45; 20:7).

Pentecost
So those who received his (Peter's) word were baptized, and there were added that day about three thousand souls. Acts 2:41

The first community
And they devoted themselves to the apostles' teaching and fellowship, to the breaking of bread and the prayers. Acts 2:42

In this activity directed towards the forming (baptism) and maintaining (the breaking of the bread) of the community, there is the
basic nucleus of what we now call the sacramental life of the
Church.

In pursuing our observation of this earliest Church, we note that
its baptismal and eucharistic life is the result of the combination of
three elements: faith, the rite and the memorial.

Faith

Faith comes first. None of this activity would exist without it. The
baptisms of Pentecost took place only because Peter's speech led
the hearers to join in: 'What are we to do? Be converted and let
every one be baptized' (Acts 2:37–38). The breaking of the bread
at home took place only because the disciples wanted to make
memorial of the living Lord. The Emmaus episode is an astonish-
ing confirmation of this in its remark that the Lord disappeared
from the sight of his disciples the moment they recognized him.
One cannot believe if one sees, for in that case there is no room for
faith. It is because one does not see that one is led to believe.

The rite

Neither bathing in water nor sacred communal meals are the
inventions of Jesus or the first Christians. These two practices form
part of the universal heritage of religion (as anthropology proves)
and more particularly of the heritage of the religious life of the
Jewish people.

Thus we know (to keep to the period before Jesus) that there was
baptism of proselytes (pagans who converted to Judaism), and
certainly the baptism of John. Furthermore religious meals were
held not only in ardent groups (like the Essenes and the
Therapeutae) but in all Jewish families, on the sabbath and all the
great festivals. The paschal meal was the most important of them.

Following Jesus, who himself underwent baptism and presided
over numerous religious meals with his disciples (of which the
Supper was the last), the first Christians resorted to these two ritual
practices to give communal expression to their relationship to the
Lord.

The memorial

Faith, which is the gift of God, and the rite, which is a human action, come together to result in a memorial. The memorial is based on a past event (the death and resurrection of the Lord Jesus), affirming its permanent efficacy and reviving it by the symbolic performance of the rite so as to announce its future fulfilment. As human beings, the first Christians could only continue their relationship with the 'Invisible Living Lord' by the visible mediation of these rites, which were the memorials of baptism and the breaking of bread. These are not rites that they invented – as we have seen – but through Christ and the Holy Spirit they gave them an absolutely new meaning and content.

Anamnesis = Memorial
These words have the same meaning, but one comes from Greek and the other from Latin.

'The Lord, God of your Fathers, God of Abraham, God of Isaac and God of Jacob has sent me to you. That is my name for ever, it is my memorial' (Ex 3:15).
That day (of the feast of the Passover) will serve as a memorial for you (Ex 12:14).
Glory be to the Father and to the Son and to the Holy Spirit, to the God who is, was and is to come.
Glory to you, the one who was dead; Glory to you, the one who is alive, our Saviour and our God.
Come, Lord Jesus!

This new way of using these rites consisted not only of remembering the one who had 'disappeared' (see Emmaus), as Jesus had asked of them (hence the institution), but of 'doing this in remembrance of him', i.e. of allowing the living Jesus to continue to act among them by making them benefit from his Pasch which was historically past, but mystically always present.

It is of the Eucharist only that Jesus said, 'Do this in remembrance of me', but baptism (and all the other sacraments) is as much a memorial of Christ's *Pasch* as the 'broken bread'.

So what we call the basic nucleus of the sacramental life of the Church was in place. This nucleus did not yet have any other name than those of the two acts which made it up, baptism and the breaking of the bread (the Lord's supper, for Paul in I Cor. 11:20; chronologically, he is the first to talk of the Eucharist).

However, alongside these, we can see the presence of a certain number of actions in the service of the faith of the first communities. But their practices remain shrouded in the mists of history, and moreover there was still no precise name to designate them or,

even more important, theological conception (like that of sacrament) under which to bring them. This is what made Maurice
Jourjon, a patristic specialist, say that 'the sacraments were born
before there was a term with which to describe them'. To live out
all situations of life from Christ and with him was the sole preoccupation of the first Christians.

The sacraments – before the term was used
Some actions of the first Christian communities were already sacraments, even before the term was used:

- acts of exclusion from the community or reintegration into it
  (Matt 18:15–18 implies this; I Cor 5 proves it);
- acts of handing on a responsibility from the leader of the
  community (Matt 16:18 to Peter; to bishops or elders (presbyters) in I Tim 3:2; 5:17, etc.);
- acts of a giving of the Spirit, apparently distinct from baptism
  (Acts 8:17);
- acts of prayer and the anointing of the sick (James 5:14);
- without forgetting that at this time, as at all others, men and
  women were getting married, and that Christians married in
  the spirit of Genesis, which Jesus had recalled (Matt 19:4), and
  of which Paul had given a very high Christian interpretation
  (Eph 5:32).

The development of sacramental life

Granted that baptism and the Eucharist have been constantly lived
out by the Church down the centuries with a remarkable constancy
and fidelity, albeit with unimportant developments in the ritual
sphere, we must now ask in connection with the other sacraments
how we have arrived at our present situation, after what we have
seen of the first Christians.

One might say that in a way necessity was the main factor. It
was the life of the Church and the vital needs which it came to
feel which allowed what was there in embryo in the person of
Jesus and the New Testament to come clearly and precisely into
existence.

Three factors helped this sacramental development to come
about:

a.   the work of history;
b.   the quest for a precise vocabulary;

c.   the need for a definition of the function and number of the
        sacraments.

The work of history

Let's take a few examples:
    Confirmation. During the first three centuries of the Church,
Christianity was essentially urban (Jerusalem, Antioch, Alexandria,
Rome, Lyons . . .) and the communities were quite small in size,
particularly as a result of persecutions. The bishop was almost the
local priest. He was there. He was near. At Easter he baptized the
catechumens, performing all the rites which preceded or followed
the actual immersion in water. He, too, laid hands on neophytes
after baptism, calling on the Spirit, and anointed them with oil. It
would not occur to anyone that there were two distinct operations
here.
    However, when Christianity began to be able to expand into the
countryside round the great cities after the peace of Constantine
in 313, the bishop came to be increasingly remote from those who
were baptized in the distant communities. The priest certainly
baptized the catechumens from the community for which he was
responsible, but it was necessary to wait for the bishop for him to
lay on hands and anoint. It was only in 465 that Faustus, bishop of
Riez, spoke of 'confirmation' in this connection.
    Penance. The history of penance is the most eventful of all the
sacraments. In the West, penance had at least three different and
successive forms (without counting the periods when there was a
vacuum), and the general practice of private confession dates only
from the beginning of the seventeenth century. Saint Augustine
never had recourse to it between his conversion and his death, but
St John Bosco made his confession every day.
    Marriage. Of course Christians have always married, but in the
first centuries there was no particular ceremony or religious
approach. Faith and law consisted of marriage 'according to the
local custom'.
    Little by little, it became customary for the permission of the
bishop to be asked for the marriage of the clergy and for there to
be a Mass and a blessing of the bride at the time of a marriage. But
it was only in 1536, and to combat the abuse of illegitimate
marriages, that the Council of Trent for the first time produced an
obligatory canonical form, which is what is still used: the appearance of the couple before their parish priest and the exchange of
vows in his presence.

Ordination. It was not until 1947 and Pope Pius XII that it was made clear that the act of ordination of a priest was not the porrection (touching) of the chalice and paten, but the laying on of hands by the bishop and the prayer of consecration that goes with it.

So do we have to speak of the institution of the sacraments by Christ? If that meant that during his earthly life Jesus established the practice of the various sacraments, it would be doubly wrong: first because all the rites which developed into the sacraments existed before him, and secondly because it was not until a number of centuries after Jesus that several of these rites (all of them except baptism and the Eucharist) clearly revealed their sacramental value.

That Christ instituted the sacraments means that each of them is rightly considered an act of Christ corresponding to a particular gift of grace which Christ expressly willed, while leaving it to the Church to specify the specific forms of human action which would allow it.

The quest for a precise vocabulary

As we have seen, the first preoccupation of the earliest Christians was to live out their relationship with the Lord Jesus and not to define or classify their actions and gestures. As the years passed, the reflection of pastors and theologians led to questions being asked about a certain number of actions, perhaps because they had to be explained (in pre- or post-baptismal catechesis) or because important questions arose in connection with them. (Does the Church have the right to forgive those who have abjured their faith or committed a murder? Is baptism administered by heretics valid?)

In this reflection, the first word used for all of what we now call sacraments was the Greek word *mysterion* and above all its plural *mysteria*, the mysteries. It is a word which comes from pagan religious vocabulary. The mysteries were the non-public cults to which a person was introduced through rites of initiation which had to be kept absolutely secret and by which the salvation of the initiates was guaranteed.

In fact this word was not new in Christianity. It was already present in the Old Testament, notably in the book of Wisdom, which was originally written in Greek (Wisdom 2:22). But it is above all St Paul who gave it its full Christian sense. For him, the word denotes 'God's plan' (Eph 1:9), and even Christ in person, as one who reveals this plan (I Cor 2:1; Col 2:2).

When one begins gradually to call baptism *mysterion,* or speak of the *mysteria* of the body and blood of Christ, as does Eusebius of Caesarea (267–340) in his *Demonstration of the Gospel* (5.3), there is a concern to indicate that baptism and the Eucharist are bound up with the whole work of salvation which God accomplishes for us through Christ and that they are seen as the privileged realization of this work.

However, from the third century this word *mysterion* and its Latin transcription *mysterium* came to seem suspect to Tertullian (160-240) because of possible confusion with the pagan mysteries. He preferred the Latin term *sacramentum.*

The sacramentum

In Latin this word has two meanings. First it is a legal term which denotes the money of the party who loses a trial and which is dedicated to the deity. Second, it is the word which denotes the action by which a soldier commits himself by taking an oath to this leader and to the emperor.It is above all this notion of commitment by oath which makes Tertullian speak of baptism in terms of *sacramentum.*

But not all the Latin theologians were as intransigent as Tertullian. *Mysterium* and *sacramentum* were used indiscriminately by St Ambrose and even still by Paschasius Radbertus in the ninth century. It was only with scholasticism that *sacramentum* decisively took on the technical meaning which it has retained to our day. That, however, happened only in the Latin part of the Church; the East has always kept the word 'mystery'.

That is how things are and one cannot regret the quest for precision that this development reveals. Each word has its advantages and its disadvantages, and we know that the term 'mystery' is not without risks. However, it has to be recognized that in its concern to look at the *sacramentum* and the *sacramenta* in increasing detail and in legal terms, the Latin Church made them lose something of their openness to the Mystery, sometimes seeing them more as the means (the instrument, the tool, the thing) than the end.

'Mystery' in St Paul

For he has made known to us in all wisdom and insight the mystery of his will, according to his purpose which he set forth in Christ, as a plan for the fullness of time, to unite all things in him, things in heaven and things on earth. Eph 1:9

I want their hearts to be encouraged as they are knit together in

love, to have all the riches of assured understanding and the knowledge of God's mystery, of Christ, in whom are hidden all the
treasures of wisdom and knowledge. Col 2:2

The need for a definition of the function and number of the sacraments

If baptism and the Eucharist have a clear place in the life of the
Church of the first centuries, in the midst of other Christian acts
which came gradually to find a place in the course of the following
centuries, how was it that seven particular rites and only seven
came to be called sacraments?

We have seen that first the word 'mystery' and then the word
'sacrament' served to bring out the meaning of certain ritual
actions in connection with the whole plan of God. The idea is a
fine one. It ended up, for example, in an affirmation by Paschasius
Radbertus (790–865) which Vatican II was to take over.

Mystery and Sacrament in Paschasius Radbertus (790–865)
The nativity of Christ and all the economy of salvation form a great
sacrament, for in the visible man, the divine majesty accomplishes
invisibly and secretly what will serve for our consecration and sanctification. That is why the incarnation of God is rightly called
mystery or sacrament. (*Liber de corpore et sanguine domini*, PL 120, col.
1725)

But this admirable theology also concealed a considerable
vagueness of definition. What is a mystery? St John Chrysostom
replies: 'There is a mystery when we consider other things than
what we see.' That is very true and well said. But it is not enough
for a systematic reflection.

What is a sacrament? For St Ambrose, both baptism and foot-
washing. For St Augustine both the creed and the Our Father, and
baptism and the Eucharist.

However, it was St Augustine who brought the first clarification
in reflecting on the sacrament as a sign. He said that the sacrament
is the tangible sign of a holy thing.

With a few nuances, Augustine's definition was to hold until the
Middle Ages. But the vagueness remained. For St Peter Damien
(1072), sacraments are tangible signs of a holy thing, and so the
anointing of kings, the canonicate, the dedication of Churches,
funerals, the monastic habit are sacraments.

It was at this stage that the great theologians of the Middle Ages
appeared. First of all, Augustine's definition appeared inadequate

to Hugh of Saint Victor (died 1141). It seemed to him that while one can say that every sacrament is a tangible sign of a holy thing, one cannot say that every tangible sign of a holy thing is a sacrament. The sacrament of baptism is certainly the tangible sign of a holy thing, but blessed water, which is also the tangible sign of a holy thing, cannot be a sacrament with the same status as baptism. So he adds to the definition of Augustine the need for the sign to be of divine institution to be a sacrament.

The mystery in St John Chrysostom

There is a mystery when we consider things other than those that we see . . . The non-believer who sees baptism thinks that it is only water; I, not just considering what I see, contemplate the purification of the soul brought about by the Holy Spirit . . . (*Homily 1 on I Corinthians*, PG 61, col. 55)

The sign in St Augustine

The sign is something which, over and above the image whose meaning it nurtures, brings forth from itself something else in thought. (*De doctrina Christiana II.1*)

Abelard (1079–1142) distinguished between the *sacramenta majora*, useful to salvation: baptism, Eucharist, order, penitence; and the *sacramenta minora*, to increase devotion: blessed water, ashes. The unknown author of the *Summa Sententiarum* (thirteenth century) also adds that to be a sacrament the tangible sign must be efficacious. In this way he comes to mark out six tangible signs which are efficacious and thus sacraments: our six (not including marriage). Finally Peter Lombard, in his *Sentences*, written in 1150, included everything: sign, institution, efficacy. He added that the tangible sign, to be a sacrament, has to be the cause of the grace which it signifies. Starting from there, he examined all the sacred rites (from blessed water to the Eucharist), finally decreeing that seven only can be called sacraments: the number seven was established.

The first Council officially to name the seven sacraments was the Fourth Lateran Council in 1215. But it was not until the seventh session of the Council of Trent in 1547 that it was defined as being a matter of faith that there are seven sacraments, no more and no less.

However, between Peter Lombard and the Council of Trent mention has to be made of the work of a tremendous theologian, St Thomas Aquinas (died 1274). He did not add anything to Peter Lombard's seven sacraments, but pushed the analysis of the sacraments as far as a theological synthesis which on a number of points will never be surpassed, despite the literary form and vocabulary characteristic of scholasticism. Some of it is quoted below.

The composition of the sacraments

To take account of the way in which the sacraments are composed, Thomas Aquinas borrows from Aristotle the distinction between matter and form. The basis of each sacrament is a human action which gives material expression to the intervention of Christ by means of the form offered by words.

The sacrament of the Eucharist is the taking of bread and wine and saying the words of institution over them. Both are necessary.

Another Aristotelian concept allowed Thomas Aquinas to distinguish in the Eucharist between substance and accidents. At consecration the substance of bread gives place to the substance of the body of Christ (hence the idea of 'trans-substantiation'), but the accidents of bread (composition, taste, perishable character) remain.

The function of the sacraments

In reflecting on the function of the sacraments as signs, Thomas Aquinas ends up with the following definition: 'A sacrament is a sign of some sacred reality for the sanctification of human beings.' His analysis of the relationship between sign and sacrament thus brings out that a sacrament is made up of:

1.   The sign itself (*sacramentum tantum*): that is the tangible rite. In the Eucharist, this is taking bread and wine and saying the words of consecration over them.
2.   The sign and the reality signified (*res et sacramentum*): this is the immediate effect of the tangible rite. In the Eucharist this is the fact that the body of Christ is present in the consecrated bread (the real presence).
3.   The reality alone (*res tantum*): that is the finality of the sacrament, its grace. In the Eucharist this is the unity of the mystical body of Christ.

The hierarchical organization of the sacraments

Not all the sacraments are equal. They can be considered according to two systems:

The linear system (with an anthropological basis). Here baptism has priority because it conditions all the rest, since it is a birth. The others are like the rest of life: growth (confirmation), food (Eucharist), social organization (order, marriage), etc.

The circular system. Here it is the Eucharist which has priority, because it is the only sacrament which directly contains the person of Christ. It is as it were the nucleus around which the other sacraments gravitate and are ordered to it: one is baptized to be 'incorporated', one is 'ordained' to serve the body of Christ, and so on.

Some features of the doctrine of St Thomas Aquinas on the sacraments

Summa theologiae III, questions 60–65:

> The term sacrament is properly applied to that which is a sign of some sacred reality pertaining to human beings. (*Question 60, article 2*)

> Three factors of our sanctification can be taken into consideration: the actual cause, which is the passion of Christ; the form, which consists in grace and the virtues, and the ultimate end which it is designed to achieve, which is eternal life (*Question 60, article 3*)

> Just as in the mystery of the Incarnation the Word of God is united to the flesh which we can perceive with our senses, so too in the sacraments words are applied to sensible materials. (*Question 60, article 6*)

> In the sacraments the words act as the formal principle while the sensible realities act as the material one (*Question 60, article 7*)

> With regard to the direct achieving of a positive further fullness of life this takes place in three ways: first through generation, for it is through this that human beings begin to be and to live, and the factor corresponding to this in the life of the spirit is baptism ... The second way is through growth, for it is by this that the individual is brought to due fullness in size, weight and strength. And the factor corresponding to this in the life of the spirit is confirmation, for it is in this that the Holy Spirit and strength are conferred . . . The third way of directly achieving some positive further fullness of life at the physical level is through nutrition, for it is by this that life and strength in human beings are maintained. And the factor corresponding to this in the life of the spirit is the eucharist. (*Question 65, article 1*)

> The sacrament of the Eucharist is, in an absolute sense, the greatest
> of all the sacraments . . . in this sacrament Christ himself is present
> substantially. All the other sacraments are ordered to this one as to
> their end. (*Question 65, article 3*)

These extracts from the doctrine of St Thomas on the sacraments
must inevitably seem just scholarly (scholastic!) dissection.

In this connection intellectual honesty calls for three remarks,
particularly for the reader who knows little of the history of theological thought.

First, the work of St Thomas Aquinas has provided sacramental
theology with 'monumental' richness. Its construction no longer
corresponds to the architecture that one would use today, but it is
a cathedral which the Church cannot ignore if it is to understand
its history, and particularly the history of its faith. One can even
regret that recent centuries have forgotten its existence. If people
had always referred to St Thomas Aquinas, they would have never
arrived at the fragmented conception which presents the seven
sacraments as seven distinct actions separate from one another.
Nor would the aim of the Eucharist have been thought to be the
real presence, but the unity of the mystical body which it realizes
in communion.

Second, it might appear disturbing that it was necessary to wait
until the twelfth century to know that there were seven sacraments
and even until the sixteenth for this to be defined *de fide*. That is
part of the lovely mystery of the Church which is not a monolithic
block but a living organism. It reveals to us above all that, in the
Church, life is superior to reflection. Such a remark does not mean
that there is no need for reflection and study, but it does remind
us that with or without words and definitions, millions and millions
of faithful over time (twenty centuries) and space (the whole
world) have not ceased to live out their faith and that it is thanks
to them that this faith has been handed down to us and that we
experience it in our turn.

Third, it is worth recalling that our twentieth century has seen a
marked return to Thomistic theology, and that this return clearly
had an influence on the preparation and development of the
theology of the Second Vatican Council. But before we get to
Vatican II we have to say something about the Reformers and the
Council of Trent.

The Reformers

There is something almost offensive in attempting to sum up the position of the Reformers on the sacraments in a few lines. We hope that members of the Reformation Churches will forgive us, and note that we are doing the same thing for the whole history of theological thought.

Two preliminary remarks need to be made. We owe it to the truth to point out that the attitude of the Reformers was largely caused by a certain number of abuses for which the Church was responsible (the excessive increase in Masses for the dead, recourse to doubtful means in the practice of indulgences, and so on).

It also has to be said that from the beginning there were differences between the positions of Luther, Calvin and above all Zwingli, and that differences remain today, particularly over the sacraments, their number and their functions. That having been said, the essential position of the Reformers, which provoked the reaction of the Catholic Church, can be presented as two points:

First, in the name of the scripture, only those sacraments were retained which were explicitly mentioned in the New Testament, baptism and the Eucharist. The Augsburg Confession of 1530 also retained penitence, but specifically stated that confirmation, extreme unction and marriage are only ceremonies. As for the priesthood, there could be no question who is the sole priest in the Church of Christ.

Second in the name of justification by faith alone, the sacrament can only be an external sign. It may provoke faith, but in that case it is faith given by God which justifies, and not the sacrament. Calvin was even more radical than Luther in subjecting the saving action of the sacraments entirely to the preaching of the word. For his part, Luther states that it is not the sacrament but the faith of the sacrament which justifies.

The Council of Trent (The Nineteenth Ecumenical Council)

Seventh Session (1547)   Twenty-first Session (1562)

Canons on the sacraments
1.   If anyone says that the sacraments of the new Law were not all instituted by our Lord Jesus Christ; or that there are less or more than seven, namely baptism, confirmation, the Eucharist, penitence, extreme unction, order and marriage; or that one of these seven is not truly and strictly speaking a sacrament, let him be anathema.

6.   If anyone says that the sacraments of the new law do not contain the grace that they signify or that they do not confer this grace on those who do not put any obstacle in the way, as if they were only external signs of grace or justice received by faith, and marks of Christian profession, which also allow people to distinguish the faithful from the unfaithful, let him be anathema.

(NB This extract from the second chapter of this session is a reply to the still very topical question of whether one can or cannot change anything in the administration and celebration of the sacraments.)

The Holy Council declares: in the dispensation of the sacraments, their substance being saved, the Church has always had the power to decide or to modify what it judges best fitted to the spiritual utility of those who receive them and in respect of the sacraments themselves, depending on the variety of circumstances, times and places.

The Council of Trent

The Council of Trent presented its doctrine of the sacraments at the seventh session (1547). It did so not only to condemn the errors of the Reformers but also to correct the abuses which it noted in the Church and to enlighten and strengthen the faith of the faithful.

For the first time in the history of the Church, then, it was defined as dogma that there are seven sacraments, no more and no less, that they are all instituted by Christ, and that they all confer the grace that they signify.

As we said in the case of St Thomas Aquinas, the literary genre, which here is even legalistic, hardly matches our present-day

mentality and may sometimes even seem shocking (the anathemas!). But the Council of Trent must not be judged by today's
criteria. The state of the Church at the time really called for reor-
ganization, and the crisis provoked by the Reformers was a serious
one. The work of the Council of Trent was indispensable, and on
closer inspection appears less negative than some of its formulations might suggest.

That having been said, a present-day Christian will always ask
why there seems to be such a difference between what the Council
of Trent says about the sacraments and the way in which they are
talked about by Vatican II.

Contemporary theology of the sacraments

Precisely four centuries divide the end of the Council of Trent
(1563) from the beginning of the Second Vatican Council (1962).
It is not surprising that responses to the way to present the doctrine
of the Church, developments in attitudes and changes of tone are
numerous. Among all those which are possible (it would take a
whole book to analyse just this question), we shall consider only
one: it is not the only one, but it is determinative and positive.

Since roughly the beginning of the twentieth century, the
Church has benefited from the incredible leap forward made by
archeology, history, and linguistic and literary studies. The discoveries in each of these areas are innumerable, and one cannot
criticize our sixteenth-century ancestors for not having benefited
from them. Still, particularly in theological work, they have led to
a considerable advance in questions of biblical and patristic exegesis. That does not mean that we have more faith than our
predecessors, but it does mean that we are in a better position to
know about the founding period of the Church than they were.

Acknowledgements

The editors gratefully acknowledge the following permissions to reproduce copyright material. All possible attempts have been made to contact copyrights holders and to acknowledge their copyright correctly. We are grateful to: SPCK for Chapters 1, 15,16, & 25, 'Revelation (*Dei Verbum*)' by Robert Murray SJ, 'The Church (*Lumen Gentium*)' by Richard McBrien, 'The Church in the Modern World (*Gadium et Spes*)' by Enda McDonagh, 'Liturgy (*Sacrosanctum Concilium*)' by Adrian Kavanagh OSB, which were taken from *Modern Catholicism, Vatican II and After*, Adrian Hastings, Editor, 1991; St Anthony Messenger Press for Chapter 2 which was taken from *Reading the Gospels With the Church: From Christmas Through Easter* by Raymond E. Brown, 1996, the Appendix 'The Historical Truth of the Gospels' – *Instruction of the Pontifical Biblical Commission* (1964), translated by J.A. Fitzmyer, is used with permission of the translator; Paulist Press for Chapters 9, 10, 12, 17, 18, & 24 which have been taken from the following: 'The Spiritual Journey of St Paul' in *According to Paul: Studies in the Theology of the Apostle* by Joseph A. Fitzmyer S.J., Paulist Press, 1993; 'The Present State of Christology' in '*Models of Jesus Revisited*' by John F. O'Grady, Paulist Press, 1994; 'Jesus, Savior and Son of God' in *Understanding Catholicism* by Monika K. Hellwig, Paulist Press, 1981; 'The Church We Believe In' in *The Church We Believe In* by Francis A. Sullivan SJ, Gill and Macmillan, 1988; 'Evaluation and Interpretation of the Documents of Vatican II' in *Creative Fidelity – Weighing and Interpreting Documents of the Magisterium* by Francis A. Sullivan SJ, Gill and Macmillan, 1996; 'From Symbol to Sacrament' in *The Book of Sacramental Basics* by Tad Guzie, Paulist Press, 1981; The Liturgical Press for Chapters 4, 7, 14, & 23 which have been taken from the following: 'Returning to the Sources: The Hebrew Bible' by Daniel L. Smith-Christopher, 'Introduction to the Study of the New Testament' by Jeffrey Siker, in Thomas P. Rausch SJ *The College Student's Introduction to Theology* Copyright © 1993 by The Order of St. Benedict, Inc. Published by The Liturgical Press, Collegeville, Minnesota. Used with permission.

'The Church and the Council' and 'Sexual Morality and Social Justice' by Thomas P. Rausch SJ, in *Catholicism at the Dawn of the Third Millennium,* Copyright © 1996 by The Order of St Benedict, Inc. Published by The Liturgical Press, Collegeville, Minnesota. Used with permission; The Associated Sulpicians of the U.S. for Chapter 3 'Historical-Critical Exegesis of the Bible in Roman Catholicism' which has been taken from *Biblical Exegesis and Church Doctrine* by Raymond E. Brown SS, Paulist Press, 1985; Abingdon Press for Chapter 5 ' The Canon of the Old Testament' which has been taken from *An Introduction To Old Testament Study* by John H. Hayes, SCM Press Ltd, 1982; SCM Press for Chapters 6, 26, & 27 which have been taken from the following: 'What is a Prophet' in *How to Read the Prophets* by Jean-Pierre Prévost, translated by John Bowden, SCM Press Ltd., 1996; 'The Development of the Catholic Sacraments' in *Doors to the Sacred* by Joseph Martos, SCM Press Ltd., 1981; 'The Sacraments in the History of the Church' in *How to Understand the Sacraments* by Philippe Béguerie and Claude Duchesneau, translated by John Bowden and Margaret Lydamore, SCM Press Ltd., 1991.

We are grateful to E.J. Dwyer (Australia) Pty Ltd. for Chapter 8 'The Gospel Stories' which has been taken from *Studying the Gospels – an introduction* by Gideon Goosen and Margaret Tomlinson, E.J. Dwyer (Australia) Pty Ltd., 1994; Veritas Publications for Chapter 11 'The Doctrine of the Incarnation: Human and Cosmic Considerations' which has been taken from *Christ at the Centre – Selected Issues In Christology* by Dermort A. Lane, © First published by Veritas Publications. Used with permission; The Columba Press for Chapter 13 'His Own Person or Divine Puppet?' which has been taken from *Jesus: Self-portrait by God* by Enda Lyons, The Columba Press, 1994; Darton, Longman, & Todd for Chapter 19 *Ecumenism* taken from The Theology of Vatican II by Christopher Butler, published and copyright 1981, Darton, Longman, & Todd; The Furrow for Chapter 20 'What's 'Special' About Christian Morality?' by Denis O'Callaghan, *Furrow,* volume 28, number 8 August 1977; Gill and Macmillan for Chapter 21 'Approaching Christian Morality' which has been taken from *The Truth in Love – Reflections On Christian Morality* by Vincent MacNamara, Gill and Macmillan, 1988.

We are grateful to HarperCollins Publishers for Chapter 22 'The History of Moral Theology' which has been taken from *Principles For A Catholic Morality* (Revised Edition) by Timothy E. O'Connell, HarperCollins Publishers, 1990.

We are also grateful to Bishop John Rawsthorne, Fr. Andrew Faley and members of the Board of Studies for the Catholic Certificate in Religious Studies in the numerous centres where the Certificate is taught for their helpful suggestions. To Dr. Bernadette Porter, Frances Spackman, Káren North, and Mike Castelli from Digby Stuart College, Roehampton Institute London for their encouragement in this project. To Professor Stanley Porter for useful hints in publishing a Reader. To Fr. Steven Porter from Rancho Cucamonga, California, for his help in tracing some of the authors. To Kate Rhodes for secretarial assistance and especially to Heather Ferguson-Gow who typed all the chapters and retyped many of the chapters. We would very much want to thank Tom Longford and Jo Ashworth of Gracewing for their careful assistance in the publication of this Reader.

Michael A Hayes
Liam Gearon
23 April 1998
Feast of St George

Index